Immigration: the law and practice

Immigration: the law and practice

3rd Edition

Michael Supperstone QC, MA, BCL (*Oxon*)
of the Middle Temple, Barrister

and

Declan O'Dempsey MA (*Cantab*), Dip Law
of the Middle Temple, Barrister

© Longman Group Ltd 1994

ISBN 0851 21874 1

Published by
Longman Group Ltd
21-27 Lamb's Conduit Street
London WC1N 3NJ

Associated offices
Australia, Hong Kong, Malaysia, Singapore and USA

First Edition 1983
Second Edition 1988

A CIP catalogue record for this book is available
from the British Library.

All rights reserved. No part of this publication may be
reproduced, stored in a retrieval system, or transmitted,
in any form or by any means, electronic, mechanical,
photocopying, recording or otherwise, without the prior
written permission of the publishers, or a licence
permitting restricted copying issued by the Copyright
Licensing Agency Ltd, 90 Tottenham Court Road,
London W1P 9HE.

Printed and bound in Great Britain by
Biddles Ltd, Guildford and King's Lynn

Contents

Preface	xiv
Table of Abbreviations	xvi
Table of Cases	xvii
Table of Statutes	xli
Table of Statutory Instruments	xlvii
Table of Immigration Rules	li
Table of EC Cases	lv
Table of EC Legislation	lix
Table of European Treaties and Conventions	lxi

Part I Background

1 General Background	3
1 The British Nationality Act 1948	5
2 The Commonwealth Immigrants Acts 1962 and 1968	5
3 The Immigration Act 1971	6
4 The British Nationality Act 1981	6
5 Use of Parliamentary materials	7
2 The Immigration Act 1971	9
1 The concept of patriality and right of abode before the 1981 Act	9
2 The right of abode after the 1981 Act	13
3 Settlement	13
4 Rights of appeal	15
5 Illegal entry	16

CONTENTS

3 The British Nationality Act 1981   24
  1 Categories of citizenship defined by the 1981 Act   25
  2 Other relevant categories of citizenship   27
  3 Acquisition of British citizenship from
    1 January 1983   29
  4 Loss of British citizenship   35

4 Statutory Developments Since 1981   37
  1 Immigration (Carriers' Liability) Act 1987   37
  2 The Immigration Act 1988   41
  3 British Nationality (Hong Kong) Act 1990   43
  4 The Asylum and Immigration Appeals Act 1993   50

5 The Immigration Rules   51
  1 Introduction   51
  2 The 1994 Rules   51
  3 Commonwealth citizens settled in the UK in 1973   52
  4 Status of the rules   52
  5 Decisions taken outside the rules: concessions
    and policies   54
  6 Judicial review of the rules   55

Part II Immigration Control

6 The Immigration Rules: Introduction and Interpretation   59
  1 Introduction   59
  2 Interpretation   61
  3 General provisions regarding leave to enter or
    remain in the UK   62
  4 Returning residents   69
  5 Holders of restricted travel documents and
    passports   71
  6 Entry clearance   72
  7 Variation of leave to enter or remain   75
  8 Undertakings   79
  9 Medical   80

7 Part 2 of HC 395: Persons Seeking to Enter or Remain
  in the UK for visits   82
  1 Requirements for leave to enter   82
  2 'is genuinely seeking entry as a visitor'   83

CONTENTS vii

	3 'intends to leave the UK'	86
	4 'does not intend to take employment in the UK'	88
	5 'Will maintain and accommodate himself'	89
	6 Extensions of stay	90
	7 Visitors in transit	91
	8 Private medical treatment	92
8	Part 3 of HC 395: Students	96
	1 Students: leave to enter or remain	96
	2 Extensions	104
	3 Student nurses	106
	4 Post graduate doctors and dentists	109
	5 Spouses of students	110
	6 Children of students	111
	7 Prospective students	112
9	Part 4 of HC 395: Au pairs, Working Holiday-makers and Training or Work Experience	115
	1 Au pair	115
	2 Working holiday-makers	117
	3 Children of working holiday-makers	121
	4 Seasonal workers at agricultural camps	122
	5 Teachers and language assistants coming to the UK under approved exchange schemes	124
	6 DoE approved training or work experience	126
	7 Spouses of persons with limited leave to remain	131
	8 Children of persons admitted or allowed to remain	132
10	Persons Seeking to Enter or Remain in the UK for employment	135
	1 Introduction: entry for work	135
	2 Work permit holders	137
	3 Representatives of overseas media	143
	4 Representatives of overseas firms (sole representatives)	145
	5 Extensions	146
	6 Private servants in diplomatic households	148
	7 Overseas government employees	151
	8 Ministers of religion, missionaries and members of religious orders	152
	9 Airport staff	156
	10 Exception on grounds of UK ancestry	158

CONTENTS

	11	Indefinite leave to remain on grounds of UK ancestry	160
	12	Spouses of persons with limited leave to enter or remain	161
	13	Children of persons with limited leave to enter or remain	163

11 Persons Seeking to Enter or Remain in the UK as Businessmen, Self-Employed Persons, Investors or Creative Artists — 166
- 1 Business entry — 166
- 2 Extensions — 173
- 3 EC association agreements — 175
- 4 Investors — 181
- 5 Creative artists — 184
- 6 Spouses of persons with limited leave to enter or remain — 186
- 7 Children of persons with limited leave to enter or remain — 188
- 8 Exercise of a right of access to a child resident in the UK — 190
- 9 Holders of special vouchers — 191
- 10 EEA nationals and their families — 194
- 11 Retired persons of independent means — 194
- 12 Spouses of retired persons with independent means — 196
- 13 Children of retired persons with independent means — 198

12 Family Members — 201
- 1 Spouses — 201
- 2 Para 201: primary purpose test — 207
- 3 Fiancé(e)s — 216
- 4 Children — 218
- 5 Children born in the UK who are not British citizens — 228
- 6 Adopted children — 230
- 7 Adopted children: settlement — 235
- 8 Parents, grandparents and other dependant relatives of persons present and settled in the UK — 237

CONTENTS

13	General Grounds for the Refusal of Leave to Enter or Remain in the UK	244
	1 Grounds on which entry clearance or leave to enter the UK is to be refused	246
	2 Exclusion conducive to the public good	247
	3 Grounds on which entry clearance or leave to enter the UK should normally be refused	248
	4 Persons in possession of an entry clearance	252
	5 Refusal of variation of leave to enter or remain or curtailment of leave	254
	6 Para 323 – curtailment	258
	7 Registration with the police	258
	8 Asylum	260
	9 Rights of appeal	261
14	Deportation	262
	1 Introduction	262
	2 Long residence policies	263
	3 Deportation: rules	265
	4 Considerations to be taken into account in considering deportation action	272
	5 Deportation of family members	275
	6 Deportation: appeals	278
	7 Procedure	281
	8 Revocation of deportation order	283

Part III European free movement

15	EEA Nationals and their Families	289
	1 Introduction	289
	2 The European Economic Area agreement	290
	3 European Economic Area Act 1993	292
	4 Personal scope of the right to free movement	293
	5 Rights of admission	294
	6 The nature of permitted derogation	303
	7 UK provisions: s 7 of the 1988 Act	305
16	The right of EEA Nationals to Residence and Settlement	307
	1 Introduction	307
	2 EC provisions	307

	3	Directive 68/360: residence rights	307
	4	Residence in relation to services	308
	5	Students	309
	6	Other residence rights	309
	7	Retired or incapacitated	310
	8	Expulsion	312
	9	Appeals	314
	10	UK implementation of free movement: HC 395, paras 255–262	316
	11	The EEA family permit	319
17	Third Country Agreements and other Provisions		320
	1	Agreement with Turkey	320
	2	Co-operation agreements with Algeria, Morocco and Tunisia	322
	3	Third Country nationals employed in EA undertakings	325
	4	Agreement on the external frontiers of the EC	325
18	Application and Enforcement of the EEA and EC Law		328
	1	Introduction	328
	2	Injunctions	331
	3	Preliminary rulings	331
	4	Procedure for applying for a preliminary ruling	332

Part IV Asylum

19	Asylum		335
	1	Asylum applications	335
	2	Refusal of asylum	344
	3	Consideration of cases	352
	4	Children	363
	5	Exceptional leave to remain and settlement housing and social security	365
	6	EU asylum law	367
20	Asylum Appeals and Removal		372
	1	Rights of appeal	372
	2	Appeal rules	375
	3	Determination of an appeal	377

CONTENTS xi

4	Special appeals procedure for claims without foundation	378
5	Appeal from the special adjudicator to the IAT	381
6	Appeals from the IAT	383
7	General procedure under the 1993 Rules	383
8	Deportation and removal of asylum seekers	388

Part V Procedure

21	Procedure on Examination, Detention and Release	393
1	Examination by the immigration authorities	393
2	Detention of persons liable to examination or removal	398
3	Temporary admission and release	399
4	Bail pending an appeal	401

22	Procedure on deportation	404
1	Orders for deportation by the S of S	404
2	Recommendations by the criminal courts	406
3	Effect of a deportation order	407
4	Detention of persons before deportation	407
5	Revocation of deportation orders	408

Part VI Remedies

23	Appeal Procedures I	411
1	HC 395, Part 12	411
2	Deportation orders	418
3	Circumstances in which there is no right of appeal	425

24	Appeal Procedures II: Instituting and Conducting an Appeal to the Adjudicator	434
1	Notification of rights of appeal	434
2	Methods of service	435
3	Launching an appeal	438
4	Interlocutory matters before hearing of appeal	440
5	Preliminary points and further opportunity to appeal	443
6	Other interlocutory matters	445
7	The hearing	450

xii   CONTENTS

25 Appeal Procedures III: Instituting and Conducting an
    Appeal to the IAT and CA   464
    A   Appeals to the IAT   464
        1   Criteria to be satisfied before leave will be granted 465
        2   How to appeal to the IAT   467
        3   Refusal of leave to appeal and grounds of appeal   469
        4   Evidence and documents on appeal to the IAT   470
    B   Reference of cases to the S of S
        for further consideration   470
    C   Appeals to the CA   471

26 The impact of the European Convention on
    Human Rights   473
    1   Introduction   473
    2   The Convention as an interpretative guide   473
    3   The Convention as a remedy   475
    4   The Convention under EC law   478
    5   Procedure for making an application to the
        Commission   479

27 Judicial Review   481
    1   The remedy of judicial review   481
    2   The nature of immigration decision amenable
        to judicial review   482
    3   Grounds for judicial review   486
    4   Restrictions on judicial review   495
    5   Remedies   499
    6   Procedure for applying for judicial review   500

28 Habeas Corpus   510

Part VII   Criminal Offences

29 Criminal Offences   517
    1   Criminal offences under the 1971 Act   517
    2   Illegal entry and similar offences   517
    3   Assisting illegal entry and harbouring   522
    4   General offences in connection with the
        administration of the 1971 Act   523

CONTENTS xiii

5	Offences by persons connected with ships, aircraft, ports or with the Channel Tunnel	526
6	Criminal offences under the British Nationality Act 1981	526
7	Liability to deportation	527
8	Criminal offences under the Housing Act 1985 and the 1993 Act	528
9	Police station interviews	529

Appendix: The Immigration (European Economic Area Order) 1994   531

Index   545

Preface

There have been substantial developments in this area since the last edition, in terms of legislation (the Immigration Act 1988 and the Asylum and Immigration Appeals Act 1993), radical changes in the Immigration Rules and in terms of decisions of the courts. There have been two drastic reductions in the rights of immigrants and one significant enlargement. The Immigration Act 1988 removed from most persons overstaying their leave, or being found to be in breach of their conditions of leave, any right of effective appeal against deportation. The Asylum and Immigration Appeals Act 1993 removes rights of appeal from large numbers of persons. This was done on the basis that the waiting times for appeals were too long, and that the purpose of most visits was past by the time the appeal was determined. Several former Law Lords spoke against these provisions of the 1993 Act, predicting gloomily the number of judicial reviews the lack of appeal rights will inspire. The curate's egg of an Act provides a much needed right of appeal in all asylum cases, but the time limits for bringing the appeals and the schedule for the determination of the appeals which it contains will place advisers in difficulties about obtaining sensitive evidence from overseas. However, the Geneva Convention relating to the Status of Refugees is given primacy in UK law for the first time.

The Court of Appeal in *Mokuolu v S of S* and *Ex parte Chan* has emphasised the administrative nature of illegal entry, which includes the case of persons who enter without leave, albeit innocently. In *Muboyayi* the Court of Appeal emphasised the use of habeas corpus as an aid to judicial review and considered the possibility of placing a stay on the actions of the Crown in removing persons.

The notorious primary purpose rule remains, but has been mitigated by a concession made in Parliament relating to established marriages, and, to a certain extent by the decision of the European Court of Justice in *Surinder Singh*. Other developments in EC law have been included in an expanded chapter on EC law. In an increasingly discretionary area there have also been several important policy statements. In relation to Article 8 of the European Convention on Human Rights, the Home Office has finally drawn up proper guidelines for the avoidance of breaches of the right to respect for family life in deportation cases.

We would like to express our thanks to the Home Office and the many people who assisted us in the preparation of this edition by their helpful comments and suggestions. In particular we are grateful to Fiona Lindsley and Sue Shutter for reading and commenting on the book, and to ILPA and Clare Cozens for the provision (often at short notice) of much valuable material. We are indebted to the editorial staff of Longman for all their hard work in the production of this book. We dedicate this book to our wives Dianne Supperstone and Clare Cozens. We thank them and our editors for their patience and assistance during the preparation of this edition, protracted as it was by the passage of the 1993 Act and by the introduction of the 1994 Rules.

We have attempted to state the law and practice as at 17 May 1994 although, where possible, we have incorporated important decisions after that date. In an Appendix to this book we have commented upon the Immigration (European Economic Area) Order 1994.

Michael Supperstone QC	Declan O'Dempsey
11 Kings Bench Walk	4 Brick Court
Temple	Temple
London EC4	London EC4Y 9AD

Abbreviations

BDTC	British Dependent Territories Citizen
BOC	British Overseas Citizen
BPP	British Protected Persons
CA	Court of Appeal
CUKC	Citizens of the UK and Commonwealth
EC	European Community
EU	European Union
HL	House of Lords
IAT	Immigration Appeal Tribunal
IND	Immigration and Nationality Department
Para	Paragraph
S of S	Secretary of State (for the Home Department unless context indicates otherwise)

References to paragraph numbers without more are references to the Immigration Rules HC 395.

Where a case name commences 'R v Secretary of State for the Home Department, ex parte', this has been abbreviated to 'ex p' throughout.

Table of Cases

A (A minor) (Wardship), Re [1991] Imm AR 606; [1992] Fam Law 151; [1992] 1 FLR 427 459
Abassi (Saleem v Secretary of State for the Home Department [1992] Imm AR 349, CA 505
Ach-Charki v ECO Rabat [1991] Imm AR 162 460
Adaah v Secretary of State for the Home Department [1993] Imm AR 197 ... 462
Adejumoke v Secretary of State for the Home department [1993] Imm AR 265 119
Adesina v Secretary of State for the Home Department [1988] Imm AR 442 ... 20
Afful v Secretary of State for the Home Department [1983] Imm AR 236 492
Afful v Secretary of State [1986] Imm AR 230 268
Ahmad v Secretary of State for the Home Department [1990] Imm AR 61 ... 342, 343
Ahmed (Sagir) (8260) 212
Ahmed (Mahtab) v Secretary of State for the Home Department [1992] Imm AR 538, CA 505
Ahmed v ECO Islamabad [1977] Imm AR 25 451
Akbar (8670) 209
Akdag v Secretary of State for the Home Department [1993] Imm AR 172, CA 341
Akhtar (Nasreen) (2166) 206
Akhtar v Governor of Pentonville Prison [1993] Imm AR 424 512
Akhtar (Jan) v ECO, Islamabad [1977] Imm AR 107 441
Akhtar (Tahzeem) v IAT [1991] Imm AR 326; (1990) The Times, 4 December, CA 250
Alam (Mahzar) v ECO Lahore [1973] Imm AR 79 222
Al-Ahbari v Secretary of State for the Home Department [1988] Imm AR 567, CA 436
Alassini (Zibrilla) v Secretary of State [1991] Imm AR 367 486
Al-Hasani (Falah) (4670) 168
Al-Hasani v Secretary of State for the Home Department [1986] Imm AR 363 174
Ali (Ifzal) v Secretary of State [1994] Imm AR 69 502
Al-Sabah (Sheikh Mohammed Nasser) v IAT, sub nom R v Secretary of State for the Home Department, ex p Al-Sabah [1992] Imm AR 223; [1992] COD 212; (1992) The Times, 27 January 269, 340
Alsawaf v Secretary of State for the Home Department [1988] Imm AR 410 .. 348

xvii

TABLE OF CASES

Ameyaw (Elvis) v Secretary of State for the Home Department [1992] Imm AR 206, CA 344
Amin v ECO, Bombay see R v ECO, Bombay, ex p Amin
Amoah v Secretary of State for the Home Department [1987] Imm AR 236 ... 257
Anand v Secretary of State for the Home Department [1978] Imm AR 36 277
Ancharaz v Immigration Officer, London (Heathrow) Airport [1976] Imm AR 49 449
Andronicou v Chief Immigration Officer, London (Heathrow) Airport [1974] Imm AR 87 252
Andereh (91331) 433
Anisminic Ltd v Foreign Compensation Commission [1969] 2 AC 147; [1967] 2 WLR 163; [1969] 1 All ER 208, HL revsg [1968] 2 QB 862 ...... 44, 45, 486
Arshad v Immigration Officer, London (Heathrow) Airport [1977] Imm AR 19 253
Asante v Secretary of State for the Home Department [1991] Imm AR 78 342
Asfaw (5339) 454
Ashnan v British Coal [1990] 2 WLR 1437 380
Ashrafi v IAT [1989] Imm AR 234, CA 414
Ashraf (Mohammed v IAT [1988] Imm AR 101, CA 457
Asiedu v Secretary of State for the Home Department [1988] Imm AR 186 ... 483
Assam Railways & Trading Co Ltd v IRC [1945] AC 445 7
Associated Provincial Picture Houses Ltd v Wednesbury Corporation [1948] 1 KB 223; [1947] 2 All ER 680; (1948) 177 LT 641, CA 55, 466, 482, 486, 488, 489, 508
Attorney-General v Ryan [1980] AC 718; [1980] 2 WLR 143; (1979) 123 SJ 621, PC 44
Awosika v Secretary of State [1989] Imm AR 35 99
Awuku (4220) 228
Ayettey v Secretary of State for the Home Department [1972] Imm AR 261 .. 103
Azid (Abdul) v ECO Dhaka [1991] Imm AR 578 461
Badmus v Secretary of State for the Home Department [1994] Imm AR 137 .. 374
Baig (1886) 87
Baijal v Secretary of State for the Home Department [1976] Imm AR 34 120
Balasingham, Re (1987) The Times, 22 July 497
Baldachino v Secretary of State for the Home Department [1972] Imm AR 14 . 89
Bamgbose, Re [1990] Imm AR 135; [1990] COD 97; (1989) The Independent, 16 November, CA 17, 66
Bari v IAT [1987] Imm AR 13, CA 120, 121
Bashir v Immigration Officer, Dover [1976] Imm AR 96 71
Bashirotyo v IAT [1990] Imm AR 461 406
Baydur (5442) 146, 148
Begum (Ihayat) v Visa Officer, Islamabad [1978] Imm AR 174 206
Begum (Kalsoom) v Visa Officer, Islamabad [1988] Imm AR 325 154
Begum (Nazir) v ECO, Islamabad [1976] Imm AR 31 206
Behrooz v Secretary of State [1991] Imm AR 82 64
Berthiaume v Dastons [1930] AC 79 206
Bhagat v Secretary of State [1972] Imm AR 189 ...... 103, 440
Bhatia v IAT [1985] Imm AR 50, CA 213
Bi (Alam) v IAT [1979–80] Imm AR 146 467
Bibi (Taj) v ECO Islamabad [1977] Imm AR 25 451
Bibi (Hasan) v ECO Bombay [1976] Imm AR 28 240
Bila v Secretary of State for the Home Department [1994] Imm AR 130 361
Blair (1797) 87

TABLE OF CASES

BOC Ltd v Ministry of Technology [1971] AC 610; [1970] 3 WLR 488; [1970] 3
All ER 165, HL...487
Boehm-Bradley v Visa Officer, Washington [1986] Imm AR 305.............185
Bonzeid v Secretary of State for the Home Department [1991] Imm AR 204,
CA 348, 349
Britto v Secretary of State for the Home Department [1984] Imm AR 93......14
Bugdaycay v Secretary of State for the Home Department [1987] AC 514; [1987]
Imm AR 250; [1987] 2 WLR 606, HL 19, 20, 337, 347, 399, 474, 482
Butt v Secretary of State [1979–80] Imm AR 82 268
C (an infant) v ECO Hong Kong [1976] Imm AR 165......................159
Caballero (4605) 228
CCSU v Minister for the Civil Service [1985] AC 274; [1984] 1 WLR 1174;
[1984] 3 All ER 935 ....45, 486, 489, 490, 493
Celik (Ali) v Secretary of State for the Home Department [1991] Imm AR 8,
CA..490
Chahal v Secretary of State for the Home Department [1994] Imm AR 107...366
Chanda v ECO, Bombay [1978] Imm AR 40 ....53, 240, 241
Cheema (M A) v IAT [1982] Imm AR 46, CA 444
Choong (6162)..243
Choudury (Mohammed) v IAT [1990] Imm AR 211, CA 210
Chief Constable of the North Wales Police v Evans [1982] 3 All ER 141; [1982]
1 WLR 1155; (1982) 126 SJ 549.......................................481
Conteh v Secretary of State for the Home Department [1992] Imm AR 594,
CA..350
Corinaldesi (2957)..305
Covent Garden Community Association v GLC [1981] JPL 183.............495
Dagdalen v Secretary of State for the Home Department [1988] Imm AR 425.435
Dagdar (2101) 99
Darch v Weight [1984] 1 WLR 659; [1984] 2 All ER 245; (1984) 128 SJ 315...523
De Clive Lowe (Kenneth) v Immigration Officer, Heathrow [1992] Imm AR
91 ....120, 121
Deen v Secretary of State for the Home Department [1987] Imm AR 543 257,
455
Dhillon v Secretary of State for the Home Department [1987] Imm AR 222;
(1988) 86 Cr App R 14, CA 403
Dial v Secretary of State for the Home Department [1987] Imm AR 36 77
Din (Mohammed) v ECO, Karachi [1978] Imm AR 56 87
Ding (3304) 256
Dungarwalla v Secretary of State for the Home Department [1989] Imm AR
476...79
Durojaiye v Secretary of State for the Home Department [1991] Imm AR 307,
CA 21, 99
Dursun v Secretary of State for the Home Department [1993] Imm AR 189,
CA..349
ECO, Antananviro v Popat (Hansa) [1990] Imm AR 598 465
ECO, Bombay v Joshi [1975] Imm AR 1.................................71
ECO, Bombay v Patel (Khalid) [1991] Imm AR 553 470
ECO, Bombay v Patel (Vali) [1991] Imm AR 147 ....458, 464
ECO, Dhaka v Bibi (Rayful) [1993] Imm AR 63 448
ECO, Bombay v Sacha [1973] Imm AR 5...........................243, 248
ECO, Bombay v Seedat [1975] Imm AR 121.............................241
ECO, Canberra v Ward [1975] Imm AR 129.............................183
ECO, Colombo v Hanks [1976] Imm AR 74..............................87

TABLE OF CASES

ECO Hong Kong v Lai [1974] Imm AR 98............................84, 86
ECO, Islamabad v Ahmed (Bashir) [1991] Imm AR 130...................457
ECO, Islamabad v Ishfaq (Mohammed) [1992] Imm AR 289............441, 450
ECO, Islamabad v Hussain (Mohamed) [1991] Imm AR 476............207, 461
ECO, Islamabad v Khan (Ajaib) [1993] Imm AR 68.......................454
ECO, Islamabad v Thakurdas [1990] Imm AR 288........................450
ECO, Karachi v Ahmed [1989] Imm AR 254..........................98, 458
ECO, Kingston v Holmes [1975] Imm AR 20.............................227
ECO, Kingston v Martin [1978] Imm AR 100............................226
ECO, Lagos v Samanda [1975] Imm AR 16...............................85
ECO, Lagos v Sobanjo [1978] Imm AR 22..............................100
ECO, Manila v Magalso [1993] Imm AR 293.............................85
ECO, New Delhi v Bhambra [1973] Imm AR 14.......................98, 464
ECO, New Delhi v Kaur (Parkas) [1979-80] Imm AR 114.................241
ECO, New Delhi v Kumar [1978] Imm AR 185............................87
ECO, New Delhi v Malham [1978] Imm AR 209..........................241
ECO, New Delhi v Sibal [1973] Imm AR 50............................243
ECO, New Delhi v Singh (Balbir) [1977] Imm AR 109..................234
ECO, Nicosia v Georgiou [1976] Imm AR 151...........................83
ECO, Port Louis v Grenade [1978] Imm AR 143........................240
ECO, Rome v Rahman (Hussein) [1991] Imm AR 102.....................170
Edusi (6598)...250
Edwards v Bairstow [1956] AC 14; [1955] 3 WLR 410; [1955] 3 All ER 48,
 HL..466, 483
Ejaz (Mohammed) v Secretary of State for the Home Department (21 December
 1978, unreported)..457
Elu v Secretary of State for the Home Department [1989] Imm AR 568.......76
Emmanuel v Secretary of State for the Home Department [1972] Imm AR 69.226
Eugene v ECO, Bridgetown, Barbados [1975] Imm AR 111.................225
Eusebio (4739)...250
Fairmonnt Investments Ltd v Secretary of State for the Environment [1976] 1
 WLR 1255; [1976] 2 All ER 865; (1976) 120 SJ 801, HL................492
Fanons v Secretary of State for the Home Department [1993] Imm AR 200...174
Farinha, Re [1992] Imm AR 174; [1992] COD 202; [1992] Crim LR 438, DC .263
Fawehinmi v Secretary of State for the Home Department [1991] Imm AR 1;
 [1990] COD 388, CA..66
Foon v Secretary of State for the Home Department [1983] Imm AR 29......93
Francis v Secretary of State for the Home Department [1972] Imm AR 162...441
Friends of the Earth Ltd, Re [1988] JPL 93, CA......................498
Gaima v Secretary of State for the Home Department [1989] Imm AR 205 ...484
Ganu (Aviva) v Secretary of State [1993] Imm AR 20...................95
Ghassemiah and Mirza v Home Office [1989] Imm AR 42, CA...............78
Ghosh v ECO, Calcutta [1976] Imm AR 60.............................102
Giangregorio v Home Secretary [1983] Imm AR 104; [1983] 3 CMLR 472 ...295,
 308
Gillegao (Grenda) [1989] Imm AR 174................................463
Goffar v ECO, Dacca; Dey v ECO, Dacca [1975] Imm AR 142..........98, 101
Goodison v Secretary of State for the Home Department [1979-80] Imm AR
 122...71
Grant v Borg [1982] 1 WLR 638; [1982] 2 All ER 257; (1982) 126 SJ 311, HL.518,
 519
Grazales (Jorge) v Secretary of State for the Home Department [1990] Imm AR
 505, CA..496, 497

Guinaban (3475)...149
Gunatilake v ECO, Colombo [1975] Imm AR 23..........................119
Gupta v Secretary of State for the Home Department [1979–80] Imm AR 52..266
Gyeabour (Domfeh) [1989] Imm AR 94 ....264, 493
H, Re [1990] The Guardian, 17 May 507
Haji v Secretary of State for the Home Department [1978] Imm AR 26 170
Halil v Davidson [1979–80] Imm AR 164...................................76
Hamid (Abdul) v ECO, Dhaka [1986] Imm AR 469 154
Hamid (Sultan) v Secretary of State for the Home Department [1993] Imm AR
  216, CA 19
Hamilton v ECO, Kingston, Jamaica [1974] Imm AR 43 85
Hanit v Secretary of State for the Home Department [1985] Imm AR 57 267
HK (An infant), Re [1967] 2 QB 617; [1967] 2 WLR 962; 111 SJ 296 .....64, 490
Hope (832)..146, 148
Hossain v Immigration Officer, Heathrow [1990] Imm AR 520...........85, 253
Hoth v Secretary of State for the Home Department [1985] Imm AR 20......295
HTV Ltd v Price Commission [1976] ICR 170; 120 SJ 298, CA 491
Huda v ECO, Dacca [1976] Imm AR 109 88
Hussein (Mohammed) v IAT and Secretary of State for the Home Department
  [1991] Imm AR 413, CA 264, 483, 493
Hussain v Secretary of State for the Home Department [1972] Imm AR 264 ..442
Hussain v Secretary of State for the Home Department [1993] Imm AR 353 ..381
Hussain (Basharat) v Visa Officer, Islamabad [1991] Imm AR 182...........206
Hussain (Shabir) v ECO, Islamabad [1991] Imm AR 483 460
Hussein v Secretary of State for the Home Department [1975] Imm AR 69 11
Hussein (Abid) v ECO Islamabad [1989] Imm AR 46...................88, 248
Hussein (Aliya) v Hussain (Shahid) [1983] Fam 1; [1982] 3 WLR 679; [1982]
  3 All ER 369 204
Hyrapiet (2232)..95
IAT v Chelliah [1985] Imm AR 192; (1986) 83 LS Gaz, CA..................14
Ibrahim v Visa Officer, Islamabad [1978] Imm AR 18.....................225
Immigration Officer, Birmingham v Sadiq (Mohammed) [1978] Imm AR 115..88,
  393
Immigration Officer, Heathrow v Ekinci [1989] Imm AR 346 450
Immigration Officer, Heathrow v Mirani (Neil) [1990] Imm AR 132 455
Immigration Officer, Heathrow v Salmak [1991] Imm AR 191 253
Immigration Officer, Heathrow v Yuvraj Kapoor [1991] Imm AR 357 .....75, 92
Immigration Officer, London (Heathrow) Airport v Schonenburger [1975] Imm
  AR 7 84
Immigration Officer, Ramsgate v Cooray [1974] Imm AR 38................440
Iqbal v ECO, Islamabad [1992] Imm AR 255 453
Irawo-Ogan v Secretary of State for the Home Department [1992] Imm AR 337,
  CA 504, 505
IRC v Lysaght [1928] AC 234 14
IRC v National Federation of Self-employed and Small Businesses Ltd [1982]
  AC 617; [1981] 2 WLR 722; [1982] 2 All ER 93, HL 445, 503, 507
Islam v ECO, Dacca [1974] Imm AR 83 102
Islam v Secretary of State for the Home Department [1975] Imm AR 106 404
Issa (4011) 99
Jabeen (4925)..212
Jamhadas (6597)...171, 174
Jan (Said Mar) v Secretary of State for the Home Department (1983) 133 New
  LJ 44...242

TABLE OF CASES

Jones v Chief Adjudication Officer [1990] IRLR 533; (1990) *The Independent*,
  16 August 302, 310
Jordan v Secretary of State for the Home Department [1972] Imm AR 201 ... 266
Juma v Secretary of State for the Home Department [1974] Imm AR 96 105
Kaefer and Proacci v France (C-100/89 and C-101/89) (1991) *The Times*, 25
  February 293, 294
Kanda v Government of Malaya [1962] AC 322; [1962] 2 WLR 1153, CA 492
Kandiya v IAT [1990] Imm AR 377; (1990) *The Times*, 24 March, CA 210
Karantoni v Secretary of State [1987] Imm AR 518, CA 278
Karim (Mohammed) v Visa Officer, Islamabad [1986] Imm AR 224 464
Kassam v Secretary of State for the Home Department [1976] Imm AR 20 ... 457,
  458
Kasuji (5956) 212
Kaur (Amar) (2517) 241
Kaya (Tahir) v Secretary of State [1992] Imm AR 591, CA 68
Kelada (Sehan) v Secretary of State [1991] Imm AR 400 85
Kelzani v Secretary of State for the Home Department [1978] Imm AR 193 ... 422
Kerali (Kemal) v Secretary of State [1991] Imm AR 199 .... 349, 368
Keshwani v Secretary of State for the Home Department [1975] Imm AR 38 ... 11
Kenng v Secretary of State for the Home Department [1992] Imm AR 201,
  CA 17
Khan v Secretary of State for the Home Department [1977] 3 All ER 538 19
Khan (Asif) v IAT [1984] Imm AR 68; [1984] 1 WLR 1337; [1985] 1 All ER 40,
  CA 493
Khan (Fauzia Wamar Din Bagga) v Secretary of State [1987] Imm AR 173,
  CA 448, 498, 501
Khan (Sett) v ECO, Karachi [1975] Imm AR 64 101
Khan (Tosir) v ECO, Dacca [1974] Imm AR 55 432
Khanom v ECO, Dacca [1979-80] Imm AR 182 206
Kongar (6601) 148
Kpoma v Secretary of State for the Home Department [1973] Imm AR 25 105
Kroohs v Secretary of State for the Home Department [1978] Imm AR 15 424
Kuku v Secretary of State for the Home Department [1990] Imm AR 27 78
Kus v Landeshauptstadt Wiesbaden (C-237/91) 16 December 1992, ECJ 322
Labiche v Secretary of State for the Home Department [1991] Imm AR 263;
  [1991] COD 302; (1991) *The Times*, 24 January, CA 437
Ladd v Marshall [1954] 3 All ER 745; [1954] 1 WLR 1489; 98 SJ 870, CA 509
Lake (3393) 30
Lal (Sushma) v Secretary of State for the Home Department [1992] Imm AR
  303, CA 502
Lamptey v Owen [1982] Crim LR 42; (1981) 125 SJ 725, DC 518
Latiff v Secretary of State for the Home Department [1972] Imm AR 76 432
Layne v Secretary of State for the Home Department [1987] Imm AR 243 295
Leahy (7981) 160
Lee v Secretary of State for the Home Department [1975] Imm AR 75 105
Levene v IRC [1928] AC 217; [1928] All ER Rep 746 14
Liberto v Immigration Officer, London (Heathrow) Airport [1975] Imm AR
  61 251
Liew (Vun) v Secretary of State [1989] Imm AR 62 494
Lokko v Secretary of State for the Home Department [1990] Imm AR 111 ... 441,
  449
Lubberseh v Secretary of State for the Home Department [1984] Imm AR 56;
  [1984] 3 CMLR 77 .... 308, 314

TABLE OF CASES

Lubetkin v Secretary of State [1979–80] Imm AR 162 77
Lui v Secretary of State for the Home Department [1986] Imm AR 287 14
M v Home Office and Baker [1993] WLR 433; [1993] 3 All ER 537; (1993) The Times, 28 July, HL 501
Mahendrah v Secretary of State for the Home Department [1988] Imm AR 492 106
Makinde v Secretary of State for the Home Department [1991] Imm AR 469 .420
Manickavasager v Metropolitan Police Commissioner [1987] Crim LR 50, DC 519
Marler (E T) Ltd v Robertson [1974] ICR 72 380
Martin v Secretary of State for the Home Department [1972] Imm AR 71 226
Martin v Secretary of State for the Home Department [1993] Imm AR 161 ...270
Marwah (7422) 145, 160
Masood (Sumeina) v IAT [1992] Imm AR 69, CA......................209, 210
Masud (Naved) v IAT [1992] Imm AR 129, CA............................76
Mauji v Secretary of State for the Home Department [1986] Imm AR 290 437
Maybasan (Serif), Re [1991] Imm AR 89 ....445, 510
Meharbath (Mohd) v ECO, Islamabad [1989] Imm AR 57 213
Mehmet v Secretary of State for the Home Department [1977] Imm AR 68 ...266
Mehta (B K D) v IAT [1979–80] Imm AR 16 468
Memi v Secretary of State for the Home Department [1976] Imm AR 129 154
Mendis (Viraj) v IAT and Secretary of State [1989] Imm AR 6; (1989) The Times, 20 January, CA 338, 342
Mendoza v Secretary of State for the Home Department [1992] Imm AR 122 .136
Miah (Fozlu) v Secretary of State for the Home Department [1991] Imm AR 581, CA 463, 505
Miah (Hassan) v Secretary of State for the Home Department [1991] Imm AR 437, CA 224
Miah (Mohammed Moyha) v Secretary of State for the Home Department [1992] Imm AR 106, CA...264, 483
Miah (Rahim) v Secretary of State [1989] 1 WLR 806......................22
Miller v Lenton (1981) Cr App R(S) 171 270
Minton v Secretary of State for the Home Department [1990] Imm AR 199; [1990] COD 101, CA 19
Mobley (5368) 154
Mohammed v Knowll [1968] 2 All ER 563 203
Mohammed Ach-Ccharki v ECO, Rabat [1991] Imm AR 162 206
Mokuolo v Secretary of State for the Home Department [1989] Imm AR 51; (1988) The Times, 5 October, CA 18, 66, 485
Moussavi v Secretary of State for the Home Department [1986] Imm AR 39 ..77, 414, 460
Munasinghe v Secretary of State for the Home Department [1975] Imm AR 79...121
Mundowa v Secretary of State [1992] Imm AR 80; [1992] 3 All ER 606; [1992] COD 127, CA 421
Murgai v ECO, New Delhi [1975] Imm AR 86 103
Mushtaq (9343)...212
Musisi (Samuel) v Secretary of State for the Home Department [1992] Imm AR 520...341
Mustafa v Secretary of State for the Home Department [1979–80] Imm AR 32 ....278, 422
Mustafaraj v Secretary of State for the Home Department [1994] Imm AR 78...379

xxiv TABLE OF CASES

Mustun v Secretary of State for the Home Department [1972] Imm AR 97 ...250
Mutengu v Secretary of State [1992] Imm AR 419, CA.....................505
Muthulakshmi v Secretary of State [1972] Imm AR 23 441
Narin (Unal) v Secretary of State [1990] Imm AR 403; [1990] 2 CMLR 233;
 [1990] COD 417, CA 321
Needham v ECO, Kingston, Jamaica [1973] Imm AR 75 227
Nijssen v Immigration Officer, London (Heathrow) Airport [1978] Imm AR
 226..304
Nisa v Secretary of State [1979–80] Imm AR 20............................91
Nkiti v Immigration Officer, Gatwick [1989] Imm AR 585, CA 488, 494
NSH v Secretary of State, ex p [1988] Imm AR 389.........................499
Nottinghamshire CC v Secretary of State for the Environment [1986] AC 240;
 [1986] 2 WLR 1; [1986] 1 All ER 199, HL.............................486
O v Immigration Officer, Heathrow [1992] Imm AR 584 464
Oberoi v Secretary of State [1979–80] Imm AR 175.........................452
Obeyesekere v Secretary of State [1976] Imm AR 16........................85
Ofuajoku v Secretary of State [1991] Imm AR 68..........78, 106, 249, 256, 461
Ogunde v Secretary of State [1990] Imm AR 257 443
Oke (8557)...98
Oladehinde v Secretary of State [1990] 3 All ER 393; [1991] 1 AC 254; [1990]
 3 WLR 797, HL...262, 404, 420, 487
Olusanya (Olugbenga), Re [1988] Imm AR 117, DC.....................88, 510
Olashehinde v Secretary of State [1992] Imm AR 443 506
Oloniluyi v Secretary of State [1989] Imm AR 135.........................494
Oral (Mehmet) v Secretary of State [1991] Imm AR 208; (1990) The Times, 28
 November, CA 503
O'Reilly v Mackman [1983] 2 AC 237; [1982] 3 WLR 1096; [1982] 3 All ER
 1124, HL 490
Otani (3224)..168
Owusu v Secretary of State [1976] Imm AR 101......................105, 256
Owusu-Sekyere's Application, Re [1987] Imm AR 425, CA 267
Ozter v Secretary of State [1978] Imm AR 137 278
Padmore v Secretary of State [1972] Imm AR 1 458
Paet v Secretary of State [1979–80] Imm AR 185......................257, 455
Parekh v Secretary of State [1976] Imm AR 84..........................168
Parsayiah v Visa Officer, Karachi [1986] Imm AR 155 435
Parvez v Immigration Officer, London (Heathrow) Airport [1979–80] Imm AR
 84..248
Patal (Chhagahbhai) v Visa Officer, Bombay [1991] Imm AR 97 450
Patal (Jivahlal) (4895) 169
Patel v ECO, Bombay [1973] Imm AR 30 88
Patel v ECO, Bombay [1991] Imm AR 273 85
Patel v ECO, Nairobi [1987] Imm AR 116...............................168
Patel v IAT [1983] Imm AR 76, CA............................100, 101, 106
Patel v Secretary of State [1986] Imm AR 457 268
Patel (Aiyub) v ECO, Bombay [1991] Imm AR 273.......................450
Patel (Dawood) v Secretary of State for the Home Department [1990] Imm
 AR 478 ....156, 459, 494
Patel (Girishkumar) v Secretary of State for the Home Department [1989]
 Imm AR 246 211
Patel (M R) v ECO, Bombay [1978] Imm AR 154 87
Pearlman v Keepers and Governor of Harrow School [1979] QB 56; [1978] 3
 WLR 736; [1979] 1 All ER 365 45

TABLE OF CASES

Pearson v IAT [1978] Imm AR 212 .... 135, 432
Pecastaing v Belgium State (No 98/79) [1980] ECR 891; [1980] 3 CMLR 685 .. 315
Pepper v Hart [1992] 3 WLR 1032; [1993] AC 593; [1993] 1 All ER 42, HL 7
Perera v Immigration Officer, London (Heathrow) Airport [1979-80] Imm AR
  58 396
Petrovski v Secretary of State [1993] Imm AR 134 343
Pickstone v Freemans plc [1989] AC 66; [1988] 3 CMLR 221, HL 7
Pinnock v ECO, Kingston, Jamaice [1974] Imm AR 22 225
Pinnock (M E) v ECO, Kingston, Jamaica [1977] Imm AR 4 227
Poh, Re [1983] 1 WLR 2; [1983] 1 All ER 287; 127 SJ 16, HL 505
Pondel (Giri) v Secretary of State [1991] Imm AR 567 455
Pour (1479) 105
Practice Direction [1979] 2 All ER 880 501
Practice Note (QBD) (Judicial Review: Affidavit in Reply) [1989] 1 WLR 358;
  [1989] 1 All ER 1024; (1989) 153 JP 363 .... 506, 508
Prajpati v IAT [1982] Imm AR 56, CA 74, 75
Puri v Secretary of State [1972] Imm AR 21 100
Purwal v ECO, New Delhi [1977] Imm AR 98 432
Puttick v Secretary of State [1985] Imm AR 118 .... 251, 304
Quereshi v Immigration Officer, London [1978] Imm AR 176 250
R v An adjudicator, ex p Secretary of State [1989] Imm AR 423 ..... 55, 442, 453
R v An adjudicator, ex p Umeloh (Chuks) [1991] Imm AR 602 .... 401, 424
R v An adjudicator (Care), ex p Secretary of State [1989] Imm AR 423 483
R v Antypas (1972) 57 Cr App R 207; [1973] Crim LR 130, CA 269
R v Ariquat (1987) Cr App R(S) 83 270
R v Barnet LBC, ex p Shah [1983] 2 AC 309; [1983] 2 WLR 16; [1983] 1 All ER
  226, HL 14
R v Bello (1978) 67 Cr App Rep 288; [1978] Crim LR 551, CA 518
R v Caird (1970) 54 Cr App R 499; [1970] Crim LR 656; 114 SJ 652 289
R v Chief Constable of Merseyside Police, ex p Calveley [1986] 2 WLR 144;
  [1986] QB 424; [1986] 1 All ER 257 495
R v Chief Immigration Officer, Bradford Airport, ex p Hussain (Ashiq) [1989]
  3 All ER 1601; [1970] 1 WLR 9; 113 SJ 836 98
R v Chief Immigration Officer, Gatwick Airport, ex p Kharrazzi [1980] 1 WLR
  1396; [1980] 3 All ER 373; (1980) 124 SJ 629, CA 99, 483, 486, 497
R v Chief Immigration Officer, London (Heathrow) Airport, ex p Bibi (Salamat)
  [1976] 3 All ER 843; [1976] 1 WLR 979; 120 SJ 405, CA 52, 53, 474
R v Chief Immigration Officer, Manchester Airport, ex p Begum (Insah) [1973] 1
  All ER 594; [1973]
  1 WLR 141; (1972) 116 SJ 884, CA 396, 436
R v Civil Service Appeal Board, ex p Cunningham, [1991] 4 All ER 310; [1992]
  ICR 817; [1991] IRLR 297, CA 490
R v Clarke (Ediakpo) [1985] AC 1037; [1985] 3 WLR 113; [1985] 2 All ER 777,
  HL 524, 525
R v Compassi (1987) 9 Cr App R(S) 270 269
R v Cornwall CC, ex p Huntingdon [1992] 3 All ER 566; [1992] COD 223;
  (1992) 142 New LJ 348, DC 45
R v Criminal Injuries Compensation Board, ex p Cummins (1992) *The Times*, 21
  January; [1992] PIQR 281; [1992] COD 297 .... 469, 490
R v Crown Court at Knightsbridge, ex p International Sporting Club (London)
  Ltd [1982] QB 304; [1987] 3 WLR 640; [1981] 3 All ER 417 487
R v Dairy Produce Quotas Tribunal, ex p Caswell [1990] 2 AC 738; [1990] 2
  WLR 1320; [1990] 2 All ER 434, HL 498, 499

TABLE OF CASES

R v Department of Employment, *ex p* Allen [1991] Imm AR 336........135, 482
R v Diggines, *ex p* Rahmani [1986] AC 475; [1986] 2 WLR 530; [1986] 1 All E 921, HL 450
R v ECO Bombay, *ex p* Amin [1983] 2 AC 818; [1983] 3 WLR 258; [1983] 2 All ER 864, HL...............................74, 192, 194, 481, 482
R v Foreign and Commonwealth Office, *ex p* Everett [1989] 1 All ER 655; [1989] 2 WLR 224 ....65, 482
R v Governor of Ashford Remand Centre, *ex p* Bonzagon [1983] Imm AR 69; (1983) 127 SJ 596, CA...18
R v Governor of Brixton Prison, *ex p* Soblen [1963] 2 QB 243 263
R v Governor of Haslar Prison, *ex p* Egbe (1991) *The Times*, 4 June, CA.....403
R v Governor of Pentonville Prison, *ex p* Herbage (No 2) [1987] QB 872; [1986] 3 WLR 504;
[1986] 3 All ER 209 507
R v Hallstrom, *ex p* Waldron [1986] 1 QB 824; [1985] 3 WLR 1090; [1985] 3 All ER 775, CA...496
R v Hampstead and St Pancras Rent Tribunal, *ex p* Goodman [1951] 1 All ER 170; [1951] 1 KB 541; [1951] 1 TLR 37 448
R v Hillingdon London BC, *ex p* Puklhoffer [1986] AC 484; [1986] 2 WLR 259; [1986] 1 All ER 467, HL..483
R v IAT, *ex p* Ahluwalia [1979–80] Imm AR 1........................257, 437
R v IAT, *ex p* Akhtar [1991] Imm AR 326; (1990) *The Times*, 4 December, CA..486
R v IAT, *ex p* Alexander [1982] 1 WLR 1076; (1982) 126 SJ 512; [1982] 2 All ER 766; [1982] Imm AR 50, HL 53
R v IAT, *ex p* Alghali [1984] Imm AR 106 401
R v IAT, *ex p* Ali [1990] Imm AR 531; [1991] COD 37 471
R v IAT, *ex p* Ali (Faifor) [1990] Imm AR 531; [1991] COD 37..........74, 224
R v IAT, *ex p* Ali (Khatoon) [1979–80] Imm AR 195 71
R v IAT, *ex p* Ali (Tohur) [1988] Imm AR 237, (1988) 18 Fam Law 289, CA.233, 276, 460
R v IAT, *ex p* Al-Sabah [1992] Imm AR 223; [1992] COD 212; (1992) *The Times*, 27 January, CA...272
R v IAT, *ex p* Alsairaf [1988] Imm AR 410; (1987) *The Times*, 29 August, DC 338
R v IAT, *ex p* Amin [1993] Imm AR 367................................508
R v IAT, *ex p* Amirbeaggi (1982) *The Times*, 25 May 457
R v IAT, *ex p* Antonissen [1992] Imm AR 196....................295, 304, 305
R v IAT, *ex p* Aradi [1987] Imm AR 359................................315
R v IAT, *ex p* Armstrong [1977] Imm AR 80 468
R v IAT, *ex p* A-V (1989) *The Times*, 22 August..........................268
R v IAT, *ex p* B [1989] Imm AR 166; [19899] COD 270, DC 360
R v IAT, *ex p* Bastiampillai [1983] 2 All ER 844; [1983] Imm AR 1 ..76, 241, 242
R v IAT, *ex p* Begum (Mahshoora) [1986] Imm AR 385 ....53, 55, 483
R v IAT, *ex p* Begum (Rehana) [1993] Imm AR 1 212
R v IAT, *ex p* Begum (Suily) [1990] Imm AR 226; [1990] COD 170..........250
R v IAT, *ex p* Bernstein [1987] Imm AR 182; [1988] *The Times*, 11 June, CA .135
R v IAT, *ex p* Bhanji [1977] Imm AR 89 76
R v IAT, *ex p* Bhatia [1985] Imm AR 50 207
R v IAT, *ex p* Bi (Rashida) [1990] Imm AR 348..........................465
R v IAT, *ex p* Bibi [1989] Imm AR 1 ....203, 206

TABLE OF CASES   xxvii

R v IAT, ex p Bibi (Rashida) [1988] Imm AR 290; (1988) The Times, 22 February, CA 225
R v IAT, ex p Bouchtaoni [1992] Imm AR 433 466
R v IAT, ex p Cheema [1982] Imm AR 124; (1983) 133 New LJ 1100, CA 267
R v IAT, ex p Chiew [1981] Imm AR 102; (1981) 125 SJ 463 183
R v IAT, ex p Chundawadra [1988] Imm AR 161, CA 474
R v IAT, ex p Chundawadra (Surendra Jessa) [1987] Imm AR 227 ...... 270, 271, 273, 474
R v IAT, ex p Coomasaru [1983] 1 WLR 14; [1983] 1 All ER 208; [1982] Imm AR 77, CA 18, 71
R v IAT, ex p Desai [1987] Imm AR 18 460
R v IAT, ex p De Sousa [1977] Imm AR 6 11
R v IAT, ex p Dukobu [1990] Imm AR 390 438
R v IAT, ex p El Hassanin [1986] 1 WLR 1448, CA 420
R v IAT, ex p Florent [1985] Imm AR 141, CA 269
R v IAT, ex p Fuller [1993] Imm AR 177 420
R v IAT, ex p Gethva (Mahjula) [1990] Imm AR 450 213
R v IAT, ex p Gondalia [1991] Imm AR 519 .... 210, 461
R v IAT, ex p Hassanin [1986] Imm AR 502; [1986] 1 WLR 1448; [1987] 1 All ER 74, CA 456
R v IAT, ex p Hirani (2 July 1981, unreported, DC) 171
R v IAT, ex p Hoque and Singh [1988] Imm AR 216; [1988] 2 FLR 542; [1989] Fam Law 71, CA 207, 209, 218, 459
R v IAT, ex p Hubbard [1985] Imm AR 110 .... 435, 441, 460
R v IAT, ex p Hussain [1999] Imm AR 382 467
R v IAT, ex p Ibrahim [1989] Imm AR 111; [1989] COD 272, CA 276
R v IAT, ex p Idiaro [1991] Imm AR 546 .... 98, 99
R v IAT, ex p Ihovejas [1983] Imm AR 204 142
R v IAT, ex p Iqbal [1993] Imm AR 270; [1993] COD 226; (1992) The Times, 24 December 210, 454
R v IAT, ex p Islam [1992] Imm AR 452 508
R v IAT, ex p Jonah [1985] Imm AR 7 341
R v IAT, ex p Jones (Ross Wayne) [1986] Imm AR 496; [1988] 1 WLR 477; [1982] 2 All ER 65, CA 451
R v IAT, ex p Joseph [1977] Imm AR 70; (1977) 121 SJ 203 169
R v IAT, ex p Joseph [1988] Imm AR 329 243
R v IAT, ex p Kandiah (Rasiah) [1991] Imm AR 431; [1991] COD 472 454
R v IAT, ex p Kaur [1991] Imm AR 107 .... 209, 210
R v IAT, ex p Khan (Ahmad) [1982] Imm AR 134 .... 466, 469, 490
R v IAT, ex p Khan (Perween) [1972] 3 All ER 297; [1972] 1 WLR 1058; 116 SJ 600 100
R v IAT, ex p Khan (S G H) [1975] Imm AR 26 .... 459, 466
R v IAT, ex p Khatab (Mohammed) [1989] Imm AR 313 209
R v IAT, ex p Kirimetiyane (1982) The Times, 17 June 466
R v IAT, ex p Kotecha [1982] Imm AR 88; [1983] 1 WLR 487; [1983] 2 All ER 289, CA 456
R v IAT, ex p Kumar [1986] Imm AR 446; [1987] 1 FLR 444; (1987) 17 Fam Law 197, CA 207, 209, 211
R v IAT, ex p Kwok on Tong [1981] Imm AR 214 170
R v IAT, ex p Lakhani [1988] Imm AR 474 397
R v IAT, ex p Lila [1978] Imm AR 50; (1977) The Times, 29 October 449, 455
R v IAT, ex p Lokko [1990] Imm AR 359; [1990] The Guardian, 20 September 146, 148

TABLE OF CASES

R v IAT, *ex p* Mahmood (Sajid) [1988] Imm AR 121 226
RR v IAT, *ex p* Malik (1987) *The Times*, 18 November 461
R v IAT, *ex p* Manek [1978] 3 All ER 641; [1978] 1 WLR 1190; (1978) 122 SJ 714, CA 239
R v IAT, *ex p* Marchon (1993) *The Times*, 23 February, CA, *affg* [1993] Imm AR 98 313
R v IAT, *ex p* Martin [1972] Imm AR 275 (1972) 116 SJ 697; (1972) *The Times*, 20 July 170, 461
R v IAT, *ex p* Masood (Sumeina) [1992] Imm AR 69, CA, *affg* [1991] Imm AR 283 .... 461, 495
R v IAT, *ex p* Mawji [1982] Imm AR 97 168
R v IAT, *ex p* Mehmet (Ekrem) [1977] 2 All ER 602; [1977] 1 WLR 795; (1976) 121 SJ 255 .... 404, 422, 435, 441, 444
R v IAT, *ex p* Mehra [1983] Imm AR 156 455
R v IAT, *ex p* Mehta (V M) [1976] Imm AR 174 444
R v IAT, *ex p* Miah (Jasmine) [1991] Imm AR 184 .... 457, 461
R v IAT, *ex p* Miah (Lulu) [1987] Imm AR 143 .... 457, 483
R v IAT, *ex p* Miller [1988] Imm AR 358 347
R v IAT, *ex p* Minta [1992] Imm AR 380 .... 23, 64, 67
R v IAT, *ex p* Nathwani [1979–80] Imm AR 9 216
R v IAT, *ex p* Ozkurtulus [1986] Imm AR 80 98
R v IAT, *ex p* Palomeno [1987] Imm AR 42 284
R v IAT, *ex p* Patel (Anilkumar Ravindrabhai) [1988] AC 910; [1988] 2 WLR 1165; [1988] 2 All ER 378, HL 252, 267, 269, 493
R v IAT, *ex p* Patel (Girishkumar) [1990] Imm AR 153 .... 459, 474
R v IAT, *ex p* Peikazadi [197–80] Imm AR 191 169
R v IAT, *ex p* Pollicino [1989] Imm AR 531 439
R v IAT, *ex p* Rafique [1990] Imm AR 235; [1990] COD 98 .... 71, 210
R v IAT, *ex p* Rahman [1987] Imm AR 313, CA 53, 168, 170
R v IAT, *ex p* Rashid (Abdul) [1978] Imm AR 71 456
R v IAT, *ex p* Razaque (Kalsoom) [1989] Imm AR 451 .... 16, 438, 458, 482
R v IAT, *ex p* Rocha [1982] Imm AR 12 439
R v IAT, *ex p* Samaraweera [1974] 2 All ER 171; [1974] 1 WLR 487; 118 SJ 221 468
R v IAT, *ex p* Secretary of State [1990] Imm AR 652 416
R v IAT, *ex p* Secretary of State [1992] Imm AR 554; [1993] COD 56; (1992) *The Times*, 7 September 420
R v IAT, *ex p* Secretary of State (1993) *The Times*, 15 July, CA *affg* [1993] Imm AR 298; [1993] COD 319 225
R v IAT, *ex p* Shaikh [1981] 1 WLR 1107; [1981] 3 All ER 29; (1981) 125 SJ 240 100
R v IAT, *ex p* Sheikh [1988] *The Times*, 17 March, CA 267
R v IAT, *ex p* Singh (Ajaib) [1978] Imm AR 59 .... 251, 252
R v IAT, *ex p* Singh (Bakhtaur) [1986] Imm AR 352; [1986] 1 WLR 910; [1986] 2 All ER 721, HL 52, 272, 277, 421, 483, 487
R v IAT, *ex p* Singh (Chhinderpal) [1989] Imm AR 69 240
R v IAT, *ex p* Singh (Mahendra) [1984] Imm AR 1 467
R v IAT, *ex p* Singh (Swarah) [1987] 1 WLR 1394; [1987] 3 All ER 690; [1987] Imm AR 563, CA 241, 242
R v IAT, *ex p* Subramanium [1977] QB 190; [1976] 3 WLR 630, CA 76
R v IAT, *ex p* Suleman [1976] Imm AR 147 468
R v IAT, *ex p* Takeo [1987] Imm AR 522 54
R v IAT, *ex p* Tobon (Martinez) [1987] Imm AR 536 460

TABLE OF CASES

R v IAT, ex p Tong [1981] Imm AR 214; (1981) The Times, 8 December 460
R v IAT, ex p Uddin [1986] Imm AR 203 225
R v IAT, ex p Uddin (Shafique) [1990] Imm AR 104, CA 30
R v IAT, ex p Wali [1989] Imm AR 86..................................209
R v IAT, ex p Weerasuriya [1982] Imm AR 23; [1983] 1 All ER 195 456
R v IAT, ex p Zandfani [1984] Imm AR 213.............................196
R v IAT and an adjudicator, ex p Secretary of State [1990] Imm AR 166 468
R v IAT and Singh (Surinder), ex p Secretary of State (C-370/90) [1992] Imm AR 565; (1992) The Times, 31 August; (1992) The Guardian, 15 July 201, 275, 315
R v Immigration Officer, ex p Ali [1982] Imm AR 1; (1983) 80 LS Gaz 99, CA..417
R v Immigration Officer ex p Chan [1992] 1 WLR 541; [1992] 2 All ER 738; [1992] Imm AR 233, CA...18
R v Immigration Officer, ex p Shah [1982] 1 WLR 544; [1982] 2 All ER 264..397, 407
R v IRC, ex p Preston [1985] AC 835; [1985] 2 WLR 836; [1985] 2 All ER 327, HL 491, 497
R v Kahapathipillai (1988) The Times, 26 March 270
R v Kensington Commissioners, ex p Polignac [1917] 1 KB 486 502
R v Khan (S G H) [1975] Imm AR 26 101
R v Lympne Airport Chief Immigration Officer, ex p Singh (Amrik) [1968] 3 All ER 63..87, 100
R v Mayor and Burgesses of the London Borough of Tower Hamlets, ex p Begum (Jalika) [1991] Imm AR 86; (1990) 24 HLR 230 462
R v Medical Appeal Tribunal, ex p Gilmore [1957] 1 QB 574; [1957] 2 WLR 498; 101 SJ 248, CA..45
R v Mental Health Review Tribunal, ex p Clatworthy [1985] 3 All ER 699....492
R v Mistry, R v Asare [1980] Crim LR 177, CA..........................523
R v Monomai (Sorraseakh) [1991] Imm AR 29............................21
R v Naillie [1993] AC 674; [1993] 2 WLR 927; [1993] 2 All ER 782, HL ..17, 522
R v Nazari [1980] 3 All ER 880; [1980] 1 WLR 1366; (1980) 71 Cr App R 87, CA..269
R v Omajudi [1992] Imm AR 104; (1992) 94 Cr App R 224; [1992] Crim LR 377, CA 406
R v Peterkin (adjudicator), ex p Soni [1972] Imm AR 253 460
R v Police Complaints Board, ex p Madden [1983] 1 WLR 447; [1983] 2 All ER 353; [1983] Crim LR 263 488
R v Secretary of State for Education, ex p Avon CC (No 2) [1991] 2 WLR 702; [1991] 1 QB 558; [1991] 1 All ER 282, CA 500
R v Secretary of State for Health, ex p Luff [1991] Imm AR 382; [1992] 1 FLR 59; [1991] Fam Law 472 234
R v Secretary of State for the Foreign and Commonwealth Office, ex p Everett [1989] QB 811; [1989] 2 WLR 224; [1989] 1 All ER 655, CA...........11, 45
R v Secretary of State for the Home Department, ex p Abassi [1992] Imm AR 349; (1992) The Times, 6 April, CA......................................442
R v Secretary of State for the Home Department, ex p Abdi (1994) The Times, 25 April 384
R v Secretary of State for the Home Department, ex p Abdullah [1992] Imm AR 438..352, 371
R v Secretary of State for the Home Department, ex p Adebodun [1991] Imm AR 60 106

TABLE OF CASES

R v Secretary of State for the Home Department, *ex p* Ademuyiwa [1986] Imm AR 1 70
R v Secretary of State for the Home Department, *ex p* Akhtar [1975] 1 WLR 1717; [1975] 3 All ER 1087; 62 Cr App R 167 239
R v Secretary of State for the Home Department, *ex p* Akhtar [1991] Imm AR 232; [1991] COD 298; *The Times*, 14 January, CA 417
R v Secretary of State for the Home Department, *ex p* Akyol [1990] Imm AR 571 .... 349, 368
R v Secretary of State for the Home Department, *ex p* Ali [1992] Imm AR 316 264
R v Secretary of State for the Home Department, *ex p* Ali (Mohammed Fazor) [1988] Imm AR 274; (1988) *The Times*, 23 January 66, 484
R v Secretary of State for the Home Department, *ex p* Ali (Momin) [1984] 1 WLR 663; [1984] 1 All ER 1009; [1984] Imm AR 23, CA 509
R v Secretary of State for the Home Department, *ex p* Allegret [1989] Imm AR 211 .... 495, 498
R v Secretary of State for the Home Department, *ex p* Al-Mehdawi [1990] 1 AC 876; [1989] 3 WLR 1294; [1989] 3 All ER 843, HL 452, 492
R v Secretary of State for the Home Department, *ex p* Alupo [1991] Imm AR 538 361
R v Secretary of State for the Home Department, *ex p* Amoa [1992] Imm AR 218 489
R v Secretary of State for the Home Department, *ex p* Animashun [1990] Imm AR 70; [1990] COD 176; (1989) *The Times*, 12 October 105
R v Secretary of State for the Home Department, *ex p* Aouiche (1991) *The Times*, 4 June, CA 338, 343
R v Secretary of State for the Home Department, *ex p* Arjumand [1983] Imm AR 123 84
R v Secretary of State for the Home Department, *ex p* Arora (Rakesh) [1990] Imm AR 89 459
R v Secretary of State for the Home Department, *ex p* Attivor [1988] Imm AR 109 .... 495, 498
R v Secretary of State for the Home Department, *ex p* Avci (Zeynal) [1994]   Imm AR 35 352
R v Secretary of State for the Home Department, *ex p* Awuku [1988] Imm AR 606 492
R v Secretary of State for the Home Department, *ex p* Ayoola [1992] Imm AR 170 .... 85, 103
R v Secretary of State for the Home Department, *ex p* B (1991) *The Independent*, 29 January; (1991) *The Guardian*, 30 January 431
R v Secretary of State for the Home Department, *ex p* Bagga [1990] 3 WLR 1013; [1991] 1 QB 485; [1991] 1 All ER 777, CA 266, 396
R v Secretary of State for the Home Department, *ex p* Bakar (Abu) (1981) unreported 14
R v Secretary of State, *ex p* Balogun [1989] Imm AR 603 .... 74, 493
R v Secretary of State for the Home Department, *ex p* Begum [1989] Imm AR 302; (1989) *The Times*, 3 April, CA 506
R v Secretary of State for the Home Department, *ex p* Begum (Angur) and Begum (Rukshanda) [1990] Imm AR 1; [1990] COD 107, CA 225, 239, 253, 503
R v Secretary of State for the Home Department, *ex p* Berko [1991] Imm AR 127 502

TABLE OF CASES   xxxi

R v Secretary of State for the Home Department, ex p Betancourt [1988] Imm
  AR 78 396
R v Secretary of State for the Home Department, ex p Bhatti (Fida) [1989] Imm
  AR 189 494
R v Secretary of State for the Home Department, ex p Binbasi [1989] Imm AR
  595 342
R v Secretary of State for the Home Department, ex p Bokele [1991] Imm AR
  124 349
R v Secretary of State for the Home Department, ex p Bolat [1991] Imm AR
  417 361
R v Secretary of State for the Home Department, ex p Botta [1987] Imm AR
  80; [1987] 2 CMLR 189 294
R v Secretary of State for the Home Department, ex p Brakwah [1989] Imm AR
  366 ....21, 84
R v Secretary of State for the Home Department, ex p Brind [1991] 1 AC 696;
  [1991] 2 WLR 588; [1991] 1 All ER 720, HL 474, 484, 489, 490
R v Secretary of State for the Home Department, ex p Bugdaycay [1987] AC
  514; [1987] 2 WLR 606; [1987] 1 All ER 940; HL 483, 484
R v Secretary of State for the Home Department, ex p Chahal [1994] Imm AR
  107 ....337, 381, 432
R v Secretary of State for the Home Department, ex p Chan (Kwong Fai)
  [1992] 1 WLR 541; [1992] 2 All ER 738; [1992] Imm AR 233 ....19, 394
R v Secretary of State for the Home Department, ex p Cheblak [1991] 2 All
  ER 319; [1991] 1 WLR 890; [1991] COD 394, CA 431, 499, 512
R v Secretary of State for the Home Department, ex p Chomsuk (Saichon)
  [1991] Imm AR 29 ....20, 462
R v Secretary of State for the Home Department, ex p Chong (Su-San) [1990]
  Imm AR 397 ....495, 497
R v Secretary of State for the Home Department, ex p Choudhary [1978] 3 All
  ER 790; [1978] 1 WLR 1177; 122 SJ 539, CA 510
R v Secretary of State for the Home Department, ex p Choudhary (1981) The
  Times, 16 December, PC 511
R v Secretary of State for the Home Department, ex p Colak [1993] Imm AR
  581; 137 SJ (LB) 187; (1993) The Times, 6 July, CA 367
R v Secretary of State, ex p Coonhye (1988) The Independent, 20 April 92
R v Secretary of State for the Home Department, ex p Cox [1992] COD 72;
  (1991) The Times, 10 September; (1991) The Times, 8 October 474
R v Secretary of State for the Home Department, ex p Crew [1982] Imm AR
  94, CA 29
R v Secretary of State for the Home Department, ex p Dhahan [1988] Imm AR
  257; (1988) The Times, 15 January 234
R v Secretary of State for the Home Department, ex p Dinesh [1987] Imm AR
  131 440
R v Secretary of State for the Home Department, ex p Direk (Halil) [1992] Imm
  AR 330 341
R v Secretary of State for the Home Department, ex p Doorga [1990] Imm AR
  98; [1990] COD 109, CA 496, 497, 503
R v Secretary of State for the Home Department, ex p Dordas [1992] Imm AR
  99; [1992] COD 126; (1991) The Times, 18 October 21
R v Secretary of State for the Home Department, ex p Dyfan [1993] Imm AR
  180 503
R v Secretary of State for the Home Department, ex p Ejaz (1993) The Times,
  7 December; (1993) The Independent, 22 December 18, 35

TABLE OF CASES

R v Secretary of State for the Home Department, ex p El-Tanonkhi [1993] Imm AR 71 362
R v Secretary of State for the Home Department, ex p Fahmi (1994) The Times, 2 March 364
R v Secretary of State for the Home Department, ex p Fawehimi [1991] Imm AR 1; [1990] COD 388, CA 504, 507
R v Secretary of State for the Home Department, ex p Fernando [1987] Imm AR 377 101
R v Secretary of State for the Home Department, ex p Gallagher (1994) The Times, 16 February 313
R v Secretary of State for the Home Department, ex p Ghebretatios [1993] Imm AR 585; (1993) The Times, 19 July, CA 367
R v Secretary of State for the Home Department, ex p Giambi [1982] 1 All ER 434 408
R v Secretary of State for the Home Department, ex p Gomez (unreported, 17 January 1991) 101
R v Secretary of State for the Home Department, ex p Guiled [1993] Imm AR 236 502
R v Secretary of State for the Home Department, ex p Gulbacke [1991] Imm AR 526 342
R v Secretary of State for the Home Department, ex p Gunes [1991] Imm AR 278; [1991] COD 301 .... 338, 362
R v Secretary of State for the Home Department, ex p H [1988] Imm AR 389 431
R v Secretary of State for the Home Department, ex p Hindjou [1989] Imm AR 24 .... 496, 497, 498
R v Secretary of State, ex p Hosenball [1977] 3 All ER 452 ...... 52, 53, 431, 499
R v Secretary of State for the Home Department, ex p Husseyin [1988] Imm AR 129 266
R v Secretary of State for the Home Department, ex p Ibrahim (Eid Mohammed) [1993] Imm AR 124 395
R v Secretary of State for the Home Department, ex p Jaifrey (Mohammed) [1990] Imm AR 6, CA 483, 488
R v Secretary of State for the Home Department, ex p Jayakody [1982] 1 WLR 405, [1982] 1 All ER 461; (1981) 125 SJ 588, CA 19
R v Secretary of State for the Home Department, ex p Jeyakumaran [1994] Imm AR 45 .... 342, 343
R v Secretary of State for the Home Department, ex p Jibril [1993] Imm AR 308 474
R v Secretary of State for the Home Department, ex p K [1991] 1 QB 270; [1990] 3 WLR 755; [1990] 3 All ER 562, CA 361
R v Secretary of State for the Home Department, ex p Kamara [1991] Imm AR 423 436
R v Secretary of State for the Home Department, ex p Kaur [1987] Imm AR 278 216
R v Secretary of State for the Home Department, ex p Kaur (Mahvinder) [1991] Imm AR 426 269
R v Secretary of State for the Home Department, ex p Ken'aan [1990] Imm AR 544 413
R v Secretary of State for the Home Department, ex p Ketowoglo [1992] Imm AR 268; (1992) The Times, 6 April, CA 499, 502
R v Secretary of State for the Home Department, ex p Khaled [1987] Imm AR 67 18

TABLE OF CASES xxxiii

R v Secretary of State for the Home Department, ex p Khan (Asif) [1984] Imm
AR 68 234
R v Secretary of State for the Home Department, ex p Khan (Haggan) [1991]
Imm AR 174 497
R v Secretary of State for the Home Department, ex p Khan (Hiran) [1990] 1
WLR 798; [1990] 2 All ER 531, CA 22
R v Secretary of State for the Home Department, ex p Khan (Taj Mohammed)
[1985] Imm AR 104, CA 17
R v Secretary of State for the Home Department, ex p Khawaja [1984] AC 74;
[1983] 2 WLR 321; [1983] 1 All ER 765, HL 16, 17, 20, 22, 66, 267, 393,
397, 484, 485, 504, 510
R v Secretary of State for the Home Department, ex p Kumar [1990] Imm AR
265 396
R v Secretary of State for the Home Department, ex p Kumar [1993] Imm AR
401 463
R v Secretary of State for the Home Department, ex p Kusi-Boahem [1988]
Imm AR 540; (1988) The Times, 18 June 407
R v Secretary of State for the Home Department, ex p Kyomya [1993] Imm AR
331 357
R v Secretary of State for the Home Department, ex p Lapinid [1984] 3 All ER
257; [1984] 1 WLR 1289; [1984] Imm AR 101, CA 78, 397
R v Secretary of State for the Home Department, ex p Lateef [1991] Imm AR
334 397
R v Secretary of State for the Home Department, ex p Lawson (Vera) [1994] Imm
AR 58 395
R v Secretary of State for the Home Department, ex p Mahoney [1992] Imm
AR 275 22
R v Secretary of State for the Home Department, ex p Malhi [1990] 1 WLR
933; [1991] QB 194; [1990] 2 All ER 357, CA 420
R v Secretary of State for the Home Department, ex p Margueritte [1983] 2
AC 309; [1983] QB 180; [1982] 3 WLR 754; [1982] 3 All ER 909, CA 14
R v Secretary of State for the Home Department, ex p Mesirionye [1993] Imm
AR 119 264
R v Secretary of State for the Home Department, ex p Miah [1983] Imm
AR 91 22
R v Secretary of State for the Home Department, ex p Minton [1990] Imm AR
199; [1990] COD 101, CA 397
R v Secretary of State for the Home Department, ex p Maezzi, 6 October
1988, CA 342
R v Secretary of State for the Home Department, ex p Mohammed (Khushi)
and Khawaja [1990] Imm AR 439 437
R v Secretary of State for the Home Department, ex p Mohan [1989] Imm AR
436 .... 18, 65
R v Secretary of State for the Home Department, ex p Muboyayi [1992] 1 QB
244; [1991] 3 WLR 442; [1991] 4 All ER 72, CA 500, 501, 512
R v Secretary of State for the Home Department, ex p Mudzengi [1993] Imm
AR 320 502
R v Secretary of State for the Home Department, ex p Munongo [1991] Imm
AR 616 361
R v Secretary of State for the Home Department, ex p Mughal [1974] QB 313;
[1973] 3 WLR 647; [1973] 3 All ER 796, CA 492
R v Secretary of State for the Home Department, ex p Murali [1993] Imm AR
311 349

R v Secretary of State for the Home Department, ex p Musa [1993] Imm AR 210...361
R v Secretary of State for the Home Department, ex p Muse [1992] Imm AR 282 ....22, 492, 504
R v Secretary of State for the Home Department, ex p Muslu [1993] Imm AR 151...365
R v Secretary of State for the Home Department, ex p Mussawir [1989] Imm AR 297..17, 485
R v Secretary of State for the Home Department, ex p Nkiti [1989] Imm AR 182, CA 252
R v Secretary of State for the Home Department, ex p NSH [1988] Imm AR 389...381
R v Secretary of State for the Home Department, ex p Nwasu [1993] Imm AR 206...502
R v Secretary of State for the Home Department, ex p Nzamba-Liloneo [1993] AR 140...489
R v Secretary of State for the Home Department, ex p Ogunlande [1992] COD 46..395
R v Secretary of State for the Home Department, ex p Okusanya [1993] Imm AR 13..395
R v Secretary of State for the Home Department, ex p Olokodana [1992] Imm AR 499...504
R v Secretary of State for the Home Department, ex p Omishore [1990] Imm AR 582..424, 443
R v Secretary of State for the Home Department, ex p Onay [1992] Imm AR 320...342
R v Secretary of State for the Home Department, ex p O'Shea [1988] Imm AR 484; (1988) *The Times*, 1 April, CA.................................266
R v Secretary of State for the Home Department, ex p Ouakkonche [1991] Imm AR 5..421
R v Secretary of State for the Home Department, ex p Ounejma [1989] Imm AR 75; [1989] COD 278, DL 55, 74, 483, 487
R v Secretary of State for the Home Department, ex p P [1992] COD 295 341
R v Secretary of State for the Home Department, ex p Panchah (1991) *The Times*, 6 May..421
R v Secretary of State for the Home Department, ex p Patel [1986] Imm AR 208...525
R v Secretary of State for the Home Department, ex p Patel [1986] Imm AR 515, CA 250
R v Secretary of State for the Home Department, ex p Patel (1987) *The Times*, 24 October 21
R v Secretary of State for the Home Department, ex p Patel (Pushpabeh) [1993] Imm AR 257 499
R v Secretary of State for the Home Department, ex p Phansopkar [1975] 3 All ER 497; [1976] QB 606; [1975] 3 WLR 322, CA...........53, 67, 510
R v Secretary of State for the Home Department, ex p Prajpati [1990] Imm AR 513...211, 457
R v Secretary of State for the Home Department, ex p Pulgarin [1992] Imm AR 96..497
R v Secretary of State for the Home Department, ex p Ram [1979] 1 WLR 148; [1979] 1 All ER 687; (1978) 123 SJ 112, DC.......................18
R v Secretary of State for the Home Department, ex p Razak [1986] Imm AR 44..397

TABLE OF CASES

R v Secretary of State for the Home Department, *ex p* Rehal [1989] Imm AR 576; [1990] COD 40; (1989) *The Times*, 3 July, CA 396
R v Secretary of State for the Home Department, *ex p* Rofathallah [1988] 3 WLR 591; [1988] 3 All ER 1; (1988) 132 SJ 1182, CA...................201
R v Secretary of State for the Home Department, *ex p* Rubanra [1993] Imm AR 447...348
R v Secretary of State for the Home Department, *ex p* Saffu-Mensah (Kuradwo) [1991] Imm AR 43 250
R v Secretary of State for the Home Department, *ex p* Saftar [1992] Imm AR 1...209
R v Secretary of State for the Home Department, *ex p* Sakala [1994] Imm AR 143...494
R v Secretary of State for the Home Department, *ex p* Salamat [1993] Imm AR 239...497
R v Secretary of State for the Home Department, *ex p* Salim [1990] Imm AR 316 ....21, 250
R v Secretary of State for the Home Department, *ex p* Santillo [1981] 2 WLR 362; [1981] QB 778; [1981] 2 All ER 897; (1980) 125 SJ 100, CA 313, 491
R v Secretary of State for the Home Department, *ex p* Satta [1978] Imm AR 190..252
R v Secretary of State for the Home Department, *ex p* Selo Wa-Selo [1990] Imm AR 76, CA 417
R v Secretary of State for the Home Department, *ex p* Shami (Shrokh) [1992] Imm AR 542 366
R v Secretary of State for the Home Department, *ex p* Sholola [1992] Imm AR 135; [1992] COD 226 506
R v Secretary of State for the Home Department, *ex p* Siddique [1992] Imm AR 127..396
R v Secretary of State for the Home Department, *ex p* Singh (Atruinder) [1993] Imm AR 450 502
R v Secretary of State for the Home Department, *ex p* Singh (Bahadur) [1976] Imm AR 143 445
R v Secretary of State for the Home Department, *ex p* Singh (Baljib) [1994] Imm AR 42 344
R v Secretary of State for Home Affairs, *ex p* Singh (Bhajah) [1975]   2 All ER 1081..53
R v Secretary of State for the Home Department, *ex p* Singh (Gurmeet) [1987] Imm AR 489 341
R v Secretary of State for the Home Department, *ex p* Singh (Harnaik) [1989] 2 All ER 867...84
R v Secretary of State for the Home Department, *ex p* Singh (Mangal) [1992] Imm AR 376 ....348, 352
R v Secretary of State for the Home Department, *ex p* Singh (Parshottam) [1989] Imm AR 469; [1989] COD 454...............................397
R v Secretary of State for the Home Department, *ex p* Singh (Roj) [1992] Imm AR 607 352
R v Secretary of State for the Home Department, *ex p* Sivakumaeran [1988] 2 WLR 92; [1988] AC 958; (1987) *The Independent*, 25 February......338, 341
R v Secretary of State for the Home Department, *ex p* Sritharan [1993] Imm AR 184..337
R v Secretary of State for the Home Department, *ex p* Swati [1986] 1 WLR 477, CA; [1986] Imm AR 88; [1986] 1 All ER 717 ....86, 402, 435, 437, 483, 488, 496, 497

R v Secretary of State for the Home Department, *ex p* Tahi [1992] Imm AR 157..........460
R v Secretary of State for the Home Department, *ex p* Tarrant [1985] QB 251; [1984] 2 WLR 613; [1984] 1 All ER 799..........487
R v Secretary of State for the Home Department, *ex p* Thavathevathasan, 22 December 1993, CA..........350, 379
R v Secretary of State for the Home Department, *ex p* Thirakumar [1989] Imm AR 270; [1989] COD 458; (1989) *The Times*, 10 March, CA..........396
R v Secretary of State for the Home Department, *ex p* Tolba [1988] Imm AR 78..........71
R v Secretary of State for the Home Department, *ex p* Tombofa [1988] Imm AR 400; [1988] LS Gaz, 18 May 42, CA..........315
R v Secretary of State for the Home Department, *ex p* Tuglaci [1993] Imm AR 47..........424
R v Secretary of State for the Home Department, *ex p* Turkoglu [1988] QB 398; [1987] Imm AR 484; [1987] 2 All ER 823, CA..........402, 507
R v Secretary of State for the Home Department, *ex p* Uddin (Noor) [1990] Imm AR 181; [1990] COD 252; (1989) *The Times*, 18 October..........224, 471
R v Secretary of State for the Home Department, *ex p* Ul-Haq [1993] Imm AR 144..........490, 493
R v Secretary of State for the Home Department, *ex p* V [1988] Imm AR 561..........496
R v Secretary of State for the Home Department, *ex p* Veigho (Alavi) (1989) *The Times*, 22 August..........488
R v Secretary of State for the Home Department, *ex p* Vigna [1993] Imm AR 93..........362
R v Secretary of State for the Home Department, *ex p* Yassine [1990] Imm AR 354; [1990] COD 339; (1990) 134 SJ 638..........38, 347, 348
R v Secretary of State for the Home Department, *ex p* Yeboah [1987] 1 WLR 1586; [1987] 3 All ER 999; [1987] Imm AR 414, CA..........436
R v Secretary of State for the Home Department, *ex p* Yeshfu [1987] Imm AR 366..........284, 493
R v Secretary of State for the Home Department, *ex p* Yildaz [1991] Imm AR 354..........348
R v Secretary of State for the Home Department, *ex p* Yurekli [1990] Imm AR 334..........362
R v Secretary of State for the Home Department, *ex p* Zamir [1980] AC 930; [1980] 3 WLR 249; (1980) 124 SJ 527, HL..........510
R v Secretary of State for the Home Department, *ex p* Zib [1993] Imm AR 350..........340
R v Secretary of State for the Home Department, *ex p* Zibrila-Alassini [1991] Imm AR 367..........343
R v Secretary of State for Transport, *ex p* Factortame Ltd [1990] 2 AC 85; [1989] 2 WLR 997; [1989] 2 All ER 892, HL..........7, 500, 512
R v Serry (1980) 3 Cr App R(S) 336; (1980) *The Times*, 31 October, CA..........270
R v Singh (Hardial) [1983] Imm AR 198..........408
R v Singh and Meeuwsen [1972] 1 WLR 1600; [1973] 1 All ER 122; 116 SJ 863, CA..........522
R v Special adjudicator, *ex p* Guei, 31 January 1994..........380
R v Special adjudicator, *ex p* Kandasamy (1994) *The Times*, 11 March..........349
R v Special adjudicator, *ex p* Mehan, 8 October 1993, DC..........379
R v Spura [1988] 10 Cr App R(S) 376..........304

TABLE OF CASES xxxvii

R v Stratford upon Avon DC, *ex p* Jackson [1985] 1 WLR 1319; [1985] 3 All
    ER 769; (1985) 129 SJ 854, CA 499
R v Tshuma (1981) 3 Cr App R(S) 97 270
R v Williams, *ex p* Phillips [1914] 1 QB 608 499
R v Windsor Licensing Justices, *ex p* Hodes [1983] 1 WLR 685; [1983] 2 All
    ER 551; (1983) 127 SJ 378, CA 496
R v Zamah (1975) 6 Cr App Rep 227, CA 525
Raeal Communications, *Re* [1981] AC 374, [1980] 3 WLR 181; [1980] 2 All ER
    634, HL 45
Rahman v Qadir [1993] Crim LR 874 523
Rahman (Jihah) v Secretary of State [1989] Imm AR 325 .... 366, 432
Rajendrah v Secretary of State [1989] Imm AR 512 .... 78, 249, 256
Rajput v IAT [1989] Imm AR 350 .... 55, 201
Ram (Tilak) v ECO New Delhi [1978] Imm AR 123 241
Ramjane v Chief Immigration Officer, Gatwick Airport [1973] Imm AR 84 ... 117
Ramzan v Visa Officer, Islamabad [1978] Imm AR 111 451
Randhawa v Secretary of State [1972] Imm AR 158 183
Rashid (Myeen) v ECO, Dacca [1976] Imm AR 12 99
Ravat v ECO, Bombay [1974] Imm AR 79 225
Regina (8973) 136
Rehal v Secretary of State [1989] Imm AR 576; [1990] COD 40; (1989) *The
    Times*, 3 July 18
Rehman v Secretary of State [1978] Imm AR 80 .... 266, 304, 436
Rennie v ECO, Kingston [1979–80] Imm AR 117 227
Rhemtulla v IAT [1979–80] Imm AR 168 .... 404, 435, 444
Ridge v Baldwin [1964] AC 40; [1963] 2 WLR 935; [1963] 2 All ER 66, HL ... 491
Ross-Clunis v Secretary of State for the Foreign and Commonwealth Office
    [1991] Imm AR 595; [1991] 2 AC 439; [1991] 3 WLR 146, HL 25
Roy v Secretary of State [1988] Imm AR 53 131
Rudolph v ECO, Colombo [1985] Imm AR 84 .... 225, 226, 228
Ryoo (Soon Ok) v Secretary of State [1992] Imm AR 59; [1992] COD 134;
    (1991) *The Independent*, 5 July 496, 497, 505
Sae-Heng v Visa Officer, Bangkok [1979–80] Imm AR 69 451
Saemian v Immigration Officer, Heathrow [1991] Imm AR 489 432
Saffa-Mensah v Secretary of State [1992] Imm AR 185; [1992] COD 215, CA .. 21
Said (Hukan) v IAT [1989] Imm AR 372 .... 269, 488
Saini (Jagtar) v Secretary of State [1993] Imm AR 96 454
Saleh v Secretary of State [1975] Imm AR 154 448
Sashiharan v Secretary of State [1993] Imm AR 253 420
Schele v Immigration Officer, Harwich [1976] Imm AR 1 251
Secretary of State v Abdel (Razaq) [1992] Imm AR 152 463
Secretary of State v Agyen-Frempong [1986] Imm AR 108 70
Secretary of State v Akinrajomu [1988] Imm AR 590 71
Secretary of State v Ally [1972] Imm AR 258 169
Secretary of State v Aluko [1974] Imm AR 90 266
Secretary of State v Behrooz [1991] Imm AR 82 .... 397, 417
Secretary of State v Brizmohun [1972] Imm AR 122 131
Secretary of State v Campbell [1972] Imm AR 115 227
Secretary of State v Croning [1972] Imm AR 51 424
Secretary of State v Durojaiye [1991] Imm AR 248 105
Secretary of State v Evgenion [1978] Imm AR 89 183
Secretary of State v Fardy [1972] Imm AR 192 463
Secretary of State v Glean [1972] Imm AR 84 461

Secretary of State v Gomes [1990] Imm AR 576..........................135
Secretary of State v Grant [1974] Imm AR 64............................120
Secretary of State v Ibrahim [1994] Imm AR 1...........................443
Secretary of State v Idowu [1972] Imm AR 197 252
Secretary of State v Jones [1978] Imm AR 161 185
Secretary of State v Lakdawalla [1972] Imm AR 26 ....11, 65
Secretary of State for the Home Department v Mowla [1991] Imm AR 210;
  [1992] 1 WLR 70; [1991] COD 304, CA........................79, 488, 494
Secretary of State v Otchere [1988] Imm AR 21 342
Secretary of State v Patel [1988] Imm AR 75 256
Secretary of State v Peters [1993] Imm AR 187...........................75
Secretary of State v Petron [1978] Imm AR 87............................76
Secretary of State v Pope [1987] Imm AR 10 119
Secretary of State v Purushothaman [1972] Imm AR 176 459
Secretary of State v Pusey [1972] Imm AR 240...........................226
Secretary of State v Raval [1975] Imm AR 72............................183
Secretary of State v Razaq Abdel [1992] Imm AR 152 ....348, 462
Secretary of State v Rohr [1983] Imm AR 95 ....183, 196
Secretary of State v Riaz [1987] Imm AR 88..............................90
Secretary of State v Sidique [1976] Imm AR 69 ....257, 453
Secretary of State v Stillwaggon [1975] Imm AR 132.....................186
Secretary of State v Thaker [1976] Imm AR 114..........................105
Secretary of State v Two Citizens of Chile [1977] Imm AR 36............347
Secretary of State v Virdee [1972] Imm AR 215 102
Secretary of State v Wedad [1979–80] Imm AR 27.........................257
Selo Wa-Selo v Secretary of State [1990] Imm AR 76, CA.................444
Seyed v Secretary of State [1987] Imm AR 303...........................171
Shabir v Visa Officer, Islamabad [1989] Imm AR 185 240
Shah (4618) 193
Shah v Secretary of State [1972] Imm AR 56 193
Shevey v Secretary of State [1987] Imm AR 453..........................185
Shomali (3451) 99
Sing and Kaur v Secretary of State [1993] Imm AR 382 452
Singa (Marchano) v Secretary of State [1992] Imm AR 160, CA.......508, 509
Singh (4620)...171
Singh (Balbir) v Secretary of State [1992] Imm AR 426, CA 347, 352
Singh (Baljinder) v ECO, New Delhi [1975] Imm AR 34....................234
Singh (Bhagat) v ECO, New Delhi [1978] Imm AR 134 87
Singh (Hardial), Re [1983] Imm AR 198 511
Singh (Harmail) v IAT [1978] Imm AR 140 466
Singh (Jaswant) v Secretary of State [1993] Imm AR 4 508
Singh (Mahjit).........Secretary of State [1990] Imm AR 124, CA........494
Singh (Manmohan) v ECO, New Delhi [1975] Imm AR 118 ....84, 88
Singh (Matwinder) (23 March 1987, unreported, Div Ct) 209
Singh (Nachtar) v Secretary of State [1991] Imm AR 195 448
Singh (Pargan) v Secretary of State [1992] 1 WLR 1052; (1992) 142 New LJ
  1575; (1992) The Times, 26 October..............................422, 443
Singh (Piara) v ECO, New Delhi [1977] Imm AR 1 154
Singh (Pritpal) v Secretary of State [1972] Imm AR 154 170
Singh (Yadvinder) v Secretary of State [1988] Imm AR 480 507
Sloley v ECO, Kingston [1973] Imm AR 54................................226
Smith (Thelma) (8642) 160
Sokha v Secretary of State [1992] Imm AR 14 403

TABLE OF CASES xxxix

Somasundaram v ECO, Bombay [1990] Imm AR 16................... 240, 433
Somasundaram v Melchior (Julius) [1988] 1 WLR 1394; [1989] 1 All ER 129..380
Soyemi v Secretary of State [1989] Imm AR 564 76
Suarez (Johnny) v Secretary of State for the Home Department [1991] Imm
  AR 54, CA 486, 495
Suthendran v IAT [1977] AC 359, HL 76, 77
Tadimi (Mohammed) v Secretary of State for the Home Department [1993]
  Imm AR 90, CA 20, 503
Tahir (Nadeem) v IAT [1989] AR 98, CA 435, 455
Tambimuttu v Secretary of State [1979–80] Imm AR 91 441
Teame v Aberash (1994) *The Times*, 8 April
Teflisi (3522) 253
Tekle v Visa Officer Prague [1986] Imm AR 71 337
Thamathirampillai v Secretary of State [1981] Imm AR 47, CA 402
Thevarajah (David) v Secretary of State [1991] Imm AR 371, CA 349, 505
Thomas v Chief Adjudication Officer and Secretary of State for Social Security
  [1991] 2 QB 164; [1991] 2 WLR 886; [1991] 3 All ER 315 490
Uche (Ubakanwas) v Secretary of State [1991] Imm AR 252, CA 504
Uddin (Hawa) v IAT [1991] Imm AR 134, CA....................... 460, 461
Uddin (Sunam) v Secretary of State [1991] Imm AR 587, CA 224
Ulrich (4129) 295
Umarji (Anima) v Secretary of State [1989] Imm AR 285.................. 458
Uppal v Home Office (1978) *The Times*, 20 October 477
Villone v Secretary of State [1979–80] Imm AR 23....................... 268
Vilvarajah v Secretary of State [1990] Imm AR 457, CA...399, 402, 446, 483, 508
Visa Officer, Aden v Thabet [1977] Imm AR 75.......................... 463
Visa Officer, Cairo v Ashraf [1979–80] Imm AR 45...................... 456
Visa Officer, Islamabad v Altaf (Mohammed) [1979–80] Imm AR 141........ 457
Visa Officer, Islamabad v Bashir [1978] Imm AR 77 243
Visa Officer, Islamabad v Begum (Kalsoom) [1978] Imm AR 206............ 206
Visa Officer, Islamabad v Bi (Channo) [1978] Imm AR 182 .... 66, 206, 454
Visa Officer, Islamabad v Hussain [1987] Imm AR 39.................... 463
Visa Officer, Islamabad v Sindhu [1978] Imm AR 147 243
Visa Officer, Karachi v Mohammed (Hasan) [1978] Imm AR 168 .... 456, 457
Waddington v Miah [1974] 1 WLR 683; 118 SJ 365....................... 517
Wadia v Secretary of State [1977] Imm AR 92...................... 453, 455
Wah (Yau Yak) v Home Office [1982] Imm AR 16, CA
Walid (1662) 75
Watson v Immigration Officer, Gatwick Airport [1986] Imm AR 75 284
Williams v Immigration Officer, Heathrow [1986] Imm AR 186 466
Williams v Secretary of State [1972] Imm AR 207................... 225, 227
Wiseman v Borneman [1971] AC 297; [1969] 3 WLR 706; [1969] 3 All ER 255,
  HL.. 491
Wong (5991) 67
Yeong Hoi Yuen v Secretary of State [1977] Imm AR 34................ 105, 131
Yosef v Secretary of State [1979–80] Imm AR 72........................ 456
Yousuf (Mohammed) v ECO, Karachi [1990] Imm AR 191 .... 42, 463
Zaman (Mohammad) v ECO, Lahore [1973] Imm AR 71.................... 240
Zamir v Secretary of State [1980] AC 930; [1980] 3 WLR 249; 124 SJ 527, HL .20
Zia (Raja) v Secretary of State [1993] Imm AR 404...................... 454

Table of Statutes

Asylum and Immigration Appeals
  Act 1993 ....3, 37, 38, 40, 50,
            374, 382, 385, 387, 399,
            474, 475, 481, 491
  s 1 335
  s 2 .... 335, 340
  s 3 358
    (4) 359
    (5) 359
    (6) 359
    (7) 359
  s 4 366
  s 5 366
    (8) 366
  s 6 .... 388, 398
  s 7 .... 42, 78, 255
    (1) 78, 420
    (2) 255, 340
  s 8 .... 372, 414
    (1) 389
    (2) 388
    (3)(*a*) 389
    (4) 389
  s 9 .... 383, 471
    (1) 427
    (2) 471
  s 10 .... 400, 413
    (2) 427
  s 11 .... 97, 119, 126
  s 12 38
  s 13 426
  Sched 1, para 5 529
  Sched 2, para 1 373
          para 2 .... 373, 388
          para 5(2) 380
              (3) 378, 485
              (5) 380
          para 7 .... 388, 398

Asylum and Immigrations Appeals
  Act 1993—*contd*
  Sched 2, para 8 .... 388, 389, 398
Backing of Warrants (Republic of
  Ireland) Act 1965 263
Bill of Rights 1689—
  art 8 7
British Nationality Act 1948 .. 3, 5, 10,
                       25, 27, 36
  s 1 5
  s 2 28
  s 4 5
  s 5 5
  s 7 26
  s 12 25
    (6) 25, 26
    (7) 25
British Nationality Acts
  1948-1964 36
British Nationality Act 1965 27
British Nationality Act 1981 ... 3, 4, 5,
             6, 7, 9, 12, 13, 24, 25, 27,
            28, 29, 37, 41, 49, 50, 425
  s 3 31
  s 3 .... 31, 32, 522
    (2) 32
  s 5 .... 31, 33
  s 6 .... 33, 34
    (1) 34
    (2) 34
  s 7 .... 28, 31, 33
  ss 8–10 31
  s 12 35
  s 13(1) 35
  s 14 .... 30, 31
  s 23 26
  s 26 27

British Nationality Act 1981—*contd*
Pt IV 49, 293
s 30 27
  (*a*) 69
s 31 27
  (2) 28
Pt V 6
s 37(1) 27
s 38 27
s 39 .... 6, 9
  (2) 13
  (3) 13
s 40 .... 18, 31
  (1) 36
  41(1)(*f*) 527
s 46 524
  (1)(*a*), (*b*) 526
  (2) 527
s 50(1) 14, 259
  (2) 13, 29
  (3)–(5) 13, 14, 29
  (9)(*a*) 29
Sched 1 .... 33, 34
Sched 3 24
Sched 4 9
Sched 6 25
British Nationality (No 2) Act
  1964 25
British Nationality (Hong Kong)
  Act 1990 .... 37, 43
  s 1 44
    (1) 46, 49
    (4) 49
    (5) 44
  s 3(3) 45
    (4) 45
  s 6(2) 49
  Sched 1 .... 46, 48
    para 4 44
  Sched 2 .... 42, 49
    para 4(1) 49
    para 5 49
Channel Tunnel Act 1987—
  s 12 393
Children Act 1989............. 275
Commonwealth Immigrants Act
  1962 .... 5, 11
Commonwealth Immigrants Act
  1968 .... 5, 11
Criminal Appeals Act 1968
  s 50 421
Diplomatic Privileges Act 1964 .. 266

Domicile and Matrimonial Proceedings
  Act 1973—
  s 3 203
Education Act 1944 114
Employment Protection (Consolidation) Act 1978
  s 136 472
European Communities Act 1972 473
  s 1(2) 177, 292
European Communities Act 1972
  s 2 .... 28, 178, 289, 320
    (1) 328
    (2) 42, 305, 338, 330
    (4) 328
  s 3(1) 329
Extradition Act 1989 263
European Economic Area Act
  1993 292
  s 3 .... 305, 306
Forgery and Counterfeiting Act 1981—
  s 9 525
Housing Act 1985—
  Pt II....................... 62
  Pt III...................... 89
  s 74 528
    (3) 528
  s 326 212
Housing (Scotland) Act 1987—
  Pt II....................... 89
Immigration Act 1971 .. 3, 4, 6, 9, 10,
            13, 14, 16, 19, 22, 24,
            25, 27, 28, 38, 41, 55,
            68, 69, 75, 136, 250, 271,
            289, 382, 385, 390, 395,
            437, 443, 454, 491, 510
  s 1 6
    (1) 9, 17, 201
  Pt I 6, 527
    (3) 247
    (5) 52, 421
  s 2 .... 6, 9, 10, 13, 25
    (1) 17
    (*c*) 66
    (2) 67
  s 3 .... 6, 12, 378
    (*a*) 11
    (2) 6, 51
    (*b*) 360
    (3)(*b*) 74, 79, 420, 494
    (5) 265, 372, 380, 389,
                   404, 418, 438, 527
    (*a*)........... 265, 266, 419
    (*b*)........ 265, 269, 372, 389,
                   404, 406, 527

TABLE OF STATUTES   xliii

Immigration Act 1971—*contd*
s 3(5)(*c*) 265, 277, 419
   (6) 265, 269, 372, 389,
                    404, 406, 527
   (7) 521
   (8) 10, 17, 22, 66
   (9) 13, 22, 23, 64, 67
     (*a*) 64
     (*b*) 66
s 4 12
   (1) 54, 396, 486
   (3) 259, 525
   (4) 259, 525
s 5 .... 276, 404, 528
   (1), (2) 265
   (3) 265, 276, 278
   (4) 265, 278, 419
   (6) 405
s 6 528
   (5)(*a*) 421
   (6) 405
s 7 28
   (1) 305, 406, 418
s 8 .... 12, 15, 417, 519
   (1) 378, 519
   (2) 14, 373
   (3) 14, 266, 373
     (*a*) 373
     (*b*) 373, 378
   (3A) 266
   (4) 378
     (*b*) 14
     (*c*) 14
s 11 .... 17, 65, 92, 203
   (1) 399
   (1A) 65
Pt II 6, 15, 372, 374
s 12 .... 15, 425
s 13 .... 413, 414, 415, 424,
                    426, 434, 439
   (1) 314, 423, 424
   (3) 414, 440
   (3A) 414, 425
   (3AA) 431, 491
   (3B) 119, 126, 414, 426
   (3C) 427
   (5) 283, 435
s 14 .... 126, 340, 413, 416,
                  417, 426, 427
   (1) 76, 264, 314, 417,
                              418
   (2) 418
   (2A) 417, 426

Immigration Act 1971—*contd*
s 14(2B) 427
   (5) 417, 426
s 15 .... 413, 418, 420, 423,
                        424, 431
   (1) 314
   (2) 405, 418
   (3) 418
   (7) 15
     (*a*) 421
     (*b*) 421
     (*c*) 421
   (8) 421
   (9) 421
s 16 .... 413, 422, 423
   (1)(*a*), (*b*) 372
s 17 .... 413, 423
   (1), (2) 415
s 18 .... 15, 434
   (1)(*a*) 435
   (2) 434
s 19 .... 53, 54, 432, 433, 459
   (1)(*a*)(i) 433
   (2) 54, 432
s 20 464
   (1) 464
s 21 .... 384, 452, 470, 517
s 22(2)(*a*) 464
   (3) 453
   (4) 452, 453
   (5) 465
   (6) 447
s 23 453
Pt III 6
s 24 .... 64, 519, 520
   (1)(*a*) 518
     (*b*) 518, 520, 523
       (i) 518
       (ii) 519
     (*c*) 519, 523
     (*d*) 517, 520
     (*e*) 520
     (*f*) 521
     (*g*) 521
   (1A) 519
   (2) 517
   (4) 518
s 25 .... 517, 522
   (1) 522, 523
   (2) 523
   (6) 522, 523
   (7) 522
s 26 .... 517, 523

TABLE OF STATUTES

Immigration Act 1971—*contd*
s 26(1)(*a*) 524
    (*c*) 518, 524, 525, 526, 527
    (*d*) 525
    (1)(*e*) 525
    (*f*) 259, 525
    (*g*) 525
s 27 526
    (*a*)(i) 526
    (ii) 526
    (*b*)(i) 526
    (ii) 526
    (iii) 526
    (*c*) 526
    (*d*) 526
s 28(1) 517
s 33(1) 16, 17, 74, 192, 404
    (4) 413, 421, 428
Sched 2 .... 65, 203, 360, 393, 394, 445, 520, 524, 525, 526
    para 1 520
    (2) 520
    (3) 487
    para 2 .... 521, 524, 525
    para 3 .... 524, 525
    para 4(1) 63
    (2A) 394
    para 5 378
    para 6 434
    (1) 396, 397
    para 8 .... 347, 422
    (1)(*c*) 398
    para 9 .... 397, 422, 485
    para 10 .... 422, 521
    (1) 398
    para 11 .... 422, 521
    para 12 .... 422, 526
    para 13 .... 422, 526
    para 14 .... 79, 422
    para 15 422
    para 16 ...... 398, 448, 521
    (1) 399, 445
    (2) 445
    para 18(4) 512
    para 19 398
    para 21 .... 216, 399
    (1) 521
    (2) 521
    para 22 ...... 400, 402, 445
    para 24(1) 400
    (2) 401

Immigration Act 1971—*contd*
    Sched 2, para 24(3) 401
    para 28(5) 389
    para 29 .... 375, 445
    para 30(2)(*a*)–(*e*) 402
    para 88 398
    Sched 2, Pt II
Sched 3 .... 388, 407, 408, 520, 521, 526
    para 2(5) 521
    para 8 521
    para 9 380
Sched 5 15
Immigration Act 1988 .... 3, 37
s 1 .... 41, 52
    (5) 41
s 2 204
    (2) 41
    (4) 42
    (7) 42
s 3 .... 64, 66
s 5 .... 42, 419, 420
    (1) 433
    (4) 419
s 7 ....28, 305, 306, 318, 330
    (1) 42
    (2) 330
s 8 .... 42, 394
    (4) 42
    (5) 394
s 9 429
Schedule 43
    paras 1, 3 43
    para 6 .... 43, 65
    para 7 43
    para 8 .... 19, 396
    para 10 399
Immigration Appeals Act 1993... 15
Immigration (Carriers' Liability) Act 1987 .... 37, 39, 41, 50, 346
    s 1(1) 37
    s 1A(2)(*a*) 38, 92
Ireland Act 1947—
    s 2 28
Magna Carta 1297—
    Chap 39 512
    40 512
Matrimonial Causes act 1973—
    s 11(*d*) 204
Police and Criminal Evidence Act 1984 395
Prevention of Terrorism (Temporary Provisions) Act 1974 528

Prevention of Terrorism (Temporary Provisions) Act 1976 528
Prevention of Terrorism (Temporary Provisions) Act 1989 314
  Sched 2 314
Race Relations Act 1976 376
Rehabilitation of Offenders Act 1974 .... 251, 284
Sex Discrimination Act 1975 . 135, 376
Single European Act 1986 ..... 42, 367
Social Security Act 1986 .... 79, 89
Supreme Court Act 1981
  s 31 .... 481, 498
    (2) 500
    (6) 498
  s 34 482
  s 51(6) 505

Table of Statutory Instruments

Asylum Appeals (Procedure) Rules 1984
  r 8 384
  r 11(4) 376
  r 20 384
  r 22 383
    (3) 385
  r 23 .... 383, 385
  r 25 .... 383, 385, 386
  r 26 383
  r 27 .... 383, 386
    (1) 385
  r 28 .... 383, 386, 387
  r 29 383
  r 31 384
  r 32 .... 384, 386
  r 33 384
  r 34 384
  r 35 384
  r 36 384
    (*a*) 384
  r 38 384
  r 40 384
  r 41 384
  r 44 384
  r 45 384
  r 52 384
Asylum Appeals (Procedure) Rules 1993 (SI 1993 No 1661) 375, 491
  r 3 375
  r 5(1) 375
    (2) 378, 379, 380
    (3) 375
    (5)–(8) 376
  r 6 377
    (2) 378
  r 7 377
  r 8 376
  r 9 .... 377, 378

Asylum Appeals (Procedure) Rules 1993 (SI 1993 No 1661)—*contd*
    (2) 378
    (3) 382
    (4) 377
  r 10 378
  r 11(2) 377
    (3) 378
    (4) 377
  r 13 381
  r 14 381
    (1) 381
  r 15 382
  r 16 382
  r 17 382
    (3) 382
  r 18 382
  r 19 382
  r 21(5) 471
  r 29 387
    (6) 387
  r 30 .... 381, 383, 471
  r 31 .... 378, 380, 382
  r 32 387
    (3) 378
  Schedule 375
British Nationality (Hong Kong) (Selection Scheme) Order 1990 (SI 1990 No 2292) 43
  art 5 48
  art 27 48
  art 29 45
Channel Tunnel (Fire Services, Immigration and Prevention of Terrorism) Order 1990 (SI 1990 No 2227) 526

TABLE OF STATUTORY INSTRUMENTS

European Communities (Definition of Treaties) (European Agreement establishing an Association between the European Communities and their Member States and the Republic of Hungary) Order 1992 (SI 1992 No 2871).................... 177
European Communities (Definition of Treaties) (European Agreement establishing an Association between the European Communities and their Member States and the Republic of Poland) Order 1992 (SI 1992 No 2872).................... 177
European Convention on Extradition Order 1990 (SI 1990 No 1507) . 263
Hong Kong (British Nationality) Order 1986 (SI 1986 No 948) 26
Housing (Northern Ireland) Order 1986 Pt II........................ 89
Immigration Appeals (Notices) Regulations 1984 (SI 1984 No 2040)... 16, 434
   reg 3 434
      (3) 436
      (4) 436, 437, 443
   reg 4 437
   reg 6 .... 435, 442
Immigration Appeals (Procedure) (Amendment) Rules 1993 (SI 1993 No 1662).................... 472
Immigration Appeals (Procedure) Rules 1984 (SI 1984 No 2041) 413
   r 4 .... 416, 443
      (7) 422
      (8) 422
      (9) 423
      (10) 424
      (11) 436
         (a).................... 436
   r 5 444
   r 6 438
      (1) 439
      (2) 438
      (3)(c).................... 438
      (6)(a).................... 448
   r 8 .... 413, 440, 443
      (2) 440
      (3) 444, 450
      (4) 452
   r 10 442
   r 11 .... 413, 443, 444
      (3) 452

Immigration Appeals (Procedure) Rules 1984 (SI 1984 No 2041)—*contd*
   r 11(4) 422
   r 12 450
   r 13 465
   r 14 465
      (2) 465
   r 18 470
   r 20 450
      (c) 451
   r 21 464
   r 21B 472
   r 23 445
   r 24 448
   r 25 441
   r 26 453
   r 27 447
   r 28 452
   r 29 455
   r 30 442
      (2) 442
   r 31 454
   r 32 453
   r 33 447
   r 35 451
   r 36 .... 447, 448
   r 37(6) 442
   r 38 454
   r 39 454
   r 40 453
   r 44 .... 442, 443
   Pt III 472
   Sched 472
Immigration (Carriers' Liability Prescribed Sum) Order 1991 (SI 1991 No 1497) 37
Immigration (Control of Entry through the Republic of Ireland) Order 1972 (SI 1972 No 1610)
   art 4........................ 68
Immigration (European Economic Area) Order 1994 ..62, 64, 290, 292, 293, 306, 318, 319
Immigration (Landing and Embarkation Cards) Order 1975 (SI 1975 No 65)..................295, 525
Immigration (Registration with the Police) Regulations 1972 (SI 1972 No 1758).................... 259
   reg 2(1) 259
   reg 5 260
   reg 7 260
   reg 8 260

TABLE OF STATUTORY INSTRUMENTS

Immigration (Registration with the Police) Regulations 1972 (SI 1972 No 1758)—*contd*
  reg 8(*b*) 260
  reg 9 260
  reg 10 260
Immigration (Registration with Police) (Amendment) Regulations 1990 (SI 1990 No 400) 259
Immigration (Registration with Police) (Amendment) Regulations 1991 (SI 1991 No 965) 259
Immigration (Registration with Police) (Amendment) (No 2) Regulations 1982 (SI 1982 No 1024) 259
Immigration (Restricted Right of Appeal Against Deportation) (Exemption) Order 1988 (SI 1988 No 1203) . 420
Immigration (Restricted Right of Appeal Against Deportation) (Exemption) Order 1993 (SI 1993 No 1656). 42, 281, 420
Immigration (Transit Visas) Order 1993 (SI 1993 No 1678) 38, 92
Immigration (Variation of Leave) (Amendment) Order 1989 (SI 1989 No 1005).................... 76
Immigration (Variation of Leave) (Amendment) Order 1993 (SI 1993 No 1657).................. 78, 417
Immigration (Variation of Leave) Order 1976 (SI 1976 No 1572) ..76, 77, 79, 417
  art 3....................... 78
    (1) 77
    (2) 78
    (*c*) 77

Immigration (Variation of Leave) Order 1976 (SI 1976 No 1572)—*contd*
  art 3(3) 77
  art 4........................ 78
Income Support (General) Regulations 1987 (SI 1987 No 1971)—
  reg 71(1) 367
Social Security (Northern Ireland) Order 1986........................79, 89
Rules of the Supreme Court 1965 (SI 1965 No 1776)—
  Ord 18, r 19 380
  Ord 32, r 6 506
  Ord 41, r 5(2) 501
  Ord 45, r 5 500
  Ord 52, r 1 500
  Ord 53, r 2 481
    r 3 .... 376, 501
    (5) 504
    (6) 506
    (7) 495
    (10)(*a*)............. 500
    r 4 498
    (2) 500
    r 5(5) 508
    r 6(1) 508
    (2) 501
    r 8 .... 507, 508
    r 10(*a*) 506
  Ord 54...................... 510
  Ord 58...................... 508
  Ord 59...................... 509
    r 10 509
  Ord 62, r 11 502
  Ord 114, r 2 332
    (2) 332

Table of Immigration Rules

HC 169 201
  para 49 213
HC 251 .... 60, 70, 89, 117,
                        212, 250
HC 395 (Statement of Changes in
  Immigration Rules) 52, 94, 106,
                  154, 212, 290, 349
  paras 2, 3 .... 59, 60
  para 4 .... 59, 61
  para 5 60
  para 6 .... 13, 61, 88, 89,
                          122, 222
  Pt 1 62
  paras 7, 8 62
  paras 9–11 63
  paras 12, 13 65
  para 14 66
  para 15 .... 67, 247
  para 16 68
  paras 17, 18 69
  para 19 .... 69, 70
  para 20 69
  paras 21, 22 .... 71, 254
  para 23 .... 72, 254
  paras 24, 25 72
  para 26 .... 73, 247
  paras 27–29 73
  para 30 .... 73, 74
  para 31 75
  paras 32, 33 75
  para 34 78
  para 35 .... 79, 249
  para 36 .... 80, 254
  para 37 .... 80, 93, 254
  para 38 .... 80, 247, 254
  para 39 .... 80, 254
  Pt 2 82

HC 395—*contd*
  Pts 2–8 .... 247, 255, 258
  paras 40–56 425
  para 40 82
  para 41 82
    (i) 83, 90
  para 42 83
  para 43 .... 83, 90
  paras 44–46 90
  paras 47–50 91
  para 51 .... 85, 92, 93
    (v) 93
  para 52 94
  para 53 93
  para 54 .... 85, 94
  paras 55, 56 94
  Pt 3 96
  paras 57–62 425
  para 57 .... 96, 98, 99
  paras 58, 59 97
  para 60 .... 105, 488
  paras 61, 62 104
  para 63 106
  para 64 .... 107, 108
  paras 65, 66 107
  para 67 .... 107, 108
  para 68 .... 108, 330
  para 69 .... 108, 330
  para 70 .... 109, 330
  para 71–73 .... 109, 330
  para 74 .... 110, 330
  paras 75–77 110
  para 78 111
  paras 79–81 425
  paras 79, 80 111
  paras 81, 82 112
  paras 82–87 425
  paras 83–87 113

TABLE OF IMMIGRATION RULES

HC 395—*contd*
Pt 4	115
para 88	115
para 89	115, 117
(ii)	429
para 90–93	116
para 94	117
para 95	117, 429
(ii)	429
paras 96–98	118
para 99	119
para 100	119
para 101	121, 122
para 102–104	122
para 105, 106	123
para 107	123
(iv)	124
para 108	123
paras 109, 110	124
para 111	125
para 112	125
paras 110–121	131, 132
para 113–115	125
para 116	126
para 117	127, 129
para 118	127
para 119	129
para 120	130
para 121	130
paras 122, 123	131
para 124	132
para 125	132
(vi)	134
paras 126, 127	133
paras 128–193	161, 163
Pt V	137
para 128	137, 138
paras 129, 130	137
paras 131–134	141
para 135	142
para 136–138	143
paras 139–142	144
para 143	145
para 144	145
(ii)	146, 148
(iii)–(vi)	147
(iv)	146
para 145	145
para 146	146, 330
para 147	146, 148, 330
para 148–151	147, 330
para 152	148, 150, 312, 330
para 153	149, 330

HC 395—*contd*
para 154	149, 330
para 155	149, 150
paras 156–159	150
paras 160–164	151
paras 165–169	152
para 170–172	153
paras 173–175	155
para 176	155, 156
para 177	155
para 178	156
para 179–183	157
para 184	158
para 185	158
para 186	158, 429
para 187	158
para 188–191	159
para 192	160
para 193	160
para 194	161
para 195	161
para 196	162
para 197	163
para 198	163
para 199	164
Pt 6	166
paras 200–210	85
paras 200–239	186, 188
para 200	166, 177
para 201	166, 171, 172
(ii)	169
(iii)	170
(vi)	170
(vii)	171
(ix)	170
(x)	170
para 202	167, 171
(iii)	172
para 203	167
para 204	167
para 205	168
para 206, 207	173
para 208–210	174
para 211	175
para 212	175
(v)	177
para 213	175, 176
(iv)	177
para 214	176, 178
para 215, 216	176
para 217	178
para 218	179
para 219	179, 180

TABLE OF IMMIGRATION RULES

HC 395—*contd*
para 220–222	179
para 223	180
paras 224, 225	181
paras 226–230	182
para 231	173
paras 232–236	184
paras 237–239	185
para 240	186
para 241	187
para 242	187
para 243	188
para 244	189
para 245	189
Pt 7	190
para 246	190
para 247–249	191
paras 250–254	192
paras 255–262	194, 316
para 255	316, 318
para 256	316, 318
para 257	316
(ii)	318
para 258	317
para 259	317
(iii)	319
para 260	316
para 261	317
para 262	318
para 263–265	194
paras 266–270	195
para 271	196
para 272	196
para 273	197
para 274	198
para 275	199
para 276	199
Pt 8	202
paras 277–279	202
para 280	203
para 281	294, 296
para 282	72, 205
para 283	205
para 284	205, 215, 216
(vi)	216
paras 285–289	215
para 290	216
paras 291–295	217
para 296	218, 222, 253
para 297	218, 224, 253
para 298	219, 228, 253
para 299	220, 253
para 300	220, 253

HC 395—*contd*
para 301	220, 253
(i)–(v)	228
para 302	221, 228, 253
para 303	221, 253
para 304	228, 253
para 305	228, 253
paras 306–308	229, 253
para 309	230, 253
para 310	230, 253
para 311	231, 253
para 312	232, 253
para 313	233, 253
para 314	235, 237, 253
(xi)	237
para 315	236, 237, 253
para 316	236, 253
para 317	237, 239, 240
(i)	239, 241
(*d*)	239
(*e*)	239, 240
(iii)	241
(iv)	240
paras 318, 319	238
Pt 9	244, 246, 258
para 320	244, 246
(16)	251
(19)	251
para 321	252
para 322	254, 258
(11)	258
para 323	255
para 324	255
Pt 10	258, 319
para 325	258
para 326	259
Pt 11	260, 335, 356
para 327	335, 336
paras 328–333	338
para 328	335, 338
paras 329–331	336
para 332	336, 338
para 333	336, 339, 372, 388
para 334	336, 339, 340, 364
(ii)	340
para 335	339, 344
para 336	344
para 337	344, 346
para 338	340, 345
para 339	340, 345
para 340	352, 358
para 341	353, 358, 360
para 342	353, 358, 360

HC 395—contd
- para 343 .... 353, 358, 361
- para 344 .... 353, 358
- para 345 .... 345, 347
- para 346 .... 345, 352
- para 347 .... 345, 352
- para 348 .... 345, 414
- paras 349–351 364
- para 352 .... 364, 434
- Pt 12 .... 261, 411
- paras 353–361 411
- para 353 .... 411, 413
- para 354 .... 411, 414
- para 355 .... 411, 414, 415
- para 356 412
- para 357 412
- para 358 .... 412, 417
- para 359 412
- para 360 412
- para 361 413
- Pt 13 .... 265, 404
- paras 362–395 404
- paras 362, 363 265
- para 364 .... 272, 340
- para 365 275

HC 395—contd
- para 366 276
- para 367 276
- para 368 276
- para 369 278
- paras 370–373 279
- para 374 .... 279, 281
- para 375–378 280
- para 379 .... 280, 372, 373
- para 380 280
- paras 381–387 262
- para 381 .... 281, 282
- paras 382–385 281
- paras 386–388 282
- para 389 .... 278, 282
- para 390 .... 283, 408
- para 391 .... 283, 284, 408
- para 392 .... 283, 408
- para 393 .... 283, 408
- paras 394, 395 .... 284, 408
- Appendix 74, 285
- para 1 285
- para 2 .... 74, 285
- HC 503 201

Table of EC Cases

Abdulazia, Cabales and Balkandali v UK [1985] 11 EHRR 459; [1984] EHRR
451 ....201, 478
Adoni v Belgian State (115, 116/81) [1982] ECR 1665; [1982] 3 CMLR 631 ...304
Allue v Universita degli Studi di Venezia [1989] ECR 1591 ....302, 310
Amministrazione delle Finanze dello Stato v Simmenthal SpA (106/77) [1978]
ECR 629; [1978] 3 CMLR 263 328
Beldjoudi v France (1992) 14 EHRR 801; (1992) *The Times*, 10 April.........271
Berrehab v Netherlands (1988) 11 EHRR 322 ....271, 274, 475, 476
Bettray v Statsecretaris van Justitie (344/87) [1989] ECR 1621; [1991] 1 CMLR
459..295
Blum (Lawrie) v Land Baden-Wurttemberg (C-66/85) [1987] ICR 483 295
Bourgoin SA v Ministry of Agriculture Fisheries and Food [1985] 3 All ER
585..331
Caprino v UK [1982] 4 EHRR 97 476
Centre Public d'Aide Social de Courcelles v Lebon (316/85) [1989] 1 CMLR
337; [1987] ECR 2811 295
City of Wiesbaden v Baralli [1968] CMLR 329 304
Commission v Germany (249/86) [1989] ECR 1263; [1990] 3 CMLR 540 297
Costa v ENEL (6/64) [1964] ECR 585; [1964] CMLR 425 329
Cowan v Le Trésor Public (186/87) [1990] 2 CMLR 613; [1989] ECR 195 300
Demirel v Stadt Schwabisch Gmund (12/86) [1989] 1 CMLR 421; [1987] ECR
3719 ....321, 479
Diatta v Land Berlin (267/83) [1986] 2 CMLR 164; [1985] ECR 567 294
Dzodzi v Belgium (C-297/88, 197/89) [1990] ECR I-3763 (1991) *The Times*, 7
January..330
Employees of National Research Council v Italy, Re [1988] 3 CMLR 635.....296
ERTAE v Plioroforissis and Konvelas (C-260/89) [1991] ECRI-2925 ....327, 478
Eunomia di Parro v Ministry of Education [1971] ECR 811..................330
Francovich v Italian Republic (C-6, C-9/90) [1992] IRLR 84 331
Generics (UK) Ltd v Smith Kline & French Laboratories Ltd [1990] 1 CMLR
416..332
Haegen v Fratelli & Moretti SNC [1980] 3 CMLR 253 332
Henn and Darby v DPP (34/79) [1980] 2 CMLR 229; [1980] 2 WLR 597;
[1980] 2 All ER 166, HL...478
Hoechst v EC Commission (46/87, 227/88) [1989] ECR 2859; [1991] 4 CMLR
10 ....327, 478
Ianelli v Meroni (74/76) [1977] ECR 557 330

lv

TABLE OF EC CASES

Johnston v Chief Constable of RUC (222/84) [1987] QB 129; [1986] 3 WLR 1038; [1986] 3 CMLR 240..327, 478
Kamel v UK [1982] 4 EHRR 244..475
Kempf v Staatssecretaris van Justitie (139/85) [1987] 1 CMLR 764; [1986] ECR 1741..294, 304
Knoors v Secretary of State for Economic Affairs (No 115/78) [1979] ECR 399; [1979] 2 CMLR 357..315
Levin v Staatsecretaris van Justitie (53/81) [1982] ECR 1035; [1982] 2 CMLR 454..295
Luisi and Carbone v Ministero del Tesoro (286/82, 26/83) [1985] 3 CMLR 52; [1984] ECR 377..300
Marleasing SA v La Commercial Internacional de Alimentacion SA (C-106/89) [1992] 1 CMLR 305; [1990] ECR I-4135.............................330
Morson and Jhanjan v State of the Netherlands (35, 36/82) [1982] ECR 3723; [1983] 2 CMLR 221..315
Moustaquim v Belgium (1991) 13 EHRR 802..............................475
Nold v EC Commission (4/73) [1974] ECR 491; [1974] 2 CMLR 338.........478
ONEM v Kziber (C-18/90) [1991] ECR I-199.................117, 323, 234, 325
Parliament v Council (C-295/90), 7 July 1992.........................301, 309
Procureur de la Republique v Waterkeyn (314-6/81) [1982] ECR 4337; [1983] 2 CMLR 145..479
Pubblico Ministero v Ratti (148/78) [1979] ECR 1629......................330
R v Bonchereau (30/77) [1978] 2 WLR 250; [1978] 1 QB 732; [1977] 2 CMLR 800; [1978] ECR 1999..................................79, 251, 304, 313
R v Escauriaza [1989] 3 CMLR 281; (1988) 87 Cr App R 344; (1988) 9 Cr App R(S)..251, 304
R v Pieck (157/79) [1981] 1 QB 571; [1981] 3 All ER 46; [1981] 2 WLR 960; [1981] ECR 2171; [1980] 3 CMLR 220....................260, 305, 313, 314
R v Secretary of State for the Home Department, ex p Sandhu [1983] 3 CMLR 131..294
R v Secretary of State for the Home Department, ex p Santillo (131/79) [1981] 2 All ER 897; [1987] QB 778; [1981] 2 WLR 362; [1981] 1 CMLR 569.....29, 251
R v Secretary of State for Transport, ex p Factortame Ltd [1990] 2 AC 85; [1989] 2 WLR 997; [1989] 2 All ER 692; [1989] 3 CMLR 1, HL ...7, 500, 512
R v Secretary of State for Transport, ex p Factortame (No 2) (C-213/89) [1991] 1 AC 603; [1990] 3 WLR 818; [1991] 1 All ER 70; [1990] 3 CMLR 375..331
Reed v Staatsecretariat van Justitie [1987] 2 CMLR 164....................297
Rush Portuguesa LDA v Office National d'Immigration (C-113/89) [1990] [1991] 2 CMLR 818; [1990] ECR 1-1417; *The Times*, 12 April................325
Rutili v Minster of the Interior (36/75) [1975] ECR 1219; [1976] 1 CMLR 140..478
SACE v Italian Minsitry for Finance (33/70) [1970] ECR 1213; [1971] CMLR 123..330
Salgoil SpA v Italian Ministry for Foreign Trade (13/68) [1968] ECR 453; [1969] CMLR 181..329
Sevince v Staatssecretariat van Justitie (C-192/89) [1990] ECR I-34-61; [1992] 2 CMLR 57..321
Soering v UK (1988) 11 EHRR 439..477
SPUC v Grogan (159/90) [1991] 3 CMLR 849 (1991) *The Independent*, 15 October..479
State, The v Rover [1976] ECR 497..295

State, The v Watson and Belmann [1976] ECR 1185 478
Uppal v UK [1981] 3 EHRR 391 476
Van Duyn v Home Office [1974] 3 All ER 178; [1974] 1 WLR 1107; [1974] 1
    CMLR 347..28
Van Duyn v Home Office (No 2) (41/74) [1975] 3 All ER 190; [1975] Ch 358;
    [1975] 2 WLR 760; [1974] ECR 1337; [1975] 1 CMLR 1 ....289, 303, 307, 330
Van Gend en Loos v Nederlandse Administratie der Belastingen (No 26/62)
    [1963] ECR 1; [1963] CMLR 105....................................329
Vilvarajah v UK (1991) *The Independent*, 5 November 477
W v UK (1988) 10 EHRR 29 477
Wachauf v State, The (C-5/88) [1989] ECR 2609; [1991] 1 CMLR 328 327

Table of EC Legislation

Council of Association Decision 2/76 . 321
  art 2(1)(b) 321, 322
Council of Association Decision 2/78 . 320
Council of Association Decision 1/80 . 320, 321
  art 6 322
    (1) 322
Directive 63/360 297
  art 3 298
    (2) 75
  art 4 307
  art 5 298
  art 6 308
  art 7 308
  art 8 298
  art 10 298
Directive 64/2 247
Directive 64/221 [1984] OJ 056/850... 28, 29, 81, 251, 291, 297, 303, 305, 311, 312, 315, 319, 321, 322
  art 2 303
    (2) 303, 313
  art 3 303
  art 6 .... 313, 314
  art 8 314
  art 9 .... 313, 314
    (2) 303, 315
  Annexe 305
Directive 1408/71 323
Directive 73/148 .... 292, 299
  art 1 .... 299, 300
  art 3 300
    (2) 300
  art 4 .... 300, 308
    (1) 309

Directive 73/148—contd
  art 55 300
Directive 75/34 .... 299, 303, 310
  art 2, 3 310
  art 5 311
Directive 75/35 311
Directive 76/207 323
Directive 90/364 .... 292, 302, 310
  art 1 302
    (2) 302
Directive 90/365 ... 292, 298, 303, 311
  art 1 311
Directive 90/366 .... 292, 301
  art 1 .... 301, 309
  art 2 309
    (1) 301
Directive 90/366 309
  art 1 309
  art 2 309
Directive 93/96 [1993] OJ L317/59 .... 103, 301, 309
Regulation 1612/68 .... 135, 291, 296, 298, 301
  arts 1, 2 296
  arts 3, 4 297
  art 7 297
    (2) 297
  art 8 297
  art 9 297
  art 10 .... 296, 298, 307, 312
    (1) 297
  art 11 .... 297, 307
  art 12 307
Regulation 1251/70 .... 291, 298, 303, 311
  arts 1–4 312
Regulation 72/194 303

lix

Regulation 2210/78 323	Rules of Procedure of EC Commission	
Regulation 2211/78 323		
Regulation 2212/78 323	r 37 479	

Table of European Treaties and Conventions

Agreement establishing an Association between the European Economic Community and Turkey (Ankara, 12 September 1963) OJ C113 320
Convention and Protocol relating to the Status of Refugees 1951 (Cmnds 9171 and 3906).........42, 74, 337, 346, 372
  art 1 340
  art 1A......................340
  art 1C......................343
  art 1E......................344
  art 1F......................344
  art 31 337
  art 31.2....................337
  art 32 ....337, 366
  art 33..............337, 347, 348
Convention on the External Frontiers of the EC (draft).........326, 327
Council of Europe Agreement on the Abolition of Visas for Refugees 1959..........................74
Dublin Convention 346, 368
  art 4 351
  art 5 368
  art 6 ....368, 369
  art 7 ....368, 369
  art 8 368
  art 9 369
  art 10 ....370, 371
  art 11 370
  arts 14, 15 371
European Convention on Establishment
  art 3(3).....................263
European Convention on Extradition 1957........................263

European Convention on Human Rights and Fundmental Freedoms 1953.........53, 270, 271, 339, 473
  art 1 474
  art 2 475
  art 3 ....473, 476
  art 5 473
  art 8 ....201, 271, 273, 473, 475, 476, 480
    (2)......................477
  art 10 ....327, 478
  art 12 473
  art 13 ....191, 201, 271, 473
  art 14................201, 473, 476
  art 25 479
First Protocol...................275
  art 2 274
Fourth Protocol
  art 2 478
European Convention on the Supression of Terrorism........263
European Economic Area Agreement 290, 305, 307, 328
  art 2(b).....................290
  art 4 290
    (2)......................291
  art 28 291
    (3)......................291
  art 30 291
  art 31 ....291, 292
  art 33 292
  art 34 292
  art 36 292
  Pt III 290
  Annex V 291
  Annex VIII 292
Geneva Convention on Refugees 1951........................326

TABLE OF EUROPEAN TREATIES AND CONVENTIONS

Treaty of Rome 1957 .....29, 135, 287
  art 5 328
  art 7 ....289, 367
  art 89 ....326, 367, 369
  arts 40–50 320
  arts 48–60 289
  art 48 ....289, 294, 295, 314, 321
    (3)........................28
    (4).......................296
  art 49 294
  art 50 294
  art 51 294
  arts 52–59 299
  art 52.................289, 299, 315
  art 56 327
    (1)........................28
  arts 59–66 299
  art 59 ....289, 325
  art 60 ....299, 325
  art 66 327

Treaty of Rome 1957—*contd*
  art 169 329
  art 177 332
  art 189 329
  art 238 ....290, 320
  art 227 293
Treaty on European Union 1993 ...42, 289
  art 3(c) 28
  art 7 ....64, 68
  art 8a 290
    (1).......................289
  art 48 28
    (3).......................251
  Title VI, art K1 325
    art K2 326
UN Convention on Torture 339
Vienna Convention on the Law of Treaties 1969 (Cmnd 7964)
  art 31(3)(b) 337

Part I

Background

Chapter 1

General Background

The Immigration Act 1971 and the British Nationality Act 1981 are authority for, and the main sources of, the network of subordinate legislation and administrative discretion which is the basic law of immigration control. In addition significant modifications to rights of appeal and immigration control have been effected by the Immigration Act 1988 and the Asylum and Immigration Appeals Act 1993. The ramifications of the rule-making powers given to the S of S by these Acts are extensive.

Immigration control results from a few substantive rights granted by statute and subordinate legislation, and from procedural rules governing the grant and refusal of leave to enter and remain. As a result of the large areas of discretion granted to the S of S, substantive rights have to be derived from the procedural mechanism governing that discretion.

The 1971 Act is concerned with the control of travel to and from the UK, and the control of settlement within the UK. Before the British Nationality Act 1948 the basic distinction (which still remains today) was between those persons with and those without the right of entry. They were divided broadly into British subjects who had that right, and aliens and British Protected Persons (BPP) who were born in or had a connection with a British Protectorate, who did not.

The 1948 Act made a division within the category of British Subjects. It created three categories: citizens of the UK and Commonwealth (CUKC), citizens of independent Commonwealth countries (such as India, Ghana or Jamaica), and British subjects without citizenship. All these had the right of entry. By the time of the 1971 Act further distinctions had been made within these categories. Certain persons who previously had the right of entry lost it. British subjects without citizenship lost the right of entry, ironically being called 'British Subjects' thereafter.

The 1971 Act removed the right of entry by means of the concept of patriality. Within the categories of those who had previously had the right of entry, it made the distinction between 'patrials' who were not subject to immigration control, and 'non-patrials' who were. This distinction remains in the separation of those who have and those who do not have the 'right of abode'. It further split the category of CUKC, into 'patrial' CUKCs (those CUKCs with the right of abode), and 'non-patrial' CUKCs (without the right of abode). The category of citizens of independent Commonwealth countries was similarly split. They were thereafter known as 'patrial Commonwealth citizens' and 'non-patrial Commonwealth citizens'.

By the 1981 Act, citizenship rights were equated with freedom from immigration control. Thus CUKCs with the right of abode (patrial CUKCs) became known as British citizens. Patrial Commonwealth citizens became known as 'Commonwealth citizens patrial on 31 January 1982'. Both of these categories were free from immigration control and could enter the UK after any length of absence. Non-patrial CUKCs became further subdivided into British Dependent Territories citizens (BDTCs) and British overseas citizens (BOCs). Commonwealth citizens who were non-patrial became known as 'Commonwealth citizens not patrial on 31 January 1982'. Before the 1981 Act the right of abode in the UK was defined by reference to the concept of patriality. Since the 1981 Act the right of abode is determined by reference to the categories of citizenship which were created at that time (see Chapter 3). It is characteristic of this area of law that what seems to be a substantive right of citizenship in fact flows from a person's relation to immigration control, and not vice versa.

The illogical process of assimilating citizenship to immigration control is the result of a gradual retreat by successive British governments from the imperial stance which recognised all citizens of the Empire as British subjects. Various pressures have led governments to withdraw some of the full rights of citizenship (ie the right freely to enter and settle in the UK) from members of the Commonwealth. At the same time governments have been reluctant to renounce symbolic labels such as 'citizen of the UK and colonies' and 'Commonwealth citizen'. The 1981 Act finally acknowledged the hypocrisy of offering a citizenship which entails

GENERAL BACKGROUND 5

subjection to immigration control inconsistent with the titular status of that citizenship.

1 The British Nationality Act 1948

Until the BNA 1948, everyone who owed allegiance to the Crown was a British subject. All others were aliens. The BNA 1948 divided the category of British subject (which was interchangeable with 'Commonwealth citizen' under that Act) into two categories, CUKCs and persons who had citizenship of independent Commonwealth countries (s 1).

Citizenship of the United Kingdom and Colonies (CUKC)

A person acquired the status of CUKC either by birth in the UK and colonies, or by descent from a father who was born there (ss 4 and 5). The intention seems to have been that as gradually the remaining colonies became independent a large number of CUKCs would lose that citizenship on acquiring the citizenship of their newly independent country. The position would eventually be reached where the CUKC category would be reduced to citizens of the UK. All other former members of that category would be citizens of independent Commonwealth countries, and therefore British subjects (or Commonwealth citizens).

2 The Commonwealth Immigrants Acts 1962 and 1968

Not all British colonies became independent. Some persons, particularly Asians living in East Africa, did not automatically acquire the citizenship of the country in which they lived when it became independent, and they remained CUKCs. The result was that persons who had strong ties with the UK shared the same citizenship status as those who did not. Some critics believed that this was anomalous. Consequently the gradual effect of legislation since 1948 has been to subdivide the category of CUKC by subjecting its members to differential immigration control. This in turn has come to seem anomalous. The 1981 Act dispersed the category of CUKC to the four winds. The first steps on this road were taken by the 1962 Act, the first Act to impose immigration control on British subjects. One group that had not been subject to that control, the East African Asians, were subsequently caught in the expanding net of control by the 1968 Act.

3 The Immigration Act 1971

The structure of the 1971 Act is relatively simple. It has four parts and six schedules. The key parts of the Act are Parts I–III. Part I provides for the control of entry into and stay within the UK. The effect of this Part and the rules made under it are examined in Part II of this book. Part II of the Act sets up the statutory appeals machinery examined in Chapters 23 ff. Part III of the Act deals with criminal offences, which are discussed in Part VII of this book.

The pivotal sections of the Act are ss 1–3. Section 1 sets out the travellers and the journeys which are subject to immigration control. The right of abode in the UK (previously known as patriality) is defined in s 2. This section was substantially amended by the 1981 Act so that the right of abode is defined by reference to the categories of citizenship set up under the 1981 Act, instead of by reference to the concept of patriality. Section 3 of the Act makes general provision as to immigration control, with subs 3(2) being the source of the S of S's power to make the crucial immigration rules.

4 The British Nationality Act 1981

The pattern of the 1981 Act is superficially simple. There are five parts. The first four create four new categories of citizenship: British citizenship, British Dependent Territories citizen (BDTC), British Overseas Citizen, and British subject. These new categories and their consequences are discussed in Chapter 3. Part V is a miscellany, which among other things makes, by s 39, amendments to the 1971 Act.

In the case of British citizenship and BDTCs the 1981 Act sets out how these categories of citizenship may be acquired: both at the commencement and after commencement of the Act. As to BOCs and British subjects, there are only limited statutory mechanisms for the acquisition of citizenship after commencement, since it was intended that these categories would die out. The Act makes provision for the loss of citizenship.

The main change to the pre-existing law made by the 1981 Act in connection with citizenship was that it was no longer possible to acquire the citizenship which is crucial to freedom from immigration control simply by being born in the UK. Before the 1981 Act anyone who was born in the UK became a CUKC and had the right of abode (ie was patrial), simply by virtue of place of birth. Since the 1981 Act, however, birth in the UK, is not sufficient and the clearest traditional means of acquiring citizenship (*jus soli*) is abolished.

The apparently simple structure of the 1981 Act is complicated by the necessity of cross-reference to earlier nationality laws. The question of who belongs to the four categories of citizenship under the 1981 Act cannot be determined simply by looking at that Act. It is necessary first to look at the categories of citizenship which preceded those set out in the 1981 Act: they are the foundation upon which that Act is built.

5 Use of Parliamentary materials

In general, reference to parliamentary materials has not been permitted as an aid to the construction of statutes, but there are a number of exceptions to this rule. It is permissible when construing primary or secondary legislation to use the reports of Commissions and to refer to White Papers solely in order to ascertain the mischief which a provision is intended to cure (*Assam Railways & Trading Co Ltd v Commissioners of Inland Revenue* [1935] AC 445 at 457–8). In *R v S of S for Transport, ex p Factortame Ltd* [1990] 2 AC 85, the HL was prepared to look at a Law Commission's Report for the purpose of drawing an inference as to the intention of Parliament from the fact that Parliament had not implemented one of its recommendations. The HL in *Pickstone v Freemans plc* [1989] AC 66 departed from the general rule when construing a statutory instrument, in order to ascertain the intention of Parliament at the time the instrument had been presented to Parliament by the responsible Minister.

The general prohibition on reference to Parliamentary materials stems from the view that such reference might infringe Article 8 of the Bill of Rights 1689, prohibiting the questioning of proceedings in Parliament in any other place. However, in *Pepper v Hart* [1992] 3 WLR 1032, the HL held that the use of clear ministerial statements by the courts as a guide to the construction of ambiguous legislation would not infringe the Bill of Rights. Lord Browne-Wilkinson said (at p 1056) that reference to 'parliamentary materials should only be permitted where such material clearly discloses the mischief aimed at or the legislative intent behind the ambiguous or obscure words'. He thought it unlikely that any statement other than the statement of the Minister or other promoter of a Bill would meet these criteria.

It is therefore possible to use *Hansard* as a guide to the interpretation of legislation in the following circumstances:
- (*a*) where the legislative provision is ambiguous or obscure or leads to absurdity;
- (*b*) where the materials which are relied upon consist of one or more statements by Ministers or other promoters of a Bill;
- (*c*) where other parliamentary materials are needed to understand the statements of the Ministers and their effects.

Where words in a statute are capable of bearing more than one meaning, and Parliament considered what interpretation should be placed upon those words, the court should look at Parliamentary materials in appropriate cases regardless of the practical difficulties that may be created by such a practice. Where the interpretation previously given to ambiguous words by a court conflicts with that expressed by the Minister at the time of the promotion of a Bill, the Minister's interpretation should in the future prevail. It is possible to refer to statements made by way of a concession by a Minister in Parliament in addition to such interpretive references.

Chapter 2

The Immigration Act 1971

The 1971 Act distinguishes between those categories of person who are subject to immigration control and those who are not. The key phrase used by the 1971 Act is 'right of abode in the UK'. This is not a phrase which appears in the passport of a person who is not subject to immigration control. The 1971 Act, s 1(1) provides that all those who have a right of abode in the UK shall be free to live in and to come and go into or from the UK without let or hindrance except in so far as may be necessary to establish that right. Section 2 defines who is to have a right of abode and provides that such persons are to be described as 'patrials'. This section was amended by the 1981 Act, s 39 and Sched 4. The right of abode remains the crucial factor which distinguishes those who are and those who are not subject to immigration control. However, the 1981 Act also redefined by reference to the categories of citizenship the persons who do or do not have a right of abode in the UK.

The 1971 Act also introduces the concepts of 'illegal entry' and 'settlement'. These continue to have relevance, and are discussed below.

1 The concept of patriality and right of abode before the 1981 Act

Patriality was a characteristic of CUKCs and citizens of independent Commonwealth countries only. Once a person had established his patriality to the satisfaction of the authorities and obtained his passport, in which was stamped the phrase 'holder has right of abode in the UK', he was free to come and go as he pleased. In practical terms, he would have been subject to immigration control in the sense that he would probably have been asked to show his passport when he entered and left the country.

There were, however, no restrictions on how long he could stay and or on his right to work. There was no requirement to undergo examination or register with the police. The practice of stamping the passport in this way has now ceased, because the holder would have those rights automatically as a British citizen.

(a) The right of abode (patriality)

Methods of acquisition Patriality is now known as the right of abode in the UK. After the 1971 Act a CUKC or Commonwealth citizens either had the right of abode (was patrial) or did not have it (was non-patrial). Before 1983 patriality was acquired by various routes:

(1) The first and most obvious route to patriality was to have been born, adopted, naturalised or registered (with some exceptions) in the UK and Islands (Channel Islands or the Isle of Man).

(2) The second way was by descent from or adoption by a father who was born etc in the UK and Islands, or was himself descended from or adopted by a father who was born etc in the UK or Islands.

(3) A third method of acquiring patriality was by being a CUKC who was settled at any time in the UK and Islands, and having been at that time ordinarily resident in the UK for five years or more.

(4) Patriality could be acquired by being a Commonwealth citizen born to or adopted by a parent who was a CUKC by virtue of his or her birth in the UK or Islands.

(5) The 1971 Act, s 2 made provision for certain women to be patrials by virtue of their marriage, namely, those women who were Commonwealth citizens and married to, were the widows of, or the ex-wives of men who were patrials by virtue either of birth in the UK and Islands, or were adopted, naturalised or registered in the UK, or had patriality by any of the other means. Widows and ex-wives of British subjects under the pre-BNA 1948 law, who would have been patrials either because they were born etc in the UK or were descended from a patrial, were also patrials.

(b) The burden of proving patriality

Under the 1971 Act, s 3(8), if any question arises as to whether a person does or does not have the right of abode (is or is not a patrial), the burden of proving that fact is on the person who asserts that he has the right. In the past a passport which said 'holder has right of abode in the UK' would have been sufficient proof. Difficulties arose in the case of a person who did not hold such a passport. The case of *S of S v Lakdawalla* [1972] Imm AR 26 underlines the problems experienced by persons who did not possess the appropriate passport. The IAT accepted that there was no entitlement as of right to a passport: the issue of passports is within the royal prerogative. However, the refusal to issue a new passport is amenable to judicial review (*R v S of S for the Foreign and Commonwealth Office, ex p Everett* [1989] QB 811). *Lakdawalla* was a case under the Commonwealth Immigrants Acts 1962–68, but the principle is the same today. The IAT reached the conclusion, under the immigration rules in force at the time, that 'eligible to hold a passport' did not (and presumably could not) mean 'legally eligible to hold a passport'. The IAT then directed itself in accordance with the administrative practices followed in passport offices in deciding whether or not the respondent was 'eligible' to hold a passport.

The 1971 Act, s 3(a) provided that persons who claimed patriality either by virtue of ordinary residence (route (3)) or marriage (route (4)) should prove it by means of a certificate of patriality by marriage. He needed no certificate if his claim was made by his spouse, who was a patrial either by virtue of birth in the UK or Islands, or by virtue of descent (routes (1) and (2)). Changes were introduced to this by the 1981 Act (see Chapter 3 below).

The cases on patriality show a tendency to deny patriality to potential holders. In *R v IAT ex p De Sousa* [1977] Imm AR 6, the appellant was refused entry to the UK. She appealed on the basis that she was naturalised in the UK and so did not require leave to enter at all. She was a BPP resident in Kenya who was granted a certificate of naturalisation by the Kenyan Governor. The certificate bore the signature of a Colonial Office functionary in London, and was registered at the Home Office. However, the Divisional Court held that she was not 'naturalised in the UK', and so not a patrial. A similar conclusion was reached in *Keshwani v S of S* [1975] Imm AR 38 in relation to an appellant naturalised by virtue of a certificate granted by the Ugandan Governor.

In *Hussein v S of S* [1975] Imm AR 69 it was held that patriality by virtue of descent (route (2) above) could not be acquired unless the grandparent from whom citizenship was traced had that citizenship by virtue of his own birth, adoption or naturalisation or registration in the UK. The appellants, one of whose maternal great-grandfathers had been born in Derby, were not patrials because their grandfather, although a British subject, was born in Madras, and their mother in Bombay.

In summary, before the 1981 Act came into force, there were two main categories for the purposes of nationality law. This was the distinction between British subjects (or Commonwealth citizens) and aliens. This was, however, a superficial division, since most Commonwealth citizens were for the purposes of immigration control in almost the same position as aliens, as most of them were non-patrial and therefore had no right of entry. The same patrial/non-patrial division existed within the CUKC category. CUKCs, and Commonwealth citizens who were not patrial, BPPS and aliens were subject to immigration control and required leave to enter and remain.

Limited exceptions to this wide general rule were provided for in the 1971 Act, s 8. In summary, there were exemptions from immigration control under that section in favour of seamen and aircrews in certain circumstances, anyone in whose favour the S of S had made an order, members of diplomatic missions, their families and households, and members of certain armed forces. (The position of nationals of EEA countries and of the Republic of Ireland is different from that of other aliens: see Chapters 15 and 16 below).

The result was that before the commencement of the 1981 Act non-patrial CUKCs and other Commonwealth citizens, despite the ties of their citizenship with the UK, were not free to enter and remain as they chose as the 1971 Act makes clear. Section 3 provided that non-patrials could not enter the UK without leave to enter. They could be given limited or indefinite leave to enter and remain; and such leave might be given subject to conditions such as restrictions on employment. Non-Commonwealth citizens could also be required to register with the police.

This meant that a large number of persons seeking to enter and stay in the UK had no right or entitlement to do so. They could only do so as the result of an administrative discretion which is vested by the 1971 Act in the S of S (who makes the rules) and the immigration officers (who administer those rules). Section 4 provides that the power of giving or refusing leave to enter the UK is to be exercised by immigration officers. Leave once given can be varied. This power is vested in the S of S (s 4).

2 The right of abode after the 1981 Act

The 1981 Act amended the 1971 Act, s 2. The definition of who is to have the right of abode was changed.

The 1981 Act, s 39(2) provides that for s 2 of the 1971 Act there shall be substituted:

A person is under this Act to have the right of abode in the UK if—
 (*a*) he is a British citizen; or
 (*b*) he is a Commonwealth citizen who—
   (i) immediately before the commencement of the British Nationality Act 1981 was a Commonwealth citizen having the right of abode in the UK by virtue of s 2(1)(*d*) or s 2(2) of this Act as then in force; and
   (ii) has not ceased to be a Commonwealth citizen in the meanwhile.

The new categories of citizenship under the 1981 Act are discussed in Chapter 3.

The 1981 Act, s 39(3) amends the 1971 Act s 3(9), and provides for certificates of patriality to be replaced by certificates of entitlement where such certificates may be required under the 1981 Act. The documentation that may be necessary to obtain entry is discussed in Chapter 6.

3 Settlement

'Settlement' was first defined in the 1971 Act, the 1981 Act and s 50(2)–(5) largely repeat the effect of the provisions of the 1971 Act. Clearly cases decided under the 1971 Act and cases decided under the 'returning residents' rule (see Chapter 6 below) will be authoritative in relation to the concept. There are two aspects to being settled:
 (1) A person is not settled until he is free of any restriction under the immigration laws as to the length of his stay in the UK.
 (2) He must be ordinarily resident in the UK.

Reference may also be made to the interpretation sections of the Immigration Rules, para 6 (see page 61). A person who is settled is no longer bound by the particular purpose for which he was admitted. So, for example, a person who had entered on a work permit to take up a particular job, may take up a completely different type of work when settled. Persons who are settled are also described as having 'indefinite leave to remain' or as having been granted 'permanent stay'. A person with this kind of leave may have a stamp in his passport stating that he has 'indefinite leave to remain in the UK'. Under the immigration rules there is a qualifying period of leave to remain after which an entrant may apply for indefinite leave to remain.

(a) Ordinary residence

Ordinary residence is partially defined in the 1981 Act, s 50(5). A person cannot be ordinarily resident if he is in the UK in breach of the immigration laws (see *Ex p Margueritte* [1983] 2 AC 309). 'Immigration laws' includes past immigration laws (see the 1981 Act s 50(1) and *Lui v S of S* [1986] Imm AR 287). Clearly if he has committed an offence under the 1971 Act or the 1981 Act he is in breach; but the concept of breach is wider than that, and embraces presence in the UK as an illegal entrant. Breach of the immigration laws also includes breaches of administrative directions under the legislation, such as a deportation order, and conditions of leave to enter or remain in the UK. It is irrelevant that such a breach is innocent and inadvertant (*IAT v Chelliah* [1985] Imm AR 192).

Ordinary residence is a concept used in other areas such as tax legislation and the Education Acts. It refers to a person's abode in a particular place or country which he has adopted voluntarily, or for settled purposes (which can include education), as part of the regular order of his life for the time being, whether of short or long duration (*R v Barnet LBC, ex p Shah* [1983] 2 AC 309, per Lord Scarman at p 343). A person can be ordinarily resident in the UK while absent for not insignificant periods, so long as he maintains some tie or connection with the UK. There must be 'an element of having a home here' (*Ex p Abu Bakar* (1981) unreported, per Woolf J). However, a person may be ordinarily resident in two places as once (*Britto v S of S* [1984] Imm AR 93). It is a question of fact in every case. The decided cases give broad guidance, but are not to be regarded as decisive precedents (see, for example, *IRC v Lysaght* [1928] AC 234 and *Levene v IRC* [1928] AC 217).

Exceptions to the general rule about settlement are contained in the 1981 Act, s 50(3), (4). A person who would otherwise fall to be regarded as settled, is not in fact settled for the purposes of the legislation, if he is subject to an exemption under the 1971 Act s 8(2), (3), (4)(*b*) and (*c*). That section confers exemption from immigration control on various categories of person, such as those in respect of whom the S of S has made an order, diplomatic agents (and members of their families and households) and members of visiting Commonwealth forces. A person who falls within one of these exemptions is not 'settled' in the UK, even if he meets all the other requirements of settlement. There is an exception to this rule in the case of a person to whom a child is born while he or she is apparently settled but subject to a s 8 exemption unless the person is entitled to diplomatic immunity.

4 Rights of appeal

Until 1969 there was no statutory machinery for appeals in connection with immigration. The 1971 Act, s 12 continued the existence of the IAT and of the adjudicators first set up under the Immigration Appeals Act 1969. Schedule 5 to the 1971 Act makes provision for the appointment, administration and organisation of these appellate bodies. Adjudicators and the members of the IAT are now appointed by the Lord Chancellor. Further changes have been made to rights of appeal by the Asylum and Immigration Appeals Act 1993, according a right of appeal to the CA provided that the IAT has granted leave but withdrawing rights of appeal from persons entering as visitors or short-term students and from persons whose application for leave must under the immigration rules be refused, either because they do not have the correct documentation or because they do not fulfil mandatory requirements of the immigration rules (see Chapter 23).

Part II of the 1971 Act sets out the rights of appeal to these bodies. An appeal is usually in the first instance to the adjudicator, and then to the IAT. Exceptionally, the adjudicator may be leapfrogged (for instance under s 15(7)). It is to be noted that there is generally no right of appeal against a decision to deport made on the grounds of national security (see pages 431–432 below).

Appeals may be made against
 (a) refusal of entry clearance;
 (b) refusal of leave to enter;
 (c) conditions of leave to enter and remain;
 (d) a decision to make a deportation order;
 (e) the validity of directions for removal;
 (f) refusal to revoke a deportation order; and
 (g) treatment as an illegal entrant.

Under s 18 the S of S may by regulations make provision for written notice of a decision which is appealable under the 1971

Act to be given to the potential appellant. This power was exercised by the Immigration Appeals (Notices) Regulations 1984 (SI 1984 No 2040). The notice must give reasons for the decision, but it is conclusive of the person by whom and the reasons for which the decision has been taken. The notice must also inform the person concerned of his rights of appeal under the Act. It must contain enough information to identify the basis of the decision made by the S of S. The sufficiency of the information will vary with the type of decision being taken. In a notice of a decision to deport based upon the allegation that it would be conducive to the public good, more information (such as the offence for which the deportee is being deported, or the conduct complained of by the S of S) is required, than if the decision is based upon a breach of a condition of leave, such as overstaying (*R v IAT, ex p Kalsoom Razaque* [1989] Imm AR 451).

5 Illegal entry

An 'illegal entrant' is defined in the 1971 Act, s 33(1) as 'a person unlawfully entering or seeking to enter in breach of a deportation order, or of the immigration laws, and includes a person who has so entered.' Under the 1971 Act, the S of S is only entitled to order the detention and removal of an immigrant who entered the UK under an apparently valid permission if the immigrant is in fact an illegal entrant.

In *Ex p Khawaja* [1984] AC 74, the HL decided that on an application to the court for judicial review of an immigration officer's order detaining a person in the UK as an illegal entrant, the court had a duty to enquire whether there had been sufficient evidence to justify the immigration officer's belief that the entry had been illegal. It is not enough for the immigration officer reasonably to believe that the person is an illegal entrant: if the S of S cannot prove that on the balance of probabilities the facts relied upon by the immigration officer show that the entrant is an illegal entrant, he has no power to remove him on that basis. The burden of proving that the person is an illegal entrant falls on the S of S, provided that the applicant can produce evidence of leave to enter having been granted. This will usually take the form of a genuine passport stamp. It is enough for the S of S to prove the facts which establish that entry was not in accordance with the immigration laws. For example, if the stamp in the passport is not genuine, it is not necessary for the S of S to prove how the person entered the country (*Ex p Mussawir* [1989] Imm AR 297).

A British citizen does not require leave to enter and may enter, and remain under the 1971 Act, ss 1(1) and 2(1). Anyone who does not have the right of abode in the UK requires leave to enter under s 3(1) of that Act. The onus is on a person who asserts that he is a British citizen to prove that he is (s 3(8); and see *In Re Bamgbose* [1990] Imm AR 135).

The definition of 'illegal entrant' is a broad one, and the categories of illegal entrants are not closed. Three categories may be identified:
  (*a*) those who enter the UK clandestinely; or
  (*b*) those who obtain leave to enter either by themselves practising fraud, or by someone practising fraud on their behalf, or by concealing material facts; or
  (*c*) those who obtain leave to enter by the use of a materially false document (*R v Naillie* [1993] Imm AR 462).

Under the 1971 Act, s 11 provision is made for persons who disembark to be deemed not to have entered the UK if they remain within an area approved by an immigration officer for persons to remain in pending a decision being made on their entry. A person does not enter the UK merely by disembarking, so that a person who disembarks without a right of entry is not automatically an illegal entrant. Asylum seekers, who may arrive with forged documents or no documents at all, will not be considered to have entered if they remain in such an area before making their application for asylum. In *Naillie* the HL held that as long as a person disembarking is an asylum seeker, and does not attempt otherwise to seek entry or obtain entry by fraud such as by the use of false documentation or without any documentation at all, but remains within a designated area when he claims asylum, he is not an illegal entrant.

Anyone who is subject to British immigration control and does not have leave to enter and enters the UK will be an illegal entrant, however innocent that entry may be (*Keung v S of S* [1992] Imm AR 201). It includes those who enter clandestinely, those who have entered by deception (see below (b) and *Ex p Khawaja* [1984] AC 14), and a person who has absconded having been granted temporary admission, for such a person has not been granted leave to enter (*Ex p Taj Mohammed Khan* [1985] Imm AR 104). More importantly, the definition includes a person who requires leave under the immigration laws to enter and enters without it. He is an illegal entrant whether or not he intended to enter by deception, or was aware that he was entering illegally (*Ex p Abdul Khaled* [1987] Imm AR 67, following *R v Governor of Ashford Remand Centre, ex p Bouzagou* [1983] Imm AR 69 (CA)). No element of *mens rea* is involved.

In *Abdul Khaled* a 13-year-old boy was brought into the country by British citizens who falsely claimed that he was their son. Their deception rendered the entry illegal. In *Bouzagou* a person was held to be an illegal entrant, when having overstayed his limited leave, and travelled to the Republic of Ireland, he entered the UK by the port of Liverpool at which no immigration control operated. However a person who was naturalised by registration or by issue of a certificate cannot be declared an illegal entrant unless deprived of his status as a British citizen under s 40 of the 1981 Act (*ex p Ejaz* (1993) *Times*, 7 December).

(a) Mistake

The general principle is that those who require leave to enter, but enter without leave, are illegal entrants. It is not necessary for the S of S to prove that a deception has occurred (*R v Immigration Officer, ex p Chan* [1992] 1 WLR 541). In *Mokuolo v S of S* [1989] Imm AR 51, two Nigerian sisters were held to be illegal entrants when they were admitted without the grant of leave because their passports mistakenly stated that they were British citizens. Further, an entrant may be an illegal entrant where the passport clearly gives the correct status of the entrant, shows that he requires leave to enter, and the immigration officer mistakenly believes that the entrant does not require leave to enter. In *Rehal v S of S* [1989] Imm AR 576 the immigration officer failed to grant leave to enter, because he believed the entrants to be British citizens, whilst their passports clearly stated that they were BOCs. The applicants were guilty of no misrepresentation of any kind, but nevertheless were illegal entrants because they lacked leave to enter when they needed to have it (see also *Ex p Mohan* [1989] Imm AR 436).

The position is slightly different where the entrant is innocent of any deception, and the immigration officer places a stamp in his passport granting him leave to enter. In *Ex p Ram* [1979] 1 WLR 148 the immigration officer, in the mistaken belief that the entrant had the right to indefinite leave to remain, stamped his passport to that effect. The effect of that stamp was that the entrant did receive indefinite leave to remain, as the immigration officer was acting within his powers. The entry was not therefore illegal (see also *R v IAT, ex p Coomasaru* [1983] 1 WLR 14).

Where the immigration officer puts a stamp in a person's passport which is illegible, the person obtains six months' leave to enter (Immigration Act 1988, Schedule, para 8). Such leave is deemed to be subject to a condition prohibiting employment. In *Minton v S of S* [1990] Imm AR 199 the length of the period of a visit could not be determined from the stamp in the passport. The CA took the view that the statutory provisions should be construed strictly. Extrinsic evidence as to the meaning of the stamp could not be introduced, so as to avoid six months' leave being deemed to have been granted.

(b) Entry by deception

One way in which an entrant may be in breach of the immigration laws is if he secures entry by means of a deception. The deception may be that of the entrant or of another person. In *Khan v S of S* [1977] 3 All ER 538 a husband produced an incorrect passport on behalf of his wife. The deception, of which she was ignorant, vitiated her leave. In *Chan* [1992] 1 WLR 541, the entrant innocently produced false documents of a kind required under the 1971 Act. Where a person produces a passport which is in fact a forgery, it does not matter whether he knows that it is a forgery or not. The leave obtained by means of its production is vitiated (*Hamid v S of S* [1993] Imm AR 216). Any deception must, however, be a material deception. The facts involved in the deception must be decisive to the grant of leave to enter in that if they were disclosed to the immigration officer he would in all probability refuse entry. Thus a deception operates to vitiate consent, if it is in relation to material facts and leave would in all probability not have been granted but for the deception (*Ex p Jayakody* [1982] 1 WLR 405). However, the entrant may not gain leave to enter on the basis of deceptive information, and thereafter admit to his true purpose and claim that he could have obtained leave on the basis of the true facts unless he claims to be a refugee (see chapter 19).

The question of whether facts are material or not must be seen in the context of the leave being sought. An entrant must not give a version of his intentions which is in fundamental respects at variance with his true intention (*Bugdaycay v S of S* [1987] AC 514). Thus in *Jayakody* the CA asked itself whether the Home Secretary would have been bound to refuse entry or whether he would in all probability have refused entry to a man who had applied for leave to remain for two months as a visitor. He had failed to disclose that he was married to a woman who was on a nursing course in the UK, and after he had obtained leave he applied for leave to remain until she completed the course. The CA held that even if the immigration officer had known about the marriage he might still have granted leave to enter as a visitor, so that the deception was not material. In *Bugdaycay*, the deception was that the entrant maintained that he wanted leave to enter the UK for a short period, whereas the true facts were that he wanted to apply for asylum. Thus if the entrant obtains leave to enter in one capacity, but secretly intends to remain in another capacity, the deception used to obtain leave is likely to be material, and it does not matter that had the truth been told, leave might have been granted.

A person seeking asylum who has entered the UK illegally will not be removed from the UK before he has had the opportunity to appeal against any refusal of asylum (see Chapter 20).

In *Adesina v S of S* [1988] Imm AR 442, the entrant sought leave to enter as a visitor, but in fact intended to study in the UK. Likewise in *Ex p Chomsuk* [1991] Imm AR 29 a concealed intention to work vitiated leave to enter granted for the purpose of studying. Finally, in *Mohammed Tadimi v S of S* [1993] Imm AR 90, the CA held that the applicant had deceived the immigration officer where he had entered as a student, was a student, but was also a chef. His nominal role as a student was not his real role or occupation.

In *Zamir v S of S* [1980] AC 930, the HL decided that apparently legal entry through the system of immigration control could be rendered illegal by non-disclosure of material facts. The case concerned an entrant who after obtaining entry clearance for settlement to join his parents on the basis that he was unmarried, got married. He did not disclose this fact on entry. He was not asked about marriage at that time. He was detained with a view to removal when his marriage was discovered by the S of S. The HL held that he had entered by deception, and his entry was illegal. This decision suggested that there was a duty of candour on entrants amounting to a requirement of utmost good faith to disclose all material facts. However, the facts which are material to the immigration authorities may not be appreciated as being important by the entrant. In *Ex p Khawaja* [1984] AC 74 the HL decided that there is no duty of candour upon an entrant amounting to a duty of utmost good faith. The HL accepted that silence as to a material fact is capable of amounting to deception so as to render entry gained thereby illegal. Actions such as the presentation of a passport known to contain false information may amount to deception (*Ex p Patel* (1987) *The Times*, 24 October). Thus in *Durojaiye v S of S* [1991] Imm AR 307 an extension of leave was obtained after entry by deception. The stamp resulting from that was later relied upon when the passport holder presented his passport on re-entry. Presentation of the passport alone amounted to deception.

If the S of S cannot prove that the entrant or his agent concealed a materially deceptive intention at the time that he obtained entry, he will be unable to show that the entry was vitiated by deception (see eg *Sorraseakh Monomai* [1991] Imm AR 29 (note)). However, if the entrant was given leave to enter for one purpose, but intended to follow another purpose if that was possible, he will be taken to intend to pursue that other purpose. Thus in *Ex p Brakwah* [1989] Imm AR 366 the entrant obtained leave to enter as a visitor, but intended to study if the conditions were favourable to that course of action. Glidewell LJ sitting in the Divisional Court stated that the basic question was

Has the Home Office proved to the required standard that the Applicant lied when he said that he wished to enter for a few weeks as a visitor and was that lie the effective means of obtaining leave to enter?

The CA in *Saffu-Mensah v S of S* [1992] Imm AR 185 stated that those who apply for leave to enter are required to tell the truth in the statements they make to the immigration officer which are material to their application. The critical date for the consideration of whether the representation made by the entrant is true or not is the date on which the representation is made, and there is nothing in the rules to suggest that the S of S should consider only whether the representation is true or false at the date of the application to enter (*Ex p Salim* [1990] Imm AR 316).

If the entrant made no representations at all, but fails to correct something said by someone else, which he may or may not have known about, he may in certain circumstances not be treated as an illegal entrant by reason of deception. In *Ex p Dordas* [1992] Imm AR 99, Kennedy J held that a Filipino servant, entering with her employer, who harboured an intention at the time of entry to run away from her employer but who did not disclose this, made no representation on this basis. She had not been asked to make any representations, and had played no real part in the preparations for coming to the UK.

Where the entrant entered before the coming into force of the

1971 Act, and his entry was secured by a third party's deception, he is entitled to be treated as settled in the UK by virtue of the returning residents' rule. After his settlement, later deceptions on re-entry, although possibly criminal offences, would not alter his status as a legal entrant (*Hiran Khan v S of S* [1990] 1 WLR 798). However if he is not lawfully settled, the position is different. The CA has held that if a minor entered the UK before the coming into force of the 1971 Act by virtue of a third party's deception (of which he knew) that entry was not lawful (*Rahim Miah v S of S* [1989] 1 WLR 806). Subsequent re-entries were not lawful where he relied upon the same deception, even if he satisfied para 56 of HC 169.

(c) Proving illegal entry

The S of S must prove that the entry is illegal. The standard of proof remains a civil one, but where there is an allegation that entry was obtained by means of a deception, a high degree of probability is necessary for the S of S to succeed (*Ex p Miah* [1983] Imm AR 91). Since a person declared to be an illegal entrant is liable to detention as such, the court must be satisfied that the facts of the case are as stated by the immigration officer. The S of S must prove to a high degree of probability that the facts leading to the conclusion that the entrant was an illegal entrant were in existence at the time that conclusion was reached by the immigration officer. A statement by the immigration officer that there were reasonable grounds for believing that the entrant was an illegal entrant does not by itself satisfy the burden of proof. The court must look at the evidence relied upon by the immigration officer to see whether or not it satisfied the burden of proof (*Khawaja v S of S* [1984] AC 74). The court will look at all the evidence, and not merely that which was available at the time of the decision of the S of S (see *Ex p Mahoney* [1992] Imm AR 275 and *Ex p Muse* [1992] Imm AR 282).

If a person asserts his right of entry on the basis of being a British citizen, the burden of proof that he is a British citizen falls on him by the 1971 Act, s 3(8). By s 3(9) of the Act a person entering the UK and claiming to have the right of abode must prove that he has that right by means either of a UK passport describing him as a British citizen or as a CUKC having the right of abode, or by a certificate of entitlement certifying that he has the right. An immigration officer may be satisfied that a would-be entrant is a British citizen on evidence other than a passport. That evidence may be oral or documentary (*Ex p Minta* [1992] Imm AR 380). If, however, the entrant produces a passport describing him as a British citizen, the immigration officer must accept that as proof. If the immigration officer does not accept that the passport is genuine, the burden is on the S of S to prove that it is a false passport, but the burden of showing that he is a British citizen remains on the entrant. A British Visitor's passport will not qualify under s 3(9) as conclusive proof that the bearer is a British citizen, because it is not one of the documents specified under that subsection.

As a result of the decision of the CA in *R v S of S for the Environment, ex p LB Tower Hamlets* [1993] 3 All ER 439, a local authority may determine whether a person is an illegal entrant for the purposes of s 33(1) of the 1971 Act. If it concludes that he is, it must notify the Home Office. The (draft) Homelessness Code of Guidance indicates that local authorities' enquiries need not be limited to housing matters.

Chapter 3

The British Nationality Act 1981

By virtue of the 1981 Act, CUKCs are divided into three groups: British citizens, British Dependent Territories citizens (BDTCs) and British Overseas citizens (BOCs). Residual classes of British subjects under the Act and British protected persons continue to exist. The label of Commonwealth citizen is also continued: it is applied to all categories of citizen created by the 1981 Act, to British subjects under the Act and to all citizens of the countries listed in Sched 3 to the Act. It is a citizenship of little more than symbolic value.

The 1981 Act changes the definition of right of abode in the UK. Further, it ends the equation between right of abode and the description 'patrial'. That ungainly word now disappears from immigration law. The distinction between 'patrial' and 'non-patrial' no longer exists. However there is still a distinction between those who have and those who do not have the right of abode.

It might have been thought logical that right of abode would be determined under the 1981 Act simply by the fact of British citizenship. However, the concept of 'patrial' under the unamended 1971 Act did not quite coincide with that of 'British citizen' under the 1981 Act. In the same way there is no total identity between 'British citizenship' and 'right of abode' under the 1981 Act. Those who have a right of abode under the 1981 Act are British citizens and those Commonwealth citizens who were patrials under the 1971 Act. This means that no nominally 'British' citizenships under the 1981 Act entail freedom from immigration control, apart from British citizenship itself. By contrast certain Commonwealth citizens, who are not even nominally 'British', are free from immigration control altogether. These, on the whole, are citizens of 'white' Commonwealth countries whose parents were born in the UK and Islands.

THE BRITISH NATIONALITY ACT 1981

1 Categories of citizenship defined by the 1981 Act

(a) British citizens

Broadly speaking, British citizens are those who under the 1971 Act were CUKCs and patrials. There are two exceptions to this generalisation:
  (*a*) persons who were registered as CUKCs under the British Nationality (No 2) Act 1964. These were stateless persons registered on the ground that their mothers were CUKCs at the time of their birth. They are not British citizens unless either
      (i) their mothers became (or if alive would have become) British citizens at the commencement of the Act; or
      (ii) they were patrials by virtue of being a CUKC settled at any time in the UK or Islands, ordinarily resident there for five or more years, at the commencement of the 1981 Act;
  (*b*) persons excluded from patriality under the 1971 Act, s 2 apparently by mistake. They are British subjects without any citizenship who on commencement of the BNA 1948 would have become CUKCs but for their citizenship of (or potential citizenship of) a Commonwealth country.

Under the 1948 Act s 12(6) they could apply to be registered as CUKCs and the S of S could in his discretion accept or refuse the application. If the application was made in an independent Commonwealth country the UK High Commissioner was to exercise the powers of the S of S. Under the 1981 Act persons became British citizens if they were registered under the BNA 1948, s 12(7), and were so registered by virtue of their descent by the male line from someone who was born or naturalised in the UK or colonies.

The wording of the 1948 Act is to be strictly interpreted and the status of a person under the Act will depend upon his status under s 12 at the date of commencement of the Act (*Ross-Clunis v S of S for the Foreign and Commonwealth Office* [1991] Imm AR 595).

(b) British Dependent Territories citizens (BDTCs)

The second category of 'British' citizens created by the 1981 Act on the abolition of CUKC status is that of BDTCs. This is a class of CUKCs who have some form of connection with a dependent territory, for example by birth, descent, naturalisation or registration. Those territories are listed in the 1981 Act, Sched 6.

They include Gibraltar. Initially the Falkland Islands were included in the list, but in 1985 citizens of the Falklands were made British citizens (British Nationality (Falklands Islands) Act 1983).

The methods by which this citizenship is acquired are laid down in the 1981 Act s 23. The first group of persons who hold this citizenship are CUKCs who are such by virtue of their birth, naturalisation or registration in a dependent territory; CUKCs who are born to a parent who at the time of the birth was a CUKC by virtue of birth, naturalisation or registration in a dependent territory, or were themselves born to a parent who held such citizenship; and women who were CUKCs and have at some time been married to men in either of the above categories. Those who were CUKCs by virtue of a connection with a British Dependency (such as Hong Kong at 31 December 1982) became BDTCs on 1 January 1983.

The second group of persons who are BDTCs are broadly those who were registered as CUKCs under BNA 1948, s 7 or s 12(6), and have some form of connection by descent with a dependent territory.

Since 1 January 1983, a BDTC can pass on that status to a child at birth if the child is born after that date in the dependent territory. Likewise the child of a person who is settled in a dependent territory will be a BDTC. If he is not, he will have to register or be registered.

(c) British Nationals (Overseas) (Hong Kong)

A person who but for a connection with Hong Kong would not be a BDTC will lose his citizenship on 1 July 1997, when the territory passes to China (Hong Kong (British Nationality) Order 1986 SI 1986 No 948). The Order creates a new form of citizenship: British Nationals (Overseas), for persons connected with Hong Kong. If, but for a connection with Hong Kong, a person would not be a BDTC, he may before 1 July 1997 register as a British National (Overseas). This category is an illusory category of citizenship; the Chinese do not recognise it. The system whereby Hong Kong BDTCs can acquire the right of abode is described in Chapter 4 below.

(d) British Overseas citizens (BOCs)

Those CUKCs who are not either British citizens or BDTCs are BOCs. This is the residual class of 'British' citizenship. It is not defined in the 1981 Act, except negatively in s 26. It covers those persons who, when the colony in which they lived became independent, did not acquire citizenship of that new country, but retained their CUKC status. They are therefore in the odd position of not really belonging anywhere. They are not citizens of the country in which they live, and yet their citizenship is of a type which gives them no right to enter the UK, the country which gives them nominal citizenship.

(e) British subjects

There is a further category of citizenship under the 1981 Act, that of 'British subject under the Act'. This does not coincide with the class of British subject under the BNA 1948, but was the new name for the category of British subjects without citizenship. Under the 1981 Act, British subjects without citizenship, women who registered as British subjects under the BNA 1965 and Irish citizens born before 1949 who chose to retain their status as British subjects, continue as 'British subjects under the Act' (ss 30 and 31).

(f) British Protected Persons (BPPs)

The final category of citizenship under the 1981 Act is that of BPP. Under s 38 the Queen may by Order in Council declare, in relation to any territory which has at any time been a protectorate or protected state for the purposes of the BNA 1948 or a UK Trust Territory under that Act, that any group of persons in that territory shall be BPPs. This is subject to the proviso that they are not citizens of any Commonwealth country which consists of, or includes, the territory in question. Most BPPs currently live in Brunei. BPPs are not included in the definition of Commonwealth citizenship (see the 1981 Act, s 37(1)). They are in a citizenship limbo because they are not aliens either.

2 Other relevant categories of citizenship

There are two other categories of citizenship which although not defined in the 1981 Act are relevant for immigration purposes. These are citizenship of an EU country, and of the Republic of Ireland. Such persons are aliens. They have, however, many advantages over the persons categorised as 'British' citizens above, apart from British citizens themselves. They are not subject to immigration control under the rules or the 1971 Act.

(a) Citizens of the Republic of Ireland

Citizens of Eire are aliens. However, by virtue of the Ireland Act 1949, s 2 they are not to be regarded as such. Thus an Irish citizen may vote in a UK Parliamentary election.

Citizens of Eire born before 1948 were British subjects. The BNA 1948, s 2 enabled them, if they wished, to opt formally to remain British subjects. The 1981 Act, s 31(2) enables them to remain British subjects even if they live in Eire. Irish citizens who had been settled in the UK since before 1 January 1973 could register as British citizens under the 1981 Act before 31 December 1987 (s 7). Citizens of Eire are liable to deportation. However, their liability is affected by the fact that they are EU nationals, and may only be deported in accordance with EC Directive 64/221 ([1964] OJ 056/850) (see Chapter 15). In any event, Irish citizens who were ordinarily resident in the UK on the day the 1971 Act came into force are not liable to deportation (1971 Act s 7).

(b) EU citizens

The UK, as a result of its accession to the European Community, is obliged by the Treaty on European Union to allow freedom of movement to EU citizens, and to permit them to work, study, reside, and establish themselves in self-employment without restriction in the UK (European Communities Act 1972 s 2 and the Treaty on European Union arts 3(c), 48). Although there is no reflection of this in any amendment to either the 1971 Act or 1981 Act, special provision in the immigration rules has been made for the admission of EU nationals and for the admission of their dependants. It is arguable that even this provision contravenes the Treaty on European Union. The Immigration Act 1988, s 7 provides that EU nationals do not require leave to enter under UK domestic law. In the meanwhile the EC provisions discussed in Chapter 15 may be relied upon to override any provision of UK law with which they are incompatible.

EU nationals can be refused entry to a member state on the ground of personal unacceptability (EC Directive 64/221). Examples of this are that the presence of the person is a threat to public policy, national security, or public health. In *Van Duyn v Home Office* [1974] 3 All ER 178, the plaintiff, who was Dutch, was refused entry to the UK on the basis that she wanted to take a job as a secretary with the Church of Scientology. The European Court of Justice accepted that her exclusion was valid because the terms of EC Directive 64/221 were satisfied, even though the organisation in that case, which the government described as 'socially harmful', was not actually illegal.

The power to deport EC nationals who under the Treaty of Rome have the right to live in the country where they are workers or self-employed persons, has been considered in *R v Bouchereau* [1978] 2 WLR 251 and *Ex p Santillo* [1981] 2 All ER 897. In both cases the court emphasised that a deportation order should not be lightly made, and that the court should inquire carefully into all the circumstances. The order should only be made if the court is satisfied that the person in question represents a real threat to society. (The same rules apply to EEA nationals exercising free movement rights, see generally, Chapter 15.)

(c) Aliens

Aliens are all those persons who do not fall into any of the categories of British nationality and are not citizens of any other Commonwealth country. No elaborate definition is necessary. They have no claim or right to enter or remain in the UK unless they fall into one of the two privileged classes discussed above. However, in practice they may be given unlimited leave to remain just as may any member of the categories of British nationality. Aliens are just as much potential victims or beneficiaries of the discretionary system of control as are the holders of other kinds of British nationality, that is, of course, apart from British citizens themselves.

3 Acquisition of British citizenship from 1 January 1983

There are four ways in which British citizenship may be acquired under the 1981 Act. These are by birth or adoption, by descent, by registration and by naturalisation. Birth in the UK from 1 January 1983 by itself is no longer an automatic route to citizenship.

(a) By birth or adoption

Birth A child born in the UK to a parent, living or dead, who is either a British citizen or settled in the UK, is a British citizen. 'Settled' is defined at some length in s 50(2), (3), (4) and (5) of the Act and is discussed in Chapter 2. Where the parents are not married, only the mother counts as a 'parent' for these purposes (see s 50(9)(*a*) and *Ex p Crew* [1982] Imm AR 94). Where there is a suggestion that the child may be legitimated by some rule of foreign law, the legitimacy of the child is determined by the father's domicile (*Lake* (3393)).

There is a rebuttable presumption in the case of a child abandoned in the UK that one of his parents satisfies the requirements necessary to confer British citizenship by birth. A child born in the UK whose parents are known not to satisfy the requirements is nevertheless entitled to register as a British citizen if one of his parents subsequently meets one of the requirements and an application is made so to register him.

A child born in the UK to parents who at no time satisfy the requirements is nevertheless entitled to apply to be registered as a British citizen after the age of ten if in each year of his life he has not been absent from the UK for more than 90 days. The S of S may in his discretion register any person who has been absent for longer.

Adoption If an adoption order is made by a British court in respect of a minor who is not a British citizen, he will be a British citizen if his adopter, or one of his adopters, is a British citizen. He retains that citizenship even if subsequently the adoption order ceases to have effect.

(b) By descent

A person born outside the UK may be a British citizen if when he is born one of his parents is a British citizen, in three situations. The first is if one parent is a British citizen otherwise than by descent (see British Nationality Act 1981, s 14). The second is when one parent is a British citizen serving abroad either in Crown service or in any service designated by the S of S (ie working at a British Embassy etc, or serving in the armed forces abroad, or in one of a number of listed jobs such as working for the British Council or the Medical Research Council). Recruitment for that service must have taken place in the UK. The third occurs when one parent is serving in an institution of the EC; recruitment for that service must have taken place in a country which was at the time of recruitment a member of the EC.

Whether or not citizenship by descent arises will be determined by the status of the relevant parent at the time of the birth (the father only if the birth was before 1983). In *R v IAT, ex p Uddin* [1990] Imm AR 104, the CA held that where the father of the applicant for leave to enter registered as a CUKC after the birth of the applicant the applicant had become a citizen of Pakistan, and therefore did not obtain British citizenship on his father's registration. The fact that his father had been issued with a British Seaman's identity card and National Registration card was irrelevant.

The principal disadvantage suffered by a British citizen by descent, in comparison to British citizens by any other means, is that he will not automatically pass his citizenship on to a child born abroad. It will be possible, however, for the child to obtain British citizenship by registration (see below).

(c) By registration

It has been noted above that the 1981 Act, s 3, provides that in two cases children born in this country can be registered as British citizens. Registration is a method of acquiring citizenship by administrative grant. In most instances, provided that statutory conditions are met, there is a right to registration. This is not to be confused with naturalisation, which is a wholly discretionary grant of citizenship. There is thus a right to challenge a refusal of registration in the courts, whereas there is no such right to appeal from the withholding of naturalisation. British citizens who acquire their citizenship by registration or naturalisation can be deprived of it by the S of S (British Nationality Act 1981, s 40).

Acquisition of citizenship by registration is governed by ss 3, 4 and 5 of the Act. Sections 7-10 make provision for transitional cases. There are four main areas to be considered:

Minors Under s 3 the S of S has a discretion to register a minor as a British citizen if an application for registration is made on his behalf. In addition to this broad discretion, s 3 confers certain entitlements to registration as a British citizen on children born outside the UK.

The first such entitlement is in the case of a child born outside the UK on whose behalf an application is made within 12 months of his date of birth. One of the child's parents, or the mother if the parents are not married, must be a British citizen by descent (defined in s 14). In turn, one of the grandparents must have been a British citizen otherwise than by descent at the date of birth, or is now such a citizen (or would be if alive). Finally, the child's parent must have spent a period of three years in the UK before the date of birth, and during that period have been absent from the UK for not more than 270 days. In other words, the entitlement to registration only accrues if a child's parent has both ties of descent and residence with the UK. The S of S may, in his discretion, consider an application made up to six years from the date of birth. Once registered, the child will become a British citizen by descent.

There is a further entitlement to registration in the case of a child born outside the UK if an application is made while he is a minor and one of his parents meets the following statutory requirements:

  (1) One parent must be a British citizen by descent at the date of birth.
  (2) The child and his parents (or parent if the marriage has ended or led to a legal separation or one of the parents is dead) must have lived in the UK for three years preceding the application, and not have been absent from the UK for more than 270 days in that period.
  (3) The consent of the parents (or parent) to the registration must have been signified in the prescribed manner.

Thus, if one parent to a subsisting marriage objects to the application on well-founded grounds, the registration cannot go through. Equally, if the parents are living apart, in different countries, but there has been no formal divorce or legal separation, the child is not entitled to be registered, unless both parents have been in the country for the stipulated three-year period (with permitted absences). If the parents are not married the requirements must be met by the mother. Again, once he is registered, the child will become a British citizen by registration.

BDTCs and others Section 4 applies to applications for registration by BDTCs, BNOs, BOCs, British subjects under the 1981 Act and BPPs. If the conditions laid down by the section are met, the applicant is entitled to be registered a British citizen.

Under the 1981 Act, s 4(2), to qualify the applicant must have been in the UK at the beginning of the period of five years ending with the date of the application, and the number of days on which he was absent from the UK must not exceed 450. In addition he must not have been absent in the 12 months leading up to the application for more than 90 days. In that latter period he must have been free from restrictions on the period of his stay under the immigration laws. Lastly, he must not have been in breach of the immigration laws in the five-year period.

In the case of such applications the S of S has a discretion to register even if the requirements as to length of absence from the UK are not met. Equally, he may disregard restrictions on the period of stay if they are not in force at the date of the application. Finally, he may even disregard breaches of the immigration laws.

The S of S also has a discretion to register applicants under this section who have served in Crown service under the government of a dependent territory or in paid or unpaid service in other government institutions established by law in a dependent territory.

UK nationals for the purposes of Community treaties On accession to the EC the UK defined the meaning of 'UK national' for the purposes of the Community treaties in a unilateral declaration which is annexed to the Treaty of Accession. The legal status of this declaration is uncertain. The definition is framed in such a way as to include citizens of the UK and Colonies by virtue of birth, registration or naturalisation in Gibraltar, as well as patrial citizens of the UK and Colonies. Under the 1981 Act, s 5 the former are entitled to registration as British citizens without needing to have lived in the UK at all, and for a nominal fee. For the purposes of EC law nationality is determined by the domestic law of each member state. In certain cases nationality is defined by ethnicity and may include persons with no other connection with the member state (see Chapter 15).

Transitional provisions There are cases in which persons are entitled to registration if they applied, in most instances, within five years of commencement of the 1981 Act. In essence this applies to persons who had acquired a right under previous legislation to be registered: but if they do not exercise this right in time, they will lose it. The 1981 Act came into force on 1 January 1983 and so the five-year period ended on 31 December 1987.

Section 7 The first case under s 7 is that of Commonwealth and Irish citizens settled in this country on 1 January 1973 (the date of commencement of the 1971 Act). Provided they have been settled since that date, they are entitled to registration if they applied before 1 January 1988, though the S of S has a discretion in any particular case to entertain an application before 1 January 1991. Commonwealth citizens settled in the UK before 1 January 1973, except those under 18 on 1 January 1983, who retain this right will have five years after their 18th birthday to register. The right will finally expire at the end of 1995.

(d) By naturalisation

The final way of acquiring British citizenship is by naturalisation. This is entirely discretionary. Naturalisation is governed by the 1981 Act, s 6 and Sched 1. The S of S may in his discretion grant a certificate of naturalisation to a person of full age and capacity if he considers that he satisfies the conditions set out in Sched 1.

The major change reflected in s 6 was that all spouses of British citizens became eligible to apply for naturalisation. Before the 1981 Act, wives of patrial CUKCs were entitled to registration as such citizens. Wives have now lost that right. They must now apply, like husbands, for naturalisation. Sex equality has been produced by withdrawing a right from one sex rather than by extending it to the other.

General requirements The requirements in Sched 1 differ according to whether the application is made under s 6(1) or (2). The requirements to be met by a spouse of a British citizen are less stringent than those affecting other applicants for naturalisation. The members of the latter group must have a sufficient knowledge of English, Welsh or Scots Gaelic and be of good character. They must intend either to live mainly in the UK if they are naturalised, or to enter or continue in Crown service, service in an international organisation of which the UK is a member, or employment in a company or association established in the UK. They must also have been in the UK for five years before the application, and absent for less than 450 days in that period. They must not have been absent from the UK for more than 90 days in the 12 months immediately before the application, nor in that period can they have been subject under the immigration laws to any restriction on their length of stay. In the five years leading up to the application, they must not have been in breach of the immigration laws. The S of S has a discretion to waive or modify all or any of the foregoing conditions except those relating to linguistic ability, good character and intention to remain in the UK. However, the S of S may, at his discretion, refuse to grant naturalisation to a person who is subject to a restriction on his length of stay or at the date of application for naturalisation.

Spouses of British citizens The requirements affecting the spouse of an existing British citizen are similar to those outlined above. However, the residence requirement is only three years (with not more than 270 days' absence in that period). In the year before the application he must not be absent for more than 90 days; the couple must be settled by the date of the application. There are no language qualifications for such applicants, nor need they intend to reside in the UK or enter or continue in Crown service. They need only be of good character. The S of S again has discretion to waive or modify the conditions, except that relating to good character.

4 Loss of British citizenship

There are two ways in which British citizenship may be lost under the 1981 Act. The first is by renunciation—this is an act of the citizen himself. The second is by deprivation—this is an act of the S of S. The first can be exercised by all persons who have acquired British citizenship by whatever method. The second only affects British citizens who acquired their citizenship by registration or naturalisation. Once registered or naturalised a person cannot lose citizenship by being declared an illegal entrant (*Ex p Ejaz* (1993) *Times*, 7 December).

(a) Renunciation

British citizenship can only be renounced by a declaration of renunciation made in the prescribed manner. Under the 1981 Act s 12, the renunciation is not effective unless and until it is registered by the S of S. The S of S must refuse to register the declaration unless he is satisfied that the person concerned will have, or will acquire an alternative citizenship. If a registration is made, and it transpires that the person concerned has no alternative citizenship at the date of registration, and did not acquire one within six months of that date, he is to be deemed always to have been a British citizen, despite the registration of his declaration. The S of S also has a discretion to refuse to register declarations made in time of war.

If a renunciation is made in order to acquire a different citizenship, the person concerned has a right to resume his British citizenship subsequently by registration under s 13(1). However, he may only do so once. Anyone who has made a declaration of renunciation for whatever reason may apply by registration to resume his British citizenship; such registration is in the S of S's discretion.

(b) Deprivation

British citizens who have acquired their citizenship by registration or naturalisation may be deprived of their citizenship by the S of S. Broadly there are two statutory justifications for this: either that the citizen acquired his status by deception or that while holding that citizenship he has acted in a way which is thought to make him unfit to hold it any longer.

The S of S may deprive of citizenship anyone who has exhibited disloyalty or disaffection towards Her Majesty, or anyone who has unlawfully traded, or communicated with or assisted the enemy in time of war, or has, within five years of his acquisition of citizenship, been sentenced anywhere in the world to a year's imprisonment or more. The S of S's discretion to make an order of deprivation is subject to two overriding considerations. First, the order must not be made unless it is 'not conducive to the public good' for the person concerned to remain a citizen. Secondly, no-one is to be deprived of British citizenship if as a result he becomes stateless. The person concerned has the right to be notified if the S of S intends to make an order and has a right to an inquiry before a committee appointed by the S of S. The S of S's power in relation to 'unfit' citizens extends to all those registered or naturalised under the 1981 Act and all those naturalised under previous legislation.

The S of S may also make an order of deprivation under s 40(1) in respect of anyone whom he is satisfied obtained his registration or naturalisation by fraud, false representation or the concealment of a material fact. This wide power makes it crucial for an applicant for citizenship to be completely honest in his application. Any false representation can mean that the applicant may find that his status is abruptly changed. Section 40(1) applies not only to citizens registered or naturalised under the 1981 Act, but also to those registered under the British Nationality Acts 1948–1964 and anyone naturalised before the commencement of the 1981 Act.

Chapter 4

Statutory Developments Since 1981

The chief statutory developments since the 1981 Act are the Immigration (Carriers' Liability) Act 1987, the Immigration Act 1988, the British Nationality (Hong Kong) Act 1990, and finally the Asylum and Immigration Appeals Act 1993.

1 Immigration (Carriers' Liability) Act 1987

The Immigration (Carriers' Liability) Act 1987 contains a system for levelling fines against airlines carrying persons without proper documentation. The fine currently stands at £2,000 per person arriving without the proper documentation (Immigration (Carriers' Liability Prescribed Sum) Order 1991 (SI No 1497)). If a person who requires leave to enter the UK arrives in the UK by ship or aircraft, the owners or agents of the ship or aircraft shall be liable to pay the S of S on demand £2,000 in respect of that person (CLA 1987, s 1(1)) if he fails to produce the following documents when required to do so by an immigration officer:

(*a*) a valid passport with photograph or some other document satisfactorily establishing his identity and nationality or citizenship; and

(*b*) in the case of a visa national, a valid entry or transit visa.

However, no liability is incurred if the carrier can show that the person produced to the carrier the above documents when embarking on the aircraft or ship for the UK journey. The carrier is also not liable if shown a document which purports to be one of the appropriate documents unless its falsity is reasonably apparent. The Channel Tunnel concessionaires will be exempt from fines (see HL debs, 1 April 1993 cols 1003–6).

The IND pursue an active role in the training of airlines and shipping companies to ensure that passengers arriving in the UK are properly documented. Airline staff have to act as informal immigration filters for the UK. Schiemann J made the point in *Ex p Yassine* [1990] Imm AR 359 that the 1987 Act together with requirements imposed by the S of S relating to visas pose substantial obstacles in the path of refugees wishing to come to the UK in that a visa national needs a visa before travelling to the UK; refugee visas are not available in the country of persecution as a person needs to be outside his country of habitual residence or origin before claiming that status; and carriers are disinclined to carry those without visas in the light of the 1987 Act. The refugee therefore has the following options:

(*a*) lying to the UK authorities in his own country to obtain, eg a visitor's or student's visa;
(*b*) obtaining a credible forgery of a passport;
(*c*) obtaining a ticket to a third country with a stopover in the UK.

Under the Asylum and Immigration Appeals Act 1993 the S of S may by order require persons of any description who, on arrival in the UK, intend to pass through to another country or territory without entering the UK, to hold a visa for that purpose. The order may specify a description of persons by reference to nationality, citizenship, origin or other connection with any particular country or territory, but not by reference to race, colour or religion (1987 Act, s 1A(2)(*a*), as inserted by the 1993 Act, s 12). However, the order shall not permit the requirement of a transit visa to apply to any person who has the right of abode under the 1971 Act. Further, any category of person may be exempted from the operation of the order. From 22 July 1993 citizens of Afghanistan, Iran, Iraq, Lebanon, Libya, Somalia, Sri Lanka, Turkey, Uganda and Zaire require transit visas; other visa nationals do not, if there is less than 24 hours between their flights (Immigration (Transit Visas) Order 1993 (SI 1678)).

New guidelines for the operation of the 1987 Act have been issued by the Home Office in order to permit a greater degree of discretion in the operation of the Act to the local immigration officers at ports of entry. The guidelines explain the procedure for dealing with passengers with inadequate documentation on arrival, for notifying a carrier that it is liable for a charge, for making representations against the charge, and for recovering the charge. The guidelines also explain the criteria applied by the Immigration Service for waiving the charge. (See Immigration (Carriers' Liability) Act 1987; and *Charging Procedures: A Guide for Carriers*.)

STATUTORY DEVELOPMENTS SINCE 1981

Carriers are expected to ensure
(a) that a passport or travel document presented by a passenger is acceptable for entry to the UK;
(b) that the passenger is the rightful holder;
(c) that it is valid;
(d) if the passenger needs a visa, that the visa is valid for the holder and any other accompanying passengers named in the passport.

The IND provides guidance on UK document requirements and on forgery detection. A forgery is reasonably apparent for the purposes of the 1987 Act if it is of a standard which a trained representative of a carrying company, examining it carefully but briefly and without the use of technological aids, could reasonably be expected to detect. A trained representative is expected to have a basic level of knowledge of how to identify fraudulent documents, but not to be expert nor to have the resources for a highly detailed examination.

If a passenger has no documents on arrival, the carrier is liable unless it can show that the passenger presented proper documents on embarkation. In any case where the documents presented raise doubts in the carrier's mind, the IND take the view that it is generally advisable to take all possible steps to resolve those doubts before deciding to carry the passenger. If it is not possible to resolve the doubts (eg by reference to the UK Immigration Service or embassy), a contemporaneous record of the document and details of the steps taken to check it is recommended. The carrier is advised to photocopy the document, showing the pages containing the holder's personal details and photograph and visa. The carrier is expected to keep a record of the details on those pages. If the carrier can show a proper system, has a record of relatively few inadequate document cases, and the record or photocopy does not reveal an obvious forgery, the charge may be waived. If the passenger arrives with insufficient or false documents, and is detected by the immigration service, the carrier is notified, given the opportunity to examine the documentation and to interview the passenger if the passenger agrees. At this stage the port inspector may decide that there is no liability. If he decides that there is, Form IS80(b) is sent to the carrier, indicating that a charge will be levied. The port inspector will consider the standard of the forgery, or any exceptional circumstances (such as whether the flight was diverted). Once the carrier receives the notification it has 30 days in which to make representations to the port inspector, who may allow further time if it is difficult to obtain evidence in that time, and there is good cause for the delay.

The carrier may make representations as to the standard of the forgery, or give details of exceptional circumstances at the time of the embarkation which prevented a full document check, or make representations concerning the endorsements. A non-exhaustive list of cases in which the inspectors will normally be prepared to waive a charge is given in the guidance note. The charge may be waived in the case of visa national passengers if the visa is not endorsed as valid for the number of persons travelling and included in the same document. However, if the visa is endorsed 'holder only' a charge will be levied in respect of any other person travelling with the holder and included in the document. The charge may also be waived if the visa is used and the immigration officer's endorsement was not placed on the same page, or placed so that no more than one page of the document need be turned either way in order to see the endorsement. If the endorsement is unclear or obscure the charge may also be waived. However, if the visa itself has expired the charge will be maintained.

Finally, the charge may be waived where the visa national passenger arrives by air, and the carrier genuinely believed that the passenger's sole purpose in the UK was transit, and that he qualified for a visa waiver under the International Civil Aviation Organisation's terms, ie at the time of booking in he was in possession of a confirmed onward booking by air within 24 hours of scheduled arrival, and the necessary documentation such as a genuine valid visa for his destination.

Nationals of Iraq and Sri Lanka are not entitled to the concession of transition without a visa. Nationals of Iran, Lebanon, Libya, Somalia, Syria and Turkey may only transit through the UK if they remain in airside transit areas. Liability may also be incurred if they approach and apply to immigration control. The carrier is warned that many UK airports do not allow passengers to remain in airside areas overnight. It is likely that more countries will be added to the list of transit visa countries under regulations to be made under the Asylum and Immigration Appeals Act 1993.

Where the port inspector waives the charge formal notification is sent, and if the charge is maintained, a Notification of Formal Demand (IS80(d)) is issued. This informs the carrier that there are 30 days in which to pay. Further representations may then be made to the immigration inspectors at the Carriers' Liability Section at the Immigration Service Headquarters within 30 days.

The carrier should mention all relevant information and explain why the decision is wrong. Initially the port inspector may reconsider at this stage, but if the decision is again maintained the representations are forwarded to the Carriers' Liability Section. Time may be extended to obtain necessary information.

There is no right of appeal against the notice. However, the immigration service cannot enforce the prescribed sum as a fine, but only as a civil debt. The Act provides no means of enforcement. The carriers' remedy in respect of a charge may take the form solely of a judicial review of the decision to impose the charge. Alternatively the 1987 Act may be viewed as creating a statutory duty. The court would then have some scope for intervention as to the sum payable.

2 The Immigration Act 1988

The Immigration Act 1988 introduced further restrictions on the rights of Commonwealth citizens, restricted rights of appeal in deportation cases, and amended the 1971 Act. The 1988 Act, s 1, repealed s 1(5) of the 1971 Act, which provided that the Immigration Rules should be so framed that Commonwealth citizens settled in the UK on 1 January 1973, their wives and children were not less free to come into and go from the UK by virtue of those rules than if the 1971 Act had not been passed. If the application for entry clearance to come to the UK for settlement by the wife or child was made before the date on which the section came into force (1 August 1988) the right was not affected.

A woman with a right of abode by virtue of marriage to a man to whom she is or was polygamously married, and who was a CUKC with a right of abode at the commencement date of the 1981 Act, and who has not since her marriage been in the UK before 1 August 1988, is not entitled to enter the UK in certain circumstances. She is not entitled if there is another woman living who is the wife or widow of that husband who:

(a) is or has been in the UK at any time since marrying the husband; or
(b) has a certificate of entitlement in respect of the right of abode as his wife; or
(c) has an entry clearance to enter the UK as the wife of the husband (1988 Act, s 2(2)). If since her marriage she has been in the UK, and at that time there was no other wife of the husband satisfying the above conditions, she shall

not be precluded from re-entering the UK (s 2(4)). The woman has the burden of proving she had been in the UK before 1 August 1988, and since her marriage. However, only the legal presence of a woman in the UK other than as a visitor will affect the rights of a woman claiming to be able to enter (s 2(7)).

The 1988 Act, s 5 restricted the right of appeal against deportation in cases where the applicant had broken the terms of his limited leave, or was a family member of such a person's family. In those cases a person could only appeal against the decision to make a deportation order on the ground that on the facts of his case there is in law no power to make the deportation order for the reasons stated in the notice of the decision. The restriction only applied to a person who was last given leave to enter the UK less than seven years before the date of the decision, and does not apply to persons whose leave to enter or remain has been curtailed under the Asylum and Immigration Appeals Act 1993, s 7 alleging that their deportation would breach the UK's obligations under the Convention and Protocol relating to the Status of Refugees of 1951 (Immigration (Restricted Right of Appeal Against Deportation) (Exemption) Order 1993 (SI No 1656)). Unless the person proves that he had not been given leave to enter less than seven years before the decision, it is presumed that he was given leave within seven years (see Chapter 23).

The 1988 Act, s 7(1), provides that a person shall not require leave to enter or remain in any case in which he is entitled to do so by virtue of an enforceable Community right or of any provision made under the European Communities Act 1972, s 2(2). Until this provision is brought into operation, such persons may rely on the various free movement rights granted under the Treaty of Rome as amended by the Single European Act of 1986 and under the Treaty on European Union 1993. EEA nationals exercising rights to free movement require no leave to enter (see Chapter 15).

Section 8 provides for the examination of passengers before their arrival in the UK. Where a person arrives in the UK with a passport or travel document bearing a stamp placed there by an immigration officer before his departure on, or during, his journey to the UK, and the stamp states that he may enter the UK, he is deemed to have been given on arrival in the UK the leave specified in the stamp together with such conditions (if any) as are imposed by its terms. Such a person is not subject to examination on arrival, save to establish that he satisfies these conditions (s 8(4)). However, the leave may be cancelled by notice in writing from the immigration officer, refusing him leave to enter. The leave may be cancelled in this way at any time before the end of a period of 24 hours from his arrival at the port of entry, or the conclusion of the examination conducted to verify that he carries the appropriate stamp. The port of entry includes the terminal area of the Channel Tunnel system in the UK, and the service and maintenance area of the system in the UK. The provision only applies to the first occasion that the person arrives in the UK after his passport is stamped, where that arrival is not later than seven days after the stamping of his passport.

The Schedule to the 1988 Act provides for the continuation of limitations and conditions on a leave which is granted to a person who has leave, but who obtains a subsequent leave within the period of the earlier leave (para 1). Where a deportation order is made against a person appealing in respect of a limited leave, any appeal pending in respect of that limited leave lapses (para 3). Immigration officers are given the power to detain any passport or other document produced by a person pursuant to an examination until the person is either given leave to enter, or is about to depart or be removed following a refusal of leave to enter (para 6). The time limit for giving or refusing or cancelling leave to enter has been extended to 24 hours, and the default leave obtained by the person entering, if a decision was not made within that time, was reduced from indefinite leave to remain to six months' leave to remain with a condition prohibiting employment (paras 7 and 8).

3 British Nationality (Hong Kong) Act 1990

The British Nationality (Hong Kong) Act 1990 provides a scheme for registration which operates by way of a points system, enabling Hong Kong heads of households, their spouses and children to register as British citizens. It favours those with education, special skills, necessary skills, or those who have done voluntary service for the community. The scheme also provides for entrepreneurs and members of the sensitive services to be invited to register as British citizens.

(a) Qualification

Selection is in accordance with a scheme set out in the schedule to the British Nationality (Hong Kong) (Selection Scheme) Order

1990 (SI No 2292). By the 1990 Act, Sched 1, para 4, to qualify for registration an applicant must:
- (*a*) be settled in Hong Kong by reason of being ordinarily resident and lacking any restriction on the duration of his stay; and
- (*b*) fall within one of the following categories:
    - (i) a BDTC by virtue of a connection with Hong Kong; or
    - (ii) a BN(O); or
    - (iii) a BOC; or
    - (iv) a British Protected Person; or
    - (v) a British subject; or
    - (vi) a person who is not a British national who has applied for naturalisation or registration as a BDTC in Hong Kong before 26 July 1990, and whose application for registration as a BDTC is ultimately successful; and
- (*c*) where the application is made under the General Occupational Class or the Disciplined Services Class (police, etc), the applicant is engaged in one of the occupations covered by those classes.

Under the 1990 Act the Governor may make recommendations that persons in the various categories mentioned above be registered as having the right of abode.

The British Nationality (Hong Kong) Act 1990, s 1, is concerned with the decision of the S of S in relation to the grant or refusal of an application for British citizenship. The Governor and the S of S shall not be required to give reasons for decisions made in the exercise of a discretion vested in either of them by the Act. Further, 'no such decision shall be subject to appeal or liable to be questioned in any court' (s 1(5)). Some commentators take the view that these words exclude an application for judicial review of any such decision. This is arguably not so. Ouster clauses of this kind do not prevent the court from intervening in the case of excess of jurisdiction (*Anisminic Ltd v Foreign Compensation Commission* [1969] 2 AC 147). Action in contravention of the principles of natural justice amounts to an excess of jurisdiction. Thus in *Attorney General v Ryan* [1980] AC 718, where a Minister refused an application for citizenship without giving the applicants a fair hearing, the Privy Council held his decision invalid, notwithstanding the relevant statute providing that it 'shall not be subject to appeal or review in any court'. Moreover, as every error of law is jurisdictional, all 'shall not be questioned' clauses are arguably ineffective. (But see *Pearlman v Harrow School Governors* [1979] QB 56 and *Re Racal Communications* [1981] AC 374 in relation to decisions of judicial bodies.) Where it is a judicial act which is in issue, an ouster clause may be effective, particularly where it is a decision of an inferior court that is involved; but in relation to an administrative decision which arguably grant of citizenship would be, the *Anisminic* approach would still prevail.

The supervisory powers of the court may only be restricted by the most clear and explicit words (*R v Medical Appeal Tribunal, ex p Gilmore* [1957] 1 QB 574 at 583, per Denning LJ). Nevertheless, where a statute lays down the way in which a measure may be challenged and the grounds on which this may be done, and expressly prohibits any other form of legal challenge, a court may decide that it has no jurisdiction to entertain claims on grounds or in a manner not set out in the statute (for a recent example, see *R v Cornwall CC, ex p Huntingdon* [1992] 3 All ER 566, Div Ct). The critical distinction between that type of situation and that under the 1990 Act is that in the latter the legislation gives no opportunity of questioning the validity of the decision in the High Court at all. Where there is no statutory right of appeal to the courts, judicial review should not be excluded. However, the extent of the review is likely to be limited to procedural as opposed to substantive grounds (*CCSU v Minister for the Civil Service* [1985] AC 374; and *R v S of S for Foreign and Commonwealth Affairs, ex p Everett* [1989] 2 WLR 224, CA).

Under s 3(3) the Governor appoints a committee to advise him on matters arising under the scheme for registration of applicants, and may authorise public officers to exercise functions in respect of applications, but no recommendation can be made except by the Governor. It is thus possible that the decisions taken by the committee, or the advice given by such a committee could be susceptible to judicial review even where the advice given relates to a decision which is ultimately within the discretion of the Governor.

Decisions taken by public officers exercising the Governor's discretionary decision making function are not susceptible to appeal or liable to be questioned by a court by the 1990 Act, s 3(4). This provision is subject to the qualifications mentioned above in relation to such ouster clauses. Public officers involved in administering the scheme may be applicants themselves, and therefore the Order provides, under art 29, that they, along with committee members and staff members on the establishment of Government House, may not deal in an official capacity with their own application, or any application in which they have a personal interest. The Governor is under a duty to provide an annual report on the discharge of his duties under the 1990 Act to the S of S, but there is no requirement for the publication of the report beyond that.

(b) The scheme

The 1990 Act, Sched 1, provides for the scheme for the selection of persons to be recommended by the Governor for registration under s 1(1). The scheme set up under the Sched prescribes criteria or quotas for persons of different classes or descriptions, selection methods as between persons of different classes or descriptions, and areas of discretion. The scheme also permits recommendations on the basis of special contributions by a person to the economy of Hong Kong.

Under the scheme there are four classes. Places are allocated as follows:

General Occupational Class (GOC)	36,200
Disciplined Services Class (DSC)	7,000
which are filled on the basis of points allocated to a person (see below)	
Sensitive Services Class (SSC)	6,300
Entrepreneurs Class	500
which are filled either by invitation or by an application by a person to be considered under that heading.	

There are two parts to the scheme, one for the head of the household, and one for minor children and the spouse of the head of the household. In relation to the first of these there are various classes and quotas. Applications are made on specific forms (BN(HK)1), and the information is placed on computer, which produces an initial profile on the basis of points scored for each occupational group. Once the initial profile is obtained, the steering committee which advises the Governor recommends for each group the criteria by which special circumstance points will be awarded. This process results in a revised ranking, and the number of places available in relation to that group are then filled in ranking order. Those thus selected are then interviewed by immigration officers to verify the information they have supplied, and to check that they are of good character. Where a candidate is refused at this stage, he is replaced by the next person down in the list.

Heads of households The Governor may treat an application under one class as an application under another, if it appears more appropriate, provided that if the application is refused under that class, it must be reconsidered under the original class. If there is a tie between two equally qualified applicants the Governor has a discretion as to which of the two should be chosen in order not to exceed the quota for that class.

The four categories

1 General Occupational Class The GOC covers occupations which have an important role to play in the prosperity or administration of Hong Kong. There are 20 occupational groups in the GOC. The numbers of places allocated to each occupational group is calculated according to the estimated number of persons working in each group, and their estimated emigration rate over the three years before the scheme was introduced. A person applying under the GOC must study a series of job descriptions given in a series of manuals published by the Hong Kong government and choose which most accurately reflects the duties he performs. An applicant is recommended by the Governor if he reaches a sufficiently high total on a points system to bring him within the quota fixed for the occupational group under which he has applied. There are quotas within the occupational class.

Approved occupations 500 places go to those in an occupation approved by the Governor as requiring technical or professional skills or qualifications such as are considered necessary or desirable for the continued successful administration of Hong Kong.

The allocation of points for the GOC The applicant can be awarded between –200 and +200 points in relation to age. A maximum of 150 points may be awarded for working experience. A maximum of 150 points may be awarded in respect of education and training. Proficiency in the English language attracts a maximum of 50 points.

A maximum of 50 points are allocated for each connection which the applicant has with the UK. Up to 50 points may be scored for service with the Legislative Council, the Executive Council and other approved public bodies. Points are awarded for each year of service subject to a maximum of ten years of service. Additional points (up to 150) may be awarded as a matter of discretion.

2 The Disciplined Services The Disciplined Services form another class under art 5 of the Order. This class is only open to public sector workers. Each disciplined service has a quota. Locally enlisted persons with service in the navy, army or as a uniformed member of the Hong Kong Auxiliary Air Force, together with disciplined members of the customs and excise, fire services, immigration services, the police, the Correctional Services Department and the Operations Department, Independent Commission Against Corruption form a separate group, in which points are allotted under a similar system to that used for the GOC.

3 The sensitive service class A person may be recommended under this head if the Governor considers a recommendation justified in view of his service in the interests of the Crown either in the private or public sector, or his activities of a sensitive nature. This class is merely subject to a numerical quota.

4 The entrepreneurs class The Governor may offer up to 500 places for well-known and respected entrepreneurs whom he regards as having made a special contribution to the economy of Hong Kong.

Third country citizenship Where the applicant has a citizenship status other than of Hong Kong or the Republic of China, by virtue of which he has the right of abode in that country, 200 points will be deducted (art 27) if an application is being dealt with under the general occupational class or disciplined services class. If the application is being dealt with under the sensitive services or entrepreneurs classes, the Governor shall take that citizenship into account in making the decision whether to make a recommendation. No points are deducted if the status of the applicant in the third country gives a right of either temporary or permanent residence in that country but does not give citizenship.

(c) Spouses and minor children

Under the 1990 Act, Sched 2, provision is made for the registration (on recommendation) of the spouse and minor children of a person registered under the scheme for heads of households under Sched 1. They are eligible for registration, regardless of whether they are settled in Hong Kong or of their nationality.

Family members

Spouses Spouses may be registered on recommendation, whether the marriage took place before or after the registration of the head of the household. If it took place after the registration of the principal, the spouse will not be registered unless settled in Hong Kong at the time of the marriage. Where a marriage takes place after the applicant has ceased to be settled in Hong Kong, or where the marriage took place after 30 June 1997, the spouse will not be eligible for registration.

Children By the 1990 Act, s 1(4), the spouse and minor children of a person who is registered as a British citizen in accordance with the scheme, may acquire British citizenship by registration before 30 June 1997. If registered in accordance with the scheme the spouse or child is not counted for registration purposes under the quota system. By Sched 2, para 4(1), only the children of a registered person who are minors at the date they apply for registration may be registered. The scheme also extends to an adopted minor child if a Hong Kong court made the adoption order. Illegitimate minor children of a woman may be registered.

Finally the Scheme contained in the Schedule will only apply to post registration marriages if the spouse applying to be registered under it was settled in Hong Kong at the time of the marriage. By para 5 it is provided that it is immaterial whether the spouse or a child applying for registration is settled in Hong Kong or has any citizenship or nationality otherwise than under the British Nationality Act 1981.

Exceptions to registration By the 1990 Act, s 6(2), a person whom the Governor or S of S has reason to believe is not of good character shall not be recommended or registered. Registration may not take place if the S of S has reason to believe that the applicant to be registered has ceased, after the date of a recommendation, either to be settled in Hong Kong and a BDTC by virtue of a connection with Hong Kong, or to be a British National (Overseas), a BOC, a British Protected Person or a British subject by virtue of Part IV of the British Nationality Act 1981.

Consequences of registration When the applicant is registered as a British citizen under the 1990 Act, s 1(1), he is treated as a British citizen otherwise than by descent, and thus his children born after registration will be British citizens. Those who are registered under the children and spouses scheme in the 1990 Act, Sched 2 are to be treated as British citizens by descent, so that unless their children are born in the UK they will not be British citizens. Those whose status before registration was that of a BDTC cease to be BDTCs if they become British citizens under the 1990 Act. Persons registered become subject to the scheme of the British Nationality Act 1981 relating to Commonwealth citizenship, deprivation of citizenship, legitimated and posthumous children, evidence and offences.

4 The Asylum and Immigration Appeals Act 1993

The Asylum and Immigration Appeals Act 1993 came into force on 26 July 1993. It performs the following functions:
(1) It gives primacy to the Convention and Protocol on the Status of Refugees.
(2) It makes provision for the treatment of asylum seekers.
(3) It provides asylum seekers with a right of appeal in all cases.
(4) It removes the right of appeal from persons seeking to come as visitors and short term students, from those whose appeal would have to be refused under the Immigration Rules, and from those who do not have certain documents required under the Immigration Rules. This provision caused the most debate, with several serving and former Law Lords warning of the dangers of an increase in the number of judicial review applications with which the courts would have to deal.
(5) It provides a right of appeal (with leave) to the Court of Appeal in all immigration cases, save asylum applications certified to be without foundation.
(6) It provides for a streamlined and abbreviated appeal process in cases which are certified to be without foundation. Persons whose cases are so certified may appeal to the adjudicator, but not to the IAT. Their remedy will thereafter be an application for judicial review.
(7) It amends the Immigration (Carriers' Liability) Act 1987 so as to extend the liability of carriers in respect of persons who are required to have transit visas, and who are specified by Order.

The 1993 Act provided for the introduction of amendments to the Immigration Rules which dealt with asylum claims. The subject is discussed in detail in Chapters 19 and 20, and the new right of appeal to the Court of Appeal is dealt with in Chapter 25.

Chapter 5

The Immigration Rules

1 Introduction

The immigration rules are not, like most delegated legislation under Acts of Parliament, statutory instruments. They take the form of statements placed by the S of S before Parliament, and take effect subject to a negative resolution by either House within 40 days of the date they are laid before Parliament.

The system of control is very much an administrative, discretionary one, and the language of the rules underlines this. It is an area in which legal principles are made difficult to formulate. The first tier of the statutory appeal procedure, too, exhibits many of the characteristics of an administrative rather than a judicial process. Adjudicators are appointed by the Lord Chancellor, and paid by his department. Adjudications are not reported. IAT decisions are retained in the library at Thanet House, London. The Immigration Appeal Reports (Imm AR) are published by HMSO in volumes which are known for the obvious reason as 'Green Books'. Unreported decisions of the High Court and the IAT are often summarised in *Tolley's Immigration and Nationality Law and Practice* (INL&P), the journal of the Immigration Law Practitioners Association and the Legal Action Group Bulletin. The Joint Council for the Welfare of Immigrants also produces a quarterly bulletin which provides useful updating information and reports of cases.

2 The 1994 rules

The 1971 Act, s 3(2) requires the Home Secretary to make rules

as to the practice to be followed in the administration of this Act for regulating the entry into and stay in the United Kingdom of persons required by this Act to have leave to enter, including any rules as to the period for which leave is to be given and the conditions to be attached in different circumstances.

The current rules are contained in the *Statement of Changes in Immigration Rules* (HC 395) which takes effect from 1 October 1994. They cover control on and after entry in respect of all persons required by the Act to have leave to enter. The rules have a new format in which the rules controlling immigration on entry and post-entry are grouped together under categories of persons. New categories of person are introduced: those intending to establish themselves in business pursuant to EC Association Agreements, investors, those exercising rights of access to a child resident in the UK and EEA nationals. Detailed changes are discussed under Part II below.

3 Commonwealth citizens settled in the UK in 1973

The rules in operation before 1989 were framed so that Commonwealth citizens settled in the UK at the coming into force of the 1971 Act, their wives and children were not by virtue of anything in the rules, any less free to enter and leave the UK than if the 1971 Act had not been passed. This protection derived from s 1(5) of the 1971 Act, but the subsection was repealed by the 1988 Act s 1. After 8 July 1989 wives and children of Commonwealth citizens have to show that they can maintain and accommodate themselves in accordance with the current immigration rules.

4 Status of the rules

In *R v Chief Immigration Officer, London (Heathrow) Airport, ex p Salamat Bibi* [1976] 3 All ER 843, Roskill LJ observed (at p 848) that the immigration rules 'are just as much delegated legislation as any other form of rule making activity or delegated legislation which is empowered by Act of Parliament ... they are just as much part of the law of England as the 1971 Act itself.' However, all three members of the CA in *R v S of S, ex p Hosenball* [1977] 3 All ER 452 disapproved of this observation and in *R v IAT, ex p Bakhtaur Singh* [1986] Imm AR 352, [1986] 1 WLR 910, Lord Bridge, at p 359, said:

'Immigration rules ... are quite unlike ordinary delegated legislation ... The rules do not purport to enact a precise code having statutory force.

They are discursive in style, in part merely explanatory and, on their face, frequently offer no more than broad guidance as to how discretion is to be exercised in different typical situations. Insofar as they lay down principles to be applied they generally do so in loose and imprecise terms ...

In *Hosenball's* case (above) Lord Denning MR said (at p 459) that the immigration rules were not rules of law but were 'rules of practice laid down for the guidance of immigration officers and tribunals who are entrusted with the administration of this Act'. He recognised that to some extent the courts must have regard to them because there are provisions in the Act itself, particularly in s 19, which show that in appeals to an adjudicator, if the immigration rules have not been complied with, then the appeal is to be allowed. In addition the courts always have regard to the rules: not only in matters where there is a right of appeal, but also in cases under prerogative writs where there is a question whether the officers have acted fairly.

It follows from the present approach to the rules that the strict canons of construction applicable to statutes cannot be properly applied to the rules. They are not statutory instruments but are designed under the 1971 Act, s 3(2) to be 'rules as to the practice to be followed in the administration of the Act'. Thus regard must be had to the purpose for which the rules were made in interpreting them (*Chauda v ECO Bombay* [1978] Imm AR 40). They must be construed sensibly according to the natural meaning of the language which is employed (*R v IAT, ex p Alexander* [1982] 1 WLR 1076 and *R v IAT, ex p Manshoora Begum* [1986] Imm AR 385). Although they are to be given a commonsense construction looking at the rules altogether, it is not proper to disregard a requirement in a rule which is specific and expressed in plain and unambiguous language (see, *R v IAT, ex p Rahman* [1987] Imm AR 313).

As the Convention on Human Rights and Fundamental Freedoms is not formally part of the law of England, immigration officers are under no duty to bear in mind the principles stated in the Convention when exercising their powers under the rules (but see p 273). Their decisions are to be made solely in accordance with the rules (*R v Chief Immigration Officer, London (Heathrow) Airport, ex p Salamat Bibi* [1976] 3 All ER 843, per Lord Denning MR at p 847; dicta of Lord Denning MR in *R v S of S for Home Affairs, ex p Bhajan Singh* [1975] 2 All ER at p 873 and of Scarman LJ in *R v S of S, ex p Phansopkar* [1975] 3 All ER at p 511 disapproved).

It should be borne in mind that the S of S retains a residual discretion in these matters, and may be requested by an appellant to depart, or to authorise an officer to depart, from the rules (see ss 4(1) and 19(2) of the Act). The appellate authorities are able to review the exercise of the S of S's discretion in relation to a decision taken outside the rules. A restrictive interpretation of the rules should not be employed so as to exclude a person from appealing (*R v IAT, ex p Takeo* [1987] Imm AR 522).

5 Decisions taken outside the rules: concessions and policies

Where the proper course under the immigration rules would be to refuse an application either for leave to enter or to remain, the Home Office may make an exception to the rules and grant leave. Practices that have been defined in Parliamentary answers or MPs' correspondence are consistently applied. The Joint Council for the Welfare of Immigrants (JCWI) and the Immigration Law Practitioners' Association (ILPA) and other organisations have in the past been able to assist in the clarification of such practices by requesting information from the Home Office, who then set out the concession in letters to them. Adjudicators can only allow an appeal, however, where the decision is not accordance with the law or the immigration rules applicable (1971 Act, s 19). In all other cases they must dismiss the appeal. Where a decision is made outside the immigration rules, an appeal may fail, but an adjudicator is entitled to make a recommendation, in a case which should fall within a concession, that the usual practice should be followed. In certain circumstances it is possible to apply for judicial review of a decision not to apply a concession (see Chapter 27 below).

Where the Home Office's concessions are less well defined or are not consistently applied, they are more likely to be known as either policies or principles. The more important of these concessions are mentioned in the text at the appropriate place. They relate to

(*a*) private domestic servants;
(*b*) 'common law' spouses;
(*c*) indefinite leave to remain based on lengthy residence of ten or 14 years;
(*d*) entry clearance or leave to remain for children under 12 applying to join a lone parent;
(*e*) exceptional leave to enter or remain for those refused asylum;
(*f*) policies on third safe countries; and
(*g*) bringing children for adoption.

THE IMMIGRATION RULES 55

An applicant's awareness of a relevant concession may give rise to a legitimate expectation on his part that he will be treated in accordance with it. Some of the concessions will relate purely to the practice of the Home Office and may change rapidly. JCWI and ILPA of 115 Old Street London ECIV 9JR, are the best sources of information on concessions, and information relating to Home Office practices. Both issue bulletins and newsletters, providing the practitioner with a good way of keeping up to date with developments, especially in this area. (For a useful discussion of such concessions see *Home Office discretion outside the Immigration Rules* by F Webber in Legal Action, February 1994 p 18.)

6 Judicial review of the Rules

Since the immigration rules are made by the S of S pursuant to powers granted to him by the Immigration Act 1971, the rules themselves may be subject to judicial review. They may be struck down as *ultra vires* if they are unreasonable on the test laid down in *Associated Provincial Picture Houses Ltd v Wednesbury Corporation* [1948] 1 KB 223. In *R v IAT, ex p Manshoora Begum* [1986] Imm AR 385 Simon Brown J struck down as unreasonable, thus *ultra vires*, a requirement in the rules that in considering whether there were exceptional compassionate circumstances justifying the admission of relatives aged under 65 of persons settled in the UK, the immigration officer should satisfy himself that the applicant had a standard of living substantially below that of his own country as well as being financially dependent on someone in the UK. (See also *R v S of S, ex p Ounejma* [1989] Imm AR 75, *Rajput v IAT* [1989] Imm AR 350, *R v An adjudicator, ex p S of S* [1989] Imm AR 423, and Chapter 27 below.)

Part II

Immigration Control

Chapter 6

The Immigration Rules: Introduction and Interpretation

GENERAL PROVISIONS

1 Introduction

INTRODUCTION

The Home Secretary has made changes in the Rules laid down by him as to the practice to be followed in the administration of the Immigration Acts for regulating entry into and the stay of persons in the United Kingdom and contained in the statement laid before Parliament on 23 March 1990 (HC 251) (as amended). This statement contains the Rules as changed and replaces the provisions of HC 251 (as amended).

2. Immigration Officers, Entry Clearance Officers and all staff of the Home Office Immigration and Nationality Department will carry out their duties without regard to the race, colour or religion of persons seeking to enter or remain in the United Kingdom.

3. In these Rules words importing the masculine gender include the feminine unless the contrary intention appears.

Implementation and transitional provisions

4. These Rules come into effect on 1 October 1994 and will apply to all decisions taken on or after that date save that any application made before 1 October 1994 for entry clearance, leave to enter or remain or variation of leave to enter or remain shall be decided under the provisions of HC 251, as amended, as if these Rules had not been made.

COMMENTARY

The new Immigration Rules are contained in HC 395. This makes a number of substantive changes to the Rules and presents them in a new format in which the on-entry and after-entry rules are grouped together. Thus the provisions for visitors about requirements for entry and the provisions about requirements for an extension of leave are all to be found in the same place. The Rules explain the practice to be followed in the administration of the Immigration Acts for regulating entry into and the stay in the UK of persons who do not have the right of abode in the UK. Immigration officers and entry clearance officers will carry out their duties without regard to the race, colour or religion of persons seeking to enter the UK (para 2). In the Rules, words importing the masculine gender include the feminine, unless the contrary intention appears (para 3). The Rules came into effect on 1 October 1994. They apply to all decisions taken on or after that date, except where the application for entry clearance, leave to enter, or leave to remain was made before 1 October 1994. Applications made before that date are decided under the provisions of HC 251 as amended.

The Rules represent a codification of many of the pre-existing practices of the Home Office. Refusal of leave to enter or remain under the new rules is in many cases mandatory unless certain conditions are met. Cutting down the area of the immigration officer's discretion creates perhaps too rigid a framework. In this part we have set out a restatement of the rules together with commentary. Unfortunately the Home Office has not taken the opportunity to publish the various concessions and policies by which immigration officers in fact operate so as to make them part of the immigration rules. This is particularly unfortunate as the Rules are supposed to represent the S of S's guidelines for the exercise of the immigration officer's discretion. The result may be an increase in decisions taken outside the rules under these concessions.

Application

5. Save where expressly indicated, these Rules do not apply to a European Economic Area (EEA) national or the family member of such a national who is entitled to enter or remain in the United Kingdom by virtue of the provisions of the Immigration (European Economic Area) Order 1994. But an EEA national or his family member who is not entitled to rely on the provisions of that Order is covered by these Rules.

COMMENTARY

The European Economic Area is dealt with in Chapter 15 (for the EEA Order see the Appendix). It should be noted, however, that if a conflict were to arise between the UK legislation and that of the EU, including any treaties with non-EU countries, the law of the EU would prevail. This principle would not be affected

GENERAL PROVISIONS 61

by the apparent reservation of para 5. Further the last sentence of the para does not alter this principle.

2 Interpretation

By para 6 of the Rules the following interpretations apply:

INTERPRETATION

6. In these Rules the following interpretations apply:
'the Immigration Acts' mean the Immigration Act 1971 and the Immigration Act 1988.
'the 1993 Act' is the Asylum and Immigration Appeals Act 1993.
'the 1994 EEA Order' is the Immigration (European Economic Area) Order 1994.
'United Kingdom passport' bears the meaning it has in the Immigration Act 1971.
'Immigration Officer' includes a Customs Officer acting as an Immigration Officer.
'public funds' means
   (a)   housing under Part III of the Housing Act 1985, Part II of the Housing (Scotland) Act 1987 or Part II of the Housing (Northern Ireland) Order 1988;
   (b)   income support, family credit, council tax benefit and housing benefit under Part VII of the Social Security Contributions and Benefits Act 1992; and
   (c)   income support, family credit and housing benefit under the Social Security Contributions and Benefits (Northern Ireland) Act 1992.
'Department of Employment' includes, where appropriate, the equivalent Government Department for Northern Ireland.
'settled in the United Kingdom' means that the person concerned:
   (a)   is free from any restriction on the period for which he may remain save that a person entitled to an exemption under Section 8 of the Immigration Act 1971 (otherwise than as a member of the home forces) is not to be regarded as settled in the United Kingdom except in so far as Section 8(5A) so provides; and
   (b)   is either:
       (i)   ordinarily resident in the United Kingdom without having entered or remained in breach of the immigration laws; or
       (ii)   despite having entered or remained in breach of the immigration laws, has subsequently entered lawfully or has been granted leave to remain and is ordinarily resident.
'a parent' includes
   (a)   the stepfather of a child whose father is dead;
   (b)   the stepmother of a child whose mother is dead;

(c) the father as well as the mother of an illegitimate child where he is proved to be the father;
(d) an adoptive parent but only where a child was adopted in accordance with a decision taken by the competent administrative authority or court in a country whose adoption orders are recognised by the United Kingdom (except where an application for leave to enter or remain is made under paragraphs 310–316);
(e) in the case of a child born in the United Kingdom who is not a British citizen, a person to whom there has been a genuine transfer of parental responsibility on the ground of the original parent(s)' inability to care for the child.

'visa nationals' are the persons specified in the Appendix to these Rules who need a visa for the United Kingdom.

'employment', unless the contrary intention appears, includes paid and unpaid employment, self-employment and engaging in business or any professional activity.

'EEA national' means a national of a State which is a Contracting Party to the European Economic Area Agreement other than the United Kingdom, but until the EEA Agreement comes into force in relation to Liechtenstein does not include a national of the State of Liechtenstein.

'family member' in relation to an EEA national has the same meaning as in the 1994 EEA Order.

COMMENTARY

The 1994 EEA Order is intended to give effect to the European Community law relating to the European Economic Area. Under it rights to free movement are granted to citizens of the EEA states (see Chapter 15). The concepts of settlement and ordinary residence are dealt with at pages 13 and 14.

Housing under Part III of the Housing Act 1985 and similar provisions for Scotland and Northern Ireland is the provision of local authority housing to a person classed as homeless.

3 General provisions regarding leave to enter or remain in the United Kingdom

PART 1

General Provisions Regarding Leave to Enter or Remain in the United Kingdom

Leave to enter the United Kingdom

7. A person who is neither a British citizen nor a Commonwealth citizen with the right of abode nor an EEA national or the family member of such a national who is entitled to enter or remain in the United Kingdom

GENERAL PROVISIONS 63

by virtue of the provisions of the Immigration (European Economic Area) Order 1994 requires leave to enter the United Kingdom.

8. Under Sections 3 and 4 of the Immigration Act 1971 an Immigration Officer when admitting to the United Kingdom a person subject to control under that Act may give leave to enter for a limited period and, if he does, may impose conditions restricting or prohibiting employment or occupation in the United Kingdom or requiring the person to register with the police or both. He may also require him to report to the appropriate Medical Officer of Environmental Health. Under Section 24 of the 1971 Act it is an offence knowingly to remain beyond the time limit or to fail to comply with such a condition or requirement.

9. The time limit and any conditions attached will be made known to the person concerned by a written notice which will normally be given to him or be endorsed by the Immigration Officer in his passport or travel document.

Exercise of the power to refuse leave to enter the United Kingdom

10. The power to refuse leave to enter the United Kingdom is not to be exercised by an Immigration Officer acting on his own. The authority of a Chief Immigration Officer or of an Immigration Inspector must always be obtained.

Requirement for persons arriving in the United Kingdom or seeking entry through the Channel Tunnel to produce evidence of identity and nationality

11. A person must, on arrival in the United Kingdom or when seeking entry through the Channel Tunnel, produce on request by the Immigration Officer:
   (i) a valid national passport or other document satisfactorily establishing his identity and nationality; and
   (ii) such information as may be required to establish whether he requires leave to enter the United Kingdom and, if so, whether and on what terms leave to enter should be given.

COMMENTARY

A person whose passport records that he is a British citizen should have no difficulty in entering the UK. Problems arise in the case of persons who are British citizens but have no passport evidencing the fact, and persons who are not British citizens and seek entry under the discretionary powers vested in the immigration authorities.

A person must on arrival in the UK produce on request by an immigration officer, a valid national passport or other document satisfactorily establishing his identity and nationality (1971 Act,

Sched 2, para 4(1)). Anyone arriving in the UK is liable to be examined and must furnish an immigration officer with such information as may be required for the purpose of deciding whether he requires leave to enter, and if so on what terms leave should be given. An immigration officer is under a duty to act fairly at all times (*Re HK (an infant)* [1967] 2 QB 617). The rules make clear that the power to refuse leave to enter may only be exercised by an immigration officer with the consent of a Chief Immigration Officer. A person seeking entry to the UK and claiming to have a right of abode may prove that he has that right, by producing a UK passport describing him as a British citizen, or as a CUKC with the right of abode (1971 Act, s 3(9)(*a*), as amended by the Immigration Act 1988, s 3). In *R v IAT, ex p Minta* [1992] Imm AR 380 it was held that a British Visitor's passport was not sufficient to discharge the burden under s 3(9), because it does not describe the bearer as a British citizen. It is therefore not proof of citizenship under s 3(9). While the immigration officer may be satisfied by other evidence of citizenship, he is only bound to accept a valid full British passport or certificate of entitlement as proof of citizenship under s 3(9).

Of course EEA nationals, diplomats immune under the provisions of the 1971 Act, crew members and Commonwealth citizens with the right of abode do not require leave to enter the UK. EU nationals can only be required to produce a valid identity document and under Article 7 of the Treaty of European Union such border controls as there are for travelers between member states, are of doubtful validity. Again it should be noted that the express provision in para 7 restricting entry to those who do not require leave under the EEA Order will be of no effect if the provisions of the EEA Order conflict with EC law on free movement.

The time limit and any condition attached, for example a condition restricting employment, will be made known to the passenger by a written notice. This will normally be given to the passenger or be endorsed by the immigration officer in the passenger's passport or travel document. Any ambiguity in such an endorsement should be resolved in favour of the passenger. Where a notice contains two dates, either of which might denote the date from which leave might run, the later date will be taken if it is more favourable to the passenger (*Behrooz v S of S* [1991] Imm AR 82 (IAT)). The Rules specify that it is an offence under s 24 of the 1971 Act for a person knowingly to remain beyond the time limit or to fail to comply with a condition or requirement imposed on his leave.

Leave to enter must be given by an immigration officer. The fact that a person may be examined by a police officer on arrival does not give rise to any leave being granted, for police officers in such situations cannot be treated as having the implied authority to grant leave to enter (*R v S of S, ex p Mohan* [1989] Imm AR 436).

The issue of a passport by the UK government is a matter within the Royal Prerogative. It is a question of discretion, and the government cannot be compelled to grant a passport to a person even if he is apparently eligible to hold one (*S of S v Lakdawalla* [1972] Imm AR 26). However, the CA has held that the refusal to issue a new passport, though part of the prerogative power, is amenable to judicial review (*R v Foreign & Commonwealth Office, ex p Everett* [1989] 1 All ER 655).

Under para 6 of the Schedule to the Immigration Act 1988, the immigration officer has the power to detain a passport or other document establishing the identity and nationality or citizenship of the holder until the holder is given leave to enter, or is about to depart following a refusal of leave.

'Arrival' in the UK is not the same as entry to the UK. A person arriving in the UK on a ship or aircraft is deemed not to have entered the UK until he has disembarked and left any area approved by an immigration officer for persons to remain pending a decision on entry, or while he is on temporary admission to the UK pending the decision (1971 Act, s 11 and Sched 2). Where a person comes to the UK via the Channel Tunnel system he is deemed not to have entered the UK unless and until he leaves the Channel Tunnel system (1971 Act, s 11(1A)).

Requirement for a person not requiring leave to enter the United Kingdom to prove that he has the right of abode

12. A person claiming to be a British citizen must prove that he has the right of abode in the United Kingdom by producing either:
    (i) a United Kingdom passport describing him as a British citizen or as a citizen of the United Kingdom and Colonies having the right of abode in the United Kingdom; or
    (ii) a certificate of entitlement duly issued by or on behalf of the Government of the United Kingdom certifying that he has the right of abode.

13. A person claiming to be a Commonwealth citizen with the right

of abode in the United Kingdom must prove that he has the right of abode by producing a certificate of entitlement duly issued to him by or on behalf of the Government of the United Kingdom certifying that he has the right of abode.

14. A Commonwealth citizen who has been given limited leave to enter the United Kingdom may later claim to have the right of abode. The time limit on his stay may be removed if he is able to establish a claim to the right of abode, for example by showing that:
(i) immediately before the commencement of the British Nationality Act 1981 he was a Commonwealth citizen born to or legally adopted by a parent who at the time of the birth had citizenship of the United Kingdom and Colonies by his birth in the United Kingdom or any of the Islands; and
(ii) he has not ceased to be a Commonwealth citizen in the meanwhile.

COMMENTARY

Burden of proof Where a person claims a right to enter by reason of citizenship or the right of abode, the burden of proof on the balance of probabilities rests with him (1971 Act, s 3(8) and *Bamgbose* above). It rests with the applicant throughout (*Fawehinmi v S of S* [1991] Imm AR 1 and see *R v S of S, ex p Ali* [1988] Imm AR 274 and *Visa Officer Islamabad v Channo Bi* [1978] Imm AR 182). The immigration officer is not bound to accept proof by production of a copy birth certificate (*Re Bamgbose* [1990] Imm AR 135). Where, however, a person presents a passport or certificate of entitlement, the evidential burden shifts and it is for the S of S to prove that the document has been forged or fraudulently obtained or that the person is for some other reason an illegal entrant (*R v S of S, ex p Khawaja* [1984] AC 74 see eg Ld. Fraser at 97F). In *Mokuolu v S of S* [1989] Imm AR 51 it was held that despite *Khawaja* the legal burden of proof does not shift where the ground on which the applicant seeks to rebut an allegation that he is an illegal entrant is that he has a right of abode or British citizenship. S 3(8) requires proof on the balance of probabilities, and the mere production of a birth certificate may not discharge it, if there are any discrepancies in the applicant's case which render it unlikely that he is a British citizen or has the right of abode.

Passport (see page 65).

Certificate of entitlement A person who seeks to enter the UK and claims to have the right of abode proves that right by means of a certificate of entitlement issued by or on behalf of the government of the UK certifying that he has such a right of abode

(1971 Act, s 3(9)(*b*) as amended by 1988 Act s 3, and see *R v IAT, ex p Minta* [1992] Imm AR 380). A statement that the holder of a passport has a right of abode written in a UK passport can constitute a certificate of entitlement (*Wong* (5991)).

A person who claims to be a British citizen because he was on 31 December 1982 a CUKC with a right of abode under s 2(1)(*c*) or 2(2) of the 1971 Act as then in force, must, however, prove that he has the right of abode by producing the certificate of entitlement duly issued to him by a British government representative overseas, or by the Home Office unless he can meet the requirements of s 3(9) of the 1971 Act as amended.

A commonwealth citizen who is not a British citizen but has a right of abode must prove that he has the right of abode by producing a certificate of entitlement duly issued to him by a British Government representative overseas or by the Home Office (para 8).

As in the case of entry certificates, the queue for certificates of entitlement were very long. The problems caused by the length of queues in India were considered by the CA in *R v S of S, ex p Phansopkar* [1976] QB 606. The appellant was married to a patrial and wished to join him in the UK. Issue of certificates of entitlement was subject to a 14-21 month delay. She sought entry without one and was refused. On being detained she sought habeas corpus and judicial review of the decision. The CA granted these remedies and the S of S was ordered to grant her application for a certificate of patriality in the UK as opposed to India. The court observed that patrials had the right to leave and enter the UK without let or hindrance subject only to the question of proof of patriality. That right could not be taken away by delaying the issue of the certificate without good cause. Since 1985 the queues in the Indian subcontinent have been divided into four groups, with those claiming the right of abode having the shortest time to wait.

Common travel area

Common Travel Area

15. The United Kingdom, the Channel Islands, the Isle of Man and the Republic of Ireland collectively form a common travel area. A person who has been examined for the purpose of immigration control at the point at which he entered the area does not normally require leave to enter any other part of it. However certain persons subject to the Immigration (Control of Entry through the Republic of Ireland) Order 1972 (as amended) who enter the United Kingdom through the Republic of Ireland do require leave to enter. This includes:

(i) those who merely passed through the Republic of Ireland;
(ii) persons requiring visas;
(iii) persons who entered the Republic of Ireland unlawfully;
(iv) persons who are subject to directions given by the Secretary of State for their exclusion from the United Kingdom on the ground that their exclusion is conducive to the public good;
(v) persons who entered the Republic from the United Kingdom and Islands after entering there unlawfully or overstaying their leave.

COMMENTARY

The 1971 Act establishes what is called the 'common travel area', as defined above. A person who does not have leave to enter or remain in the UK does not benefit from this para. Travel from the Republic to the UK is governed by the provisions of Article 7 of the Treaty of European Union, whereby free movement of persons travelling within the internal market is guaranteed. A person who enters from the Republic of Ireland does not pass through immigration control. The Immigration (Control of Entry through the Republic of Ireland) Order 1972 provides by article 4 that such a person may remain for a period of not more than three months from the date on which he entered the UK. A person entering the UK from Eire does not require and is not given leave by the Order, but he is automatically put under a restriction as to the length of permitted stay and if he disregards that restriction, he will become an overstayer (*Tahira Kaya v S of S* [1991] Imm AR 572). The new provision spells out the categories of person requiring leave to enter from the Republic, by means of an inclusive list. The absence of a category from that list will not render an otherwise unlawful entry lawful. Note that a person who breaches a condition of his leave (that does not relate to the length of his stay) and then travels to the Republic does not require leave if he returns within his period of leave.

Admission of certain British passport holders

Admission of certain British passport holders

16. A person in any of the following categories may be admitted freely to the United Kingdom on production of a United Kingdom passport issued in the United Kingdom and Islands or the Republic of Ireland prior to 1 January 1973, unless his passport has been endorsed to show that he was subject to immigration control:
(i) a British Dependent Territories citizen;
(ii) a British National (Overseas);
(iii) a British Overseas citizen;

GENERAL PROVISIONS 69

   (iv) a British protected person;
   (v) a British subject by virtue of Section 30(a) of the British Nationality Act 1981, (who, immediately before the commencement of the 1981 Act, would have been a British subject not possessing citizenship of the United Kingdom and Colonies or the citizenship of any other Commonwealth country or territory).

17. British Overseas citizens who hold United Kingdom passports wherever issued and who satisfy the Immigration Officer that they have, since 1 March 1968, been given indefinite leave to enter or remain in the United Kingdom may be given indefinite leave to enter.

COMMENTARY

A BDTC, a BOC, a BNO, a BPP or a British subject by virtue of s 30(a) of the 1981 Act who holds a UK passport should be admitted freely on production of a British passport which was issued in the common travel area before 1 January 1973. He will not be admitted freely if the passport is endorsed to show that he is subject to immigration control. The effect of demanding the production of the passport which was issued before the introduction of the 1971 Act is that persons falling within this category must have the out-of-date passport with them on entering the UK, in addition to their current passport. The Home Office have indicated that only the production of the expired passport will establish the right not to be subjected to immigration control. BOCs who hold UK passports whenever issued, and who satisfy the immigration officer that since 1 March 1968 they have been granted indefinite leave to enter or remain in the UK will be given indefinite leave to enter.

4 Returning residents

Returning Residents

18. A person seeking leave to enter the United Kingdom as a returning resident may be admitted for settlement provided the Immigration Officer is satisfied that the person concerned:
   (i) had indefinite leave to enter or remain in the United Kingdom when he last left; and
   (ii) has not been away from the United Kingdom for more than 2 years; and
   (iii) did not receive assistance from public funds towards the cost of leaving the United Kingdom; and
   (iv) now seeks admission for the purpose of settlement.

19. A person who does not benefit from the preceding paragraph by reason only of having been away from the United Kingdom too long may nevertheless be admitted as a returning resident if, for example, he has lived here for most of his life.

20. The leave of a person whose stay in the United Kingdom is subject to a time limit lapses on his going to a country or territory outside the common travel area. Such a person who returns after a temporary absence abroad within the period of this earlier leave has no claim to admission as a returning resident. His application to re-enter the United Kingdom should be considered in the light of all the relevant circumstances. The same time limit and any conditions attached will normally be reimposed if he meets the requirements of these Rules, unless he is seeking admission in a different capacity from the one in which he was last given leave to enter or remain.

COMMENTARY

Under HC 251, the following factors were considered:
(a) the length of the original residence in the UK of the person;
(b) the length of time that he had been out of the UK;
(c) the reasons for the absence exceeding two years; was it at the applicant's wish or through no fault of his own;
(d) the nature of any family ties in the UK, how close they are and the extent to which the person has maintained those family members during his absence from the UK;
(e) the purpose and intent of the person returning to the UK at the time he returned (it had to be at least for the purposes of settling in the UK);
(f) whether the person has a home in the UK, and if he was admitted to the UK, whether he intended to live in that home (see *ex p Ademuyiwa* [1986] Imm AR 1, and *S of S v Agyen-Frempong* [1986] Imm AR 108).

The underlying principle of the previous rule was that if a person could not establish that he had not been away from the UK for longer than two years, he had to show strong connections with the UK, by a combination of length of residence and family or other ties. Para 19 permits the immigration officer to exercise his discretion about the readmission of a person. The only example it gives of a factor to be taken into account in the exercise of that discretion is that the person has lived in the UK for most of his life. Other factors may be taken into account, and the factors listed under the previous rules are all clearly relevant in determining whether a person is a resident primarily of the UK who is returning to settle here.

The returning resident must have been settled in the UK on the last occasion that he was in the UK. 'Settlement' (see Chapter 2) requires the applicant to be ordinarily resident (*ECO Bombay v Joshi* [1975] Imm AR 1) in the UK without any conditions attached to his stay and without having entered or remained in breach of the immigration laws (*Bashir v Immigration Officer, Dover* [1976] Imm AR 96). A person with indefinite leave to remain may lose the right to settle under the provisions of the returning residents rule, if he returned to the UK and was granted limited leave at any stage before making the application to enter as a returning resident. *S of S v Akinrujomu* [1988] Imm AR 590 was authority under the previous set of rules for the proposition that has now been incorporated into HC 395. Where a person enters the UK and is granted leave as a visitor for the purposes of a short visit he will not be able to rely on the returning residents rule thereafter.

The person entering must have a present intention to settle in the UK. Returning resident status must therefore be claimed on entry (echoing *R v IAT ex p Coomasaru* [1983] 1 WLR 14 under earlier rules). However, if a person seeks admission only as a visitor or as a student for a limited period, there is no obligation on an immigration officer to advise him of his right to be admitted for settlement (*Ex p Tolba* [1988] Imm AR 78). The status of returning resident does not extend to a person who has already returned in a different capacity (*Goodison v S of S* [1979–80] Imm AR 122, *R v IAT, ex p Khatoon Ali* [1979–80] Imm AR 195). It is a question of the entrant's current intentions. In this regard some guidance as to 'an intention to settle' may be had from Simon Brown J in *R v IAT, ex p Rafique* [1990] Imm AR 235, a primary purpose case (see page 207) where he stated that if there is uncertainty about the duration of a person's stay, but a claim is made to enter for the purposes of marriage, it is proper to consider the application as an application for settlement as if ordinary residence is contemplated. If a person seeks entry as a returning resident, but expresses uncertainty about the duration of his stay it would be appropriate similarly to consider him as intending ordinary residence sufficient for settlement.

5 Holders of restricted travel documents and passports

Holders of restricted travel documents and passports

21. The leave to enter or remain in the United Kingdom of the holder

of a passport or travel document whose permission to enter another country has to be exercised before a given date may be restricted so as to terminate at least two months before that date.

22. If his passport or travel document is endorsed with a restriction on the period for which he may remain outside his country of normal residence, his leave to enter or remain in the United Kingdom may be limited so as not to extend beyond the period of authorised absence.

23. The holder of a travel document issued by the Home Office should not be given leave to enter or remain for a period extending beyond the validity of that document. This paragraph and paragraphs 21-22 do not apply to a person who is eligible for admission for settlement or to a spouse who is eligible for admission under paragraph 282 or to a person who qualifies for the removal of the time limit on his stay.

COMMENTARY

Under the previous immigration rules a person could be refused entry on the grounds he would not be admitted to his country of normal residence if he stayed more than a certain period. HC 395 retains that power where the person holds a document which requires entry to another country in less than two months. Otherwise the current rule merely permits a limitation on the leave which can be granted. Under para 282 a person seeking leave to enter the UK as the spouse of a person present and settled in the UK or who is being admitted on the same occasion for settlement may be admitted for an initial period of up to 12 months. Such a person must have an entry clearance for this purpose. The fact that his travel documents may indicate that his permission to enter another country has to be exercised before a certain date does not permit the S of S to terminate his leave at least two months before that date. Further if his passport permits him to remain outside his country of normal residence only for a limited period, his leave cannot be limited so as not to extend beyond the period of the absence authorised by his country of normal residence.

6 Entry clearance

Entry Clearance

24. A visa national and any other person who is seeking entry for a purpose for which prior entry clearance is required under these Rules must produce to the Immigration Officer a valid passport or other identity document endorsed with a United Kingdom entry clearance issued to him for the purpose for which he seeks entry. Such a person will be refused

GENERAL PROVISIONS

leave to enter if he has no such current entry clearance. Any other person who wishes to ascertain in advance whether he is eligible for admission to the United Kingdom may apply for the issue of an entry clearance.

25. Entry clearance takes the form of a visa (for visa nationals) or an entry certificate (for non-visa nationals). These documents are to be taken as evidence of the holder's eligibility for entry into the United Kingdom, and accordingly accepted as 'entry clearances' within the meaning of the Immigration Act 1971.

26. An application for entry clearance will be considered in accordance with the provisions in these Rules governing the grant or refusal of leave to enter. Where appropriate, the term 'Entry Clearance Officer' should be substituted for 'Immigration Officer'.

27. An application for entry clearance is to be decided in the light of the circumstances existing at the time of the decision, except that an applicant will not be refused an entry clearance where entry is sought in one of the categories contained in paragraphs 296–316 solely on account of his attaining the age of 18 years between receipt of his application and the date of the decision on it.

28. An applicant for an entry clearance must be outside the United Kingdom and Islands at the time of the application. An applicant for an entry clearance who is seeking entry as a visitor must apply to a post designated by the Secretary of State to accept applications for entry clearance for that purpose and from that category of applicant. Any other application must be made to the post in the country or territory where the applicant is living which has been designated by the Secretary of State to accept applications for entry clearance for that purpose and from that category of applicant. Where there is no such post the applicant must apply to the appropriate designated post outside the country or territory where he is living.

29. For the purposes of paragraph 28 'post' means a British Diplomatic Mission, British Consular post or the office of any person outside the United Kingdom and Islands who has been authorised by the Secretary of State to accept applications for entry clearance. A list of designated posts is published by the Foreign and Commonwealth Office.

30. An application for an entry clearance is not made until any fee required to be paid under the Consular Fees Act 1980 (including any Regulations or Orders made under that Act) has been paid.

COMMENTARY

The term 'entry clearance' is defined in s 33(1) of the 1971 Act. Entry clearances are visas, entry certificates (for non-visa

Commonwealth citizens) or other documents which in accordance with the immigration rules are to be taken as evidence or the requisite evidence of a person's eligibility for entry into the UK, although he is not a British citizen. Other documents may not be treated as such evidence of eligibility to enter (see *R v S of S, ex p Balogun* [1989] Imm AR 603). Documents such as work permits (s 33(1)) or special quota vouchers (*Amin v ECO Bombay* [1983] 2 All ER 864) are not entry clearances. 'Visa exempt' stamps issued under s 3(3)(b) of the 1971 Act are not entry clearances. They are no longer issued, but they are in any event merely a declaration of the provision of the Immigration Rules that in certain circumstances citizens of some countries do not require visas. They do not confer any greater rights than were granted to the bearer at the time the extension of his leave is granted (*Balogun* (above)).

Entry clearance officers are not mentioned in the 1971 Act, but no significance has been attached to that omission (*R v S of S, ex p Ounejma* [1989] Imm AR 75). HC 359 makes clear that the term 'Entry Clearance Officer' should be substituted for 'Immigration Officer' in the rules governing the grant of leave to enter, as these govern the grant of entry clearance.

An application for an entry clearance will not be considered to have been made until all the appropriate fees have been paid (para 30).

An application for entry clearance need not be made in any prescribed form; however, there must be a request in quite unambiguous terms for entry clearance to be issued to a particular person (*Prajpati v IAT* [1982] Imm AR 56). A letter from a solicitor stating 'we would be grateful if you would review our client's case and authorise the Entry Clearance Officer to grant entry clearance' was held by Kennedy J not to constitute an application in *R v IAT, ex p Jaifor Ali* [1990] Imm AR 531. He held that an application had to follow a prescribed form. *Prajpati* was not cited to him.

Visa nationals Nationals of certain countries are required to produce to the immigration officer a passport or other identity document endorsed with a UK visa issued for the purpose for which the individual seeks entry. Such nationals, known as 'visa nationals', may either be foreign nationals, or Commonwealth citizens who are specified in the Appendix to HC 395, and at page 285 below. They must produce to the immigration officer a passport or other identity document endorsed with a UK entry clearance issued for the purpose for which they seek entry. They must be refused leave to enter if they have no such current entry clearance. Holders of refugee travel documents issued under the 1951 Convention relating to the Status of Refugees by countries who signed the Council of Europe Agreement of 1959 on the Abolition of Visas for Refugees do not need visas if they are visiting the UK for three months or less. Para 2 of the Appendix to the Rules exempts such persons from the requirement of a visa. There is no discretion to grant leave to enter to a visa national if he does not have a current visa (*Walid* (1662)). A visa national needs a visa even if he is a transit passenger (*Immigration Officer Heathrow v Yuvraj Kapoor* [1991] Imm AR 357). Where an EEA national is accompanied by a non-EU family member, the family member may be required to show a visa (Art 3(2) Directive EC 68/360). Every facility must be provided to such a person to enable him to obtain the necessary visa, and impediments put in the way of such a family member such as a requirement that the visa be obtained in the country of the person's origin will be a breach of the Directive.

7 Variation of leave to enter or remain

Variation of leave to enter or remain in the United Kingdom

31. Under Section 3(3) of the 1971 Act a limited leave to enter or remain in the United Kingdom may be varied by extending or restricting its duration, by adding, varying or revoking conditions or by removing the time limit (whereupon any condition attached to the leave ceases to apply). When leave to enter or remain is varied an entry is to be made in the applicant's passport or travel document (and his registration certificate where appropriate) or the decision may be made known in writing in some other appropriate way.

32. After admission to the United Kingdom any application for an extension of the time limit on or variation of conditions attached to a person's stay in the United Kingdom must be made to the Home Office before the applicant's current leave to enter or remain expires.

33. Where the application is in respect of employment for which a work permit or a permit for training or work experience is required or is in respect of the spouse or child of a person who is making such an application, the application should be made direct to the Department of Employment Overseas Labour Service.

COMMENTARY

For an application for variation of leave to be made for the purposes of the 1971 Act, the applicant must prove that the Home Office received the application (*S of S v Peters* [1993] Imm AR

187). The question of whether an application is an application for a variation of leave to remain is a question of fact (*Soyemi v S of S* [1989] Imm AR 564). Merely sending a passport, without any covering letter, generally will not be sufficient to qualify as an application for a variation of leave (*Elu v S of S* [1989] Imm AR 568). The application must be in unambiguous terms (*Prajpati v IAT* [1982] Imm AR 56). However, if the Home Office acts upon the sending of a passport, it will be difficult for it to argue that no application has been made (see *Soyemi*). The application must be made to the correct S of S. Unless the rules indicate otherwise, as in the case of applications for extensions of work permits which are made to the Department of Employment, the correct S of S will be for the Home Department. No valid application will be made if an application is sent to another Department (*Naved Masud v IAT* [1992] Imm AR 129).

Extension of leave: *the rule in Suthendran's case* There is one very important point to be borne in mind when applications for a variation of leave are made. This arises from the decisions of the CA and the HL in *R v IAT ex p Subramaniam* [1977] QB 190 and in *Suthendran v IAT* [1977] AC 359 respectively. Applications must be made before the current leave, which it is sought to vary, expires. If this is not done, rights of appeal against a refusal of that leave are lost (see also *R v IAT ex p Bastiampillai* [1983] 2 All ER 844). The strictness of the decision in *Suthendran's* case was mitigated by the operation of the Immigration (Variation of Leave) Order 1976 (SI 1976 No 1572).

In *Suthendran's* case the majority of the HL, following *Subramaniam*, held that if an application for variation of leave is made after that leave expires, there is no right of appeal against the refusal. Section 14(1) of the 1971 Act only gives a right of appeal to someone who has limited leave to remain. The majority also held that if an application is made before a person's leave expires, but it is not refused until after the expiration of leave, there is no right of appeal either (see also *R v IAT, ex p Bhanji* [1977] Imm AR 89 considered in *Halil v Davidson* [1979–80] Imm AR 164).

The 1976 Order now provides that if an application for variation is made before leave expires but is dealt with after expiration, that person's leave is to continue until 28 days after the refusal of the variation. From 8 July 1989 where a person has applied for a variation of a current leave and withdraws that application, his leave must be extended for a period of 28 days after the withdrawal

(Immigration (Variation of Leave) (Amendment) Order 1989 (SI 1989 No 1005)).

The 1976 Order has been considered in several cases. In *S of S v Petrou* [1978] Imm AR 87 the IAT held that if a person's leave expires on a Sunday and an application for a variation is not made until the following Monday, that person is not protected by the provisions of the 1976 Order. However, an application for a variation of leave is to be deemed to be made on the date it is posted (*Lubetkin v S of S* [1979–80] Imm AR 162). So where an application was posted on the day leave expired, the applicant was protected by the 1976 Order. This is a broad interpretation of the Order, but a just one, in view of the delays which can be experienced in the postal system. The application must not be too vague: it must be reasonably clear that the communication is an application for leave (*Dial v S of S* [1987] Imm AR 36). The date of the decision for the purposes of the 28-day period is either:

(*a*) the date on which notice of the decision is posted;

(*b*) the date on which the notice of the decision is otherwise served (Art 3(3)).

The position where a person who is enjoying extended leave under the operation of the Order makes a fresh application for an extension of leave on new grounds is complicated. The relevant principles have been summarised in *Moussavi v S of S* [1986] Imm AR 39:

(i) Para 3(1) of the Order extends the duration of an applicant's leave when he makes an application during the currency of leave granted to him otherwise than by virtue of the Order.

(ii) Such extension operates so that a further application made during the period of the extension will be made during the currency of leave.

(iii) By virtue of para 3(2)(*c*) the Order does not apply to the further application so as to extend yet again the appellant's leave because of the further application.

(iv) In consequence of the decision in *Suthendran* and the non-extension of the appellant's leave because of the further application, a right of appeal will be attracted to a refusal of the further application only if that refusal is made during the extension of the leave operating by the Order because of the first application.

(v) The extension of leave conferred by para 3(1) of the Order terminates 28 days after an application which causes that extension to come into operation is withdrawn.

It is not possible for a person to extend his leave indefinitely by making successive applications for variation and consequent appeals. During the course of an extension under the Variation of Leave Order (VOLO) provisions, the conditions attached to the original grant of leave continue to be attached (*R v S of S, ex p Lapinid* [1984] 1 WLR 1269, *Rajendran v S of S* [1989] Imm AR 512 and *Ofoajoku v S of S* [1991] Imm AR 68).

The Order does not apply where:
(*a*) the date of the decision is more than 28 days before the end of the period of leave;
(*b*) where the leave expired before the Order came into operation;
(*c*) where there is no other concurrent period of leave save that granted by an operation of the Order;
(*d*) where the duration of a person's leave has been curtailed by the S of S under s 7(1) of the 1993 Act (Article 3(2) as amended).

By Article 4 (inserted by the Immigration (Variation of Leave) (Amendment) Order 1993 (SI 1993 No 1657)) where the duration or a person's leave has been extended by Article 3, and the duration of his leave has been curtailed under s 7 of the 1993 Act, the extension has no effect after the date on which leave is curtailed.

Withdrawn applications for leave to remain in the United Kingdom

Withdrawn applications for variation of leave to enter or remain in the United Kingdom

34. Where a person whose application for variation of leave to enter or remain is being considered requests the return of his passport for the purpose of travel outside the common travel area, the application for variation of leave shall, provided it has not already been determined, be treated as withdrawn as soon as the passport is returned in response to that request and the provisions of the Immigration (Variation of Leave) Order 1976 (as amended) will apply.

COMMENTARY

On departure from the common travel area the limited leave held by an entrant lapses. The entrant must satisfy the authorities each time of his right to enter the UK (*Channo Bi* (above) *Ghassemian v Home Office* [1989] Imm AR 42 and *Kuku v S of S* [1990] Imm AR 27). The S of S cannot be estopped from refusing entry on a second or subsequent occasion. If the applicant requests the return of his passport for the purposes of travel outside the common travel area, any application he has pending before the immigration service will be taken to be withdrawn (although the Home Office has no power unilaterally to cancel the application, see *Dungarwalla v S of S* [1989] Imm AR 476). Woolf LJ in *Kuku* thought that it would be desirable for the Home Office to issue documents dealing with the effects of leaving the common travel area during the currency of a leave to remain. Stamps which are issued under s 3(3)(*b*) of the 1971 Act do not give rise to a legitimate expectation that the person bearing the stamp will be readmitted if he leaves the common travel area and returns before the expiration of his leave (*S of S v Mowla* [1991] Imm AR 210). The stamps are merely an attempt to set out the effects of the 1971 Act (Sched 2, para 14); they do not grant any extra rights.

The leave of a person who withdraws his application for an extension will be extended for 28 days after the withdrawal by the Immigration (Variation of Leave) Order 1976 (as amended). Under the new rule he will have 28 days in which to travel, but as soon as he leaves the common travel area, he must obtain fresh leave to re-enter whether or not he returns within that 28-day period. Leave also lapses when a person's application has been treated as withdrawn because his passport has been returned in response to his request for it. The new rule makes it clear that the provisions of the Immigration (Variation of Leave) Order 1976 (as amended) apply to the person's leave (see page 76).

8 Undertakings

Undertakings

35. A sponsor of a person seeking leave to enter or variation of leave to enter or remain in the United Kingdom may be asked to give an undertaking in writing to be responsible for that person's maintenance and accommodation for the period of any leave granted, including any further variation. Under the Social Security Administration Act 1992 and the Social Security Administration (Northern Ireland) Act 1992, the Department of Social Security or, as the case may be, the Department of Health and Social Services in Northern Ireland may seek to recover from the person giving such an undertaking any income support paid to meet the needs of the person in respect of whom the undertaking has been given.

COMMENTARY

Undertaking relating to maintenance and accommodation A relative or friend of an applicant for variation of leave may be asked to give an undertaking to be responsible for that person's maintenance and accommodation. Under the Social Security Act 1986 or the

Social Security (Northern Ireland) Order 1986, the Department of Social Security or the Department of Health and Social Services in Northern Ireland, may recover from the person who gave the undertaking any income support subsequently paid to the applicant. The undertaking must be written before such enforcement action can be taken against the relative or friend.

9 Medical

Medical

36. A person who intends to remain in the United Kingdom for more than 6 months should normally be referred to the Medical Inspector for examination. If he produces a medical certificate he should be advised to hand it to the Medical Inspector. Any person seeking entry who mentions health or medical treatment as a reason for his visit, or who appears not to be in good mental or physical health, should also be referred to the Medical Inspector; and the Immigration Officer has discretion, which should be exercised sparingly, to refer for examination in any other case.

37. Where the Medical Inspector advises that a person seeking entry is suffering from a specified disease or condition which may interfere with his ability to support himself or his dependants, the Immigration Officer should take account of this, in conjunction with other factors, in deciding whether to admit that person. The Immigration Officer should also take account of the Medical Inspector's assessment of the likely course of treatment in deciding whether a person seeking entry for private medical treatment has sufficient means at his disposal.

38. A returning resident should not be refused leave to enter on medical grounds. But where a person would be refused leave to enter on medical grounds if he were not a returning resident, or in any case where it is decided on compassionate grounds not to exercise the power to refuse leave to enter, or in any other case where the Medical Inspector so recommends, the Immigration Officer should give the person concerned a notice requiring him to report to the Medical Officer of Environmental Health designated by the Medical Inspector with a view to further examination and any necessary treatment.

39. The Entry Clearance Officer has the same discretion as an Immigration Officer to refer applicants for entry clearance for medical examination and the same principles will apply to the decision whether or not to issue an entry clearance.

COMMENTARY

Under paragraph 37 the role of the medical inspector is to advise whether a person seeking entry is suffering from a specified disease or condition which may interfere with his ability to support himself or his dependants. The immigration officer has discretion in the face of that advice to admit the person.

A person who satisfies the rules relating to returning residents is not to be refused entry on medical grounds alone, but may be required to report to the Medical Officer of Environmental Health with a view to further examination and any necessary treatment.

Immigration officers are only to refer EEA nationals (when they are exercising rights of free movement) to a medical inspector if they show 'obvious signs of mental or physical ill-health'. They may only be refused leave to enter if the medical inspector certifies that they are suffering from one of the diseases listed in the annex to EC directive 64/221. Similarly members of the family of an EEA national may only be refused leave to enter for medical reasons if they are suffering from such a disease.

Chapter 7

Part 2 of HC 395: Persons Seeking to Enter or Remain in the United Kingdom for Visits

Part 2 of the Immigration Rules deals with the general requirements on those who seek to enter or remain in the UK as visitors for the purposes of
  (a) transit;
  (b) private medical treatment; or
  (c) transacting business.
EEA nationals wishing to visit are not subject to the requirement of leave to enter when they are exercising an EEA free movement right. EU citizens may not be subject to controls at the border (see Chapter 15).

1 Requirements for leave to enter

PART 2:

Persons Seeking to Enter or Remain in the United Kingdom for Visits

VISITORS

Requirements for leave to enter as a visitor

40. For the purpose of paragraphs 41–46 a visitor includes a person living and working outside the United Kingdom who comes to the United Kingdom to transact business (such as attending meetings and briefings, fact finding, negotiating or making contracts with United Kingdom businesses to buy or sell goods or services). A visitor seeking leave to enter or remain for private medical treatment must meet the requirements of paragraphs 51 or 54.

41. The requirements to be met by a person seeking leave to enter the United Kingdom as a visitor are that he:

PERSONS SEEKING TO ENTER THE UK FOR VISITS

(i) is genuinely seeking entry as a visitor for a limited period as stated by him, not exceeding 6 months; and
(ii) intends to leave the United Kingdom at the end of the period of the visit as stated by him; and
(iii) does not intend to take employment in the United Kingdom; and
(iv) does not intend to produce goods or provide services within the United Kingdom, including the selling of goods or services direct to members of the public; and
(v) does not intend to study at a maintained school; and
(vi) will maintain and accommodate himself and any dependants adequately out of resources available to him without recourse to public funds or taking employment; or will, with any dependants, be maintained and accommodated adequately by relatives or friends; and
(vii) can meet the cost of the return or onward journey.

Leave to enter as a visitor

42. A person seeking leave to enter the United Kingdom as a visitor may be admitted for a period not exceeding 6 months, subject to a condition prohibiting employment, provided the Immigration Officer is satisfied that each of the requirements of paragraph 41 is met.

Refusal of leave to enter as a visitor

43. Leave to enter as a visitor is to be refused if the Immigration Officer is not satisfied that each of the requirements of paragraph 41 is met.

COMMENTARY

For general grounds of refusal of leave see Chapter 13.

The requirements of para 41 are all mandatory. Leave to enter is to be refused if they are not all fulfilled (para 43). A person may not be admitted as a visitor if it is his intention to study at a maintained school during his visit. A seasonal agricultural worker cannot extend his time in the UK by applying for an extension of stay as a visitor.

2 'is genuinely seeking entry as a visitor for a limited period as stated by him not exceeding 6 months'

(a) Period of admission (HC 395, para 41(i))

A visitor and any dependants accompanying him will normally be given leave to enter for a period of six months unless the immigration officer is satisfied that there are particular circumstances which justify the giving of a shorter period of leave.

Restricted returnability (see page 71) would be such a factor. The applicant must state the length of the intended visit (see *ECO Nicosia v Georgiou* [1976] Imm AR 151). The immigration officer must be satisfied that the applicant will genuinely seek entry for that period alone. The applicant must satisfy the immigration officer that he is genuinely seeking entry for a particular period not in excess of six months. He must also be able to satisfy the immigration officer that he will be able to maintain and accommodate himself for that period. The immigration officer is not obliged to consider whether he could grant leave to enter for a period shorter than that stated by the applicant (*Immigration Officer, London (Heathrow) Airport v Schonenburger* [1975] Imm AR 7, and *Ex p Harnaik Singh* [1969] 2 All ER 867). The immigration officer may not refuse an application because the applicant is likely to apply for an extension of leave once admitted (*Ex p Arjumand* [1983] Imm AR 123). The immigration office is entitled to consider whether the stated period for which leave is sought is the period for which the applicant genuinely seeks to be in the UK. However, if the entrant genuinely seeks entry for a shorter period, but there is a chance that his purposes may not be completed within that time and he will need to seek an extension, leave to enter should not be refused on that basis.

(b) Purpose of visit

The only requirement is that the person genuinely seeks entry as a visitor. An immigration officer when considering whether an applicant is a genuine visitor or not will take into consideration the circumstances of the person seeking entry. Thus a person of means and position in his country of origin may well be accepted as a genuine visitor even if his declared intention is 'only to visit the maze at Hampton Court'. However, when a considerable sum of money is to be expended by a family with limited resources, close scrutiny will be given to the reasons for the expenditure (*Manmohan Singh v ECO New Delhi* [1975] Imm AR 118).

A person who does not fall into the other categories within the immigration rules may seek entry as a visitor. Where an applicant has a wish to study if a place becomes available to him that may be seen as an intention to study. Leave to enter as a visitor will be refused (*Ex p Brakwah* [1989] Imm AR 366). However, it is the current intention of the applicant which must be assessed (see *ECO Hong Kong v Lai* [1974] Imm AR 98). On the other hand there is no category in the rules of persons visiting the UK 'for family reasons'. Such a visit may be permissible depending on what the substantive purpose of the visit is to be. A visit for the purposes of maintaining family relationships while the applicant's children are being educated in the UK is to be dealt with under the rules governing visitors (*Sehan Kelada v S of S* [1991] Imm AR 400). A person entering for the purposes of attending his own appeal will also be dealt with under the visitor rules (*Patel v ECO Bombay* [1991] Imm AR 273). However, it is important to distinguish between, on the one hand, an application to visit with a view to assisting relatives in times of illness or a mother with the care of her children so as to enable her to attend a course of training or study (*Hamilton v ECO Kingston Jamaica* [1974] Imm AR 43, and *ECO Lagos v Samanda* [1975] Imm AR 16), which is acceptable; and on the other hand, an application to enter as a visitor to relieve the mother of the care of her children so that she can be gainfully employed (*Obeyesekere v S of S* [1976] Imm AR 16) which is not acceptable. An application for a work permit should have been made in this latter type of case (see also *ECO Manila v Magalso* [1993] Imm AR 293). Otherwise the reasons for entry may be unimportant, or even frivolous.

Persons entering for private medical treatment must satisfy the conditions set out in para 51 and those seeking an extension of stay should satisfy the conditions in para 54. A distinction is drawn also between persons entering to transact business as visitors and those seeking to establish themselves in the UK in business. The latter have to satisfy the conditions set out at paras 200–210.

Business visitors A business visitor is a person based and employed outside the UK who comes to the UK to transact business (such as attending meetings and briefings, observing or checking facts, negotiating or making contracts with UK businesses to buy or sell goods or services) and who then leaves the UK.

Where a person bought an off-the-shelf company and registered it to process goods he was regarded as having ceased merely to transact business, and to be engaging in business (*Ex p Ayoola* [1992] Imm AR 170). In *Hossain v Immigration Officer Heathrow* [1990] Imm AR 520 the IAT held that a person with a multiple visit stamp in his passport who set up a company in the UK, and was the driving force behind it, was engaged in business rather than merely transacting it on each of the visits he made on the stamp.

The rules are likely to be operated in accordance with the previous practice of the Home Office. Whether a visitor is engaging in business or merely transacting business will be a matter of fact and degree. A person will be regarded as transacting business if he is attending meetings, signing contracts, or arranging deals, or activities of a similar nature, and not taking a job which could be done by a resident worker or doing any 'productive work' (Home Office letter to ILPA in (1991) 5 INL&P No 1).

More recently the Home Office identified these basic requirements used to identify a 'bona fide' business visitor:

(1) The person should live and work abroad, and should not be attempting to base himself in the UK, even temporarily. The visit should therefore be short.
(2) He should continue to be paid by his overseas employer.
(3) He should not be providing a service to a UK firm, but his work should arise from his employment for the overseas employer.
(4) He must not do a job which might otherwise be taken by an EU worker and if his work entails a product of some kind (goods or services), it should at all times be produced abroad, otherwise he will be doing 'productive work'. Productive work means work which is capable of producing goods or services which have a monetary or exchange value, and can include attending a meeting if it involves preparing a report, collecting and analysing data, and making recommendations to the UK company.

The nature of the work to be done determines whether a visitor is transacting business or should seek entry under the rules relating to business persons. Thus a person providing a service for a fee would have to gain admission under the business rules, whereas a person attached temporarily to a UK company in an advisory capacity only would be admitted as a business visitor (see Anne Balcombe 'Business visitors: Home Office Practice (1993) 7 INL&P 19).

3 'intends to leave the United Kingdom at the end of his visit'

The immigration officer must be satisfied that the applicant intends to leave the UK at the end of his visit (see *Swati v S of S* [1986] 1 WLR 4772). It is only the applicant's intentions at the time of seeking leave to enter and not intentions no longer held by him that are relevant (see *ECO Hong Kong v Lai* (above)). If there are doubts as to the intention of the applicant regarding leaving the UK, leave to enter must be refused (see HC 395 para 43).

The fact that a sponsor is willing to give an undertaking that the applicant will leave will not resolve those doubts (*ECO New Delhi v Kumar* [1978] Imm AR 185). However, unsuccessful applications to enter the UK may be taken into account in deciding whether the applicant will leave at the end of his visit.

(b) Factors taken into account

Any factor may be considered. However, mere suspicion that a person will not return to his country at the end of his visit is not sufficient grounds for refusal of leave to enter (*R v Lympne Airport Chief Immigration Officer, ex p Amrik Singh* [1968] 3 All ER 63). Suspicions should be supported by tangible evidence (*Baig* (1886)). Thus in *Bhagat Singh v ECO New Delhi* [1978] Imm AR 134 (IAT) the only matter which aroused suspicion as to the intention of the applicant, a 74-year-old widower, was his reply to repeated questions as to whether he would apply to remain with his son, that he would see what the position was when he arrived and then he might apply. However, the ECO should have weighed that factor against the fact that he was financially independent, that he had three brothers and sisters living in his home village, that he had returned from the UK previously, and that his health would suffer if he lived in a cold climate. Had he done so he would not have found that the applicant was not a genuine visitor.

In the absence of any bad faith, the fact that the person is the holder of a UK passport issued outside the UK should not lead to the presumption that he would not leave at the end of the visit (*Mohammed Din v ECO Karachi* [1978] Imm AR 56), but it is a factor which may be taken into account among other factors (*Patel (MR) v ECO Bombay* [1978] Imm AR 154).

The mere lack of incentive to leave the UK at the end of the visit is an insufficient reason for not being satisfied that the applicant intends to leave the UK at the end of the visit (*Blair* (1797)). However, the so-called 'economic incentive' for an applicant to leave his country and 'better himself' in the UK may be taken into account by immigration officers. In *ECO Colombo v Hanks* [1976] Imm AR 74 one applicant was granted an entry certificate to enable her to visit the UK whilst her son and daughter were refused entry certificates. By reason of her age and the expectancy that she would inherit a family house, the mother was said not to have the same incentive as her children to leave Sri Lanka permanently. The daughter's previous applications to enter the UK had failed, and she had applied to emigrate to Australia. The son had been practically unemployed save for casual work for a period of nearly four years. These matters were held to disclose a strong intention on their part not to return to Sri Lanka.

In *Patel v ECO Bombay* [1973] Imm AR 30 an elderly widow was granted an entry certificate to visit her son, daughter and grandchildren. Various factors pointed to the genuine nature of the visit. It was cheaper for her to visit her relatives than the other way round. She had lived in India all her life, and spoke no English. She was of an age at which it was unlikely she would want to uproot herself and settle in a country with a different climate. She would not gain very much financially by coming to the UK, and she had a return air fare paid for by her son who lived in India. He had saved up for five years to pay for it.

The mere possession of a return air fare on the other hand is not by itself conclusive evidence that the passenger will leave the UK at the end of his stay (*Immigration Officer Birmingham v Mohammed Sadiq* [1978] Imm AR 115).

Persons of limited means, without substantial positions, may have more difficulty in persuading an immigration officer that they have a real intention to leave at the end of their stay (*Manmohan Singh* (above)). The presence of relatives in the home country, and evidence that the applicant is or will be employed in that country, are other factors taken as a guide to whether the applicant will leave (*Huda v ECO Dacca* [1976] Imm AR 109). The undertaking of a person to maintain and accommodate a person of limited means may assist in removing the suspicion that he will not leave at the end of the visit.

Refusal to answer questions put by the ECO or immigration officers, for example in relation to family details, gives reasonable grounds for the immigration officer not to be satisfied that the applicant intends to leave at the end of the proposed visit (*Immigration Officer Birmingham v Mohammad Sadiq* [1978] Imm AR 115, and *Abid Hussain v ECO Islamabad* [1989] Imm AR 46). The cumulative effect of suspicious matters may justify refusal (*In Re Olusanya (Olugbenga)* [1988] Imm AR 117).

4 'does not intend to take employment in the United Kingdom'

(a) Employment, production of goods and services and study

The definition of 'employment' Para 6 defines 'employment' as including paid and unpaid employment, self-employment and engaging in any business or any professional activity, unless a contrary intention appears in rules. Visitors must not intend to engage in any of those activities. If the applicant intends to take employment, whether paid or unpaid, or to engage in business or professional activity, leave to enter as a visitor will be inappropriate, and the requirements relating to those seeking to enter for employment or to engage in business or professional activity should be satisfied (see page 166). Entry will be refused if the applicant comes to the UK with the definite purpose of seeking employment, even if that purpose is secondary to the main purpose of the visit (*Baldachino v S of S* [1972] Imm AR 14).

5 'Will maintain and accommodate himself and any dependants out of the resources available to him, without working or recourse to public funds'

'Public funds' means:
(*a*) housing under Part III of the Housing Act 1985, Part II of the Housing (Scotland) Act 1987, or Part II of the Housing (Northern Ireland) Order 1988; and
(*b*) income support, family credit and housing benefit under the Social Security Act 1986 and the Social Security (Northern Ireland) Order 1986 (see para 6).

A relative or friend may be asked to give an undertaking in writing to be responsible for the person's maintenance and accommodation for the period of any leave granted, including any variation. They are rarely sought in practice, but any income support paid to an entrant may be recovered from the person giving the undertaking. If the relative or other sponsor of a person seeking entry to the UK refuses to give, when requested to do so, an undertaking in writing to be responsible for that person's maintenance and accommodation for the period of leave granted, leave may be refused to the person seeking entry on the ground that the person cannot maintain himself without recourse to public funds. The phrase 'available to him' should include monies other than the applicant's own. In HC 251 the rule relating to business persons joining UK businesses required the applicant to show that he would be bringing money 'of his own'. No similar intention is contained in this rule.

Where the immigration officer is not satisfied as to the above, leave to enter as a visitor must be refused under the immigration rules (para 43).

6 Extensions of stay

(a) Extension of stay as a visitor

Requirements for an extension of stay as a visitor

44. Six months is the maximum permitted leave which may be granted to a visitor. The requirements for an extension of stay as a visitor are that the applicant:
  (i) meets the requirements of paragraph 41 (ii)–(vii); and
  (ii) has not already spent, or would not as a result of an extension of stay spend, more than 6 months in total in the United Kingdom as a visitor.

Any period spent as a seasonal agricultural worker is to be counted as a period spent as a visitor.

Extension of stay as a visitor

45. An extension of stay as a visitor may be granted, subject to a condition prohibiting employment, provided the Secretary of State is satisfied that each of the requirements of paragraph 44 is met.

Refusal of extension of stay as a visitor

46. An extension of stay as a visitor is to be refused if the Secretary of State is not satisfied that each of the requirements of paragraph 44 is met.

COMMENTARY

A person seeking an extension of leave to remain as a visitor must satisfy the immigration officer that he intends to leave the UK at the end of his visit, and that he does not intend to take paid or unpaid employment or engage in business or professional activity. He must also satisfy the immigration officer that he will maintain and accommodate himself and any dependants out of the resources available to him, without working or recourse to public funds. He must show that he can meet the cost of his return or onward journey. Once the applicant is admitted any application for an extension must be considered under these paragraphs. The aggregate stay may not exceed six months (para 44). However, where an application is made for a period which would exceed that aggregate it may be treated as an application for an extension for the remainder of the six-month period if it is related to some specific event such as being able to see the Christmas lights (*S of S v Riaz*

[1987] Imm AR 88). It is not *necessary* for the applicant to specify a further limited period, as he is not required to satisfy the requirement contained in para 41(i), although the applicant would be best advised to specify such a period so as to satisfy the immigration officer that he intends to leave the UK at the end of the visit. The application must be refused if the result of *an* extension would be that the aggregate period of the visit exceeded six months. A refusal on the sole basis that the period of the extension sought would result in a visit exceeding six months would be unlawful. Extensions may be granted to non-visa nationals to remain in some other temporary capacity such as student or working holiday maker, or on marriage or as a dependant (*Nisa v S of S* [1979–80] Imm AR 20).

7 Visitors in transit

VISITORS IN TRANSIT

Requirements for admission as a visitor in transit to another country

47. The requirements to be met by a person (not being a member of the crew of a ship, aircraft, hovercraft, hydrofoil or train) seeking leave to enter the United Kingdom as a visitor in transit to another country are that he:
 (i) is in transit to a country outside the common travel area; and
 (ii) has both the means and the intention of proceeding at once to another country; and
 (iii) is assured of entry there; and
 (iv) intends and is able to leave the United Kingdom within 48 hours.

Leave to enter as a visitor in transit

48. A person seeking leave to enter the United Kingdom as a visitor in transit may be admitted for a period not exceeding 48 hours with a prohibition on employment provided the Immigration Officer is satisfied that each of the requirements of paragraph 47 is met.

Refusal of leave to enter as a visitor in transit

49. Leave to enter as a visitor in transit is to be refused if the Immigration Officer is not satisfied that each of the requirements of paragraph 47 is met.

Extension of stay as a visitor in transit

50. The maximum permitted leave which may be granted to a visitor

in transit is 48 hours. An application for an extension of stay beyond 48 hours from a person admitted in this category is to be refused.

COMMENTARY

The S of S has made an order under section 1A(2)(*a*) of the Immigration (Carriers' Liability) Act 1987 that citizens of Afghanistan, Iran, Iraq, Lebanon, Libya, Somalia, Sri Lanka, Turkey, Uganda, and Zaire require transit visas for all entries to the UK. Other visa nationals only require them if there is more than 24 hours between their arrival and departure flights (Immigration (Transit Visa) Order 1993 SI No 1678/1993).

If he does not leave the transit lounge a transit passenger will be deemed not to have entered the UK (1971 Act, s 11). A transit *visitor* must have the means and the intention of proceeding at once to another country. 'Means' is not confined to financial means. Where no airline will carry a transit passenger, he does not have the means of proceeding to another country (*R v S of S, ex p Coonhye The Independent,* 20 April 1988).

A visa national in transit to another country requires a current visa in order to be given leave to enter the UK (*Immigration Officer, Heathrow v Yuvraj Kapoor* [1991] Imm AR 357).

8 Visitors seeking to enter or remain for private medical treatment

VISITORS SEEKING TO ENTER OR REMAIN FOR PRIVATE MEDICAL TREATMENT

Requirements for leave to enter as a visitor for private medical treatment

51. The requirements to be met by a person seeking leave to enter the United Kingdom as a visitor for private medical treatment are that he:
   (i) meets the requirements set out in paragraph 41 (iii)–(vii) for entry as a visitor; and
   (ii) in the case of a person suffering from a communicable disease, has satisfied the Medical Inspector that there is no danger to public health; and
   (iii) can show, if required to do so, that any proposed course of treatment is of finite duration; and
   (iv) intends to leave the United Kingdom at the end of his treatment; and
   (v) can produce satisfactory evidence, if required to do so, of:
      (*a*) the medical condition requiring consultation or treatment; and
      (*b*) satisfactory arrangements for the necessary consultation or treatment at his own expense; and
      (*c*) the estimated costs of such consultation or treatment; and

(*d*) the likely duration of his visit; and
(*e*) sufficient funds available to him in the United Kingdom to meet the estimated costs and his undertaking to do so.

Leave to enter as a visitor for private medical treatment

52. A person seeking leave to enter the United Kingdom as a visitor for private medical treatment may be admitted for a period not exceeding 6 months, subject to a condition prohibiting employment, provided the Immigration Officer is satisfied that each of the requirements of paragraph 51 is met.

Refusal of leave to enter as a visitor for private medical treatment

53. Leave to enter as a visitor for private medical treatment is to be refused if the Immigration Officer is not satisfied that each of the requirements of paragraph 51 is met.

COMMENTARY

For the general grounds of refusal see Chapter 13. Refusal of leave to enter is mandatory if the immigration officer is not satisfied about any of the conditions specified in para 51 (para 53). The evidential requirements of para 51(v) should be noted when making any application. He must not intend to take paid or unpaid employment or engage in business or professional activity. He must maintain and accommodate himself and any dependants out of the resources available to him, without taking work or recourse to public funds. He must not intend to study at a maintained school. He must be able to meet the cost of the return or onward journey. It is not necessary for the applicant to show that he can meet the cost of his medical treatment out of personal funds (*Foon v S of S* [1983] Imm AR 29). He must be able to show that he can meet the cost of the treatment from funds which are *available* to him. The applicant must now show evidence if required of a medical condition requiring treatment in the UK.

The likely costs of the treatment will continue to be assessed by the medical inspector, and the immigration officer is obliged to take account of that assessment when considering whether the applicant's means are adequate (para 37). The length of the visit may exceed six months. Initially the applicant is likely to receive six months' leave to enter. After entry, if further medical treatment is necessary, an extension may be sought.

A person seeking entry for the purposes of private medical treatment need not show that he intends to leave the UK at the end of the period stated by him for his visit. He must, however, show that he intends to leave the UK at the end of his course of treatment. By para 52 the leave granted to such a person will not initially exceed six months. The person may, however, apply for an extension of leave if necessary. A major change introduced by HC 395 is that the treatment must be of finite duration, so that an applicant must have some information on the duration of his treatment. It is not clear whether a provisional duration will be considered sufficient for this requirement. During the first six months the applicant may receive treatment from a general practitioner, or practitioner of alternative medicine. However, he will require the support of an NHS consultant to obtain an extension (see para 54).

Requirements for an extension of stay as a visitor for private medical treatment

54. The requirements for an extension of stay as a visitor to undergo or continue private medical treatment are that the applicant:
   (i) meets the requirements set out in paragraph 41 (iii)–(vii) and paragraph 51 (ii)–(v); and
   (ii) has produced evidence from a registered medical practitioner who holds an NHS consultant post of satisfactory arrangements for private medical consultation or treatment and its likely duration; and, where treatment has already begun, evidence as to its progress; and
   (iii) can show that he has met, out of the resources available to him, any costs and expenses incurred in relation to his treatment in the United Kingdom; and
   (iv) has sufficient funds available to him in the United Kingdom to meet the likely costs of his treatment and intends to meet those costs.

Extension of stay as a visitor for private medical treatment

55. An extension of stay to undergo or continue private medical treatment may be granted, with a prohibition on employment, provided the Secretary of State is satisfied that each of the requirements of paragraph 54 is met.

Refusal of extension of stay as a visitor for private medical treatment

56. An extension of stay as a visitor to undergo or continue private medical treatment is to be refused if the Secretary of State is not satisfied that each of the requirements of paragraph 54 is met.

COMMENTARY

HC 395 introduced a restriction on the scope of the rule relating to extensions of leave to remain by a person undergoing private medical treatment. An application for an extension of stay for medical treatment must now be supported by a registered medical practitioner who holds an NHS consultant post. A person seeking an extension of leave for the purposes of private medical treatment must not intend to take paid or unpaid employment or engage in business or professional activity. He must maintain and accommodate himself and any dependants out of the resources available to him, without taking work or recourse to public funds. He must be able to meet the cost of the return or onward journey. If the disease is a communicable disease he must have satisfied the medical inspector that there is no danger to public health. He must be able to show the course of treatment he is to undergo is of finite duration. The visit must have some finite end. It is unlikely that an extension will be granted 'until treatment is concluded' where there is no known date for that event (*Hyrapiet* (2232)). The rule provides for the granting of an extension of stay for private medical treatment at the discretion of the S of S.

The discretion will not be exercised if:
(*a*) the applicant does not produce evidence from a registered medical practitioner who holds an NHS consultant post of satisfactory arrangements for private medical consultations or treatment and its likely duration. Where treatment has begun, he must also give evidence of its progress;
(*b*) there is reason to believe that the treatment would be at the public expense.

The duration of the treatment, particularly whether it is finite or not, is a factor. The S of S may take account of the fact that the treatment is available in the applicant's country in the exercise of his discretion (*Aviva Ganu v S of S* [1993] Imm AR 20).

Chapter 8

Part 3 of HC 395: Students

1 Students: leave to enter or remain

Part 3 of the Rules makes provision for persons seeking to enter or remain in the UK for studies. HC 395 provides that all students are expected to be enrolled for at least 15 hours a week of full-time daytime study. The only exception relates to students enrolled on a full-time degree course at a publicly funded institution of further or higher education. Students are no longer allowed to enroll on a variety of part-time courses at a variety of establishments in order to make up the 15 hours. HC 395 requires a student to enroll for a single subject or directly related subjects at a single institution. The student must be intending to study at an independent fee paying school outside the maintained sector. A child under 16 who seeks leave to enter or remain for studies must be in full-time education which meets the requirements of the Education Act 1944 at an independent fee paying school. Children under 16 may not therefore enroll on secretarial courses, for example.

PART 3:

PERSONS SEEKING TO ENTER OR REMAIN IN THE UNITED KINGDOM FOR STUDIES

STUDENTS

Requirements for leave to enter as a student

57. The requirements to be met by a person seeking leave to enter the United Kingdom as a student are that he:
   (i) has been accepted for a course of study at:
      (*a*)   a publicly funded institution of further or higher education; or

STUDENTS

    (b) a *bona fide* private education institution which maintains satisfactory records of enrolment and attendance; or
    (c) an independent fee paying school outside the maintained sector; and
  (ii) is able and intends to follow either:
    (a) a recognised full-time degree course at a publicly funded institution of further or higher education; or
    (b) a weekday full-time course involving attendance at a single institution for a minimum of 15 hours organised daytime study per week of a single subject or directly related subjects; or
    (c) a full-time course of study at an independent fee paying school; and
  (iii) if under the age of 16 years is enrolled at an independent fee paying school on a full-time course of studies which meets the requirements of the Education Act 1944; and
  (iv) intends to leave the United Kingdom at the end of his studies; and
  (v) does not intend to engage in business or to take employment, except part-time or vacation work undertaken with the consent of the Secretary of State for Employment; and
  (vi) is able to meet the costs of his course and accommodation and the maintenance of himself and any dependants without taking employment or engaging in business or having recourse to public funds.

Leave to enter as a student

58. A person seeking leave to enter the United Kingdom as a student may be admitted for an appropriate period depending on the length of his course of study and his means, and with a condition restricting his freedom to take employment, provided the Immigration Officer is satisfied that each of the requirements of paragraph 57 is met.

Refusal of leave to enter as a student

59. Leave to enter as a student is to be refused if the Immigration Officer is not satisfied that each of the requirements of paragraph 57 is met.

COMMENTARY

For general grounds of refusal see Chapter 13. Section 8 of the Asylum and Immigration Appeals Act 1993 provides that if a person is refused entry as a student for a period of study up to six months and he does not have a prior entry clearance for the purpose or is refused entry as a prospective student, he may not appeal against the decision to refuse him entry. Where he seeks an entry clearance in order to follow a course of study of not more than six months' duration for which he has been accepted or seeks an entry clearance with the intention of studying, but without being accepted for any course of study, he may not appeal against a refusal of that entry clearance. Such decisions are now amenable to judicial review (see further Chapter 27). The period of leave granted under the entry rules may be of any appropriate period depending on the length of the course of study and the student's means.

Educational establishments It is necessary for the course to be at a bona fide educational establishment (*R v IAT, ex p Idiaro* [1991] Imm AR 546, an example of one which was not). Whether the establishment is a bona fide establishment is a question of fact, and the immigration officer should consider whether the educational establishment can conceivably provide what it claims to provide for students. The individual establishment should be considered and general assumptions about the character of particular educational establishments should not be made (*Oke* (8557)). The educational establishment is required by para 57 to keep satisfactory records of enrolment.

(a) Able and intends to follow

In assessing the ability of the applicant to follow the course, it is likely that the intellectual abilities of the applicant will be considered as under the old rules; however, the express mention of consideration being given to the applicant's 'qualifications' has disappeared. The immigration officer will consider whether the applicant's knowledge of English is sufficient for the type of course on which he is enrolled (*ECO Karachi v Ahmed* [1989] Imm AR 254). A poor knowledge of English will indicate an inability to follow a computer course (*Goffar v ECO Dacca* [1975] Imm AR 142), and the need for an interpreter will indicate inability to follow a highly technical course (*R v IAT, ex p Ozkurtulus* [1986] Imm AR 80). Where the applicant clearly does not appear to understand sufficient English, or, for example, mathematics, to attend a course of studies at a college of further education, the immigration officer may contact the college to make sure that they will have the applicant (*R v Chief Immigration Officer, Bradford Airport, ex p Ashiq Hussain* [1969] 3 All ER 1601).

Lack of ability may be taken to be evidence of lack of intention to follow the course. However, there must be evidence and not mere suspicion that the applicant cannot and/or does not intend to follow the course (*ECO New Delhi v Bhambra* [1973] Imm AR

14). Ability, conversely, does not indicate that a person's intention, for example to study English, is any less realistic (*Dagdar* (2101)).

(b) Full time course of study

The concept covers a 'coherent and definite educational proposal which the student could reasonably be expected to complete' (*R v Chief Immigration Officer, Gatwick Airport, ex p Kharrazzi* [1980] 1 WLR 1396). Thus it can include, as in that case, ten years of education including 'O' and 'A' levels and the attainment of a university degree, even before the student has been guaranteed or accepted for a place at university. The phrase 'full-time course of study' may include more than one course, provided that they are specific parts of a coherent whole (Ibid, per Waller LJ at p 1406). Each case must depend upon its own facts and the ability of the individual concerned (*Myeen Rashid v ECO Dacca* [1976] Imm AR 12). A three year old, however, may not be a student (*Issa* (4011)).

In *Patel v IAT* [1983] Imm AR 76, the CA stated, obiter, that the wider meaning given to studies in *Kharrazzi* should include 'the gaining of experience' and 'any activity which is related to the studies' (per Lawton LJ at 81). Paragraph 57 now requires that if there is more than one course involved in the studies, the subjects studied must be 'directly related'.

In *Awosika v S of S* [1989] Imm AR 35, the IAT held that where a course had organised classes which did not take up the whole or a substantial part of the student's time, but were supplemented by private study which did, the rule may be satisfied. Thus two part-time courses can constitute a full-time course of day time study for the purposes of this rule (*Shomali* (3451)). However, the rule requires attendance for 15 hours. The discretion present in HC 251 has been removed by the requirement that leave must be refused if any of the requirements of para 57 is not satisfied.

Organised When considering the general rule that there must be 15 hours of organised study per week, consideration must be given to whether the study is organised. In *R v IAT, ex p Idiaro* [1991] Imm AR 546 Henry J held that to be 'organised' study there must be both (a) an organiser making the rules, and (b) the organised, who adhere to those rules, have tasks set for them, do them at specific times and places and under supervision. A course which was not structured in this way might nevertheless satisfy the rule in the paragraph which is merely setting out a general rule. Certain obiter in *Durojaiye v S of S* [1991] Imm AR 307 suggest that the meaning of 'organised daytime study' encompasses more than merely formal teaching time at an institution. However the 15 hours referred to in the paragraph are those hours which are compulsory under the course and for which the applicant must attend and study. Merely attending for 15 hours may not result in fulfilling the conditions in the paragraph.

(c) Intention to leave

Occasionally there will be direct evidence of an intention not to leave. For example, where the applicant firmly states that he intends to remain in the UK after the course and take employment entry will be refused (*ECO Lagos v Sobanjo* [1978] Imm AR 22).

In most cases the intention of the applicant will be ascertained by reference to indirect evidence, and by looking at all the circumstances surrounding the application. It is a question of fact (*Patel v IAT* [1983] Imm AR 76). Lack of plans by an applicant to take up employment in his home country after completion of his course of training and a complete vagueness on the subject of future employment anywhere may suggest to an immigration officer that an applicant will not leave the UK after he has concluded his studies. However, on the authority of *R v Lympne Airport Chief Immigration Officer, ex p Amrik Singh* [1968] 3 All ER 163, such a suspicion would not form a valid reason for refusing to grant an entry certificate or to grant admission for present study (*Puri v S of S* [1972] Imm AR 21).

Although the immigration officer may refuse entry if satisfied that the applicant intends not to leave at the end of the course, the fact that the applicant has in mind the possibility, among other things, of being allowed to stay in the UK after his course should not affect his right of entry, provided that the course of study is the primary purpose for which entry to the UK is made (*R v IAT, ex p Perween Khan* [1972] 3 All ER 297). Thus the fact that the applicant harbours a hope which he expresses of being able to remain after completion of his studies does not necessarily nullify the intention which the applicant has at the time of entry to leave at the end of his studies (*R v IAT, ex p Shaikh* [1981] 1 WLR 1107). On the other hand if the intention to undergo a course of studies is a mere device to gain entry so as to be able to stay in circumstances in which he knows he would be unlikely to be permitted to remain he should not be permitted to enter (*Perween Khan* (above) pages 273-4 per Bridge J). An intention to leave is not exhibited if the applicant intends to leave only if by no lawful means can he avoid it (*Patel v IAT* (above)). The immigration officer may also take account of the applicant's immigration history, and the fact that he has failed to complete his study plans on previous visits (*Ex p Fernando* [1987] Imm AR 377). Similarly, a history of examinations failed or unattempted may be evidence of lack of ability and/or lack of intention to leave the UK after study terminates (*Ex p Gomez, CA 17.1.91*).

Lack of realism is not a proper ground for refusing entry clearance or admission. The Divisional Court in *R v Khan (SGH)* [1975] Imm AR 26 allowed an application for certiorari where an ECO refused an entry certificate to a Pakistani citizen who applied to attend a short computer course. The officer took the view that it was unrealistic that the applicant should have involved his first cousin in expenditure for the course fees plus the cost of his return air ticket, particularly as there were local computer operator schools in Karachi, much cheaper than in the UK. The applicant had not made any specific inquiries with companies as regards employment on his return. However, the officer misdirected himself. May J said at p 30:

that it might in the circumstances have been foolhardy, and certainly less than thrifty to come all the way from Karachi to London for the course without making inquiries may be so and perhaps this may be said to be unrealistic, but in my judgment it in no way follows that it was dishonest or that the applicant was not genuine.

Nevertheless in assessing whether an application is genuine it is often necessary to take into account factors which would also need to be considered when considering whether an application is realistic. On an application to attend a computer operator's course such factors as the applicant's background, and whether he had made inquiries about suitable courses and employment prospects in the computer field in his home country, may well be material factors in determining whether the applicant intended to leave the UK on completion of his course (*Goffar v ECO Dacca: Dey v ECO Dacca* [1975] Imm AR 142). The absence of any inquiries about job opportunities locally or concern about material benefits to be gained by taking a short vocational course, coupled with such matters as a large expenditure of money by a poor family to enable an applicant to attend a course in the UK, will be taken to be highly relevant matters when considering whether the applicant will leave the UK on completion of his course (*Khan (SGH) v ECO Karachi* [1975] Imm AR 64 at 68). Thus an application by a rickshaw puller to study the Egyptian scarabs in the British Museum would be likely to create an immediate doubt which would be for the applicant to dispel as to his intentions. A university graduate making the same application would not have such difficulty (*Islam v ECO Dacca* [1974] Imm AR 83 at p 86).

Save in so far as doubts are raised as to the intention to leave the UK after completion of his study, as long as the immigration rules are complied with it is a matter of indifference, first as to the nature of the study proposed, and secondly, the use to which the applicant proposes to put the knowledge thereby gained (*Islam* at p 85).

The IAT in *Ghosh v ECO Calcutta* [1976] Imm AR 60 held that there was nothing objectionable in the ECO's request that the applicant obtain written confirmation from his present employers (who he claimed had given him leave of absence) that the qualifications he would acquire from attendance at a 16-week course in computer programming would be 'acceptable' to them for employment in that field. Such a request was considered to be very different from asking an applicant for an assurance that he would be employed as a computer programmer after his proposed training (*S of S v Virdee* [1972] Imm AR 215). Moreover when substantial sums of money are paid out for a short vocational course, the source of those funds is 'clearly not an irrelevant matter and one not to be disregarded' (*Ghosh* at p 65).

(d) Employment

Students will have been admitted with a condition prohibiting or restricting their permission to take employment. With the consent of the Department of Employment (DoE), bona fide students may work in their free time. If the course involves employment the educational establishment should agree with the local Jobcentre that all its overseas students on that course should be permitted to engage in the employment required for the course. The educational establishment may also ask his employer to obtain a permit for the student.

Where a student wishes to take a job which is not integral to the course in this way, the student should apply to the DoE to obtain a variation of any prohibition there may be on him taking employment. If the student cannot show that he does not need to take employment to finance his studies, a variation is unlikely to be granted.

Where the condition stamped on the passport is a restriction on working, the student should apply for permission from his local

Jobcentre, which will need to see the passport stamp, and will give the student form OSS1. The student should ensure that the form is properly completed by himself, his educational establishment and the prospective employer. Permission is more likely if the job has been advertised and is in some way relevant to his course. Employment taking up more than 20 hours is very unlikely to be permitted.

The student's means from free-time employment are not to be taken into account in deciding whether his means are adequate.

Students are not allowed to engage in business (*Ex p Ayoola* [1992] Imm AR 170).

(e) Adequate means

The applicant must be able to meet the costs of his course and accommodation and the maintenance of himself and any dependants without working or recourse to public funds. It is a question of fact whether the applicant can meet these costs. Detailed documentary evidence will be important, including communications from banks, and bank statements showing that funds are available, and where appropriate can be transferred to the UK (*Murgai v ECO New Delhi* [1975] Imm AR 86). Letters of sponsorship and other documentary evidence must be specific and unambiguous. In *Ayettey v S of S* [1972] Imm AR 261, neither a letter from the applicant's father stating that he was financially responsible for his son and was able to bear the costs of the course, nor one from a solicitor testifying that the father was of substance who owned property abroad were held to be sufficient (see also *Bhagat v S of S* [1972] Imm AR 189). There must be evidence available showing how the total costs can be met.

EU students The position of students who are EU citizens is governed by the freedom of movement provisions (Article 48) of the Treaty of Rome which take precedence over the immigration rules. Under the Treaty the position of students has been dealt with by Directive 93/96 OJ No L317/59. This gives the nationals of member states who have been accepted on a vocational training course the right to pursue it. The right of free movement is also given to the spouse and children of a person pursuing such a course. The student must have sickness insurance, and satisfy the national authority that he will not place a burden on the national social assistance scheme during his residential period. The right of residence is restricted to the period of study. Non-EU national members of his family will receive visas for the same duration as the course of the student, and may engage in employment or self-employment in the host state. This Directive is discussed in detail in Chapter 15.

2 Extensions

Requirements for an extension of stay as a student

60. The requirements for an extension of stay as a student are that the applicant:
   (i) was admitted to the United Kingdom with a valid student entry clearance if he is a person specified in the Appendix to these Rules; and
   (ii) meets the requirements for admission as a student set out in paragraph 57 (i)–(vi); and
   (iii) has produced evidence of his enrolment on a course which meets the requirements of paragraph 57; and
   (iv) can produce satisfactory evidence of regular attendance during any course which he has already begun; or any other course for which he has been enrolled in the past; and
   (v) can show evidence of satisfactory progress in his course of study including the taking and passing of any relevant examinations; and
   (vi) would not, as a result of an extension of stay, spend more than 4 years on short courses (ie courses of less than 2 years duration, or longer courses broken off before completion); and
   (vii) has not come to the end of a period of government or international scholarship agency sponsorship, or has the written consent of his original sponsor for a further period of study in the United Kingdom and satisfactory evidence that sufficient sponsorship funding is available.

Extension of stay as a student

61. An extension of stay as a student may be granted, subject to a restriction on his freedom to take employment, provided the Secretary of State is satisfied that the applicant meets each of the requirements of paragraph 60.

Refusal of extension of stay as a student

62. An extension of stay as a student is to be refused if the Secretary of State is not satisfied that each of the requirements of paragraph 60 is met.

COMMENTARY

(f) Extensions

A person applying for an extension of his leave as a student must continue to satisfy the admission criteria above, and must also satisfy all of the requirements of para 60, failing which his application must be refused. However, a person who had been properly admitted to the UK as a student and received extensions as such for studies at a technical college on an HND course in business studies, lost his student status when he subsequently entered into a four-year training contract with a firm of chartered accountants (*Yeong Hoi Yuen v S of S* [1977] Imm AR 34). To fulfil the requirement that the applicant for an extension of leave be enrolled, it is sufficient that the applicant is entitled to an unconditional, confirmed place on a course which satisfies the rules (*Chinwo v S of S* [1985] Imm AR 74). The requirement of regular attendance is a mandatory requirement of the rule, showing the good faith of the student. It does not require the student to attend without absences. However, there must be satisfactory explanations for those absences (*Pour* (1479)). If the requirement is not satisfied the application must be refused (*S of S v Durojaiye* [1991] Imm AR 248). If an application for an extension has been properly refused by reason of the applicant's unsatisfactory attendance record the applicant cannot succeed on appeal against the refusal by showing that his attendance since that refusal has improved (*Juma v S of S* [1974] Imm AR 96). It is for the S of S to decide whether to accept certificates of attendance from an educational establishment as evidence of regular attendance (*Kpoma v S of S* [1973] Imm AR 25).

(g) Intention to leave at the end of the course of studies

This requirement applies both on entry and on application for extensions. Thus a student who deliberately ignored the time limit and conditions subject to which he was admitted was refused an extension of his stay (*Lee v S of S* [1975] Imm AR 75). Where a student entrusted his passport to a college on the understanding that they would look after his immigration matters, and it failed to do so, the S of S was entitled to take account of the student's own inertia (*Ex p Animashaun* [1990] Imm AR 70). Similarly a student who had taken ordinary full-time employment in breach of the conditions of his admission was refused an extension to remain as a student (*S of S v Thaker* [1976] Imm AR 114), as was an applicant who had falsely represented herself only as a holiday visitor when she had applied for an entry certificate, whereas her intention was to pursue a course of study (*Owusu v S of S* [1976] Imm AR 101) and also a student who deceived the immigration authorities as to his examination history (*Ex p Adebodun* [1991] Imm AR 60). An applicant does not have the necessary intention to leave if he intends to leave only if by no lawful means can he avoid it (*Patel v IAT* [1983] Imm AR 76).

The new rules make clear that where a period of government or international scholarship agency scholarship has ended, no further extensions may be granted. Under HC 251 if the same course of study was being followed after the end of the period of scholarship, the S of S could exercise his discretion to extend leave.

(h) Satisfactory progress

A prolonged lack of examination success will be taken into account. Thus an appellant's total lack of success in his four years' study in the UK justified the doubts of the S of S that the appellant intended to return to his own country on the completion of his studies (*Mahendran v S of S* [1988] Imm AR 492). Further if the person has not taken any exams over a three-year period, the S of S may take that into account (*Adebodun* [1991] Imm AR 60). Moreover, there is no obligation on the S of S to warn a student that a lack of academic success can be taken into account in considering his application for extension of leave (*Ofoajoku v S of S* [1991] Imm AR 68).

A visa national will only be granted an extension if he was admitted to the UK with an entry clearance for the purposes of studying.

(i) Student nurses

HC 395 defines what is meant by a student nurse. A person seeking leave to remain in the UK as a student nurse must satisfy the immigration officer or ECO that he intends to leave the UK at the end of his studies. Student nurses are not allowed to switch to work permit employment once they have qualified. They must qualify under the Training and Work Experience Scheme provisions if they wish to take post-registration courses. This change brought about by HC 395 is a result of the Department of Employment no longer regarding nursing as a shortage occupation.

3 Student nurses

Definition of student nurse

63. For the purposes of these Rules the term student nurse means

a person accepted for training as a student nurse or midwife leading to a registered nursing qualification; or an overseas nurse or midwife who has been accepted on an adaptation course leading to registration as a nurse with the United Kingdom Central Council for Nursing, Midwifery and Health Visiting.

Requirements for leave to enter as a student nurse

64. The requirements to be met by a person seeking leave to enter the United Kingdom as a student nurse are that the person:
   (i) comes within the definition set out in paragraph 63 above; and
   (ii) has been accepted for a course of study in a recognised nursing educational establishment offering nursing training which meets the requirements of the United Kingdom Central Council for Nursing, Midwifery and Health Visiting; and
   (iii) did not obtain acceptance by misrepresentation; and
   (iv) is able and intends to follow the course; and
   (v) does not intend to engage in business or take employment except in connection with the training course; and
   (vi) intends to leave the United Kingdom at the end of the course; and
   (vii) has sufficient funds available for accommodation and maintenance for himself and any dependants without engaging in business or taking employment (except in connection with the training course) or having recourse to public funds. The possession of a Department of Health bursary may be taken into account in assessing whether the student meets the maintenance requirement.

Leave to enter the United Kingdom as a student nurse

65. A person seeking leave to enter the United Kingdom as a student nurse may be admitted for the duration of the training course, with a restriction on his freedom to take employment, provided the Immigration Officer is satisfied that each of the requirements of paragraph 64 is met.

Refusal of leave to enter as a student nurse

66. Leave to enter as a student nurse is to be refused if the Immigration Officer is not satisfied that each of the requirements of paragraph 64 is met.

Requirements for an extension of stay as a student nurse

67. The requirements for an extension of stay as a student nurse are that the applicant:
   (i) was admitted to the United Kingdom with a valid student entry clearance if he is a person specified in the Appendix to these Rules; and
   (ii) meets the requirements set out in paragraph 64 (i)–(vii); and

(iii) has produced evidence of enrolment at a recognised nursing educational establishment; and
(iv) can provide satisfactory evidence of regular attendance during any course which he has already begun; or any other course for which he has been enrolled in the past; and
(v) would not, as a result of an extension of stay, spend more than 4 years in obtaining the relevant qualification; and
(vi) has not come to the end of a period of government or international scholarship agency sponsorship, or has the written consent of his original sponsor for a further period of study in the United Kingdom and evidence that sufficient sponsorship funding is available.

Extension of stay as a student nurse

68. An extension of stay as a student nurse may be granted, subject to a restriction on his freedom to take employment, provided the Secretary of State is satisfied that the applicant meets each of the requirements of paragraph 67.

Refusal of extension of stay as a student nurse

69. An extension of stay as a student nurse is to be refused if the Secretary of State is not satisfied that each of the requirements of paragraph 67 is met.

COMMENTARY

For general grounds of refusal see Chapter 13. An application for leave to enter or for an extension must satisfy the requirements of para 64 and of para 67 respectively. In either case if the requirements are not all satisfied, refusal is mandatory. When applying for an extension of leave to remain as a student nurse, the applicant must satisfy the immigration officer that he falls within the definition of 'student nurse'. He must be accepted for training as a student nurse leading to a registered nursing qualification. If a qualified nurse or midwife he must be accepted on an adaptation course leading to registration as a nurse with the UK Central Council for Nursing Midwifery and Health Visiting. He must be accepted for a course of study in a nursing educational establishment and must not have obtained that acceptance by misrepresentation. He must be able and intend to follow the course. He must not intend to take employment except in connection with a training course. He must intend to leave the UK at the end of the course. He must have sufficient funds available for accommodation and maintenance for himself and any dependants without doing work other than in connection with the training course, or recourse to

STUDENTS

public funds (see page 61). The student nurse's means will include the possession of a Department of Health bursary. He must not as a result of the extension spend more than four years obtaining the relevant qualification.

4 Post-graduate doctors and dentists

POSTGRADUATE DOCTORS AND DENTISTS

Requirements for leave to enter as a postgraduate doctor or dentist

70. The requirements for leave to enter the United Kingdom for the purpose of training as a postgraduate doctor or dentist are that the applicant:
- (i) (a) is a graduate from a United Kingdom medical school intending to undertake Pre-Registration House Officer employment for up to 12 months, as required for full registration with the General Medical Council; and
  - (b) has not spent more than 12 months in aggregate in Pre-Registration House Officer employment; or
- (ii) (a) is a doctor or dentist eligible for full or limited registration with the General Medical Council or with the General Dental Council who intends to undertake postgraduate training in a hospital; and
  - (b) has not spent more than 4 years in aggregate in the United Kingdom as a postgraduate doctor or dentist, excluding any period spent in Pre-Registration House Officer employment; and
- (iii) intends to leave the United Kingdom on completion of his training period.

Leave to enter as a postgraduate doctor or dentist

71. A person seeking leave to enter the United Kingdom to study as a postgraduate doctor or dentist may be admitted for a period not exceeding 12 months provided the Immigration Officer is satisfied that each of the requirements of paragraph 70 is met.

Refusal of leave to enter as a postgraduate doctor or dentist

72. Leave to enter as a postgraduate doctor or dentist is to be refused if the Immigration Officer is not satisfied that each of the requirements of paragraph 70 is met.

Requirements for extension of stay as a postgraduate doctor or dentist

73. The requirements for an extension of stay as a postgraduate doctor or dentist are that the applicant:
- (i) (a) meets the requirements of paragraph 70 (i)(a); and
  - (b) would not, as a result of an extension of stay, spend more

than 12 months in aggregate in Pre-Registration House Officer employment; or
 (ii) (a) is a doctor or dentist who can provide satisfactory evidence of limited or full registration with the General Medical Council or registration with the General Dental Council and intends to undertake postgraduate training in a hospital; and
 (b) would not, as a result of an extension of stay, spend more than 4 years in aggregate in the United Kingdom as a postgraduate doctor or dentist excluding any period spent in Pre-Registration House Officer employment; and
 (iii) intends to leave the United Kingdom on completion of his training period.

Extension of stay as a postgraduate doctor or dentist

74. An extension of stay as a postgraduate doctor or dentist may be granted for a period not exceeding 12 months provided the Secretary of State is satisfied that each of the requirements of paragraph 73 is met.

Refusal of extension of stay as a postgraduate doctor or dentist

75. An extension of stay as a postgraduate doctor or dentist is to be refused if the Secretary of State is not satisfied that each of the requirements of paragraph 73 is met.

5 Spouses of students

SPOUSES OF STUDENTS

Requirements for leave to enter or remain as the spouse of a student

76. The requirements to be met by a person seeking leave to enter or remain in the United Kingdom as the spouse of a student are that:
 (i) the applicant is married to a person admitted to or allowed to remain in the United Kingdom under paragraphs 57–75; and
 (ii) each of the parties intends to live with the other as his or her spouse during the applicant's stay and the marriage is subsisting; and
 (iii) there will be adequate accommodation for the parties and any dependants without recourse to public funds; and
 (iv) the parties will be able to maintain themselves and any dependants adequately without recourse to public funds; and
 (v) the applicant does not intend to take employment except as permitted under paragraph 77 below; and
 (vi) the applicant intends to leave the United Kingdom at the end of any period of leave granted to him.

Leave to enter or remain as the spouse of a student

77. A person seeking leave to enter or remain in the United Kingdom

as the spouse of a student may be admitted or allowed to remain for a period not in excess of that granted to the student provided the Immigration Officer or, in the case of an application for limited leave to remain the Secretary of State, is satisfied that each of the requirements of paragraph 76 is met. Employment is to be prohibited except where the period of leave being granted is 12 months or more.

Refusal of leave to enter or remain as the spouse of a student

78. Leave to enter or remain as the spouse of a student is to be refused if the Immigration Officer or, in the case of an application for limited leave to remain, the Secretary of State is not satisfied that each of the requirements of paragraph 76 is met.

COMMENTARY

For general grounds of refusal see Chapter 13. The spouse of a student should not have their freedom to work restricted, where the student's course is longer than 12 months. However, a person must show that he can maintain and accommodate himself without recourse to public funds or without working in order to gain admission as a spouse of a student.

6 Children of students

CHILDREN OF STUDENTS

Requirements for leave to enter or remain as the child of a student

79. The requirements to be met by a person seeking leave to enter or remain in the United Kingdom as the child of a student are that he:
  (i) is the child of a parent admitted to or allowed to remain in the United Kingdom as a student under paragraphs 57–75; and
  (ii) is under the age of 18 or has current leave to enter or remain in this capacity; and
  (iii) is unmarried, has not formed an independent family unit and is not leading an independent life; and
  (iv) can, and will, be maintained and accommodated adequately without recourse to public funds; and
  (v) will not stay in the United Kingdom beyond any period of leave granted to his parent.

Leave to enter or remain as the child of a student

80. A person seeking leave to enter or remain in the United Kingdom as the child of a student may be admitted or allowed to remain for a period of leave not in excess of that granted to the student provided the Immigration Officer or, in the case of an application for limited leave

to remain, the Secretary of State is satisfied that each of the requirements of paragraph 79 is met. Employment is to be prohibited except where the period of leave being granted is 12 months or more.

Refusal of leave to enter or remain as the child of a student

81. Leave to enter or remain in the United Kingdom as the child of a student is to be refused if the Immigration Officer or, in the case of an application for limited leave to remain, the Secretary of State is not satisfied that each of the requirements of paragraph 79 is met.

COMMENTARY

For general grounds of refusal see Chapter 13. A student's under 18-year-old child will be granted entrance for the period of the student's authorised stay if he can be maintained and accommodated without recourse to public funds. His freedom to take employment will not be restricted. It must be shown that he has not formed an independent family unit, and that he is not leading an independent life. He must be maintained and accommodated adequately without recourse to public funds. He must be admitted with his parent who is the spouse of the student. The exceptions to this rule are either where the only parent still alive is the student, or the parent allowed to remain has sole responsibility for his upbringing, or there are serious and compelling family or other considerations which make exclusion undesirable. Suitable arrangements must have been made for his care.

The maximum period of his leave must not exceed the maximum period granted to the student parent.

7 Prospective students

PROSPECTIVE STUDENTS

Requirements for leave to enter as a prospective student

82. The requirements to be met by a person seeking leave to enter the United Kingdom as a prospective student are that he:
   (i) can demonstrate a genuine and realistic intention of undertaking, within 6 months of his date of entry, a course of study which would meet the requirements for an extension of stay as a student set out in paragraphs 60 or 67; and
   (ii) intends to leave the United Kingdom on completion of his studies or on the expiry of his leave to enter if he is not able to meet

the requirements for an extension of stay as a student set out in paragraphs 60 or 67; and
  (iii) is able without working or recourse to public funds to meet the costs of his intended course and accommodation and the maintenance of himself and any dependants while making arrangements to study and during the course of his studies.

Leave to enter as a prospective student

83. A person seeking leave to enter the United Kingdom as a prospective student may be admitted for a period not exceeding 6 months with a condition prohibiting employment, provided the Immigration Officer is satisfied that each of the requirements of paragraph 82 is met.

Refusal of leave to enter as a prospective student

84. Leave to enter as a prospective student is to be refused if the Immigration Officer is not satisfied that each of the requirements of paragraph 82 is met.

Requirements for extension of stay as a prospective student

85. Six months is the maximum permitted leave which may be granted to a prospective student. The requirements for an extension of stay as a prospective student are that the applicant:
  (i) was admitted to the United Kingdom with a valid prospective student entry clearance if he is a person specified in the Appendix to these Rules; and
  (ii) meets the requirements of paragraph 82; and
  (iii) would not, as a result of an extension of stay, spend more than 6 months in the United Kingdom.

Extension of stay as a prospective student

86. An extension of stay as a prospective student may be granted, with a prohibition on employment, provided the Secretary of State is satisfied that each of the requirements of paragraph 85 is met.

Refusal of extension of stay as a prospective student

87. An extension of stay as a prospective student is to be refused if the Secretary of State is not satisfied that each of the requirements of paragraph 85 is met.

COMMENTARY

The course of study must be at either an independent fee paying school or a college outside the maintained sector. It must be either a recognised full-time degree course at a publicly funded institution of further or higher education, or a weekday daytime course involving attendance for a minimum of 15 hours' organised study per week of a single subject or directly related subjects, or a full-time course of study at an independent fee paying school or college. Also, if the applicant is under 16, he must be enrolled on a full time course of studies which meets the requirements of the Education Act 1944. The prospective student must satisfy the immigration officer that he intends to leave the UK on completion of his studies or on the expiry of his leave to enter the UK if he cannot satisfy the requirements of an extension of stay as a student.

The maximum period of leave as a prospective student is six months. Thus, if he cannot produce evidence of enrolment on a suitable course, or has failed to give regular attendance during the course if it has started; or if he cannot show that he has given regular attendance at past courses for which he has been enrolled, his application for an extension must be refused. Also if he cannot show evidence of satisfactory progress in his course of study or if the extension would result in him spending more than four years of courses of less than two years or courses which are longer, but which have been broken off before completion, the application must be refused. If he has come to the end of a period of government or international scholarship agency scholarship, the application must be refused. He must also be able to meet the costs of his intended course and accommodate and maintain himself and his dependants while making arrangements to study and during the course of his studies, without working or recourse to public funds.

Chapter 9

Part 4 of HC 395: Persons Seeking to Enter or Remain in the UK in an 'Au Pair' Placement, as a Working Holidaymaker, or for Training or Work Experience

1 Au pair

PART 4:

PERSONS SEEKING TO ENTER OR REMAIN IN THE UNITED KINGDOM IN AN 'AU PAIR' PLACEMENT, AS A WORKING HOLIDAYMAKER, OR FOR TRAINING OR WORK EXPERIENCE

'AU PAIR' PLACEMENTS

Definition of an 'au pair' placement

88. For the purposes of these Rules an 'au pair' placement is an arrangement whereby a young person:
  (a) comes to the United Kingdom for the purpose of learning the English language; and
  (b) lives for a time as a member of an English speaking family with appropriate opportunities for study; and
  (c) helps in the home for a maximum of 5 hours per day in return for a reasonable allowance and with two free days per week.

Requirements for leave to enter as an 'au pair'

89. The requirements to be met by a person seeking leave to enter the United Kingdom as an 'au pair' are that he:
  (i) is seeking entry for the purpose of taking up an arranged placement which can be shown to fall within the definition set out in paragraph 88; and
  (ii) is aged between 17–27 inclusive or was so aged when first given leave to enter in this capacity; and
  (iii) is unmarried; and

(iv) is without dependants; and
(v) is a national of one of the following countries: Andorra, Bosnia-Herzegovina, Croatia, Cyprus, Czech Republic, The Faeroes, Greenland, Hungary, Liechtenstein, Macedonia, Malta, Monaco, San Marino, Slovak Republic, Slovenia, Switzerland, or Turkey; and
(vi) does not intend to stay in the United Kingdom for more than 2 years as an 'au pair'; and
(vii) intends to leave the United Kingdom on completion of his stay as an 'au pair; and
(viii) if he has previously spent time in the United Kingdom as an 'au pair', is not seeking leave to enter to a date beyond 2 years from the date on which he was first given leave to enter the United Kingdom in this capacity.

Leave to enter as an 'au pair'

90. A person seeking leave to enter the United Kingdom as an 'au pair' may be admitted for a period not exceeding 2 years with a prohibition on employment except as an 'au pair', provided the Immigration Officer is satisfied that each of the requirements of paragraph 89 is met. (A non-visa national who wishes to ascertain in advance whether a proposed 'au pair' placement is likely to meet the requirements of paragraph 89 is advised to obtain an entry clearance before travelling to the United Kingdom).

Refusal of leave to enter as an 'au pair'

91. An application for leave to enter as an 'au pair' is to be refused if the Immigration Officer is not satisfied that each of the requirements of paragraph 89 is met.

Requirements for an extension of stay as an 'au pair'

92. The requirements for an extension of stay as an 'au pair' are that the applicant:
    (i) was given leave to enter the United Kingdom as an 'au pair' under paragraph 90; and
    (ii) is undertaking an arranged 'au pair' placement which can be shown to fall within the definition set out in paragraph 88; and
    (iii) meets the requirements of paragraph 89 (ii)–(vii); and
    (iv) would not, as a result of an extension of stay, remain in the United Kingdom as an 'au pair' to a date beyond 2 years from the date on which he was first given leave to enter the United Kingdom in this capacity.

Extension of stay as an 'au pair'

93. An extension of stay as an 'au pair' may be granted with a prohibition on employment except as an 'au pair', provided the Secretary of State is satisfied that each of the requirements of paragraph 92 is met.

Refusal of extension of stay as an 'au pair'

94. An extension of stay as an 'au pair' is to be refused if the Secretary of State is not satisfied that each of the requirements of paragraph 92 is met.

COMMENTARY

HC 395 removes the discrimination against men present in HC 251. HC 395 now requires that 'au pairs' have two free days per week and their maximum period of leave (two years) is not an aggregate but continuous period. The requirements under paragraph 89 must be satisfied, and if they are not the immigration officer has no discretion to grant leave under the rules. The arrangement must be the sole reason that the person wishes to visit the UK. If it appears at interview that his ultimate intention is to take up full-time employment, he will be refused entry (*Ramjane v Chief Immigration Officer Gatwick Airport* [1973] Imm AR 84). Evidence should be produced to satisfy the immigration service that the arrangement has been made. A letter from the host family should be provided confirming the arrangement, and describing the au pair's duties. It should indicate that he will have to study English and how much pocket money he will be paid. EU citizens may work as au pairs exercising their right to free movement. They do not need leave to enter for this or any other purpose. Nationals of states which are parties to the European Economic Area Agreement do not require leave to enter (or to remain in the UK when exercising free movement rights). The EEA countries are listed on page 290.

Extensions A woman whose current leave to enter or remain was granted before 5 July 1992 may be granted an extension of leave as an au pair even if she did not enter in that capacity. Similarly under Co-operation Agreements in the Field of Labour which are directly effective between the EU and several countries (Turkey, Morocco, Algeria and Tunisia) the rule may discriminate against workers from those countries wishing to continue in employment as 'au pairs' (see *ONEM v Kziber* C18/90).

2 Working holidaymakers

WORKING HOLIDAYMAKERS

Requirements for leave to enter as a working holidaymaker

95. The requirements to be met by a person seeking leave to enter the United Kingdom as a working holidaymaker are that he:

(i) is a Commonwealth citizen; and
(ii) is aged 17-27 inclusive or was so aged when first given leave to enter in this capacity; and
(iii) is unmarried or is married to a person who meets the requirements of this paragraph and the parties to the marriage intend to take a working holiday together; and
(iv) has the means to pay for his return or onward journey; and
(v) is able and intends to maintain and accommodate himself without recourse to public funds; and
(vi) is intending to take employment incidental to a holiday but not to engage in business, provide services as a professional sportsman or entertainer or pursue a career in the United Kingdom; and
(vii) does not have dependent children any of whom are 5 years of age or over or who will reach 5 years of age before the applicant completes his working holiday; or commitments which would require him to earn a regular income; and
(viii) intends to leave the United Kingdom at the end of his working holiday; and
(ix) if he has previously spent time in the United Kingdom as a working holidaymaker, is not seeking leave to enter to a date beyond 2 years from the date he was first given leave to enter in this capacity; and
(x) holds a valid United Kingdom entry clearance for entry in this capacity.

Leave to enter as a working holidaymaker

96. A person seeking leave to enter the United Kingdom as a working holidaymaker may be admitted for a period not exceeding 2 years with a condition restricting his freedom to take employment, provided he is able to produce to the Immigration Officer, on arrival, a valid United Kingdom entry clearance for entry in this capacity.

Refusal of leave to enter as a working holidaymaker

97. Leave to enter as a working holidaymaker is to be refused if a valid United Kingdom entry clearance for entry in this capacity is not produced to the Immigration Officer on arrival.

Requirements for an extension of stay as a working holidaymaker

98. The requirements for an extension of stay as a working holidaymaker are that the applicant:
(i) entered the United Kingdom with a valid United Kingdom entry clearance as a working holidaymaker; and
(ii) meets the requirements of paragraph 95(i)-(viii); and
(iii) would not, as a result of an extension of stay, remain in the United Kingdom as a working holidaymaker to a date beyond 2 years

from the date on which he was first given leave to enter the United Kingdom in this capacity.

Extension of stay as a working holidaymaker

99. An extension of stay as a working holidaymaker may be granted with a condition restricting his freedom to take employment, provided the Secretary of State is satisfied that the applicant meets each of the requirements of paragraph 98.

Refusal of extension of stay as a working holidaymaker

100. An extension of stay as a working holidaymaker is to be refused if the Secretary of State is not satisfied that each of the requirements of paragraph 98 is met.

COMMENTARY

HC 395 introduces a mandatory requirement of an entry clearance. A person who entered in another capacity cannot switch to the category of working holidaymaker. A person who does not have an entry clearance may not appeal against a refusal of entry under this category (section 13(3B) of 1971 Act as amended by 1993 Act, s 11). For the definition of 'Commonwealth citizen'. The rule permits married couples to take a working holiday together. However, the dependent spouse must also qualify independently as a working holidaymaker.

A working holidaymaker may not engage in business, pursuing a career, or providing services as a professional sportsman or entertainer. The rule is designed to accommodate persons within the age bracket who have not yet settled down in the sense of becoming established in a more or less permanent abode or place or way of life. Therefore where a woman had previously married, had a child for which she was responsible, taken a job and finished her academic training she was taken to have settled down. A different conclusion would be reached if her settled pattern of life was disrupted (*Adejumoke v S of S* [1993] Imm AR 265). The primary purpose for such a person must be a holiday, with employment only incidental to that purpose. The leave granted under this rule is different from leave granted for the purpose of taking employment, and different considerations apply (*S of S v Pope* [1987] Imm AR 10). An intention to obtain a full-time job rather than to take on a job or jobs which would be occasional and subordinate to the holiday would not be acceptable (*Gunatilake v ECO Colombo* [1975] Imm AR 23). The Home Office have indicated that working holidaymakers may work part time for the whole of the holiday or full time for part of the holiday. They stated that out of the two years only one could be spent working, otherwise a work permit should be sought. However, the rule does not preclude the applicant from taking full-time work provided it is not for the duration of the holiday. The IAT gave a broader interpretation to the paragraph as worded in HC 251 than the Home Office. Such full-time work as being a director of a company on a fixed contract lasting more than 12 months may be consistent with the rule (*Kenneth De Clive Lowe v Immigration Officer, Heathrow* [1992] Imm AR 91). The rule as it appears in HC 395 provides that the applicant must not have 'commitments' which would require him *to earn a regular income*, and specifically mentions dependent children who will attain five years of age during the period of the working holiday. The Immigration Officer will refuse leave to enter if the person does not have the means to pay for his return journey or if he has reason to believe that recourse to public funds is likely. To be a genuine working holidaymaker, a person must initially have some resources with which to finance his holiday, augmenting his resources from time to time by taking employment (*S of S v Grant* [1974] Imm AR 64). There is no obligation, however, on an intending working holidaymaker to show that he will work at all during his holiday (*Bari v IAT* [1987] Imm AR 13). He must, however, show that he has an intention to take employment incidental to a holiday.

(a) Extensions

In addition to satisfying the requirements for applications for entry, a person applying to extend his leave as a working holidaymaker must show that he entered with a valid entry clearance as a working holidaymaker. Where a visitor had no funds with him on arrival and had been working for his sponsor more or less full time it appeared that his holiday was not incidental to his work and, therefore, he did not meet the requirements of the rules (*S of S v Grant* [1974] Imm AR 64). The IAT similarly dismissed an appeal on the facts as they indicated that the freelance work in the textile industry taken by an appellant could not, by reason of her high earnings on commission, be accepted as an employment incidental only to her holiday (*Baijal v S of S* [1976] Imm AR 34). Nor where on the evidence it was plain that an appellant had been a hard working full-time member of the staff of a departmental store could 'her work properly be described as employment which was only incidental to a holiday' (*Munasinghe v S of S* [1975] Imm AR 79). The rule does not forbid the taking of full-time work. Periods of such work are permitted, as is involvement in the ownership of a limited company in certain circumstances (*de Clive Lowe v Immigration Officer, Heathrow* [1992] Imm AR 91). Conversely the rules do not require the person to work at all for the duration of his leave as a working holidaymaker. He must not, however, become a charge on public funds (*Badrul Bari v IAT* [1987] Imm AR 13). HC 395 introduces a restriction on the maximum period of leave a person may have as a working holidaymaker. The maximum period of two years is now to be continuous, not aggregated.

3 Children of working holidaymakers

CHILDREN OF WORKING HOLIDAYMAKERS

Requirements for leave to enter or remain as the child of a working holidaymaker

101. The requirements to be met by a person seeking leave to enter or remain in the United Kingdom as the child of a working holidaymaker are that:
   (i) he is the child of a parent admitted to or allowed to remain in the United Kingdom as a working holidaymaker; and
   (ii) he is under the age of 5 and will leave the United Kingdom before reaching that age; and
   (iii) he can and will be maintained and accommodated adequately without recourse to public funds or without his parent(s) engaging in business or taking employment except as provided by paragraph 95 above; and
   (iv) both parents are being or have been admitted to or allowed to remain in the United Kingdom save where:
      (a) the parent he is accompanying or joining is his sole surviving parent; or
      (b) the parent he is accompanying or joining has had sole responsibility for his upbringing; or
      (c) there are serious and compelling family or other considerations which make exclusion from the United Kingdom undesirable and suitable arrangements have been made for his care; and
   (v) if seeking leave to enter, he holds a valid United Kingdom entry clearance for entry in this capacity or, if seeking leave to remain, was admitted with a valid United Kingdom entry clearance for entry in this capacity.

Leave to enter or remain as the child of a working holidaymaker

102. A person seeking leave to enter or remain in the United Kingdom as the child of a working holidaymaker may be admitted or allowed to remain for the same period of leave as that granted to the working holidaymaker provided that, in relation to an application for leave to enter, a valid United Kingdom entry clearance for entry in this capacity is produced to the Immigration Officer on arrival or, in the case of an application for leave to remain, he was admitted with a valid United Kingdom entry clearance for entry in this capacity and is able to satisfy the Secretary of State that each of the requirements of paragraph 101(i)–(iv) is met.

Refusal of leave to enter or remain as the child of a working holidaymaker

103. Leave to enter or remain in the United Kingdom as the child of a working holidaymaker is to be refused if, in relation to an application for leave to enter, a valid United Kingdom entry clearance for entry in this capacity is not produced to the Immigration Officer on arrival or, in the case of an application for leave to remain, the applicant was not admitted with a valid United Kingdom entry clearance for entry in this capacity or is unable to satisfy the Secretary of State that each of the requirements of paragraph 101(1)–(iv) is met.

COMMENTARY

Paragraph 101 provides that the child must not during the time of the holiday attain five years. Note the definition of 'parent' in para 6 (page 61). Both parents must be admitted, or have been admitted save where only one parent survives and he accompanies that parent. He may also accompany a single parent or join a single parent where the parent he is accompanying has sole responsibility for his upbringing (see page 225). The child may accompany one parent also where there are serious and compelling family or other considerations which make exclusion from the UK undesirable and suitable arrangements have been made for his care (see page 226). He may be maintained by recourse to employment which is incidental to the holiday.

4 Seasonal workers at agricultural camps

SEASONAL WORKERS AT AGRICULTURAL CAMPS

Requirements for leave to enter as a seasonal worker at an agricultural camp

104. The requirements to be met by a person seeking leave to enter the United Kingdom as a seasonal worker at an agricultural camp are that he:

(i) is a student in full-time education aged between 18–25 years inclusive, except if returning for another season at the specific invitation of a farmer; and
(ii) holds a valid Home Office work card issued by the operator of a scheme approved by the Secretary of State; and
(iii) intends to leave the United Kingdom at the end of his period of leave as a seasonal worker; and
(iv) does not intend to take employment except in the terms of this paragraph.

Leave to enter as a seasonal worker at an agricultural camp

105. A person seeking leave to enter the United Kingdom as a seasonal worker at an agricultural camp may be admitted with a condition restricting his freedom to take employment for a period not exceeding 3 months or until 30 November of the year in question, whichever is the shorter period, provided the Immigration Officer is satisfied that each of the requirements of paragraph 104 is met.

Refusal of leave to enter as a seasonal worker at an agricultural camp

106. Leave to enter the United Kingdom as a seasonal worker at an agricultural camp is to be refused if the Immigration Officer is not satisfied that each of the requirements of paragraph 104 is met.

Requirements for extension of stay as a seasonal worker at an agricultural camp

107. The requirements for an extension of stay as a seasonal worker at an agricultural camp are that the applicant:
(i) entered the United Kingdom as a seasonal worker with a valid Home Office work card under paragraph 105; and
(ii) meets the requirements of paragraph 104 (iii)–(iv); and
(iii) can show that there is further farm work available under the approved scheme; and
(iv) would not, as a result of an extension of stay, remain in the United Kingdom as a seasonal worker for longer than 6 months in aggregate or beyond 30 November of the year in question, whichever is the shorter period.

Extension of stay as a seasonal worker at an agricultural camp

108. An extension of stay as a seasonal worker may be granted with a condition restricting his freedom to take employment for a further period not exceeding 3 months or until 30 November of the year in question, whichever is the shorter period, provided the Secretary of State is satisfied that the applicant meets each of the requirements of paragraph 107.

Refusal of extension of stay as a seasonal worker at an agricultural camp

109. An extension of stay as a seasonal worker at an agricultural camp is to be refused if the Secretary of State is not satisfied that each of the requirements of paragraph 107 is met.

COMMENTARY

A person applying for an extension must have been granted leave to enter as a seasonal worker at an agricultural camp. He will therefore be a student between 18–25 years, or returning for another season at the specific invitation of a farmer. He will therefore have to provide evidence of such an invitation. He must also hold a valid Home Office camp card issued by the operator of the scheme which has been approved by the S of S. He must intend to leave the UK at the end of his period of leave as a seasonal worker, and must not intend to take other work. He must also have been given leave for a period of three months or until 30 November of the year in question whichever is the shorter period. He must be able to show that there is further farm work available under the approved scheme. A letter from the person organising the camp should be sufficient evidence of this. Leave must in any event expire on 30 November of the year in question or after a further three months, so that the maximum period of leave is six months (para 107(iv)).

5 Teachers and language assistants coming to the UK under approved exchange schemes

TEACHERS AND LANGUAGE ASSISTANTS COMING TO THE UNITED KINGDOM UNDER APPROVED EXCHANGE SCHEMES

Requirements for leave to enter as a teacher or language assistant under an approved exchange scheme

110. The requirements to be met by a person seeking leave to enter the United Kingdom as a teacher or language assistant on an approved exchange scheme are that he:
(i) is coming to an educational establishment in the United Kingdom under an exchange scheme approved by the Education Departments or administered by the Central Bureau for Educational Visits and Exchanges or the League for the Exchange of Commonwealth Teachers; and
(ii) intends to leave the United Kingdom at the end of his exchange period; and
(iii) does not intend to take employment except in the terms of this paragraph; and

(iv) is able to maintain and accommodate himself and any dependants without recourse to public funds; and
(v) holds a valid United Kingdom entry clearance for entry in this capacity.

Leave to enter as a teacher or language assistant under an exchange scheme

111. A person seeking leave to enter the United Kingdom as a teacher or language assistant under an approved exchange scheme may be given leave to enter for a period not exceeding 12 months provided he is able to produce to the Immigration Officer, on arrival, a valid United Kingdom entry clearance for entry in this capacity.

Refusal of leave to enter as a teacher or language assistant under an approved exchange scheme

112. Leave to enter the United Kingdom as a teacher or language assistant under an approved exchange scheme is to be refused if a valid United Kingdom entry clearance for entry in this capacity is not produced to the Immigration Officer on arrival.

Requirements for extension of stay as a teacher or language assistant under an approved exchange scheme

113. The requirements for an extension of stay as a teacher or language assistant under an approved exchange scheme are that the applicant:
  (i) entered the United Kingdom with a valid United Kingdom entry clearance as a teacher or language assistant; and
  (ii) is still engaged in the employment for which his entry clearance was granted; and
  (iii) is still required for the employment in question, as certified by the employer; and
  (iv) meets the requirements of paragraph 110 (ii)–(iv); and
  (v) would not, as a result of an extension of stay, remain in the United Kingdom as an exchange teacher or language assistant for more than 2 years from the date on which he was first given leave to enter the United Kingdom in this capacity.

Extension of stay as a teacher or language assistant under an approved exchange scheme

114. An extension of stay as a teacher or language assistant under an approved exchange scheme may be granted for a further period not exceeding 12 months provided the Secretary of State is satisfied that each of the requirements of paragraph 113 is met.

Refusal of extension of stay as a teacher or language assistant under an approved exchange scheme

115. An extension of stay as a teacher or language assistant under

an approved exchange scheme is to be refused if the Secretary of State is not satisfied that each of the requirements of paragraph 113 is met.

COMMENTARY

There is a mandatory requirement of an entry clearance for the purpose of this category. A person may not appeal against a refusal of leave to enter, without an entry clearance (section 13(3B) of the 1971 Act as amended by section 11 of the 1993 Act). A person seeking an extension of leave as a teacher or language assistant must have entered the UK with a valid UK entry clearance in that category. He must still be in the employment for which the entry clearance was granted, although the rule would appear to envisage a person being granted leave where the establishment at which he was still employed had ceased to be approved for exchanges since his original leave was granted. He must produce a certificate from his employer stating that he is still required for the employment in question. He must intend to leave the UK at the end of the exchange period. He must not intend to take other employment than under the exchange. The aggregate total of his leave in this capacity, including the extension should not exceed two years. A person who did not have an entry clearance for the purpose may not appeal against a refusal to extend his leave under this category (section 14 of the 1971 Act as amended by section 11 of the 1993 Act).

6 Department of Employment approved training or work experience

DEPARTMENT OF EMPLOYMENT APPROVED TRAINING OR WORK EXPERIENCE

Requirements for leave to enter for Department of Employment approved training or work experience

116. The requirements to be met by a person seeking leave to enter the United Kingdom for Department of Employment approved training or work experience are that he:
  (i) holds a valid work permit from the Department of Employment issued under the Training and Work Experience Scheme; and
  (ii) is not of an age which puts him outside the limits for employment; and
  (iii) is capable of undertaking the training or work experience as specified in his work permit; and
  (iv) intends to leave the United Kingdom on the completion of his training or work experience; and

(v) does not intend to take employment except as specified in his work permit; and
(vi) is able to maintain and accommodate himself and any dependants adequately without recourse to public funds.

Leave to enter for Department of Employment approved training or work experience

117. A person seeking leave to enter the United Kingdom for approved training may be admitted to the United Kingdom for a period not exceeding 3 years and a person seeking entry for approved work experience may be admitted for a period not exceeding 12 months, provided the Immigration Officer is satisfied that each of the requirements of paragraph 116 is met. Leave to enter is to be subject to a condition permitting the person to take or change employment only with the permission of the Department of Employment.

Refusal of leave to enter for Department of Employment approved training or work experience

118. Leave to enter the United Kingdom for Department of Employment approved training or work experience is to be refused if the Immigration Officer is not satisfied that each of the requirements of paragraph 116 is met.

COMMENTARY

The applicant must have a permit from the DoE issued under the Training and Work Experience Scheme. Application is made on form WP2. The Department of Employment requirements are set out below, including those relating to age for each of work experience and training. The maximum leave to enter available for a person seeking training is three years. The maximum leave to enter available to a person seeking approved work experience is 12 months. HC 395 prohibits visitors switching into the Training and Work Experience Scheme after arrival. However, those granted leave to enter as students may switch.

(a) Department of Employment requirements

The post must genuinely be for training and work experience. If the application is in fact to employ an overseas national in a vacant post, application should be made for a work permit on form WP1. Permits are not required for:
   (*a*) business persons, and the self-employed including writers and artists;

(b) ministers of religion;
(c) representatives of overseas newspapers, news agencies and broadcasting organisations;
(d) private servants of diplomatic staff;
(e) sole representatives of overseas firms;
(f) teachers and language assistants under approved schemes;
(g) employees of an overseas government or international organisation;
(h) seamen under contract to join a ship in British waters;
(i) operational ground staff of overseas owned airlines;
(j) seasonal workers at agricultural camps under approved schemes;
(k) doctors and dentists in postgraduate training;
(l) business visitors.

Permission is given to enable a national of any country to come to the UK for training towards a professional or specialist qualification, or to undertake a short period of work experience. The applicant must have sufficient command of English to enable him to benefit from the training or work experience. The applicant must return overseas at the end of the training. The DoE will not approve a transfer to ordinary employment in the UK. The applicant must then work abroad, usually for a minimum of two years before an application can be made for approval of further TWES training. He will normally have to work abroad for a period of at least two years before applying for a work permit.

Training The training should lead to a professional or specialist qualification. The trainee must be 18 years or older. He must have qualifications equivalent to UK degree level or NVQ level 4 or higher. The employer must be able to show that the training is relevant to the qualifications of the trainee. The training period must be agreed in advance. If qualifications take a number of years to obtain, approval will be given for an initial period. That period will be extended if the trainee is making satisfactory progress. The trainee will be allowed a maximum of three attempts (or chances) to take any one examination before the DoE approval will be affected. The trainee should be training for a minimum of 30 hours per week. No approval will be given for supplementary qualifications to be taken once the agreed course of training is completed. The trainee must receive the same terms and conditions, and salary, as UK or EU trainees receive. If the qualification is a professional one, the employer must be registered or approved by the appropriate professional body.

Work experience The overseas national should be 18–25. He must be employed in a supernumerary capacity, and should not be filling a job which would otherwise be available to a UK or EU national. In those cases an application for a work permit should be made. An exception is made for recognised exchange arrangement exchanges. The person must have the appropriate experience or the appropriate academic qualifications to enable him to benefit from the proposed work experience being offered. Only in very exceptional circumstances will a period of time longer than 12 months be approved by the DoE. Under para 117 the maximum period of leave on entry is 12 months. The work experience must be of an acceptable level to the DoE. It must be at least NVQ 4 or higher, and should last 30 or more hours per week.

Any payment made to the overseas national should only be a modest personal spending allowance. A person working under an exchange agreement where rates of pay are reciprocal may be paid a full wage. Where a person is transferred from an overseas branch of a company to the UK for the purposes of work experience, he may receive a full wage. If he is employed in a senior position an application should be made for a work permit on Form WP1.

If an application for a Training and Work Experience position has not been made in the previous four years the employer should send a copy of the latest audited accounts and a copy of the latest annual report or any publicity or marketing material. If these are not available evidence of the tenure of the business premises, details of staff employed in the UK, and a copy of the incorporation documents for the company should be sent.

The company must show that it is already providing goods or services, or is contractually committed to doing so. Applications for Training and Work Experience Form WP2 are dealt with at the Overseas Labour Section, the Employment Department, W5 Moorfoot, Sheffield S1 4PQ. The application will generally be dealt with within six to eight weeks of receipt.

(b) Extensions of stay for DoE approved training or work experience

Requirements for extension of stay for Department of Employment approved training or work experience

119. The requirements for an extension of stay for Department of Employment approved training or work experience are that the applicant:
 (i) entered the United Kingdom with a valid work permit under

paragraph 117 or was admitted or allowed to remain in the United Kingdom as a student; and
(ii) has written approval from the Department of Employment for an extension of stay in this category; and
(iii) meets the requirements of paragraph 116 (ii)–(vi); and
(iv) would not as a result of an extension of stay spend more than 2 years in the United Kingdom for Department of Employment approved work experience.

Extension of stay for Department of Employment approved training or work experience

120. An extension of stay for approved training may be granted for a further period not exceeding 3 years; and an extension of stay for approved work experience may be granted for a further period not exceeding 12 months provided the Secretary of State is satisfied that each of the requirements of paragraph 119 is met. An extension of stay is to be subject to a condition permitting the applicant to take or change employment only with the permission of the Department of Employment.

Refusal of extension of stay for Department of Employment approved training or work experience

121. An extension of stay for Department of Employment approved training or work experience is to be refused if the Secretary of State is not satisfied that each of the requirements of paragraph 119 is met.

COMMENTARY

The maximum period a person may remain in the UK on approved training is three years. The maximum period a person may remain in the UK on approved work experience is two years. If the person wishes to change employer, or the employer wishes to change the type of work the person is doing, permission must be obtained. It will only be given to a new employer if he offers the same training or work experience as the first employer. The new employer must apply separately. Applications for extensions should be made well in advance. The employer should explain why he wishes to keep the overseas national.

Training The employer should give details of the dates and number of attempts at each examination taken by the trainee, together with his result and future examination dates.

Work experience Extensions beyond 12 months are not usually approved without agreement at the commencement of the work experience period. Exceptionally an extension may be granted if a fully reasoned application is made. A programme of further work should be sent to the DoE.

The application must show that the training is continuing on a training and work experience scheme, and that the applicant is making satisfactory progress (*S of S v Brizmohun* [1972] Imm AR 122). An extension will be refused without the appropriate approval from the DoE (see *Yeong Hoi Yueng v S of S* [1977] Imm AR 34 and *Roy v S of S* [1988] Imm AR 53).

7 Spouses of persons with limited leave to remain under paras 110–121

SPOUSES OF PERSONS WITH LIMITED LEAVE TO ENTER OR REMAIN UNDER PARAGRAPHS 110–121

Requirements for leave to enter or remain as the spouse of a person with limited leave to enter or remain in the United Kingdom under paragraphs 110–121

122. The requirements to be met by a person seeking leave to enter or remain in the United Kingdom as the spouse of a person with limited leave to enter or remain in the United Kingdom under paragraphs 110–121 are that:
 (i) the applicant is married to a person with limited leave to enter or remain in the United Kingdom under paragraphs 110–121; and
 (ii) each of the parties intends to live with the other as his or her spouse during the applicant's stay and the marriage is subsisting; and
 (iii) there will be adequate accommodation for the parties and any dependants without recourse to public funds in accommodation which they own or occupy exclusively; and
 (iv) the parties will be able to maintain themselves and any dependants adequately without recourse to public funds; and
 (v) the applicant does not intend to stay in the United Kingdom beyond any period of leave granted to his spouse; and
 (vi) if seeking leave to enter, the applicant holds a valid United Kingdom entry clearance for entry in this capacity or, if seeking leave to remain, was admitted with a valid United Kingdom entry clearance for entry in this capacity.

Leave to enter or remain as the spouse of a person with limited leave to enter or remain in the United Kingdom under paragraphs 110–121

123. A person seeking leave to enter or remain in the United Kingdom as the spouse of a person with limited leave to enter or remain in the United Kingdom under paragraphs 110–121 may be given leave to enter or remain in the United Kingdom for a period of leave not in excess of that granted to the person with limited leave to enter or remain under paragraphs 110–121 provided that, in relation to an application for leave

to enter, he is able, on arrival, to produce to the Immigration Officer a valid United Kingdom entry clearance for entry in this capacity or, in the case of an application for limited leave to remain, was admitted with a valid United Kingdom entry clearance for entry in this capacity and is able to satisfy the Secretary of State that each of the requirements of paragraph 122(i)–(v) is met.

Refusal of leave to enter or remain as the spouse of a person with limited leave to enter or remain in the United Kingdom under paragraphs 110–121

124. Leave to enter or remain in the United Kingdom as the spouse of a person with limited leave to enter or remain in the United Kingdom under paragraphs 110–121 is to be refused if, in relation to an application for leave to enter, a valid United Kingdom entry clearance for entry in this capacity is not produced to the Immigration Officer on arrival or, in the case of an application for limited leave to remain, if the applicant was not admitted with a valid United Kingdom entry clearance for entry in this capacity or is unable to satisfy the Secretary of State that each of the requirements of paragraph 122(i)–(v) is met.

COMMENTARY

The spouse of a person on approved training or on work experience, or the spouse of a person who has leave as a teacher or language assistant under an approved exchange scheme, must satisfy the requirements of para 122. The first of these requirements is that the couple are married. They must intend to live together as spouses during the applicant's stay, and the marriage must be subsisting. Some evidence should therefore be available to show that the marriage is subsisting. The requirements of para 122 are mandatory, as is possession or production of an entry clearance.

8 Children of persons admitted or allowed to remain under paras 110–121

CHILDREN OF PERSONS ADMITTED OR ALLOWED TO REMAIN UNDER PARAGRAPHS 110–121

Requirements for leave to enter or remain as the child of a person with limited leave to enter or remain in the United Kingdom under paragraphs 110–121

125. The requirements to be met by a person seeking leave to enter or remain in the United Kingdom as the child of a person with limited leave to enter or remain in the United Kingdom under paragraphs 110–121 are that:

(i) he is the child of a parent who has limited leave to enter or remain in the United Kingdom under paragraphs 110–121; and
(ii) he is under the age of 18 or has current leave to enter or remain in this capacity; and
(iii) he is unmarried, has not formed an independent family unit and is not leading an independent life; and
(iv) he can, and will, be maintained and accommodated adequately without recourse to public funds in accommodation which his parent(s) own or occupy exclusively; and
(v) he will not stay in the United Kingdom beyond any period of leave granted to his parent(s); and
(vi) both parents are being or have been admitted to or allowed to remain in the United Kingdom save where:
    (*a*)   the parent he is accompanying or joining is his sole surviving parent; or
    (*b*)   the parent he is accompanying or joining has had sole responsibility for his upbringing; or
    (*c*)   there are serious and compelling family or other considerations which make exclusion from the United Kingdom undesirable and suitable arrangements have been made for his care; and
(vii) if seeking leave to enter, he holds a valid United Kingdom entry clearance for entry in this capacity or, if seeking leave to remain, was admitted with a valid United Kingdom entry clearance for entry in this capacity.

Leave to enter or remain as the child of a person with limited leave to enter or remain in the United Kingdom under paragraphs 110–121

126. A person seeking leave to enter or remain in the United Kingdom as the child of a person with limited leave to enter or remain in the United Kingdom under paragraphs 110–121 may be given leave to enter or remain in the United Kingdom for a period of leave not in excess of that granted to the person with limited leave to enter or remain under paragraphs 110–121 provided that, in relation to an application for leave to enter, he is able, on arrival, to produce to the Immigration Officer a valid United Kingdom entry clearance for entry in this capacity or, in the case of an application for limited leave to remain, he was admitted with a valid United Kingdom entry clearance for entry in this capacity and is able to satisfy the Secretary of State that each of the requirements of paragraph 125(i)–(vi) is met.

Refusal of leave to enter or remain as the child of a person with limited leave to enter or remain in the United Kingdom under paragraphs 110–121

127. Leave to enter or remain in the United Kingdom as the child of a person with limited leave to enter or remain in the United Kingdom under paragraphs 110–121 is to be refused if, in relation to an application for leave to enter, a valid United Kingdom entry clearance for entry in this capacity is not produced to the Immigration Officer on arrival or,

in the case of an application for limited leave to remain, if the applicant was not admitted with a valid United Kingdom entry clearance for entry in this capacity or is unable to satisfy the Secretary of State that each of the requirements of paragraph 125(i)–(vi) is met.

COMMENTARY

The applicant must be the child of a person who has limited leave as a person on approved training or on work experience, or a person who has leave as a teacher or language assistant under an approved exchange scheme. The child must be under 18. He must not have formed an 'independent family unit'. He must not be married. He must not be living an independent life. The child must be maintained and adequately accommodated without recourse to public funds. For the definition of 'public funds' see page 61. There is no requirement that the parents themselves maintain the child. However, there is a requirement that he is maintained and accommodated in accommodation which his parent(s) own or occupy *exclusively*. Thus the parent(s) must either own the accommodation exclusively, or occupy it exclusively. No definition is offered of 'accommodation'. Both parents must be admitted or have been admitted, unless the conditions set out in paragraph 125(vi) apply. For 'sole responsibility' see page 225, and for 'serious and compelling family or other considerations', see page 226.

Chapter 10

Persons Seeking to Enter or Remain in the United Kingdom for Employment

1 Introduction: entry for work

Possession of a work permit does not automatically result in leave to enter, nor can it be treated as the same thing (*S of S v Gomes* [1990] Imm AR 576). If the DoE refuses to grant a permit, there is no appeal against the decision (*Pearson v IAT* [1978] Imm AR 212). It may be possible to apply for judicial review of a decision to refuse a work permit in appropriate circumstances. Thus a decision of the DoE regarding the grant of a work permit may be reviewed if the DoE does not take account of the latest information which is available to it at the time of the decision but merely that which is available at the time of the application (*R v Department of Employment, ex p Barry Allan* [1991] Imm AR 336); but not it seems on the basis that the grant or refusal of a work permit is an act of sexual discrimination under the Sex Discrimination Act 1975 (*R v IAT, ex p Bernstein* [1987] Imm AR 182). Moreover where a policy statement is issued it may give rise to a legitimate expectation on the part of the entrant that its terms will be observed until the Department announces a change in its policy (for judicial review, see Chapter 27).

EEA citizens The position of EEA citizens and their dependents is dealt with in detail in Chapter 15. However, an EU citizen is permitted to enter without obtaining leave by virtue of the free movement provisions of the Treaty of Rome, and Regulation 1612/68 and Directives made pursuant to that treaty. Further, freedom of movement may apply to non-EU citizens employed by undertakings from a EU state whilst it is carrying out a project in the UK (*Rush Portuguesa LDA v Office National d'Immigration*, (1990) *The Times*, 12 April). Thus a requirement that the non-

EU national employee of an EU undertaking must be in possession of a work permit cannot be imposed on such employees.

Domestic work No rule covers the position of those in domestic work for persons of independent means. Frequently they are given a visitor stamp, which, as the Home Office knows, does not reflect what they are actually doing. By way of a concession, the Home Office produces a leaflet which is given to the worker and his employer. This formalises the earlier practice of the Home Office. The following requirements need to be fulfilled for the concession to apply:

(a) the domestic servant must be 17 years or older;
(b) in the case of an employer visiting the UK, the servant must have been employed by him for at least 12 months before entry to the UK;
(c) in any other case the employment must have been for at least 24 months;
(d) the domestic servant must have entry clearance.

When considering whether to grant or refuse entry clearance, the ECO will investigate the sort of work the servant will do, and the hours involved. The servant will be asked whether he wishes to go to the UK. The servant is told, and it is stressed in the leaflet, that he will not be permitted to change employment after entry. The servant's leave will be granted in line with that of his employer. The practice of granting visitor's stamps in these circumstances was criticised by the IAT in *Mendoza v S of S* [1992] Imm AR 122 where it was said that such stamps failed to make clear, as they are required to by the 1971 Act, the terms of the grant of leave. Where a domestic worker had been admitted to the UK pursuant to this concession and her application for an extension refused because she was trying to change from one employer to a different one, the adjudicator and the IAT had jurisdiction to consider whether the decision was in accordance with the law. If the domestic worker's legitimate expectation under the concession has been infringed the appellate authorities may find that the decision is not in accordance with the law. However, a domestic worker's legitimate expectation under this concession can only be that he will be allowed to remain in the UK as long as the employer with whom he arrived remains (*Regina* (8973)). The Home Office issue a leaflet (*Information for Domestic Servants Travelling to the UK* (C150 56 00 10170)) for domestic workers dealing with their rights whilst in the UK, including whether they may change employer, and what to do if they are ill treated.

2 Work permit holders

PART 5:

PERSONS SEEKING TO ENTER OR REMAIN IN THE UNITED KINGDOM FOR EMPLOYMENT

WORK PERMIT EMPLOYMENT

Requirements for leave to enter the United Kingdom for work permit employment

128. The requirements to be met by a person coming to the United Kingdom to seek or take employment (unless he is otherwise eligible for admission for employment under these Rules or is eligible for admission as a seaman under contract to join a ship due to leave British waters) are that he:
(i) holds a valid Department of Employment work permit; and
(ii) is not of an age which puts him outside the limits for employment; and
(iii) is capable of undertaking the employment specified in the work permit; and
(iv) does not intend to take employment except as specified in his work permit; and
(v) is able to maintain and accommodate himself and any dependants adequately without recourse to public funds; and
(vi) in the case of a person in possession of a work permit which is valid for a period of 12 months or less, intends to leave the United Kingdom at the end of his approved employment.

Leave to enter for work permit employment

129. A person seeking leave to enter the United Kingdom for the purpose of work permit employment may be admitted for a period not exceeding 4 years (normally as specified in his work permit), subject to a condition restricting him to employment approved by the Department of Employment, provided the Immigration Officer is satisfied that each of the requirements of paragraph 128 is met.

Refusal of leave to enter for employment

130. Leave to enter for the purpose of employment is to be refused if the Immigration Officer is not satisfied that each of the requirements of paragraph 128 is met (unless he is otherwise eligible for admission for employment under these Rules or is eligible for admission as a seaman under contract to join a ship due to leave British waters).

COMMENTARY

The requirements for a work permit are set out below. The person must not be of an age which puts him outside the limits for employment. Where a person is not eligible under any of the following categories he must meet the requirements of para 128 before entering to work.

The categories are:
(a) post graduate doctor or dentist;
(b) working holidaymakers;
(c) seamen;
(d) seasonal workers at agricultural camps;
(e) training or work experience;
(f) representatives of overseas newspapers, news agencies and broadcasting organisations;
(g) sole representatives of overseas firms;
(h) private servants of diplomatic staff;
(i) overseas government employees;
(k) ministers of religion etc;
(l) airport based operational ground staff of overseas airlines;
(m) exceptions based on UK ancestry.

(a) Department of Employment requirements

Form WP1 must be filled out by the prospective employer, and should be filled out as soon as the person is identified for a post. The application should not be made more than six months before the date upon which the employer wishes to bring the employee to the UK, or three months before the person's current leave expires. Permits will only be issued for posts requiring either recognised degree level or equivalent professional qualifications, with normally two years' post qualification experience. Time spent in the UK in a permit-free capacity (see above) will not normally be taken into account for the purposes of calculating such experience. Where a worker is employed under a work permit the employer must take responsibility for the employee's pay, tax and national insurance. The terms and conditions relating to the employment must be equal to those offered to UK employees for doing similar work.

Keyworkers Keyworkers are persons having technical or specialised skills and expertise essential to the day-to-day running of the company. A keyworker must have specialised skills, knowledge or experience not readily available in the EU, and the jobs of others must depend upon them. Their permits are issued for short periods only. Catering and hotel specialists may also be key workers. If the worker has extensive knowledge of languages

PERSONS SEEKING EMPLOYMENT IN THE UK 139

and cultures which are not readily available in the UK or EU he may be processed as a keyworker if at least 60 per cent of his time is spent in contact work using his cultural or linguistic knowledge.

Work permits will not be issued for certain categories of employment. Thus no permits will be issued for manual, craft, clerical, secretarial or similar levels or for resident domestic work, such as nannies or housekeepers.

Persons in the following categories need only fill in the first part of WP1:
 (a) a senior post in an international company which requires an existing employee to transfer from abroad or for a post designed to develop the career of an existing employee;
 (b) a post at board level or equivalent for which there is no other suitable candidate;
 (c) a new post essential to an inward investment project bringing jobs and capital to the UK;
 (d) occupations which are acknowledged by the industry or profession as being in acute short supply nationally and likely to be so within the EC. The DoE may vary the 'shortage occupations' in accordance with the changing labour market, and inquiries should be addressed to the DoE at the time of the application.

Form WP1 asks for details of the following in Part 1:
 (a) the person to be employed;
 (b) the UK employer;
 (c) the employment offered; including how long the person is expected to be employed in the UK (specifying a period). If a period of more than four years is specified, reasons for the longer period must be given. The form must specify the duties involved in the job the pay and hours;
 (d) the qualifications of the employee, including any bodies with whom the person is registered; and the qualifications required by the job;
 (e) the employee's employment record, including whether the person has held a Training and Work Experience Scheme permit within two years;
 (f) the reasons for recruiting from outside the EU; including whether it is a transfer within an international company, and the reasons for making the offer to the person in terms of heads (a) to (d) above;
 (g) if it is said that the occupation is one requiring high level

skills, qualifications and experience acknowledged to be in acute short supply within the EU, where the employer has had difficulty in recruiting, evidence to show that there is no suitable candidate available in the EU, and details of any recruitment methods tried by the employer.

In all other cases Part II of the Form WP1 must be filled in, and in particular where the person:
  (a) has held a Training and Work Experience Scheme permit in the last two years; or
  (b) has held a permit for a career development post in the last six months; or
  (c) is already in the UK; or
  (d) is a keyworker.

The whole of the Form must be filled in. Thus in relation to such persons the following details must be given:
  (a) evidence of the need to recruit from outside the EU;
    (i) why training or transfer cannot fill the need;
    (ii) why the job cannot be filled by an EU worker;
  (b) in relation to keyworkers:
    (i) special skills, experience or qualifications which the worker has making him uniquely qualified to do the job;
    (ii) the way in which the jobs of workers in the UK, and the success of the business, depend on the recruitment of the person;
    (iii) the relevant knowledge of language or cultural skills which are not readily available in the EU, together with reasons why these skills are essential for the job.

The prospective employer must supply:
  (a) evidence of the qualifications of the person;
  (b) original references on letter headed paper covering the last two years;
  (c) copies of all advertisements, showing the name and date of publication;
  (d) if the person is in the UK and not in approved employment, his passport.

If no application for a work permit has been made in the last four years the following also must be supplied:
  (a) the employer's latest audited accounts with the accountant's name clearly shown;
  (b) copy of the latest annual report or publicity or internal marketing.

In default of the above, evidence of the tenure of the business premises, the staff employed in the UK, copies of any company incorporation documents should be provided.

Advertisements should identify a specific post and must have been placed within the last six months before the application being made in a quality newspaper with national or EU circulation, or in a trade journal. For keyworker posts the advert must be available in all EU countries.

(b) Extension of stay for work permit employment

Requirements for an extension of stay for work permit employment

131. The requirements for an extension of stay to seek or take employment (unless the applicant is otherwise eligible for an extension of stay for employment under these Rules) are that the applicant:
- (i) entered the United Kingdom with a valid work permit under paragraph 129; and
- (ii) has written approval from the Department of Employment for the continuation of his employment; and
- (iii) meets the requirements of paragraph 128 (ii)–(v).

Extension of stay for work permit employment

132. An extension of stay for work permit employment may be granted for a period not exceeding the period of approved employment recommended by the Department of Employment provided the Secretary of State is satisfied that each of the requirements of paragraph 131 is met. An extension of stay is to be subject to a condition restricting the applicant to employment approved by the Department of Employment.

Refusal of extension of stay for employment

133. An extension of stay for employment is to be refused if the Secretary of State is not satisfied that each of the requirements of paragraph 131 is met (unless the applicant is otherwise eligible for an extension of stay for employment under these Rules).

Indefinite leave to remain for a work permit holder

134. Indefinite leave to remain may be granted, on application, to a person admitted as a work permit holder provided:
- (i) he has spent a continuous period of 4 years in the United Kingdom in this capacity; and
- (ii) he has met the requirements of paragraph 131 throughout the 4 year period; and
- (iii) he is still required for the employment in question, as certified by his employer.

Refusal of indefinite leave to remain for a work permit holder

135. Indefinite leave to remain in the United Kingdom for a work permit holder is to be refused if the Secretary of State is not satisfied that each of the requirements of paragraph 134 is met.

COMMENTARY

A person who holds a work permit may apply for an extension of leave to remain as a work permit holder. He must be in possession of a valid permit. He must not intend to take employment except as specified in the permit. He must be able to maintain and accommodate himself and any dependants without recourse to public funds (see pages 61). The DoE must approve the continuation of the employment.

A work permit is issued in relation to a specific job and with a specific employer, so that if the person wishes to change employers, the new employer must apply for a work permit, and satisfy the above requirements. In any event changes of employer are only allowed for the same kind of work for which the permit was originally issued. If the employer or person wishes the person to change jobs within the company, a fresh permit application must be made. Applications for extensions of work permits are made on Form WP5. The passport must be sent, and the DoE will need to be satisfied as to why the employer needs to keep the overseas national; that efforts have been made to fill the post with an EU national, stating the results of those efforts; the period of the employer's need for the overseas national. An application should not be made earlier than three months before the permit expires, but before the permit does expire. Form WP5 also seeks details of why training or transfer will not fill the employer's need during the extended period.

Under Co-operation Agreements in the Field of Labour between the EU and Turkey, Morocco, Algeria, and Tunisia workers from those countries may not need an extension of a work permit to remain working in the UK (see Chapter 17).

In relation to indefinite leave to remain, the applicant must show that he has spent a continuous period of four years in the UK as a work permit holder. He must show that he is still required for the employment in question. Indefinite leave to remain is not now automatic after service of the four-year period. Where the claim for indefinite leave is based upon approved employment, all four years must be approved (*R v IAT, ex p Inovejas* [1983] Imm AR 204).

3 Representatives of overseas newspapers, news agencies and broadcasting organisations

(a) Requirements for leave to enter as a representative of an overseas newspaper, news agency or broadcasting organisation

REPRESENTATIVES OF OVERSEAS NEWSPAPERS, NEWS AGENCIES AND BROADCASTING ORGANISATIONS

Requirements for leave to enter as a representative of an overseas newspaper, news agency or broadcasting organisation

136. The requirements to be met by a person seeking leave to enter the United Kingdom as a representative of an overseas newspaper, news agency or broadcasting organisation are that he:
 (i) has been engaged by that organisation outside the United Kingdom and is being posted to the United Kingdom on a long-term assignment as a representative; and
 (ii) intends to work full-time as a representative of that overseas newspaper, news agency or broadcasting organisation; and
 (iii) does not intend to take employment except within the terms of this paragraph; and
 (iv) can maintain and accommodate himself and any dependants adequately without recourse to public funds; and
 (v) holds a valid United Kingdom entry clearance for entry in this capacity.

Leave to enter as a representative of an overseas newspaper, news agency or broadcasting organisation

137. A person seeking leave to enter the United Kingdom as a representative of an overseas newspaper, news agency or broadcasting organisation may be admitted for a period not exceeding 12 months provided he is able to produce to the Immigration Officer, on arrival, a valid United Kingdom entry clearance for entry in this capacity.

Refusal of leave to enter as a representative of an overseas newspaper, news agency or broadcasting organisation

138. Leave to enter as a representative of an overseas newspaper, news agency or broadcasting organisation is to be refused if a valid United Kingdom entry clearance for entry in this capacity is not produced to the Immigration Officer on arrival.

COMMENTARY

The rules require the person entering to have an entry clearance as a representative. He will have no right of appeal without one. If a representative of an overseas newspaper, news agency or broadcasting organisation is on a long-term assignment to the UK, he will not require a work permit. The Home Office interpret the word 'newspaper' broadly to include magazines concerned with news (see INL&P October 1986, p 92).

(b) Requirements for an extension of stay as a representative of an overseas newspaper, news agency or broadcasting organisation

Requirements for an extension of stay as a representative of an overseas newspaper, news agency or broadcasting organisation

139. The requirements for an extension of stay as a representative of an overseas newspaper, news agency or broadcasting organisation are that the applicant:
 (i) entered the United Kingdom with a valid United Kingdom entry clearance as a representative of an overseas newspaper, news agency or broadcasting organisation; and
 (ii) is still engaged in the employment for which his entry clearance was granted; and
 (iii) is still required for the employment in question, as certified by his employer; and
 (iv) meets the requirements of paragraph 136 (ii)–(iv).

Extension of stay as a representative of an overseas newspaper, news agency or broadcasting organisation

140. An extension of stay as a representative of an overseas newspaper, news agency or broadcasting organisation may be granted for a period not exceeding 3 years provided the Secretary of State is satisfied that each of the requirements of paragraph 139 is met.

Refusal of extension of stay as a representative of an overseas newspaper, news agency or broadcasting organisation

141. An extension of stay as a representative of an overseas newspaper, news agency or broadcasting organisation is to be refused if the Secretary of State is not satisfied that each of the requirements of paragraph 139 is met.

Indefinite leave to remain for a representative of an overseas newspaper, news agency or broadcasting organisation

142. Indefinite leave to remain may be granted, on application, to a representative of an overseas newspaper, news agency or broadcasting organisation provided:
 (i) he has spent a continuous period of 4 years in the United Kingdom in this capacity; and
 (ii) he has met the requirements of paragraph 139 throughout the 4 year period; and
 (iii) he is still required for the employment in question, as certified by his employer.

PERSONS SEEKING EMPLOYMENT IN THE UK   145

Refusal of indefinite leave to remain for a representative of an overseas newspaper, news agency or broadcasting organisation

143. Indefinite leave to remain in the United Kingdom for a representative of an overseas newspaper, news agency or broadcasting organisation is to be refused if the Secretary of State is not satisfied that each of the requirements of paragraph 142 is met.

COMMENTARY

Where an application for indefinite leave is based on permit-free employment, the applicant must have been 'on call' for duties for his employers for a period of time for it to count towards settlement (*Marwah* (7422)).

4 Representatives of overseas firms which have no branch, subsidiary or other representative in the UK (sole representatives)

REPRESENTATIVES OF OVERSEAS FIRMS WHICH HAVE NO BRANCH, SUBSIDIARY OR OTHER REPRESENTATIVE IN THE UNITED KINGDOM (SOLE REPRESENTATIVES)

Requirements for leave to enter as a sole representative

144. The requirements to be met by a person seeking leave to enter the United Kingdom as a sole representative are that he:
  (i) has been recruited and taken on as an employee outside the United Kingdom as a representative of a firm which has its headquarters and principal place of business outside the United Kingdom and which has no branch, subsidiary or other representative in the United Kingdom; and
  (ii) seeks entry to the United Kingdom as a senior employee with full authority to take operational decisions on behalf of the overseas firm for the purpose of representing it in the United Kingdom by establishing and operating a registered branch or wholly-owned subsidiary of that overseas firm; and
  (iii) intends to be employed full-time as a representative of that overseas firm; and
  (iv) is not a majority shareholder in that overseas firm; and
  (v) does not intend to take employment except within the terms of this paragraph; and
  (vi) can maintain and accommodate himself and any dependants adequately without recourse to public funds; and
  (vii) holds a valid United Kingdom entry clearance for entry in this capacity.

Leave to enter as a sole representative

145. A person seeking leave to enter the United Kingdom as a sole representative may be admitted for a period not exceeding 12 months

provided he is able to produce to the Immigration Officer, on arrival, a valid United Kingdom entry clearance for entry in this capacity.

Refusal of leave to enter as a sole representative

146. Leave to enter as a sole representative is to be refused if a valid United Kingdom entry clearance for entry in this capacity is not produced to the Immigration Officer on arrival.

COMMENTARY

The firm must be bona fide, and a person will only be regarded as a representative of an overseas firm if there is an active trading concern in existence outside the UK. If the base office has effectively ceased trading, the applicant will need a work permit (*R v IAT, ex p Lokko* [1990] Imm AR 111). The new para 144(ii) provides a definition of 'sole representative' as a senior employee with the authority to take operational decisions on behalf of the overseas firm for the purpose of representing it in the UK by establishing and operating a registered branch or wholly owned subsidiary of that overseas firm. This encapsulates the effect of a series of cases under previous rules. Thus a sole representative will generally have considerable plenipotentiary powers and will be fully versed in all aspects of the company's activities and policies. He will have responsibility for making important decisions on behalf of the firm (*Hope* (832)). However, such plenipotentiary powers are not necessary in the light of modern communications. The firm's affairs should occupy a visible part of his time and effort and his duties should be required so that the firm may function properly (*Baydur* (5442)). He must, however, intend to be employed full time as a representative of the overseas firm, and it is not clear whether being 'on call' for the firm would be enough. The decision in *Lokko*, in so far as it suggests that a majority shareholder in an overseas organisation may enter as its sole representative, is overturned by para 144(iv).

5 Extensions

Requirements for an extension of stay as a sole representative

147. The requirements for an extension of stay as a sole representative are that the applicant:
 (i) entered the United Kingdom with a valid United Kingdom entry clearance as a sole representative of an overseas firm; and

PERSONS SEEKING EMPLOYMENT IN THE UK

(ii) can show that the overseas firm still has its headquarters and principal place of business outside the United Kingdom; and
(iii) is employed full-time as a representative of that overseas firm and has established and is in charge of its registered branch or wholly-owned subsidiary; and
(iv) is still required for the employment in question, as certified by his employer; and
(v) meets the requirements of paragraph 114 (iii)–(vi).

Extension of stay as a sole representative

148. An extension of stay not exceeding 3 years as a sole representative may be granted provided the Secretary of State is satisfied that each of the requirements of paragraph 147 is met.

Refusal of extension of stay as a sole representative

149. An extension of stay as a sole representative is to be refused if the Secretary of State is not satisfied that each of the requirements of paragraph 147 is met.

Indefinite leave to remain for a sole representative

150. Indefinite leave to remain may be granted, on application, to a sole representative provided:
   (i) he has spent a continuous period of 4 years in the United Kingdom in this capacity; and
   (ii) he has met the requirements of paragraph 147 throughout the 4 year period; and
   (iii) he is still required for the employment in question, as certified by his employer.

Refusal of indefinite leave to remain for a sole representative

151. Indefinite leave to remain in the United Kingdom for a sole representative is to be refused if the Secretary of State is not satisfied that each of the requirements of paragraph 150 is met.

COMMENTARY

Where a person establishes a branch or subsidiary or other representation in the UK, an extension will be granted if he can show that at the time of the application he is in charge of that branch etc, and his employer confirms he wishes to continue to employ him. He must satisfy the requirements of para 144 (iii)–(vi). Thus he must intend to be employed full time as a representative of that overseas firm and must not be a majority shareholder in it. He must not intend to take employment except as a sole representative of that overseas firm in the UK. He must be able to maintain himself, and any dependants adequately without recourse to public funds, and he must have had a valid entry clearance for entry as a sole representative.

The applicant will have to show that he acts as the sole representative of a trading concern whose activities remain centred overseas (*Lokko v S of S* [1990] Imm AR 111). He will still need to satisfy the requirements on entry, and the S of S will need information as to:

(*a*) the time and effort he puts into the business;
(*b*) what he has achieved;
(*c*) what he is expected to achieve; and
(*d*) the role his activities play in the overall commercial activities of the firm he represents (*Kongar* (6601)).

He must still satisfy the definition of 'sole representative'. Although a representative need not have considerable plenipotentiary powers in the light of modern communications, the affairs of the company must continue to occupy a considerable part of his time and effort (*Baydur* (5442)). The representative's authority must be more than that of a distributor or sales agent (*Hope* (832)). He must be a senior employee with the authority to take operational decisions on behalf of the overseas firm for the purpose of representing it in the UK by establishing a branch or wholly owned subsidiary of that firm (para 144(ii)).

Indefinite leave Indefinite leave is granted after a continuous period of four years spent in the UK as a sole representative. The rule stresses that throughout that period the applicant must have satisfied the requirements of para 147, which require that the applicant had an entry clearance as a sole representative. He must have been able to show that the overseas firm has its headquarters and principal place of business outside the UK. He must show that he was throughout that time in charge of the UK branch, and that his services were required throughout that period, as certified by his employer. The employer must certify that he is still required for the employment.

6 Private servants in diplomatic households

PRIVATE SERVANTS IN DIPLOMATIC HOUSEHOLDS

Requirements for leave to enter as a private servant in a diplomatic household

152. The requirements to be met by a person seeking leave to enter the United Kingdom as a private servant in a diplomatic household are that he:

(i) is aged 18 or over; and
(ii) is employed as a private servant in the household of a member of staff of a diplomatic or consular mission who enjoys diplomatic privileges and immunity within the meaning of the Vienna Convention on Diplomatic and Consular Relations or a member of the family forming part of the household of such a person; and
(iii) intends to work full-time as a private servant within the terms of this paragraph; and
(iv) does not intend to take employment except within the terms of this paragraph; and
(v) can maintain and accommodate himself and any dependants adequately without recourse to public funds; and
(vi) holds a valid United Kingdom entry clearance for entry in this capacity.

Leave to enter as a private servant in a diplomatic household

153. A person seeking leave to enter the United Kingdom as a private servant in a diplomatic household may be given leave to enter for a period not exceeding 12 months provided he is able to produce to the Immigration Officer, on arrival, a valid United Kingdom entry clearance for entry in this capacity.

Refusal of leave to enter as a private servant in a diplomatic household

154. Leave to enter as a private servant in a diplomatic household is to be refused if a valid United Kingdom entry clearance for entry in this capacity is not produced to the Immigration Officer on arrival.

COMMENTARY

HC 395 introduces a requirement that the private servant must be 18 or over, as a result of proposed EC legislation relating to the employment of young workers. To satisfy the requirement of full-time work it is insufficient if the person works two mornings per week (*Guinaban* (3475)).

Extensions

Requirements for an extension of stay as a private servant in a diplomatic household

155. The requirements for an extension of stay as a private servant in a diplomatic household are that the applicant:
(i) entered the United Kingdom with a valid United Kingdom entry clearance as a private servant in a diplomatic household; and
(ii) is still engaged in the employment for which his entry clearance was granted; and

(iii) is still required for the employment in question, as certified by the employer; and
(iv) meets the requirements of paragraph 152 (iii)–(v).

Extension of stay as a private servant in a diplomatic household

156. An extension of stay as a private servant in a diplomatic household may be granted for a period not exceeding 12 months provided the Secretary of State is satisfied that each of the requirements of paragraph 155 is met.

Refusal of extension of stay as a private servant in a diplomatic household

157. An extension of stay as a private servant in a diplomatic household is to be refused if the Secretary of State is not satisfied that each of the requirements of paragraph 155 is met.

Indefinite leave to remain for a servant in a diplomatic household

158. Indefinite leave to remain may he granted, on application, to a private servant in a diplomatic household provided:
  (i) he has spent a continuous period of 4 years in the United Kingdom in this capacity; and
  (ii) he has met the requirements of paragraph 155 throughout the 4 year period; and
  (iii) he is still required for the employment in question, as certified by his employer.

Refusal of indefinite leave to remain for a servant in a diplomatic household

159. Indefinite leave to remain in the United Kingdom for a private servant in a diplomatic household is to be refused if the Secretary of State is not satisfied that each of the requirements of paragraph 158 is met.

COMMENTARY

HC 395 makes provision for a private servant to apply for indefinite leave to remain. Throughout a period of four years he must continually have satisfied the requirements of para 155. Thus he must have entered the UK with a valid UK entry clearance as a private servant in a diplomatic household. He must remain in the employment for which that entry clearance was granted. His employer must require him for that employment throughout the period, and must provide a certificate to that effect. Additionally for the whole of the period of four years the applicant must intend to work full time as a private servant within the terms of para 152. He must not intend to take employment except as a private servant in the household of a member of staff of a diplomatic or consular mission. He must be able to maintain and accommodate himself and any dependants without recourse to public funds throughout the period. If any of these requirements is not satisfied, indefinite leave to remain must be refused.

7 Overseas government employees

OVERSEAS GOVERNMENT EMPLOYEES

Requirements for leave to enter as an overseas government employee

160. For the purposes of these Rules an overseas government employee means a person coming for employment by an overseas government or employed by the United Nations Organisation or other international organisation of which the United Kingdom is a member.

161. The requirements to be met by a person seeking leave to enter the United Kingdom as an overseas government employee are that he:
   (i) is able to produce either a valid United Kingdom entry clearance for entry in this capacity or satisfactory documentary evidence of his status as an overseas government employee; and
   (ii) intends to work full time for the government or organisation concerned; and
   (iii) does not intend to take employment except within the terms of this paragraph; and
   (iv) can maintain and accommodate himself and any dependants adequately without recourse to public funds.

Leave to enter as an overseas government employee

162. A person seeking leave to enter the United Kingdom as an overseas government employee may be given leave to enter for a period not exceeding 12 months, provided he is able, on arrival, to produce to the Immigration Officer a valid United Kingdom entry clearance for entry in this capacity or satisfy the Immigration Officer that each of the requirements of paragraph 161 is met.

Refusal of leave to enter as an overseas government employee

163. Leave to enter as an overseas government employee is to be refused if a valid United Kingdom entry clearance for entry in this capacity is not produced to the Immigration Officer on arrival or if the Immigration Officer is not satisfied that each of the requirements of paragraph 161 is met.

Requirements for an extension of stay as an overseas government employee

164. The requirements to be met by a person seeking an extension of stay as an overseas government employee are that the applicant:

152 IMMIGRATION CONTROL

  (i) was given leave to enter the United Kingdom under paragraph 162 as an overseas government employee; and
  (ii) is still engaged in the employment in question; and
  (iii) is still required for the employment in question, as certified by the employer; and
  (iv) meets the requirements of paragraph 161 (ii)–(iv).

Extension of stay as an overseas government employee

165. An extension of stay as an overseas government employee may be granted for a period not exceeding 3 years provided the Secretary of State is satisfied that each of the requirements of paragraph 164 is met.

Refusal of extension of stay as an overseas government employee

166. An extension of stay as an overseas government employee is to be refused if the Secretary of State is not satisfied that each of the requirements of paragraph 164 is met.

Indefinite leave to remain for an overseas government employee

167. Indefinite leave to remain may be granted, on application, to an overseas government employee provided:
  (i) he has spent a continuous period of 4 years in the United Kingdom in this capacity; and
  (ii) he has met the requirements of paragraph 164 throughout the 4 year period; and
  (iii) he is still required for the employment in question, as certified by his employer.

Refusal of indefinite leave to remain for an overseas government employee

168. Indefinite leave to remain in the United Kingdom for an overseas government employee is to be refused if the Secretary of State is not satisfied that each of the requirements of paragraph 167 is met.

8 Ministers of religion, missionaries and members of religious orders

MINISTERS OF RELIGION, MISSIONARIES AND MEMBERS OF RELIGIOUS ORDERS

169. For the purposes of these Rules:
  (i) a minister of religion means a religious functionary whose main regular duties comprise the leading of a congregation in performing the rites and rituals of the faith and in preaching the essentials of the creed;
  (ii) a missionary means a person who is directly engaged in spreading a religious doctrine and whose work is not in essence administrative or clerical;

(iii) a member of a religious order means a person who is coming to live in a community run by that order.

Requirements for leave to enter as a minister of religion, missionary or member of a religious order

170. The requirements to be met by a person seeking leave to enter the United Kingdom as a minister of religion, missionary or member of a religious order are that he:
- (i) (*a*) if seeking leave to enter as a minister of religion has either been working for at least one year as a minister of religion or, where ordination is prescribed by a religious faith as the sole means of entering the ministry, has been ordained as a minister of religion following at least one year's full-time or two years' part-time training for the ministry; or
  - (*b*) if seeking leave to enter as a missionary has been trained as a missionary or has worked as a missionary and is being sent to the United Kingdom by an overseas organisation; or
  - (*c*) if seeking leave to enter as a member of a religious order is coming to live in a community maintained by the religious order of which he is a member and, if intending to teach, does not intend to do so save at an establishment maintained by his order; and
- (ii) intends to work full-time as a minister of religion, missionary or for the religious order of which he is a member; and
- (iii) does not intend to take employment except within the terms of this paragraph; and
- (iv) can maintain and accommodate himself and any dependants adequately without recourse to public funds; and
- (v) holds a valid United Kingdom entry clearance for entry in this capacity.

Leave to enter as a minister of religion, missionary or member of a religious order

171. A person seeking leave to enter the United Kingdom as a minister of religion, missionary or member of a religious order may be admitted for a period not exceeding 12 months provided he is able to produce to the Immigration Officer, on arrival, a valid United Kingdom entry clearance for entry in this capacity.

Refusal of leave to enter as a minister of religion, missionary or member of a religious order

172. Leave to enter as a minister of religion, missionary or member of a religious order is to be refused if a valid United Kingdom entry clearance for entry in this capacity is not produced to the Immigration Officer on arrival.

COMMENTARY

HC 395 introduces a definition of 'minister of religion', 'missionary' and 'member of a religious order'. An ordained minister is now expected to have followed a period of one year full-time study or two years' part-time study before ordination. Ministers of religion and members of religious orders do not require work permits if they are coming to work full time as such (*Piara Singh v ECO New Delhi* [1977] Imm AR 1). Entry clearance is in practice only issued after due enquiry is made in the UK as to the need for such an appointment and other matters (*Memi v S of S* [1976] Imm AR 129). Applicants must be able to maintain and accommodate themselves and their dependants without recourse to public funds. Members of religious orders engaged in teaching at establishments maintained by their own order will not require work permits, but if they teach at outside institutions they will require work permits. The phrase 'religious orders' means monastic orders (*Abdul Hamid v ECO Dhaka* [1986] Imm AR 469), although para 169 defines a member of a religious order as a person who is coming to live in a community run by the order. The IAT in *Mobley* (5368) considered that the phrases 'ministers of religion, and missionaries' included those who organised the propagation of a faith as well as those who actually propagate that faith. It is necessary to see what the person's purpose is in seeking to do the work which he seeks to enter to perform. He must be undertaking the work in order to spread doctrine. However, the new rule now requires that the missionary should be directly engaged in spreading a religious doctrine, and whose work is not essentially administrative or clerical. Thus a person whose work is essentially administrative will not be a missionary, but it is likely that if the main purpose of his role included administrative tasks and the writing and dissemination of materials designed to spread a religious doctrine, he would still be covered by this rule. The extent to which his experience or qualifications make him a minister of religion is a question of fact, to be interpreted in the light of the customs of the faith in question. A minister of religion will be someone whose main regular duties comprise the leading of a congregation in performing the rites and rituals of the faith and in preaching the essentials of the creed. Thus a person who officiates and who leads in matters of religion will be a minister of religion (*Kalsoom Begum v Visa Officer Islamabad* [1988] Imm AR 325). A full-time Imam will be a minister of religion (*Abdul Hamid* (above)).

Extensions

Requirements for an extension of stay as a minister of religion, missionary or member of a religious order

173. The requirements for an extension of stay as a minister of religion, missionary or member of a religious order are that the applicant:
   (i) entered the United Kingdom with a valid United Kingdom entry clearance as a minister of religion, missionary or member of a religious order; and
   (ii) is still engaged in the employment for which his entry clearance was granted; and
   (iii) is still required for the employment in question as certified by the leadership of his congregation, his employer or the head of his religious order; and
   (iv) meets the requirements of paragraph 170 (ii)–(iv).

Extension of stay as a minister of religion, missionary or member of a religious order

174. An extension of stay as a minister of religion, missionary or member of a religious order may be granted for a period not exceeding 3 years provided the Secretary of State is satisfied that each of the requirements of paragraph 173 is met.

Refusal of extension of stay as a minister of religion, missionary or member of a religious order

175. An extension of stay as a minister of religion, missionary or member of a religious order is to be refused if the Secretary of State is not satisfied that each of the requirements of paragraph 173 is met.

Indefinite leave to remain for a minister of religion, missionary or member of a religious order

176. Indefinite leave to remain may be granted, on application, to a person admitted as a minister of religion, missionary or member of a religious order provided:
   (i) he has spent a continuous period of 4 years in the United Kingdom in this capacity; and
   (ii) he has met the requirements of paragraph 173 throughout the 4 year period; and
   (iii) he is still required for the employment in question as certified by the leadership of his congregation, his employer or the head of the religious order to which he belongs.

Refusal of indefinite leave to remain for a minister of religion, missionary or member of a religious order

177. Indefinite leave to remain in the United Kingdom for a minister of religion, missionary or member of a religious order is to be refused

156   IMMIGRATION CONTROL

if the Secretary of State is not satisfied that each of the requirements of paragraph 176 is met.

COMMENTARY

A person seeking an extension under this head must have had an entry clearance for this purpose on entry. He must still be engaged in the employment for which the visa was granted. His employer or the head of the religious order of which he is a member must certify that he is still required for the employment in question. He must also show that he intends to work full time as a minister of religion, missionary or for the religious order of which he is a member, and that he does not intend to take any other employment. He must maintain and accommodate himself without recourse to public funds.

A person who enters in another capacity may not under the rules change his status to that of minister of religion. In practice such an application may not be rejected out of hand. Outside the rules a person may be permitted to remain in a religious position. The S of S will refer to a panel of advisers as to the need for the person (*Dawood Patel v S of S* [1990] Imm AR 478, and see letter of 1 June 1982 at page 481 ff). However, there must be compelling reasons why the person cannot apply for an entry clearance abroad. Generally a person seeking to switch from another category to that of a minister of religion will be refused the variation, and will be expected to return abroad and apply (see *Dawood Patel*, p 484 and Ministerial letter dated 31 March 1987 (ibid)).

9 Airport-based operational ground staff of overseas-owned airlines

AIRPORT-BASED OPERATIONAL GROUND STAFF OF OVERSEAS-OWNED AIRLINES

Requirements for leave to enter the United Kingdom as a member of the operational ground staff of an overseas-owned airline

178. The requirements to be met by a person seeking leave to enter the United Kingdom as a member of the operational ground staff of an overseas-owned airline are that he:
  (i) has been transferred to the United Kingdom by an overseas-owned airline operating services to and from the United Kingdom to take up duty at an international airport as station manager, security manager or technical manager; and
  (ii) intends to work full-time for the airline concerned; and
  (iii) does not intend to take employment except within the terms of this paragraph; and

PERSONS SEEKING EMPLOYMENT IN THE UK

(iv) can maintain and accommodate himself and any dependants without recourse to public funds; and

(v) holds a valid United Kingdom entry clearance for entry in this capacity.

Leave to enter as a member of the operational ground staff of an overseas-owned airline

179. A person seeking leave to enter the United Kingdom as a member of the operational ground staff of an overseas-owned airline may be given leave to enter for a period not exceeding 12 months, provided he is able to produce to the Immigration Officer, on arrival, a valid United Kingdom entry clearance for entry in this capacity.

Refusal of leave to enter as a member of the operational ground staff of an overseas-owned airline

180. Leave to enter as a member of the operational ground staff of an overseas-owned airline is to be refused if a valid United Kingdom entry clearance for entry in this capacity is not produced to the Immigration Officer on arrival.

Requirements for an extension of stay as a member of the operational ground staff of an overseas-owned airline

181. The requirements to be met by a person seeking an extension of stay as a member of the operational ground staff of an overseas-owned airline are that the applicant:
   (i) entered the United Kingdom with a valid United Kingdom entry clearance as a member of the operational ground staff of an overseas-owned airline; and
   (ii) is still engaged in the employment for which entry was granted; and
   (iii) is still required for the employment in question, as certified by the employer; and
   (iv) meets the requirements of paragraph 178 (ii)–(iv).

Extension of stay as a member of the operational ground staff of an overseas-owned airline

182. An extension of stay as a member of the operational ground staff of an overseas-owned airline may be granted for a period not exceeding 3 years, provided the Secretary of State is satisfied that each of the requirements of paragraph 181 is met.

Refusal of extension of stay as a member of the operational ground staff of an overseas-owned airline

183. An extension of stay as a member of the operational ground staff of an overseas-owned airline is to be refused if the Secretary of State is not satisfied that each of the requirements of paragraph 181 is met.

Indefinite leave to remain for a member of the operational ground staff of an overseas-owned airline

184. Indefinite leave to remain may be granted, on application, to a member of the operational ground staff of an overseas-owned airline provided:
   (i) he has spent a continuous period of 4 years in the United Kingdom in this capacity; and
   (ii) he has met the requirements of paragraph 181 throughout the 4 year period; and
   (iii) he is still required for the employment in question, as certified by the employer.

Refusal of indefinite leave to remain for a member of the operational ground staff of an overseas-owned airline

185. Indefinite leave to remain in the United Kingdom for a member of the operational ground staff of an overseas-owned airline is to be refused if the Secretary of State is not satisfied that each of the requirements of paragraph 184 is met.

COMMENTARY

Paragraphs 178–185 limit the posts which qualify airport based operational ground staff for permit-free employment to station managers, or technical managers.

10 Exception on grounds of United Kingdom ancestry

PERSONS WITH UNITED KINGDOM ANCESTRY

Requirements for leave to enter on the grounds of United Kingdom ancestry

186. The requirements to be met by a person seeking leave to enter the United Kingdom on the grounds of his United Kingdom ancestry are that he:
   (i) is a Commonwealth citizen; and
   (ii) is aged 17 or over; and
   (iii) is able to provide proof that one of his grandparents was born in the United Kingdom and Islands; and
   (iv) is able to work and intends to take or seek employment in the United Kingdom; and
   (v) will be able to maintain and accommodate himself and any dependants adequately without recourse to public funds; and
   (vi) holds a valid United Kingdom entry clearance for entry in this capacity.

Leave to enter the United Kingdom on the grounds of United Kingdom ancestry

187. A person seeking leave to enter the United Kingdom on the grounds of his United Kingdom ancestry may be given leave to enter for a period

PERSONS SEEKING EMPLOYMENT IN THE UK

not exceeding 4 years provided he is able to produce to the Immigration Officer, on arrival, a valid United Kingdom entry clearance for entry in this capacity.

Refusal of leave to enter on the grounds of United Kingdom ancestry

188. Leave to enter the United Kingdom on the grounds of United Kingdom ancestry is to be refused if a valid United Kingdom entry clearance for entry in this capacity is not produced to the Immigration Officer on arrival.

Requirements for an extension of stay on the grounds of United Kingdom ancestry

189. The requirements to be met by a person seeking an extension of stay on the grounds of United Kingdom ancestry are that he is able to meet each of the requirements of paragraph 186 (i)–(v).

Extension of stay on the grounds of United Kingdom ancestry

190. An extension of stay on the grounds of United Kingdom ancestry may be granted for a period not exceeding 4 years provided the Secretary of State is satisfied that each of the requirements of paragraph 186 (i)–(v) is met.

Refusal of extension of stay on the grounds of United Kingdom ancestry

191. An extension of stay on the grounds of United Kingdom ancestry is to be refused if the Secretary of State is not satisfied that each of the requirements of paragraph 186 (i)–(v) is met.

COMMENTARY

Proof of descent is the main requirement of the rule. The entrant will need the following documents:

(a) the grandparent's birth certificate;
(b) the grandparents' marriage certificate;
(c) the birth certificate of the parent of the applicant who is descended from the relevant grandparents;
(d) the parents' marriage certificate; and
(e) the applicant's birth certificate.

The term 'grandparents' does not include the paternal grandparents of an illegitimate child (*C (an infant) v ECO Hong Kong* [1976] Imm AR 165). However, in a letter dated 14 March 1991 the Home Office stated that it is the S of S's practice to accept legitimate and illegitimate lines of descent, and adoptive lines as qualifying an applicant to seek entry clearance as a person who does not need a work permit on the grounds of UK ancestry.

In *Leahy* (7981) the IAT held that where the applicant is employable and proposes to take employment if that becomes necessary he satisfies the requirement of this paragraph that he wishes to take or seek employment. The intention to find work must be a genuine intention, even if it is unrealistic. Indeed it does not matter whether the person has an undisclosed further intention such as to secure the admission of relatives (*Thelma Smith* (8642)).

The main requirement of rules relating to permit free employment based on UK ancestry is that the applicant must be at least 17 years old. He must be able to work, and not likely to fall a charge on public funds. The rules permit a person to change to this category from another category.

11 Indefinite leave to remain on the grounds of United Kingdom ancestry

Indefinite leave to remain on the grounds of United Kingdom ancestry

192. Indefinite leave to remain may be granted, on application, to a Commonwealth citizen with a United Kingdom born grandparent provided:
  (i) he meets the requirements of paragraph 186 (i)–(v); and
  (ii) he has spent a continuous period of 4 years in the United Kingdom in this capacity.

Refusal of indefinite leave to remain on the grounds of United Kingdom ancestry

193. Indefinite leave to remain in the United Kingdom on the grounds of a United Kingdom born grandparent is to be refused if the Secretary of State is not satisfied that each of the requirements of paragraph 192 is met.

COMMENTARY

The applicant for indefinite leave to remain under this head must prove that he has spent a continuous period of four years in the UK in this capacity. He must also show that he has found work, and that the employer wishes to continue to employ him. If these conditions are not satisfied refusal is mandatory. This represents a significant tightening of the provisions relating to UK ancestry.

Where the claim is based upon permit-free employment, the applicant must have been 'on call' for the employer during a period for it to count towards the period (*Marwah* (7422)).

12 Spouses of persons with limited leave to enter or remain under paragraphs 128-193

SPOUSES OF PERSONS WITH LIMITED LEAVE TO ENTER OR REMAIN UNDER PARAGRAPHS 128-193

Requirements for leave to enter or remain as the spouse of a person with limited leave to enter or remain in the United Kingdom under paragraphs 128-193

194. The requirements to be met by a person seeking leave to enter or remain in the United Kingdom as the spouse of a person with limited leave to enter or remain in the United Kingdom under paragraphs 128-193 are that:
   (i) the applicant is married to a person with limited leave to enter or remain in the United Kingdom under paragraphs 128-193; and
   (ii) each of the parties intends to live with the other as his or her spouse during the applicant's stay and the marriage is subsisting; and
   (iii) there will be adequate accommodation for the parties and any dependants without recourse to public funds in accommodation which they own or occupy exclusively; and
   (iv) the parties will be able to maintain themselves and any dependants adequately without recourse to public funds; and
   (v) the applicant does not intend to stay in the United Kingdom beyond any period of leave granted to his spouse; and
   (vi) if seeking leave to enter, the applicant holds a valid United Kingdom entry clearance for entry in this capacity or, if seeking leave to remain, was admitted with a valid United Kingdom entry clearance for entry in this capacity.

Leave to enter or remain as the spouse of a person with limited leave to enter or remain in the United Kingdom under paragraphs 128-193

195. A person seeking leave to enter or remain in the United Kingdom as the spouse of a person with limited leave to enter or remain in the United Kingdom under paragraphs 128-193 may be given leave to enter or remain in the United Kingdom for a period of leave not in excess of that granted to the person with limited leave to enter or remain under paragraphs 128-193 provided that, in relation to an application for leave to enter, he is able, on arrival, to produce to the Immigration Officer a valid United Kingdom entry clearance for entry in this capacity or, in the case of an application for limited leave to remain, he was admitted with a valid United Kingdom entry clearance for entry in this capacity and is able to satisfy the Secretary of State that each of the requirements of paragraph 194 (i)-(v) is met. An application for indefinite leave to remain in this category may be granted provided the applicant was admitted with a valid United Kingdom entry clearance for entry in this capacity and is able to satisfy the Secretary of State that each of the requirements

of paragraph 194 (i)–(v) is met and provided indefinite leave to remain is, at the same time, being granted to the person with limited leave to enter or remain under paragraphs 128–193.

Refusal of leave to enter or remain as the spouse of a person with limited leave to enter or remain in the United Kingdom under paragraphs 128–193

196. Leave to enter or remain in the United Kingdom as the spouse of a person with limited leave to enter or remain in the United Kingdom under paragraphs 128–193 is to be refused if, in relation to an application for leave to enter, a valid United Kingdom entry clearance for entry in this capacity is not produced to the Immigration Officer on arrival or, in the case of an application for limited leave to remain, if the applicant was not admitted with a valid United Kingdom entry clearance for entry in this capacity or is unable to satisfy the Secretary of State that each of the requirements of paragraph 194 (i)–(v) is met. An application for indefinite leave to remain in this category is to be refused if the applicant was not admitted with a valid United Kingdom entry clearance for entry in this capacity or is unable to satisfy the Secretary of State that each of the requirements of paragraph 194 (i)–(v) is met or if indefinite leave to remain is not, at the same time, being granted to the person with limited leave to enter or remain under paragraphs 128–193.

COMMENTARY

The spouses of the following persons are subject to these paragraphs:
(a) Persons with work permits;
(b) Representatives of overseas newspapers, news agencies and broadcasting organisations;
(c) Representatives of overseas firms which have no branch, subsidiary or other representative in the UK (sole representatives);
(d) Private servants in diplomatic households;
(e) Overseas government employees;
(f) Ministers of religion, missionaries and members of religious orders;
(g) airport-based operational ground staff of overseas-owned airlines; and
(h) persons with UK ancestry.

Such persons must show that each of the parties to the marriage intend to live with the other as his or her spouse during the applicant's stay in the UK. The spouse must show that there will be adequate accommodation for the parties and any dependants without recourse to public funds in accommodation which they own or occupy exclusively (see page 211). The parties must be able

PERSONS SEEKING EMPLOYMENT IN THE UK

to maintain themselves and any dependants adequately without recourse to public funds. The spouse must have a valid entry clearance for the purpose.

13 Children of persons with limited leave to enter or remain in the UK under paragraphs 128-193

CHILDREN OF PERSONS WITH LIMITED LEAVE TO ENTER OR REMAIN IN THE UNITED KINGDOM UNDER PARAGRAPHS 128-193

Requirements for leave to enter or remain as the child of a person with limited leave to enter or remain in the United Kingdom under paragraphs 128-193

197. The requirements to be met by a person seeking leave to enter or remain in the United Kingdom as a child of a person with limited leave to enter or remain in the United Kingdom under paragraphs 128-193 are that:
   (i) he is the child of a parent with limited leave to enter or remain in the United Kingdom under paragraphs 128-193; and
   (ii) he is under the age of 18 or has current leave to enter or remain in this capacity; and
   (iii) he is unmarried, has not formed an independent family unit and is not leading an independent life; and
   (iv) he can and will be maintained and accommodated adequately without recourse to public funds in accommodation which his parent(s) own or occupy exclusively; and
   (v) he will not stay in the United Kingdom beyond any period of leave granted to his parent(s); and
   (vi) both parents are being or have been admitted to or allowed to remain in the United Kingdom save where:
      (a) the parent he is accompanying or joining is his sole surviving parent;
      (b) the parent he is accompanying or joining has had sole responsibility for his upbringing; or
      (c) there are serious and compelling family or other considerations which make exclusion from the United Kingdom undesirable and suitable arrangements have been made for his care; and
   (vii) if seeking leave to enter, he holds a valid United Kingdom entry clearance for entry in this capacity or, if seeking leave to remain, was admitted with a valid United Kingdom entry clearance for entry in this capacity.

Leave to enter or remain as the child of a person with limited leave to enter or remain in the United Kingdom under paragraphs 128-193

198. A person seeking leave to enter or remain in the United Kingdom as the child of a person with limited leave to enter or remain in the United Kingdom under paragraphs 128-193 may be given leave to enter or remain

in the United Kingdom for a period of leave not in excess of that granted to the person with limited leave to enter or remain under paragraphs 128-193 provided that, in relation to an application for leave to enter, he is able to produce to the Immigration Officer, on arrival, a valid United Kingdom entry clearance for entry in this capacity or, in the case of an application for limited leave to remain, he was admitted with a valid United Kingdom entry clearance for entry in this capacity and is able to satisfy the Secretary of State that each of the requirements of paragraph 197 (i)-(vi) is met. An application for indefinite leave to remain in this category may be granted provided the applicant was admitted with a valid United Kingdom entry clearance for entry in this capacity and is able to satisfy the Secretary of State that each of the requirements of paragraph 197 (i)-(vi) is met and provided indefinite leave to remain is, at the same time, being granted to the person with limited leave to enter or remain under paragraphs 128-193.

Refusal of leave to enter or remain as the child of a person with limited leave to enter or remain in the United Kingdom under paragraphs 128-193

199. Leave to enter or remain in the United Kingdom as the child of a person with limited leave to enter or remain in the United Kingdom under paragraphs 128-193 is to be refused if, in relation to an application for leave to enter, a valid United Kingdom entry clearance for entry in this capacity is not produced to the Immigration Officer on arrival or, in the case of an application for limited leave to remain, if the applicant was not admitted with a valid United Kingdom entry clearance for entry in this capacity or is unable to satisfy the Secretary of State that each of the requirements of paragraph 197 (i)-(vi) is met. An application for indefinite leave to remain in this category is to be refused if the applicant was not admitted with a valid United Kingdom entry clearance for entry in this capacity or is unable to satisfy the Secretary of State that each of the requirements of paragraph 197 (i)-(vi) is met or if indefinite leave to remain is not, at the same time, being granted to the person with limited leave to enter or remain under paragraphs 128-193.

COMMENTARY

These provisions apply to the child of a person who falls within the categories on page 162.

The person seeking to bring a child to the UK must show that:
(*a*) there will be
    (i) adequate accommodation for the person admitted for work, and children
    (ii) without recourse to public funds
(*b*) that they will be able to maintain themselves adequately without recourse to public funds.

Children will not be admitted under these rules to join or

accompany a parent if the spouse of that parent is not admitted under this rule, save as set out above.

Employment The spouse's and children's freedom to take employment is not restricted.

The child must be under 18 or have current leave to enter the UK. He must not be married, and must not have formed an independent family unit. He must not be leading an independent life. He must be accommodated and maintained adequately without recourse to public funds in accommodation which his parent(s) own or occupy exclusively.

Chapter 11

Persons Seeking to Enter or Remain in the United Kingdom as Businessmen, Self-employed Persons, Investors or Creative Artists

1 Business entry

PART 6:

PERSONS SEEKING TO ENTER OR REMAIN IN THE UNITED KINGDOM AS A BUSINESSMAN, SELF-EMPLOYED PERSON, INVESTOR, WRITER, COMPOSER OR ARTIST

PERSONS INTENDING TO ESTABLISH THEMSELVES IN BUSINESS

Requirements for leave to enter the United Kingdom as a person intending to establish himself in business

200. For the purpose of paragraphs 201–210 a business means an enterprise as:
— a sole trader; or
— a partnership; or
— a company registered in the United Kingdom.

201. The requirements to be met by a person seeking leave to enter the United Kingdom to establish himself in business are:
    (i) that he satisfies the requirements of either paragraph 202 or paragraph 203; and
    (ii) that he has not less than £200,000 of his own money under his control and disposable in the United Kingdom which is held in his own name and not by a trust or other investment vehicle and which he will be investing in the business in the United Kingdom; and
    (iii) that until his business provides him with an income he will have sufficient additional funds to maintain and accommodate himself

PERSONS SEEKING TO ENTER OR REMAIN IN THE UK

and any dependants without recourse to employment (other than his work for the business) or to public funds; and
(iv) that he will be actively involved full-time in trading or providing services on his own account or in partnership, or in the promotion and management of the company as a director; and
(v) that his level of financial investment will be proportional to his interest in the business; and
(vi) that he will have either a controlling or equal interest in the business and that any partnership or directorship does not amount to disguised employment; and
(vii) that he will be able to bear his share of liabilities; and
(viii) that there is a genuine need for his investment and services in the United Kingdom; and
(ix) that his share of the profits of the business will be sufficient to maintain and accommodate himself and any dependants without recourse to employment (other than his work for the business) or to public funds; and
(x) that he does not intend to supplement his business activities by taking or seeking employment in the United Kingdom other than his work for the business; and
(xi) that he holds a valid United Kingdom entry clearance for entry in this capacity.

202. Where a person intends to take over or join as a partner or director an existing business in the United Kingdom he will need, in addition to meeting the requirements at paragraph 201, to produce:
   (i) a written statement of the terms on which he is to take over or join the business; and
   (ii) audited accounts for the business for previous years; and
   (iii) evidence that his services and investment will result in a net increase in the employment provided by the business to persons settled here to the extent of creating at least 2 new full-time jobs.

203. Where a person intends to establish a new business in the United Kingdom he will need, in addition to meeting the requirements at paragraph 201 above, to produce evidence:
   (i) that he will be bringing into the country sufficient funds of his own to establish a business; and
   (ii) that the business will create full-time paid employment for at least 2 persons already settled in the United Kingdom.

Leave to enter the United Kingdom as a person seeking to establish himself in business

204. A person seeking leave to enter the United Kingdom to establish himself in business may be admitted for a period not exceeding 12 months with a condition restricting his freedom to take employment provided he

is able to produce to the Immigration Officer, on arrival, a valid United Kingdom entry clearance for entry in this capacity.

Refusal of leave to enter the United Kingdom as a person seeking to establish himself in business

205. Leave to enter the United Kingdom as a person seeking to establish himself in business is to be refused if a valid United Kingdom entry clearance for entry in this capacity is not produced to the Immigration Officer on arrival.

COMMENTARY

HC 395 provides a definition of 'a business'. It is an enterprise as a sole trader, or a partnership or a company registered in the UK. A passenger seeking admission for the purpose of establishing himself in the UK in business or in self-employment, whether on his own account or in partnership must hold a current entry clearance for that purpose. An application on Form IM2A and IM2C may be made to a British Consulate, embassy or High Commission.

The wording of the rule must be observed, and if one requirement is not fulfilled, it is not possible to claim that the overall purpose of it is satisfied and so gain admission (*R v IAT, ex p Mohammed Rahman* [1987] Imm AR 313 (CA)). Thus if the applicant does not have entry clearance, then no matter how much money he may be proposing to invest in the UK, he will not be granted leave to enter as a business person (*Falah Al-Hasani* (4670)). However, it is not necessary to identify in detail the exact nature of the business which it is intended to operate if leave is granted (*R v IAT, ex p Mawji* [1982] Imm AR 97). Of course in practice it will be difficult if not impossible to obtain leave unless fairly specific proposals are put forward (*Patel v ECO, Nairobi* [1987] Imm AR 116).

A passenger who has obtained an entry clearance should be admitted provided there are no general grounds for refusing entry (*Parekh v S of S* [1976] Imm AR 84). Admission will be for 12 months or less with a condition restricting his freedom to take employment. The applicant must show that he will be occupied full time running the business. This requirement may be satisfied if the applicant will be occupied full time running two businesses; it is a matter of degree. He must also show that there is a genuine need for his services and investment. The ECO should consider the criterion of likely commercial survival on a competitive basis to be an important factor, but also should consider the national benefit to trade and social need and the impact the business will have on already existing businesses (*Otani* (3224)). It will be helpful if the applicant has undertaken market research, and it may be difficult for the applicant to convince the ECO that there is a genuine need for his services and investment in a business without it (*Jivanlal Patel* (4895)). However, it is not essential, as the Home Office have taken the view that the way the test is applied depends upon the nature of the business. The main concern is whether the business is likely to be successful and whether it will make a profit (see *Business and Self-Employment: an Analysis of the Immigration Rules*—Part 1, by David Webb in INL&P Vol 7 No 1 (1993) p 12).

(a) His own money (para 201(ii))

The applicant must show that he will be bringing money of his own to put into the business and in no case should the amount of money to be invested by the applicant be less than £200,000. The rules require that the money should be under the applicant's control and disposable in the UK. The money must be held in his own name, and not by a trust or other investment vehicle. The money must be invested in the business in the UK. Evidence that this amount or more is under his control and disposable in the UK must be produced. The phrase 'money of his own' will include monies freely given to him by his wife for their mutual benefit over which he has unfettered control (*S of S v Ally* [1972] Imm AR 258). The rules require the investment of 'monies' which are immediately available at the time of the decision. The monies do not have to be lodged in a UK financial institution, but must be freely transferable to the UK, and not, for example, subject to exchange controls which prevent this. Whether the money is his own or not has to be looked at 'in the round' (*R v IAT, ex p Joseph* [1977] Imm AR 70). The intention of the rules is that the applicant should be the controller of the business; that he shall not 'front' for someone else; and that he shall have a stake in the business so that he has an incentive to make certain the business is viable (*R v IAT, ex p Peikazadi* [1979-80] Imm AR 191 at 193). If the applicant holds family monies it is important to consider the basis on which he holds those monies: whether as a free gift and therefore in his unfettered control and disposition, or as a loan, in which case there would have to be consideration as to the length of the term of the loan (*Peikazadi's* case). Where a long-term loan is made by a family the rule will be satisfied (*R v IAT, ex p Kwok on Tong* [1981] Imm AR 214). The rules do not contemplate that an entrant should be allowed to set up in business on borrowed money over which he has no control or ability to service the loan (*Haji v S of S* [1978] Imm AR 26). The rules will not be satisfied if the applicant simply inherits a business, worth in excess of £200,000 which is already established in the UK (*R v IAT, ex p Mohammed Rahman* (above)), nor will it be satisfied by money invested in a freehold property which may be difficult to sell or may be used for some other purpose. The money must be immediately available for investment at the time of the decision by the ECO (*ECO Rome v Hussain Rahman* [1991] Imm AR 102). The Home Office will normally expect the monies to be invested in the business within 12 months of admission (see *Business and Self-Employment: an Analysis of the Immigration Rules*—Part 1, by David Webb in INL&P Vol 7 No 1 (1993)). The monies must also be invested in the business and the rule will not be satisfied if a part of the monies required to be invested in the business is in fact invested for living expenses (*Devshi Patel* (above)).

(b) Maintenance and accommodation (para 201(iii), (ix) and (x))

The applicant must show that until the business provides him with an income he will have sufficient additional funds to maintain and accommodate himself and any dependants without recourse to public funds or employment other than work for the business. He must also show that once the business is established, his share of the profits will be sufficient to maintain and accommodate himself and any dependants without recourse to public funds or employment other than his work for the business. He must also show that he does not intend to supplement his business activities by taking or seeking employment in the UK other than his work for the business. He must show that he can obtain a livelihood without having to supplement his business activities by employment of any kind (*R v IAT, ex p Martin* [1972] Imm AR 275).

(c) Disguised employment (para 201(vi))

The proposed partnership or directorship must not amount to 'disguised employment'. On the facts in *Pritpal Singh v S of S* [1972] Imm AR 154 the IAT concluded that the appellant was in reality a paid employee. He was a director and secretary of a private limited company trading in sports equipment on a salary of £1,200 per annum. He loaned money to the company and held 15 £1 shares out of the company's share capital of £100. He received no share of the profits and there was no agreement in writing as to the future of the company. He could be removed from the board and from his secretarial duties at any time by the majority shareholders.

(d) Meeting liabilities (para 201(vii))

It is only those liabilities of a business which are reasonably foreseeable of which the applicant must be able to meet his share (*R v IAT, ex p Hirani* (2.7.81 Unrept Div Ct)). It is not necessary for an applicant who intends to join a partnership to show that he can meet all its liabilities, but he must be able to show that he could bear his proportionate share of the liabilities. Where the business is to be conducted through investment in a company, the Home Office have stated that ideally what is sought is an investment of £200,000 by way of share capital (see INL&P Vol 7 No 1, (1993), p 10).

(e) Taking over or joining an existing business (para 202)

In addition to the requirements under paragraph 201, the person who wishes to take over or join as a partner or a director an existing business in the UK will need to produce the terms of the take over, audited accounts for the business for the previous years and evidence that his services and investment will result in a net increase in the employment provided by the business to persons settled in the UK. He must produce evidence of the likely creation of at least two new jobs.

It is a mandatory requirement of the paragraph that the applicant provide accounts and evidence that they have been audited. If it is not satisfied, entry will be refused (*Seyed v S of S* [1987] Imm AR 303). There must be some evidence that the presence of the applicant will require the employment of employees who are settled in the UK (*Singh* (4620)). The creation of self-employment will not satisfy the rule (*Seyed* (above)). There must be evidence that normally the structure of the business is such that there will be in post those persons whose employment under a contract of service or apprenticeship has come about because of the establishment of the new business (*Jamnadas* (6597)).

Where a person is joining an existing partnership or company, the Home Office has stated in the past that if this does not result in the creation of new employment, but the maintenance of existing employment, the rule is not satisfied. The previous practice was that each case was examined in the light of all its circumstances, particularly the number of jobs involved, and leave could be granted (see INL&P (above), p 13). Such leave was exceptional and outside the immigration rules. It is not clear that this practice will continue under HC 395 para 202(iii). Thus an overseas business person would not be able to obtain leave under the rules to enter the UK to ensure that a business and its attendant jobs continue to exist if he could not show that there would also be a net increase in employment.

Establishing a new business A person who intends to establish a new business in the UK must satisfy the requirements of para 201 and must also produce evidence that he will be bringing into the country sufficient funds of his own to establish a business. He must also show that the business will create full-time paid employment for at least two persons already settled in the UK.

Concession relating to lawyers The Home Office on 21 March 1991 in a letter to a legal publisher stated that solicitors, barristers and consultants in overseas law coming to the UK to work, generally will not need to invest £200,000 as required by these rules. If they are coming as employees they will need permits, but if they are entering as partners or to set up practice, they are admitted on a concessionary basis outside the immigration rules. An applicant must have:

(*a*) entry clearance before travelling;
(*b*) the ability to maintain and accommodate himself without recourse to public funds or taking other work;
(*c*) evidence from the Law Society, Bar Council or Chambers of his eligibility to practise in the UK;
(*d*) evidence that he has permission from the Bar Council to practise from home if he is a barrister intending to do so;
(*e*) evidence of his qualifications, and a letter from the appropriate Law Society confirming that there is no objection to his application (in the case of consultants in foreign law);
(*f*) evidence of his financial means if he is intending to establish a new practice in the UK.

Such a concession may give rise to a legitimate expectation that its terms will be observed, and may in certain circumstances give rise to a judicial review of the decision to refuse entry.

2 Extensions

Requirements for an extension of stay in order to remain in business

206. The requirements for an extension of stay in order to remain in business in the United Kingdom are that the applicant can show:
   (i) that he entered the United Kingdom with a valid United Kingdom entry clearance as a businessman; and
   (ii) audited accounts which show the precise financial position of the business and which confirm that he has invested not less than £200,000 of his own money directly into the business in the United Kingdom; and
   (iii) that he is actively involved on a full-time basis in trading or providing services on his own account or in partnership or in the promotion and management of the company as a director; and
   (iv) that his level of financial investment is proportional to his interest in the business; and
   (v) that he has either a controlling or equal interest in the business and that any partnership or directorship does not amount to disguised employment; and
   (vi) that he is able to bear his share of any liability the business may incur; and
   (vii) that there is a genuine need for his investment and services in the United Kingdom; and
   (viii) (*a*) that where he has established a new business, new full-time paid employment has been created in the business for at least 2 persons settled in the United Kingdom; or
   (*b*) that where he has taken over or joined an existing business, his services and investment have resulted in a net increase in the employment provided by the business to persons settled here to the extent of creating at least 2 new full-time jobs; and
   (ix) that his share of the profits of the business is sufficient to maintain and accommodate him and any dependants without recourse to employment (other than his work for the business) or to public funds; and
   (x) that he does not and will not have to supplement his business activities by taking or seeking employment in the United Kingdom other than his work for the business.

Extension of stay in order to remain in business

207. An extension of stay in order to remain in business with a condition restricting his freedom to take employment may be granted for a period not exceeding 3 years provided the Secretary of State is satisfied that each of the requirements of paragraph 206 is met.

Refusal of extension of stay in order to remain in business

208. An extension of stay in order to remain in business is to be refused if the Secretary of State is not satisfied that each of the requirements of paragraph 206 is met.

Indefinite leave to remain for a person established in business

209. Indefinite leave to remain may be granted, on application, to a person established in business provided he:
    (i) has spent a continuous period of 4 years in the United Kingdom in this capacity and is still engaged in the business in question; and
    (ii) has met the requirements of paragraph 206 throughout the 4 year period; and
    (iii) submits audited accounts for the first 3 years of trading and management accounts for the 4th year.

Refusal of indefinite leave to remain for a person established in business

210. Indefinite leave to remain in the United Kingdom for a person established in business is to be refused if the Secretary of State is not satisfied that each of the requirements of paragraph 209 is met.

COMMENTARY

(f) Extensions and indefinite leave

The minimum capital requirement must be in the business by this stage, and there must be evidence of employees engaged and working (*Jamnadas* (6597)). The requirement is for employment to have been created for more than one person. The employment of the same person at different times did not satisfy the rule (*Fanous v S of S* [1993] Imm AR 200).

Persons given limited leave to enter or remain in some other capacity have no claim to establish themselves in the UK for the purpose of setting up in business whether on their own account or as partners in a new or existing business, or to be self-employed. Their applications for extension of stay or leave to remain for these purposes are to be refused (*Al-Hasani v S of S* [1986] Imm AR 363).

If the requirements set out above are met then the applicant's stay may be extended for a further period on a condition restricting his freedom to take employment, provided that the aggregate of his period of stay in the capacity of businessman or self-employed person does not exceed the qualifying period for settlement of four years. After four years' residence, the person may apply for permanent settlement.

3 Persons intending to establish themselves in business under provisions of EC Association Agreements

PERSONS INTENDING TO ESTABLISH THEMSELVES IN BUSINESS UNDER PROVISIONS OF EC ASSOCIATION AGREEMENTS

Requirements for leave to enter the United Kingdom as a person intending to establish himself in business under the provisions of an EC Association Agreement

211. For the purpose of paragraphs 212-223 a business means an enterprise as:
— a sole trader; or
— a partnership; or
— a company registered in the United Kingdom.

212. The requirements to be met by a person seeking leave to enter the United Kingdom to establish himself in business are that:
 (i) he satisfies the requirements of either paragraph 213 or paragraph 214; and
 (ii) the money he is putting into the business is under his control and sufficient to establish himself in business in the United Kingdom; and
 (iii) until his business provides him with an income he will have sufficient additional funds to maintain and accommodate himself and any dependants without recourse to employment (other than his work for the business) or to public funds; and
 (iv) his share of the profits of the business will be sufficient to maintain and accommodate himself and any dependants without recourse to employment (other than his work for the business) or to public funds; and
 (v) he does not intend to supplement his business activities by taking or seeking employment in the United Kingdom other than his work for the business; and
 (vi) he holds a valid United Kingdom entry clearance for entry in this capacity.

213. Where a person intends to establish himself in a company in the United Kingdom which he effectively controls he will need, in addition to meeting the requirements at paragraph 212, to show:
 (i) that he is a national of Hungary or Poland; and
 (ii) that he will have a controlling interest in the company; and
 (iii) that he will be actively involved in the promotion and management of the company; and
 (iv) that the company will be registered in the United Kingdom and be trading or providing services in the United Kingdom; and
 (v) that the company will be the owner of the assets of the business; and

(vi) where he is taking over an existing company, a written statement of the terms on which he is to take over the business and audited accounts for the business for previous years.

214. Where a person intends to establish himself in self-employment or in partnership in the United Kingdom he will need, in addition to meeting the requirements at 212 above, to show:
   (i) that he is a national of Poland; and
   (ii) that he will be actively involved in trading or providing services on his own account or in partnership in the United Kingdom; and
   (iii) that he, or he together with his partners, will be the owner of the assets of the business; and
   (iv) in the case of a partnership, that his part in the business will not amount to disguised employment; and
   (v) where he is taking over or joining an existing business a written statement of the terms on which he is to take over or join the business and audited accounts for the business for previous years.

Leave to enter the United Kingdom as a person seeking to establish himself in business under the provisions of an EC Association Agreement

215. A person seeking leave to enter the United Kingdom to establish himself in business may be admitted for a period not exceeding 12 months with a condition restricting his freedom to take employment provided he is able to produce to the Immigration Officer, on arrival, a valid United Kingdom entry clearance for entry in this capacity.

Refusal of leave to enter the United Kingdom as a person seeking to establish himself in business under the provisions of an EC Association Agreement

216. Leave to enter the United Kingdom as a person seeking to establish himself in business is to be refused if a valid United Kingdom entry clearance for entry in this capacity is not produced to the Immigration Officer on arrival.

COMMENTARY

A section was added to the immigration rules by HC 395. It provides for persons intending to establish themselves in pursuance of the EC Association Agreements. Nationals of Poland and Hungary are affected at present. They do not have to show that they are investing a minimum of £200,000 in the UK when entering as persons intending to establish themselves in companies in which they have controlling interests (para 213). The provisions of para 214 apply to nationals of Poland who intend to establish themselves in self-employment or a partnership. A national of Hungary who

PERSONS SEEKING TO ENTER OR REMAIN IN THE UK 177

intends to establish himself in self-employment or partnership must satisfy the requirements of paras 200 ff as a foreign national.

(a) A national of Hungary or Poland establishing himself in a company

The agreements between EC states and Hungary and Poland are declared to be Community Treaties for the purposes of s 1(2) of the ECA 1972 (The European Communities (Definition of Treaties) (European Agreement establishing an Association between the European Communities and their Member States and the Republic of Hungary) Order 1992 (SI 1992 No 2871), and Poland (SI 1992 No 2872)). The aims of the Treaty with Hungary are:
  (*a*) to provide a framework for political dialogue;
  (*b*) a free trade area;
  (*c*) the promotion of economic, financial and cultural co-operation; and
  (*d*) supporting the efforts of Hungary to become a market economy.

The agreement between EC states and Poland is declared to be a Community Treaty for the purposes of s 1(2) of the ECA 1972 (The European Communities (Definition of Treaties) (European Agreement establishing an Association between the European Communities and their Member States and the Republic of Poland (SI 1992 No 2872)). The aims of the Treaty with Poland are:
  (*a*) to provide a framework for political dialogue;
  (*b*) the promotion of cultural, trade and economic relations;
  (*c*) the provision of financial and technical assistance; and
  (*d*) the creation of an appropriate framework for Poland's gradual integration into the EC.

As a result of these agreements a national of one of these states does not have to show that he will be investing at least £200,000 of his own money in the company, or that he will be occupied full time in the running of the company. He does have to show that he will be actively involved in the promotion and management of the company (para 213(iv)) and he must show that he does not intend to supplement his business activities by taking or seeking employment in the UK other than his work for the business (para 212(v). He does not need to show that his services and investment are needed and will create paid full-time employment in the company for persons already settled in the UK. Where taking over or joining as a partner an existing company he does not need to show evidence that the creation of full-time employment will result in a corresponding increase in the numbers of employees of the company.

Section 2 of the ECA 1972 provides all such rights, powers, liabilities, obligations and restrictions from time to time created or arising by or under the Treaties and all such remedies and procedures from time to time provided for under the Treaties as in accordance with the Treaties are, without further enactment, to be given legal effect or used in the UK. They are to be recognised and available in the UK and shall be enforced as enforceable Community rights. Quite apart from their introduction by domestic legislation, the rights created under the Agreements may have direct effect where they are clear and precise enough. One of the requirements of HC 395 is that a person relying on the rule must show that he is a national of the relevant country. As a result of the Association Agreement's status as part of the EC legal framework, the question of a person's nationality is a matter of law, but it is to be determined by the national law of the relevant country. Thus a person claiming to be Polish could rely on provisions of Polish nationality law to prove his nationality. Further an error by the S of S regarding a person's nationality would be an error of law.

Nationals of Poland who are self employed must comply with the provisions of paragraph 214. A national of Poland is not required to show that he will invest at least £200,000 of his own money in the business. He does not need to show that he will be occupied full time in the running of the business, nor that his services and investment are needed and will create new paid full time employment in the business for persons already settled in the UK.

Extensions and indefinite leave

Requirements for an extension of stay in order to remain in business under the provisions of an EC Association Agreement

217. The requirements for an extension of stay in order to remain in business in the United Kingdom are that the applicant can show that:
    (i) he has established himself in business in the United Kingdom; and
    (ii) his share of the profits of the business is sufficient to maintain and accommodate himself and any dependants without recourse to employment (other than his work for the business) or to public funds; and
    (iii) he does not and will not supplement his business activities by taking or seeking employment in the United Kingdom other than his work for the business; and

PERSONS SEEKING TO ENTER OR REMAIN IN THE UK

(iv) in addition he satisfies the requirements of either paragraph 218 or paragraph 219.

218. Where a person has established himself in a company in the United Kingdom which he effectively controls he will need, in addition to meeting the requirements at paragraph 217 above, to show:
  (i) that he is a national of Hungary or Poland; and
  (ii) that he is actively involved in the promotion and management of the company; and
  (iii) that he has a controlling interest in the company; and
  (iv) that the company is registered in the United Kingdom and trading or providing services in the United Kingdom; and
  (v) that the company is the owner of the assets of the business; and
  (vi) the current financial position in the form of audited accounts for the company.

219. Where a person has established himself as a sole trader or in partnership in the United Kingdom he will need, in addition to meeting the requirements at 217 above, to show:
  (i) that he is a national of Poland; and
  (ii) that he is actively involved in trading or providing services on his own account or in partnership in the United Kingdom; and
  (iii) that he, or he together with his partners, is the owner of the assets of the business; and
  (iv) in the case of a partnership, that his part in the business does not amount to disguised employment; and
  (v) the current financial position in the form of audited accounts for the business.

Extension of stay in order to remain in business under the provisions of an EC Association Agreement

220. An extension of stay in order to remain in business with a condition restricting his freedom to take employment may be granted for a period not exceeding 3 years provided the Secretary of State is satisfied that each of the requirements of paragraphs 217 and 218 or 219 is met.

Refusal of extension of stay in order to remain in business under the provisions of an EC Association Agreement

221. An extension of stay in order to remain in business is to be refused if the Secretary of State is not satisfied that each of the requirements of paragraphs 217 and 218 or 219 is met.

Indefinite leave to remain for a person established in business under the provisions of an EC Association Agreement

222. Indefinite leave to remain may be granted, on application, to a person established in business provided he:

(i) has spent a continuous period of 4 years in the United Kingdom in this capacity and is still so engaged; and
(ii) has met the requirements of paragraphs 217 and 218 or 219 throughout the 4 years; and
(iii) submits audited accounts for the first 3 years of trading and management accounts for the 4th year.

Refusal of indefinite leave to remain for a person established in business under the provisions of an EC Association Agreement

223. Indefinite leave to remain in the United Kingdom for a person established in business is to be refused if the Secretary of State is not satisfied that each of the requirements of paragraph 222 is met.

COMMENTARY

A person who has obtained leave to enter may also obtain an extension of stay in order to remain in business under the terms of an EC Association Agreement. A national of either Poland or Hungary must show that he has established himself in business in the UK. He must also show that his share of the profits is sufficient to maintain and accommodate him and his dependants without recourse to public funds or employment other than his work for the business. He must show that he does not supplement his business activities by seeking or taking employment in the UK. When seeking an extension of his leave in this capacity he does not need to show that he entered the UK with an entry clearance as a business person, nor satisfy the investment criterion, nor the employment creation criteria. He does not need to show that he will be occupied full time in running the company.

The Association Agreements require separate provision to be made under the immigration rules for nationals of Poland and nationals of Hungary. A Hungarian needs to satisfy the capital investment requirement rule if he is seeking entry or an extension to be self-employed. If he effectively controls a company which he has established in the UK he will not need to satisfy the capital investment rule. It appears that nationals of either Poland or Hungary entering in some other capacity can apply for an extension of their leave to establish themselves in business. The rules do not require an applicant to show that he entered with an entry clearance for the purpose of establishing himself in business. Such a person has to show that he has established a business.

Extensions: nationals of Poland (para 219) He does not need to have invested at least £200,000 of his own money in the business. He does not need to show that he will be occupied full time in the running of the business, nor that his services and investment are needed and will create new paid full-time employment in the business for persons already settled in the UK. He does not have to produce evidence that his creation of new full-time employment will result in a corresponding increase in the numbers of employees of the business.

Indefinite leave to remain The applicant must have spent a continuous period of four years in the UK established in business under an EC Association Agreement. For the whole of the four years he must have satisfied the requirements of the rules. He must also submit audited accounts for the first three years of trading and management accounts for the fourth year.

4 Investors

(a) Requirements for leave to enter the United Kingdom as an investor

INVESTORS

Requirements for leave to enter the United Kingdom as an investor

224. The requirements to be met by a person seeking leave to enter the United Kingdom as an investor are that he:
  (i) has money of his own under his control and disposable in the United Kingdom amounting to no less than £1 million; and
  (ii) intends to invest not less than £750,000 of his capital in the United Kingdom by way of United Kingdom Government bonds, share capital or loan capital in active and trading United Kingdom registered companies (other than those principally engaged in property investment and excluding investment by the applicant by way of deposits with a bank, building society or other enterprise whose normal course of business includes the acceptance of deposits); and
  (iii) intends to make the United Kingdom his main home; and
  (iv) is able to maintain and accommodate himself and any dependants without taking employment (other than self-employment or business) or recourse to public funds; and
  (v) holds a valid United Kingdom entry clearance for entry in this capacity.

Leave to enter as an investor

225. A person seeking leave to enter the United Kingdom as an investor may be admitted for a period not exceeding 12 months with a restriction on his right to take employment, provided he is able to produce to the

Immigration Officer, on arrival, a valid United Kingdom entry clearance for entry in this capacity.

Refusal of leave to enter as an investor

226. Leave to enter as an investor is to be refused if a valid United Kingdom entry clearance for entry in this capacity is not produced to the Immigration Officer on arrival.

Requirements for an extension of stay as an investor

227. The requirements for an extension of stay as an investor are that the applicant:
   (i) entered the United Kingdom with a valid United Kingdom entry clearance as an investor; and
   (ii) has no less than £1 million of his own money under his control in the United Kingdom; and
   (iii) has invested not less than £750,000 of his capital in the United Kingdom on the terms set out in paragraph 224(ii) above and intends to maintain that investment on the terms set out in paragraph 224(ii); and
   (iv) has made the United Kingdom his main home; and
   (v) is able to maintain and accommodate himself and any dependants without taking employment (other than his self-employment or business) or recourse to public funds.

Extension of stay as an investor

228. An extension of stay as an investor, with a restriction on the taking of employment, may be granted for a maximum period of 3 years, provided the Secretary of State is satisfied that each of the requirements of paragraph 227 is met.

Refusal of extension of stay as an investor

229. An extension of stay as an investor is to be refused if the Secretary of State is not satisfied that each of the requirements of paragraph 227 is met.

Indefinite leave to remain for an investor

230. Indefinite leave to remain may be granted, on application, to a person admitted as an investor provided he:
   (i) has spent a continuous period of 4 years in the United Kingdom in this capacity; and
   (ii) has met the requirements of paragraph 227 throughout the 4 year period including the requirement as to the investment of £750,000 and continues to do so.

Refusal of indefinite leave to remain for an investor

231. Indefinite leave to remain in the United Kingdom for an investor is to be refused if the Secretary of State is not satisfied that each of the requirements of paragraph 230 is met.

COMMENTARY

The rules introduce a new category of investor in order to enable persons who wish to invest substantial amounts in the UK to engage in business. Unfortunately the sums involved are so large that the rules will only benefit a very few people and may act as a disincentive to investment in the UK from those who do not have such large amounts of capital.

There is no requirement that the investor has a close connection with the UK. He must have £1 million or more under his control and disposal in the UK. He must have the intention to invest not less than £750,000 of his capital in the UK by way of UK Government Bonds, share capital or loan capital in active and trading UK registered companies. He must intend to make the UK his home. He must have an entry clearance for the purpose for which he seeks entry.

(b) money of his own under his control

It is insufficient for the purposes of this rule that the applicant has funds available to him, but which are not his in the sense of his having a right which can be enforced in law against anyone. Thus access to a father's wealth will not meet the requirements (*R v IAT, ex p Chiew* [1981] Imm AR 102). Income from a guaranteed pension may be taken into account (*S of S v Raval* [1975] Imm AR 72), as may income from a separation agreement, enforceable abroad (*S of S v Rohr* [1983] Imm AR 156).

(c) 'maintenance'

The provision of accommodation (whether free or subsidised) and keep by relatives of the applicant should be disregarded (*S of S v Evgeniou* [1978] Imm AR 89). The financial position must be assessed on its own without taking into account any assistance provided by the applicant's family (*Randhawa v S of S* [1972] Imm AR 158; *ECO Canberra v Ward* [1975] Imm AR 129).

In order to obtain settlement the investor must for the period of four years have £750,000 invested in the UK in Government Bonds, share or loan capital in UK companies.

5 Creative artists

WRITERS, COMPOSERS AND ARTISTS

Requirements for leave to enter the United Kingdom as a writer, composer or artist

232. The requirements to be met by a person seeking leave to enter the United Kingdom as a writer, composer or artist are that he:
   (i) has established himself outside the United Kingdom as a writer, composer or artist primarily engaged in producing original work which has been published (other than exclusively in newspapers or magazines), performed or exhibited for its literary, musical or artistic merit; and
   (ii) does not intend to work except as related to his self-employment as a writer, composer or artist; and
   (iii) has for the preceding year been able to maintain and accommodate himself and any dependants from his own resources without working except as a writer, composer or artist; and
   (iv) will be able to maintain and accommodate himself and any dependants from his own resources without working except as a writer, composer or artist and without recourse to public funds; and
   (v) holds a valid United Kingdom entry clearance for entry in this capacity.

Leave to enter as a writer, composer or artist

233. A person seeking leave to enter the United Kingdom as a writer, composer or artist may be admitted for a period not exceeding 12 months, subject to a condition restricting his freedom to take employment, provided he is able to produce to the Immigration Officer, on arrival, a valid United Kingdom entry clearance for entry in this capacity.

Refusal of leave to enter as a writer, composer or artist

234. Leave to enter as a writer, composer or artist is to be refused if a valid United Kingdom entry clearance for entry in this capacity is not produced to the Immigration Officer on arrival.

Requirements for an extension of stay as a writer, composer or artist

235. The requirements for an extension of stay as a writer, composer or artist are that the applicant:
   (i) entered the United Kingdom with a valid United Kingdom entry clearance as a writer, composer or artist; and
   (ii) meets the requirements of paragraph 232 (ii)–(iv).

Extension of stay as a writer, composer or artist

236. An extension of stay as a writer, composer or artist must be granted for a period not exceeding 3 years with a restriction on his freedom to

take employment, provided the Secretary of State is satisfied that each of the requirements of paragraph 235 is met.

Refusal of extension of stay as a writer, composer or artist

237. An extension of stay as a writer, composer or artist is to be refused if the Secretary of State is not satisfied that each of the requirements of paragraph 235 is met.

Indefinite leave to remain for a writer, composer or artist

238. Indefinite leave to remain may be granted, on application, to a person admitted as a writer, composer or artist provided he:
   (i) has spent a continuous period of 4 years in the United Kingdom in this capacity; and
   (ii) has met the requirements of paragraph 235 throughout the 4 year period.

Refusal of indefinite leave to remain for a writer, composer or artist

239. Indefinite leave to remain for a writer, composer or artist is to be refused if the Secretary of State is not satisfied that each of the requirements of paragraph 238 is met.

COMMENTARY

HC 395 introduces the sub-category of 'composer' to this category. HC 395 also requires the person seeking entry or leave to remain to show that he has established himself abroad before applying. The applicant will only be admitted as a writer, composer or an artist if he can show, on the balance of probabilities, that he will be able to generate income from his work. He must show that for the preceding year before entry he has been able to maintain and accommodate himself and any dependants from his own resourses without working except as a writer. However it is not necessary to show that his work has been profitable in the past (*Boehm-Bradley v Visa Officer, Washington* [1986] Imm AR 305). It will not be enough if he can only show that he will receive support from his family (*S of S v Jones* [1978] Imm AR 161). He must be able to show that he will be able to maintain and accommodate himself and any dependants from his own resources without working save as a writer, composer or artist. In some cases it will be difficult to draw the line between a self-employed journalist who writes mainly promotional articles, and a self-employed writer who is engaged upon small literary works. If the writer is living off the proceeds of his own composition he will be classified as a writer (*Shevey v S of S* [1987] Imm AR 453). He must, however, show that he has established himself outside the UK as a writer engaged in producing original work which has been published (other than exclusively in newspapers or magazines).

The word 'artist' is a reference to persons in the category of painter or sculptor rather than to singers (*S of S v Stillwaggon* [1975] Imm AR 132). Such entertainers must apply for work permits.

The following evidence should be provided in support of the application:
 (a) the applicant's curriculum vitae;
 (b) bank statements;
 (c) other evidence of his resources;
 (d) invoices from past sales;
 (e) examples of past work;
 (f) evidence relating to present and future commissions, stating the number per annum, and the approximate fee per work; and
 (g) letters of recommendation by past tutors or recipients of work.

(For a fuller discussion see INL & P April 1990 p 73, *Practical Problems for Businessmen: Writers and Artists* by P Trott).

The effect of the new rule will in practice be that only established artists will be able to qualify for entry.

6 Spouses of persons with limited leave to enter or remain under paras 200–239

SPOUSES OF PERSONS WITH LIMITED LEAVE TO ENTER OR REMAIN UNDER PARAGRAPHS 200–239

Requirements for leave to enter or remain as the spouse of a person with limited leave to enter or remain under paragraphs 200–239

240. The requirements to be met by a person seeking leave to enter or remain in the United Kingdom as the spouse of a person with limited leave to enter or remain in the United Kingdom under paragraphs 200–239 are that:
 (i) the applicant is married to a person with limited leave to enter or remain in the United Kingdom under paragraphs 200–239; and
 (ii) each of the parties intends to live with the other as his or her spouse during the applicant's stay and the marriage is subsisting; and
 (iii) there will be adequate accommodation for the parties and any dependants without recourse to public funds in accommodation which they own or occupy exclusively; and

(iv) the parties will be able to maintain themselves and any dependants adequately without recourse to public funds; and
(v) the applicant does not intend to stay in the United Kingdom beyond any period of leave granted to his spouse; and
(vi) if seeking leave to enter, the applicant holds a valid United Kingdom entry clearance for entry in this capacity or, if seeking leave to remain, was admitted with a valid United Kingdom entry clearance for entry in this capacity.

Leave to enter or remain as the spouse of a person with limited leave to enter or remain in the United Kingdom under paragraphs 200-239

241. A person seeking leave to enter or remain in the United Kingdom as the spouse of a person with limited leave to enter or remain in the United Kingdom under paragraphs 200-239 may be given leave to enter or remain in the United Kingdom for a period of leave not in excess of that granted to the person with limited leave to enter or remain under paragraphs 200-239 provided that, in relation to an application for leave to enter, he is able, on arrival, to produce to the Immigration Officer a valid United Kingdom entry clearance for entry in this capacity or, in the case of an application for limited leave to remain, he was admitted with a valid United Kingdom entry clearance for entry in this capacity and is able to satisfy the Secretary of State that each of the requirements of paragraph 240(i)-(v) is met. An application for indefinite leave to remain in this category may be granted provided the applicant was admitted with a valid United Kingdom entry clearance for entry in this capacity and is able to satisfy the Secretary of State that each of the requirements of paragraph 240(i)-(v) is met and provided indefinite leave to remain is, at the same time, being granted to the person with limited leave to remain under paragraphs 200-239.

Refusal of leave to enter or remain as the spouse of a person with limited leave to enter or remain in the United Kingdom under paragraphs 200-239

242. Leave to enter or remain in the United Kingdom as the spouse of a person with limited leave to enter or remain in the United Kingdom under paragraphs 200-239 is to be refused if, in relation to an application for leave to enter, a valid United Kingdom entry clearance for entry in this capacity is not produced to the Immigration Officer on arrival or, in the case of an application for limited leave to remain, if the applicant was not admitted with a valid United Kingdom entry clearance for entry in this capacity or is unable to satisfy the Secretary of State that each of the requirements of paragraph 240(i)-(v) is met. An application for indefinite leave to remain in this category is to be refused if the applicant was not admitted with a valid United Kingdom entry clearance for entry in this capacity or is unable to satisfy the Secretary of State that each of the requirements of paragraph 240(i)-(v) is met or if indefinite leave to remain is not, at the same time, being granted to the person with limited leave to remain under paragraphs 200-239.

COMMENTARY

Spouses of the following are affected by these rules:
(a) persons intending to establish themselves in business;
(b) persons intending to establish themselves in business under provisions of EC Association Agreements;
(c) investors;
(d) writers, composers and artists.

A person entering as the spouse of a person in one of these categories must show that each of the parties intends to live with the other as his spouse during the applicant's stay and that the marriage is subsisting. For accommodation and maintenance requirements see page 211. He must have an entry clearance for this purpose.

7 Children of persons with limited leave to enter or remain under paragraphs 200–239

CHILDREN OF PERSONS WITH LIMITED LEAVE TO ENTER OR REMAIN UNDER PARAGRAPHS 200–239

Requirements for leave to enter or remain as the child of a person with limited leave to enter or remain in the United Kingdom under paragraphs 200–239

243. The requirements to be met by a person seeking leave to enter or remain in the United Kingdom as a child of a person with limited leave to enter or remain in the United Kingdom under paragraphs 200–239 are that:
  (i) he is the child of a parent who has leave to enter or remain in the United Kingdom under paragraphs 200–239; and
  (ii) he is under the age of 18 or has current leave to enter or remain in this capacity; and
  (iii) he is unmarried, has not formed an independent family unit and is not leading an independent life; and
  (iv) he can and will be maintained and accommodated adequately without recourse to public funds in accommodation which his parent(s) own or occupy exclusively; and
  (v) he will not stay in the United Kingdom beyond any period of leave granted to his parent(s); and
  (vi) both parents are being or have been admitted to or allowed to remain in the United Kingdom save where:
    (a) the parent he is accompanying or joining is his sole surviving parent; or
    (b) the parent he is accompanying or joining has had sole responsibility for his upbringing; or

PERSONS SEEKING TO ENTER OR REMAIN IN THE UK

(c) there are serious and compelling family or other considerations which make exclusion from the United Kingdom undesirable and suitable arrangements have been made for his care; and

(vii) if seeking leave to enter, he holds a valid United Kingdom entry clearance for entry in this capacity or, if seeking leave to remain, was admitted with a valid United Kingdom entry clearance for entry in this capacity.

Leave to enter or remain as the child of a person with limited leave to enter or remain in the United Kingdom under paragraphs 200–239

244. A person seeking leave to enter or remain in the United Kingdom as the child of a person with limited leave to enter or remain in the United Kingdom under paragraphs 200–239 may be admitted to or allowed to remain in the United Kingdom for the same period of leave as that granted to the person given limited leave to enter or remain under paragraphs 200–239 provided that, in relation to an application for leave to enter, he is able to produce to the Immigration Officer, on arrival, a valid United Kingdom entry clearance for entry in this capacity or, in the case of an application for limited leave to remain, he was admitted with a valid United Kingdom entry clearance for entry in this capacity and is able to satisfy the Secretary of State that each of the requirements of paragraph 243(i)–(vi) is met. An application for indefinite leave to remain in this category may be granted provided the applicant was admitted with a valid United Kingdom entry clearance for entry in this capacity and is able to satisfy the Secretary of State that each of the requirements of paragraph 243(i)–(vi) is met and provided indefinite leave to remain is, at the same time, being granted to the person with limited leave to remain under paragraphs 200–239.

Refusal of leave to enter or remain as the child of a person with limited leave to enter or remain in the United Kingdom under paragraphs 200–239

245. Leave to enter or remain in the United Kingdom as the child of a person with limited leave to enter or remain in the United Kingdom under paragraphs 200–239 is to be refused if, in relation to an application for leave to enter, a valid United Kingdom entry clearance for entry in this capacity is not produced to the Immigration Officer on arrival or, in the case of an application for limited leave to remain, if the applicant was not admitted with a valid United Kingdom entry clearance for entry in this capacity or is unable to satisfy the Secretary of State that each of the requirements of paragraph 243(i)–(vi) is met. An application for indefinite leave to remain in this capacity is to be refused if the applicant was not admitted with a valid United Kingdom entry clearance for entry in this capacity or is unable to satisfy the Secretary of State that each of the requirements of paragraph 243(i)–(vi) is met or if indefinite leave to remain is not, at the same time, being granted to the person with limited leave to remain under paragraphs 200–239.

COMMENTARY

The children of the following are provided for by these paragraphs:
   (a) persons intending to establish themselves in business;
   (b) persons intending to establish themselves in business under provisions of EC Association Agreements;
   (c) investors;
   (d) writers, composers and artists.

The accommodation which must be provided for him must be accommodation which his parents either own exclusively or occupy exclusively. For 'sole responsibility', see page 225. For 'serious and compelling family or other considerations', see page 226. He must have an entry clearance for this purpose.

8 Persons exercising rights of access to a child resident in the UK

PART 7:

OTHER CATEGORIES

PERSONS EXERCISING RIGHTS OF ACCESS TO A CHILD RESIDENT IN THE UNITED KINGDOM

Requirements for leave to enter the United Kingdom as a person exercising rights of access to a child resident in the United Kingdom

246. The requirements to be met by a person seeking leave to enter the United Kingdom to exercise access rights to a child resident in the United Kingdom are that he:
   (i) produces evidence that a court in the United Kingdom has granted him access rights to his child; and
   (ii) is seeking leave to enter for the purpose of exercising access rights to his child; and
   (iii) is either divorced or legally separated from the other parent of the child; and
   (iv) intends to leave the United Kingdom at the expiry of his leave to enter; and
   (v) does not intend to take employment in the United Kingdom; and
   (vi) does not intend to produce goods or provide services within the United Kingdom, including the selling of goods or services direct to members of the public; and
   (vii) will maintain and accommodate himself and any dependants adequately out of resources available to him without recourse to public funds or taking employment; or will, with any dependants,

PERSONS SEEKING TO ENTER OR REMAIN IN THE UK 191

    be maintained and accommodated adequately by relatives or friends; and
(viii) can meet the cost of the onward or return journey; and
 (ix) holds a valid United Kingdom entry clearance for entry in this capacity.

Leave to enter as a person exercising rights of access to a child resident in the United Kingdom

247. A person seeking leave to enter the United Kingdom to exercise rights of access to a child resident in the United Kingdom may be granted leave to enter for a period which will enable him to exercise his access rights but in any case for no longer than 12 months provided he is able to produce to the Immigration Officer, on arrival, a valid United Kingdom entry clearance for entry in this capacity. Leave to enter is to be subject to a condition prohibiting employment.

Refusal of leave to enter as a person exercising rights of access to a child resident in the United Kingdom

248. Leave to enter as a person exercising rights of access to a child resident in the United Kingdom is to be refused if a valid United Kingdom entry clearance for entry in this capacity is not produced to the Immigration Officer on arrival.

COMMENTARY

HC 395 introduces this category as a result of the ECtHR judgment in *Yousef* (App No 14830/89 np). In that case the Court found that the UK was in breach of Article 13 of the Convention (the right of redress). HC 395 provides for a parent who is either divorced or legally separated to come to the UK for up to 12 months for the purpose of exercising access rights granted by a court in the UK to a child resident in the UK. Immigration enforcement often takes place in the context of family breakdown or itself results in family breakdown. It is difficult to see how a person who has been removed could benefit from this rule in practice, given the general grounds for refusal (see Chapter 13).

9 Holders of special vouchers

HOLDERS OF SPECIAL VOUCHERS

Requirements for indefinite leave to enter as the holder of a special voucher

249. The requirements for indefinite leave to enter as the holder of a special voucher are that the person concerned:
    (i) is a British Overseas citizen; and

(ii) is in possession of a special voucher issued to him by a British Government representative overseas or a valid United Kingdom entry clearance for settlement in the United Kingdom in this capacity.

Indefinite leave to enter as the holder of a special voucher

250. A British Overseas citizen may be granted indefinite leave to enter the United Kingdom provided he is able to produce to the Immigration Officer, on arrival, either a special voucher issued to him by a British Government representative or a valid United Kingdom entry clearance for settlement in this capacity.

Refusal of indefinite leave to enter as the holder of a special voucher

251. Indefinite leave to enter as the holder of a special voucher is to be refused if neither a special voucher issued by a British Government representative nor a valid United Kingdom entry clearance for settlement in this capacity is produced to the Immigration Officer on arrival.

Requirements for indefinite leave to enter as the spouse or child of a special voucher holder

252. The requirements for indefinite leave to enter the United Kingdom as the spouse or child of a special voucher holder are that the person concerned:
    (i) is in possession of a valid United Kingdom entry clearance for settlement in the United Kingdom in this capacity; and
    (ii) can and will be maintained and accommodated adequately by the special voucher holder without recourse to public funds.

Indefinite leave to enter as the spouse or child of a special voucher holder

253. Indefinite leave to enter as the spouse or child of a special voucher holder may be granted provided a valid United Kingdom entry clearance for settlement is produced to the Immigration Officer on arrival.

Refusal of indefinite leave to enter as the spouse or child of a special voucher holder

254. Indefinite leave to enter as the spouse or child of a special voucher holder is to be refused if a valid United Kingdom entry clearance for settlement is not produced to the Immigration Officer on arrival.

COMMENTARY

There is no claim as of right to a voucher, nor appeal against the refusal to issue one as it is not an entry clearance for the purposes of s 33(1) of the 1971 Act (*R v ECO Bombay, ex p Amin* [1983]

2 AC 818). The following conditions must be fulfilled before a special voucher is issued:
(a) A male applicant must be over 18 to qualify as a 'head of household';
(b) a female must be over 18; and
   (i) single or widowed or divorced; or
   (ii) married to a man who, for medical reasons, is not able to act as the 'head of household';
in order to qualify as the 'head of household';
(c) the applicant must have no other citizenship;
(d) the applicant must have a connection with East Africa;
(e) the applicant must be 'under pressure' to leave his country of residence;
(f) the applicant must have no other country to which he could go save the UK;
(g) the applicant must have an intention to settle in the UK.

If the applicant or his parents were born in Kenya, Tanzania, Uganda, Malawi, Zambia, Zimbabwe or Aden or have been settled at any time in one of those countries, he will be deemed (a) as having a connection with East Africa; and (b) as being under pressure to emigrate if he normally resides in Kenya, Tanzania, Malawi, Zambia or India.

A refusal to issue a special voucher is amenable to judicial review in certain circumstances. A guidance leaflet defining the conditions on which special vouchers will be issued has been published. Such a leaflet gives rise to a legitimate expectation that its terms will be observed. Moreover a failure to follow its own guidance will lay the decision maker open to the criticism that he acted inconsistently. The term 'dependant' is to be construed by reference to the various classes of other relatives and dependants defined in the immigration rules (*Shah* (4618)). These are spouses, children, children over 18 and parents, grandparents and other relatives. Unmarried children under 25 will also be admitted under the terms of the guidance if they are fully dependent upon the BOC at the time the voucher is offered. Vouchers are issued by British representatives overseas. The scheme is administered by the Foreign and Commonwealth Office, not the Home Office. A guidance leaflet has been issued for persons applying for a special voucher, available from the Home Office (Form OF2). Vouchers cannot be issued in the UK (*Shah v S of S* [1972] Imm AR 56). The refusal to issue a voucher is not appealable under the 1971 Act (*R v ECO, ex p Amin* [1983] 2 AC 818).

10 EEA nationals and their families

The paragraphs (255–262) relating to EEA nationals and their families are set out in Chapter 15 together with a detailed discussion of the applicable EU law. HC 395 sets out the criteria in national law for EEA nationals and their family members to obtain an EEA family permit, and settlement. These provisions supplement the provisions of the Immigration (European Economic Area) Order 1994.

11 Retired persons of independent means

RETIRED PERSONS OF INDEPENDENT MEANS

Requirements for leave to enter the United Kingdom as a retired person of independent means

263. The requirements to be met by a person seeking leave to enter the United Kingdom as a retired person of independent means are that he:
  (i) is at least 60 years old; and
  (ii) has under his control and disposable in the United Kingdom an income of his own of not less than £25,000 per annum; and
  (iii) is able and willing to maintain and accommodate himself and any dependants indefinitely in the United Kingdom from his own resources with no assistance from any other person and without taking employment or having recourse to public funds; and
  (iv) can demonstrate a close connection with the United Kingdom; and
  (v) intends to make the United Kingdom his main home; and
  (vi) holds a valid United Kingdom entry clearance for entry in this capacity.

Leave to enter as a retired person of independent means

264. A person seeking leave to enter the United Kingdom as a retired person of independent means may be admitted subject to a condition prohibiting employment for a period not exceeding 4 years, provided he is able to produce to the Immigration Officer, on arrival, a valid United Kingdom entry clearance for entry in this capacity.

Refusal of leave to enter as a retired person of independent means

265. Leave to enter as a retired person of independent means is to be refused if a valid United Kingdom entry clearance for entry in this capacity is not produced to the Immigration Officer on arrival.

PERSONS SEEKING TO ENTER OR REMAIN IN THE UK

Requirements for an extension of stay as a retired person of independent means

266. The requirements for an extension of stay as a retired person of independent means are that the applicant:
   (i) entered the United Kingdom with a valid United Kingdom entry clearance as a retired person of independent means; and
   (ii) meets the requirements of paragraph 263(ii)–(iv); and
   (iii) has made the United Kingdom his main home.

Extension of stay as a retired person of independent means

267. An extension of stay as a retired person of independent means, with a prohibition on the taking of employment, may be granted so as to bring the person's stay in this category up to a maximum of 4 years in aggregate, provided the Secretary of State is satisfied that each of the requirements of paragraph 266 is met.

Refusal of extension of stay as a retired person of independent means

268. An extension of stay as a retired person of independent means is to be refused if the Secretary of State is not satisfied that each of the requirements of paragraph 266 is met.

Indefinite leave to remain for a retired person of independent means

269. Indefinite leave to remain may be granted, on application, to a person admitted as a retired person of independent means provided he:
   (i) has spent a continuous period of 4 years in the United Kingdom in this capacity; and
   (ii) has met the requirements of paragraph 266 throughout the 4 year period and continues to do so.

Refusal of indefinite leave to remain for a retired person of independent means

270. Indefinite leave to remain in the United Kingdom for a retired person of independent means is to be refused if the Secretary of State is not satisfied that each of the requirements of paragraph 266 is met.

COMMENTARY

HC 395 limits the persons of independent means category to retired persons. Thus the minimum age for this category is now 60. A further change brought about by these rules is that a person must now have an income of not less than £25,000 per year. Under HC 251 an applicant might be admitted if he had a capital sum of £200,000 or more.

Close connection In addition to satisfying the immigration officer of the maintenance and accommodation requirements, and investment requirements relating to investors, the applicant must satisfy him that he has a close connection with the UK. A very long period of residence in the UK may in itself amount to a close connection (*R v IAT, ex p Zandfani* [1984] Imm AR 213). In most cases it will be relevant whether the applicant has formed a strong sense of belonging and community as a result of his residence in the UK. However, possessions or business connections or previously having held British nationality may be sufficient (see, for example, *S of S v Rohr* [1983] Imm AR 156).

12 Spouses of persons with limited leave to enter or remain in the UK as retired persons of independent means

SPOUSES OF PERSONS WITH LIMITED LEAVE TO ENTER OR REMAIN IN THE UNITED KINGDOM AS RETIRED PERSONS OF INDEPENDENT MEANS

Requirements for leave to enter or remain as the spouse of a person with limited leave to enter or remain in the United Kingdom as a retired person of independent means

271. The requirements to be met by a person seeking leave to enter or remain in the United Kingdom as the spouse of a person with limited leave to enter or remain in the United Kingdom as a retired person of independent means are that:
    (i) the applicant is married to a person with limited leave to enter or remain in the United Kingdom as a retired person of independent means; and
    (ii) each of the parties intends to live with the other as his or her spouse during the applicant's stay and the marriage is subsisting; and
    (iii) there will be adequate accommodation for the parties and any dependants without recourse to public funds in accommodation which they own or occupy exclusively; and
    (iv) the parties will be able to maintain themselves and any dependants adequately without recourse to public funds; and
    (v) the applicant does not intend to stay in the United Kingdom beyond any period of leave granted to his spouse; and
    (vi) if seeking leave to enter, the applicant holds a valid United Kingdom entry clearance for entry in this capacity or, if seeking leave to remain, was admitted with a valid United Kingdom entry clearance for entry in this capacity.

Leave to enter or remain as the spouse of a person with limited leave to enter or remain in the United Kingdom as a retired person of independent means

272. A person seeking leave to enter or remain in the United Kingdom as the spouse of a person with limited leave to enter or remain in the

United Kingdom as a retired person of independent means may be given leave to enter or remain in the United Kingdom for a period not in excess of that granted to the person given limited leave to enter or remain as a retired person of independent means provided that, in relation to an application for leave to enter, he is able to produce to the Immigration Officer, on arrival, a valid United Kingdom entry clearance for entry in this capacity, or, in the case of an application for limited leave to remain, he was admitted with a valid United Kingdom entry clearance for entry in this capacity and is able to satisfy the Secretary of State that each of the requirements of paragraph 271(i)–(v) is met. An application for indefinite leave to remain in this category may be granted provided the applicant was admitted with a valid United Kingdom entry clearance for entry in this capacity and is able to satisfy the Secretary of State that each of the requirements of paragraph 271(i)–(v) is met and provided indefinite leave to remain is, at the same time, being granted to the person with limited leave to enter or remain as a retired person of independent means. Leave to enter or remain is to be subject to a condition prohibiting employment except in relation to the grant of indefinite leave to remain.

Refusal of leave to enter or remain as the spouse of a person with limited leave to enter or remain in the United Kingdom as a retired person of independent means

273. Leave to enter or remain in the United Kingdom as the spouse of a person with limited leave to enter or remain in the United Kingdom as a retired person of independent means is to be refused if, in relation to an application for leave to enter, a valid United Kingdom entry clearance for entry in this capacity is not produced to the Immigration Officer on arrival or, in the case of an application for limited leave to remain, if the applicant was not admitted with a valid United Kingdom entry clearance for entry in this capacity or is unable to satisfy the Secretary of State that each of the requirements of paragraph 271(i)–(v) is met. An application for indefinite leave to remain in this category is to be refused if the applicant was not admitted with a valid United Kingdom entry clearance for entry in this capacity or is unable to satisfy the Secretary of State that each of the requirements of paragraph 271(i)–(v) is met or if indefinite leave to remain is not, at the same time, being granted to the person with limited leave to enter or remain as a retired person of independent means.

COMMENTARY

The requirements placed upon a person seeking leave to enter or remain in the UK as the spouse of a person with limited leave to enter as a retired person of independent means are that he is married to that person; that each intends to live with the other as the other's spouse; and that the marriage is subsisting (see page 216). He must show that there will be adequate accommodation for them and their dependants without recourse to public funds in accommodation which they own or occupy exclusively (see page 211). He must have a valid entry clearance, and must intend to leave at the end of the period granted to his spouse. Indefinite leave can only be obtained in this category if at the same time the principal applicant is being granted indefinite leave to remain.

13 Children of persons with limited leave to enter or remain in the UK as retired persons of independent means

CHILDREN OF PERSONS WITH LIMITED LEAVE TO ENTER OR REMAIN IN THE UNITED KINGDOM AS RETIRED PERSONS OF INDEPENDENT MEANS

Requirements for leave to enter or remain as the child of a person with limited leave to enter or remain in the United Kingdom as a retired person of independent means

274. The requirements to be met by a person seeking leave to enter or remain in the United Kingdom as the child of a person with limited leave to enter or remain in the United Kingdom as a retired person of independent means are that:
 (i) he is the child of a parent who has been admitted to or allowed to remain in the United Kingdom as a retired person of independent means; and
 (ii) he is under the age of 18 or has current leave to enter or remain in this capacity; and
 (iii) he is unmarried, has not formed an independent family unit and is not leading an independent life; and
 (iv) he can, and will, be maintained and accommodated adequately without recourse to public funds in accommodation which his parent(s) own or occupy exclusively; and
 (v) he will not stay in the United Kingdom beyond any period of leave granted to his parent(s); and
 (vi) both parents are being or have been admitted to or allowed to remain in the United Kingdom save where:
  (*a*) the parent he is accompanying or joining is his sole surviving parent; or
  (*b*) the parent he is accompanying or joining has had sole responsibility for his upbringing; or
  (*c*) there are serious and compelling family or other considerations which make exclusion from the United Kingdom undesirable and suitable arrangements have been made for his care; and
 (vii) if seeking leave to enter, he holds a valid United Kingdom entry clearance for entry in this capacity or, if seeking leave to remain, was admitted with a valid United Kingdom entry clearance for entry in this capacity.

PERSONS SEEKING TO ENTER OR REMAIN IN THE UK

Leave to enter or remain as the child of a person with limited leave to enter or remain in the United Kingdom as a retired person of independent means

275. A person seeking leave to enter or remain in the United Kingdom as the child of a person with limited leave to enter or remain in the United Kingdom as a retired person of independent means may be given leave to enter or remain in the United Kingdom for a period of leave not in excess of that granted to the person with limited leave to enter or remain as a retired person of independent means provided that, in relation to an application for leave to enter, he is able to produce to the Immigration Officer, on arrival, a valid United Kingdom entry clearance for entry in this capacity or, in the case of an application for limited leave to remain, he was admitted with a valid United Kingdom entry clearance for entry in this capacity and is able to satisfy the Secretary of State that each of the requirements of paragraph 274(i)–(vi) is met. An application for indefinite leave to remain in this category may be granted provided the applicant was admitted to the United Kingdom with a valid United Kingdom entry clearance for entry in this capacity and is able to satisfy the Secretary of State that each of the requirements of paragraph 274(i)–(vi) is met and provided indefinite leave to remain is, at the same time, being granted to the person with limited leave to enter or remain as a retired person of independent means. Leave to enter or remain is to be subject to a condition prohibiting employment except in relation to the grant of indefinite leave to remain.

Refusal of leave to enter or remain as the child of a person with limited leave to enter or remain in the United Kingdom as a retired person of independent means

276. Leave to enter or remain in the United Kingdom as the child of a person with limited leave to enter or remain in the United Kingdom as a retired person of independent means is to be refused if, in relation to an application for leave to enter, a valid United Kingdom entry clearance for entry in this capacity is not produced to the Immigration Officer on arrival, or in the case of an application for limited leave to remain, if the applicant was not admitted with a valid United Kingdom entry clearance for entry in this capacity or is unable to satisfy the Secretary of State that each of the requirements of paragraph 274(i)–(vi) is met. An application for indefinite leave to remain in this category is to be refused if the applicant was not admitted with a valid United Kingdom entry clearance for entry in this capacity or is unable to satisfy the Secretary of State that each of the requirements of paragraph 274(i)–(vi) is met or if indefinite leave to remain is not, at the same time, being granted to the person with limited leave to enter or remain as a retired person of independent means.

COMMENTARY

For 'own or occupy exclusively', see page 211. For 'public funds', see page 61. For 'sole responsibility', see page 225. For 'serious and compelling family or other considerations', see page 226.

Chapter 12

Family Members

1 Spouses

Marriage to a British citizen does not result in a right under s 1(1) of the 1971 Act for a wife or husband to join his or her spouse in the UK (*Ex p Rofatullah* [1988] 3 WLR 591). In *Abdulaziz, Cabales and Balkandali v UK* [1985] 11 EHRR 459, the European Court of Human Rights held that the provisions of HC 169 which made it more difficult for a husband to join his wife settled here than for a wife to join her husband, discriminated on the grounds of sex and contravened Arts 8, 13 and 14 of the European Convention on Human Rights. In response to this decision, the rules were amended by HC 503. There is now no differentiation between the rules for husbands and for wives. It is now more difficult for both to join their spouses than formerly. A more recent set of rules has been challenged as being *ultra vires* the 1971 Act, but this challenge failed in the CA on the basis that the present rules are not so unreasonable, uncertain or unfair in their application that Parliament could not have intended them (*Rajput v IAT* [1989] Imm AR 350).

EEA nationals A member state must grant leave to enter and reside in its territory to the spouse, whether an EU national or not, of a national of that state who has travelled to another member state in order to exercise a Community right in that other state and who returns in order to exercise a Community right in the state of which he is a national (*R v IAT and Surinder Singh, ex p S of S* [1992] Imm AR 565). It is necessary to show that there is a factor linking the circumstances with any of the situations governed by EU law. Therefore if a UK national marries a non-EEA national, it is necessary for the couple to exercise a right, for example of establishment in France, before they return to the UK in order to exercise a Community right in the UK. Other EEA nationals, will of course be able to enter with their spouses in order to exercise a Community right. Polygamous marriages, if valid in the EEA member state of origin of the EEA national, would not be subject to the restrictions placed upon such marriages under domestic law (see below).

PART 8:

FAMILY MEMBERS

SPOUSES

277. Nothing in these Rules shall be construed as permitting a person to be granted entry clearance, leave to enter, leave to remain or variation of leave as a spouse of another if either party to the marriage will be aged under 16 on the date of arrival in the United Kingdom or (as the case may be) on the date on which the leave to remain or variation of leave would be granted.

278. Nothing in these Rules shall be construed as allowing a woman to be granted entry clearance, leave to enter, leave to remain or variation of leave as the wife of a man ('the husband') if:
   (i) her marriage to the husband is polygamous; and
   (ii) there is another woman living who is the wife of the husband and who:
       (a) is, or at any time since her marriage to the husband has been, in the United Kingdom; or
       (b) has been granted a certificate of entitlement in respect of the right of abode mentioned in Section 2(1)(a) of the Immigration Act 1988 or an entry clearance to enter the United Kingdom as the wife of the husband.
For the purpose of this paragraph a marriage may be polygamous although at its inception neither party had any other spouse.

279. Paragraph 278 does not apply to any woman who seeks entry clearance, leave to enter, leave to remain or variation of leave where:
   (i) she has been in the United Kingdom before 1 August 1988 having been admitted for the purpose of settlement as the wife of the husband; or
   (ii) she has, since her marriage to the husband, been in the United Kingdom at any time when there was no such other woman living as is mentioned in paragraph 278(ii),
but where a woman claims that paragraph 278 does not apply to her because she has been in the United Kingdom in circumstances which cause her to fall within sub-paragraphs (i) or (ii) of that paragraph it shall be for her to prove that fact.

FAMILY MEMBERS

280. For the purposes of paragraphs 278 and 279 the presence of any wife in the United Kingdom in any of the following circumstances shall be disregarded:
(i) as a visitor; or
(ii) an illegal entrant; or
(iii) in circumstances whereby a person is deemed by Section 11(1) of the Immigration Act 1971 not to have entered the United Kingdom.

COMMENTARY

Section 11 of the 1971 Act provides that a person is deemed not to have entered the UK where he remains in a disembarkation approved area, nor while detained, nor while on temporary admission, nor while released but liable to detention under schedule 2 to the 1971 Act.

(a) Under 16

A spouse will not be admitted to the UK where either of the parties to the marriage is under 16. Therefore although a valid marriage may have been contracted abroad, which will be valid for the purposes of UK law, until the under age party becomes of age, the spouse will be unable to enter. Further, s 3 of the Domicile and Matrimonial Proceedings Act 1973 has the effect that a child under 16 has the domicile of its father, so that a marriage before that age may be valid for the purposes of UK law by virtue of its domicile before the marriage. The paragraph prevents the spouse's entry until she becomes of age.

(b) Polygamy

Only a polygamous marriage which is:
(*a*) in a form valid in the country in which it is celebrated; and
(*b*) valid according to the law of the country in which each party is domiciled will be recognised as a valid marriage for the purposes of the immigration rules.

(*Mohammed v Knowll* [1968] 2 All ER 563). A marriage's validity may often be tested by reference to the law of the country with which it has the most real and substantial connection (*R v IAT, ex p Rafika Bibi* [1989] Imm AR 1). However, this test will only be used where it upholds the validity of the marriage.

A polygamous marriage or a potentially polygamous marriage is void in UK law if it was entered into outside the UK but at a time when either party was domiciled in the UK (see Matrimonial Causes Act 1973, s 11(*d*)). Where the marriage is legal, and the father is a British citizen, the children of a polygamous marriage will have the father's nationality.

The 1988 Act made it impossible for a wife in a polygamous marriage, whose husband has already brought another wife into the UK as his wife, to enter on that footing (s 2 1988 Act). She has a right of abode in the UK, but is prevented from exercising it if the other wife has already done so, or if there is another wife of the marriage who is or any time since her marriage to the husband has been in the UK.

The marriage may be polygamous, although at its inception neither party has any spouse additional to the other. However not every marriage which takes place where polygamy is legal is potentially polygamous. In *Hussain (Aliya) v Hussain (Shahid)* [1983] Fam 26, the CA held that a marriage is potentially polygamous only if at least one party has the capacity to marry a second spouse while the marriage subsists. In that case the husband could not contract a second marriage due to being domiciled in the UK, and his wife was not able to contract a second marriage under Islamic law. Therefore the marriage was not potentially polygamous and was not invalid by virtue of s 11(*d*) of the Matrimonial Causes Act 1973.

SPOUSES OF PERSONS PRESENT AND SETTLED IN THE UNITED KINGDOM OR BEING ADMITTED ON THE SAME OCCASION FOR SETTLEMENT

Requirements for leave to enter the United Kingdom with a view to settlement as the spouse of a person present and settled in the United Kingdom or being admitted on the same occasion for settlement

281. The requirements to be met by a person seeking leave to enter the United Kingdom with a view to settlement as the spouse of a person present and settled in the United Kingdom or who is on the same occasion being admitted for settlement are that:
    (i) the applicant is married to a person present and settled in the United Kingdom or who is on the same occasion being admitted for settlement; and
    (ii) the marriage was not entered into primarily to obtain admission to the United Kingdom; and
    (iii) the parties to the marriage have met; and
    (iv) each of the parties intends to live permanently with the other as his or her spouse and the marriage is subsisting; and
    (v) there will be adequate accommodation for the parties and any dependants without recourse to public funds in accommodation which they own or occupy exclusively; and

(vi) the parties will be able to maintain themselves and any dependants adequately without recourse to public funds; and

(vii) the applicant holds a valid United Kingdom entry clearance for entry in this capacity.

For the purposes of this paragraph, a member of HM Forces based in the United Kingdom but serving overseas is to be regarded as present and settled in the United Kingdom.

Leave to enter as the spouse of a person present and settled in the United Kingdom or being admitted for settlement on the same occasion

282. A person seeking leave to enter the United Kingdom as the spouse of a person present and settled in the United Kingdom or who is on the same occasion being admitted for settlement may be admitted for an initial period not exceeding 12 months provided a valid United Kingdom entry clearance for entry in this capacity is produced to the Immigration Officer on arrival.

Refusal of leave to enter as the spouse of a person present and settled in the United Kingdom or being admitted on the same occasion for settlement

283. Leave to enter the United Kingdom as the spouse of a person present and settled in the United Kingdom or who is on the same occasion being admitted for settlement is to be refused if a valid United Kingdom entry clearance for entry in this capacity is not produced to the Immigration Officer on arrival.

Requirements for an extension of stay as the spouse of a person present and settled in the United Kingdom

284. The requirements for an extension of stay as the spouse of a person present and settled in the United Kingdom are that:

(i) the applicant has limited leave to remain in the United Kingdom; and

(ii) is married to a person present and settled in the United Kingdom; and

(iii) the marriage was not entered into primarily to obtain settlement here; and

(iv) the parties to the marriage have met; and

(v) the applicant has not remained in breach of the immigration laws; and

(vi) the marriage has not taken place after a decision has been made to deport the applicant or he has been recommended for deportation or been given notice under Section 6(2) of the Immigration Act 1971; and

(vii) each of the parties intends to live permanently with the other as his or her spouse and the marriage is subsisting; and

(viii) there will be adequate accommodation for the parties and any dependants without recourse to public funds in accommodation which they own or occupy exclusively; and

(ix) the parties will be able to maintain themselves and any dependants adequately without recourse to public funds.

COMMENTARY

The onus is on the applicant to satisfy the ECO on the balance of probabilities that a valid marriage has taken place (*Visa Officer Islamabad v Kalsoom Begum* [1978] Imm AR 206). If there is any doubt a full investigation into family relationships and everyday family matters will be conducted. If substantial discrepancies are discovered in the accounts of the sponsor and the applicant, entry clearance may be refused. It is not necessary, however, to pinpoint the date of the marriage. If there is evidence to show that the applicant and sponsor are now married, they should obtain entry clearance despite having claimed falsely that they had married at an earlier time than they actually did (*Khanom v ECO Dacca* [1979–80] Imm AR 182).

The validity of the marriage is determined by the law of the place in which it is celebrated (*Berthiaume v Dastous* [1930] AC 83). Capacity to marry is determined by the law of each party's domicile immediately before the marriage (*R v IAT, ex p Rafika Bibi* [1989] Imm AR 1). If the marriage is invalid but the couple state that they would marry if necessary in the UK, the application should be treated as an application by a fiancé or fiancee (*Mohammed Ach-Ccharki v ECO, Rabat* [1991] Imm AR 162). Islamic law may be taken into account in determining the validity of a marriage, but it is not binding. Thus a marriage may be presumed from 'prolonged and continual cohabitation as husband and wife' according to s 268 in *Mulla's Principles of Muhammedan Law* (6th Edn) provided that the cohabitation is proven (*Inayat Begum v Visa Officer, Islamabad* [1978] Imm AR 174). For marriage by proxy see *Nazir Begum v ECO Islamabad* [1976] Imm AR 31. Thus a marriage by telephone or letter may be valid in form (*Nasreen Akhtar* (2166)). The tradition of Rukhsati is not necessary for a Muslim marriage's validity (*Basharat Hussain v Visa Officer, Islamabad* [1991] Imm AR 182). The evidence of independent witnesses that the applicant had, when previously in the UK, lived with the sponsor as his wife satisfied the IAT in one case that the relationship claimed was genuine, in view of the Muslim custom whereby such cohabitation would have been inconceivable if the applicant had not been the sponsor's wife (*Visa Officer, Islamabad v Channo Bi* [1978] Imm AR 182).

Where the applicant or spouse has been married before,

consideration should be given to whether the first marriage is finished. A customary marriage will result in a valid marriage. If that marriage is not dissolved properly it may render the marriage on the basis of which entry is sought bigamous, and therefore invalid. A customary divorce will be effective if that form of divorce is recognised in the country of the parties' domicile.

2 Para 281: primary purpose test

Where a person seeks leave to enter the UK with a view to settlement as the spouse of a person present and settled in the UK or of someone who is being admitted for settlement on the same occasion, the immigration authorities will need to be satisfied of the following:

(a) that the couple are married; and
(b) that the marriage was not entered into primarily to obtain admission to the UK; and
(c) that the parties to the marriage have met; and
(d) each of the parties intends to live permanently with the other as his or her spouse and the marriage is subsisting; and
(e) that there will be adequate accommodation for the couple and their dependants in accommodation which either the couple own or occupy exclusively; and
(f) the couple and their dependants will be able to maintain themselves without recourse to public funds; and
(g) the applicant has a valid entry clearance for entry as the spouse of a person settled in the UK or being admitted for settlement in the UK.

Without an entry clearance the applicant will not have a right of appeal against a decision to refuse entry. The primary purpose of the marriage must not be to obtain admission to the UK. The burden is on the applicant to satisfy the ECO on a balance of probabilities that the marriage was not entered into primarily to obtain admission to the UK (*R v IAT, ex p Kumar* [1986] Imm AR 446). The factors listed are of equal importance and the burden in each case remains on the applicant (*ECO Islamabad v Mohamed Hussain* [1991] Imm AR 476 and *R v IAT, ex p Bhatia* [1985] Imm AR 50).

The leading case on primary purpose is *R v IAT ex p Hoque & Singh* [1988] Imm AR 216 which sets out ten propositions by way of guidance relating to the application of the test:

(a) the onus falls on the applicant to satisfy the ECO that it is not the primary purpose of the marriage to obtain admission to the UK, and that the other requirements of the rule are satisfied;
(b) in considering an application the ECO is not limited to such evidence as the applicant may put before him, but is entitled to make inquiries of his own and test such evidence as the applicant chooses to put forward;
(c) it is the intention on the part of the applicant which is the central consideration: however, the intention of both parties will be relevant in assessing the purpose of the marriage: where it is an arranged marriage the reasons of those who arranged the marriage will also be relevant;
(d) the mere fact that the parties prove an intention to live together does not by itself suffice to enable an applicant to show that the primary purpose of the marriage was not to obtain admission:
   (i) in the case of a prospective marriage the intention at the present time is the relevant consideration; however,
   (ii) in the case of a concluded marriage the intention of the parties at the time of the celebration of the marriage is the relevant consideration;
(e) whether the parties intend to live together permanently as spouses, and whether they have previously met, 'spell out' matters relevant to whether the primary purpose of the marriage was admission to the UK; in the case of married couples intervening devotion (see below) may make it easier to satisfy the ECO on the question of whether the primary purpose of the marriage was to gain admission;
(f) the fact that a marriage is an arranged marriage, although a circumstance to be taken into account, does not, where arranged marriages are the norm, show that the purpose of the marriage was to obtain admission to the UK;
(g) the fact that the applicant is applying for an entry clearance under these paragraphs usually presupposes an intention to settle in the UK with the spouse: admissions on the applicant's part that he seeks to obtain admission to the UK should not be taken as evidence that this was the primary purpose of the marriage.

An ECO may make inquiries as to the circumstances in which the marriage was entered into, and may not shut his eyes to evidence which shows that the primary purpose of the marriage is to gain admission. On the other hand he should not scratch around for evidence to show that the marriage was entered into primarily for admission purposes. It is easy but wrong to treat the desire of the applicant to gain admission as evidence that this is the primary purpose of the marriage (*Kumar* (above), and *Hoque & Singh*). The fact that other parts of the rule are satisfied, so that there is an intention to live together permanently, will often cast a flood of light on the primary purpose of the marriage. The ECO should act as a kind of jury assessing the evidence as a whole without fine analysis in order to ascertain the real purpose of the marriage.

(a) Cases on primary purpose marriages

The *Hoque & Singh* guidelines have been considered in a number of cases. A sponsor to a marriage may make it a condition that she will only marry someone who is prepared to live in the UK (*R v IAT, ex p Shameem Wali* [1989] Imm AR 86, and *R v IAT, ex p Mohammed Khatab* [1989] Imm AR 313). Without more, such a condition would not show that the primary purpose of the marriage was to gain admission. Farquharson J in *Wali* observed that 'there is no reason why a British citizen, a woman, living in this country, should not wish to make it a condition of her marrying that she would only do so to somebody who, like herself, was going to live in the UK.' (at p 91).

There is something inherently unlikely in the proposition that two people would, as Simon Brown J stated in *Matwinder Singh* (Unrept DC 23 March 1987), 'bind and commit themselves together for life in a marriage with all that implies primarily in order to achieve the husband's settlement in the United Kingdom.' The Court of Session thought Simon Brown J's view to be a factor which an adjudicator could not ignore in assessing primary purpose cases (*Ex p Saftar* [1992] Imm AR 1). See also McCullough J in *R v IAT ex p Kaur* [1991] Imm AR 107.

Such general improbability does not prevent the ECO from considering the question of whether the marriage was entered into primarily for the purposes of gaining admission where appropriate, and where one party to the marriage intends to live permanently with the other only if the other is able to gain the necessary consent to enter the UK, he will not be regarded as having a proper intention to live with that other person at all (*Sumeina Masood v IAT* [1992] Imm AR 69). However, the IAT in *Akbar* (8670) stated that *Masood* should not be read as equating a precondition of residence in the

UK by the sponsor with a conclusion that the primary purpose of the marriage was admission. Limiting *Masood* to its own facts, the IAT held that it showed how, on particular facts, a condition of residence can lead to the conclusion that the marriage was primarily for admission. Such a conditional intention would only become an intention to live together (as opposed to a mere wish) if there was some reasonable prospect of its being fulfilled. Where no such prospect exists, an ECO will be justified in taking the view that if the husband's intention to live permanently with his wife is contingent on entry, the primary purpose of the marriage is to gain entry.

Caution should be exercised over answers given in interviews with ECOs concerning the strength of an applicant's desire to gain admission. It is wrong to treat the fact that a person has lied about the strength of such a desire to gain admission as evidence that the desire to gain admission was the primary purpose of the marriage (*R v IAT, ex p Kaur* [1991] Imm AR 107). However, an adjudicator will be entitled to take into account general factors such as whether during the course of an interview the applicant and sponsor had lied, if the taint of those earlier lies is not removed on his hearing the oral evidence (*R v IAT, ex p Gondalia* [1991] Imm AR 519).

Where the only dispute is whether the primary purpose of the marriage was to gain entry, the satisfaction of the requirement that the parties intended to live together does not by itself settle that dispute (*Mohammed Choudhury v IAT* [1990] Imm AR 211).

The rules require an intention to settle. However, they do not exclude those who are genuinely undecided about their long-term intentions, and where there is uncertainty as to the duration of the couple's stay, the application should be treated as an application as if ordinary settlement was contemplated (*R v IAT, ex p Najma Rafique* [1990] Imm AR 235).

There is no duty on an adjudicator to make specific findings in relation to the intention to live together, but it is usually desirable if he makes such findings as it will make clear that he has taken into account the matters which he should take into account. He should indicate the reasoning on which his conclusion is based, so as to show which factors he balanced in determining the question of the parties' motivation (*Kandiya v IAT* [1990] Imm AR 377 and *R v IAT, ex p Iqbal* [1993] Imm AR 270).

(b) Evidence of intervening devotion

Cases from the Indian subcontinent form the bulk of refused applications. There is a suspicion among immigration officers as to love matches in this context. In *R v IAT, ex p Kumar* [1986] Imm AR 446 the CA held that events which have happened since a marriage has been entered into may be material to the evaluation of the purpose of the marriage. If the couple can show evidence of affectionate contact between them during any time they have been separated, it may be easier for them to satisfy the requirement that the primary purpose of the marriage was not to gain admission. Such evidence has become known as 'intervening devotion'. Evidence of such intervening devotion will include communications since meeting, such as letters, telephone calls and other contact, and presents being given or received. If the couple have lived together for a time that will be taken as evidence of such devotion. However, it is only a factor, and may be outweighed by other factors such as deceit over the primary purpose of the marriage (*Girishkumar Patel v S of S* [1989] Imm AR 246).

Devotion in cases of fiancés and fiancees may not be in keeping with the cultural traditions of the couple, or an arranged marriage. In those cases post-decision evidence of devotion since the engagement may be considered irrelevant (*Ex p Prajpati* [1990] Imm AR 513, a case of post-decision pregnancy).

(c) Concession on intervening devotion in established marriages

In reply to a Parliamentary Question on 30 June 1992 (210 HC (Official Reports 6th Series) Col. 523–524) the Home Office Minister stated that in principle an application from a spouse for an entry clearance or leave to remain should be allowed when it is accepted that the marriage is genuine and subsisting and either the couple have been married for at least five years, or one or more children of the marriage have the right of abode in the UK. An application could be refused, however, if the applicant's criminal record would make exclusion conducive to the public good, or where the sponsor in the UK is unable to meet the maintenance and accommodation requirements of the immigration rules. It is likely that a couple who satisfied this concession would in any event be able successfully to appeal against a decision against them; however it does indicate that the ECO's investigation in such cases should be less rigorous than the investigation in any ordinary case need be.

(d) Finances and accommodation

The rules require that there will be adequate accommodation for the parties to the marriage and their dependants without recourse to public funds. The new rules do not require that the accommodation is 'accommodation of their own', a phrase which caused needless litigation under HC 251. However HC 395 does require that the couple have adequate accommodation for the parties and any dependants in accommodation *which they own or occupy exclusively*.

The IAT in *Saghir Ahmed* (8260) concluded that the correct test of adequacy was that recognised in UK law in relation to accommodation, ie the criterion of overcrowding. The IAT stated that all that was required by the rule was that the couple should be able to live at least part of their lives in accommodation which they exclusively occupy. The IAT construed this in turn in its minimal sense of there needing to be a room which the couple occupy. It could not see why an applicant should be refused entry because he would have to share a bathroom with, or live in a house with, another family. In *Mushtaq* (9343) the IAT held that the proper approach to assessing whether accommodation is adequate is to use the test of overcrowding under UK housing law. Thus they had reference to the room standard and space standard of s 326 of the Housing Act 1985. They recommended that evidence on these aspects should be provided. With the addition in the new Rules of the requirement of exclusive ownership or occupation of the accommodation, there will now have to be some area which the couple occupy exclusively.

HC 395 does not represent a change in policy in relation to spouses, and the previous case law serves therefore as a guide to the future interpretation of the accommodation provisions. The sponsor must show that there will be adequate accommodation for the couple. The rule can be satisfied by proof of any form of ownership of the accommodation, but is also satisfied by proof that the sponsor occupies the accommodation (*Kasuji* (5956) and *Jabeen* (4925)). The rules require that the applicant and sponsor can and will maintain and accommodate themselves without recourse to public funds (see page 61 for public funds). The obligation upon an applicant is to show that his admission will not cause any additional recourse to public funds. The appellate authorities will look at the state of affairs at the time the decision was taken, whether or not presented to the ECO, which would suggest that within a foreseeable period of the applicant's arrival, adequate maintenance will be available (see, for example, *R v IAT, ex p Rehana Begum* [1993] Imm AR 1).

The parties must have met There is no requirement that the parties should have met in the context of marriage or marriage arrangements, but merely that there should be an appreciation of the other party to the marriage in the sense of appearance or personality. The IAT in *Mohd Meharban v ECO, Islamabad* [1989] Imm AR 57 accepted that the rule required that at the date of the decision each party could point to the other as a person known and identified by the other.

Evidence in primary purpose cases An adjudicator has to consider motive in marriage cases (*R v IAT, exp Manjula Gethva* [1990] Imm AR 450). He is entitled to make an analysis of the parties' motives. In some cases there may be one simple factor which can be described as *the* motive for the marriage, however, in other cases there may be many motives for the marriage. Ignorance of cultural traditions has led to assumptions being made about applications particularly from the Indian subcontinent (*Bhatia v IAT* [1985] Imm AR 50). A helpful study of social practices of the Indian subcontinent has been made by Mr Philip Powell, a sociologist (Notes for UK Lawyers on Custom and Practice in the Indian Subcontinent available from 1 Horton Road, London E8). This evidence can be used to rebut some of the more subjective assumptions of ECOs and immigration officers regarding traditions relating to marriage. The study contains digests of erroneous views expressed by ECOs regarding marriage traditions.

(e) Cohabitants

Where a couple have been living in permanent association with each other, the partner without a right of abode has no claim to enter, but may be admitted as if he or she was the spouse of the other partner. Since the deletion of para 49 of HC 169 with effect from 26 August 1985, such applications fall to be considered on a discretionary basis outside the immigration rules. An instruction was issued to immigration officers on 8 November 1985 providing guidance on the exercise of that discretion (see [1986] 1 INL & P 89–90). The concession was limited in terms to personal relationships outside marriage between members of the opposite sex, one of whom must be present and settled in the UK. All the circumstances of the relationship will be considered in each case to decide whether the discretion will be exercised in the applicant's favour. Immigration officers should be satisfied as to the following:

(*a*) that the couple have been living together in a stable relationship and intend to continue doing so permanently;

(b) any previous marriage or similar relationship has broken down permanently;
(c) that there is adequate maintenance and accommodation available for the couple and their dependants without recourse to public funds.

The fact that the couple have chosen not to marry is not a conclusive reason for refusing leave to enter, although the discretion is more often exercised in the case of couples where one of the parties is temporarily unable to marry. Where the couple cannot prove either that they have been living in a stable relationship or that one of them is not free to marry, if the sponsor would suffer undue hardship by being required to live in the partner's country overseas, the discretion may be exercised in the couple's favour. The immigration officer will take the following into account in assessing such hardship:

(a) the length of the sponsor's connection with the UK;
(b) the relationship with other family members in the UK;
(c) the sponsor's prospects of finding work overseas;
(d) the difficulty the sponsor may have in living in the partner's country.

The marriage rules are applied to the couple as if they were married. Therefore leave to enter may be refused where an applicant remained in the UK in breach of the immigration rules before the application is made.

The partner seeking entry should obtain an entry clearance granted for the purpose of joining a person present and settled in the UK. Where an application for leave to remain is based upon this concession it will be refused where it is made after a decision to deport has been made. Since grant of leave under this concession is discretionary, and outside the rules, any appeal against the exercise of that discretion will be certain to fail. In certain circumstances it may be possible to take proceedings for judicial review. If the applicant is in the UK, the Home Office usually grant permanent residence at the end of 12 months; otherwise the couple are likely to be treated initially as a married couple are treated.

In the past the length of cohabitation required before the Home Office in practice exercised their discretion was two years. However, recently the practice seems to have become more flexible and the discretion may be exercised in cases where cohabitation has been for a shorter period.

When considering deportation and the guidance provided for immigration officers on marriage and children, cohabitants are treated as married (see page 273).

Extensions

Extension of stay as the spouse of a person present and settled in the United Kingdom

285. An extension of stay as the spouse of a person present and settled in the United Kingdom may be granted for a period of 12 months in the first instance, provided the Secretary of State is satisfied that each of the requirements of paragraph 284 is met.

Refusal of extension of stay as the spouse of a person present and settled in the United Kingdom

286. An extension of stay as the spouse of a person present and settled in the United Kingdom is to be refused if the Secretary of State is not satisfied that each of the requirements of paragraph 284 is met.

Requirements for indefinite leave to remain for the spouse of a person present and settled in the United Kingdom

287. The requirements for indefinite leave to remain for the spouse of a person present and settled in the United Kingdom are that:
   (i) the applicant was admitted to the United Kingdom or given an extension of stay for a period of 12 months and has completed a period of 12 months as the spouse of a person present and settled here; and
   (ii) the applicant is still the spouse of the person he or she was admitted or granted an extension of stay to join and the marriage is subsisting; and
   (iii) each of the parties intends to live permanently with the other as his or her spouse.

Indefinite leave to remain for the spouse of a person present and settled in the United Kingdom

288. Indefinite leave to remain for the spouse of a person present and settled in the United Kingdom may be granted provided the Secretary of State is satisfied that each of the requirements of paragraph 287 is met.

Refusal of indefinite leave to remain for the spouse of a person present and settled in the United Kingdom

289. Indefinite leave to remain for the spouse of a person present and settled in the United Kingdom is to be refused if the Secretary of State is not satisfied that each of the requirements of paragraph 287 is met.

COMMENTARY

Paragraph 284 provides that the applicant for an extension of leave to remain based on marriage to a person settled in the UK must not have remained in breach of the immigration laws. Thus a person who has overstayed cannot rely on this rule to obtain an extension of his leave. Similarly, para 284(vi) provides that the marriage must not have taken place after a decision to deport the applicant has been made, or a criminal court has made a recommendation for his deportation.

Where a person is refused entry but is granted temporary admission under para 21 of Sched 2 to the 1971 Act, he is not granted leave to enter in a temporary capacity. He cannot rely on para 284 to obtain an extension of a leave he does not possess. Further, he may be refused indefinite leave to remain in the UK upon marriage to a person settled in the UK (*ex p Kaur* [1987] Imm AR 278). The marriage must not have been entered into with the purpose of obtaining settlement (*R v IAT ex parte Nathwani* [1979-80] Imm AR 9). Where the marriage is genuine and subsisting, leave to remain should be granted having regard to the Ministerial statement of 30th June 1992 (see page 211) and see also the Home Office guidelines on enforcement action (pages 273).

The spouse seeking indefinite leave must have completed a 12-month period as the spouse of the settled person. The grounds on which an extension may be refused generally, and must be refused if the S of S is not satisfied regarding them, are set out on page 244 ff.

3 Fiancé(e)s

FIANCÉ(E)S

Requirements for leave to enter the United Kingdom as a fiancé(e) (ie with a view to marriage and permanent settlement in the United Kingdom)

290. The requirements to be met by a person seeking leave to enter the United Kingdom as a fiancé(e) are that:
 (i) the applicant is seeking leave to enter the United Kingdom for marriage to a person present and settled in the United Kingdom or who is on the same occasion being admitted for settlement; and
 (ii) it is not the primary purpose of the intended marriage to obtain admission to the United Kingdom; and
 (iii) the parties to the proposed marriage have met; and
 (iv) each of the parties intends to live permanently with the other as his or her spouse after the marriage; and
 (v) adequate maintenance and accommodation without recourse to public funds will be available for the applicant until the date of the marriage; and

(vi) there will, after the marriage, be adequate accommodation for the parties and any dependants without recourse to public funds in accommodation which they own or occupy exclusively; and
(vii) the parties will be able after the marriage to maintain themselves and any dependants adequately without recourse to public funds; and
(viii) the applicant holds a valid United Kingdom entry clearance for entry in this capacity.

Leave to enter as a fiancé(e)

291. A person seeking leave to enter the United Kingdom as a fiancé(e) may be admitted, with a prohibition on employment, for a period not exceeding 6 months to enable the marriage to take place provided a valid United Kingdom entry clearance for entry in this capacity is produced to the Immigration Officer on arrival.

Refusal of leave to enter as a fiancé(e)

292. Leave to enter the United Kingdom as a fiancé(e) is to be refused if a valid United Kingdom entry clearance for entry in this capacity is not produced to the Immigration Officer on arrival.

Requirements for an extension of stay as a fiancé(e)

293. The requirements for an extension of stay as a fiancé(e) are that:
   (i) the applicant was admitted to the United Kingdom with a valid United Kingdom entry clearance as a fiancé(e); and
   (ii) good cause is shown why the marriage did not take place within the initial period of leave granted under paragraph 291; and
   (iii) there is satisfactory evidence that the marriage will take place at an early date; and
   (iv) the requirements of paragraph 290(ii)–(vii) are met.

Extension of stay as a fiancé(e)

294. An extension of stay as a fiancé(e) may be granted for an appropriate period with a prohibition on employment to enable the marriage to take place provided the Secretary of State is satisfied that each of the requirements of paragraph 293 is met.

Refusal of extension of stay as a fiancé(e)

295. An extension of stay is to be refused if the Secretary of State is not satisfied that each of the requirements of paragraph 293 is met.

COMMENTARY

For the general grounds for refusal of entry, see Chapter 13.

For commentary on the primary purpose test, accommodation and maintenance requirements, see page 207 above. The burden is on the applicant to show that the primary purpose of the proposed marriage is not to gain admission, but the ECO should not scratch around for evidence upon which to base a refusal, and should consider the evidence for and against as a whole. A series of propositions were put forward in *Hoque & Singh* (above pages 207–208) as to the proper approach to the question of primary purpose. A mere desire to live in the UK with the wife does not amount to an attempt to use the marriage to the wife as a vehicle for entry to the UK. If the applicant and sponsor live in a community in which arranged marriages are the norm, the fact that the marriage was arranged is not significant.

It is possible to obtain an extension of leave as a fiancé if there was good cause why the marriage did not take place within the initial period of leave granted under the rules. There must also be evidence that the marriage will take place at an early date.

4 Children

CHILDREN

296. Nothing in these Rules shall be construed as permitting a child to be granted entry clearance, leave to enter or remain, or variation of leave where his mother is party to a polygamous marriage and any application by her for admission or leave to remain for settlement or with a view to settlement would be refused pursuant to paragraph 278.

LEAVE TO ENTER OR REMAIN IN THE UNITED KINGDOM AS THE CHILD OF A PARENT, PARENTS OR A RELATIVE PRESENT AND SETTLED OR BEING ADMITTED FOR SETTLEMENT IN THE UNITED KINGDOM

Requirements for indefinite leave to enter the United Kingdom as the child of a parent, parents or a relative present and settled or being admitted for settlement in the United Kingdom

297. The requirements to be met by a person seeking indefinite leave to enter the United Kingdom as the child of a parent, parents or a relative present and settled or being admitted for settlement in the United Kingdom are that he:
    (i) is seeking leave to enter to accompany or join a parent, parents or a relative in one of the following circumstances:
        (*a*) both parents are present and settled in the United Kingdom; or
        (*b*) both parents are being admitted on the same occasion for settlement; or
        (*c*) one parent is present and settled in the United Kingdom and the other is being admitted on the same occasion for settlement; or

FAMILY MEMBERS

    (d)   one parent is present and settled in the United Kingdom or being admitted on the same occasion for settlement and the other parent is dead; or

    (e)   one parent is present and settled in the United Kingdom or being admitted on the same occasion for settlement and has had sole responsibility for the child's upbringing; or

    (f)   one parent or a relative is present and settled in the United Kingdom or being admitted on the same occasion for settlement and there are serious and compelling family or other considerations which make exclusion of the child undesirable and suitable arrangements have been made for the child's care; and

(ii) is under the age of 18; and

(iii) is not leading an independent life, is unmarried, and has not formed an independent family unit; and

(iv) can, and will, be maintained and accommodated adequately without recourse to public funds in accommodation which the parent, parents or relative own or occupy exclusively; and

(v) holds a valid United Kingdom entry clearance for entry in this capacity.

Requirements for indefinite leave to remain in the United Kingdom as the child of a parent, parents or a relative present and settled or being admitted for settlement in the United Kingdom

298. The requirements to be met by a person seeking indefinite leave to remain in the United Kingdom as the child of a parent, parents or a relative present and settled in the United Kingdom are that he:

(i) is seeking to remain with a parent, parents or a relative in one of the following circumstances:

    (a)   both parents are present and settled in the United Kingdom; or

    (b)   one parent is present and settled in the United Kingdom and the other parent is dead; or

    (c)   one parent is present and settled in the United Kingdom and has had sole responsibility for the child's upbringing; or

    (d)   one parent or a relative is present and settled in the United Kingdom and there are serious and compelling family or other considerations which make exclusion of the child undesirable and suitable arrangements have been made for the child's care; and

(ii) has limited leave to enter or remain in the United Kingdom, and

    (a)   is under the age of 18; or

    (b)   was given leave to enter or remain with a view to settlement under paragraph 302; and

(iii) is not leading an independent life, is unmarried, and has not formed an independent family unit; and

(iv) can, and will, be maintained and accommodated adequately without recourse to public funds in accommodation which the parent, parents or relative own or occupy exclusively.

Indefinite leave to enter or remain in the United Kingdom as the child of a parent, parents or a relative present and settled or being admitted for settlement in the United Kingdom

299. Indefinite leave to enter the United Kingdom as the child of a parent, parents or a relative present and settled or being admitted for settlement in the United Kingdom may be granted provided a valid United Kingdom entry clearance for entry in this capacity is produced to the Immigration Officer on arrival. Indefinite leave to remain in the United Kingdom as the child of a parent, parents or a relative present and settled in the United Kingdom may be granted provided the Secretary of State is satisfied that each of the requirements of paragraph 298 is met.

Refusal of indefinite leave to enter or remain in the United Kingdom as the child of a parent, parents or a relative present and settled or being admitted for settlement in the United Kingdom

300. Indefinite leave to enter the United Kingdom as the child of a parent, parents or a relative present and settled or being admitted for settlement in the United Kingdom is to be refused if a valid United Kingdom entry clearance for entry in this capacity is not produced to the Immigration Officer on arrival. Indefinite leave to remain in the United Kingdom as the child of a parent, parents or a relative present and settled in the United Kingdom is to be refused if the Secretary of State is not satisfied that each of the requirements of paragraph 298 is met.

Requirements for limited leave to enter or remain in the United Kingdom with a view to settlement as the child of a parent or parents given limited leave to enter or remain in the United Kingdom with a view to settlement

301. The requirements to be met by a person seeking limited leave to enter or remain in the United Kingdom with a view to settlement as the child of a parent or parents given limited leave to enter or remain in the United Kingdom with a view to settlement are that he:
    (i) is seeking leave to enter to accompany or join or remain with a parent or parents in one of the following circumstances:
        (*a*) one parent is present and settled in the United Kingdom or being admitted on the same occasion for settlement and the other parent is being or has been given limited leave to enter or remain in the United Kingdom with a view to settlement; or
        (*b*) one parent is being or has been given limited leave to enter or remain in the United Kingdom with a view to settlement and has had sole responsibility for the child's upbringing; or

(c) one parent is being or has been given limited leave to enter or remain in the United Kingdom with a view to settlement and there are serious and compelling family or other considerations which make exclusion of the child undesirable and suitable arrangements have been made for the child's care; and
(ii) is under the age of 18; and
(iii) is not leading an independent life, is unmarried, and has not formed an independent family unit; and
(iv) can, and will, be maintained and accommodated adequately without recourse to public funds in accommodation which the parent or parents own or occupy exclusively; and
(v) (where an application is made for limited leave to remain with a view to settlement) has limited leave to enter or remain in the United Kingdom; and
(vi) if seeking leave to enter, holds a valid United Kingdom entry clearance for entry in this capacity or, if seeking leave to remain, was admitted with a valid United Kingdom entry clearance for entry in this capacity.

Limited leave to enter or remain in the United Kingdom with a view to settlement as the child of a parent or parents given limited leave to enter or remain in the United Kingdom with a view to settlement

302. A person seeking limited leave to enter the United Kingdom with a view to settlement as the child of a parent or parents given limited leave to enter or remain in the United Kingdom with a view to settlement may be admitted for a period not exceeding 12 months provided he is able, on arrival, to produce to the Immigration Officer a valid United Kingdom entry clearance for entry in this capacity. A person seeking limited leave to remain in the United Kingdom with a view to settlement as the child of a parent or parents given limited leave to enter or remain in the United Kingdom with a view to settlement may be given limited leave to remain for a period not exceeding 12 months provided the Secretary of State is satisfied that each of the requirements of paragraph 301(i)–(v) is met.

Refusal of limited leave to enter or remain in the United Kingdom with a view to settlement as the child of a parent or parents given limited leave to enter or remain in the United Kingdom with a view to settlement

303. Limited leave to enter the United Kingdom with a view to settlement as the child of a parent or parents given limited leave to enter or remain in the United Kingdom with a view to settlement is to be refused if a valid United Kingdom entry clearance for entry in this capacity is not produced to the Immigration Officer on arrival. Limited leave to remain in the United Kingdom with a view to settlement as the child of a parent or parents given limited leave to enter or remain in the United Kingdom with a view to settlement is to be refused if the Secretary of State is not satisfied that each of the requirements of paragraph 301(i)–(v) is met.

COMMENTARY

For 'maintained and accommodated adequately without recourse to public funds in accommodation... own or occupy exclusively' see page 211.

Polygamous marriages (see page 203). The child of a polygamous marriage may not obtain leave to enter or remain or indefinite leave to remain under HC 395 (para 296). The rule as currently drafted would prevent the entry of a child who otherwise has good grounds to enter, for example, because he is a British citizen by descent, or because he qualifies for asylum. For these reasons, the rule can probably be challenged as a fetter on the discretion of the S of S.

(a) Definition of 'a parent'

Paragraph 6 (see page 61) provides the definition of 'a parent': 'a parent' includes the stepfather of a child whose father is dead, the stepmother of a child whose mother is dead, and the father as well as the mother of a child of an unmarried couple, where he is proved to be the father. It also includes an adoptive parent, but only where a child was adopted in accordance with a decision taken by the competent administrative authority or court in a country whose adoption orders are recognised by the UK. In the case of a child born in the UK who is not a British citizen, a person to whom there has been a genuine transfer of parental responsibility on the grounds of the original parents' inability to care for the child is included in the definition of 'a parent'. A step parent cannot be taken into account therefore where a dependent child's parents are both living (*Manzar Alam v ECO Lahore* [1973] Imm AR 79).

(b) Proving blood relationships

Where the parentage of the child is disputed it may be necessary for the applicant to establish it. For first time applicants for entry clearance there is a government scheme of DNA testing of relationships between parents and children applying to join them. The policy was set out to the House of Commons in a written answer (see 154 HC Official Report (6th Series) Written Answers Cols 463–465 (14 June 1989)). The following points should be noted:

    (*a*)   DNA testing is recognised to be the most accurate method of determining parentage in immigration cases;

    (*b*)   the results of tests commissioned by an applicant and performed by a recognised tester will be accepted;

(c) ECOs will offer tests in cases where the relevant relationship cannot be proved easily by other means;
(d) refusal to take a test will not by itself be a ground for refusing entry clearance;
(e) fees are charged for the service, except where the family agrees to take the test and is applying for entry clearance for the first time on this ground.

ECOs have also been issued with instructions concerning the use of DNA results:

(a) if both parents have been tested, and the result shows the disputed relationship to be two to three times more likely than another relationship, the tests should be regarded as conclusive;
(b) the result of the test creates a presumption in its favour in any event, but if the likelihood of the relationship is less than two to three times more likely than another relationship, the immigration officer should look also at the surrounding circumstances;
(c) care should be taken over the identity of the donor of blood, and information as to the donor should be obtained direct from the independent expert rather than the applicant;
(d) where what is being tested is the applicant's relationship to one parent, the result should be more than 60 per cent accurate if it is to be relied upon. There should be good reason for testing only one of the parents;
(e) if a relationship to one parent alone is established, disclosure of the result to other members of the family should be treated with utmost caution.

The Home Office has approved Cellmark Diagnostics of Blacklands Way Abingdon Business Park, Abingdon Oxon, OX 141DY and University Diagnostics, University College, London, Gower St, London WC1E 6BT for private tests. Such tests may be helpful to those who are applying to enter for a second or subsequent time, and by those preparing for appeals.

Policy on adults refused entry as children, whose relationship is proved In the written answer referred to above (14 June 1989), the S of S set out a policy on adults whose applications as children were refused on the basis that they could not prove that they were related as claimed to the sponsor, but who, in the light of a DNA test, have now been proved to be related as claimed. Some such adults may have fulfilled all the other requirements of the rules for admission as children, but as adults no longer fulfill them.

The S of S stated that the rules relating to admission as adults would not be waived in such cases. However, he also stated that in relation to outstanding and future reapplications the requirements of the rules would be waived in certain circumstances. In order to qualify for such consideration, a person aged 18 or over reapplying has to show:
- (*a*) that he was refused entry clearance as a child on the ground that he was not related as claimed to the sponsor;
- (*b*) that DNA evidence establishes that he was after all related as claimed;
- (*c*) that he is still wholly or mainly dependent on his sponsor in the UK; and
- (*d*) that there are compassionate circumstances in his case; however, the mere fact of the childhood refusal and subsequent inability therefore to join the sponsor will not be regarded as a compassionate circumstance.

The S of S went on to state that all the circumstances of the case would be considered, including:
- (*a*) the degree and nature of the dependency;
- (*b*) the nature and extent of the compassionate circumstances;
- (*c*) the reapplicant's present age and marital status;
- (*d*) whether other close family members such as siblings are already settled in the UK;
- (*e*) the lapse of time between the original application and the reapplication.

Greater weight is attached to compassionate circumstances relating to the situation of the reapplicant abroad than to those relating to the sponsor.

In *Hassan Miah v S of S* [1991] Imm AR 437, the CA refused to interfere with this policy on the basis that it was essentially a matter within the discretion of the S of S of a decision by the S of S referring the matter to adjudication (*Ex p Noor Uddin* [1990] Imm AR 181). However, there is no obligation on the S of S to refer such cases in this way (*Sunam Uddin v S of S* [1991] Imm AR 587), and the court will not compel a reference (*R v IAT, ex p Jaifor Ali* [1990] Imm AR 531).

(c) Indefinite leave to enter

A person seeking indefinite leave to enter the UK as the child of a parent(s) or relative present and settled in the UK or being admitted for settlement must be in the circumstances set out in para 297.

Both parents present and settled in the UK The intention of this provision is that the child would be coming to the UK to be united with both his parents. It is not sufficient that both parents reside in the UK if they are separated (*Pinnock v ECO Kingston Jamaica* [1974] Imm AR 22). However, the Home Office in practice allow children to enter if both parents are settled in the UK but are separated.

'On the same occasion admitted for settlement' Either both parents must accompany the child and be admitted for settlement or if one parent is settled in the UK, the other must accompany the child and be admitted for settlement. The child will be unable to gain admission for settlement if the parent who is not settled does not accompany him (*Ex p Rukshanda Begum* [1990] Imm AR 1). Similarly the accompanying parent must intend to settle (*R v IAT, ex p Rashida Bibi* [1988] Imm AR 298). The purpose of the provisions is the reunification of families. Thus where a child's mother accompanied him from Pakistan although she would not settle as the sponsor's wife, and the sponsor's intention was to return to Pakistan on arranging employment for his son with a view to his son contributing to the support of himself and his wife in Pakistan, entry clearance was properly refused (*Ibrahim v Visa Officer, Islamabad* [1978] Imm AR 18). The phrase 'admitted for settlement' does not include a person who was entitled to settlement or had applied for it, and was clearly going to obtain it (*R v IAT, ex p S of S* [1993] Imm AR 298).

Sole responsibility A child may join a single parent when it is shown that the parent has had sole responsibility for the child's upbringing for a not insubstantial period to time. Further the fact that others play a part in the day-to-day care of the child does not prevent the parent having sole responsibility for the purposes of this rule (*R v IAT, ex p Uddin* [1986] Imm AR 203). Where there is a sharing of responsibility for the child's upbringing between father and mother, entry clearance will not be granted (*Eugene v ECO Bridgetown Barbados* [1975] Imm AR 111). There is such a sharing if the child ordinarily lives with the mother even if his sponsoring father always maintained him financially (*Williams v S of S* [1972] Imm AR 207). The assumption of financial responsibility is not by itself conclusive (*Ravat v ECO Bombay* [1974] Imm AR 79). There must also be cogent evidence of genuine interest in and affection for the child by the parent (*Rudolph v ECO Colombo* [1984] Imm AR 84). Similarly there is a sharing of responsibility where the child does not actually live with the mother, but with her maternal grandmother, even if there is close and regular contact with the mother (*S of S v Pusey* [1972] Imm AR 240). However, the words 'sole responsibility' do not mean absolute responsibility of the parent in the UK for the upbringing of the child concerned. Some form of responsibility must in nearly all cases be exercised in practical matters by the relative with whom the child is living outside the UK. This of itself does not prevent the parent in the UK having sole responsibility (*Emmanuel v S of S* [1972] Imm AR 69; *Rudolph v ECO Colombo* (above)). The evidence taken over all must show that the sponsor remains ultimately in sole control of the child's upbringing (*R v IAT ex p Sajid Mahmood* [1988] Imm AR 121). However, it is important that a broad approach be taken to the evidence and checklists should be avoided: it is unclear that asking whether a parent is ultimately in sole control of the child's upbringing adds anything to the approach of considering the evidence as a whole in accordance with the rule (*Ramos v IAT* [1989] Imm AR 148).

The decision in each case will depend upon its own particular facts. It will involve consideration of the sources and degree of financial support of the child and whether there is coherent evidence of genuine interest in and affection for the child by the sponsoring parent in the UK (see *Emmanuel's* case (above); *Sloley v ECO Kingston* [1973] Imm AR 54; and *ECO Kingston v Martin* [1978] Imm AR 100). The issue of sole responsibility for the upbringing of a child is not, however, to be decided only as between one parent and the other parent. The position of every member of the family contributing to the child's upbringing must be taken into account when deciding whether or not the sponsoring parent has 'sole responsibility' for that upbringing (*Martin v S of S* [1972] Imm AR 71).

Concession relating to children under 12 The sole responsibility test of this paragraph will not be applied where the child is aged under 12, by virtue of a concession made by the Home Office. The concession applies where one only of the parents is settled in the UK, and the other is overseas. Children under 12 will be permitted without difficulty to join one parent if there is adequate accommodation and maintenance, and (if the parent is the father) that there is a female relative (in practice including a partner) who is resident in the household, and who is willing and able to look after the child (see Home Office leaflet RON2(D) and *Hansard* for 11 December 1979 Col 220).

Serious and compelling family or other considerations A child may join one parent or relative, even where that person has not had sole responsibility for the upbringing of the child, if there are 'serious and compelling family or other considerations which make exclusion undesirable'. The words 'serious and compelling' have been added to the present rules. It is clear from the old rules that only the most serious and compelling considerations were accepted in practice. A teenage boy living in overcrowded conditions in Jamaica and moving from household to household as relatives were reluctant to accept responsibility for him, was refused entry clearance. Although he may have been bitterly disappointed at not being allowed to come to this country, there was no evidence that he was particularly unhappy (*Rennie v ECO Kingston* [1979-80] Imm AR 117). The conditions under which the child is living in the home country are not to be weighed against the conditions available for the child in the UK (*S of S v Campbell* [1972] Imm AR 115).

In *Pinnock (ME) v ECO Kingston* [1977] Imm AR 4, for example, entry clearance was refused although it was not in dispute that the sponsor and his wife in this country have a comfortable and well-maintained home and would be able to look after the appellant child satisfactorily. In Jamaica, by contrast, she had to share a bed with an 11-year-old half-brother and a room with another half-brother. Similarly, the fact that the child might be better off in the UK, because he was unable to obtain employment in his home country, was not *per se* a relevant consideration (*Williams v S of S* [1972] Imm AR 207).

An example of domestic overcrowding which was held to be an important qualifying factor leading to the admission of an applicant to the UK can be found in the facts of *ECO Kingston v Holmes* [1975] Imm AR 20. A 12-year-old girl lived with her mother and her five younger half-brothers in a house in a depressed area in Jamaica. Her family occupied a single room in the house where the kitchen and sanitary facilities were shared by five other families who were also tenants. The small room was furnished with two beds, one double and one single, a vanity dresser and a china cabinet, all in dilapidated condition. The fact that there were far worse conditions elsewhere in Jamaica was not relevant, since bad conditions were not made better by the existence of even worse conditions (ibid, p 23). When assessing 'family or other considerations' the authorities will take into account, *inter alia*, the accommodation available, the age and health of the relative with whom the child is residing and the general state of relations between that person and the child (*S of S v Campbell* [1972] Imm

AR 115; *Needham v Entry Certificate Officer, Kingston, Jamaica* [1973] Imm AR 75). Where that relative is incapable of looking after the child, it is likely that the child will be admitted into the UK (*Rudolph v ECO Colombo* [1984] Imm AR 84). Once the relative's incapability is show there must be strong countervailing factors to show that despite the incapability no serious and compelling considerations making the child's exclusion undesirable exist (*Awuku* (4220)). Serious and compelling family or other considerations may arise out of factors other than mental or physical incapacity. An example would be where a person was unable to look after the child due to being deserted (*Caballero* (4605)).

(d) Indefinite leave to remain

A person seeking indefinite leave to remain as the child of a parent or relative present and settled in the UK must satisfy the requirements under para 298. Note that he must either be under 18 years of age or must have been given leave to enter or remain with a view to settlement under para 302. That paragraph provides for admission for a period not exceeding 12 months for such a person, if he can produce a valid entry clearance for entry in this capacity on arrival. He must also satisfy the requirements of para 301(i)–(v) (pages 220–221).

5 Children born in the United Kingdom who are not British citizens

CHILDREN BORN IN THE UNITED KINGDOM WHO ARE NOT BRITISH CITIZENS

304. This paragraph and paragraphs 305–309 apply only to unmarried dependent children under 18 years of age who were born in the United Kingdom on or after 1 January 1983 (when the British Nationality Act 1981 came into force) but who, because neither of their parents was a British citizen or settled in the United Kingdom at the time of their birth, are not British citizens and are therefore subject to immigration control. Such a child requires leave to enter where admission to the United Kingdom is sought, and leave to remain where permission is sought for the child to be allowed to stay in the United Kingdom. If he qualifies for entry clearance, leave to enter or leave to remain under any other part of these Rules, a child who was born in the United Kingdom but is not a British citizen may be granted entry clearance, leave to enter or leave to remain in accordance with the provisions of that other part.

Requirements for leave to enter or remain in the United Kingdom as the child of a parent or parents given leave to enter or remain in the United Kingdom

305. The requirements to be met by a child born in the United Kingdom who is not a British citizen who seeks leave to enter or remain in the

United Kingdom as the child of a parent or parents given leave to enter or remain in the United Kingdom are that he:
  (i) (a) is accompanying or seeking to join or remain with a parent or parents who have, or are given, leave to enter or remain in the United Kingdom; or
      (b) is accompanying or seeking to join or remain with a parent or parents one of whom is a British citizen or has the right of abode in the United Kingdom; or
      (c) is a child in respect of whom the parental rights and duties are vested solely in a local authority; and
  (ii) is under the age of 18; and
  (iii) was born in the United Kingdom; and
  (iv) is not leading an independent life, is unmarried, and has not formed an independent family unit; and
  (v) (where an application is made for leave to enter) has not been away from the United Kingdom for more than 2 years.

Leave to enter or remain in the United Kingdom

306. A child born in the United Kingdom who is not a British citizen and who requires leave to enter or remain in the circumstances set out in paragraph 304 may be given leave to enter for the same period as his parent or parents where paragraph 305(i)(*a*) applies, provided the Immigration Officer is satisfied that each of the requirements of paragraph 305(ii)–(v) is met. Where leave to remain is sought, the child may be granted leave to remain for the same period as his parent or parents where paragraph 305(i)(*a*) applies, provided the Secretary of State is satisfied that each of the requirements of paragraph 305(ii)–(iv) is met. Where the parent or parents have or are given periods of leave of different duration, the child may be given leave to whichever period is longer except that if the parents are living apart the child should be given leave for the same period as the parent who has day to day responsibility for him.

307. If a child does not qualify for leave to enter or remain because neither of his parents has a current leave (and neither of them is a British citizen or has the right of abode), he will normally be refused leave to enter or remain, even if each of the requirements of paragraph 305(ii)–(v) has been satisfied. However, he may be granted leave to enter or remain for a period not exceeding 3 months if both of his parents are in the United Kingdom and it appears unlikely that they will be removed in the immediate future, and there is no other person outside the United Kingdom who could reasonably be expected to care for him.

308. A child born in the United Kingdom who is not a British citizen and who requires leave to enter or remain in the United Kingdom in the circumstances set out in paragraph 304 may be given indefinite leave to enter where paragraph 305(i)(*b*) or (i)(*c*) applies provided the Immigration Officer is satisfied that each of the requirements of paragraph 305(ii)–(v) is met. Where an application is for leave to remain, such a child may

be granted indefinite leave to remain where paragraph 305(i)(*b*) or (i)(*c*) applies, provided the Secretary of State is satisfied that each of the requirements of paragraph 305(ii)–(iv) is met.

Refusal of leave to enter or remain in the United Kingdom

309. Leave to enter the United Kingdom where the circumstances set out in paragraph 304 apply is to be refused if the Immigration Officer is not satisfied that each of the requirements of paragraph 305 is met. Leave to remain for such a child is to be refused if the Secretary of State is not satisfied that each of the requirements of paragraph 305(i)–(iv) is met.

COMMENTARY

Scope   Children under the age of 18 born in the UK on or after 1 January 1983 who are not BCs are subject to these paragraphs.

For the general grounds of refusal of leave to enter or remain see Chapter 13.

The previous rules advised that a child in this category should obtain leave to remain before any travel outside the Common Travel Area. The child still has to obtain leave to enter on his return, but the fact of the previous leave to remain was of use in assessing the application. HC 395 also introduces a requirement that the child should not have been absent from the UK for more than two years, and if the child has been more than two years away from the UK, leave to enter must be refused. Given that the child's parents may be settled in the UK, it may be that this provision could be challenged by way of judicial review as being unreasonable.

6 Adopted children

ADOPTED CHILDREN

Requirements for indefinite leave to enter the United Kingdom as the adopted child of a parent or parents present and settled or being admitted for settlement in the United Kingdom

310. The requirements to be met in the case of a child seeking indefinite leave to enter the United Kingdom as the adopted child of a parent or parents present and settled or being admitted for settlement in the United Kingdom are that he:
- (i) is seeking leave to enter to accompany or join an adoptive parent or parents in one of the following circumstances;
    - (*a*) both parents are present and settled in the United Kingdom; or
    - (*b*) both parents are being admitted on the same occasion for settlement; or

FAMILY MEMBERS

(c) one parent is present and settled in the United Kingdom and the other is being admitted on the same occasion for settlement; or
(d) one parent is present and settled in the United Kingdom or being admitted on the same occasion for settlement and the other parent is dead; or
(e) one parent is present and settled in the United Kingdom or being admitted on the same occasion for settlement and has had sole responsibility for the child's upbringing; or
(f) one parent is present and settled in the United Kingdom or being admitted on the same occasion for settlement and there are serious and compelling family or other considerations which make exclusion of the child undesirable and suitable arrangements have been made for the child's care; and

(ii) is under the age of 18; and
(iii) is not leading an independent life, is unmarried, and has not formed an independent family unit; and
(iv) can, and will, be maintained and accommodated adequately without recourse to public funds in accommodation which the adoptive parent or parents own or occupy exclusively; and
(v) was adopted in accordance with a decision taken by the competent administrative authority or court in his country of origin or the country in which he is resident; and
(vi) was adopted at a time when:
  (a) both adoptive parents were resident together abroad; or
  (b) either or both adoptive parents were settled in the United Kingdom; and
(vii) has the same rights and obligations as any other child of the marriage; and
(viii) was adopted due to the inability of the original parent(s) or current carer(s) to care for him and there has been a genuine transfer of parental responsibility to the adoptive parents; and
(ix) has lost or broken his ties with his family of origin; and
(x) was adopted, but the adoption is not one of convenience arranged to facilitate his admission to or remaining in the United Kingdom; and
(xi) holds a valid United Kingdom entry clearance for entry in this capacity.

Requirements for indefinite leave to remain in the United Kingdom as the adopted child of a parent or parents present and settled in the United Kingdom

311. The requirements to be met in the case of a child seeking indefinite leave to remain in the United Kingdom as the adopted child of a parent or parents present and settled in the United Kingdom are that he:

(i) is seeking to remain with an adoptive parent or parents in one of the following circumstances:
  (a) both parents are present and settled in the United Kingdom; or
  (b) one parent is present and settled in the United Kingdom and the other parent is dead; or
  (c) one parent is present and settled in the United Kingdom and has had sole responsibility for the child's upbringing; or
  (d) one parent is present and settled in the United Kingdom and there are serious and compelling family or other considerations which make exclusion of the child undesirable and suitable arrangements have been made for the child's care; and
(ii) has limited leave to enter or remain in the United Kingdom, and
  (a) is under the age of 18; or
  (b) was given leave to enter or remain with a view to settlement under paragraph 315; and
(iii) is not leading an independent life, is unmarried, and has not formed an independent family unit; and
(iv) can, and will, be maintained and accommodated adequately without recourse to public funds in accommodation which the adoptive parent or parents own or occupy exclusively; and
(v) was adopted in accordance with a decision taken by the competent administrative authority or court in his country of origin or the country in which he is resident; and
(vi) was adopted at a time when:
  (a) both adoptive parents were resident together abroad; or
  (b) either or both adoptive parents were settled in the United Kingdom; and
(vii) has the same rights and obligations as any other child of the marriage; and
(viii) was adopted due to the inability of the original parent(s) or current carer(s) to care for him and there has been a genuine transfer of parental responsibility to the adoptive parents; and
(ix) has lost or broken his ties with his family of origin; and
(x) was adopted, but the adoption is not one of convenience arranged to facilitate his admission to or remaining in the United Kingdom.

Indefinite leave to enter or remain in the United Kingdom as the adopted child of a parent or parents present and settled or being admitted for settlement in the United Kingdom

312. Indefinite leave to enter the United Kingdom as the adopted child of a parent or parents present and settled or being admitted for settlement in the United Kingdom may be granted provided a valid United Kingdom entry clearance for entry in this capacity is produced to the Immigration Officer on arrival. Indefinite leave to remain in the United Kingdom as

FAMILY MEMBERS 233

the adopted child of a parent or parents present and settled in the United Kingdom may be granted provided the Secretary of State is satisfied that each of the requirements of paragraph 311 is met.

Refusal of indefinite leave to enter or remain in the United Kingdom as the adopted child of a parent or parents present and settled or being admitted for settlement in the United Kingdom

313. Indefinite leave to enter the United Kingdom as the adopted child of a parent or parents present and settled or being admitted for settlement in the United Kingdom is to be refused if a valid United Kingdom entry clearance for entry in this capacity is not produced to the Immigration Officer on arrival. Indefinite leave to remain in the United Kingdom as the adopted child of a parent or parents present and settled in the United Kingdom is to be refused if the Secretary of State is not satisfied that each of the requirements of paragraph 311 is met.

COMMENTARY

HC 395 contains a number of additional requirements as a result of the Resolution on the Harmonisation of National Policies on Family Reunification agreed by EC Ministers in Copenhagen June 1993. Broadly the scheme is that overseas adoptions must be in accordance with a decision taken by the appropriate administrative authority or court in the child's country of origin or residence. Both adoptive parents must be resident together abroad, or one or both must be settled in the UK, at the time of the adoption. The adopted child has the same rights as a child of the marriage, and he must have lost or broken his ties with his family of origin (see *R v IAT, ex p Tohur Ali* [1988] Imm AR 237).

Note that the requirements (i) to (xi) all have to be satisfied. One of the circumstances specified in (i) must therefore apply.

(a) Adoption of foreign children

The person seeking indefinite leave to enter as an adopted child must satisfy the immigration authorities that he is under the age of 18, and is unmarried, not having previously formed an independent family unit, and not leading an independent life.

He must be joining or accompanying the adoptive parent in one of the following circumstances:

(*a*) both adoptive parents are settled in the UK; or
(*b*) both parents are being admitted on the same occasion for settlement; or
(*c*) one parent is settled in the UK, and the other is being admitted to the UK on the same occasion for settlement;

(d) one parent is dead and the other parent is settled in the UK or being admitted at the same time for settlement;
(e) the parent who has had sole responsibility for the child is settled in the UK or being admitted on the same occasion for settlement; or
(f) one parent or a relative other than the parent is settled in the UK or being admitted on the same occasion for settlement in the UK, and there are serious compelling family or other considerations in the child's own country which make exclusion of the child undesirable and suitable arrangements have been made for the child's care.

The person being admitted must show that he will be maintained and accommodated adequately without recourse to public funds in accommodation which the parent, parents or relative own or occupy exclusively.

The general grounds for exclusion must not apply to the child (see Chapter 13).

The child must have an entry clearance for the purpose of entry as an adopted child. The adoption must have taken place in accordance with a decision taken by the competent administrative authority or court of his country of origin in which he is resident, and at a time when both parents were resident together in a third country.

The adoption must not be one of convenience arranged to facilitate the admission of the child (*ECO New Delhi v Balbir Singh* [1977] Imm AR 109; *Baljinder Singh v ECO New Delhi* [1975] Imm AR 34; and *Ex p Dhahan* [1988] Imm AR 257).

Adoption after entry There is no express provision in the rules for a child to be brought into the UK for adoption. The S of S occasionally exercises a discretion to permit entry for this purpose. When a person applies for leave to enter the UK to be adopted, any decision is made outside the rules. The S of S may grant entry clearance having taken advice from the Department of Health. The S of S will need to be satisfied that it is in the child's best interests to be adopted, and there should be no obvious reason why an adoption order should not be made in the UK. Detailed information is contained in the Home Office leaflet RON 117. It is possible to apply for judicial review of a decision made under these guidelines if it runs counter to a legitimate expectation created by them (*Ex p Asif Khan* [1984] Imm AR 68). A challenge to the exercise of the discretion under the guidelines was brought in *S of S for Health, ex p Luff* [1991] Imm AR 382. However, it could not be shown

FAMILY MEMBERS 235

that the exercise of the discretion was unreasonable because the Department of Health had not recommended the prospective adoptive parents, due to health problems which they had. Consideration is also given in this context to the provisions of the *United Nations Declaration on Social and Legal Principles relating to the protection of Children with special reference to Foster Placement and Adoption Nationally and Internationally 1986* (see [1991] Imm AR 448).

7 Leave to enter or remain for settlement as an adopted child

Requirements for limited leave to enter or remain in the United Kingdom with a view to settlement as the adopted child of a parent or parents given limited leave to enter or remain in the United Kingdom with a view to settlement

314. The requirements to be met in the case of a child seeking limited leave to enter or remain in the United Kingdom with a view to settlement as the adopted child of a parent or parents given limited leave to enter or remain in the United Kingdom with a view to settlement are that he:
- (i) is seeking leave to enter to accompany or join or remain with a parent or parents in one of the following circumstances:
  - (a) one parent is present and settled in the United Kingdom or being admitted on the same occasion for settlement and the other parent is being or has been given limited leave to enter or remain in the United Kingdom with a view to settlement; or
  - (b) one parent is being or has been given limited leave to enter or remain in the United Kingdom with a view to settlement and has had sole responsibility for the child's upbringing; or
  - (c) one parent is being or has been given limited leave to enter or remain in the United Kingdom with a view to settlement and there are serious and compelling family or other considerations which make exclusion of the child undesirable and suitable arrangements have been made for the child's care; and
- (ii) is under the age of 18; and
- (iii) is not leading an independent life, is unmarried, and has not formed an independent family unit; and
- (iv) can, and will, be maintained and accommodated adequately without recourse to public funds in accommodation which the adoptive parent or parents own or occupy exclusively; and
- (v) was adopted in accordance with a decision taken by the competent administrative authority or court in his country of origin or the country in which he is resident; and
- (vi) was adopted at a time when:

(a) both adoptive parents were resident together abroad; or
(b) either or both adoptive parents were settled in the United Kingdom; and
(vii) has the same rights and obligations as any other child of the marriage; and
(viii) was adopted due to the inability of the original parent(s) or current carer(s) to care for him and there has been a genuine transfer of parental responsibility to the adoptive parents; and
(ix) has lost or broken his ties with his family of origin; and
(x) was adopted, but the adoption is not one of convenience arranged to facilitate his admission to the United Kingdom; and
(xi) (where an application is made for limited leave to remain with a view to settlement) has limited leave to enter or remain in the United Kingdom; and
(xii) if seeking leave to enter, holds a valid United Kingdom entry clearance for entry in this capacity.

Limited leave to enter or remain in the United Kingdom with a view to settlement as the adopted child of a parent or parents given limited leave to enter or remain in the United Kingdom with a view to settlement

315. A person seeking limited leave to enter the United Kingdom with a view to settlement as the adopted child of a parent or parents given limited leave to enter or remain in the United Kingdom with a view to settlement may be admitted for a period not exceeding 12 months provided he is able, on arrival, to produce to the Immigration Officer a valid United Kingdom entry clearance for entry in this capacity. A person seeking limited leave to remain in the United Kingdom with a view to settlement as the adopted child of a parent or parents given limited leave to enter or remain in the United Kingdom with a view to settlement may be granted limited leave for a period not exceeding 12 months provided the Secretary of State is satisfied that each of the requirements of paragraph 314(i)–(xi) is met.

Refusal of limited leave to enter or remain in the United Kingdom with a view to settlement as the adopted child of a parent or parents given limited leave to enter or remain in the United Kingdom with a view to settlement

316. Limited leave to enter the United Kingdom with a view to settlement as the adopted child of a parent or parents given limited leave to enter or remain in the United Kingdom with a view to settlement is to be refused if a valid United Kingdom entry clearance for entry in this capacity is not produced to the Immigration Officer on arrival. Limited leave to remain in the United Kingdom with a view to settlement as the adopted child of a parent or parents given limited leave to enter or remain in the United Kingdom with a view to settlement is to be refused if the Secretary of State is not satisfied that each of the requirements of paragraph 314(i)–(xi) is met.

FAMILY MEMBERS 237

COMMENTARY

The child seeking limited leave to enter or remain with a view to settlement as the adopted child of parents must satisfy the requirements set out in that paragraph. He must be under 18, and not leading an independent life, unmarried, and must not have formed an independent family unit. He must satisfy the accommodation and maintenance requirements (see page 211). He must satisfy the adoption requirements (see page 231). If the child is seeking leave to enter with a view to settlement under para 314, he must have an entry clearance. If he does not have that document he will have no right of appeal against a decision not to give him leave to enter the UK. A child who has limited leave to enter or remain in the UK, for whatever reason, may apply for limited leave to remain with a view to settlement under para 314(xi). The maximum leave which can be granted under para 315 is 12 months. A person seeking limited leave to remain under that para may obtain leave not exceeding 12 months, on satisfying the requirements of para 314.

8 Parents, grandparents and other dependant relatives of persons present and settled in the United Kingdom

PARENTS, GRANDPARENTS AND OTHER DEPENDENT RELATIVES OF PERSONS PRESENT AND SETTLED IN THE UNITED KINGDOM

Requirements for indefinite leave to enter or remain in the United Kingdom as the parent, grandparent or other dependant relative of a person present and settled in the United Kingdom

317. The requirements to be met by a person seeking indefinite leave to enter or remain in the United Kingdom as the parent, grandparent or other dependent relative of a person present and settled in the United Kingdom are that the person:
  (i) is related to a person present and settled in the United Kingdom in one of the following ways:
    (a) mother or grandmother who is a widow aged 65 years or over; or
    (b) father or grandfather who is a widower aged 65 years or over; or
    (c) parent or grandparents travelling together of whom at least one is aged 65 or over; or
    (d) a parent or grandparent aged 65 or over who has remarried but cannot look to the spouse or children of the second marriage for financial support; and where the person settled in the United Kingdom is able and willing to maintain the parent or grandparent and any spouse or child of the second marriage who would be admissible as a dependant; or

 (e) a parent or grandparent under the age of 65 if living alone outside the United Kingdom in the most exceptional compassionate circumstances and mainly dependent financially on relatives settled in the United Kingdom; or

 (f) the son, daughter, sister, brother, uncle or aunt over the age of 18 if living alone outside the United Kingdom in the most exceptional compassionate circumstances and mainly dependent financially on relatives settled in the United Kingdom; and

(ii) is joining or accompanying a person who is present and settled in the United Kingdom or who is on the same occasion being admitted for settlement; and

(iii) is financially wholly or mainly dependent on the relative present and settled in the United Kingdom; and

(iv) can, and will, be maintained and accommodated adequately, together with any dependants, without recourse to public funds in accommodation which the sponsor owns or occupies exclusively; and

(v) has no other close relatives in his own country to whom he could turn for financial support; and

(vi) if seeking leave to enter, holds a valid United Kingdom entry clearance for entry in this capacity.

Indefinite leave to enter or remain as the parent, grandparent or other dependent relative of a person present and settled in the United Kingdom

318. Indefinite leave to enter the United Kingdom as the parent, grandparent or other dependent relative of a person present and settled in the United Kingdom may be granted provided a valid United Kingdom entry clearance for entry in this capacity is produced to the Immigration Officer on arrival. Indefinite leave to remain in the United Kingdom as the parent, grandparent or other dependent relative of a person present and settled in the United Kingdom may be granted provided the Secretary of State is satisfied that each of the requirements of paragraph 317(i)–(v) is met.

Refusal of indefinite leave to enter or remain in the United Kingdom as the parent, grandparent or other dependent relative of a person present and settled in the United Kingdom

319. Indefinite leave to enter the United Kingdom as the parent, grandparent or other dependent relative of a person settled in the United Kingdom is to be refused if a valid United Kingdom entry clearance for entry in this capacity is not produced to the Immigration Officer on arrival. Indefinite leave to remain in the United Kingdom as the parent, grandparent or other dependent relative of a person present and settled in the United Kingdom is to be refused if the Secretary of State is not satisfied that each of the requirements of paragraph 317(i)–(v) is met.

FAMILY MEMBERS

COMMENTARY

Ostensibly in order not to discriminate between family members on the grounds of sex, HC 395 restricts the admission of widowed parents and grandparents to those of 65 years of age or over.

The relevant relationships (para 317(i)) Para 317 first defines the relationship which must exist between the applicant and a person present and settled in the UK (sub-para (i)). The applicant may be the parent or grandparent of the settled person and must be 65 or older. The settled person's parents or grandparents travelling together of whom one is 65 or older also satisfy the requirement of the rules. Where the settled person's parent or grandparent is 65 or older and has remarried, but cannot look to the spouse or children of his second marriage for financial support, the relationship requirement is satisfied, save for an additional requirement imposed by para 317(i)(*d*). Under that sub-para the settled person must be able and willing to maintain both the applicant and any spouse or child of the second marriage who would be admissible as a dependant. Where the applicant is related to the settled person as his parent or grandparent under the age of 65, who is living alone outside the UK in the most exceptional compassionate circumstances, and who is mainly dependent financially on relatives settled in the UK, the relationship requirement of the paragraph is satisfied (para 317(i)(e)). Other dependent relatives are categorised as being the son, daughter, sister brother uncle, aunt over the age of 18 if living alone outside the UK in the most exceptional compassionate circumstances and mainly dependent financially upon relatives settled in the UK.

HC 395 provides for the admission for settlement of the dependants of a person who is:

(*a*) physically present in the UK (*Begum v S of S* [1990] Imm AR 1, and *R v IAT, ex p Manek* [1978] 3 All ER 641); and

(*b*) settled in the UK when the dependants applied for admission; or

(*c*) who is given leave to enter with a view to settlement on the same occasion.

A passenger seeking admission under the dependants' rules must hold a current entry clearance granted to him for the purpose of settlement (*Ex p Akhtar* [1975] 1 WLR 1717). The applicant must be joining the settled person. He must be financially (wholly or mainly) dependent on the settled person. Normally the sponsor and the settled person will be the same person, but the rules seem to envisage that the sponsor and the settled person might be different people (para 317(iv)). Thus although sub-para (*e*) under para 317(i) requires the settled person to maintain the applicant, such maintenance need not extend to accommodation which could be provided by a third (sponsoring) party under sub-para (iv). The applicant must have no other close relatives in his own country to whom he could turn for financial support.

Asylum seekers who have been granted exceptional leave to remain will not be regarded as settled, and therefore cannot rely on this provision in order to have their dependants admitted (*Somasundaram v ECO Bombay* [1990] Imm AR 16). An entry clearance will be refused unless the ECO is satisfied that all of the requirements of para 317 are satisfied. The prohibition on recourse to 'public funds' in this context includes the use of savings out of income support (*R v IAT, ex p Chhinderpal Singh* [1989] Imm AR 69). If the person seeking admission as a dependant does not have to depend upon the sponsor, but has chosen to be, he will not come within these rules (*Chavda v ECO Bombay* [1978] Imm AR 40).

The rules provide that the relative must be wholly or mainly dependent upon the relative settled in the UK. The rule does not permit the person on whom the applicant is dependent to be different from the person settled in the UK (*Shabir v Visa Officer, Islamabad* [1989] Imm AR 185). The purpose behind the rule is to enable widowed mothers and elderly parents (as they are defined in the rule) to join children settled in the UK who are supporting them because the resources of the parents are insufficient to meet their own needs. To make a successful application it must be shown that the parents are necessarily dependent upon their children in the UK either wholly or mainly (*Mohammad Zaman v ECO Lahore* [1973] Imm AR 71). Thus where the sponsor's father had in Pakistan two farms of his own, producing an income which he chose to distribute between the members of his family in that country, it was held that the payments he received from his sponsoring son had not been shown to be necessary to him and his wife (*Mohammad Zaman's* case). Similarly, where there was no evidence to suggest that two teenage sons were not able bodied or were unable to work to supplement the earnings coming into their mother's home, it was held that there was no necessary dependence upon the sponsor in the UK (*Bibi Hasan v ECO Bombay* [1976] Imm AR 28). Nor can a dependency be created by voluntarily giving up work (*ECO Port Louis v Grenade* [1978] Imm AR 143). However, it has been held that a mother may not be in a position to compel her sons to work. In these circumstances she and her daughter were necessarily dependent upon her sponsoring son in the UK; but her three sons who stated that they had not sought employment because they could live on the money sent to her mother were not (*Chauda v ECO Bombay* [1978] Imm AR 40). A widowed mother is entitled to look to her only son for support in preference to relatives on her side of the family. If, therefore, the only son settled in the UK voluntarily takes over the main support of his mother from her brother and father in India, the suggestion that her dependence upon him was not a 'necessary' dependence should not preclude her admission to the UK as the dependent widowed mother of this sponsoring only son (*ECO, New Delhi v Malhan* [1978] Imm AR 209).

HC 395 introduces the requirement that in certain of the categories of relationship under sub para (i), the applicant must be *'mainly dependent financially'* on the settled person. Paragraph 317(iii) places a general requirement on all categories of dependent relative applicant. The person must be *'financially wholly or mainly dependent'* on the settled person. Under HC 251 the requirement was that the applicant be *dependent* on the settled person. A necessary emotional dependence (*R v IAT, ex p Bastiampillai* [1983] 2 All ER 844) will no longer satisfy the requirements of the rule. The rule is, however, to be interpreted in a humanitarian manner (*R v IAT, ex p Swaran Singh* [1987] 1 WLR 1394).

The sponsor must show that he has sufficient means at the time of application. There should not be speculation as to what the family's income in the future may be, if, for example, the sponsoring son's wife were to obtain a teaching post (*ECO New Delhi v Parkash Kaur* [1979–80] Imm AR 114, and also *ECO Bombay v Seedat* [1975] Imm AR 121).

No other close relatives to turn to The requirement that there be no close relatives to whom the applicant can turn for support outside the UK is a very restrictive requirement on its face. No doubt if the immigration restrictions of the country in which the other close relative lived prevented the applicant from going to the other close relative, the latter would not be a close relative who is able to support the applicant.

'Close relatives' includes brothers, sisters, aunts, uncles, nephews and brothers in law. It is not limited to blood relatives (*Amar Kaur* (2517)). The fact that under the Hindu social code sisters are not responsible for brothers does not prevent sisters being regarded as close relatives to whom the applicant can turn (*Tilak Ram v*

ECO New Delhi [1978] Imm AR 123, but see below). The applicant must have no other relative who has the ability to provide some assistance so as to make it reasonable to expect the applicant to depend upon that relative rather than the child in the UK (see *Bastiampillai* (above)). The relative must be:

(a) outside the UK;
(b) able and willing to provide him with support; and
(c) a person to whom the applicant could turn in time of need (see *Swaran Singh* (above)).

The phrase 'without other close relatives in their own country to turn to' contemplates a situation where a person is isolated from his or her close relatives and is therefore unable to turn to them for those things for which a person can normally expect to turn to his family, such as companionship, affection, discussion of problems and courses of action, advice, physical help.

Dillon LJ in *Swaran Singh* [1987] 1 WLR 1394 at 1398 referring to the above factors said:

> while the factors listed—companionship, affection, discussion of problems etc—are relevant in the sense that an elderly parent who does not have even these available to him or her is indeed a person 'without other close relatives in his or her own country to turn to,' they do not, in my judgment, go far enough.
>
> I read the phrase in the rule 'without other close relatives in his or her country to turn to' as importing 'to turn to in case of need'—any sort of need which may afflict elderly parents living together, or a widowed mother or a father who is a widower aged 65 or over. What the need may be will depend on the facts of the particular case. But what has to be covered is not merely the need of loneliness and isolation, which the factors listed in *Said Mar Jan v Secretary of State for the Home Department* (unreported), add up to, and which is indeed often a burden to such elderly people. There may also, as in *Reg v Immigration Appeal Tribunal, ex p Bastiampillai* [1983] 2 All ER 844, be a need for a home and financial support. But there are many other circumstances in which elderly parents may need help and support from a child or other close relative. One obvious instance is the need for some close relative to turn to in the event of chronic illness. Another, more important in my personal view, is the need for a close relative to turn to, and who will be able and willing to cope, in the event of accident or sudden emergency to the elderly parent; it is difficult to imagine anything more worrying to a loving child settled here than the fear of an accident to a parent thousands of miles away with no one to cope. Another instance is the possibility of hostile and violent behaviour by neighbours towards the elderly parent who is not adequately protected.

(b) Sons daughters, aunts, uncles, etc: 'the most exceptional compassionate circumstances'

The provisions of the rule may only be extended to relatives over 18 but below 65 and more distant relatives where there are 'the most exceptional compassionate circumstances'. The relative must be living alone. A person will be regarded as living alone when the person with whom the applicant lives is dependent upon him (*Choong* (6162)). A previous set of rules required that the applicant have a standard of living substantially below that of his own country. This provision was held to be so manifestly unjust as to be invalid in *R v IAT, ex p Manshoora Begum* [1986] Imm AR 385. It is necessary to show the most exceptional circumstances. The word 'most' is not mere surplusage, but shows that a very strict test is being applied (*R v IAT, ex p Joseph* [1988] Imm AR 329). In each case whether the circumstances are the most exceptional compassionate circumstances will be a question of fact, and it is therefore essential that the fullest possible statement of the facts of the applicant's compassionate circumstances should be provided to the ECO. Applicants suffering from serious physical or mental disabilities with no one to look after them may normally be living in the most exceptional compassionate circumstances (*Visa Officer Islamabad v Sindhu* [1978] Imm AR 147; see also *ECO New Delhi v Sibal* [1973] Imm AR 50; and *ECO Bombay v Sacha* [1973] Imm AR 5). However, blindness by itself may not amount to the most exceptional compassionate circumstances (*Visa Officer Islamabad v Bashir* [1978] Imm AR 77).

Children aged 18 or over at the date of application must qualify for settlement in their own right unless there are the most exceptional compassionate circumstances.

Chapter 13

General Grounds for the Refusal of Leave to Enter or Remain in the United Kingdom

PART 9

GENERAL GROUNDS FOR THE REFUSAL OF ENTRY CLEARANCE, LEAVE TO ENTER OR VARIATION OF LEAVE TO ENTER OR REMAIN IN THE UNITED KINGDOM

Refusal of entry clearance or leave to enter the United Kingdom

320. In addition to the grounds for refusal of entry clearance or leave to enter set out in Parts 2–8 of these Rules, and subject to paragraph 321 below, the following grounds for the refusal of entry clearance or leave to enter apply:

Grounds on which entry clearance or leave to enter the United Kingdom is to be refused

(1) the fact that entry is being sought for a purpose not covered by these Rules;

(2) the fact that the person seeking entry to the United Kingdom is currently the subject of a deportation order;

(3) failure by the person seeking entry to the United Kingdom to produce to the Immigration Officer a valid national passport or other document satisfactorily establishing his identity and nationality;

(4) failure to satisfy the Immigration Officer, in the case of a person arriving in the United Kingdom or seeking entry through the Channel Tunnel with the intention of entering any other part of the common travel area, that he is acceptable to the immigration authorities there;

(5) failure, in the case of a visa national, to produce to the Immigration Officer a passport or other identity document endorsed with a valid and current United Kingdom entry clearance issued for the purpose for which entry is sought;

(6) where the Secretary of State has personally directed that the

GROUNDS TO ENTER OR REMAIN IN THE UK

exclusion of a person from the United Kingdom is conducive to the public good;

(7) save in relation to a person settled in the United Kingdom or where the Immigration Officer is satisfied that there are strong compassionate reasons justifying admission, confirmation from the Medical Inspector that, for medical reasons; it is undesirable to admit a person seeking leave to enter the United Kingdom.

Grounds on which entry clearance or leave to enter the United Kingdom should normally be refused

(8) failure by a person arriving in the United Kingdom to furnish the Immigration Officer with such information as may be required for the purpose of deciding whether he requires leave to enter and, if so, whether and on what terms leave should be given;

(9) failure by a person seeking leave to enter as a returning resident to satisfy the Immigration Officer that he meets the requirements of paragraph 18 of these Rules;

(10) production by the person seeking leave to enter the United Kingdom of a national passport or travel document issued by a territorial entity or authority which is not recognised by Her Majesty's Government as a state or is not dealt with as a government by them, or which does not accept valid United Kingdom passports for the purpose of its own immigration control; or a passport or travel document which does not comply with international passport practice;

(11) failure to observe the time limit or conditions attached to any grant of leave to enter or remain in the United Kingdom;

(12) the obtaining of a previous leave to enter or remain by deception;

(13) failure, except by a person eligible for admission to the United Kingdom for settlement or a spouse eligible for admission under paragraph 282, to satisfy the Immigration Officer that he will be admitted to another country after a stay in the United Kingdom;

(14) refusal by a sponsor of a person seeking leave to enter the United Kingdom to give, if requested to do so, an undertaking in writing to be responsible for that person's maintenance and accommodation for the period of any leave granted;

(15) whether or not to the holder's knowledge, the making of false representations or the failure to disclose any material fact for the purpose of obtaining a work permit;

(16) failure, in the case of a child under the age of 18 years seeking leave to enter the United Kingdom otherwise than in conjunction with an application made by his parent(s) or legal guardian, to provide the Immigration Officer, if required to do so, with written consent to the application from his parent(s) or legal guardian; save that the requirement as to written consent does not apply in the case of a child seeking admission to the United Kingdom as an asylum seeker;

(17) save in relation to a person settled in the United Kingdom. refusal to undergo a medical examination when required to do so by the Immigration Officer;

(18) save where the Immigration Officer is satisfied that admission would be justified for strong compassionate reasons, conviction in any country including the United Kingdom of an offence which, if committed in the United Kingdom, is punishable with imprisonment for a term of 12 months or any greater punishment or, if committed outside the United Kingdom, would be so punishable if the conduct constituting the offence had occurred in the United Kingdom;

(19) where, from information available to the Immigration Officer, it seems right to refuse leave to enter on the ground that exclusion from the United Kingdom is conducive to the public good; if, for example, in the light of the character, conduct or associations of the person seeking leave to enter it is undesirable to give him leave to enter.

COMMENTARY

The general grounds for refusal of leave to enter or remain in the UK are collected in Part 9 of HC 395. They apply to all the categories of person under the rules. Para 320 presents two types of grounds on which entry clearance or leave to enter the UK can be refused. Numbers (1) to (7) are grounds on which entry clearance or leave to enter *is to be* refused. Numbers (8)–(19) are grounds on which entry clearance or leave to enter *should normally be* refused. Thus (1)–(7) are mandatory grounds of refusal, and (8)–(19) are discretionary grounds of refusal. An immigration officer may examine the holder of an entry clearance so far as is necessary to determine whether any of the above grounds apply to him. In determining that question he may rely on inferences reasonably drawn from the results of that examination, and any other information which is available to him.

1 Grounds on which entry clearance or leave to enter the UK is to be refused (mandatory grounds)

(a) Currently the subject of a deportation order

Such a person becomes an illegal entrant on entry to the UK by entering in breach of the immigration laws.

(b) Failure to produce documents

If a person fails to produce to the immigration officer a valid national passport or other document satisfactorily establishing his identity and nationality, leave to enter will be refused. EEA nationals may be required to show a valid EEA passport or identity card under the Immigration (European Economic Area) Order 1994. However, this requirement may breach the EU law relating to free movement. In relation to EU citizens the requirement of submission to a border control is likely to breach art 8a of the Treaty on European Union which provides that every citizen of the Union shall have the right to move and reside freely within the territory of the Member States.

(c) Acceptability to common travel area immigration authorities

s 1(3) of the 1971 Act makes provision for the common travel area (see para 15 (page 67)).

(d) Visa nationals

A visa national must have a visa for all purposes under parts 2–8 of the rules. Without a visa he will have no right of appeal against a decision to refuse him entry or entry clearance.

2 Exclusion conducive to the public good

(a) Medical reasons

Where the medical officer confirms that it is undesirable for medical reasons to admit a person seeking leave to enter the UK, an immigration officer must refuse entry. The only exceptions to this rule are where the immigration officer is satisfied that there are strong compassionate reasons justifying admission, or where the person is settled in the UK. Paragraph 26 requires that a person who intends to remain in the UK for more than six months should normally be referred for medical inspection. Paragraph 38 provides that a returning resident should not be refused entry on medical grounds. Immigration officers may only refer EEA nationals (when they are seeking to exercise a right of free movement pursuant to the EEA) to a medical inspector if they show 'obvious signs of mental or physical ill health'. Such persons may only be refused if the medical inspector certifies that they are suffering from one of the diseases listed in the annexe to EC Directive 64/2.

Compassionate grounds Such grounds were found to exist to enable the admission of the holder of an entry clearance certificate as a fiancé notwithstanding that he was found on arrival to be suffering from tuberculosis in an active (but non-infectious) form. The IAT was clearly influenced by undertakings given by the appellant's uncles here (one of whom was the father of his fiancée) that they would pay the considerable expense of recommended private medical treatment and their ability to do so, and the feelings expressed by the appellant's fiancée after waiting for more than two years for his arrival (*Parvez v Immigration Officer, London (Heathrow) Airport* [1979–80] Imm AR 84). However, it should not be thought that a fiancé arriving for marriage and found to be suffering from tuberculosis should *ipso facto* be found to be in strong compassionate circumstances (*Immigration Officer, London (Heathrow) Airport v Bhatti* TH/57482/80 (1719) unreported, referred to in [1979–80] Imm AR at p 86, n 4).

In *Entry Certificate Officer, Bombay v Sacha* [1973] Imm AR 5, the IAT affirmed the decision of an adjudicator that a severely mentally retarded applicant in need of care and attention should not be refused admission because strong compassionate reasons existed. Her cousin in India who looked after her did so reluctantly and she would receive very much better care and attention from her half brother who was brought up with her from her birth till he came to the UK and whose affection for her was manifest.

Under the new rules it should be possible to argue that strong compassionate circumstances exist in such cases and that therefore the immigration officer has a discretion that should have been exercised differently.

3 Grounds on which entry clearance or leave to enter the UK should normally be refused (non-mandatory grounds)

(a) Failure to furnish information

An adverse inference may be drawn from any prevarication by the applicant. Thus an applicant failed to discharge the onus on him to bring himself within a rule when he was unable or unwilling to define his position in order to bring himself within one or another immigration rule. He could not successfully appeal an adverse decision by the ECO not to grant him entry clearance (*Abid Hussain v ECO Islamabad* [1989] Imm AR 46). The examination should not be carried further than is necessary for a decision to be made on the grant of entry clearance or to decide whether leave to enter should be given for a limited period and subject to any conditions.

(b) Returning residents

A returning resident may be refused admission when he fails to satisfy the immigration officer that he had indefinite leave when he last left the UK, and that he has not been away from the UK for more than two years, and that he did not receive assistance from public funds towards the costs of leaving the UK, and that he now seeks admission for the purposes of settlement (see para 18, page 69).

(c) Passport not recognised

Passports for states which are not recognised by the UK and 'world citizen' passports will not be accepted and may form the basis of a refusal of admission.

(d) Failure to observe the time limit or conditions

The S of S may rely on breaches which occurred in *any* earlier period of leave, where he is not estopped from doing so. In *Clifford Ofoajoku v S of S* [1991] Imm AR 68 the IAT considered that the S of S could take account of a breach of condition in an earlier period of leave. He is not estopped from relying on a breach merely because a period of further leave had intervened, where that latter period of leave was granted without knowledge of the breach. However it would be arguable that the S of S would be estopped where the latter period of leave was granted in the knowledge of the earlier breach (see *Ofoajoku* at p 74).

Furthermore, where the breach comes to light after the date of the refusal to grant the variation of leave, it may be relied upon before the appellate authorities (*Rajendran v S of S* [1989] Imm AR 512).

(e) Obtaining previous leave by deception

Where a person obtains leave by deception, clearly he is an illegal entrant. This provision however permits the immigration officer to consider periods of leave obtained in the past, irrespective of the bona fides of the current application.

(f) Sponsor's refusal to give an undertaking

Paragraph 35 provides that a sponsor may be required to give such an undertaking. If he refuses, the application for admission may be refused (see page 79).

(g) False representations or failure to disclose material facts

If the immigration officer refuses leave to enter because false representations were made, the representations must have been made by the applicant. Deception of an ECO suffices despite the fact that they are not mentioned in the 1971 Act (*Ex p Kwadwo Saffu-Mensah* [1991] Imm AR 43). Conduct can of itself amount to a representation. Silent presentation of a passport which the applicant knows to contain false information amounts to a false representation (*Ex p Patel* [1986] Imm AR 515). The representation is made at the time that the passport is presented (*Ex p Mohammed Salim* [1990] Imm AR 316). There is no requirement however that deceit or fraud should have been involved in the representation, just that it is false (*Eusebio* (4739)). In *Tahzeem Akhtar v IAT* [1991] Imm AR 326 the CA held in relation to the precursor of this rule under HC 251 that there was no justification for reading the word 'material' into the phrase 'false representations'. The only questions are:

(a) whether representations which were false were made;
(b) whether those representations were used for the purpose of obtaining an entry clearance; and
(c) whether they actually played a part in obtaining the entry clearance.

(h) Material non-disclosure

The non-disclosure must play a part in the obtaining of the entry clearance for it to be a 'material' non-disclosure (cf *Eusebio* above). In *Edusi* (6598) the IAT held that a failure to answer a question on a visa application form requesting information about previous periods of leave amounted to a non-disclosure of a material fact.

Material non-disclosure was held to justify refusal of leave to enter where an applicant with an entry clearance marked 'visitor' failed to inform the immigration officer that he had previously applied for an entry certificate and had been refused, and his appeal had been dismissed despite the fact that it was apparent from the passport that a previous application had been unsuccessful (*Mustun v S of S* [1972] Imm AR 97); also where a student applicant failed to disclose that he had 2 brothers in the UK (*Quereshi v Immigration Officer, London* [1978] Imm AR 176). In *R v IAT, ex p Suily Begum* (1990) Imm AR 226 (QBD) on the other hand, it was not regarded as a material non-disclosure that a minor daughter did not disclose that she had a number of prospective fiancés, one of whom she contemplated marrying at some stage in the future.

(i) Parents' consent

A child under 18 years of age who seeks admission will normally be refused leave to enter if he does not have the consent in writing of his parent(s). Paragraph 320(16) does not apply to child asylum seekers.

(j) Criminal convictions

A person who has been convicted in any country, including the UK, of certain offences may be refused leave to enter unless the immigration officer considered admission to be justified for strong compassionate reasons (for an earlier rule see *Liberto v Immigration Officer, London (Heathrow) Airport* [1975] Imm AR 61). The offences are those which, if they had been committed in the UK, would be punishable by 12 months or longer in prison. Thus a conviction for a relatively minor offence may lead to exclusion even though the offence was committed in the UK and the court did not recommend deportation. However, the Rehabilitation of Offenders Act 1974 applies to these offences.

EU nationals   EU law suggests that previous criminal convictions may not *per se* justify exclusion (see EU Treaty Art 48(3) and EC directive 64/221). Past conduct may only justify exclusion if it constitutes a present threat, but some past offences are so serious that the burden is on the applicant to show that the risk of similar conduct in the future is negligible (see *Puttick v S of S* [1984] Imm AR 118. Also see *R v Bouchereau* [1978] 2 WLR 251 and *Ex p Santillo* [1981] 2 All ER 897 on the power of a court to make a recommendation for deportation). In *R v Escauriaza* [1989] 3 CMLR 281 the ECJ held that the public policy exemption (that the deportee be a genuine and sufficient threat to the requirements of public policy) is satisfied where the presence of the deportee would be to the detriment of the UK.

(k) Discretionary exclusion conducive to the public good

Any person may be refused leave to enter on the ground that his exclusion is conducive to the public good.

It is not possible to enumerate or to define the types of circumstances in which the power should be used. Paragraph 320(19) does not provide an exclusive list (*R v IAT, ex p Ajaib Singh* [1978] Imm AR 59). According to the IAT in *Scheele v Immigration Officer, Harwich* [1976] Imm AR 1, it appears designed to deal with 'undesirables' of all kinds. As such it is not intended only to be used in rare or unusual circumstances. Nevertheless, it should not be lightly used or in trivial circumstances. However, in that case the exclusion of the appellant was justified when he was found in possession of cannabis, although the amount of cannabis was small and for personal use and he was in transit to another country. It is in the public interest that persons should not be readily admitted to this country in contravention of immigration rules (see *R v IAT, ex p Ajaib Singh* [1978] Imm AR 59). It may be conducive to the public good to exclude a person on the basis of previous periods of leave to enter which were obtained by deception (*R v IAT, ex p Anilkumar Patel* [1988] AC 910, and *Satta* [1978] Imm AR 190), although this would now be dealt with under para 320(12) (see page 245). An acquittal on a criminal charge does not preclude the immigration officer from concluding on the balance of probabilities that the person committed the offence. In such circumstances he may without making further inquiries exclude him on the basis that his exclusion would be conducive to the public good (*Ex p Nkiti* [1989] Imm AR 182). The power cannot lawfully be exercised in an arbitrary manner, and trivial occasions of its use will render the decision either amenable to review or appeal.

4 Persons in possession of an entry clearance

Refusal of leave to enter in relation to a person in possession of an entry clearance

321. A person seeking leave to enter the United Kingdom who holds an entry clearance which was duly issued to him and is still current may be refused leave to enter only where the Immigration Officer is satisfied that:
   (i) whether or not to the holder's knowledge, false representations were employed or material facts were not disclosed, either in writing or orally, for the purpose of obtaining the entry clearance; or
   (ii) a change of circumstances since it was issued has removed the basis of the holder's claim to admission, except where the change of circumstances amounts solely to the person becoming over age for entry in one of the categories contained in paragraphs 296–316 of these Rules since the issue of the entry clearance; or
   (iii) refusal is justified on grounds of restricted returnability; on medical grounds; on grounds of criminal record; because the person seeking leave to enter is the subject of a deportation order or because exclusion would be conducive to the public good.

COMMENTARY

A person who holds an entry clearance which was duly issued to him (*S of S v Idowu* [1972] Imm AR 197), and which is still current (*Andronicou v Chief Immigration Officer, London (Heathrow) Airport* [1974] Imm AR 87) is not to be refused leave to enter

GROUNDS TO ENTER OR REMAIN IN THE UK

unless the immigration officer is satisfied that one of the following grounds applies to him.

(a) False representations and non-disclosure
See page 19.

(b) Change of circumstance
A change of circumstance since the entry clearance was issued which removes the basis of the holder's claim to admission may result in refusal of leave to enter. If the holder of the entry clearance is a child entering under the paras relating to the entry of relatives and the only change of circumstance is that the holder has become an adult in the interim, leave to enter should not be refused. Where the change occurs after arrival, but before leave to enter, the immigration officer may take it into account (*Teflisi* (3522)). The question of whether there has been a change of circumstance is a matter of fact and degree (*Hossain v Immigration Officer, Heathrow* [1990] Imm AR 520). Where two Pakistani children under 18 years of age were granted entry clearances to enable them to join their parents in the UK, leave to enter was properly refused because between the time they were interviewed and the time when the entry clearances were granted, their mother had returned to Pakistan. Their admission depended upon both parents being present and settled in the UK. The mother's return removed the basis of the claim to admission, and was a change of circumstances affecting what should have been a continuing state of affairs subsisting from the time the clearances were issued until the children's arrival at the port of entry (*Arshad v Immigration Officer London (Heathrow) Airport*) [1977] Imm AR 19). In *R v S of S, ex p Rukshanda Begum* [1990] Imm AR 1 a child, who was granted entry clearance to accompany his mother to the UK, arrived in the UK without her. A change in circumstances was held to have occurred because the mother could not fulfil the requirements of the rules that she should be admitted at the same time for settlement. On the other hand where the length of a visit was all that had changed, no change of circumstance affecting the basis of the application occurred (*Immigration Officer, Heathrow v Salmak* [1991] Imm AR 191).

Where the change of circumstance since the issuing of the entry clearance is merely that the applicant has become too old for entry as a child of a settled person (paras 296 to 316) it does not give grounds for refusal of leave to enter.

IMMIGRATION CONTROL

Restricted returnability etc For the definition of 'restricted returnability' see paras 21 to 23. For medical grounds, see paras 36 to 39. For criminal convictions, see page 251. For exclusion conducive to the public good, see page 251.

5 Refusal of variation of leave to enter or remain or curtailment of leave

Refusal of variation of leave to enter or remain or curtailment of leave

322. In addition to the grounds for refusal of extension of stay set out in Parts 2–8 of these Rules, the following provisions apply in relation to the refusal of an application for variation of leave to enter or remain or, where appropriate, the curtailment of leave:

Grounds on which an application to vary leave to enter or remain in the United Kingdom is to be refused

(1) the fact that variation of leave to enter or remain is being sought for a purpose not covered by these Rules.

Grounds on which an application to vary leave to enter or remain in the United Kingdom should normally be refused

(2) the making of false representations or the failure to disclose any material fact for the purpose of obtaining leave to enter or a previous variation of leave;
(3) failure to comply with any conditions attached to the grant of leave to enter or remain;
(4) failure by the person concerned to maintain or accommodate himself and any dependants without recourse to public funds;
(5) the undesirability of permitting the person concerned to remain in the United Kingdom in the light of his character, conduct or associations or the fact that he represents a threat to national security;
(6) refusal by a sponsor of the person concerned to give, if requested to do so, an undertaking in writing to be responsible for his maintenance and accommodation in the United Kingdom or failure to honour such an undertaking once given;
(7) failure by the person concerned to honour any declaration or undertaking given orally or in writing as to the intended duration and/or purpose of his stay;
(8) failure, except by a person who qualifies for settlement in the United Kingdom or by the spouse of a person settled in the United Kingdom, to satisfy the Secretary of State that he will be returnable to another country if allowed to remain in the United Kingdom for a further period;

GROUNDS TO ENTER OR REMAIN IN THE UK

(9) failure by an applicant to produce within a reasonable time documents or other evidence required by the Secretary of State to establish his claim to remain under these Rules;

(10) failure, without providing a reasonable explanation, to comply with a request made on behalf of the Secretary of State to attend for interview;

(11) failure, in the case of a child under the age of 18 years seeking a variation of his leave to enter or remain in the United Kingdom otherwise than in conjunction with an application by his parent(s) or legal guardian, to provide the Secretary of State, if required to do so, with written consent to the application from his parent(s) or legal guardian; save that the requirement as to written consent does not apply in the case of a child who has been admitted to the United Kingdom as an asylum seeker.

Grounds on which leave to enter or remain may be curtailed

323. A person's leave to enter or remain may be curtailed on any of the grounds set out in paragraph 322(2)–(5) above or if he ceases to meet the requirements of the Rules under which his leave to enter or remain was granted.

Crew members

324. A person who has been given leave to enter to join a ship, aircraft, hovercraft, hydrofoil or international train service as a member of its crew, or a crew member who has been given leave to enter for hospital treatment, repatriation or transfer to another ship, aircraft, hovercraft, hydrofoil or international train service in the United Kingdom, is to be refused leave to remain unless an extension of stay is necessary to fulfil the purpose for which he was given leave to enter or unless he meets the requirements for an extension of stay as a spouse in paragraph 284.

COMMENTARY

The requirements in each of the immigration rules in parts 2–8 of HC 395 that have to be satisfied are supplemented by these general grounds of refusal. They are divided into one mandatory ground and ten discretionary grounds of refusal. An application for a variation of leave to enter or remain must be refused where the variation of leave to enter or remain is being sought for a purpose not covered by HC 395. Where leave is curtailed after an unsuccessful asylum application, pursuant to s 7 of the 1993 Act, the person has no right of appeal (1993 Act, s 7(2)). However, he may appeal against any decision to deport him subsequently made.

(a) Non-disclosure

A person who obtained leave for one period intending that he would make an application for extension of that leave was treated as having made false representations, where that longer period was held to have been his intention throughout (*Ding* (3304)). An application for a variation of leave to enter from visitor to student was properly refused by the S of S where a person falsely represented herself as a holiday visitor when she had applied for an entry certificate, whereas her intention was to pursue a course of study. The IAT commented that the purpose of the rules was not to allow persons, whose real purpose in coming to the UK was to study, to enter on the false pretence that they came for no purpose other than for a short visit. Such persons could not reasonably expect that, having presented the Home Office with a *fait accompli* of compliance with the formal requirements for students, they have a right to stay in that capacity (*Owusu v S of S* [1976] Imm AR 101).

(b) Breaches of earlier conditions

The S of S may rely on breaches which occurred in an earlier period of leave. In *Clifford Ofoajoku v S of S* [1991] Imm AR 68 the S of S took account of a breach of condition in an earlier period of leave. He was not estopped from relying on it because a period of further leave had intervened, where that latter period of leave was granted without knowledge of the breach. Where the breach comes to light after the date of the refusal to grant the variation of leave, it may be relied upon before the appellate authorities (*Rajendran v S of S* [1989] Imm AR 512). An application is considered in the light of the circumstances at the time of the decision and not in the light of the facts at the time of the application (*S of S v Patel* [1988] Imm AR 75). The only exception to this is where a child who applies to join his parents becomes older than 18 by the time of the decision. In *Clifford Ofoajoku v S of S* [1991] Imm AR 68 the IAT rejected the S of S's argument that estoppel can never operate in immigration cases, but stated that simply granting leave after knowledge that the applicant had worked in breach would not by itself estop the S of S from relying on the breach, since there is a discretionary power to refuse an extension of leave because of prior breaches. Although estoppel can operate against the Crown in certain cases the doctrine is of very limited application in cases involving the exercise of immigration control (see *Paet v S of S* [1979–80] Imm AR 185; and *R v IAT, ex p Ahluwalia*

[1979–80] Imm AR 1). So, for example, neither a delay of four years in instituting deportation proceedings, nor alleged assurances by the police that if the appellants co-operated in a prosecution they would not be deported, estopped the S of S from ultimately deciding to deport (*Deen v S of S* [1987] Imm AR 543). Again the S of S was not estopped from refusing an extension requested by an appellant because he granted her a number of extensions in order to enable her to find a firm of solicitors willing to accept her as an articled clerk (*S of S v Wedad* [1979–80] Imm AR 27). The immigration rules do not provide for the condonation, in the sense of full forgiveness, of past immigration offences (*S of S v Sidique* [1976] Imm AR 69).

(c) Maintenance and accommodation

See pages 211. For public funds see page 61.

(d) Character, conduct and associations

See page 251. This is a broad power to deal with undesirables of all kinds. The list is not exclusive. For the provisions relating to EEA nationals see Chapter 15.

(e) Refusal of a sponsor to give an oral or written undertaking

The sponsor can be required to give an undertaking under para 35 to be responsible for the maintenance and accommodation of the applicant (see page 79). If he refuses to give such an undertaking or fails to honour it the application may be refused.

(f) Declarations as to duration of stay

An application may be refused even if the undertaking has originally been honestly given (*Amoah v S of S* [1987] Imm AR 236). 'undertaking' is used here to mean a promise or statement by the applicant as well as a written declaration or undertaking.

(g) Restricted returnability

If a person does not qualify for settlement he must satisfy the S of S that he can be returned to another country at the end of the further period of leave he seeks. A person who qualifies for settlement (and his spouse) do not have to satisfy the S of S of this.

(h) Provision of documents and failure to attend an interview

The applicant must provide the evidence on which his application for an extension may be assessed. However, there are no guidelines on what constitutes an unreasonable time. The S of S may take into account the delay of a person's agents. These provisions mirror the rules relating to the determination of asylum claims (see Chapter 19).

(i) Written consent

Children under the age of 18 seeking leave to remain in the UK must have the written consent of their parent or guardian. Paragraph 322 only applies to the determination of applications under Parts 2-8 of HC 395. There is no need for the express disavowal of para 322(11) in relation to Part 9 applications for asylum.

6 Paragraph 323—curtailment

The Applicant's leave to enter or remain may be curtailed by virtue of any of the discretionary grounds or if at any time he ceases to satisfy the terms of the para of Parts 2-8 under which he was given leave to enter or remain. Where a person has limited leave, and he makes a claim for asylum, that limited leave may be curtailed at the same time as the asylum claim is refused. He has no right of appeal under section 14 against such curtailment but may appeal against the refusal of asylum.

7 Registration with the police

PART 10

REGISTRATION WITH THE POLICE

325. A condition requiring registration with the police should normally be imposed on any foreign national aged 16 years or over who is given limited leave to enter the United Kingdom:
  (i) for employment for longer than 3 months unless he has been admitted for permit free employment as a private servant in a diplomatic household or as a minister of religion; or
  (ii) for longer than 6 months under the following categories of these Rules:
    (*a*)   students;
    (*b*)   'au pair';
    (*c*)   businessmen and self-employed persons;

(d) investors or persons of independent means;
(e) creative artists;
(f) family members of European Economic Area nationals who are not themselves European Economic Area nationals; or

(iii) as the spouse or child of a person required to register with the police; or
(iv) exceptionally, in any other case where the Immigration Officer considers it necessary to ensure that a foreign national complies with the terms of a limited leave to enter.

326. A condition requiring registration with the police should also be imposed when a foreign national on whom a registration requirement was not imposed on arrival is granted an extension of stay which has the effect of allowing him to remain in the United Kingdom for employment for longer than 3 months, or otherwise for longer than 6 months, reckoned from the date of his arrival, save where:
  (i) the person concerned is under the age of 16; or
  (ii) the extension of stay was granted as a minister of religion or private servant in a diplomatic household; or
  (iii) the extension of stay was granted on the basis of marriage to a person settled in the United Kingdom.

COMMENTARY

When an alien aged 16 or over is given leave to enter for a limited period he may be required (under s 3(1)(c) of the 1971 Act) to register with the police if he falls into one of the above categories. Family members of EEA nationals who are not themselves EEA nationals may be required to register although this rarely happens in practice.

Pursuant to s 4(3) and (4) the S of S made regulations regarding registration with the Police and the provision of information for hotel records. The term 'alien' means a national of another country who is neither a Commonwealth citizen nor a BPP (see page 29) 1981 Act, s 50(1), and Reg 2(1) of the Immigration (Registration with the Police) Regulations 1972 (as amended)). A stamp is placed in the person's passport stating 'The holder is also required to register at once with the police'.

The current Regulations setting out particulars to be kept in the register are contained in the Immigration (Registration with the Police) Regulations 1972 (SI 1972 No 1758 (as amended by SI 1982/1024, SI 1990/400 and SI 1991/965), made pursuant to section 4(3) of the 1971 Act. Failure to register without reasonable excuse is a criminal offence under s 26(1)(f) of the 1971 Act.

(a) Registration

Within seven days of the Regulations becoming applicable to him, the alien must attend at the offices of the chief police officer for either his area of residence (if he is resident) or in any other case the chief police officer for the area in which for the time being he happens to be. In London the relevant office is the Aliens Registration Office, at 10 Lamb's Conduit Street, London WC1 3MX, otherwise it is the local central police station. If he registers within 7 days he is taken to have registered 'at once'. He must furnish such information as the officer may require, including his name, address, marital status, his employment or occupation, and the name and address of his employer (Schedule to the Regulations). He must produce a passport or other documentation establishing his identity or nationality. If he cannot do this, he must give an explanation of why he is unable to do so. Any change in address must be notified to the officer within seven days (Reg 7). Other changes in the particulars must be notified to the officer within eight days of their occurrence (Reg 8). If an alien is absent from his UK residence for a period exceeding two months he must notify the officer of his address for the time being, and of his return. Any other changes of address within that time must be notified to the officer within eight days, provided that he intends to remain at that address for more than eight days (Reg 7). The alien is provided with a certificate of registration for which he is charged a fee (Reg 10) and which he may be required to produce to any constable or immigration officer. The alien is required to provide the officer, if required, with two copies of a photograph of himself (Reg 5, 8(b), and 9). If he fails to provide a photograph the officer may cause him to be photographed (Reg 9).

(b) EEA nationals

EEA nationals exercising Community rights (see Chapter 15) are exempt from registration. Members of the EEA national's family, who are not themselves EEA nationals, are subject to registration (*R v Pieck* [1981] QB 571).

8 Asylum

The Rules relating to asylum form Part 11 of HC 395. The rules are discussed in Chapter 19, together with the separate appeal system applicable to asylum claims.

9 Rights of Appeal

The Rules relating to rights of appeal form Part 12 of HC 395. Part 12 and commentary upon it is set out in Chapter 23.

Chapter 14

Deportation

1 Introduction

Deportation is one method of removing a person from the UK. Others include removal under removal directions given in respect of an illegal entrant; and supervised and voluntary departures. In relation to deportation orders there are normally three stages before removal is effected. First, the S of S will notify the person who may be deported that he intends to deport him. Second, if an appeal against that notice is either not made or unsuccessful, the S of S will sign the deportation order. Third, the deportation order is implemented. It is important to keep the stages clear, and in particular to note that such rights of appeal as exist relate to the first part of the process. Where there is a possibility of a recommendation being made by a criminal court, a slightly different system operates: the defendant must be given the opportunity to address the court on this aspect of his sentence, and may appeal against that aspect through the criminal appeals system (see paras 381–389, pages 269–270 below).

The power to make a deportation order may be exercised by immigration officers of the rank of inspector. Following *Oladehinde v S of S* [1991] 1 AC 254, the Home Office has stated that written records of the decision, making process must be kept and that cases in which a person has been in the UK for a long time, or where there are compassionate circumstances, must be referred from the immigration officer to the Home Office for a decision. It was stressed in *Oladehinde* that the person making the decision should not have been involved in the investigation of the case at all. Immigration officers will interview a person and send a fax to an inspector for confirmation of the decision they reach.

Separate legislation governs the surrender from the UK of persons who have committed crimes in other countries. Extradition to the Republic of Ireland is covered by the Backing of Warrants (Republic of Ireland) Act 1965; to Commonwealth countries and to foreign countries by the Extradition Act 1989. These statutes apply to nationals as well as to aliens. See also the Suppression of Terrorism Act 1978, and the European Convention on the Suppression of Terrorism. The European Convention on Extradition 1957 and the European Convention on Extradition Order 1990 set procedures for extradition to, broadly, the EU countries, Israel, Turkey, Cyprus, Finland and Norway (see the full list in *Re Farinha* [1992] Imm AR 174). The Repatriation of Prisoners Act 1984 makes provision for foreign prisoners serving sentences in the UK to be returned to their own country to complete their terms of imprisonment. All parties, the prisoner, the foreign country, and the UK, must consent to the repatriation. The law of extradition, deportation, and the right of asylum are closely inter-linked (see *R v Governor of Brixton Prison, ex p Soblen* [1963] 2 QB 243).

2 Long residence policies

Finally, before turning to a statement of the Rules, it is convenient to consider the Secretary of State's policies relating to long residence. Applications for indefinite leave to remain may be made on the basis of these concessions. However, they remain primarily of use in consideration of deportation cases.

(a) Ten years

Except where the grant of leave would not be in the public interest, if a person has resided lawfully in the UK for more than ten years continuously, and makes an application based on that residence, it will be considered on its merits within the terms of a statement by the Minister of State for the Home Department (see Hansard 5 November 1987 (121 HC Official Report (6th Series) written answers cols 833–834). The Home Office will take into account among other considerations:

(*a*) strength of ties with the UK or another country;
(*b*) the total length of continuous residence;
(*c*) the proportion of that residence which was lawful.

Each case is considered on its merits. Article 3(3) of the European Convention on Establishment provides that nationals of its contracting parties who have lawfully resided for ten years in the territory of another party can only be expelled for reasons of national security, or serious reasons of public order, public health or public morality. The Home Office states that it applies the principle of the Article more widely, the question of the establishment of close ties being of greatest concern.

Indefinite leave to remain should normally be granted if the applicant has ten or more years of lawful continuous residence, and there are no strong countervailing factors.

(b) Fourteen years

Where an applicant for indefinite leave to remain has 14 years' or more continuous residence in the UK, whether legal or not in whole or in part, indefinite leave to remain will normally be granted. It may be refused however if there is an extant criminal record or a deliberate positive and blatant attempt to evade immigration control.

Long residence is also taken into account where it is less than either of the above periods when consideration is given as to whether to deport a person. Where the period of residence is long, but does not fall into the above categories, the proportion of lawful residence in the UK and the length of residence will be the primary factors in determining whether to deport.

In *Domfeh Gyeabour* [1989] Imm AR 94, the IAT considered that an overstayer who overstayed nearly 11 years had a legitimate expectation that he would be allowed to remain on the basis of an earlier ministerial statement on the removal of illegal entrants after ten years' residence. No legitimate expectation, however, that the applicant would not be deported could be raised on the Ministerial statement if the applicant was aware that the S of S intended to deport him for half his period of long residence (*Mohammed Hussain v IAT* [1991] Imm AR 413). Further, where 10 years' residence is relied upon it must be lawful residence. The person must have had leave for that period, and it is not enough that for some of the time he was protected from removal by s 14(1) of the 1971 Act because he had an appeal pending against a deportation order (*Ex p Mesirionye* [1993] Imm AR 119). Further, the residence required for 14 years must be more than merely ordinary residence (*Ex p F Ali* [1992] Imm AR 316). There have been two ministerial statements on this subject and the S of S relies on the later of the two. He is entitled to change his policy (*Mohammed Miah v S of S* [1992] Imm AR 106).

Appeals against deportation orders are dealt with in Chapter 23).

3 Deportation

PART 13

DEPORTATION

A deportation order

362. A deportation order requires the subject to leave the United Kingdom and authorises his detention until he is removed. It also prohibits him from re-entering the country for as long as it is in force and invalidates any leave to enter or remain in the United Kingdom given him before the order was made or while it is in force.

363. The circumstances in which a person is liable to deportation are set out in the Immigration Act 1971 and include:
- (i) failure to comply with a condition attached to his leave to enter or remain or remaining beyond the time limited by the leave;
- (ii) where the Secretary of State deems the person's deportation to be conducive to the public good;
- (iii) where the person is the wife or child under 18 of a person ordered to be deported; and
- (iv) where a court recommends deportation in the case of a person over the age of 17 who has been convicted of an offence punishable with imprisonment.

COMMENTARY

Under ss 3(5)–(6) and 5(1)–(4) of the 1971 Act the S of S may, if he thinks fit, make a deportation order requiring a person who does not have the right of abode to leave and to remain out of the UK:
- (a) if the person has failed to comply with a condition attached to his leave to enter or remain beyond the authorised time (see s 3(5)(a));
- (b) if the S of S deems the person's deportation to be conducive to the public good (see s 3(5)(b));
- (c) if the person is the wife or the child under 18 of a person ordered to be deported (see s 3(5)(c); and
- (d) if the person, after reaching the age of 17, is convicted of an offence for which he is punishable with imprisonment and the court recommends deportation (see s 3(6)).

The power to deport applies generally to all persons subject to control under the 1971 Act including persons who have been granted settlement. However, it does not apply to any member of a mission (within the meaning of the Diplomatic Privileges Act 1964), any person who is a member of the family and forms part of the household of such a member (*Gupta v S of S* [1979-80] Imm AR 52), or any other person entitled to the like immunity from jurisdiction as is conferred by the 1964 Act on a diplomatic agent (s 8(3) of the 1971 Act). Immunity however only applies to a member of a mission other than a diplomatic agent if he enters the UK:

(*a*) as a member of the mission; or

(*b*) in order to take up a post which was offered to him before he travelled (s 8(3A) of the 1971 Act, see also *Ex p Bagga* [1990] 3 WLR 1013.

A citizen of the Irish Republic or a Commonwealth citizen who was settled and has been ordinarily resident in the UK continuously since 1 January 1973 is not liable to be deported on the ground that his deportation is conducive to the public good; and if he was settled and ordinarily resident in the UK on 1 January 1973 and has been so resident for the last five years (*Mehmet v S of S* [1977] Imm AR 68; and *Rehman v S of S* [1978] Imm AR 80) he is not liable to deportation on any ground (s 1 of the 1971 Act). In *Ex p O'Shea* [1988] Imm AR 484 the CA held that a woman against whom a deportation order had been made could not subsequently render herself immune from deportation by marrying a British citizen, a position which is now confirmed in para 284(vi) of HC 395 (see also *Ex p Husseyin* [1988] Imm AR 129).

(a) Deportation for breach of conditions or unauthorised stay (s 3(5)(a) 1971 Act)

The rules mirror the 1971 Act in stating that the S of S may make a deportation order where a person has failed to comply with a condition attached to his leave to enter or remain. Full account is to be taken of all the relevant circumstances known to the S of S before a decision is reached. Where there had been persistent failure over a period of nearly five years to comply with the immigration rules the S of S was held to have exercised his discretion properly in ordering deportation (*S of S v Aluko* [1974] Imm AR 90). In *Jordan v S of S* [1972] Imm AR 201, the IAT emphasised that the exercise of the power of deportation should be 'consistent and fair as between one person and another'. The IAT held that were the appellants to be permitted to remain in the country it could hardly be said that such action would be 'consistent and fair' as between them and the many persons overseas subject to UK immigration control whose circumstances and background are similar to those of the appellants.

Ignorance by a person that he has overstayed is a compassionate circumstance to be taken into account (*Hanif v S of S* [1985] Imm AR 57).

Students who work in breach By a concession, genuine students do not normally merit deportation if they work in breach of their conditions. However, there must be no doubt about the quality or quantity of the studies they undertake. Deportation will still be appropriate if they have seriously broken a prohibition on employment. (See letter from Home Office to JCWI dated 18 July 1989 and *Ex p Amoa* [1992] Imm AR 218). Since rights of appeal to the adjudicator on the merits of a deportation decision have been severely limited there has been a move away from this concession in practice. There has also been an increase generally in the number of deportations and supervised departures since 1988.

(b) Deportation because 'conducive to the public good'
(1971 Act, s 3(5)(b))

The S of S has the power to deport a person if he deems it conducive to the public good. However, nowhere is the phrase 'conducive to the public good' defined. Where a person, after entry, has exercised deception in order to obtain enlarged rights of entry, this may justify deportation on public good grounds (see *Re Owusu Sekyere* [1987] Imm AR 425 and *R v IAT, ex p Cheema* [1982] Imm AR 124, where marriages of convenience were held to be against the public good). Further, a person may be deported under this head, simply because he was guilty of deception on entry (*R v IAT, ex p Patel* [1988] AC 910).

In *Patel* Lord Bridge reconsidered his views expressed in *Khawaja* that deportation on 'conducive' grounds was never intended to be invoked as a means of deporting a perfectly respectable citizen on grounds arising out of the circumstances of his original entry. Commenting on that view he said it was mistaken: 'Reading the judgment of Lord Lane CJ in *Cheema* I find myself in complete agreement with his opinion that the exercise of the power is within both the literal meaning of s 3(5)(b) and the spirit of the Act. If this is correct, there can be no possible ground to distinguish between a fraud practised in order to obtain leave to enter, and a fraud practised after entry to obtain indefinite leave' (see eg also the CA in *R v IAT, ex p Sheikh* (1988) *Times*, 17 March: original bribery to gain entry justified deportation under s 3(5)(b) despite a respectable life thereafter).

Each case is to be considered carefully in the light of the relevant circumstances known to the S of S including those general considerations listed above. In the usual case, the S of S should give a person in respect of whom deportation on this ground is contemplated an opportunity to state his case (*Afful v S of S* [1986] Imm AR 230). Both legal entrants and persons who are 'not legally here' may be deported for reasons of public good (*Villone v S of S* [1979–80] Imm AR 23).

In *Butt v S of S* [1979–80] Imm AR 82, the S of S deemed that it would be 'conducive to the public good' to deport the appellant, an illegal entrant, who was convicted of offences of theft and of criminal damage and was given a suspended sentence although the court made no recommendation for his deportation and his conviction was after several years of residence.

In *R v IAT, ex p A-V* (1989) *Times*, 22 August Rose J stated that an IAT should consider the effects of the deportation order when considering compassionate circumstances. In that case the person was to be deported to a country in which he would face the death penalty for the crime of which he had been convicted. The IAT should take into account double jeopardy, and should only compare like cases for the purposes of achieving consistency and fairness.

A decision to deport frequently arises where a person has been convicted of a criminal offence but the court has not made a recommendation for deportation (see *Patel v S of S* [1986] Imm AR 457). In *Villone*'s case (see above) the IAT considered it to be 'perfectly plain' that it was 'conducive to the public good' to make a deportation order against him. He was sentenced to three years' imprisonment for offences under the Misuse of Drugs Act 1971 and the Customs and Excise Act 1952. In addition the appellant had been charged in the USA on 14 separate occasions with drug offences, armed robbery, possessing an unlawful weapon, and being a fugitive from justice. He had been sentenced to terms totalling ten years' imprisonment. Furthermore he was currently wanted in the USA on charges of possessing stolen credit cards and a concealed weapon.

Some criminal offences are of so serious a nature as to justify deportation under this head even if there is no record of previous offences and no great likelihood of the individual reoffending (*R v IAT, ex p Florent* [1985] Imm AR 141; the CA in that case gave as an example the supply of heroin).

In order to show that a decision to deport as conducive to the public good based purely on a criminal conviction is not justified, it is necessary to show that it is either wrong in law or administratively unreasonable. The principles relating to the exercise by a court of its power to recommend deportation do not affect the S of S's power to decide to make a deportation order on conducive grounds (*Hukan Said v IAT* [1989] Imm AR 372 and *Al-Sabah v S of S* [1992] Imm AR 223).

Because of the general nature of this power it is often used in situations where a material fact has been omitted such as to deceive the S of S by the effect and implication of what has been said (*R v IAT, ex p A R Patel* [1988] Imm AR 434). A deportation order may be made on this ground notwithstanding that the deportee has an application for variation of leave to remain outstanding which has not been determined (*Ex p Manvinder Kaur* [1991] Imm AR 426).

(c) Recommendations by a criminal court

By s 3(6) of the 1971 Act any person without the right of abode, save those listed on page 266, aged 17 and over who has been convicted of a criminal offence punishable by imprisonment may be recommended for deportation by the criminal court which sentences him for the offence.

Before a criminal court makes a recommendation, the defendant must be given the opportunity to address it on the question (*R v Antypas* (1973) 57 Cr. App R 207), and the criminal court should give full reasons for its decision to make a recommendation (*R v Compassi* (1987) 9 Cr App R(S) 270). In *R v Nazari* [1980] 3 All ER 880, the CA set out the following guidelines as to the relevant matters that a criminal court considering whether to make an order recommending deportation should take into account (see also *R v Caird* (1970) 54 Cr App R 499):

(1) The court must consider whether the defendant's continued presence in the UK is to its detriment. A minor offence such as shoplifting would not normally merit recommendation of deportation.

(2) The courts are not concerned with the political systems which operate in other countries. That is a matter for the Home Secretary to take into account when deciding whether to act on the recommendation (however in *R v Walters* (1977) *Thomas's Encyclopedia of Current Sentencing Practice*

K 1.5(b) special hardship to the defendant was taken into account).
(3) The court must take into account the effect which an order recommending deportation will have on others who are not before the court and who are innocent persons. For example, will the order put an innocent spouse in the difficult position of having to choose between going abroad or remaining in the UK without the deported spouse in the interests of the children?

It may be appropriate to make a recommendation of deportation following a conviction even where the person concerned no longer has any ties to his country of origin (*R v Kanapathipillai* (1988) *Times*, 26 March). However if the defendant is an overstayer, that by itself is not a ground for the court to make a recommendation for deportation (*Miller v Lenton* (1981) Cr App R(S) 171).

Detriment The detriment must be to the community. Where a person was convicted of a single serious offence of wounding but otherwise was exemplary, a recommendation was not appropriate (*R v Idriss* (1977) Thomas's Encyclopedia of Current Sentencing Practice K1.5(a)). In *R v Ariquat* (1981) Cr App R(S) 83 the 19 year old defendant was convicted of indecent assault when he had intercourse with a 15 year old believing her to be over 16. A recommendation was quashed on appeal. Where the defendant was convicted of a serious offence of arson, the emotional stress under which he was acting was properly to be taken into account in deciding whether or not to make a recommendation (*R v Tshuma* (1981) 3 Cr App R(S) 97).

Finally, if the defendant is reliant on social security, that is not to the detriment of the community and should not be taken into consideration in deciding whether or not to make a recommendation (*R v Serry* (1980) 3 Cr App R(S) 336).

Where the court has not recommended deportation there may nevertheless be grounds, in the light of all the relevant information and subject to the right of appeal for deportation, for curtailment of stay or refusal to extend stay followed, after the supervised departure, by a prohibition on re-entry. Finally, a recommendation, or the failure to make a recommendation by a criminal court, does not in any way limit the discretionary powers of the S of S under s 3(5)(*b*). In particular, it is not *res judicata* (*Martin v S of S* [1993] Imm AR 161).

European Convention on Human Rights and Deportation In *R v IAT, ex p Chundawadra* [1987] Imm AR 227 the CA rejected the argument that the UK's signing of the European Convention on Human Rights created a legitimate expectation that the S of S would abide by its obligations under Art 8 (right to family life) and Art 13 (right to an effective remedy). The CA held that the S of S is duly obliged to take account of what was expressly or impliedly authorised by the 1971 Act and the immigration rules. However in *Beldjoudi v France* (1992) *Times,* 10 April the ECtHR held that a French deportation order made against a man who had married was in breach of Art 8. The court held that it was not justified by a pressing social need nor proportionate to the legitmate aim pursued by France of immigration control. In *Chundawadra* the CA stated that the European Court of Human Rights may give different answers to the questions 'Is the deportation conducive to the public good?' and 'Is it necessary for the protection of the public'. It may be that a deportation order may be challenged before the ECtHR on the basis of a breach of Art 8, if it breaks up a family, for example, or prevents a person having access to a child, or *vice versa*. The deportation order would also have to be necessary for the public good or for the prevention of crime. In *Berrehab v Netherlands* (1988) 11 EHRR 322, the expulsion of a father which it was sought to justify on the basis of public order was successfully challenged on the basis that it was not so necessary as to outweigh his daughter's (and his) rights to family life. Moreover in the course of the committee debates in the House of Commons on the Asylum and Immigration Appeals Act 1993, the Minister stated that exceptional leave to remain would be granted in genuine humanitarian cases in which the UK's international obligations would otherwise be broken. It is arguable therefore that if a deportation order is made in a case in which a child's rights to family life would be violated if the parent was deported, the S of S should grant the parent leave to remain exceptionally as the only way of securing the child's right to family life. A refusal to do so could be challenged by way of judicial review of the S of S's decision (see Hansard Standing Committee A 12 November 1992 Col 52). It may further be argued that in any event a deportation order which would interfere with a family unit would be in breach of the S of S's own guidelines (set out on page 273) on enforcement of deportation action where marriage or children are involved.

4 Considerations to be taken into account in considering deportation action

364. In considering whether deportation is the right course on the merits, the public interest will be balanced against any compassionate circumstances of the case. While each case will be considered in the light of the particular circumstances, the aim is an exercise of the power of deportation which is consistent and fair as between one person and another, although one case will rarely be identical with another in all material respects. Deportation will normally be the proper course where a person has failed to comply with or has contravened a condition or has remained without authority. Before a decision to deport is reached the Secretary of State will take into account all relevant factors known to him including:
   (i) age;
   (ii) length of residence in the United Kingdom;
   (iii) strength of connections with the United Kingdom;
   (iv) personal history, including character, conduct and employment record;
   (v) domestic circumstances;
   (vi) previous criminal record and the nature of any offence of which the person has been convicted;
   (vii) compassionate circumstances;
   (viii) any representations received on the person's behalf.

COMMENTARY

In considering whether deportation is the right course on the merits the public interest will be balanced against any compassionate circumstances of the case. One case will rarely be identical with another in all material aspects. So, for example, a non-EU national cannot rely on the rules applicable to EU nationals in this area (see *R v IAT ex p Al-Sabah* [1992] Imm AR 223).

The only duty the S of S has is to take account of every relevant factor known to him at the time of the decision. There is no duty on the S of S to investigate any of the above categories. The list is not exhaustive. In particular the effect of deporting a particular individual on third parties, other than his family and persons immediately connected with him, may well be a factor which is relevant to the discretionary decision whether he should or should not be deported. In *R v IAT, ex p Bakhtaur Singh* [1986] Imm AR 352, the HL held that it was relevant to take into account the loss to the Sikh community of a priest and musician with a rare talent. Similar account can be taken of the deportation of a successful businessman on the business concerned, or the effect of the loss of a scientist on important research upon which he was engaged. It is not appropriate to take into account improper pressure, such as the threat of industrial action if a person is deported.

A person who has been deported may not return to the UK while the deportation order is still in force. Where a person returns to the UK notwithstanding that a deportation order is in force against him he may lawfully be detained as an illegal entrant and deported under the original order or removed as an illegal entrant.

Cases involving marriage and children In *R v IAT, ex p Chundawadra* [1987] Imm AR 227, Taylor J held that the European Convention on Human Rights, and specifically Art 8, which requires that family life be respected was not required to be taken into account in a decision whether or not to deport. However since January 1993 Immigration Officers have been provided with guidance on cases involving marriage and children, which take into account the effect of the European Convention on Human Rights, Art 8 of which guarantees the right to respect for family life (See 1993 INL & P Vol 7, No 3). The S of S should have regard to the policy in deciding whether to deport and he may act irrationally if he fails to do so (*Ex p Amankwah* [1993] CO/2114/92). European cases have shown that however unmeritorious the applicant's immigration history the ECtHR is disposed to find a breach of Art 8 where the effect of an immigration decision is to separate an applicant from his spouse or child.

Marriage Marriage is a factor in the decision-making process relating to deportation. Enforcement action may be halted where there is a genuine and subsisting marriage to a person settled in the UK and the following conditions are satisfied:

the marriage pre-dates the decision to deport or remove; and

(a) the marriage or cohabitation has subsisted for two or more years (however, the quality of the relationship is a better positive factor than its length); or

(b) the settled spouse has lived in the UK from an early age, or it would be unreasonable to expect him to accompany the other on removal; or

(c) one or more children of the marriage have the right of abode in the UK;

    (i) once it has been concluded that the marriage is genuine and subsisting the immigration history of the person to be deported is of little relevance;

    (ii) where the spouse or the foreign national is pregnant with a child who would have the right of abode in the UK wherever born, removal is likely to be inappropriate;

(iii) the presence of the settled spouse's children by a former relationship is a factor if the children have the right of abode in the UK, are still dependent and the S of S is satisfied that either they live with or have frequent contact with the settled spouse.

The burden is on the settled spouse to show why it would be unreasonable for him to join the family outside the UK. The Home Office will in general concede this point if the settled spouse has strong family ties in the UK, or lengthy residence in the UK, or suffers from ill health. The ill health must be such that his quality of life would be significantly impaired if he were to accompany his spouse on removal. Where there are no children with the right of abode in the UK (for example, those born outside marriage to a foreign woman) there is a presumption that deportation proceedings should proceed if neither partner is settled in the UK; or the couple do not intend to live together permanently as husband and wife (a marriage of convenience); or the couple are separated.

Divorce and separation Where one parent is settled in the UK, and the removal of the other parent would result in the deprivation of frequent and regular access currently enjoyed by either parent, deportation or removal action will be abandoned by the S of S under the terms of the guidance note. The S of S cannot rely on the argument that the settled parent can travel abroad to continue access, in the light of *Berrehab v Netherlands* (1988) 11 EHRR 322. Where the person to be removed or deported has custody of a child with the right of abode (by a previous partner who is no longer in contact with the child) in the UK the guidance suggests that the factors to be considered are:

(*a*) the age of the child;
(*b*) the strength of the child's ties with the UK, including other UK resident family members;
(*c*) any medical conditions which would be better treated in the UK;
(*d*) the standard of living (including educational facilities) in the country to which the parent is to be removed.

The guidance assumes that a child of pre-school age can be expected to go to the foreign country. Article 2 of the First Protocol to the ECHR provides for the right to access to education. The assumption that a pre-school child may be expected to go to the foreign country may not be compatible with the right to access to education under the First Protocol.

Where a person has criminal convictions, but would otherwise benefit from the terms under which marriage/family relations cases are considered, removal will only be proceeded with where it can be justified as necessary in the interests of a democratic society. Thus only serious criminal convictions will justify removal, and even a long history of minor offending will not justify removal. The criminal convictions will be balanced against the other factors in the case even where they are serious.

Where a foreign national has married an EU national who is exercising Community rights in the UK he may only be removed where there are exceptionally strong grounds for suspicion that the marriage is one of convenience. This guidance refers to the exception to the right of a non-EU national who is a member of an EU national's family to free movement that was envisaged by the ECJ in *Surinder Singh* for cases of the fraudulent contraction of a marriage.

Children Where court proceedings for adoption, custodianship, wardship, or a residence order are taken to enable either the parent or child to evade immigration control, the Home Office may intervene in the proceedings only if there is strong evidence (not merely a suspicion) that there has been a serious attempt to circumvent immigration control. The Home Office will then seek to argue that the family proceedings are an abuse of process. The S of S is entitled to remove or deport a person whether there is an order relating to wardship or residence under the Children Act 1989. He does not commit a contempt of court in so doing (*Teame v Aberash* (1994) *Times*, 8 April).

5 Deportation of family members

Deportation of family members

365. Section 5 of the Immigration Act 1971 gives the Secretary of State power in certain circumstances to make a deportation order against the wife or child of a person against whom a deportation order has been made. The Secretary of State will not normally decide to deport the wife of a deportee where:
    (i) she has qualified for settlement in her own right; or
    (ii) she has been living apart from the deportee.

366. The Secretary of State will not normally decide to deport the child of a deportee where:
  (i) he and his mother are living apart from the deportee; or
  (ii) he has spent some years in the United Kingdom and is nearing the age of 18; or
  (iii) he has left home and established himself on an independent basis; or
  (iv) he married before deportation came into prospect.

367. In considering whether to require a wife or child to leave with the deportee the Secretary of State will take account of the factors listed in paragraph 364 as well as the following:
  (i) the ability of the wife to maintain herself and any children in the United Kingdom, or to be maintained by relatives or friends without charge to public funds, not merely for a short period but for the foreseeable future; and
  (ii) in the case of a child of school age, the effect of removal on his education; and
  (iii) the practicability of any plans for a child's care and maintenance in this country if one or both of his parents were deported; and
  (iv) any representations made by or on behalf of the wife or child.

368. Where the Secretary of State decides that it would be appropriate to deport a member of a family as such, the decision, and the right of appeal, will be notified and it will at the same time be explained that it is open to the member of the family to leave the country voluntarily if he does not wish to appeal or if he appeals and his appeal is dismissed.

COMMENTARY

Under s 5 of the 1971 Act there is a power to make a deportation order against the wife or children (including an adopted child (*R v IAT, ex p Tohur Ali* [1988] Imm AR 237)) under 18 of a person ordered to be deported, whether the deportation is following a conviction, for breach of a condition or unauthorised stay or on conducive grounds, unless more than eight weeks have elapsed since that person left the country following the making of an order against him (s 5(3)). If the deportation order against the principal deportee ceases to have effect then the wife or children under 18 of such a person cannot be deported under this rule (*R v IAT, ex p Ekrem Mehmet* [1977] 1 WLR 795).

The S of S can make the order to deport the family members before he makes the order to deport the principal deportee, provided he has already made the decision to deport the principal deportee (*R v IAT, ex p Ibrahim* [1989] Imm AR 111). This is based on the view that in immigration control the family is to be treated

as a unit and an interpretation of s 3(5)(c) which reads 'is or has been ordered to be' as encompassing the following situations:
  (a) where the principal deportee is deported;
  (b) where he is ordered to be deported; and
  (c) where he is to be deported.

Where the S of S decides that it would be appropriate to deport a member of a family as such, the decision, and the right to appeal, will be notified and it will at the same time be explained that it is open to the member of the family to leave the country voluntarily if he does not wish to appeal or if he appeals and his appeal is dismissed.

In considering whether to require a wife and children to leave with the 'head of the family' the S of S will take into account all relevant factors known to him including those listed in para 364 and the following (which is probably not an exclusive list (*R v IAT, ex p Bakhtaur Singh* [1986] Imm AR 352)):
  (i) The ability of the wife to maintain herself and any children in the UK or to be maintained by relatives or friends without charge to public funds, not merely for a short period, but for the foreseeable future;
  (ii) In the case of a school age child, the effect of removal on his education;
  (iii) The practicability for a child's care and maintenance in this country if one or both of his parents were deported;
  (iv) Any representations made by or on behalf of the wife or child;

The effect of removal of a school-age child on his education is designed to address the right of the child to access to education under the First Protocol to the ECHR.

The S of S must give separate consideration to each person considered for deportation (*Yan Yak Wah and Another v Home Office* [1982] Imm AR 16).

Where an appellant obtained entry to this country by deception, remained in this country unlawfully for some four years, and took employment in breach of her conditions of admission the IAT held that the public interest far outweighed the matters advanced on her behalf, inasmuch as if her conduct was to be condoned it was considered that immigration control would be rendered nugatory (*Anand v S of S* [1978] Imm AR 36).

Where the wife has qualified for settlement in the UK in her own right, for example following four years in approved employment, she has a valid claim to remain notwithstanding the expulsion of her husband and her deportation will not normally be contemplated. Where the wife has been living apart from the principal deportee it will not normally be right to include her, or any children living with her, in the deportation order.

Paragraph 389 of HC 395 provides that family members may be able to seek readmission to the UK after they cease to be members of the family. This rule reflects the 1971 Act, s 5(3) and (4). In the case of the wife, the person ceases to be a family member when the marriage comes to an end. Children cease to be 'members of the family' as defined in the Act at 18, and their deportation will not normally be contemplated if they have spent some years in the UK and are near that age. Deportation normally will not be appropriate if the child left the family home on taking employment and has established himself on an independent basis or if he is married before deportation came into prospect. In the case of children of school age it will be right to take into account, on the one hand, the disruptive effect of removal on their education and, on the other, whether plans for the care and maintenance in this country if one or both parents were deported are realistic and likely to be effective. A person who at the time a deportation order was made against him was over the age of 18, but near that age, may still be deported despite this view (*Panayiotis Karantoni v S of S* [1987] Imm AR 518).

The IAT will not readily accept that children should be permitted to remain in the UK if this results in them being separated from their parents. In *Ozter and Others v S of S* [1978] Imm AR 137, the IAT held that the disruptive effect on the children's lives, should they be sent back to Cyprus, had been grossly overstated, and to maintain the family unit the children should be with their parents. Thus the S of S in all the circumstances was justified in the decision, following the deportation orders against their parents, to deport the appellants (see also *Mustafa and Others v S of S* [1979-80] Imm AR 32).

6 Deportation: appeals

Right of appeal against destination

369. In all cases of deportation the person in respect of whom the order has been or is to be made has a right of appeal against the removal directions on the ground that he ought to be removed (if at all) to a country or territory specified by him, other than the one named in the direction (Section 17 of the 1971 Act).

DEPORTATION

Restricted right of appeal against deportation in cases of breach of limited leave

370. By virtue of Section 5(1) of the Immigration Act 1988, a person who was last given leave to enter the United Kingdom less than 7 years before the date of the decision to make a deportation order against him:
  (i) by virtue of Section 3(5)(a) of the Immigration Act 1971 (breach of limited leave); or
  (ii) by virtue of Section 3(5)(c) of that Act (as belonging to the family of a person who is or has been ordered to be deported by virtue of Section 3(5)(a))

shall not be entitled to appeal under Section 15 of the 1971 Act against that decision except on the ground that on the facts of his case there is in law no power to make the deportation order for the reasons stated in the notice of the decision.

Exemption to the restricted right of appeal

371. This restriction on the right of appeal does not apply to a person who is exempt by virtue of an order made under Section 5(2) of the 1988 Act. The Immigration (Restricted Right of Appeal against Deportation) (Exemption) Order 1993 provides that a person is exempt if he would last have been given leave to enter 7 years or more before the date of the decision to deport but for his having obtained a subsequent leave after an absence from the United Kingdom within the period limited for the duration of the earlier leave.

372. The Order also provides that a person is exempt if his limited leave has been curtailed by the Secretary of State under Section 7 of the 1993 Act.

A deportation order made on the recommendation of a Court

373. There is no appeal within the immigration appeal system against the making of a deportation order on the recommendation of a court; but there is a right of appeal to a higher court against the recommendation itself. An order may not be made while it is still open to the person to appeal against the relevant conviction, sentence or recommendation, or while an appeal is pending.

Where deportation is deemed to be conducive to the public good

374. There is no right of appeal except as to the country of destination (see paragraph 369) where a deportation order is made on the ground that the Secretary of State deems the person's deportation to be conducive to the public good as being in the interests of national security or of the relations between the United Kingdom and any other country or for other reasons of a political nature. Such cases are subject to a non-statutory advisory procedure and the person proposed to be deported on that ground will be informed, so far as possible, of the nature of the allegations against

him and will be given the opportunity to appear before the advisers, and to make representations to them, before they tender advice to the Secretary of State.

375. Where it is proposed to deport a person because it is deemed that his expulsion will be conducive to the public good on *other* than security or political grounds there is a right of appeal, under Section 15 of the 1971 Act, direct to the Immigration Appeal Tribunal.

Hearing of appeals

376. An appeal against a decision to make a deportation order against a person lies to the Tribunal.

377. Where the appeal is against a decision to make a deportation order for breach of conditions or for remaining beyond the authorised time it will be heard by an adjudicator in the first instance, unless there is pending an appeal against a decision to make an order against a person as belonging to the family of the person alleged to have broken a condition or remained beyond the authorised time, in which case both appeals will be heard by the Tribunal.

378. An order may not be made while it is still open to the person to appeal against the Secretary of State's decision, or while an appeal is pending.

Persons who have claimed asylum

379. In addition to the rights of appeal mentioned above, except where the ground of the decision to make a deportation order is that it is conducive to the public good and is certified by the Secretary of State as being in the interests of national security, a person who has claimed asylum may also appeal under Section 8 of the Asylum and Immigration Appeals Act 1993 against:
  (i) a decision to make a deportation order against him by virtue of Section 3(5) of the 1971 Act; or
  (ii) a refusal to revoke a deportation order made against him by virtue of Section 3(5) or (6) of the 1971 Act; or
  (iii) directions for his removal from the United Kingdom given under Section 16(1)(a) or (b) of the 1971 Act. In such circumstances the appeal will be before a special adjudicator who will also consider any appeal under Part II of the 1971 Act.

380. A deportation order will not be made against any person if his removal in pursuance of the order would be contrary to the United Kingdom's obligations under the Convention and Protocol relating to the Status of Refugees.

COMMENTARY

For rights of appeal see Chapter 23. For appeals against destination see page 423. For appeals in asylum cases see chapter 20. For 'no power in law' see page 419. For the Immigration (Restricted Right of Appeal against Deportation)(Exemption) Order 1993 see page 420. Appeal against a recommendation of the criminal court is made within the criminal appellate system, as it forms part of the sentence of the court (see page 269). Paragraph 374 refers to deportations deemed to be conducive for reasons of national security, relations between the UK and any other country, or for other reasons of a political nature. There is no right of appeal, but a panel of advisers reviews the decision, and the subject of the order is to be informed as far as possible of the nature of the allegations against him. For this procedure see page 431. Where such grounds are not involved there is a right of appeal against a decision that deportation is conducive to the public good to the IAT.

7 Procedure

Procedure

381. When a decision to make a deportation order has been taken (otherwise than on the recommendation of a court) a notice will be given to the person concerned informing him of the decision and of his right of appeal, or facility to make representations in the case of the security and political cases subject to the advisory procedure.

382. Following the issue of such a notice the Secretary of State may make a detention order, or any order restricting a person as to residence, employment or occupation and requiring him to report to the police, pending the making of a deportation order.

383. Where a person is detained pending an appeal, he may apply to an adjudicator for release on bail.

384. If a notice of appeal is given within the period allowed, a summary of the facts of the case on the basis of which the decision was taken will be sent to the appellate authorities, who will notify the appellant of the arrangements for the appeal to be heard.

Arrangements for removal

385. A person against whom a deportation order has been made will normally be removed from the United Kingdom. The power is to be exercised so as to secure the person's return to the country of which he is a national, or which has most recently provided him with a travel document, unless he can show that another country will receive him. In

considering any departure from the normal arrangements, regard will be had to the public interest generally, and to any additional expense that may fall on public funds.

386. The person will not be removed as the subject of a deportation order while an appeal may be brought against the removal directions or such an appeal is pending.

Supervised departure

387. A person liable to deportation may, in certain circumstances, leave the United Kingdom by means of supervised departure without having a deportation order made against him.

Returned deportees

388. Where a person returns to this country when a deportation order is in force against him, he may be deported under the original order. The Secretary of State will consider every such case in the light of all the relevant circumstances before deciding whether to enforce the order.

Returned family members

389. Persons deported in the circumstances set out in paragraph 365–368 above (deportation of family members) may be able to seek re-admission to the United Kingdom under the Immigration Rules where:
  (i) a child reaches 18 (when he ceases to be subject to the deportation order); or
  (ii) in the case of a wife, the marriage comes to an end.

COMMENTARY

The rules do not clearly distinguish between the stages of enforcement by deportation. First the decision to make a deportation order is made. The subject of the order will be informed of his right to appeal in the normal case (para 381). For rights to apply for bail, see page 445. Where there is no appeal against that decision, or the appeal fails the S of S will then sign a deportation order, and at that stage in practice there is usually an opportunity to make further representations. There is no right of appeal against the signing of the deportation order. For time limits on appeals, see Chapter 23.

Voluntary and supervised departure The applicant may renounce his right to appeal against the decision to deport him. His passport is endorsed to reflect the fact that he was served with the decision to deport. The three-year exclusion period does not apply to him. He is not automatically an illegal entrant if he attempts to return within the three-year period. He pays his own fare if the departure is voluntary.

A person who is liable to deportation may in certain circumstances leave the UK by means of a supervised departure instead of a deportation order being made against him. After his departure the S of S may direct that he should be refused leave to enter or entry clearance in order to prevent his return to the UK. Again his passport is endorsed to reflect the fact that he was served with a notice of intention to deport. The S of S pays his air fare. Obviously in any event the endorsements will be taken into account on any attempted return.

There is no limitation on the period of the prohibition, nor is there a right of appeal if the person is refused entry or entry clearance on the grounds that he is prohibited (1971 Act, s 13(5)).

8 Revocation of deportation order

Revocation of deportation order

390. An application for revocation of a deportation order will be considered in the light of all the circumstances including the following:
 (i) the grounds on which the order was made;
 (ii) any representations made in support of revocation;
 (iii) the interests of the community, including the maintenance of an effective immigration control;
 (iv) the interests of the applicant, including any compassionate circumstances.

391. In the case of an applicant with a serious criminal record continued exclusion for a long term of years will normally be the proper course. In other cases revocation of the order will not normally be authorised unless the situation has been materially altered, either by a change of circumstances since the order was made, or by fresh information coming to light which was not before the court which made the recommendation or the appellate authorities or the Secretary of State. The passage of time since the person was deported may also in itself amount to such a change of circumstances as to warrant revocation of the order. However, save in the most exceptional circumstances, the Secretary of State will not revoke the order unless the person has been absent from the United Kingdom for a period of at least 3 years since it was made.

392. Revocation of a deportation order does not entitle the person concerned to re-enter the United Kingdom; it renders him eligible to apply for admission under the Immigration Rules. Application for revocation of the order may be made to the Entry Clearance Officer or direct to the Home Office.

Rights of appeal in relation to a decision not to revoke a deportation order

393. Where an application for revocation is refused there is a right

of appeal, in the first instance to an adjudicator, unless the order was made against a person as belonging to the family of another person in which case it lies to the Tribunal.

394. No appeal lies while the person is in the United Kingdom or where the Secretary of State personally decides that continued exclusion from the United Kingdom is conducive to the public good.

395. Where an appeal does lie the right of appeal will be notified at the same time as the decision to refuse to revoke the order.

COMMENTARY

The application for the revocation of the deportation order may be made to an ECO or direct to the Home Office. Once the order is revoked the applicant for entry must satisfy the entry conditions afresh. The grant of entry clearance by an ECO who is not aware that there is a deportation order extant against the applicant cannot amount to an implied revocation of the deportation order (*Watson v Immigration Officer, Gatwick Airport*) [1986] Imm AR 75).

Applications for revocation are considered in the light of all the circumstances. The grounds on which the order was made, the community's interests, including the interest in maintaining effective immigration control, will form part of the circumstances in which the application is considered. Where a serious criminal offence is involved, it is unlikely that the order will be revoked until the offence is spent under the Rehabilitation of Offenders Act 1974, and para 391 makes it clear that exclusion for a long term of years will normally be appropriate. Otherwise the order probably will not be revoked unless the applicant can point to a change in circumstances, or to the existence of fresh information which was not available to the authorities who made or approved the original order. Marriage after the order has been signed may be taken into account (*ex p Yesufu* [1987] Imm AR, but see *R v IAT ex p Palomeno* [1987] Imm AR 42).

Passage of time itself may amount to a change in circumstances, but unless 'the most exceptional circumstances' are shown to exist, an order will not be revoked before the subject of the deportation order has been absent from the UK for a period of at least three years since it was made.

There is a right of appeal to the adjudicator where the application for revocation is refused. A family member may appeal to the IAT. There is no right of appeal against a personal decision that continued exclusion is conducive to the public good.

APPENDIX
VISA REQUIREMENTS FOR THE UNITED KINGDOM

1. Subject to paragraph 2 below the following persons need a visa for the United Kingdom:
   (a) Nationals or citizens of the following countries or territorial entities:

   Afghanistan
   Albania
   Algeria
   Angola
   Armenia
   Azerbaijan
   Bangladesh
   Belarus
   Benin
   Bhutan
   Bosnia-Herzegovina
   Bulgaria
   Burkina
   Burma
   Burundi
   Cambodia
   Cameroon
   Cape Verde
   Central African
      Republic
   Chad
   China
   Comoros
   Congo
   Cuba
   Djibouti
   Egypt
   Equatorial Guinea
   Eritrea
   Ethiopia
   Gabon
   Georgia
   Ghana
   Guinea
   Guinea-Bissau
   Haiti
   India
   Indonesia
   Iran
   Iraq
   Jordan
   Kazakhstan
   Kirgizstan
   Korea (North)
   Laos
   Lebanon
   Liberia
   Libya
   Macedonia
   Madagascar
   Mali
   Mauritania
   Moldova
   Mongolia
   Morocco
   Mozambique
   Nepal
   Nigeria
   Oman
   Pakistan
   Philippines
   Romania
   Russia
   Rwanda
   Sao Tome e Principe
   Saudi Arabia
   Senegal
   Somalia
   Sri Lanka
   Sudan
   Syria
   Taiwan
   Tajikistan
   Thailand
   Togo
   Tunisia
   Turkey
   Turkmenistan
   Uganda
   Ukraine
   Uzbekistan
   Vietnam
   Yemen
   Zaire
   The territories
      formerly comprising
      the Socialist Federal
      Republic of Yugoslavia
      excluding Croatia and
      Slovenia.

   (b) Persons who hold passports or travel documents issued by the former Soviet Union or by the former Socialist Federal Republic of Yugoslavia.
   (c) Stateless persons.
   (d) Persons who hold non-national documents.

2. The following persons do not need a visa for the United Kingdom:
   (a) those who qualify for admission to the United Kingdom as returning residents in accordance with paragraph 18;

(b) those who seek leave to enter the United Kingdom within the period of their earlier leave unless that leave:
    (i) was for a period of six months or less; or
    (ii) was extended by statutory instrument;
(c) those holding refugee travel documents issued under the 1951 Convention relating to the Status of Refugees by countries which are signatories of the Council of Europe Agreement of 1959 on the Abolition of Visas for Refugees if coming on visits of 3 months or less.

Part III

European Free Movement

Chapter 15

Nationals of EEA Countries and their Families

1 Introduction

The effect of the Treaty of Rome, which was incorporated into UK law by the European Communities Act 1972, and of the Treaty on European Union 1993 is that a national of a member state of the EC (a citizen of the EU) is entitled to admission to the UK to do any of the following activities:

(*a*) take or seek employment (Art 48);
(*b*) set up in business, become self-employed (Art 52);
(*c*) provide or receive services (Art 59).

(And see Arts 48–60 generally). By Art 7 Treaty rights are to be accorded without discrimination on the ground of nationality.

The provisions of the 1971 Act and the immigration rules may be overridden by provisions of European law to the extent that they are contrary to it (*Van Duyn v Home Office (No 2)* [1975] 3 All ER 190 and see Chapter 22). The freedom of movement provisions of the EC Treaty apply to nationals of the following countries: Belgium, Denmark, France, Greece, Ireland, Italy, Luxembourg, the Netherlands, Germany, Spain and Portugal.

Article 8a(1) of the Treaty on European Union (TEU) provides 'Every citizen of the Union shall have the right to move freely within the territory of the Member States, subject to the limitations and conditions laid down in the Treaty and by the measures adopted to give it effect'. The predecessor of this article in the Treaty of Rome was inserted by the Single European Act 1986 and guaranteed free movement within the internal market. The EC Commission expressed the view that this provision guaranteed freedom of movement to all individuals moving within the internal market whatever their nationality (see Commission Communication (Abolition of Border Controls) (Brussels 8 May 1992)). The date for the completion of the internal market was 31 December 1992. After that time all border controls, and matters arising from border controls, are in breach of Art 8a. It is clear from the wording of the provision under the TEU that free movement rights are confined to EC nationals, and those covered by co-operation agreements.

The EC entered into the European Economic Area Agreement. The immigration rules, and the Immigration (European Economic Area Agreement) Order 1994 are drafted to implement the EEA Agreement. The Agreement confers on the nationals of the EU, and the countries listed below, a right of freedom of movement equal to that enjoyed by EU citizens within the EU. The countries are: Austria, Finland, Iceland, Norway, Sweden. Liechtenstein is also a party to the agreement, but occupies a special position for the time being. In the preamble the parties express themselves to be determined to provide the fullest possible realisation of the free movement of goods, persons, services and capital within the whole Economic Area. The agreement is an association agreement under Article 238 of the EEC treaty. The preamble also states that the objective of the agreement is to arrive at and maintain a uniform interpretation and application of the agreement and (among others) the principle of free movement of persons. (For a discussion of the principles of homogeneity of application of the legal principles of the EAA Agreement, see *The Agreement on a European Economic Area* Sven Norberg, *Common Market Law Review 29, 1171* and *The EEA Agreement: an overall view* Armando Laredo, *Common Market Law Review* 29, 1199.)

2 The European Economic Area Agreement

(a) Objectives and principles

The aim of the agreement is to promote the strengthening of trade and economic relations and to create a homogeneous European Economic Area. To achieve this goal the Agreement provides for the free movement of persons (Art 2(b)). Article 4 provides that within the scope of the application of the agreement any discrimination on the grounds of nationality shall be prohibited.

(b) Free movement of persons

Part III of the Agreement makes provision for free movement of persons, services and capital. Article 28 provides for free movement of workers. Such freedom of movement within the

NATIONALS OF EEA COUNTRIES AND THEIR FAMILIES 291

territory of the EC member states and the EFTA states entails the abolition of any discrimination based on nationality between workers of EC member states and workers of EFTA states concerning employment, remuneration and other conditions of work and employment. Article 28(3) sets out the basic free movement rights for workers covered by the Agreement. The rights are:

(a) to accept offers of employment actually made;
(b) to move freely within the territory of EC Member States and EFTA States for this purpose;
(c) to stay in the territory of an EC Member State and of an EFTA State for the purpose of employment in accordance with the provisions governing the employment of nationals of that State laid down by law, or regulation or administrative action;
(d) to remain in the territory of an EC Member State or an EFTA state after having been employed there.

Annexe V Annexe V provides details of the scope of the rights of free movement. The specific Acts are dealt with in detail below. Council Directive 64/221 which deals with exclusion and deportation of those covered (see page 303) is applied save that Article 4(2), which provides that diseases or disabilities occurring after a first residence permit has been issued shall not justify refusal to renew the residence permit or expulsion, does not apply. Council Regulation EEC 1612/68 which provides for freedom of movement for workers within the Community (see page 296) is applied save for certain final provisions. Council Directive 88/360 on the abolition of restrictions on movement and residence for workers and their families is applied. Commission Regulation EEC 1251/70 on the rights of workers to remain in the territory of a signatory state after having been employed in that state is applied (see page 303).

Self-employed persons Article 30 provides for necessary measures to make it easier for persons to take up and pursue activities as workers and self-employed persons. These range from mutual recognition of qualifications to the co-ordination of the provisions laid down by law, regulations or administrative action in the EEA concerning the taking up and pursuit of activities by workers and self-employed persons.

Right of establishment Article 31 provides for a right of establishment for nationals of an EC Member State or an EFTA state in the territory of any of these states. Freedom of establishment includes the right to take up and pursue activities as self employed persons and to set up and manage undertakings (in particular companies or firms). Article 33 provides for special treatment of foreign nationals of a state on the grounds of public policy, public security or public health. Companies of undertakings formed in any one of the EC or EFTA states are entitled to exercise the right of establishment as if a natural person. A company or firm must be one constituted under civil or commercial law, co-operative societies and other legal persons governed by public or private law. Charities are not companies or firms and do not benefit from the right of establishment (Article 34).

Annexe VIII Annexe VIII gives details of the measures transposed to give effect to the right of establishment under Art 31. The General Programme for the abolition of restrictions on freedom to provide services is applied (P 0032/62 (OJ No 2 15.1.1962, p 32, English version in English Special Edition (2nd Series) IX, p 3)). The General Programme for the abolition of restrictions on freedom to provide services is applied (English Special Edition (2nd Series) IX, p 7). Council Directive 73/148 is applied. Directive 75/34 is applied. Directives 90/364, 90365, dealing with the right of residence and the right to a residence permit are applied. Directive 90/366 is applied.

Services Article 36 provides for a right to provide services within the EEA states' territory for a recipient of services in another EEA state. 'Services' means an activity provided for remuneration, and including activities:
   (a)   of an industrial character;
   (b)   of a commercial character;
   (c)   of craftsmen;
   (d)   of the professions.

A person providing such a service has the right temporarily to pursue his activity in the State in which the services are to be provided under the same conditions as those imposed by the State on its own nationals.

3 European Economic Area Act 1993

The UK made provision concerning the EEA by means of the European Economic Area Act 1993. It amended section 1(2) to include the Agreement in the list of Community Treaties. It modifies all previous relevant legislation that was limited in scope to the EC to limit its scope to the EEA, and modifies all previous provisions

NATIONALS OF EEA COUNTRIES AND THEIR FAMILIES 293

to take account of the EEA. The EEA Order 1994 makes provision for the implementation of the free movement aspects of the EEA. It is limited in scope however and should be seen in the light of the proper interpretation of the EEA and EU provisions for free movement. Detailed discussion is deferred to the Appendix to this book.

4 Personal scope of the right to free movement

(a) EEA nationals and Family members

The EEA extends the EU jurisdiction over free movement provisions to all the EEA states. Thus the case law of the EU is of assistance in the interpretation of the EEA provisions. The question whether a person is a national of a member state is to be determined by that state's domestic law. The definition of the Member States in Art 227 of the Treaty of Rome also contains reference to certain overseas territories of individual member states. Domestic definitions of 'national' may not always be coterminous with 'origin within the borders' of the country of its ex-colonies. Thus persons from certain parts of Poland of German ethnic origins are within the German definition of 'national' in Germany's Basic Law (eg from Silesia and East Prussia). A further illustration of how the nationality provisions can affect a decision is to be found in *Kaeffer and Proacci v France* (1991) *Times*, 25 February Cases C-100/1/89. A holder of a Swiss passport claimed to be of Italian nationality and became an overstayer in Polynesia after a visit. He worked. He was able to claim the EC right of establishment. A detailed discussion of the nationality provisions of the other member states is beyond the scope of this book. However, annexed to the Treaty of Rome was a definition of 'United Kingdom national' which the government has sought to revise by means of a further unilateral declaration 'On the Meaning of a UK National' (Cmnd 9062 of 1983 (TS No 67)) which indicates that where the term 'national' and cognates are used in Treaty provisions as regards the UK it means:
  (*a*) British citizens;
  (*b*) British subjects by virtue of Part IV of the 1981 Act who have a right of abode;
  (*c*) British Dependent Territories citizens who acquire their citizenship from a connection with Gibraltar.
Members of the EEA national's family entitled to admission,

whether accompanying him or joining him later, are to be admitted on the same terms whether or not they themselves are EEA nationals. However, family members who are not EEA nationals themselves and who are coming for settlement must hold a current entry clearance granted for that purpose. When the EEA national leaves the UK, any dependants who are not themselves EEA nationals lose the right to residence and so their residence permits will not be renewed (*ex p Sandhu* [1983] 3 CMLR 131). If the non-EEA national is deported, then the right to residence is lost from the date the deportation order takes effect (*Ex p Botta* [1987] Imm AR 80). Where all parties remain in the UK, however, there is no requirement that they live together under one roof (*Diatta v Land Berlin* [1986] 2 CMLR 164). Further, there is no requirement that the person entering under the free movement provisions should be able and willing to maintain and accommodate his dependants without recourse to public funds (*Kempf v Staatssecretaris van Justitie* [1987] 1 CMLR 764).

In relation to the overseas territories of EEA states, the rights applicable to freedom of establishment and to provide services, including the rights of entry and residence predicated upon the exercise of those rights, are to be applied without discrimination only to the nationals of EEA states with which the overseas country has special relations of reciprocity. If that condition is satisfied nationals of other member states are to be dealt with in a non-discriminatory manner. Whether there are relations of reciprocity between the member state and the overseas territory is a question of domestic law (see *Kaeffer* above).

5 Rights of Admission

(a) *Rights of admission under the law governing the EEA*

Workers The rights of free movement of workers are set out in Arts 48–51 of the Treaty of Rome. The right of freedom of movement for workers under Art 48 entails the right, subject to limitations, to do the following:

(*a*) accept offers of work actually made;
(*b*) move freely within the territory of a member state for this purpose;
(*c*) stay in the territory of a member state for the purpose of employment in accordance with the provisions (including

administrative action) governing the employment of nationals of the host member state;

(d) remain in the territory of the host state having been employed in that state, subject to conditions set out in regulations of the EU (Art 48).

Limitations The limitations on freedom of movement of workers are to be justified only on the following grounds:

(a) public policy;
(b) public security;
(c) public health (Art 48).

The term 'worker' is to be given a broad interpretation. A 'worker' is a person who provides services for and under the direction of another in return for remuneration (*Lawrie Blum v Land Baden-Wurttemberg* (Case 66/85) [1987] ICR 483 (ECJ)). A person coming to the UK in search of work is a 'worker', provided he seriously wishes to work (*Hoth v S of S* [1985] Imm AR 20). So is a person who is involuntarily unemployed (*Giangregorio v S of S* [1983] Imm AR 104).

In *R v IAT, ex p Antonissen* (above), the ECJ held that the UK time limit on those seeking work was not contrary to the Directive, unless the worker provides evidence that he is seeking work and has a genuine chance of obtaining it (see also [1992] Imm AR 196. An EC national who after six months cannot produce evidence that he is continuing to look for work, or that he has a genuine (or 'good', 'real', or 'more than illusory') chance of being engaged, can be required to leave the UK. The burden of proving that the unemployment is involuntary is on the EC national (*Ulrich* (4129)).

In *Levin v S of S for Justice* (No 53/81) [1982] ECR 1035, the ECJ held that a person was a 'worker' even if his job was part time and he could not hope to survive on the proceeds of his employment alone. All that was necessary was that his employment was effective and genuine (see also *Layne v S of S* [1987] Imm AR 243). However a person working in a special scheme of sheltered employment following rehabilitation was held not to be a worker as the jobs were not real, and effective, but were re-educational (*Bettray v Staatsecretarie van Justitie* 344/87). A person seeking work is entitled to rely on Art 48 (*The State v Royer* [1976] ECR 497). However he is not entitled to all the social rights accorded to workers (*Centre Public d'Aide Social de Courcelles v Lebon* [1989] 1 CMLR 337). Article 48 does not apply to those in public service, but that is narrowly circumscribed by the test for public service (Art 48(4)). To be in public service the worker must be responsible for exercising powers conferred by public law, or for safeguarding the interests of the state (*Re Employees of National Research Council v Italy* [1988] 3 CMLR 635). Such a derogation will be narrowly construed.

Regulation EEC No 1612/68   The rights of workers are given substance by Regulation 1612/68. The rights of EEA workers under these provisions and under the rules must be read in the light of Regulation (EEC) No 1612/68 which is directly enforceable. This provides for the right of an EC national to take up employment within another member state with the same priority as, and subject to the laws governing, nationals of that state.

Personal scope   The Regulation applies to any national of a member state falling within Art 1 (see below) or his family. Article 10 deals with the position of family members. It provides that the following have the right to install themselves (irrespective of their nationality) with the worker who is employed in the territory of another member state:

(*a*) his spouse and their descendants who are under the age of 21, or are dependants; and

(*b*) dependent relatives in the ascending line of the worker and his spouse.

The host state shall facilitate the admission of a dependant who does not fall within those definitions such as cohabitees of the worker in his own country, provided that they actually lived with the worker in his own country.

Rights conferred   Article 1 of the Regulation states that any national of a member state shall irrespective of his place of residence have the following rights:

(*a*) to take up an activity as an employed person;

(*b*) to pursue an activity as an employed person;

(*c*) to take up available employment in the territory of another member state; in accordance with the provisions governing the employment of nationals of the host state.

There must be no discrimination as between EC workers and the nationals of the host state in relation to contracting and performing contracts (Art 2). If immigration rules or practices:

(*a*) limit applications for and offers of employment or the right of foreign nationals to take up and pursue employment;

(*b*) impose conditions on their so doing which are not applied to UK nationals;

(*c*) impose conditions which keep nationals of other member states away from employment offered;

(d) prescribe a special recruitment procedure for foreign nationals;
(e) limit the advertising of vacancies; or
(f) subject eligibility to condition of registration with employment offices,

they are of no effect on EC nationals (Art 3).

Where there are restrictive quotas of foreign nationals in a particular type of employment, nationals of other member states are not to be counted in them (Art 4). The same facilities are to be offered to nationals of other member states as are offered to nationals of the host state, and no discriminatory medical, vocational, or other criteria may be applied, save vocational tests which the prospective employer requires to be taken when making the offer of employment. Remuneration, terms and conditions of employment and trade union rights are protected by Arts 7 and 8, and housing by Art 9.

Cohabitees are not spouses under Art 10(1) (*Reed v Staatsecretariat van Justitie* [1987] 2 CMLR 164). In the UK cohabitees of UK nationals may be considered for admission outside the immigration rules (see page 213 above). Cohabitees of EC nationals should therefore be considered under the terms of the discretion outside the immigration rules. Failure so to do would result in discriminatory treatment of EC national workers. It is not necessary for the worker to satisfy the maintenance requirement of the immigration rules, however it may be necessary for the accommodation requirements to be satisfied. The right of the family to install itself is dependent upon the worker having available housing considered as normal for national workers in the region in which he is employed. Should such housing become unavailable later, the worker's right to remain is unaffected. In particular exclusion would not be justified on public order grounds under EC 64/221 (see below and *Commission v Germany* Case No 249/86, ECJ 18 May 1989).

By Art 7(2) a worker or a member of a worker's family shall enjoy the same social advantages, such as the right to claim state benefits, as national workers.

By Art 11 the children of the national are to receive the same educational and training facilities as nationals of the host state.

Directive EEC 68/360 The Directive gives details of the abolition of restrictions on freedom of movement and residence within the Community for workers of member states and their families. The Directive is extended to EEA nationals as a result of the European

Economic Agreement. It has the same personal scope as Regulation 1612/68, and confers the right to leave and enter a member state's territory on production of a passport or valid entry card. An entry visa may only be required of a non-EC-national member of the EC national's family. Member states must allow nationals of member states to enter their territory on the production of a valid identity card or passport if they are exercising their right to take or pursue employment in that host state, and no entry visa may be demanded save from members of the family of the EC national who are not themselves EC Nationals (Art 3). Family members must prove their relationship with a document issued by the original member state and those covered by Art 10 of Reg 1612/68 need proof (issued by the original member state) of their dependency or that they lived under the same roof as the worker. The directive states that 'a relationship is proved by a document issued by a competent authority'. Thus it is not possible to look behind that document, for example, to claim that a marriage does not exist where such a document is produced.

Member states are not permitted to hinder the commencement of employment by the worker by the formalities of obtaining the evidence (Art 5).

A worker whose employment is not expected to last more than three months need only produce a statement to this effect from his employer and his entry document. Those working as intermediaries in commerce do not need the statement from the employer. A worker who commutes weekly across a border must be issued with a five-year permit. Seasonal workers have the same rights as ordinary workers. However, all such seasonal and temporary workers may be required to report their presence in the territory (Art 8), for example, to the police.

Derogation The member states may only derogate from the principles of the Directive on the following grounds:

(*a*) public policy;
(*b*) public security;
(*c*) public health (Art 10).

Retirement after employment Where an EEA worker becomes permanently incapacitated from working or retires, he and his family may remain in the host state (Commission Regulation 1250/70; see also Directive 90/365).

Entry to the UK can only be refused to a non-EEA-national member of an EEA national's family on the same grounds as an

EEA National may be excluded from a Member State (see the Appendix).

(b) Business, Self-employed persons and the provision or receipt of Services

The effect of the right of establishment created by arts 52–59 of the EEC Treaty is to confer a right of free movement on persons wishing to enter in order to set up or manage a business or to become self-employed.

Art 52 provides that freedom of establishment includes the rights:
 (*a*) to take up and pursue activities as self-employed persons; and
 (*b*) to set up and manage undertakings.

These rights are substantiated in Directives. Directive 73/148 provides for the rights of free movement of those exercising the right of establishment.

In addition, arts 59–66 give a right of free movement to persons wishing to provide services. Article 60 provides for the services that are covered. Services which are normally provided for remuneration, in so far as they are not governed by the provisions relating to freedom of movement for goods, capital and persons; and in particular:
 (*a*) activities of an industrial character;
 (*b*) activities of a commercial character;
 (*c*) activities of craftsmen; and
 (*d*) activities of the professions, are included.

Further implementation of these rights is contained in Directives 73/148 (relating to the exercise of the rights to set up a business or otherwise exercise the right of establishment or the rights relating to the provision and/or receipt of services) and 75/34, which provides for the right to remain after retiring from provision of the services or self-employment.

Directive 73/148 Scope The Directive covers EC nationals establishing themselves for self-employment or to provide services, and those wishing to go to member states as recipients of services. The EEA Agreement extends the scope of the Directive to nationals of the EEA.

Article 1 of 73/148 provides that it shall apply to the following relatives etc. of the person exercising the Community right:
 (*a*) the spouse and children under 21 years of age irrespective of their nationality; and
 (*b*) the relatives in the ascending and descending lines of the

person, who are dependent upon him, irrespective of their nationality.

Dependent relatives and other family members who lived under the same roof as the person exercising the Community right in the country of origin, irrespective of their nationality (Art 1).

Rights conferred The EC national and his family have the right to enter on the production of an identity card or valid passport (Art 3). However, non-EC-national family members may be required to produce a visa, for which they cannot be charged. They should receive the visa on proof of being the spouse or relative covered by the Directive (Art 3(2)).

Residence rights Under Directive 73/148 the right to permanent residence is granted by Art 4. If the period of the activity is to be less than three months, the person need only produce a passport or identity document. However in such cases the person may be required to report to the police. If the activity is to take longer than that the national authority must issue a residence permit when the following documents are produced:

(*a*) the passport or identity card; and

(*b*) proof that the person is within the scope of the Directive.

Derogation is on the grounds of public policy, public health, or public security (see below page 303).

If the activity is one which in the host state is connected with the exercise of official authority, Art 55 exludes it from the activities in relation to which an EC national may establish himself. As with all exceptions to Community rights, the exception is limited to that which is necessary to protect the interest of the member state.

Receipt of Services The rights extend to persons who wish to travel to receive services. In *Luisi and Carbone v Ministero del Tesoro* [1985] 3 CMLR 52, the ECJ held that tourists, persons travelling for business or educational purposes, and persons seeking medical treatment were recipients of services. Such services must normally be provided for remuneration (*Belgium v Humbel* [1989] 1 CMLR 393). Private students would therefore benefit from these rights. Such persons should have the right of free movement. Students and tourists may rely directly on EC rights (see below for students' further rights, page 301). In *Cowan v Le Tresor Public* [1990] 2 CMLR 613 the right to the same social advantages as nationals of the host state was held to require compensation by the state for an assault to be accorded to an EC national as it would be to a French national under the equivalent of the Criminal Injury Compensation Scheme.

(c) Students (Directive 90/366)

From 30 June 1992 it was possible for EC-national students in the UK to rely on Directive 90/366. They are entitled to rely on this provision whether they are in private or public education. In *Parliament v Council* Case C–295/90 the ECJ held that Directive 90/366 had a flawed juridical basis. It ruled that until a new Directive was issued it could be relied upon. Directive 93/96 has now been issued which deals with the right of residence of students. Directive 90/366 had effect up to 31 December 1993. After that time the following provisions apply under Directive 93/96.

Scope The Directive covers any student who is an EC national and who:

(*a*) has sufficient resources to avoid becoming a burden on the social security system;
(*b*) can prove that he is enrolled on a course at a recognised educational establishment for the principal purpose of following a vocational course of study;
(*c*) is covered by a sickness insurance policy covering all risks in the host state; and
(*d*) is not covered by another provision of Community law (Art 1).

The spouse and the dependent children of a national of a member state are covered by the Directive also (Art 1).

Rights conferred The student gains the right of residence for the period of his course only. The right of residence is evidenced by means of the issue of a document known as a 'residence permit for a national of a Member State of the Community', the validity of which can be limited to the duration of the course of studies or to one year where the course lasts longer. Where it is annual, it shall be renewed annually. Non-EU-national members of the family of the student receive a document of the same validity as that issued to the student on whom they depend. The residence permit or document is to be issued on the production of the person's identity card or passport, and of proof that he meets the conditions of Art 1 (Art 2.1). The spouse and the children may be entitled to work or take up self-employment in the host state if they are entitled to the right of residence in the territory of any member state, even though they may not be nationals of any member state themselves. The dependants have the same rights as are conferred on dependants of EC nationals exercising the right of freedom of movement under Regulation 1612/68.

(d) Residence (Directive 90/364)

Scope From 30 June 1992, right of residence is granted to EC nationals who are not covered by other free movement provisions. The scope is extended by the EEA Agreement to EEA nationals. Article 1 provides that the person claiming the right must show in relation to himself and his family (irrespective of their nationality) that:
  (a) they hold sickness insurance covering all risks in the host member state; and
  (b) they have sufficient resources to avoid them becoming burdens on the social security system. They will be deemed to have such resources where their resources are greater than their requirements (including those of the family) for the purposes of social security law.

The Directive also confers the right to install themselves in another Member State with the holder of the right of residence:
  (a) the spouse of the holder, and their descendants who are dependent;
  (b) dependent relatives in the ascending line of the holder of the right or the spouse, regardless of their nationality (Art 1(2)).

Rights conferred As long as they are covered by insurance and have sufficient resources those covered are entitled:
  (a) to enter without a visa on the production of a valid passport or identity card (however, non-EC-national family members must produce a visa for which they are not to be charged);
  (b) in the case of the spouse and children, to take employment regardless of their nationality.

The right is evidenced by a permit that is valid for five years. The member state may where it is thought necessary require that the permit be re-validated after the first two years. Such a requirement must only be imposed where it is necessary for the purposes set out in the preamble to the Directive of achieving an internal market without internal frontiers, and without residents becoming a burden on the host state's public finances. The requirement cannot be justified on grounds that are not necessary to achieving the purpose of the Community legislation (see e.g. *Jones v Chief Adjudication Officer* [1990] IRLR 533 and *Allue v Universita degli Studi di Venezia* [1989] ECR 1591). Non-EC-national family members are entitled to an equivalent document on production of their passport or identity card. The derogations are those in Directive 64/221 (see below).

(e) Retired persons

(Directives 75/34, 90/365 and Regs 72/194 and Council Directive 1251/70)

By Directives 75/34 (relating to the ex-self-employed), 90/35, and 1251/70 and Reg 72/194 provision is made for the free movement of those who have retired provided they are covered by their own national pension or a private pension scheme ensuring that they do not become a burden on the social security system of the host state.

6 The nature of permitted derogation (Directive 64/221)

(a) Refusal of entry to and deportation of EEA nationals

Those exercising the right to free movement may be refused entry in accordance with the provisions of Directive 64/221. The scope of the Directive has expanded to include all those exercising any of the above Community rights, together with their spouses and members of their families. The EEA Agreement extends the scope of the Directive to EEA nationals. The Directive regulates the exclusion and expulsion of persons on the following grounds:

(*a*) public policy;
(*b*) public security;
(*c*) public health (Art 2).

These grounds cannot be used to serve economic purposes (Art 2(2)). The refusal of entry or expulsion of a person may only be based upon the personal conduct of the individual against whom the action is being taken (see *Van Duyn v Home Office* [1975] 3 All ER 190). Previous criminal convictions do not in themselves constitute grounds for taking such action, nor the expiry of an identity card or passport (Art 3). EC Nationals who are refused admission may not be removed until they have had the opportunity of making representations according to Art 9(2) of EC 64/221 (*Pecastaing v Belgium State* [1980] ECR 691).

Public policy and public security Measures taken on the grounds of public policy, security, or health must be based solely on the personal conduct of the person concerned. In the case of criminal convictions there must be a present threat to public policy or security

(*Van Duyn* (above)) which must be sufficiently serious to the requirements of public policy affecting the fundamental interests of society. To the extent that criminal convictions imply the existence in the individual concerned of a propensity to act in the same way in the future, such past conduct alone may constitute a threat to the requirements of public policy or security (*R v Bouchereau* [1978] QB 732 (ECJ)). Some past offences are so serious that the burden is on the applicant to show that the risk of similar conduct in the future is negligible (*Puttick v S of S* [1984] Imm AR 118). However, in *Puttick* the IAT rejected the submission that public outrage at the past conduct of a person could of itself amount to a present threat to public policy or security. The basis of the decision to take action must be sufficiently serious as to warrant 'repressive measures' against a national of the host state (*Adoui v Belgian State* [1982] ECR 1665).

A recommendation by a criminal court for deportation is to be judged by the Directive, and in *R v Spura* [1988] 10 Cr App R(S) 376, the Court of Appeal held that the Directive and principles of natural justice require that before a recommendation is made there should be a full enquiry into the circumstances of the case. The recommending court should also give its reasons for the recommendation. The relevant test is then whether the detriment to the country justifies the recommendation in accordance with the Directive (cf. non-EC-national's position (*Al-Sabah v IAT* [1992] Imm AR 223)).

Exclusion on the grounds of public policy requires a genuine threat and one that affects the fundamental interests of the host society. However, in *R v Escauriaza* [1989] 3 CMLR 281 it was held that this requirement meant nothing more than that the continued presence of the EC national in the UK would be to its detriment.

The expiry of the passport of an EC national does not justify action being taken against him preventing him exercising rights of free movement, and the holder of a passport must be permitted to enter on a passport even where it is no longer valid and the nationality of the holder is in dispute.

Charge on public funds The EEA Order enables the S of S to exclude persons on the basis that they are going to fall a charge on public funds. It was thought that public policy justified this rule as it appeared in previous immigration rules (see *Nijssen v Immigration Officer London (Heathrow) Airport* [1978] Imm AR 226). Generally public policy will not justify the rule (*R v IAT, ex p Antonissen* (above)). However, where the question is whether a person is exercising a worker's right of free movement, it is possible to argue that a person who is an 'idle layabout' does not qualify as a worker (*City of Wiesbaden v Barulli* [1968] CMLR 329). However, *Kempf* above suggests that the requirement of satisfying the immigration officer that the EC national is not likely to become a charge on public funds is inconsistent with EC law where there is a genuine effort to find work, although it is unsuccessful. However if there is no genuine chance of the person finding work he may be expelled (*R v IAT, ex p Antonissen* [1992] Imm AR 196).

Public health The immigration rules concerning refusal of entry on medical grounds draw no distinction between EC nationals and non-EC nationals. However it would appear that immigration officers are only to refer EC nationals to a medical inspector if they show 'obvious signs of mental or physical ill-health'. They may only be refused leave to enter if the medical inspector certifies that they are suffering from one of the diseases listed in the Annexe to Directive 64/221. The same rules apply to non-EC-national family members.

Under Community provisions the residence permit is merely evidence of the right he is exercising of freedom of movement. In *R v Pieck* [1981] 3 All ER 46 the ECJ decided that the imposition of any time limit or other condition on entry is prohibited. However, the IAT in *Corinaldesi* (2957) stated that the initial period of six months conformed with EC law, as it was a 'limitation on the stay of an EEC national to test the qualifications for the right of residence on which reliance for the stay is placed'. Likewise the ECJ has held that it was not contrary to EC provision for an EC national to be required to leave if he had not found work within six months and had no genuine chance of finding it. However, the six-month period is not a time within which a person must have found work, because if the person produces evidence at the end of that period showing that he has a genuine chance of finding work, expulsion on the grounds of 64/221 will not be possible (*Antonissen*).

7 UK provisions: s 7 of the 1988 Act

A person does not require leave to enter or remain under the 1971 Act where he is entitled to enter or remain by virtue of an enforceable EC right or any provision made under section 2(2) of the European Communities Act 1972. The European Economic

Area Act 1993 provides (by section 3) that where the Agreement requires modification of a provision, which can be ascertained from the EEA Agreement, the provision has effect subject to those modifications. Section 7 of the 1988 Act must be viewed therefore as modified by section 3 of the European Economic Area Act 1993 so as to declare that EEA nationals do not require leave to enter or remain in the UK where they are exercising enforceable rights under the EEA Agreement. Section 7 of the 1988 Act has been in parallel with the Immigration (European Economic Area) Order 1994 from 20 July 1994.

Chapter 16

The Right of EEA Nationals to Residence and Settlement

1 Introduction

Where there is a conflict between the provisions of EC law, including the EEA Agreement, and the Immigration Rules, the EC provisions prevail (see *Van Duyn* above, page 289). This principle is of significance in relation to issues of residence for those who have not exercised a Community right in relation to work or self employment, but as a result of recent Directives have the right to reside in a member state, and should be borne in mind when considering the immigration rules set out below at page 316. The principles set out below are expressed by reference to EC provisions, however in the light of the EEA Agreement they have effect to ensure rights of residence to EEA nationals (see the Appendix).

2 EC provisions

(a) Persons in employment

A person admitted for six months who enters employment should be issued with a residence permit. The permit should normally be for five years unless the duration of the employment is expected to be less than 12 months in which case the permit is to be limited to that period. The family of the worker has the right to install itself with him (Arts 10 to 12 Regulation EEC 1612/68). Children of workers have a right of residence for the purposes of general education (Art 12, Regulation EEC 1612/68). Such a right may not confer a right of residence on the parent however (*Gal* (10620)).

3 Directive 68/360: residence rights

Article 4 confers on the worker the right to obtain a residence permit. To exercise the right of residence:

(a) the worker must produce:
   (i) the passport or valid identity document with which he gained entry;
   (ii) a confirmation of engagement or a certificate of employment;
(b) a member of the worker's family must produce:
   (i) his entry document;
   (ii) a document proving the relationship claimed;
   (iii) in cohabitation and dependency cases, a document issued by a competent authority of the original member state proving either their dependency or the fact that they lived under the same roof as the worker.

The family member must be issued with a residence permit which is as valid as that of the worker.

If the putative family member proves the relationship he claims by producing a document issued by a competent authority of the original state, the host state must issue a residence permit called 'Residence Permit for a National of a Member State of the EC'. This document is nothing more than evidence that the worker is exercising his Community right, and in particular cannot be made a condition of entry or residence. There may be no charge made for its issue. The residence permit is valid throughout the territory of the host member state, and must be valid for five years. Breaks in residence of up to six months are not to affect its validity. Where the employment will take more than three but less than 12 months, a temporary permit may be issued (Art 6). A valid residence permit may not be withdrawn solely on the basis that the worker is involuntarily unemployed (either through illness or accident or otherwise). The DoE in the UK is the competent national authority that confirms whether unemployment is voluntary or not (Art 7). It is sufficient however if the S of S puts the worker to proof that his unemployment was involuntary for immigration purposes (*Giangregorio v S of S* [1983] Imm AR 104). The right of residence does not depend upon the residence permit. Failure to obtain one does not affect the right of residence, nor does the expiry of limited leave in the UK, nor the refusal of a residence permit (*Lubbersen v S of S* [1984] Imm AR 56).

4 Residence in relation to services

Article 4 of Directive 73/148 grants the right of permanent residence to providers of services. It is evidenced by a residence permit for five or more years, which is not affected by gaps in the period of residence which last less than six months. The residence permit is not to be withdrawn because of involuntary unemployment or incapacity. However, the right of residence is coterminous with the provision or receipt of services in those cases. The right of abode is to be given to those who are pursuing an activity that is authorised in another member state. The right is coterminous with that authorisation (Art 4(1)). It differs from the right of abode for UK immigration law purposes only in the respect that it automatically ends on an event.

5 Students

Directive 90/366 conferred a right of residence on students and their dependants by Art 1. That right was coterminous with the duration fo the course of studies in question (Art 2). It was evidenced by a Residence permit, the validity of which was either the length of the course, or one year if the course was longer than a year. The student could obtain the permit on production of his entry document (a passport or other identity card), and proof that he was within the scope of the Directive. The Directive was held to have a flawed legal base in C-295/90 *Parliament v Council*. Directive 93/96 provides for residence rights of students. Directive 90/366 has effect up until 31 December 1993, and may be relied upon in relation to residence before that time. Directive 93/96 provides that the right of residence for students within its scope is restricted to the duration of the course of studies in question. The right of residence is evidenced by means of a 'residence permit for a national of a Member state of the Community', the validity of which may be limited to the duration of the course or one year if the course lasts longer. If the course does last longer, the permit is renewable annually. If a member of the family is not an EC national he must be issued with a residence document of the same validity as that issued to the national upon whom he depends. Member states are under an obligation to simplify as much as possible the formalities and procedure for obtaining residence documents in respect of the beneficiaries of the Directive.

6 Other residence rights

In order to harmonise provisions on the rights of EC nationals to reside in a member state other than their own, under Directive

90/364 the right of residence is conferred on residents of all member states who can comply with certain conditions (see page 301). It is evidenced by a permit which is valid for five years. The member state may, where it is thought necessary, require that the permit be re-validated after the first two years. Such a requirement must only be imposed where it is necessary for the purposes set out in the preamble to the Directive of achieving an internal market without internal frontiers, and without residents becoming a burden on the host state's public finances. The requirement cannot be justified on grounds which are not necessary to achieving the purpose of the Community legislation (see eg *Jones v Chief Adjudication Officer* [1990] IRLR 533 and *Allue v Universita degli Studi di Venezia* [1989] ECR 1591). Non-EC-national family members are entitled to an equivalent document on production of their passport or identity card.

7 Retired or incapacitated

(a) Directive 75/34

The Directive is applied by the EEA Agreement to the nationals of all EEA states. Under Directive 75/34 member states are required to recognise the rights of self-employed persons who reach the state pension age, and their family members, who pursue a self-employed activity for at least 12 months before that age. Where there is no state pension age the person may exercise the right of residence under 75/34 on reaching 65 having pursued a self-employment for at least 12 months in the member state's territory (Art 2). Where the retired person dies, the rights under the Directive may be exercised by his family members. Where a self-employed person:

(*a*) dies during his working life;
(*b*) has not yet acquired the right to remain in the member state under the Directive;
(*c*) has lived in the member state for at least two years continuously. However, absences of three months or less are acceptable;
(*d*) died from an accident at work or an occupational illness; and
(*e*) his surviving spouse is a national of the host member state or lost such nationality on marriage to the deceased,

the family member may reside in the host member state permanently (Art 3).

THE RIGHT OF EEA NATIONALS TO RESIDENCE 311

A person entitled to the right to remain must be given two years within which to exercise the right of residence, and must be able to enter or leave the member state without hindrance during those two years without affecting that right (Art 5). There is no formality to be imposed in order to exercise the right to remain. It is evidenced by the issue of a five-year permit the issue of which must be free, or cost no more than is charged to a National of the member state on issue of an identity card. The validity of the residence permit is not affected by absences of less than six months.

Persons exercising the right of residence conferred by 75/34 may be expelled under Directive 64/221 (which is applied to them by Directive 75/35).

(b) Directive 90/365

Rights of residence after retirement for persons in employment, and self employment or other occupational activities who have not exercised free movement rights during their working lives are conferred by Directive 90/365. In order to qualify for the rights the person must be:

(*a*) an EC National or a member of his family (of whatever nationality);
(*b*) in receipt of invalidity, early retirement, industrial accident or old-age benefits, of an amount sufficient to avoid him becoming a burden on the social security system of the host member state; and
(*c*) covered by sickness insurance in respect of all risks in the host member state (Art 1).

Dependent descendants, the spouse and ascendent dependent relatives of the person exercising the right or his spouse are permitted to join the person and exercise the right of residence conferred. This right expires if any of the conditions (*a*)–(*c*) ceases to apply. In particular there is no provision for the members of the family to continue to exercise a right of residence on the death of the holder of the right of residence. They may however qualify for settlement under domestic law.

(c) Regulation 1251/70

The Directive is applied to EEA nationals by the EEA Agreement. Persons who were employed in a member state may rely on the provisions of Reg 1251/70 for the right to remain in that member state after having exercised their right of freedom of movement

in that state due to their employment there. The following workers may exercise the right of residence:
  (a) a person who at the termination of his work has reached state pension age who has resided in the member state for more than three years, and who has been employed for the last 12 months there;
  (b) a worker who resided continuously in the member state for more than two years, and ceases to work due to permanent incapacity;
  (c) a worker who, after three years' continuous residence and employment, maintains a residence in his original member state where he returns at least once a week (Art 2).

The members of the person's families are defined as follows for these purposes by Art 1 (see Art 10 of Regulation 1612):
  (a) his spouse and their descendants who are under the age of 21, or are dependants; and
  (b) dependent relatives in the ascending line of the worker and his spouse;
  (c) cohabitants who were dependent upon the person and lived under the same roof.

If they are residing with the worker, they have the right to continue residing in the host member state after the death of the worker once he acquires the right to reside in the host member state. They also have that right where the worker dies from an industrial accident or occupational disease having worked and resided in the member state's territory for at least two years continuously, and where the spouse is either a national of the host state or lost the nationality of the host state on marriage to the worker (Art 3). Continuity is not broken by absences of three months or less (Art 4), nor is it broken when the worker is involuntarily unemployed during the two or three years.

8 Expulsion (Directive 64/221)

(a) EC provision

Directive 64/221 deals with removal. It is applied to nationals of EEA states by the EEA Agreement. Removal must be based on the personal conduct of the person to be deported. A deportation order cannot be based solely on the existence of a previous criminal record. It can only be justified if the presence or conduct of the individual concerned constitutes a genuine and sufficiently serious threat to the requirements of public policy or of public security. It must affect one of the fundamental interests of society additional to the disturbance of order which any infringement of the law involves (*R v Bouchereau* [1978] 1 QB 732). However, in exceptional cases where the person or the crime reveals a psychological propensity to commit offences, a single offence can justify deportation on grounds of public policy or security.

The same considerations are brought to bear by a criminal court considering whether to make a recommendation, or the IAT considering an appeal against a decision to deport. The IAT may consider that the nature and seriousness of a single offence justifies deportation (*R v IAT ex p Marchon* [1993] Imm AR 98). By Art 6 of the Directive, the person to be expelled must be informed of the grounds of public policy, security, or health upon which the decision by the S of S is based, unless it is contrary to the interests of state security. It follows that no court should make an order recommending deportation without a full enquiry into the circumstances. The court should give reasons for the recommendation, and indicate the extent to which the current previous criminal convictions of the accused have been taken into account, and the light which such convictions throw on the likely nature of the accused's personal conduct in future (*Ex p Santillo* [1981] 2 WLR 362).

It is not possible for an EEA national to be deported for breach of leave conditions, as it is not lawful to impose a requirement of leave to enter upon an EEA national or a period of leave to remain. Deportation for breach of conditions or unauthorised stay will not therefore be a permissible option, and removal will have to be on the basis of personal conduct which would warrant deportation of an EEA national on the permitted grounds (*R v Pieck* [1981] 1 QB 571). Provided that the person was genuinely exercising a Community right on entry he cannot be treated as an illegal entrant. The grounds for expulsion cannot be used to service economic ends (Art 2(2)), and therefore expulsion cannot be justified on the basis that a genuine holder of a Community right has had resort to public funds.

(b) National Security

The CA in *Ex p Gallagher* (1994) *Times*, 16 February have made a reference to the ECJ on the issue of whether Art 9 of Directive 64/221 prohibits the S of S from making an exclusion order under s 7 of the Prevention of Terrorism (Temporary Provisions) Act 1989 before receiving the opinion of a competent authority. The competent authority in such cases, argued the S of S, was the adviser appointed by him to hear objections to the exclusion order pursuant to Sched 2 of the PTA 1989. The CA have asked whether the fact that the adviser was appointed by the S of S prevented him from being a competent authority in the meaning of that term in Art 9. The CA held that the S of S was not obliged by Art 48 of the EEC Treaty or Art 6 of Directive 64/221 to give either the precise reasons for making the order or the name of the adviser if the interests of national security were affected.

9 Appeals

The rights of appeal in immigration matters of EC Nationals are in general similar to the rights of other persons. So, for example, there is an in-country right of appeal against refusal of entry under s 13(1) of the 1971 Act, and against a decision to deport under s 15(1) of the Act. Where an EC national or a member of his family of whatever nationality, wishes to appeal against a decision to require him to leave the UK or to curtail his residence, s 14(1) grants a right of appeal against a refusal to vary leave only where a person has limited leave to enter. Despite the fact that limited leave is a condition on leave on entry, and is therefore incompatible with EC law (*R v Pieck* above), the IAT held that the grant of the initial six months' residence is the grant of limited leave for the purposes of s 14(1) and so may be the subject of an appeal to the adjudicator (*Lubberson v S of S* [1984] Imm AR 56). Where a person's right of residence is (under UK law) withdrawn, the S of S's practice has been to permit a direct appeal to the IAT.

Directive 64/221 provides by Art 8 that the person to be expelled shall have the same legal remedies in respect of any decision concerning entry, or refusing the issue or renewal of a residence permit, or ordering the expulsion from their territories as are available to nationals (see Chapter 15) of the member state in respect of the acts of the administration. Article 9 provides that if there is no right of appeal on the law and the facts of a case to a court of law, or if such an appeal does not suspend any administrative action to be taken, a decision refusing a residence permit or one expelling the holder of a residence permit from the member state may not be taken by the administration (save in cases of urgency) until an opinion has been obtained from a competent authority of the host member state before which the person to be expelled

THE RIGHT OF EEA NATIONALS TO RESIDENCE 315

has rights of defence and legal representation and assistance as the domestic law provides for. It is not sufficient if the authority reviewing the decision is the same as the authority making the decision. The effect of this provision is that the decision to deport a person which the S of S refers to the IAT must be void, and subject to judicial review even if the IAT upholds the decision, as the S of S has no power to make a decision until the opining authority has been consulted. EA Nationals who are refused admission may not be removed until they have had the opportunity of making representations in accordance with Art 9(2) of EC 64/221 (*Pecastaing v Belgium State* [1980] ECR 691).

(a) Nationals of an EEA state relying on EC provisions in relation to that state

The courts have held that in order to found a EC law right the facts of the case must have some link with the kind of situation intended to be covered by EC law. Where therefore a woman became the wife of a British citizen one month after the signing of a deportation order against her, she could not claim the benefit of Directive 64/221 which deals with the rights of spouses of an EC National on deportation (*Ex p Tombofa* [1988] Imm AR 400, applying *Morson v State of the Netherlands* [1982] ECR 3723, [1983] 2 CMLR 221). In *Morson* the ECJ held that the Treaty provisions on the freedom of movement of workers cannot be applied to cases which have no factors linking them with situations governed by EC law on freedom of movement. In *R v IAT, ex p Aradi* [1987] Imm AR 359 it was held that there is no such linking factor where the right to move within the EC has not been exercised. In *Knoors v S of S for Economic Affairs* [1979] ECR 399 the ECJ held that the wording in Art 52 'nationals of one member state in the territory of another' applies so as to permit nationals of that state relying on the provisions of Art 52 of the Treaty against their own state. It is necessary to show that the person's situation had been assimilated to that of any other person enjoying rights under the Treaty. The Commission argued that an individual employed in a member state of which he is not a national can assert a right in his own state to go back to his member state and can assert a right under EC law for his spouse to be installed there with him. The Advocate General at that time was Sir Gordon Slynn (now Lord Slynn), who thought that it was neither necessary nor desirable to comment on the argument. However, the argument re-emerged in *R v IAT and Surinder Singh, ex p S of S* [1992] Imm

AR 565 where an Indian national married a British national, and they worked in the EC outside the UK. They returned to the UK to set up a business. The husband was granted limited leave to remain, during which time the marriage broke down. Before the decree absolute the S of S decided to initiate deportation proceedings against him. The ECJ held that a member state must grant leave to enter and reside in its territory to the spouse, regardless of nationality, of a national of that state who has gone to another member state in order to work there as an employed person and returns to establish himself in the state of which he is a national. The spouse must be granted the same rights as would be granted to the national under Community law if the spouse had entered and resided in another member state. It is clear that the same principle would hold good for persons exercising other EEA rights, and in particular the provisions of the immigration rules relating to the primary purpose of the marriage could not be applied to a couple entering having exercised a right to use services in another member state, who are returning to seek employment. The ECJ did state that nothing in EC law prevented the introduction of provisions which would have the effect of preventing fraudulent applications.

10 UK implementation of free movement: HC 395, paras 255–262

EEA Nationals and their Families

Settlement

255. An EEA national (other than a student) and the family member of such a person, who has been issued with a residence permit or residence document valid for 5 years, and who has remained in the United Kingdom in accordance with the provisions of the 1994 EEA Order for 4 years and continues to do so may, on application, have his residence permit or residence document (as the case may be) endorsed to show permission to remain in the United Kingdom indefinitely.

256. A self-employed EEA national who has a right to reside in the United Kingdom by virtue of having ceased such activity in the United Kingdom within the meaning of the 1994 EEA Order, and the family member of such a person, will be permitted to remain in the United Kingdom indefinitely.

257. In addition, the following persons will be permitted to remain in the United Kingdom indefinitely:
  (i) an EEA national who has been continuously resident in the United

THE RIGHT OF EEA NATIONALS TO RESIDENCE 317

Kingdom for at least 3 years, has been in employment in the United Kingdom or any other Member State of the EEA for the preceding 12 months, and has reached the age of entitlement to a state retirement pension;
(ii) an EEA national who has ceased to be employed owing to a permanent incapacity for work arising out of an accident at work or an occupational disease entitling him to a state disability pension;
(iii) an EEA national who has been continuously resident in the United Kingdom for at least 2 years, and who has ceased to be employed owing to a permanent incapacity for work;
(iv) a member of the family of an EEA national as (defined in the 1994 EEA Order) to whom (i), (ii) or (iii) above applies;
(v) a member of the family of an EEA national (as defined in the 1994 EEA Order) who dies during his working life after having resided continuously in the United Kingdom for at least 2 years, or whose death results from an accident at work or an occupational disease.

The EEA family permit

258. An 'EEA family permit' means an entry clearance issued, free of charge, to a family member (as defined in the 1994 EEA Order) who is not an EEA national and who is a visa national or a person who wishes to install himself in the United Kingdom with an EEA national who is a qualified person in the terms of the 1994 EEA Order.

Requirements for the issue of an EEA family permit

259. The requirements for the issue of an EEA family permit are that:
(i) the applicant is the family member (as defined the 1994 EEA Order) of an EEA national who is a qualified person in the terms of the 1994 EEA Order; and
(ii) the applicant is coming to the United Kingdom for a purpose provided for in the 1984 EEA Order; and
(iii) the applicant is not a person who falls to be excluded on grounds of public policy, public security or public health.

Issue of an EEA family permit

260. An application for an EEA family permit shall be granted provided the Entry Clearance Officer is satisfied that each of the requirements of paragraph 259 is met.

Refusal of an application for an EEA family permit

261. An application for an EEA family permit is to be refused if the Entry Clearance Officer is not satisfied that each of the requirements of paragraph 259 is met.

Registration with the police for family members of EEA nationals

262. The requirements relating to registration with the police are set out in Part 10.

COMMENTARY

Section 7 of the 1988 Act is brought into effect in parallel with the Immigration (EEA) Order 1994. Under section 7 of the 1988 Act, EEA nationals do not require leave to enter the UK. Para 255 of HC 395 deals with settlement conditions for EEA nationals other than students. It also makes provision for the family members of such persons. Each must have been issued with a residence permit or residence document valid for five years. He must have remained in the UK for four years. The EEA Order 1994 is intended to ensure that the EC directives on free movement and residence apply to nationals of all EEA states across the whole of the European Economic Area. It provides that a person must have been resident in the UK for four years before he qualifies for settlement in the UK. Settlement may be obtained only if the residence document of the person claiming settlement is valid for five years. The EEA national's residence document or permit is then endorsed to show permission to remain in the UK indefinitely.

Those exercising the rights of self-employed EEA nationals with a right to reside in the UK by virtue of having ceased such activity in the UK within the meaning of the 1994 Order (see the Appendix) will be permitted to remain in the UK along with his family members indefinitely (para 256). EEA nationals of pensionable age, who have been continuously resident in the UK for at least three years and have been in employment in the EEA for the preceding 12 months will receive permission to remain indefinitely. Those who have been incapacitated at work or due to an occupational disease will also have the right of permanent residence (para 257(ii)). Permission to remain indefinitely will also be granted to EEA nationals who have been continuously resident in the UK for at least two years and who have ceased to be employed because of a permanent incapacity to work. The members of the families of these categories also obtain the right of permission to remain indefinitely in those circumstances. The members of the family of a deceased EEA national who dies during his working life after having resided continuously in the UK for at least two years, or whose death results from an accident at work or occupational disease, will be permitted to remain indefinitely.

THE RIGHT OF EEA NATIONALS TO RESIDENCE

11 The EEA family permit

The family permit is an entry clearance which is issued to a family member who is not an EEA national, and who is a visa national (see page 285 for list). A person who wishes to install himself in the UK with an EEA national and who is a 'qualified person' within the terms of the 1994 Order also requires a family permit. For the definition of 'qualified person' see the Appendix. The family permit is a novel concept for the definition of 'family member' see the Appendix. The original draft of the 1994 Order was debated (and withdrawn) in the House of Lords on 29th April 1994 (see House of Lords Official Report Vol. 554 No 79, Cols. 974 to 984).

(a) Exclusion on grounds of public policy, public security or public health (para 259(iii))

The para is an attempt to implement the EEA Agreement relating to free movement. Grounds of exclusion and removal will be interpreted according to the provisions of Directive 64/221 EEC.

Family members of EEA nationals may still be required to register with the police according to the terms of Part 10 of HC 395 (para 262.).

Chapter 17

Third-Country Agreements and Other Provisions

The Member States may enter into agreements with other countries under Art 238 of the Treaty of Rome. The EEA Agreement is an example of such an agreement. Section 2 of the ECA 1972 provides that all such rights, powers, liabilities, obligations and restrictions from time to time created or arising by or under the Treaties and all such remedies and procedures from time to time provided for under the Treaties as in accordance with the Treaties are without further enactment to be given legal effect or used in the UK, and shall be recognised and available in the UK and shall be enforced as enforceable Community rights. The rights created under these Agreements may have direct effect where they are clear and precise enough.

1 The Agreement with Turkey

An Association Agreement was signed between the Member States and Turkey in 1963. It provided that the parties should be guided by Articles 48 to 50 of the Treaty of Rome in securing the free movement of workers between them (see *Agreement establishing an Association between the European Economic Community and Turkey* Ankara, 12 September 1963, Official Journal C113). Freedom of movement was to be secured by the end of 1993. The principles by which freedom of movement was to be secured were determined by the Council of Association established under the Association Agreement. Those principles were made under Council of Association decisions 2/78, 1/80. A worker from Turkey who is registered as being in the member state's work-force is entitled to the renewal of his work permit in respect of the same employer after a year of legal employment with him. After three such years he may change jobs to another registered job. After four years of legal employment he may have free access to any job of his choice which is available. His family may join him and are entitled to take work which they are offered after three years' residence, and after five years residence they may have free access to any paid employment. The limitations appearing in Directive 64/221 apply to the limitation on the rights of Turkish workers which may only be limited pursuant to public policy, public security, or public health.

In *Demirel v Stadt Schwabisch Gmund* [1989] 1 CMLR 421 the ECJ held that any Association Agreement creates special privileged links with the non-Member country, which must to a certain extent take part in the Community system. Rights of workers under the Association Agreement between a particular state and a non-memeber state fall to be considered under the Community part of the Agreement, rather than the national part of the mixed treaty. Where a provision in such an agreement concluded by the Community is clear and precise enough having regard to the wording of the agreement and the nature of the agreement, it is directly applicable. However looking at the particular Agreement between Turkey and the Member States the court ruled that its provisions were not clear and precise enough to give rise to rules of Community law which are directly applicable in the internal legal order of the member states. In *Unal Narin v Secretary of State* [1990] Imm AR 403 the UK Court of Appeal held that the Agreement did not describe clear enough obligations, and emphasised that the Agreement merely provided that the member state and Turkey would be guided by Art 48 of the Treaty of Rome. During the implementation period the Association Council had power to make such decisions as it thought fit in relation to the Agreement, and its decisions are regarded as directly associated with the Agreement, and the decisions formed an integral part of the Community legal system (*Demirel*).

The decisions of the Association Council are directly applicable where having regard to their wording and the purpose and nature of the agreement in question they contain clear and precise obligations which are not subject in their implementation or effects to the adoption of any subsequent measure. Where a state is obliged to take administrative measures as are necessary for the implementation of those decisions, that does not prevent them being directly applicable. In *Sevince v Staatssecretariat van Justitie* Case 192/89 [1990] ECR I–3473 the ECJ held that the provisions of Decisions 2/76 and 1/80 of the Council of Association were of direct application. Article 2(1)(b) of Decision 2/76 of the Association Council provided that a Turkish worker who has been in legal employment for five years in a Member State is to enjoy free access in that Member State to any paid employment of his choice in that state. Article 6(1) of Decision 1/80 provides that a Turkish worker who is duly registered as belonging to the labour force is to enjoy free access to any paid employment of his choice after four years' legal employment. The right of a Turkish worker to enjoy free access to employment after a number of years' legal employment is therefore directly applicable. It is not possible for a member state to make the rights granted by the Association Agreement conditional, or to restrict the application of the precise and unconditional right which the decisions grant to Turkish workers. The ECJ held also that the right conferred on the Turkish worker to take work of his choice after a specified period of legal employment necessarily carried with it a right of residence for the person concerned.

A person is in legal employment for the purposes of the Agreement where he is working in breach of his condition of leave to remain, as this is a permit of residence, and right to take work cannot be made conditional upon such leave. Further Turkish nationals working in member states have the right to extensions of their leave to remain and permission to take employment. For the purposes of acquiring rights under Member States' law it is irrelevant how the worker entered the member state, as long as the entry was lawful. If the Turkish worker has a stable position in the labour force and had continuing employment for one year, he can use the directly applicable Member States' law to gain an extension of leave to continue in the same employment. Article 6 of Decision 1/80 of the Association Council provides that after one year's legal employment the Turkish national is entitled to renewal of his permit to work for the same employer if the job is available. In the case of *Kus v Landeshauptstadt Wiesbaden* ECJ 16 December 1992, the Turkish national entered the state originally for the purposes of marriage to a Member State national, however, he remained to work. He was able to rely on Art 6. Further, the court indicated that the provisions relating to deportation of Turkish workers protected by Member States' law may be interpreted in the same way as Directive 64/221.

2 Co-operation Agreements with Algeria, Morocco and Tunisia

Provision is made for the treatment of workers from the Maghreb countries under the Co-operation Agreements with Algeria (Reg 2210/78), Morocco (Reg 2211/78) and Tunisia (Reg 2212). Each Agreement provides that the treatment accorded by the member state to workers from those countries employed in its territory shall be free from any discrimination based on nationality, as regards working conditions or remuneration in relation to its own nationals. Thus they prohibit discrimination on the ground of nationality in relation to the requirement of leave to remain after a limited leave has expired, the renewal of a work permit, or expulsion. Provisions of a Community Agreement whose terms are clear and precise must be regarded as directly applicable where having regard to its wording, and the purpose of the agreement, it is not necessary for there to be further measures adopted by the Member States. The terms of the Agreements with Morocco, Tunisia, and Algeria are in the above respect clear and precise in prohibiting discrimination (reference could be made to the almost identical provision in Directive 76/207 regarding sex discrimination). UK nationals do not require work permits to continue to work in the UK, and workers from Morocco, Tunisia and Algeria must not be in a worse position. Further, the Agreements provide that the workers of those countries and any family members living with them must be accorded treatment in relation to social security benefits which is free from any discrimination based on nationality in relation to nationals of the member states in which they are employed. The benefits in relation to which there must be no discrimination are those in Directive 1408/71, including maternity and illness benefits, occupational accidents and disease benefits, and unemployment. The Agreements prohibit discrimination in relation to the provision of the benefits. This would include prohibiting a person from being available for work and from taking part-time work which would enable a particular level of benefit to be claimed.

In *ONEM v Kziber* Case C-18/90 the ECJ held that in relation to the provisions concerning social security and employment, such Agreements have a direct effect. If a worker from one of the Agreement countries is unable to make contributions to the national insurance scheme he suffers direct discrimination in relation to the nationals of the UK. Similarly, if the worker cannot make those contributions from whatever source a national may, he suffers discrimination. Thus a worker from these countries cannot be prohibited from changing jobs by his immigration status. Similarly, because only certain unemployment benefits are available on the basis of purely voluntary contributions, unemployment benefit only being generated when national insurance contributions have been made, a person seeking work from one of the Agreement countries cannot be prevented from taking it even if he enters the UK in some other capacity such as that of visitor.

In *Kziber* the Advocate General considered the nature and purpose of the Moroccan Agreement. He stated, and the ECJ held, that an agreement does not have to be directed towards the integration of a country to the Member States for its provisions to have direct effect in Member States' law. The Agreement (and the other Maghreb Agreements) are reached with the purpose of adopting provisions and measures in the field, *inter alia*, of labour. The Advocate General noted that the Maghreb agreements do not have the programmatic nature which was the basis upon which the provisions of the Agreement with Turkey was held not to have direct effect. He further remarked that the provisions relating to equality in the field of labour not infrequently contain rules which are plainly designed to govern the legal situation of individuals. He concluded that the nature and purpose of the Agreement did not prevent it from being directly enforceable. He considered whether the provisions relating to discrimination in relation to working conditions or remuneration were sufficiently clear and precise to be directly enforceable and concluded that they were. The provisions of the Agreement prohibiting discrimination on the grounds of nationality between workers of the Agreement state and those of the member state, and their families, he concluded were sufficiently precise to be of direct application. Finally, he took the view that the word 'worker' must be interpreted so as to include a person who is or who has been pursuing an occupation in the territory of a member state. It would exclude however someone who was registered for a certain time with the employment agencies of a member state but without ever having been engaged in a genuine and effective occupation within the framework of an employment relationship.

The court was only concerned with the Article of that Agreement dealing with social security discrimination; however, it is clear that the provisions dealing with discrimination in relation to working conditions would also be found to be directly applicable. It held that the concept of 'worker' encompasses both an active worker and those who have left the labour market after falling subject to one or other of the risks creating entitlement under the social security system, or upon reaching pensionable age.

THIRD-COUNTRY AGREEMENTS 325

In relation to workers of the Maghreb countries (Algeria, Morocco or Tunisia) all discrimination regarding working conditions must be eliminated. This entails that workers of the Maghreb who have entered the UK may not be prevented from taking work of at least some description. They will be able to take work which would permit a UK national to continue to claim benefits as a result of the *Kziber* case itself.

3 Third-country nationals employed in EEA undertakings

Nationals of non-Member States or EEA countries who are working for Member State or EEA undertakings are entitled to exercise freedom of movement for the purposes of the undertaking for which they are employed whilst it is carrying out a project in a member state such as the UK. In *Rush Portuguesa LDA v Office National d'Immigration* (1990) *Times,* 12 April (Case C-113/89) (ECJ) a Portuguese building and public works undertaking entered into a contract to carry out works on a French Railway line. The Portuguese company brought a work-force containing third country nationals from Portugal to France. The French authorities were not entitled to require the company to obtain work permits for its employees, as a result of Arts 59 and 60 of the Treaty of Rome. The imposition of this condition, or a similar one, on a company from another member state providing services was discrimination with regard to its competitors established in the host member state, which were able freely to use their own employees. The condition would also affect the ability of the provider of services to provide its services. Foreign nationals working for an undertaking in another member state cannot be required to qualify both under the immigration conditions of the member state in which the undertaking for which they work is established, and also under the immigration requirements of the member state in which their employer requires their services in order to provide a service.

4 Agreement on the external frontiers of the Member States

The Treaty on European Union signed at Maastricht on 7 February 1992 states at Title VI Art K1 that matters such as asylum policy, the rules governing the crossing of the Member States' external borders, conditions of entry and movement, and immigration policies regarding nationals of non-Member States are to be matters of common interest. They are however to be dealt with in compliance with the European Convention for the Protection of Human Rights and Fundamental Freedoms, and the 1951 Geneva Convention on Refugees (Art K2). Thus member states are required to comply with the ECHR and the Geneva Convention on Refugees, and if Art K2 of the TEU gives rise to individual rights, asylum and immigration law must conform to all of the obligations under those Conventions. The Member States have agreed to inform and consult with one another within the Council of Ministers, with a view to co-ordinating their action. The Treaty also contains a declaration as to nationality of a Member State, which provides that wherever reference is made to nationals of the Member States, the question whether an individual possesses the nationality of a particular Member State shall be settled solely by reference to the national law of the Member State concerned. Member States may declare who are to be considered their nationals for Community purposes by way of a declaration lodged with the Presidency and may amend that declaration when necessary.

In the light of the provisions of the Treaty consideration is being given to the establishment of a common European border. The draft Convention on the External Frontiers of the EC is being considered for signature by the Member States. The draft Convention proposals require external frontiers to have established border posts, patrols, and procedures enabling the Member States to establish the authenticity of the documents carried by entrants. Carriers will be required to make enquiries of entrants as to their visa status, and eligibility. Provisions similar to those under the Carriers' Liability Act are likely whereby the carrier becomes liable for the removal of an entrant who was not entitled to enter. The proposals would require that non-Member States-nationals who are illegally present in the Member States should leave their territories at once in normal circumstances. The draft Convention makes no provision for the ECJ's intervention, but has been seen by the Commission as part of the work programme to be undertaken by the Community in order to achieve the objective set out in Article 8a of the Treaty of Rome of an internal market without internal borders (see *Commission Communication (Abolition of Border Controls)* Brussels 8 May 1992.

The draft Convention proposes the use of a common visa and a common transit visa. The common visa will be valid for one or more Member States, for a period of not more than three months in any six-month period. The common transit visa permits the non-

Member State national to travel to a non-Member State, spending not more than four days in transit in any Member State. Visas valid for more than three months would thereafter be valid only at a domestic level, and other Member States will only be obliged to permit the holder to pass in transit to the issuing state.

The common visa would be issued when the following conditions are fulfilled:

(a) the non-Member State-national holds a valid travel document for crossing frontiers and if needed a visa for the state through which he enters;

(b) the non-Member State national (i) presents documentary evidence proving the purpose of the intended stay and any conditions attached to that stay; (ii) has sufficient means of subsistence for the period of the proposed stay and his return or onward journey to a non-Member State, or can obtain those means;

(c) the non-Member State national must not be a threat to domestic public policy or security, nor may his name appear on a joint list of persons whose presence the Member States consider to be a threat to the security or public policy of particular Member States.

The draft Convention proposes that persons who are not eligible in any of the above ways, or whose names appear on the prohibitive list, may be admitted to a particular Member State on the grounds of (a) the international commitments of that State; (b) the national interests of the state; or (c) humanitarian reasons.

The ECJ has held that principles of international obligations, of which the Member States are signatories, are to be taken into account when considering questions of Member States' law (*Johnston v Chief Constable of RUC* [1987] QB 129, *Wachauf v the State* Case 5/88 and *Hoechst v EC Commission* [1989] ECR 2859). Further, a member state's power to deport or exclude a Member State national under Arts 66 and 56 of the Treaty of Rome must be read in the light of the general principle of freedom of expression embodied in Art 10 of the European Convention on Human Rights (*ERTAE v Pliroforissis & Kouvelas* Case 260/89). The ECJ held that the fundamental principles in the European Convention on Human Rights form an integral part of the general principles of law which the court enforces. Measures which are incompatible with those principles are not to be permitted in Community law. National courts interpreting Community law therefore must have regard to these principles.

Chapter 18

Application and Enforcement of the EEA and EC Law

1 Introduction

By Art 5 of the Treaty of Rome the UK has an obligation to take all appropriate measures to ensure fulfilment of its obligations arising out of the Treaty or resulting from actions taken by institutions of the EC. The UK must also abstain from any measure which could jeopardise the attainment of the objectives of the Treaty. Thus the relationship between the provisions of the Treaty and the directly applicable measures of the institutions on the one hand and national law on the other is such that directly applicable measures render automatically inapplicable any conflicting measure of current national law. They also preclude the valid adoption of national legislative measures to the extent to which they are incompatible with Community provisions (*Amministrazione delle Finanze dello Stato v Simmenthal SpA* [1978] ECR 629). The UK courts and tribunals have an obligation to apply the provisions of Community law by virtue of the European Communities Act 1972. Section 2(1) provides for the enforcement of directly effective provisions of EC law as contained in the Treaty or arising under it. By s 2(2) EC law is given further effect by the duty to enact subordinate legislation in order to implement binding provisions of EC law. Finally, statutory enactments are to be interpreted so as to give effect to the mandatory requirements of EC law (s 2(4)).

The EEA Agreement is a Treaty for the purposes of the EEC Treaty. The purpose of the Agreement is to create a common legal framework. Art 6 of the EEA Agreement states that the provisions of the Agreement in so far as they are identical in substance to corresponding rules of the EEC Treaty, or to Acts adopted in application of that Treaty shall in their implementation and application be interpreted in conformity with the relevant rulings of the Court of Justice of the EC given before 2 May 1992, which was the date of the signing of the EEA Agreement in Oporto. Any act corresponding to an EEC regulation or an EEC Directive is made part of the internal legal order of the EEA states in the same way as Regulations and Directives of the EEC are made part of the Member States' legal order. For the purposes of a claim in any of the Member States of the EU, matters of legal interpretation of the Agreement are to be dealt with in the same way as matters of the interpretation of the EEC Treaty. In the EFTA states an EFTA court will determine the interpretation of the Agreement (see Sven Norberg CML Rev 1992 at page 1188).

Any question as to the effect of the Treaties or as to the meaning or effect of any Community instrument shall be treated as a question of law and be determined as such in accordance with the principles laid down by the ECJ, if the question is not referred to the ECJ for determination by a national court (s 3(1)). Article 169 of the Treaty of Rome provides for the enforcement of EC obligations against Member States by the EC Commission through infringement proceedings. However provisions of EC law which have direct effect may be relied upon by individuals against the State. Regulations made under the Treaty are applicable in their entirety. Directives are binding only as to the result to be achieved (see Art 189, Treaty of Rome).

A provision has direct effect, and may be relied upon by an individual, where:

(a) the provision does not by its nature indicate that it concerns the Member States only in their relations *inter se* (*Costa v ENEL* [1964] ECR 585);

(b) the provision is clear and precise;

(c) the provision is unconditional and unqualified and not subject to any further measures on the part of the member states of the community (but see below);

(d) the provision is not one which leaves any or any substantial latitude to Member States (*Salgoil v Italian Ministry for Foreign Trade* [1968] ECR 453);

(e) it is irrelevant that the Commission or other member states have alternative remedies for breach of the provision in question (*Van Gend en Loos v Nederlandse Administratie der Belastingen* [1963] ECR 1).

The requirement that the provision must be unconditional and unqualified must be read in the light of a number of cases which indicate that an obligation which is originally conditional or qualified may become unconditional or unqualified by lapse of time or on the happening of an event (see, for example, *SACE v Italian Ministry for Finance* [1970] ECR 1213, *Eunomia di Parro v Ministry of Education* [1971] ECR 811 and *Ianelli v Meroni* [1977] ECR 557). Where a Member State has failed to comply with its obligations under a Treaty provision which is conditional before the end of the implementation period, that provision may become directly effective from the end of that transitional period. Where a Member State has failed to implement a directive, then providing the terms of the Directive are clear and precise, the state cannot rely on its own failure to prevent a person relying on its terms against the State (*Pubblico Ministero v Ratti* [1979] ECR 1629).

The provisions of the 1971 Act and the immigration rules may be overridden by provisions of European law to the extent that they are contrary to it (*Van Duyn v Home Office (No 2)* [1975] 3 All ER 190). Further, all national legislation, whether it was passed to implement EC obligations or not, is to be construed so as to be consistent with EC obligations (*Marleasing SA v La Commercial Internacional de Allimentacion SA* [1992] 1 CMLR 305 and *Dzodzi v Belgium* Case C–197 and 297/88 (1991) *Times*, 7 January). Special provision is made in the immigration rules for EC nationals (paras 68 to 74 (on entry) and paras 146 to 154 (after entry)). In addition there are Association and Co-operation Agreements which extend the scope of Community rights to certain non-EC nationals. They form part of Community law, so that rights created by them are actionable in the ECJ (see below). Further, it is possible to obtain interim relief such as injunctive remedies against the Crown where a question of European law is involved, and it may be possible to obtain damages for a breach by the S of S of certain provisions of European law relating to immigration control.

By s 7 of the Immigration Act 1988 a person does not require leave to enter or remain in the UK in any case where he is entitled to enter or remain by virtue of an enforceable Community right or by virtue of any provision made under s 2(2) of the ECA 1972. Section 7(2) provides that the S of S may implement statutory instruments to grant leave to enter for a limited period to any class of persons, who although EC nationals, are not entitled to enter by virtue of a Community right. If the S of S acts in breach of the provisions of Community law upon which an individual may rely, he may become liable for breach of statutory duty. However, a mere breach of Community law may not render a

Member State liable in damages for the purposes of national law, and the S of S is likely to be liable in damages for misfeasance in public office (*Bourgoin SA v Ministry of Agriculture Fisheries and Food* [1985] 3 All ER 585). Relying on another principle of Community law the applicant may be entitled to damages regardless of the position in national law. Where a member state has not implemented a piece of Community legislation which is designed to protect the monetary interests of the individual, it is liable in damages to such an individual who suffers financial loss by reason of that failure to implement the EC legislation (*Francovich v Italian Republic* [1992] IRLR 84). It is yet to be seen whether this principle will be applied in the context of immigration cases, such as that of a person seeking to exercise the right of establishment. Further it is unclear whether the principle is limited solely to cases in which the piece of legislation which has not been implemented does not have direct effect.

2 Injunctions

Where a person asserts a right of Community law against the S of S, it will be possible to obtain injunctive relief to prevent, for example, the removal of a person from the jurisdiction, or to prevent a person (eg a non-EC member of an EC national's family) being flown to his country of origin (*R v S of S for Transport, ex p Factortame (No 2)* [1991] 1 AC 603. The claim for injunctive relief should be granted by a national court where it finds the following factors:

(*a*) the case concerns a point of European law;
(*b*) the sole bar preventing it from granting interim relief is a rule of national law (ie that injunctions will not issue against the Crown);
(*c*) that damages are an insufficient remedy;
(*d*) if damages are not a sufficient remedy, where the balance of convenience lies (the court will consider the circumstances of the case, and the duty owed by the S of S to the public).

The grant of such an injunction will be an exceptional course, but it is not necessary to show a *prima facie* case that the UK law is incorrect.

3 Preliminary rulings

Where a question of EC law arises before a national court

concerning the interpretation of a provision of EC law, the court or tribunal may request the ECJ to give a ruling on the question if it is necessary for that tribunal's decision (Art 177, Treaty of Rome). If there is no reasonable scope for doubt as to the way in which the question of EC law is to be answered no reference should be made, but the national court should apply the EC law provision, or interpret the national provision so as to be consistent with the EC provision. Where there is no appeal from a decision of a court or tribunal, the court must refer to the ECJ a question of EC law necessary for its decision. Article 177 provides that the national court has a discretion to refer a question for a preliminary ruling 'if it considers that a decision on the question is necessary to enable it to give judgment'. However the Article goes on 'where any such question is raised in a case pending before a court or tribunal of a Member State against whose decision there is no judicial remedy under national law, that court or tribunal shall bring the matter before the ECJ'. Thus, the House of Lords, or the Court of Appeal when leave to appeal to the House of Lords is refused (*Haegen v Fratelli & Moretti SNC* [1980] 3 CMLR 253 and *Generics (UK) Ltd v Smith Kline & French Laboratories Ltd* [1990] 1 CMLR 416), or upon refusal of leave to move for judicial review shall refer a question of European law to the ECJ.

4 Procedure for applying for a preliminary ruling

The procedure for obtaining a preliminary reference is governed by RSC, Ord 114. Rule 2 provides that a reference may be made at any stage of the proceedings, whether before hearing evidence or having heard it. A reference cannot be made after the court has delivered judgment. The application must be made during or before the hearing (r 2(2)). The reference should contain a brief summary of the facts; the order sought by the applicant; an outline of the respondent's defence and a summary of the arguments for both parties on the issue under reference. The court in its order will include the reason it is making the reference, a statement of the relevant national law and the questions for reference.

Part IV
Asylum

Chapter 19

Asylum

1 Asylum applications

(a) Introduction

The Asylum and Immigration Appeals Act 1993 provides for the treatment of asylum seekers and the determination of their claims. Section 1 of the 1993 Act provides that a person makes a claim for asylum where he claims that it would be contrary to the UK's obligations under the Convention and Protocol relating to the Status of Refugees (Cmnd 9171 and Cmnd 3906) ('the Convention and Protocol') for him to be removed from or required to leave the UK. Nothing in the immigration rules may lay down any practice which would be contrary to the Convention and Protocol (1993 Act, s 2). The rules provide for the consideration of asylum applications in Part 11.

PART 11

ASYLUM

Definition of asylum applicant

327. Under these Rules an asylum applicant is a person who claims that it would be contrary to the United Kingdom's obligations under the United Nations Convention and Protocol relating to the Status of Refugees for him to be removed from or required to leave the United Kingdom. All such cases are referred to in these Rules as asylum applications.

Applications for asylum

328. All asylum applications will be determined by the Secretary of State in accordance with the United Kingdom's obligations under the United Nations Convention and Protocol relating to the Status of Refugees. Every

asylum application made by a person at a port or airport in the United Kingdom will be referred by the Immigration Officer for determination by the Secretary of State in accordance with these Rules.

329. Until an asylum application has been determined by the Secretary of State, no action will be taken to require the departure of the asylum applicant or his dependants from the United Kingdom.

330. If the Secretary of State decides to grant asylum and the person has not yet been given leave to enter, the Immigration Officer will grant limited leave to enter.

331. If a person seeking leave to enter is refused asylum, the Immigration Officer will then resume his examination to determine whether or not to grant him leave to enter under any other provision of these Rules.

332. If a person who has been refused leave to enter applies for asylum and that application is refused, leave to enter will again be refused unless the applicant qualifies for admission under any other provision of these Rules.

333. A person who is refused leave to enter following the refusal of an asylum application will be provided with a notice informing him of the decision and of the reasons for refusal. The notice of refusal will also explain any rights of appeal available to the applicant and will inform him of the means by which he may exercise those rights. The applicant will not be removed from the United Kingdom so long as any appeal which he may bring is pending.

Grant of asylum

334. An asylum applicant will be granted asylum in the United Kingdom if the Secretary of State is satisfied that:
   (i) he is in the United Kingdom or has arrived at a port of entry in the United Kingdom; and
   (ii) he is a refugee, as defined by the Convention and Protocol; and
   (iii) refusing his application would result in his being required to go (whether immediately or after the time limited by an existing leave to enter or remain) in breach of the Convention and Protocol, to a country in which his life or freedom would be threatened on account of his race, religion, nationality, political opinion or membership of a particular social group.

COMMENTARY

(b) Definition of asylum applicant (para 327)

The rules define an asylum applicant in para 327 as a person who claims that it would be contrary to the UK's obligations under the Convention and Protocol relating to the Status of Refugees (1951) (Cmnd 9171 and Cmnd 3906) for him to be removed or required to leave the UK. For the purposes of the rules a person may become an asylum applicant only when he is in the UK. Nothing in the Convention and Protocol prevents the S of S refusing to consider the application of a person who has not yet arrived in the UK (*Ex p Sritharan* [1993] Imm AR 184). A claim for asylum will not generally be accepted at a British Embassy (see *Tekle v Visa Officer Prague* [1986] Imm AR 71).

The UK's obligations under the Convention and Protocol The Rules are primarily concerned with the obligations arising under Art 33 of the Covention. This provides:

No Contracting State shall expel or return ('refouler') a refugee in any manner whatsoever to the frontiers of territories where his life or freedom would be threatened on account of his race, religion, nationality, membership of a particular social group or political opinion.

The UK may not impose a penalty on the refugee on account of his illegal entry if he comes directly from a country in which his life or liberty is threatened, provided that he presents himself to the authorities without delay and shows good cause for his illegal entry or presence (Art 31). The UK may not apply restrictions to the movements of refugees save for those which are necessary, and such restrictions shall only be applied until their status in the country is regularised or they obtain admission into another country (Art 31.2). Article 32 imposes an obligation on the S of S not to expel a refugee lawfully in the UK save on grounds of national security or public order (*Ex p Chahal*) [1994] Imm AR 107).

(c) Construing the Convention

In interpreting the Convention regard should be had to any subsequent practice in the application of the Convention which establishes the agreement of the parties regarding its interpretation (see Convention on the Law of Treaties, Vienna, 1969, Art 31(3)(b) (Cmnd 7964)). Such a practice is set out in the *Handbook on Procedures and Criteria for Determining Refugee Status*, which is a product of the representatives of signatory states sitting on the Executive Committee of the UNHCR. The *Handbook* was published in 1988, and is available from the UNHCR office in London, whose address is 7 Westminster Palace Gardens, Artillery Row, London SW1P 1RR.

In *Bugdaycay v S of S* [1987] AC 514 Imm AR 250, the HL held that the 1979 version of the *Handbook* had no binding force in municipal or international law, and its recommendations could not override the express terms of the 1971 Act. In *Ex p Sivakumaran* [1988] 2 WLR 92 the *Handbook* was said to amount to a statement of the points of view espoused by the High Commissioner for Refugees. The *Handbook* is an aid to the construction of the Convention, but should there be a conflict between the Hanbook and the rules, the rules prevail. In *Viraj Mendis v IAT and S of S* [1989] Imm AR 6 it was said that although the provisions of the *Handbook* have no legal status it has been cited with approval in some cases, and deserves proper consideration. In *Ex p Hidir Gunes* [1991] Imm AR 278 it was held, applying *Mendis*, that the *Handbook* provided helpful guidance as to the content and application of the Convention. In *ex p Aouiche* (1991) *Times*, 4 June, the CA held that the guidance provided in the *Handbook* concerning deserters could provide guidance in relation to the proper approach to applications for refugee status on this ground. The *Handbook* may be taken into account by special adjudicators as a 'best practice' guide to the proper way in which to approach issues such as credibility in asylum cases.

The document *Conclusions of the Executive Committee of the Office of the UNHCR* has been held to have no binding force in UK law (*R v IAT, ex p Alsawaf* [1988] Imm AR 410), nor to give rise to any legitimate expectation that it will be followed (*ex p Akyol* [1990] Imm AR 571).

(d) Applications for asylum (paras 328–333)

HC 251 made provision for applications at the port of entry and separately for applications after entry. HC 395 does not have separate rules for each category. An immigration officer at a port of entry receiving an application for asylum must refer it for determination to the S of S. Para 328 provides that all asylum applications will be determined by the S of S in accordance with the UK's obligations under the Convention and Protocol. Until that is done no action is to be taken to remove the applicant from the UK. If a person is refused asylum the immigration officer must then consider whether or not to grant him leave to enter under any other provision of HC 395. Moreover a person may apply for leave to enter, and be refused. He may then apply for asylum and be refused. Para 332 would seem to suggest that the immigration officer must then consider whether he qualifies under any other rule. A person who is refused leave to enter following the refusal of an asylum application is provided with a notice informing him of the decision and the reasons for refusal. The notice of refusal will also explain any rights of appeal available to the applicant and will inform him of the means by which he may exercise those rights. The applicant will not be removed from the UK as long as any appeal which he may bring is pending (para 333).

(e) Grant of asylum (para 334)

A person will be granted asylum in the UK if the S of S is satisfied that:
  (a) he is in the UK or has arrived at a port of entry in the UK; and
  (b) he is a refugee as defined by the Convention and Protocol; and
  (c) refusing his application would result in his being required to go (whether immediately or after the time limited by an expiring leave to enter or remain) in breach of the Convention and Protocol, to a country in which his life or freedom would be threatened on account of his race, religion, nationality, membership of a particular social group or political opinion (para 334).

If the S of S decides to grant asylum to a person who has been given leave to enter (whether or not the leave has expired) or to a person who has entered without leave, the S of S will vary the existing leave, or grant limited leave to remain (para 335).

Refusal of asylum Where a person applies for asylum and is refused because he does not fall within the definition, or for some other reason, but his removal would be in breach of another of the UK's international obligations, he should be granted exceptional leave to remain. Earl Ferrers, promoting the Asylum and Immigration Appeals Bill 1993 in the Lords stated that when a person applies for asylum and his case is considered and it is found that he cannot be granted asylum, the immigration officer has a duty to consider the UK's obligations under the UN Convention on Torture, and the European Convention on Human Rights (referred to in Chapter 26) to see whether, if the person is sent away from the UK, such action would contravene obligations under other international Conventions (HL Hansard, Vol 542, No 92 Cols 546, 548 and 551). In addition the S of S occasionally makes a concession relating to persons from a country who have leave in the UK in some capacity other than as a refugee, but who have expressed a fear of returning to the country to which they are returnable (see eg *Ex p Zib* [1993] Imm AR 350, Lebanon).

An application which does not meet the criteria set out above under para 334 will be refused. An illegal entrant liable to removal or to deportation may be notified at the same time as his asylum claim is refused of removal directions or of the appropriate deportation enforcement action (para 338). If the person has a limited leave in another immigration category his limited leave may be curtailed at the same time that his asylum application is refused. No appeal may be brought under s 14 of the 1971 Act or under the appeal provisions permitting an appeal to the special adjudicator against the curtailment of the limited leave (1993 Act, s 7(2)). When the person's leave is curtailed, he may be served with a deportation order. Full account will be taken of the factors listed in para 364.

'a refugee ... as defined by the Convention and Protocol' (para 334(ii)) A person becomes a refugee when he satisfies the definition set out in Art 1A of the Convention and Protocol relating to the Status of Refugees (1951) (Cmnd 9171 and Cmnd 3906). A refugee is anyone who

owing to a well founded fear of being persecuted for reasons of race, religion, nationality, membership of a particular social group, or political opinion, is outside his country of nationality and is unable or owing to such fear is unwilling to avail himself of the protection of that country; or who not having a nationality and being outside the country of his former habitual is unable or owing to such fear is unwilling to return to it.

The Convention and Protocol are given primacy in UK law as a result of the Asylum and Immigration Appeals Act 1993 (s 2). The 1993 Act makes provisions for the determination of claims made by a person (whether before or after its coming into force) that it would be contrary to the UK's obligations under the Convention either for him to be removed from the UK or for him to be required to leave the UK. The 1993 Act gives to asylum seekers a right of appeal. In the past many of the cases in which asylum law in the UK has been considered have been judicial review applications. The asylum seeker must satisfy the immigration authorities that he is within the definition of 'refugee' in Art 1 of the Convention and Protocol. The material date for assessing whether the person satisfies the Convention definition is the date of the decision and not that of the application. Thus if the circumstances alter, so that the applicant's fear can be said no longer to be well founded, the application will fail (*Samuel Musisi v S of S* [1992] Imm AR 520).

'owing to a well founded fear' The applicant must actually have the fear described (*Ex p Gurmeet Singh* [1987] Imm AR 489), and he must be outside his country owing to the fear. This means that the fear may arise after he has left the country. He is required to prove the causal link between the fear and his being outside the country at the time of the decision. The applicant must also show that the fear is well founded. An objective test is used to determine whether the fear is well founded. There is no obligation on the S of S to confine himself to the facts known to the applicant. The S of S may objectively determine the facts and ask whether there is a real and substantial risk of persecution for Convention reasons. His duty is to consider the application, and use his experience of similar applications and his knowledge of conditions in the country to determine whether the fear is well founded. In doing so he is entitled to rely on information supplied by the Foreign and Commonwealth Office regarding those conditions. There is no duty on him to make enquiries in the country of persecution (*Akdag v S of S* [1993] Imm AR 172). There must be 'a reasonable chance', 'substantial grounds for thinking', or 'a serious possibility' that the fear of persecution is well founded. The phrase 'real and substantial risk' was said to equate to these expressions of the test. It is satisfied by a probability well below the civil standard of proof of persecution on the balance of probabilities and could be satisfied by a one in 10 chance of persecution (*Ex p Sivakumaran* [1988] 2 WLR 92, AC 958). The fear may be well founded on the basis of past events, if they suggest that there is a risk of future illtreatment. The S of S should consider the history of the case, and relate past events to the likely interest of the persecutor in the asylum seeker in the future (*Ex p P* 23 January 1992 QBD CO 702/90 and also *R v S of S, ex p Halil Direk* [1992] Imm AR 330).

A different approach is adopted to the treatment of applications by children.

'Persecution for reasons of race, religion' etc. The dictionary definition of 'persecution' as meaning 'to pursue with malignancy or injurious action, especially to oppress for holding a heretical belief' was used in *R v IAT, ex p Jonah* [1985] Imm AR 7. Persecution requires a degree of persistence by the persecutor. Evidence of past ill treatment should be related to the likelihood that the persecutor would be interested in the asylum seeker in the future (*Ex p P* 23 January 1992 QBD CO 702/90). A series of relatively minor

incidents may not give rise to a well-founded fear of persecution (*Ex p Onay* [1992] Imm AR 320). Likewise it may not be unreasonable of the S of S to treat discrimination as not amounting to persecution (*Ex p Moezzi* 6 October 1988 CA). However it would be open to a special adjudicator to take the view that discrimination did amount on the facts of a particular case to persecution within the ordinary meaning of that word, and likewise to take the view that a series of minor incidents amounted to persecution (see *Ex p Jeyakumaran* [1994] Imm AR 45).

The passing of a law may amount to persecution depending on the extent to which it prevents the activities of the individual applicant as opposed to some members of a group of which he is a member (*Ahmad v S of S* [1990] Im AR 61). The test is the effect the legal instrument has on individual members of the group, and the application will be considered against that background. Account will be taken of the evidence he has to offer that he will feel bound to break that law. The persecution may be based on a misapprehension by the persecutors that the individual holds a political belief or was likely to commit acts in support of a political cause. The asylum seeker does not in those circumstances have to hold the belief (*Asante v S of S* [1991] Imm AR 78).

Social Group   It is not necessary for a person to have been singled out for persecution for his claim for asylum to succeed, as there may be persecution of a community or social group. However the fact that he has not been persecuted personally is a factor which the S of S may reasonably take into account (*ex p Gulbache* [1991] Imm AR 526). In *S of S v Otchere* [1988] Imm AR 21 it was held that the definition of 'membership of a particular social group' in the Convention covered former members of the Ghanaian Military Intelligence. A definition was proposed in *S of S v Binbasi* [1989] Imm AR 595 of 'possessing a common immutable characteristic which members of the group cannot change or should not be required to change'. That case turned on whether the Convention protected a person from actions which he could refrain from. There is as yet no accepted definition of 'social group'. Active homosexuals may be considered to be members of a particular social group (*Binbasi*).

In *Ex p Mendis* [1989] Imm AR 6 the CA was divided on whether future acts could found a claim for asylum on the basis that a person's views would inevitably clash with those who would then persecute him, when no events which would attract persecution have yet taken place. Balcombe LJ thought that in that case there could not be persecution for Convention reasons, but Neill LJ left open whether or not a person of settled political conviction could claim asylum because should he be returned it would be unrealistic to expect him to refrain from expressing his political views forever. Staughton LJ stated that if a person has such strong convictions that he will inevitably speak out against the regime of the country and will inevitably suffer for it, he should be treated as a refugee (and see *Ahmad* (above)).

The fear must be shown to be one which is within the Convention. In *Ex p Zibrila-Alassini* [1991] Imm AR 367 Rose J held that unless it could be shown that detrimental treatment would be meted out to the applicant and his family, because of a Convention reason, then the decision of the S of S not to grant asylum could not be challenged (however, exceptional leave to remain was granted in that case).

The persecutor need not be the authorities of the country of persecution. Sections of the population who do not respect the standards established by the laws of the country may persecute. Where serious discriminatory or other offensive acts are committed by the local populace, they can be considered as persecution if they are knowingly tolerated by the authorities, or if the authorities refuse or prove unable to offer effective protection (*Ex p Jeyakumaran* (see note [1994] Imm AR 45)). It is arguable that a deserter from an army, who is not willing to take part in activity condemned by the international community such as repressing his fellow countrymen, will be persecuted if punished for his refusal to do so (*Ex p Aouiche* (1991) *Times*, 4 June). However, it is only if there is evidence that a refusal to perform military service would result in persecution that it can form the basis for a claim for asylum (*Petrovski v S of S* [1993] Imm AR 134).

(f) Cessation of status

By cl 1C of the Convention, the Convention does not apply where a person falls into any of the following categories:
(1) He has voluntarily re-availed himself of the protection of the country of his nationality (eg by obtaining a passport).
(2) He had lost his nationality, but has voluntarily taken it up again.
(3) He has acquired a new nationality, enjoying the protection of the country of his new nationality.

(4) He has re-established himself in the country from which he fled.
(5) He can no longer, because the circumstances in connection with which he has been recognised as a refugee have ceased to exist, continue to refuse to avail himself of the protection of his country of nationality; but he can still be recognised as a refugee if he can show compelling reasons arising out of previous persecution for refusing to avail himself of that protection.
(6) If he has no nationality, he is able to return to his country of former habitual residence because the circumstances causing him to be a refugee have ceased, unless he can show compelling reason for refusing to return to that country.

Exclusion of status By cl 1E where a person has taken residence in a country in which he is recognised as having full rights and obligations of a national of that country he ceases to be a refugee. Finally, by Art 1F, if there are serious reasons for considering that a person has committed war crimes, or crimes against peace, or against humanity, or if he has committed a serious non-political crime outside the country of refuge prior to his admission as a refugee, or has been guilty of acts contrary to the purposes of the UN, he cannot be a refugee under the Convention. The S of S is entitled to distinguish between persecution and prosecution for a criminal offence, even if it is asserted that the applicant would not receive a fair trial if returned (*Elvis Ameyaw v S of S* [1992] Imm AR 594). A person linked with a terrorist organisation who faces legitimate prosecution in his country will not normally be regarded as a refugee (*Ex p Baljit Sijngh* [1994] Imm AR 42).

2 Refusal of asylum

335. If the Secretary of State decides to grant asylum to a person who has been given leave to enter (whether or not the leave has expired) or to a person who has entered without leave, the Secretary of State will vary the existing leave or grant limited leave to remain.

Refusal of asylum

336. An application which does not meet the criteria set out in paragraph 334 will be refused.

337. The Secretary of State may decide not to consider the substance

of a person's claim to refugee status if he is satisfied that the person's removal to a third country does not raise any issue as to the United Kingdom's obligations under the Convention and Protocol. More details are given in paragraphs 345 and 347.

338. When a person in the United Kingdom is notified that asylum has been refused he may, if he is liable to removal as an illegal entrant or to deportation, at the same time be notified of removal directions, served with a notice of intention to make a deportation order, or served with a deportation order, as appropriate.

339. When a person with limited leave is refused asylum the leave may be curtailed if he does not meet the requirements of the Rules under which leave was granted. When a person's leave is curtailed under Section 7 of the Asylum and Immigration Appeals Act 1993, he may at the same time be served with a notice of intention to make a deportation order. Full account will be taken of all the relevant circumstances known to the Secretary of State, including those listed in paragraph 364.

Third country cases

345. If the Secretary of State is satisfied that there is a safe country to which an asylum applicant can be sent, his application will normally be refused without substantive consideration of his claim to refugee status. A safe country is one in which the life or freedom of the asylum applicant would not be threatened (within the meaning of Article 33 of the Convention) and the government of which would not send the applicant elsewhere in a manner contrary to the principles of the Convention and Protocol. The Secretary of State shall not remove an asylum applicant without substantive consideration of his claim unless:
  (i) the asylum applicant has not arrived in the United Kingdom directly from the country in which he claims to fear persecution and has had an opportunity at the border or within the territory of a third country to make contact with that country's authorities in order to seek their protection; or
  (ii) there is other clear evidence of his admissibility to a third country.

Provided that he is satisfied that a case meets these criteria, the Secretary of State is under no obligation to consult the authorities of the third country before the removal of an asylum applicant.

Previously rejected applications

346. When an asylum applicant has previously been refused asylum in the United Kingdom and can demonstrate no relevant and substantial change in his circumstances since that date, his application will be refused.

347. When an asylum applicant has come to the United Kingdom from another country which is a party to the United Nations Convention relating to the Status of Refugees or its Protocol and which has considered and rejected an application for asylum from him, his application for asylum

in the United Kingdom may be refused without substantive consideration of his claim to refugee status. He may be removed to that country, or another country meeting the criteria of paragraph 345, and invited to raise any new circumstances with the authorities of the country which originally considered his application.

Rights of appeal

348. Special provisions governing appeals in asylum cases are set out in the Asylum and Immigration Appeals Act 1993 and the Asylum Appeals (Procedure) Rules 1993. Where asylum is refused the applicant will be provided with a notice informing him of the decision and of the reasons for refusal. At the same time that asylum is refused the applicant may be notified of removal directions or served with a notice of intention to deport, as appropriate. The notice of refusal of asylum will also explain any rights of appeal available to the applicant and will inform him of the means by which he may exercise those rights.

COMMENTARY

For rights and appeals see Chapter 13.

(a) Without consideration

Safe third country In addition to the practical difficulties put in the path of an asylum seeker coming to the UK as a result of the Immigration (Carriers' Liability) Act 1987 there is the problem that a claim for asylum will not be considered on its merits where the applicant did not come directly to the UK but travelled via a safe third country. If the S of S finds that there is a safe third country to which the asylum applicant could be sent, no consideration is given to the merits of the claim unless there is evidence that the third country will return the person to the place of persecution. With the abolition of internal frontiers in Europe, a convention on the determination of the member state responsible for considering an application for asylum has been concluded (the Dublin Convention). The effect of the Dublin Convention is that an asylum seeker will only have one chance of obtaining asylum in the EU. If one country rejects his application, no other country will consider it (see below). Although it is not yet in force, the S of S has been applying some of the principles of the Dublin Convention.

The S of S may decide not to consider the substance of a person's claim to refugee status if he is satisfied that the person's removal to a third country does not raise any issue as to the UK's obligation under the Convention and Protocol (para 337). If the S of S is satisfied that there is a safe country to which an asylum seeker can be sent his application will normally be refused without any substantive consideration of his claim to refugee status. A safe country is one in which the life or freedom of the asylum seeker would not be threatened (within the meaning of Art 33 of the Convention) and the government of which would not send the applicant elsewhere in a manner contrary to the principles of the Convention and Protocol. The S of S shall not remove an asylum seeker without substantive consideration of his claim unless:

(a) the asylum seeker has not arrived in the UK directly from the country in which he claims to fear persecution and has had an opportunity at the border or within the territory of a third country to make contact with that country's authorities in order to seek their protection; or

(b) there is clear evidence of his admissibility to a third country.

If the S of S is satisfied that a case meets these criteria he is under no obligation to consult the authorities of the third country before the removal of an asylum applicant (para 345).

Such cases may be subject to the fast-track appellate system. The rules represent the policy contained in a ministerial statement to Parliament on 25 July 1990 (see [1990] Imm AR 573 for text). The courts have taken the view that there is no obligation on the S of S to consider the application in such circumstances (*Bugdaycay v S of S* [1987] AC 514, *S of S v Two citizens of Chile* [1977] Imm AR 36, and *Ex p Yassine* [1990] Imm AR 354). The applicant is returned to the country from which he embarked unless that country is one in which his life or freedom would be threatened for a Convention reason, or would return him to the country from which he fled (see also *Balbir Singh v S of S* [1992] Imm AR 426). He may be returned to that country whether or not he wishes to go there as opposed to somewhere else (*R v IAT, ex p Miller* [1988] Imm AR 358).

The countries to which a person can be removed are set out at para 8 of Sched 2 to the 1971 Act. They are:

(a) his country of nationality;
(b) where he obtained his passport or identity document;
(c) the country of embarkation to the UK; or
(d) any other country to which there is a reason to believe he would be admitted.

In *Yassine* (above) Schiemann J held that the S of S must believe that the applicant will be admitted to the country, not merely that he should be admitted. In the absence of such a belief there is no power under (*d*) above to remove the applicant to that country. For these purposes it is only necessary that the third country should admit the applicant temporarily, including for the purposes of considering an application for asylum. It is not necessary for the S of S to have reason to believe that the applicant will be admitted for the purposes of settlement (*Alsawaf v S of S* [1988] Imm AR 410). Such a country may be one to which the applicant has not as yet gone.

When deciding whether a person will have to go to a particular country if he is required to leave the UK, the main consideration is whether he will for all practical purposes have to go to that country. This means that if he could practically go to a different country he will not have to go to the country in which he fears persecution. He should not be returned to a country if it is one which will return him in all probability to the country of persecution (*Yassine*) above). However there is no obligation to obtain the assurance of a third country that the applicant will be accepted (*Bouzeid v S of S* [1991] Imm AR 204).

Art 33 of the Convention creates an obligation on the S of S to be satisfied that the country to which removal is planned will not return the applicant to a country of persecution. The state wishing to remove an asylum seeker is obliged under the Convention to observe the principle of non-refoulment which prohibits indirect as well as direct return to the country of persecution. Any risk of return must be taken into account by the S of S (*Musisi* [1987] 2 WLR 606). Unless there is strong evidence that, in the past, asylum seekers have been returned to a country of persecution the S of S will act reasonably in relying on the third country's signature to the Convention, as an assurance that the applicant will not be returned to the country of origin without consideration of the merits of his case (*Ex p Yildiz*) [1991] Imm AR 354. Also in *ex p Mangal Singh* [1992] Imm AR 376 the S of S was held to be entitled to rely on the assessment made by the UNHCR that a country is a safe one. By contrast the S of S will not be justified in refusing to consider a claim for asylum on its merits where there is evidence that a third country said to be safe by the S of S was not a signatory to the Convention, and that there is evidence of a danger of refoulment (*S of S v Razaq Abdel* [1992] Imm AR 152). The applicant must show that the third country will not accept him or produce evidence that there is a risk of refoulment (*Ex p Rubanra* [1993] Imm AR 447). Further, the assertion by an applicant that a third country will not consider his application seriously, and therefore return him to the country of persecution, although not a ground for judicial review, will raise a factual issue for the special adjudicator to determine (cf. *R v S of S, ex p Murali* [1993] Imm AR 311).

Cases relating to the application of the third-country principle before HC 395 indicate the way in which the rule will be employed. In *Ex p Bokele* [1991] Imm AR 124, the applicant had been in Belgium for 6 weeks before entering the UK. The S of S referred to Art 5 of the Dublin Convention (which is not yet in force), but which provides that the responsibility for determining the asylum application shall lie with a member state which issues an applicant with a residence permit, as Belgium had done. Much shorter periods of time can bring the principle of the third country into play. In *ex p Akyol* [1990] Imm AR 571, Kennedy J held that the S of S's refusal to determine the applicants' applications for asylum in the UK because the applicants had spent 10–15 days in transit through other countries to the UK was not unreasonable. In *Kemal Karali v S of S* [1991] Imm AR 199 it was held that it was not unreasonable to apply this policy to applicants who hid for two days in the transit area of a Dutch airport, fleeing from Turkey (see also *Bouzeid v S of S* [1991] Imm AR 204 where the applicant spent one night in the airport transit lounge in Austria and also *David Thevarajah v S of S* [1991] Imm AR 371 where the applicants spent one night in France). It is not possible to argue that an English speaking applicant has no opportunity to claim asylum in a country where there are many English speakers (*Dursun v S of S* [1993] Imm AR 169). The Minister stated that an hour in Schipol airport would be long enough to bring this rule into use, but emphasised that it is the opportunity to seek protection which is important and not the length of stay (Official Report, Standing Committee A, 3 December 1992, Col 567). A person has the opportunity to apply for asylum in a third country if he knows that he is in a different country, is able to contact the authorities and has no reason to believe that the authorities will not receive his application for asylum (*R v Special Adjudicator ex p Kandasamy* (1994) *The Times*, March 11).

Where the country of proposed return will refuse entry to the applicants, returning them to the UK, it is not a country to which he can be removed (*Bouzeid*). HC 395 does not require the S of S to consult the authorities of the third country, but the S of S must be satisfied that the applicant can be sent to the third country. If the applicant will not be admitted there, he cannot be sent there.

The S of S's statement that he believes that the applicant will be admitted to the third country may be challenged by the applicant if he produces evidence to show that he will not be admitted. It is then a matter of fact for the special adjudicator to determine. Because the rules provide that if the S of S is satisfied that the applicant will be admitted, there is no obligation upon him to make enquiries with the third country, advisers should have access to sufficient materials about the practices of other countries on the readmissibility of asylum seekers. The proposition that the S of S must establish by direct enquiry with the third country that proper consideration will be given to the applicant's application for asylum was rejected in *Ex p Thavathevathasan*, CA 22 December 1993 FC3, 94/6744/D). However, the CA stated that if a person was returned from a third country, the S of S would be obliged to reconsider the application afresh. He would not be able to return the applicant to the third country without further enquiry.

Substantial links with the UK Where a person can be removed to a third country his application for asylum can be considered exceptionally on the grounds of his having substantial links with the UK which make it reasonable for the claim to be considered in the UK. Under the terms of a concession a person who has substantial links with the UK may present evidence of them, and the S of S may decide that it would be reasonable for the claim for asylum exceptionally to be considered in the UK (see Hansard, 25 July 1990, Written Answers, Col 263). The terms of the substantial links required were set out in a letter to the Refugee Unit on 21 March 1991 (see *Conteh v S of S* [1992] Imm AR 594 at 602). A third-country case will normally be considered substantively where the following conditions are fulfilled:

(a) the applicant's spouse is in the UK;
(b) the applicant is an unmarried minor and a parent is in the UK;
(c) the applicant has an unmarried minor child in the UK.

The relative must have either leave or temporary admission to remain in the UK as an asylum seeker. However, the S of S retains a discretion and these factors may be outweighed by other factors, such as the character of the asylum seeker (*Conteh*).

Discretion will need to be exercised according to the merits of the case where any of the following conditions are fulfilled:

(a) the minor is married but he has a parent in the UK, or has an unmarried minor child in the UK as an asylum seeker. (However, discretion will probably be exercised favourably

where the minor has a parent in the UK, rather than when he has a child in the UK);
- (b) the applicant is an elderly or otherwise dependent parent;
- (c) the family link is one which will not normally be considered, but there is clear evidence that the applicant is wholly or mainly dependent upon the relative in the UK and that there is an absence of any similar support elsewhere.

In these cases the factors which may influence the exercise of the discretion in the favour of the applicant are:
- (a) language skills: eg the applicant is fluent in English, but not in the language of the third country;
- (b) cultural links;
- (c) the number of family members the applicant has in the UK as opposed to other countries.

Where a person claims family links which do not fall within (a)–(c) above, and do not display any of the features which will be considered in the exercise of the discretion (such as dependency), the application will not be considered no matter how strong the links of language or culture. The phrase 'substantial links with the United Kindgom' in the ministerial statement of 1990 has the same meaning in substance and the same restrictions as the provisions of Art 4 of the Dublin Convention (*Ex p TK* [1993] Imm AR 231.

Statement on refugees from the former Yugoslavia In a letter to UNHCR dated 10 August 1992, the S of S stated that in the normal course of events the S of S would not make third-country returns where an applicant has merely transmitted through other countries, staying less than a day or two in any one of them. Nationals of the former Yugoslavia may still benefit from this exception under the new rules, and also from having family connections in the UK, even if they have done more than merely passed in transit through a safe country.

Earl Ferrers, promoting the 1993 Act, stated that it was the S of S's practice to waive the normal third-country policy if a person arriving in the UK can show that he has close ties with the UK, and that immediate family members may constitute such a tie, particularly if there is a degree of dependency on such family members involved (Hansard, 9 February 1993, HL Col 599). It is likely therefore that the earlier policy will continue.

Whether a country is a safe country is a matter to be considered properly in each case and in respect of each country. The S of S is entitled to take account of the assessment of the UNHCR of a country as safe, despite the hostility of non-governmental groups (see *Ex p Mangal Singh* [1992] Imm AR 376). In *ex p Abdullah* [1992] Imm AR 438 the argument of the applicant that Germany was not a safe third country because he feared persecution there from neo-Nazi groups, was rejected by the CA. Where it is suggested that a third country is not safe it is probably correct to apply the Convention test to that country. The usual procedures in asylum cases should then be followed in relation to the complaint about the third country. Under the new rules, the fact of such attacks can form the basis of an exceptional decision to consider the application substantively. Further, the evidence which the S of S received in the *Abdullah* case from the Foreign and Commonwealth Office (that there had been a decline in the number of attacks on foreigners following the policies of the German government) can now be scrutinised by the special adjudicator, subject to arguments on public interest immunity preventing disclosure of FCO reports (see also *Balbir Singh v S of S* [1992] Imm AR 426 and cf *Ex p Roj Singh* [1992] Imm AR 607).

(b) Previously rejected applications (paras 346–347)

The applicant must demonstrate that there has been a change of circumstances since the date his application was refused under para 346. Where an applicant applies for asylum in another country, which rejects his application, his claim may be refused without substantive consideration in the UK. He will be removed from the UK to that country and invited to raise any new circumstances with the authorities in the country which originally considered the application (para 347). This rule represents existing practice. Thus in *Ex p Zeynal Avci* [1994] Imm AR 35 an applicant was removed to Switzerland and invited to place the further information he had obtained before the Swiss authorities.

3 Consideration of cases

Consideration of cases

340. A failure, without reasonable explanation, to make a prompt and full disclosure of material factors, either orally or in writing, or otherwise to assist the Secretary of State to the full in establishing the facts of the case may lead to refusal of an asylum application. This includes failure to comply with a notice issued by the Secretary of State requiring the applicant to report to a designated place to be fingerprinted, or failure

to complete an asylum questionnaire, or failure to comply with a request to attend an interview concerning the application.

341. In determining an asylum application the Secretary of State will have regard to matters which may damage an asylum applicant's credibility if no reasonable explanation is given. Among such matters are:
   (i) that the applicant has failed to apply forthwith upon arrival in the United Kingdom, unless the application is founded on events which have taken place since his arrival in the United Kingdom;
   (ii) that the applicant has made false representations, either orally or in writing;
   (iii) that the applicant has destroyed, damaged or disposed of any passport, other document or ticket relevant to his claim;
   (iv) that the applicant has undertaken any activities in the United Kingdom before or after lodging his application which are inconsistent with his previous beliefs and behaviour and calculated to create or substantially enhance his claim to refugee status;
   (v) that the applicant has lodged concurrent applications for asylum in the United Kingdom or in another country.

If the Secretary of State concludes for these or any other reasons that an asylum applicant's account is not credible, the application will be refused.

342. The actions of anyone acting as an agent of the asylum applicant may also be taken into account in regard to the matters set out in paragraphs 340 and 341.

343. If there is a part of the country from which the applicant claims to be a refugee in which he would not have a well-founded fear of persecution, and to which it would be reasonable to expect him to go, the application may be refused.

344. Cases will normally be considered on an individual basis but if an applicant is part of a group whose claims are clearly not related to the criteria for refugee status in the Convention and Protocol he may be refused without examination of his individual claim. However, the Secretary of State will have regard to any evidence produced by an individual to show that his claim should be distinguished from those of the rest of the group.

COMMENTARY

(a) Preparation of asylum claims

Asylum claims call for speedy and careful preparation. An applicant's credibility can be affected by imprecise formulation of his claim. The comments set out below are based largely upon *Best Practice Guide to the Preparation of Asylum Applications from Arrival to First Interview* (Fiona Lindsley, 1992 Immigration Law Practitioners Association, London).

Initial interviews Where possible, the initial interview between the applicant and his adviser should be conducted privately, in a sympathetic manner. The adviser should not attempt to obtain all the details of the claim at this interview unless there is no other option. It should enable the adviser to see how far the claim has progressed, the social background of the applicant, and to undertake any necessary immediate work on the claim.

It is important to ascertain whether a claim for asylum has yet been made, and if so what was said in the course of it. Was a Political Asylum Questionnaire (PAQ) completed? A copy should be obtained immediately if one was. The immigration status of the applicant should be established. Has the applicant been fingerprinted? Does he have temporary admission and if so are there any reporting conditions? Has he received his Standard Acknowledgement Letter? Has a previous application for asylum been made, and if so when? What is the applicant's position in relation to housing and income support, and work? If he has been made an offer of employment, has an application been made to the Home Office for permission for him to take up work? If the asylum application was made more than six months ago, has he obtained permission to work? If the applicant is highly literate, a written statement should be obtained from him, which can be discussed and amplified in a further interview. An interpreter should be used if there are any language problems, but avoid if possible family and friends and anyone who does not have proper experience as an interpreter. The interpreter should only interpret, and should be prevented where possible from conducting his own interview. The applicant should be asked whether he is happy with the interpreter, as it sometimes happens that applicants are intimidated by an unknown person acting as interpreter, or by someone who may speak in a way which indicates an adverse political affiliation.

Port application The adviser should obtain details of the manner in which the applicant arrived in the UK, and what condition he was in at the time. He should discover whether the application is being treated as without foundation and obtain an explanation as to why no application was made in any country the applicant passed through. Details of the questions the immigration officers asked, the length of the interview and details of the interview process should be elicited.

Background materials The current situation of the country of origin should be studied in newspapers. Amnesty International reports, Watch reports and the Minority Rights Group reports. Additionally information may be available from academic sources such as the School of Oriental and African Studies which have made a study of the political situation in the country concerned or from other journalistic sources, such as the Middle East Digest.

The asylum seeker's statement The account which the applicant gives must be as detailed as possible. The account must be accurate, detailed and truthful. The primary consideration is credibility. Earl Ferrers said in Parliament:

> Ideally one could wish for conclusive independent corroboration of everything which is claimed by an applicant. That would be of benefit both to the applicant and the assessor. However in reality that is rarely possible. As a result the asylum division staff must rely on a combination of factual information which is obtained from a variety of sources and an assessment of the individual who is making the claim. In other words the credibility of the asylum seeker is a key factor (Hansard, 9 Feb 93, HL Debs Vol 542, No 92, Col 594).

It should be stressed to the applicant that the Home Office has facilities to check facts and that inaccuracies and falsehoods can be uncovered. If a copy of the statement or PAQ is submitted in advance of an interview with the Home Office and inconsistencies emerge at interview which are capable of explanation, they should be explained in a subsequent statement which should be submitted before a decision is made.

In dealing with the applicant's fear of persecution for reasons of political/religious beliefs or affiliations, or of belonging to a particular racial/national/social group the following points should be noted:

(a) details should be given of the beliefs held by the applicant and of how they were acquired, and when;

(b) details of affiliations should be given, the party or organisations to which the applicant belonged, together with any posts held or functions performed; the names of persons the applicant worked with should be given (but if the applicant is afraid to give them, this should be respected and an explanation of that fear should be obtained and noted);

(c) any activities the applicant had been involved in (demonstrations, for example) or non-compliant behaviour (avoiding conscription, for example, or refusing to be involved in the activities of another group);

(d) any detentions, torture, trials, and harassment such as restrictions on activities;

(e) any medical attention received;

(f) details of the family and their affiliations or involvement and treatment;
(g) why it was not reasonable to escape to a safe area of the country; details here should include the level and geographical extent of the control of the country of origin by the feared group;
(h) what would happen to the applicant if he were to return to the country of origin, and why it would happen; the applicant should be asked to provide details which make it credible that he would be persecuted on return, for example the fact that the airport to which he would be returned is in an area which is under the control of the feared group;
(i) what prompted the flight and details of the escape from the country of origin to the UK;
(j) any activities since coming to the UK, revealing a continued involvement or affiliation.

Under Part 11 of HC 395 the whereabouts of documentation and an explanation of such documentation as is available is important. Thus an adviser should check for:
(a) the whereabouts of passports or travel documents;
(b) details of plane tickets;
(c) documents which may support what the applicant asserts including:
    (i) membership cards for any organisation, or group;
    (ii) newspaper articles;
    (iii) photographs;
    (iv) letters from friends and family;
(d) documents which may be obtained from the country of origin, such as medical reports by doctors who have treated the applicant after torture or ill treatment.

Anything not in English should be translated. The adviser must know what it means. Nothing should be sent to the Home Office without the prior approval of the applicant. Any information disclosed should be treated in confidence by the Home Office.

Green Form assistance is available for the preparation of claims, and extensions may be granted in order to obtain a variety of information such as:
(a) expert reports on the political situation in the country of origin including any relevant area of the country of origin;
(b) medical (physical or psychiatric) reports on the applicant (for example, from the Medical Foundation for the Care

of Victims of Torture, 96–98 Grafton Road, London, NW5 3EJ);

(c) counsel's advice on the merits or evidence.

Consider obtaining a report from the Protection Officer of the UNHCR who is able to provide information in appropriate cases. Consider also referring the case to Amnesty International for comment.

The applicant will be interviewed briefly about his journey to the UK in order to ascertain whether he stopped on his journey to the UK in a third country in which he could have claimed asylum, and to establish his identity. If it is accepted that the UK is the correct country for the application to be considered one of three courses is followed:

(a) the applicant is given a Political Asylum Questionnaire (PAQ) to fill in, granted temporary admission, and required to return the completed PAQ to the port within a set period; or

(b) the applicant is detained pending determination of his claim, and the immigration officer completes a PAQ at an interview; or

(c) the applicant is released on temporary admission and required to attend an interview for a PAQ to be completed.

In the latter two cases the PAQ is an interview record. If the applicant is not detained he will be issued with a Standard Acknowledgement Letter (SAL), which will enable him to claim benefits. The letter does not give rise to a legitimate expectation that the asylum claim will be considered substantively (*Ex p Kyomya* [1993] Imm AR 331).

In all cases the applicant may be fingerprinted. Substantive asylum applications are then dealt with by the Asylum Division of the IND at the Home Office. The PAQs from port applicants are forwarded to the Asylum Division for a decision. The application may be (i) refused outright, (ii) granted or (iii) refused, but the applicant may be granted exceptional leave to remain (the applicant is not required to leave the UK because there are reasons why he should not be returned to his country). If the application is refused the applicant may appeal under the system described below. If the S of S certifies that the application is 'without foundation', the applicant has two working days in which to appeal. If the special adjudicator agrees that the application is without foundation, the applicant has no further appeal, but may in appropriate circumstances apply for judicial review of the decision that the application is without foundation. If the application is not certified to be without foundation, the applicant has ten working days in which to appeal against a refusal. He may appeal to the IAT with leave if the adjudicator refuses the appeal, and with leave of the IAT or CA he may appeal to the CA.

In country cases The application is made to the Home Office either by post or in person. The applicant may be required to attend for fingerprints to be taken by the Screening Unit at the Home Office which should not examine the merits of the claim. The PAQ will be sent to the applicant, who may be required to attend an interview if the Home Office is unable to determine the application without one. The period allowed for the return of self-completion questionnaires has been reduced from two months to four weeks. Failure without good reason to return the questionnaire within the specified time may lead to the refusal of the application. Applicants are sent one letter warning them that the application may be refused if no response is received. If for any reason some items of information or supporting documents cannot be provided within four weeks it is important that applicants provide what information is available and an explanation of the reason for their inability to provide the remainder. If the questionnaire raises further questions, particularly where the application is likely to be refused, the Home Office will interview the applicant further after receipt of the questionnaire (letter 8 July 1993 from IND to JCWI). If the application is refused the applicant has the rights of appeal outlined above in relation to port of entry applicants, but the abbreviated process for claims without foundation will generally not apply. The applicant has the right to free legal representation from the Refugee Legal Centre at appeal hearings, or may instruct solicitors or agents to represent him.

(b) Paras 340–344

A failure (whether by the asylum applicant or his agent (para 342)) without reasonable explanation to make a prompt and full disclosure of material facts either orally or in writing or otherwise to assist the S of S to the full in establishing the facts of the case may lead to the application being refused (para 340). Failing to assist the S of S includes:

    (*a*) failure to comply with a notice requiring the asylum seeker to report to a designated place to be fingerprinted (under s 3 of the 1993 Act);

    (*b*) failure to complete a PAQ; or

(c) failure to attend an interview concerning the application (para 340).

Fingerprinting of asylum seekers Section 3 of the 1993 Act gives powers to prison officers, constables and immigration officers. The powers conferred in relation to a person who has claimed asylum are:
  (a) to take reasonably necessary steps to take the fingerprints of either the asylum seeker, or any of his dependants;
  (b) by notice in writing to require the asylum seeker or any of his dependants to attend at a place which must be specified in the notice in order that fingerprints may be taken from them. The S of S may also authorise other categories of person to exercise these powers.

If the asylum seeker abandons his claim, or if the claim is determined, any notice shall cease to have effect, and the powers to fingerprint the asylum seeker or his dependants may not be exercised. By s 3(4) the notice to attend for the taking of fingerprints must give the asylum seeker at least seven days within which he is to attend. The notice may also require attendance at a particular time or between specified times of day so that fingerprinting may be carried out. If a person fails to comply with a current requirement to attend for fingerprinting, s 3(5) gives an immigration officer or constable power to arrest him without warrant. Having been arrested he may be taken to a place where his fingerprints may conveniently be taken before he is released. Further, constables and immigration officers are entitled to take such steps as may be reasonably necessary for taking the person's fingerprints before he is released, whether or not he is also brought to a place where his fingerprints may conveniently be taken. However, the section does not give the Home Office powers to fingerprint someone who has been detained in another way, for example at a DSS office (Charles Wardle, Standing Committee A, 19 November 1992, col 195). A person must be an asylum seeker for the Home Office to have the power to fingerprint him. There is no provision for the Home Office to fingerprint a person who is suspected of being an asylum seeker (Charles Wardle, Standing Committee A, 19 November 1992, col 195).

By s 3(6) and (7) the person's fingerprints, and any copies, must be destroyed either within one month of the day on which he is granted indefinite leave to remain in the UK, or ten years from the date on which they were taken, whichever is the earlier. Any data relating to the fingerprints must be rendered inaccessible by the S of S as soon as is practicable after the fingerprints are destroyed. A person may require the S of S to sign and issue a certificate to him stating that such computer data as exists in relation to his fingerprints have been rendered inaccessible. The certificate must be issued to him not later than three months from the date upon which he makes the request.

The powers under Schedule 2 to the 1971 Act, which permit a person detained for examination or removal to be photographed, and measured, and for other reasonable steps to be taken for the purposes of identifying him.

Children will not be fingerprinted as a matter of course (Earl Ferrers, HL Debs, 9 February 1993, col 627, Vol 542, No 92). A police constable, immigration or prison officer may not take steps to take the fingerprints of a child claiming asylum who is under 16, except in the presence of either the child's parent or guardian or a person other than an immigration officer, constable or prison officer or civil servant, who for the time being takes responsibility for the child. Such persons must be over 18 (s 3(2)(*b*)).

(c) Credibility

The S of S will have regard to certain matters which, if no reasonable explanation is adduced, may damage an asylum applicant's credibility, among which are that the applicant or his agent:
  (*a*) has failed to apply forthwith upon arrival in the UK, unless the application is founded upon events which have taken place since his arrival in the UK;
  (*b*) has made false representations either orally or in writing;
  (*c*) has destroyed, damaged or disposed of any passport or other documents relevant to his claim;
  (*d*) has undertaken any activities in the UK before or after lodging an application which are inconsistent with his previous beliefs and behaviour and which are calculated to create or substantially to enhance his claim to refugee status (see *R v IAT, ex p B* [1989] Imm AR 166);
  (*e*) has lodged concurrent applications for asylum in the UK and another country.

If the S of S concludes for these or any other reason, that the applicant's evidence is not credible, the application will be refused (para 341). The activities of the agent may be taken into account by the S of S (para 342).

Thus for example, the applicant is required to claim asylum in the first safe country to which he comes. He cannot avoid that duty by shielding himself behind instructions given to him by his agent to keep silent until he has reached the UK (*Ex p Musa* [1993] Imm AR 210). Under HC 395 he will probably be regarded as having had the opportunity to claim asylum in that first safe country.

As to the way in which these rules are to be interpreted, Mr Kenneth Clarke, when promoting the Bill as Home Secretary, stated:

We recognise that genuine refugees may be shocked by their experiences and may be forced to use irregular and difficult means to escape from their own countries. The draft rules make clear that wherever a reasonable explanation is provided for behaviour of this sort it will not go against the applicant. We must, however, take account of those cases where applicants have plainly been lying, behaving irregularly or deliberately destroying their own documents (Hansard Vol 213, No 64, 2 November 1992, col 35).

The rules relating to false representations by an asylum seeker should be viewed in the light of this intention, and a person's credibility should not be affected because he is mistaken about a piece of information, but only when he is plainly lying. Untrue statements by themselves are not a reason for refusal and according to the UNHCR it is the examiner's responsibility to evaluate such statements in the light of all the circumstances of the case (Handbook, para 199). Further, the Parliamentary Under S of S for the Home Department stated that the rules reflect that entirely genuine refugees may be reticent or at times actively misleading in the initial presentation of their cases, but that if there is a reasonable explanation those factors will not go against the applicant's credibility (Official Report of Standing Committee A, 17 November 1992, col 141). In deciding whether or not to grant an application for asylum the factors which the S of S may reasonably take into account include the following: the credibility of the answers given at successive interviews (*Ex p K* [1990] Imm AR 393 and see *Munongo* [1991] Imm AR 616 and *Bolat* [1991] Imm AR 417); the fact that the application for asylum was not made on arrival in the UK (*Ex p Alupo* [1991] Imm AR 538); and the delay of the applicant in making an application for asylum (*Bila v S of S* [1994] Imm AR 130).

If there is a part of the country from which the applicant claims to be a refugee in which he would not have a well-founded fear of persecution and to which it would be reasonable to expect him to go, the application may be refused (para 343). This rule reflects the practice before the Asylum and Immigration Appeals Act 1993.

In *Jonah* (above) it was held that where a man who had been a trade union official for 30 years would be forced to live in a remote part of the country away from his wife and unable to pursue being an official, he had a well founded fear of being persecuted in the sense of being oppressed. However in *ex p Yurekli* [1990] Imm AR 334, Otton J held that if it is possible for an applicant to live in another part of the country of origin without persecution, that was a factor which the S of S could reasonably take into account (and see *ex p Gunes* [1991] Imm AR 278 and *ex p El-Tanoukhi* [1993] Imm AR 71).

It is likely that in considering questions of reasonableness special adjudicators will take into account the factors held to be relevant in *Jonah's* case. The evidence of experts familiar with the political situation of a country will be needed to show that a part of a country will not be safe for the particular asylum seeker on the facts that he presents. Thus it is possible to challenge the assertion that a particular place will be safe for an applicant who has fled from a particular part of a country to another part where the persons he fears have a presence. Where it is suggested that the activity of the group feared is minimal in the allegedly safe area, a journalist or academic (for example) who has made a particular study of a country may give expert evidence of the degree of control which the feared group has over the area.

The way in which the rule will be operated was commented upon by Earl Ferrers promoting the 1993 Act in the Lords (HL Debs, Vol 543, No 106, col 801):

Refusal in those cases will not be automatic. A full assessment will be made in each case of all the circumstances of the case including any links which the asylum seeker may have here in this country; an assessment of the whole situation in the country of origin, including the extent of any alleged persecution; the ability of the national authorities to offer protection; the reasonableness of expecting the applicant to move to another part of that country and the practicalities of returning him to a safe part of his own country. Even if a person comes from a war torn part of the world in which the war is localised, it does not mean that he would necessarily be returned automatically.

Expert witnesses should have their attention drawn to these factors when their assistance is requested. Further, information from the UNHCR will be relevant. Thus in *Ex p Vigna* [1993] Imm AR 93 UNHCR's confidential memoranda of 1992 relating to returns of Tamils to the area around Colombo stated that a person could not be returned to that area in safety or dignity, although it was

ASYLUM

not affected directly by the armed conflict, unless he had a close relative living there.

4 Children

Dependants

349. A husband or wife or minor children accompanying a principal applicant may be included in an application for asylum. If the principal applicant is granted asylum any such dependants will be granted leave to enter or remain of the same duration. The case of any dependant who claims asylum in his own right and who would otherwise be refused leave to enter or remain will be considered individually in accordance with paragraph 334 above. It will not normally be necessary separately to interview or otherwise investigate the status of children accompanying a parent who is an asylum applicant except insofar as this is necessary to establish the child's identity. (In this paragraph and paragraphs 350-352 a child means a person who is under 18 years of age or who, in the absence of documentary evidence, appears to be under that age).

Unaccompanied children

350. Unaccompanied children may also apply for asylum and, in view of their potential vulnerability, particular priority and care is to be given to the handling of their cases.

351. A person of any age may qualify for refugee status under the Convention and the criteria in paragraph 334 apply to all cases. However, account should be taken of the applicant's maturity and in assessing the claim of a child more weight should be given to objective indications of risk than to the child's state of mind and understanding of his situation. An asylum application made on behalf of a child should not be refused solely because the child is too young to understand his situation or to have formed a well-founded fear of persecution. Close attention should be given to the welfare of the child at all times.

352. A child will not be interviewed about the substance of his claim to refugee status if it is possible to obtain by written enquiries or from other sources sufficient information properly to determine the claim. When an interview is necessary it should be conducted in the presence of a parent, guardian, representative or another adult who for the time being takes responsibility for the child and is not an Immigration Officer, an officer of the Secretary of State or a police officer. The interviewer should have particular regard to the possibility that a child will feel inhibited or alarmed. The child should be allowed to express himself in his own way and at his own speed. If he appears tired or distressed, the interview should be stopped.

COMMENTARY

(a) Dependants and children (paras 349, and 350–352)

The younger a child is the less one can expect him to give a comprehensive and reasoned account of why he is likely to be persecuted. It is necessary to look for information from other sources. The S of S's approach is to look at the objective likelihood of persecution in such cases. If he considers there to be a real threat, an application will not be dismissed simply because a child had not properly comprehended the risk or seemed insufficiently frightened or had inadequately articulated it (see HL Debs, 2 March 1993, Vol 543, No 104, col 575). The rules make special provision for the applications of children for asylum, whether they are accompanied or not. An unaccompanied child may also apply for asylum, and in view of their potential vulnerability, particular priority and care is to be given to the handling of their cases (para 350). A person of any age may qualify for refugee status under the Convention and the criteria in para 334 apply to all cases. However account should be taken of the applicant's maturity, and in assessing the claim of a child more weight should be given to the objective indications of risk than to the child's state of mind and understanding of his situation. An asylum application made on behalf of a child should not be refused solely because the child is too young to understand his situation or to have formed a well-founded fear of persecution. Close attention should be given to the welfare of the child at all times (para 351). The child of an asylum seeker does not lose his own claim to asylum under para 351 merely because the person on whom he is dependent has an asylum application refused. The child's claim under para 351 stands alone (*Ex p Fahmi* (1994) *Times*, 2 March).

A child means a person who is under 18 years of age, or who in the absence of documentary evidence, appears to be under that age (para 349). A child will not be interviewed about the substance of his claim to refugee status if it is possible to obtain by written enquiries or from other sources sufficient information properly to determine his claim. When an interview is necessary it should be conducted in the presence of a parent, guardian, representative or another adult, who for the time being takes responsibility for the child, and is not an immigration officer, an officer of the S of S or a police officer. The interviewer should have particular regard to the possibility that a child will feel inhibited or alarmed. The child should be allowed to express himself in his own way and at his own speed. If he appears tired or distressed, the interview should be stopped (para 352).

5 Exceptional leave to remain and settlement housing and social security

(a) Exceptional leave to remain

Where a person is not granted full refugee status, but there are compelling humanitarian reasons why he should not be required to leave the UK, he may be granted leave to remain on an exceptional basis. Such leave, known as 'exceptional leave to remain', does not carry the same security as the grant of refugee status. When a person has applied for refugee status, but has been granted exceptional leave to remain, the S of S has a policy of not giving reasons for the refusal of refugee status. It may be possible to challenge such a refusal to give reasons by way of judicial review (*Ex p Muslu* [1993] Imm AR 151). The policy on granting settlement to those granted exceptional leave to remain and on the admission of members of their families was set out in a written answer in Parliament (see Hansard, 28 July 1988 col 424 [1993] Imm AR p 152). A person given exceptional leave to remain will normally be granted settlement on making an application, after seven years' residence in the UK. Settlement may be withheld at that point, or granted earlier than that. Exceptional leave is initially granted for one year. After that time a further application may be made and the applicant is likely to be granted exceptional leave to remain for a further three years. At the end of that time he may apply for a further period of exceptional leave, and is likely to be granted a further three years' exceptional leave to remain. The dependants of a person granted exceptional leave to remain may apply to join him. Such applications from the spouse and minor children will usually be granted after four years and are subject to the general requirements of the immigration rules on the admission of spouses and dependants. If there are compelling compassionate circumstances, an application for such a family reunion may be granted at an earlier stage. If the S of S refuses to depart from this policy the decision can only be challenged by way of an application for judicial review (*Muslu* (above)).

Where the S of S refuses to extend or vary exceptional leave to remain, the applicant may appeal to the adjudicator, although it has been argued that this practice is unlawful (*Muslu* (above)).

(b) Settlement

The refugee has no right to settlement under the rules. Settlement is dealt with by way of extra-statutory discretion. The Home Office will usually grant a four-years stay. The refugee will then be able to apply for indefinite leave to remain, which is normally granted. The refugee should not be expelled save on the grounds of national security, or public order, after due process of law (Art 32 of the Convention). When considering the deportation of a person who seeks asylum, the S of S has an obligation to balance the interests of national security against those of the refugee (*Chahal v S of S* [1994] Imm AR 107).

If the refugee leaves his country of refuge, and enters another country subscribing to the European Agreement on the Transfer of Responsibility for Refugees (16 October 1980, Cmnd 8127), after two years' lawful residence there, responsibility is transferred to that country. However, residence for the purposes of study or medical treatment, or training, or imprisonment does not count towards that two-year period.

In *Jinah Rahman v S of S* [1989] Imm AR 325, the IAT considered this Agreement as a relevant circumstance which the S of S should have taken into account when considering an application for transfer of refugee status from the Netherlands to the UK in his discretion outside the rules, which the IAT have power to review. They held that the principal purpose of the Agreement was to avoid difficulties for refugees who were factually resident in one state, but have their refugee status from another state (see also *Shrokh Shami* [1992] Imm AR 542).

(c) Housing provision and social security provision for asylum seekers

Section 4 of the 1993 Act makes provision for the housing of asylum seekers and their dependants. The local authority's powers are limited to providing temporary accommodation only whilst an application for asylum is pending. By s 5 of the 1993 Act, an asylum seeker, or his dependant, acquires and ceases to have that status for the purposes of housing provision, when the S of S records that fact. Accommodation is not available for the applicant's occupation if it is not available both for the occupation of the applicant and those who might reasonably be expected to reside with him. Thus the accommodation would have to be available for his family, and any cohabitee (s 5(8)).

Asylum seekers may claim benefit once they have the Standard Acknowledgement Letter. The asylum applicant receives 90 per cent of income support, although the full levels of housing and child benefit are paid (Income Support (General) Regulations 1987 SI 1987/1971 Reg 71(1)). The letter will only be issued where the asylum seeker's fingerprints have been taken. An asylum seeker who has been admitted on a temporary basis may have been prohibited from taking work. An application must be made for the prohibition to be varied to a restriction before employment is taken. This will not usually be granted until the application has been outstanding for more than six months, except where the applicant has been offered a specific job before that time, or there are exceptional reasons (Letter from Home Office to British Refugee Council, 28 January 1988).

6 EU asylum law

Asylum law in the UK now has to be seen in the wider context of EU provisions on free movement and the internal market. The Treaty of Rome as amended by the Single European Act 1986 provided that internal frontiers be abolished by the end of 1992. Controls arising from the crossing of an internal frontier are abolished after that time. The Dublin Convention is an intergovernmental Convention, which at present is not amenable to EU jurisdiction, but which has been agreed between the Member States of the EU with a view to harmonising asylum policies in the light of Art 8a of the Treaty of Rome. The EC Commission took the view that Art 8a applies to all individuals within the internal market area, and is not restricted to nationals of EC countries. Without EC measures being adopted therefore it ought to be possible to rely on Art 8a to prevent an asylum seeker being returned to a member state through which he has travelled. However, the CA has taken the view that the provisions of Art 8a are compatible with the third-country practice employed by the S of S (*ex p Colak* [1993] Imm AR 581 and *ex p Ghebretatios* [1993] Imm AR 585). The court held in the latter case that as the Dublin Convention was negotiated with a view to the requirements of Art 8a, that Article permitted the practice of third country removals. Regardless of the correct interpretation of Art 8a, the Treaty on European Union restricts the right of free movement under the corresponding provision (Art 7) to citizens of the Union.

(a) Dublin Convention

The UK is party to the *Dublin Convention Determining the State Responsible for Examining Applications for Asylum Lodged in one of the Member States of the European Communities*, which was signed by all EC member states by 26 June 1991 (a copy of the text is at [1990] Imm AR 604). It has the effect of permitting an asylum seeker one chance to achieve recognition as a refugee in the EC states. Its purpose is that the EC may achieve an area without internal frontiers. The main provisions are considered below. Although the Dublin Convention is not yet in force, it has been referred to by the courts (see eg *Ex p Akyol* [1990] Imm AR 571 and *ex p Kemal Kerali* [1991] Imm AR 199).

Member States undertake to examine the application for asylum of any non-EC national who applies for asylum, at their border, or in their territory. The state which is to decide the application for asylum is determined in accordance with the criteria set out in Arts 4 to 8. That state will then deal with the application in accordance with its national laws and international obligations. In the case of the UK the determination will be in accordance with the Immigration Rules, and the Geneva Convention of 1951. If the asylum seeker consents a state which is not obliged to determine the application can consider the application irrespective of the criteria. The state which would have to determine the application, under Arts 4–8, is then relieved of that duty. The right to send an asylum seeker to a third state is to be exercised in accordance with the Geneva Convention.

If the applicant is an adult and has a spouse or unmarried child under 18, either of whom has been recognised as a refugee legally resident in one member state, the responsibility for determining the asylum claim falls to that state (Art 4). If the applicant does not consent to that state determining the application, it may not do so. In the case of an applicant who is an unmarried child the state will only be responsible for the determination of the asylum application if the father or the mother has been recognised there as a refugee. If the applicant has a valid visa or residence permit, the state which issued it is responsible for examining his application (Art 5). However if another Member State gave written authorisation for the visa, that other Member State is responsible. If the applicant is in possession of a transit visa, and makes his application *en route* to another Member State, where he is not subject to a visa requirement, the other Member State is responsible for determining the application. Similarly where no visas are required in the country to which a person is travelling on a transit visa in transit through a Member State, and he makes his application in that Member State, the Member State to which he is travelling will be responsible if the transit state receives written confirmation from the Member State to which the person is travelling that its entrance requirements are fulfilled by the applicant. The Convention also makes provision for an applicant who is in possession of a visa which permits him entry to more than one Member State. The Member State which has issued the longest visa, or that with the latest expiry date, will usually be responsible. Where the visas are transit visas issued on the presentation of a Member State's entry visa, the state which issued the entry visa must determine the application. Where a person had visas permitting entry and residence in more than one Member State, but which have expired more than two years previously, the state in which he lodges the application is responsible for determining it. However, where he lodges the application in one state, and it has been less than two years since one or more of those visas expired, he is treated as if he is in possession of two current visas, and the state which issued the one that expires last or is longest is responsible.

Special provision is made for persons who have entered the EC illegally from a third state under Art 6. The state to which entry is made is responsible unless it can be shown that the applicant had been living for the last six months in another member state. In all cases of entry, legal or otherwise, the first state to which the applicant comes is responsible for making the determination, unless in law the applicant has entered another member state where the requirement for him to have a visa has been waived. Until there is agreement on the definition of 'external borders' of the Community an applicant who does not leave the transit zone of an airport does not enter the Member State for the purposes of having his application for asylum determined there. However if he makes his application in the transit zone of the airport, that state is responsible for determining his claim (Art 7). A definition of 'external borders' is to be reached as part of the work programme for the implementation of the internal market under Art 8a of the Treaty of Rome. The Draft Convention on the Crossing of External Frontiers is currently awaiting agreement between Spain and the UK on the status of Gibraltar. This again will be an intergovernmental agreement which may not therefore be amenable to Community jurisdiction without being adopted by the Community.

If no Member State is identified as responsible for determining the application by the above procedure, the Member State in which the application is lodged is responsible (Art 8). Article 9 permits a Member State at the request of another Member State to examine applications for which it is not responsible, for humanitarian reasons. These will particularly be based on family or cultural grounds. If the Member State agrees, responsibility is transferred to it.

Where one Member State considers that another is responsible, it may request that other Member State to take responsibility as speedily as possible, within six months of the application being lodged. If the second state fails to take responsibility within that time, the first remains responsible. The requesting state must set out reasons why the second state is responsible under the criteria of the Convention. The second Member State must reply within three months of receipt of the request. If it fails to do so, it becomes responsible for determining the application. When the second state becomes responsible it must take charge of the applicant, and must complete the examination of the application. The applicant must be transferred to the second Member State within one month of acceptance of responsibility by that Member State. The Applicant is permitted to object to the transfer (Arts 10 and 11).

Where the applicant lodges an application in a Member State, having withdrawn it in another Member State, he may be returned to the Member State in which the application was withdrawn, with a view to having the determination completed. The following conditions must be fulfilled:

(1) The request by the second state for the first to take the applicant back contains indications enabling the first state to ascertain that it is obliged to take the applicant back, because it was determining the application or because the applicant is illegally in the state in which the new application was lodged, or because the applicant withdrew an application in the first state, or because the applicant is illegally in the second state having had his application rejected in the first state.

(2) The first state must give an answer to the request within eight days of the matter being referred to it. If it acknowledges responsibility it must take the applicant back within one month.

(b) The responsible state's duties to the asylum seeker

The state found to be responsible under the criteria set out above has the following duties under Art 10. It must take charge of the applicant; it must complete the examination; take the applicant back if he goes irregularly to another member state, or if he withdraws his application and lodges it with another member state, or if it has rejected the application, and the applicant illegally enters another member state. These responsibilities pass to a Member State which issues a residence permit for more than three months, and all but the duty to take back a rejected applicant who goes elsewhere in the EC illegally, cease to apply if the applicant left EC territory for a period of more than three months. There is no responsibility to take back an applicant who lodges an application in another EC state or one who, having been rejected, enters another EC state illegally, if the State responsible for examining following withdrawal or rejection, has taken measures to return the applicant to the country of origin, or such country as he may lawfully enter (Art 10).

Provision is made by Art 14 for the mutual exchange of information regarding legislation or practices regarding asylum, and statistics on arrivals, and their nationalities. The states may also exchange information as to trends in asylum, and circumstances in countries of origin, or the provenance of applicants for asylum. The details which may be exchanged in relation to particular applications and the determination of responsibility are dealt with in Art 15.

No express provision has been made under this Agreement for the applicant to raise particular grounds of objection, but the applicant will be able to object to a particular country dealing with the application on the grounds that it is not a safe country (see *Abdullah* [1992] Imm AR 438).

Chapter 20

Asylum Appeals and Removal

1 Rights of appeal

Where asylum is refused the applicant is provided with a notice informing him of the decision and of the reasons for refusal. At the same time that asylum is refused, the applicant may be notified of removal directions or served with a notice of intention to deport, as appropriate. The notice of refusal of asylum also explains any rights of appeal available to the applicant and will inform him of the means by which he may exercise those rights (para 333).

In addition to the other rights of appeal he may have in respect of non-asylum decisions concerning him, a person who has been refused asylum may also appeal against:

(a) a decision to make a deportation order against him by virtue of s 3(5) of the 1971 Act;

(b) a refusal to revoke a deportation order made against him by virtue of s 3(5) or 3(6) of the 1971 Act; and

(c) directions for his removal from the UK under s 16(1)(a) or (b) of the 1971 Act.

The applicant can appeal against these decisions on the basis that the action proposed would be in breach of the UK's obligations under the 1951 Convention and Protocol relating to the Status of Refugees. Such an appeal will be under s 8 of the 1993 Act. The special adjudicator will hear the application, and will also hear any non-asylum appeal under Part II of the 1971 Act (para 379, and see below). The only exception to this rule is where the ground of the decision to make the deportation order is that it would be conducive to the public good, and the order is certified by the S of S as being in the interests of national security (para 379). In those circumstances the person has only a right of review by an adviser.

The Lord Chancellor appoints special adjudicators. They are adjudicators under the 1971 Act, designated to deal with claims involving asylum issues. The Asylum Appeals (Procedure) Rules 1993 set out the procedure applicable to all asylum appeals.

The following persons may appeal to a special adjudicator on the ground that the relevant act of the S of S is contrary to the obligations of the UK under the Convention relating to Refugees:

(a) a person who is refused leave to enter;
(b) a person who has limited leave to enter or remain in the UK, against a decision or refusal on the ground that it would be against the UK's obligations for him to be required to leave the UK when his limited leave expires (s 8(2)).
(c) a person against whom a decision to make a deportation order has been made (s 8(3)(a)), or in whose case the S of S has refused to revoke a deportation order (s 8(3)(b)), may appeal to the special adjudicator on the ground that his removal in pursuance of the order would be contrary to the UK's obligations;
(d) a person against whom directions have been given for his removal as either an illegal entrant or as a person who has entered the UK in breach of a deportation order or as a member of a ship's crew, may appeal to the special adjudicator against the direction on the ground that his removal in pursuance of the order is contrary to the UK's obligations under the Convention.

A person who is both subject to a decision to deport and against whom an earlier deportation order was made, which the S of S has refused to revoke, may not bring an appeal in both capacities (s 8(3)).

Any appeal on the above grounds is heard by a special adjudicator (1993 Act Sched 2, para 1). Further, a person may not bring an appeal on any of the grounds (a)–(d) unless, before the time of the refusal, variation of decision or directions, as the case may be, he has made a claim for asylum (Sched 2, para 2). Thus a person may not bring an appeal unless he makes a claim for asylum before the time of the decision or action against which he is appealing. Earl Ferrers in promoting this late amendment in the Reports stage of the Bill in the House of Lords stated that the right course for a person who wishes to claim asylum after a notice of an immigration decision has been served upon him is to lodge an application for asylum (HL Debs, Vol 543, No 110, col 1186). A claim to asylum should be made to the immigration officer or Home Office. The asylum seeker is protected from removal while that claim is being considered. If the application is refused he will be served with a new notice of the decision and will be able to appeal to a special adjudicator at that stage. If there is any ambiguity in the wording of the paragraph, Earl Ferrers, in promoting the Act, disclosed the true intention behind the wording. Indeed he went further, and agreed that all refused asylum seekers, whatever their immigration status at the time of application or refusal, will have the right to appeal (col 1187). The wording of the paragraph does not prevent the applicant relying on any appeal grounds. It merely ensures that an appeal cannot lie in respect of a decision in relation to an asylum application which has not yet been made. It is clear also that s 8 creates a distinct right of appeal which does not in any way restrict other rights of appeal. Nothing in the 1993 Act prevents an applicant who has been refused entry for a temporary purpose claiming asylum after that decision and making an application. What he cannot do is to claim, during an appeal against refusal of entry for a temporary purpose, that the appeal should be allowed because he is an asylum seeker (see *Badmus v S of S* [1994] Imm AR 137).

Where an appeal is brought by a person on the above grounds the special adjudicator will deal with any appeal against a refusal, variation, decision or direction which the person is entitled to bring under the 1971 Act on any other ground on which he seeks to rely. The special adjudicator may also deal with any appeal brought by the person under Part II of the 1971 Act against any other decision or action.

The Immigration Appeals (Notices) Regulations 1984 apply to notices in hearings before special adjudicators. A special adjudicator must allow an appeal if he considers that the decision against which the appeal was brought was not in accordance with the law, or with any immigration rules applicable to the case or on the grounds that the discretion of the S of S should have been exercised differently, if it is a case which involves the discretion of the S of S. He is entitled to review any determination of a question of fact on which the decision was based. No decision which is in accordance with the immigration rules may be treated as having involved the exercise of a discretion by the S of S by reason only of the fact that he was requested to depart from the rules, and has refused to depart from the rules. The special adjudicator may make recommendations which the S of S must attempt to comply with if the appeal is allowed. There is a right of appeal from the special adjudicator to the IAT, save in cases which have been certified as 'without foundation' where the special adjudicator agrees with the certificate.

Bail Where a person appeals against a decision of the type (*a*), (*c*) or (*d*) on page 373, Part II of Schedule 2 to the 1971 Act will apply in relation to removal directions and bail. Thus where a person appeals against any of the determinations mentioned in (*a*), (*c*) and (*d*) above on Convention grounds, any directions previously given by virtue of the refusal for his removal from the UK shall cease to have effect, and no directions are to be given while the appeal is pending. Para 29 of Sched 2 to the 1971 Act in particular applies. This provides for the grant of bail pending appeal.

2 Appeal rules

The Asylum Appeals (Procedure) Rules (SI 1993 No 1661) (1993 Appeal Rules) govern appeals under the 1993 Act. They apply to all asylum appeals and to mixed appeals in certain respects. They apply to asylum decisions taken after the rules come into force on 26 July 1993 (Appeal Rules 1993, r 3).

A person making an asylum appeal must give notice of the appeal not later than ten working days after receiving notice of the decision against which he is appealing (r 5(1)). However, there is a special procedure to be followed in cases of decisions at the port of entry where the case is certified as without foundation.

Notice of appeal may be given by serving on an immigration officer a form prescribed in the Schedule to the 1993 Appeal Rules (Form 1), together with the notice of decision and reasons against which he is appealing in the case of a person who is refused leave to enter. In the case of a person who has limited leave to enter or remain, and who appeals against a variation, or a refusal to vary that leave on the ground that it would be contrary to the UK's obligations to require him to leave as a result of that variation or refusal to vary leave, the notice of appeal may be given by serving on the S of S the form and the notice of the decision together with reasons for the decision (r 5(3)). If the person is in custody he may serve the notice of appeal on the person having custody of him. The immigration officer or S of S must then send to the special adjudicator the documents with which the appellant has served him. He must also send any interview notes and any other document referred to in any of the documents referred to in the decision which is being appealed (r 5(6)). There is no requirement for an explanatory statement.

The appellant and the S of S are the primary parties to the appeal. However, the UK representative of the UNHCR shall be treated as a party to an appeal upon giving notice to the special adjudicator at any time during the course of the appeal that he desires to be treated as a party (r 8). The S of S has a duty to send to the UNHCR all of the documents which the appellant has served upon the S of S (r 5(6)).

Where the notice of appeal is not given within the appropriate time limit, it shall be treated for all purposes as having been given within that time limit if the person to whom it was given under the rules is of the opinion that by reason of special circumstances it is just and right for the notice to be treated as if given within the appropriate time limit (1993 Appeal Rules, r 5(5)). The special adjudicator may extend any time limit for giving notice of appeal if he considers it necessary 'in the interests of justice', whether before or after the time limit has expired (r 5(7) and (8)). This is a general power, and would enable a time limit to be extended in the event of an appellant being let down by his advisers. The extension clause used in these rules differs from and is wider than that used in the 1984 Rules. Under r 11(4) of the 1984 Rules, the adjudicator may allow an appeal out of time where he is 'of the opinion that by reason of special circumstances, it is just and right so to do'. The 1993 Appeal Rules should be construed more nearly to the provisions for extending time limits under the Sex Discrimination Act 1975 and the Race Relations Act 1976, which provide that out-of-time appeals may be considered where it is just and equitable so to do. However arguably the provisions of the 1993 Rules are broader still, and where an allegation of threat to life or liberty or the possibility of persecution is involved it would be in the interests of justice for the merits of the claim to be heard even when there has been considerable delay. There is no requirement for there to be special circumstances, rather the general interests of justice in asylum cases must be considered. The provisions of RSC Ord 53 r 3, which provide for extensions of time in judicial review cases, may also be distinguished. These provide that time may be extended where there is good reason for extending the time limits. The 1993 Appeal Rules provisions do not make reference to such a requirement.

The special adjudicator must serve on the appellant and the immigration officer or S of S as the case may be, a notice of the date, time and place fixed for the hearing of the appeal. The notice must be served by the special adjudicator within five working days of receiving a notice of appeal. Where the S of S has certified the claim to be without foundation, the notification of the date, place and time of hearing must be made within three days (r 6). Once lodged, the notice of appeal may be varied by leave of the special adjudicator (r 7).

3 Determination of an appeal

A special adjudicator will determine an appeal no later than 42 days after receiving notice of appeal. If the claim has been certified as without foundation, the determination must be made within seven working days after receiving the notice of appeal (1993 Appeal Rules, r 9).

The appeal must be determined by a hearing unless:
 (a) the special adjudicator is satisfied having regard to the material before him or to the conduct of the appellant, that the appeal has been abandoned;
 (b) the decision is withdrawn or reversed and the special adjudicator is satisfied that written notice of withdrawal or reversal has been given to the appellant;
 (c) it appears to the special adjudicator that the issues raised on the appeal have been determined by himself, or another special adjudicator in previous proceedings to which the appellant was a party on the basis of facts which did not materially differ from those to which the appeal relates.

(Appeal Rules 1993, r 9(4))

Promulgation of determination and reasons The special adjudicator must pronounce the determination and the reasons for it wherever practicable at the conclusion of the hearing. He must send to every party to the appeal written notice of the determination and reasons within ten working days of the conclusion of the hearing (r 11(2)). However if the S of S has certified the claim as without foundation and the special adjudicator agrees that it is without foundation, he must pronounce the determination and the reasons for the determination at the conclusion of the hearing. He must furnish every party to the appeal with written notice of the determination and reasons (r 11(4)).

Adjournments If the adjudicator is satisfied that there is good cause for it, he may grant an adjournment of a hearing. Where he does grant an adjournment, he must give notice of a fresh hearing date and place, either orally or in writing (r 10). The timetable for the determination of application set under r 9 must not be interfered with by the granting of an adjournment.

4 Special appeals procedure for claims without foundation

A claim for asylum is without foundation if (and only if):
(a) it does not raise any issue as to the UK's obligations under the Convention; or
(b) it is otherwise frivolous or vexatious.
(1993 Act, Sched 2, para 5(3)).

The time limit for appeals is two working days where the S of S has certified that in his opinion the applicant's claim that it would be contrary to the UK's obligations for him to be removed from the UK is without foundation. The following conditions must be satisfied. There must be personal service of the notice of refusal on the appellant and the claim must be made by a person:
(a) who was refused leave to enter the UK under the 1971 Act on the ground that his removal would be contrary to the UK's obligations under the convention (s 8(1)); or
(b) appealing against a refusal to revoke a deportation order made against him under s 3 of the 1971 Act on the ground that his removal pursuant to the order would be contrary to the UK's obligations under the convention (s 8(3)(b));
(c) appealing against removal directions on the ground that his removal in pursuance of them would be contrary to the UK's obligations under the Convention (s 8(4)).

Such cases will be determined under a special procedure (Sched 2, para 5).

(1993 Appeal Rules, r 5(2))

The time runs from the expiration of the day on which the notice of the decision is personally served on the appellant (1993 Appeal Rules, r 32(3)). The hearing must have a date assigned to it within three days of receipt of the appeal (r 6(2)). A special adjudicator will determine this kind of appeal not later than seven working days after receiving the notice of appeal (1993 Appeal Rules, r 9(2)). In practice however this time limit does not seem to have affected the length of time taken for cases to be heard. Time can be extended under r 31. If the special adjudicator agrees that the appeal is groundless, he must pronounce the determination and the reasons for the determination at the conclusion of the hearing. He must furnish every party to the appeal with written notice of the determination and reasons (r 11(3)). Removal will not take place before the written notice of the determination and reasons has been given (*R v Special Adjudicator, ex p Mehari* 8 October 1993 Div Ct).

Only where the S of S has certified the claim as being without foundation can the time limit for the applicant to appeal be abbreviated to two days. The requirement of certification may be satisfied by a statement which is not in the form of a certificate. The certification may take the form of a statement in the decision letter (*Mustafaraj v S v S* [1994] Imm AR 78). The abbreviated time limit may only be applied where the applicant has been refused leave to enter, and therefore will only apply to persons refused entry at a port of entry. It is likely that it will be used mainly in relation to third-country cases (see *Mehari* above). Most of the persons to whom the two-day time limit applies will be in custody, but the power to impose the two-day time limit is not confined to such persons. However, each of the conditions in rule 5(2) must apply before the abbreviated time limit can apply.

The test of whether the claim is without foundation must be an objective one. It must be an objective question as to whether the claim does not raise any issue as to the UK's obligations under the Convention, or is otherwise frivolous or vexatious. In *Mehari* (see above) Laws J held that a claim does not raise any issue as to the UK's obligations unless on the facts it is incumbent on the S of S to consider the substantive claim to refugee status. In third country cases no such obligation arises. Where a special adjudicator is in doubt as to whether on the facts the appellant may properly be removed under the third-country rule, the S of S will not have discharged the burden to show that the claim is without foundation in this sense. The special adjudicator has the power to find that the claim is not without foundation, and remit it for consideration by the S of S. If he remits it, the ordinary time limits will apply, so that the special adjudicator has effective control over the question. If the special adjudicator agrees with the certificate he dismisses the appeal. Where he disagrees with the certificate the appeal must either be allowed, or the case must be referred back to the S of S (see also *Ex p Thavathevathasan* 22 December 1993, *Legal Action* March 1994, p 18 (CA)). If he refers the case to the S of S for reconsideration, that is deemed to be a disposal of the appeal. However, the S of S would in those circumstances have to make a fresh decision on the case which could in turn be appealed.

Frivolous and vexatious appeals The second basis on which the

S of S may certify a claim to be without foundation is that it is frivolous or vexatious. RSC Ord 18, r 19 provides for the striking out of pleadings which are an abuse of the process of the court on (*inter alia*) these grounds (see *Somasundaram v Julius Melchior* [1988] 1 WLR 1394). The expression is also used in the rules of the industrial tribunals in relation to claims which may be struck out (see *Ashman v British Coal* [1990] 2 WLR 1437) and in relation to costs (see *Marler (ET) Ltd v Robertson* [1974] ICR 72 for the definition). In *R v a Special Adjudicator, ex p Guei* (31 January 1994, Div Ct, *Legal Action* March 1994 p 19) an applicant's claim originally did not raise an issue as to the UK's obligations, but by the time he came to appeal he mentioned facts which did raise an issue. Although this damaged his credibility, it was not appropriate for the special adjudicator to agree with the certificate on the basis that the claim was frivolous or vexatious. Arguably the appeal should not be treated as frivolous or vexatious unless it can be shown to have no prospect of success and to have been brought from an improper motive. If the special adjudicator agrees with the certificate he dismisses the appeal. Where he disagrees with the certificate the appeal must either be allowed, or the case must be referred back to the S of S.

The special procedure is inapplicable (1993 Act, Sched 2, para 5(2)) if:

(*a*) there is a non-asylum ground in the appeal;
(*b*) the person was refused leave to enter at a port of entry; and
(*c*) held a current entry clearance or work permit at that time.

Where the special adjudicator is required to determine an appeal or give written notification of a decision or the reasons therefore within a time limit under the rules, he may (before or after the time limit has expired) extend time if it is necessary in order to enable him to determine the appeal fairly or to provide notification (1993 Appeal Rules, r 31). If the special adjudicator agrees that the claim is without foundation, there shall be no right of appeal to the IAT from that decision (1993 Act Sched 2, para 5(5)). The only remedy that would remain would be judicial review in the appropriate circumstances.

National Security A person is not entitled to appeal against:
(*a*) a refusal of leave to enter;
(*b*) a variation of leave which reduces its duration;
(*c*) a decision to make a deportation order against him under s 3(5) of the 1971 Act; or

(d) a refusal to revoke a deportation order,
if the S of S certifies that the appellant's exclusion, departure, or deportation from the UK is in the interests of national security (Sched 2, para 6).

Even if the applicant satisfied the definition of 'refugee' in the Article, he could be refused the status for reasons of national security (*R v S of S, exp NSH* [1988] Imm AR 389; and see *exp Chahal* [1994] Imm AR 107, and see also *Hussain v S of S* [1993] Imm AR 353).

5 Appeal from the special adjudicator to the IAT

(a) Special procedure cases

If the special adjudicator agrees with the certificate there is no appeal against the decision. The applicant's remedy, if any, will be by way of judicial review of the special adjudicator's decision.

(b) Leave

It is necessary to obtain the leave of the IAT to appeal (1993 Appeal Rules, r 13). An application for leave to the IAT must be made not later than five working days after the appellant has received notice of the determination against which he wishes to appeal. The application is made by serving on the IAT the form (Form A2) specified in the Schedule to the 1993 Appeal Rules, together with a copy of the document in which the determination is recorded. The application must be determined by the IAT within five working days of receipt, and may be determined without a hearing. The IAT must send to the parties a notice recording the determination of the application for leave and where leave is refused, the reasons for the refusal (1993 Appeal Rules, r 13). If the IAT fails to determine the application for leave to appeal to it within five working days of receipt it is deemed to have granted the application (1993 Appeal Rules, r 30).

(c) Full hearing

The application for leave is deemed to be the notice of appeal for the appellant (1993 Appeal Rules, r 14(1)). The IAT must give notice of a hearing date and place within five working days of granting leave (1993 Appeal Rules, r 14), and the parties to the appeal are the same as the parties to the adjudication. An appeal to the IAT must be determined within 42 days after the date of service of the appellant's notice of appeal (ie from the date that the application for leave to appeal is received) (1993 Appeal Rules, r 16). Provided that time scale is observed, the IAT may grant an application for an adjournment of a hearing upon being satisfied that there is good cause for the adjournment (1993 Appeal Rules, r 18). The IAT must give written or oral notice to every party of the time and place of the adjourned hearing. The UNHCR representative may intervene at any stage in the IAT proceedings by giving notice to the IAT at any time during the course of the appeal that he desires so to do (1993 Appeal Rules, r 15).

The appellant who obtains leave to appeal has a right to a hearing before the IAT unless:
- (*a*) the IAT is satisfied, having regard to the material before it or to the conduct of the appellant, that the appeal has been abandoned by the appellant;
- (*b*) the decision has been withdrawn or reversed, and the appellant has been notified in writing of that fact;
- (*c*) the same or another IAT has determined the appeal in previous proceedings, under the 1971 or 1993 Acts, to which the appellant was a party, on the basis of facts which did not materially differ from those to which the appeal relates.

In these circumstances the IAT may determine the appeal forthwith without an oral hearing (1993 Appeal Rules, r 17). Where the IAT considers it appropriate to do so, it may remit the case to a special adjudicator instead of determining the case itself. The adjudicator must then determine the case in accordance with any directions that the IAT may have given (1993 Appeal Rules, r 17(3)). The special adjudicator must determine the appeal within 42 days of the appeal being so remitted (1993 Appeal Rules, r 9(3)).

Not later than five working days after the conclusion of the hearing the IAT must send to the parties written notice of the determination of the appeal and the reasons for it (1993 Appeal Rules, r 19). However, where the IAT is required to provide a written notification of the determination and the reasons therefor within a prescribed time, the IAT may extend time (before or after the expiration of the time limit) if it is necessary so to do in order to enable it fairly to determine the appeal or provide notification (1993 Appeal Rules, r 31). This rule will not permit the IAT to extend the time within which it may determine an appeal, nor the time within which it must determine an application for leave to appeal.

6 Appeals from the IAT

Where the IAT has made a final determination of an appeal any party may bring a further appeal to the Court of Appeal (or the Court of Sessions in Scotland) on any question of law material to that determination (s 9 1993 Act). The appellant must obtain either the leave of the IAT or, if that is refused, the Court of Appeal or Court of Sessions. The provisions extending protection from removal apply to a person appealing under s 9 of the 1993 Act to the Court of Appeal. If the IAT fails to determine an application for leave to appeal to the Court of Appeal within ten working days the application is deemed to have been granted (1993 Appeal Rules, r 30).

The application for leave to appeal must be made to the IAT or the Court of Appeal not later than 10 working days after the party seeking to appeal has received notice of the determination, and is made by the would-be appellant serving a notice of application prescribed by the 1993 Appeal Rules (Form A3) upon the IAT. A chairman or the President of the IAT may then determine the application for leave sitting alone without a hearing unless he considers that there are special circumstances making a hearing necessary or desirable. The IAT must determine the application and notify the parties of the determination and the reasons for it, within 10 working days of the IAT receiving the application for leave. If leave is refused, the applicant's only remedy is judicial review of the decision of the IAT to refuse leave.

7 General Procedure under the 1993 Rules

The special adjudicator, or IAT may take evidence as previously (see page 455) under the 1984 Rules. The 1984 Rules apply to the following *mutatis mutandis*, (see Chapter 24 (r 22)) subject to the differences outlined below:

(*a*) bail (1984 Appeal Rules, r 23 page 445);
(*b*) particulars requisite for the determination of the appeal (1984 Appeal Rules, r 25 page 441);
(*c*) representation (1984 Appeal Rules, r 26, page 453);
(*d*) summoning of witnesses (1984 Appeal Rules, r 27 page 447);
(*e*) conduct of proceedings at hearings (1984 Appeal Rules, r 28 page 452);
(*f*) evidence (1984 Appeal Rules, r 29 page 455);

(g) inspection of documentary evidence case where forgery of passports etc is alleged (1984 Appeal rules, r 20 page 442);
(h) the burden of proof (1984 Appeal Rules, r 31, page 454);
(i) the exclusion of the public (1984 Appeal Rules, r 32);
(j) transfer of proceedings (1984 Appeal Rules, r 33, page 447);
(k) hearings in the absence of the appellant or other party (1984 Appeal Rules, r 34);
(l) summary determination of appeals (1984 Appeal Rules, r 35, page 451);
(m) combined hearings of cases with a common question of law or fact arising in both of them, involving members of the same family or where it is desirable to hear certain appeals together (1984 Appeal Rules r 36 (except para (a)), page 447);
(n) irregularities (1984 Appeal Rules, r 38, page 454);
(o) the keeping of a summary of the proceedings (1984 Appeal Rules, r 40, page 453);
(p) references under s 21 of the 1971 Act (1984 Appeal Rules, r 41);
(q) delegation of functions to chairmen of the IAT sitting alone (1984 Appeal Rules, r 52, page 469);
(r) notices and forms (1984 Appeal Rules, rr 44 and 45).

(a) Disclosure

In a claim that has been certified as without foundation there is no requirement for an explanatory statement to be sent to the special adjudicator because rule 8 of the 1984 Appeal Rules does not apply. There is also no duty on the S of S to supply the special adjudicator with copies of the material which led him to conclude that the claim to asylum was without foundation (*Ex p Abdi* (1994) *The Times*, 25 April). Note however that the rules governing the supply of particulars for the determination of the case apply to the special procedure as they do to Appeals under the 1984 Appeal Rules, and asylum appeals not involving an allegation that the claim is without foundation. The CA in *Abdi* expressed the hope that it would become the practice for special adjudicators to be supplied with reports such as Amnesty International reports so that they could exercise their powers to ask for further particulars based on the contents of those reports if they felt the need for more information. Such particulars must be sought in the context of an appeal process which (in the case of appeals alleged to be without foundation) had to be operated speedily. Steyn LJ in a dissenting judgment expressed the view, correctly, that it is insufficient for the S of S simply to assert that a country is a safe country. He held that the judge was under a legal duty to disclose facts tending to prove or disprove the safety of a third country. The adjudicator under the special procedure has the power to order a witness to attend with documents (r 27(1) 1984 Appeal Rules). The special adjudicator could use this power to ensure that the applicant does have relevant documents and thus mitigate the effects of the lack of discovery.

The IAT or special adjudicator may not postpone the time fixed for the hearing of an appeal save in accordance with the 1993 Appeal Rules (r 22(3)). The special adjudicator or IAT must give the parties an opportunity to make oral representations, give evidence, call witnesses, and question any witnesses called in the proceedings, and at the conclusion of the evidence to make submissions. However, apart from this rule the appellate authority may determine its own procedure. The rule that the appellate authority must where appropriate give the respondent to an appeal the opportunity to amplify orally the written statements given at the commencement of proceedings does not apply to appeals governed by the 1993 Rules. Therefore the appellate authority may not give the respondent to an appeal the opportunity to amplify the written statement, and the respondent may be confined to closing submissions in terms of representations (r 23). The burden of proof in asylum appeals or mixed appeals is the same as under the 1984 Rules. So that if a party asserts that a decision against him taken under the 1993 Act ought not to have been made against him on the grounds that he is not a person to whom the provisions of the 1993 or 1971 Acts apply, the burden of proof is on him to prove that he is not such a person. Further, where an appellant makes an assertion which he must prove under rules made under the 1993 Act, the burden is on him to prove the assertion. Thus it is for the appellant to show that his life or liberty would be threatened on removal, and that he satisfies the Convention definition of 'refugee' (r 24).

(b) Absence of a party

Where the special adjudicator or IAT thinks it appropriate in the circumstances, the appellate authority may hear the appeal in the absence of the appellant if satisfied that:
  (*a*) he is not in the UK;
  (*b*) he is suffering from a communicable disease or from a mental disorder;

(c) by reason of illness or accident he cannot attend;
(d) it is impracticable to give him notice of the hearing, and that no person is authorised to represent him at the hearing.

Further, the special adjudicator or the IAT may hear the case in the absence of any party if satisfied that notice of the hearing was given in accordance with the 1993 Rules. However, if the absent party has furnished the authority with an explanation of his absence, it shall not pursue this course unless in the circumstances of the case it appears proper to it so to proceed (r 25). Where it does proceed with the hearing in this way the appellate authority may determine the appeal on the basis of such evidence as has been received. By r 32, any notice or other document that is sent or served under the 1993 Rules shall be deemed to have been received:

(a) on the second day after which it was sent in the case of a notice or document sent by post;
(b) on the day on which the document or notice was served; or
(c) on the day on which it was actually received by a special adjudicator or the IAT in the case of a notice sent by post to the special adjudicator or IAT as the case may be.

The President of the IAT or a chairman sitting alone may perform any of the following functions:

(a) grant bail pending an appeal to the IAT as he would under the 1984 Rules;
(b) deal with any application for leave to appeal to the IAT;
(c) remit cases to the special adjudicator with directions for its future conduct;
(d) require the attendance of witnesses (r 27).

Under the 1993 Rules there is no requirement that a document directed to an immigration officer or entry clearance officer required by the rules to be sent or given may be sent by post or registered letter to the address specified in the decision or to the IND (Appeals Section) of the Home Office (r 28). Thus any notice or document required or authorised by the Rules to be sent or given to any person or authority may be sent by post in a registered letter or by the recorded delivery service or delivered:

(a) to the secretary of the IAT where it is a document to be sent to the IAT (ie applications for leave to appeal to or from the IAT);
(b) to any clerk to an adjudicator, where the document is to be sent to the adjudicator (ie appeals forwarded by the Home

ASYLUM APPEALS AND REMOVAL

Office or immigration officer and interlocutory applications by the appellant);

(c) to the IND (Appeals Section) of the Home Office, where the document is to be sent to the S of S (ie the appellant serving a notice of appeal); or

(d) to the address for service specified in any notice given under the rules where the document is directed to any other person such as the UNHCR representative, or the asylum seeker (r 28).

Notices may be effectively served by serving the person representing a party. Where a notice is to be given to an immigration officer therefore it must be personally served on him, or may be served by post to an address specified in the notice given under the 1993 Rules, or may be served on his representative.

(c) Time

Under the 1993 Rules, where an act is to be done not later than a specified period after any event, the period of time is calculated from the expiry of the day on which the event occurred. If the time limit expires on a non-working day it will be in time if it is done on the next working day. Any non-working day is excluded from the calculation of periods of time of ten days or less (r 32). Non-working days are Saturdays, Sundays, bank holidays, Christmas day or Good Friday.

Where a person lodges his non-asylum appeal before the asylum appeal under the 1993 Act has been determined by a special adjudicator, or by the IAT, the special adjudicator or the IAT will deal with both appeals in the same proceedings. Similarly where the asylum appeal is lodged first the appellate authority will deal with both appeals (1993 Appeal Rules, r 29). To facilitate this, the adjudicator or the IAT may adjourn either an appeal so far as it is necessary or expedient for the purpose of having both dealt with together in the same proceedings. The 1993 Rules apply to both the asylum and non-asylum parts of the appeal and continue to apply to the non-asylum appeal after the asylum appeal has been determined. A person shall be taken to be appealing if he has given notice of appeal in accordance with whichever set of rules is appropriate to the kind of appeal being brought and in either case if the appeal has not been determined (r 29(6)).

8 Removal and detention of asylum seekers

During the period beginning when a person makes an asylum claim and ending when the S of S gives him notice of the decision on his claim, he may not be removed from, or required to leave the UK (s 6). Earl Ferrers, in promoting this clause in the Lords stated that the intention of the S of S is that anyone who wishes to appeal will be given the right to do so and will be able to stay in the UK in order to achieve that purpose (HL deb 2, March 1993, Vol 543, No 104, col 620). Under para 333 of HC 395 an applicant will not be removed from the UK so long as any appeal which he may bring is pending (and see 1993 Act, Sched 2 para 2). An asylum seeker is protected from deportation and removal from the time that a decision is made to the time that there ceases to be an appeal pending. When there is an appeal pending under s 8(2) of the 1993 Act by a person who has limited leave to enter or remain against a variation or refusal to vary the leave on the ground that it would be contrary to the UK's obligations under the Convention for him to be required to leave the UK after the time limited by the leave, a variation shall not take effect so long as an appeal is pending under s 8(2). An appellant can not be required to leave the UK by reason of the expiration of his leave so long as his appeal is pending under the subsection against a refusal to enlarge or remove the limit on the duration of his leave (Sched 2, para 7). Persons whose limited leave has been curtailed will not have the benefit of the VOLO provisions before making an appeal (see page 76 for VOLO). However such persons may rely on the statements of the promoters of the 1993 Act that a person will not be removed until their time for appealing has expired. An attempt to remove such a person could be challenged by judicial review of the decision of the S of S to remove the person. A pending appeal under the 1993 Act also acts as a stay of removal of a person liable to deportation. The directions which can be given under Sched 3 of the 1971 Act are stayed pending an appeal (Sched 2, para 9). The same restrictions on bail apply as apply under the 1971 Act (see page 401 below). Recognisances may be forfeited in the same way, and the same powers of arrest apply for breach of bail.

Earl Ferrers stated that the general rule under the 1971 Act was to apply under Sched 2, para 8 of the 1993 Act in the case of appeals to special adjudicators. He expressed the rule to be that an appeal is pending as long as a further appeal may be brought. The exception to that general rule was in sub-para 5 of para 28 of Sched 2 of the 1971 Act. By an amendment he introduced, the effect of that sub-paragraph was removed from all appeals under the 1993 Act. Earl Ferrers said:

> We do not intend that restriction to apply to asylum seekers. We intend that every asylum appellant shall be protected from removal for so long as he has an outstanding appeal or, if his appeal is dismissed, for so long as he has the opportunity to bring a further appeal. In other words we want all asylum seekers to be treated in accordance with the general rule on when an appeal is to be regarded as pending, which your Lordships will find set out at s 33(4) of the 1971 Act. (HL debs Vol 543 No 110, 11 March 1993 col 1188).

The Under S of S for the Home Department (Charles Wardle) stated that the intention of the provision is that an appeal shall continue to be treated as pending while an appeal may be or is being brought under the new provision (House of Commons Official Report Vol 226 No 189, Col 59–60). Thus persons who are refused at a port of entry, or persons whose leave is curtailed at the same time as the refusal of their asylum application may not be removed until they have had the opportunity of appealing, unless they have signed a disclaimer permitting them to be removed. The applicant may be able to obtain injunctive relief to prevent removal before he has had an opportunity to appeal.

A deportation order shall not be made against a person by virtue of s 3(5) of the 1971 Act so long as an appeal may be brought against the decision to make it nor if such an appeal is duly brought, so long as the appeal is pending under s 8(3)(a) of the 1993 Act (Sched 2, para 8). However when calculating the period for the making of a deportation order against a family member, any period during which there is an appeal against a decision to deport the principal deportee is discounted.

In relation to special adjudicator appeals against:
(a) exclusion (1993 Act s 8(1));
(b) a decision to make a deportation order against a person by virtue of s 3(5) of the 1971 Act;
(c) a refusal to revoke a deportation order made against a person by virtue of s 3(5) or (6) of the 1971 Act (1993 Act, s 8(3));
(d) removal directions made on the basis that the person is an illegal entrant, or has entered in breach of a deportation order, or as a member of a ship's crew (1993 Act, s 8(4)),

the system of stays on removal directions and for the grant of bail applies as if under the 1971 Act with certain exceptions.

Where a person appeals under any of the above provisions any directions previously given by virtue of a refusal of leave to enter for his removal from the UK shall cease to have effect, except in so far as they have already been carried out, and no directions may be given as long as an appeal is pending. Further, where the appeal is against directions for removal as an illegal entrant, the directions cease to have effect as long as the appeal is pending save to the extent that they have been carried out already. The family of a person who is appealing any of these decisions may not be removed either. However, persons may still be detained pending the appeal.

A person will be detained only as a last resort when it is believed that he will not comply with the terms of any temporary admission. All personal factors including an individual's health and dependent relatives are taken into account when considering detention (Charles Wardle, Official Report, 12 November 1992, col 55). Where a person has an appeal pending and is detained he may be released on bail either by an immigration officer not below the rank of inspector if the person enters into a recognisance conditioned for his appearance before an adjudicator or the IAT. An adjudicator may release an appellant on his entering into a recognisance for him to appear before another adjudicator at a time and place specified. The person fixing bail may also require sureties.

Part V

Procedure

Chapter 21

Procedure on Examination, Detention and Release

1 Examination by the immigration authorities

Under the 1971 Act, Sched 2, immigration officers have extensive powers of examination and detention. These must be exercised without regard to the race, colour or religion of prospective entrants (HC 395, Introduction, para 2). There are two types of examination by an immigration officer provided by Sched 2. First, in order to carry out an examination an immigration officer may board and search any ship, aircraft, or vehicle entering via the Channel Tunnel system. He may examine any person on board a ship, or aircraft which has landed in the UK, or in a vehicle entering through the Channel Tunnel system, whether or not he intends to enter the UK. An immigration officer may board a train entering via the Channel Tunnel system, and exercise powers of examination in relation to its passengers (Channel Tunnel Act 1987, s 12).

The purpose of the examination is:

(a) to discover whether or not any passenger is a British citizen;
(b) if not, whether he may enter the UK or not without leave; and
(c) if not, whether he should be given leave and if so for what periods and subject to what conditions.

Immigration officers may also examine persons seeking to leave the UK. The immigration officer may question an entrant in a wide-ranging way and may draw adverse inferences from a refusal to answer questions (*Immigration Officer Birmingham v Mohammad Sadiq* [1978] Imm AR 115). There is no duty of candour amounting to a requirement of utmost good faith on an entrant to disclose all material facts where he has not been specifically asked a question regarding them (*R v S of S, ex p Khawaja* [1984] AC 74). If a person has had a stamp placed in his passport before or during his journey to the UK by an immigration officer, which states that he may enter the UK either for an indefinite period or a limited period, he shall be deemed to have been given the leave on his arrival, and may only be examined at the port of entry by an immigration officer for the purposes of ascertaining whether he is such a person. He is not subject to examination under the powers conferred on the immigration officer under the 1971 Act for any other purpose (Immigration Act 1988 s 8). Such a person may have his deemed leave to enter cancelled within 24 hours of his arrival at the port at which he sought entry, or within 24 hours of his examination as to his identity. Such cancellation must be notified to the person in writing (1988 Act, s 8(5)).

The second type of examination which may carried out pursuant to Sched 2 is a medical examination. This is done in order to establish whether there are medical reasons for refusing entry. If an immigration officer gives a person leave to enter, but considers that a further medical examination may be desirable in the interests of public health, he may require the entrant, by notice in writing, to submit to one. The procedure for further examination is that the entrant is required to report his arrival to a medical officer of health, and thereafter, if that officer considers it necessary, to undergo a further examination.

Any person who is examined by an immigration officer is under a duty to provide that officer with any information or documents he may require for carrying out those duties. It will not always be sufficient simply to answer the questions asked; there may be an active obligation to disclose material facts not investigated at all.

A document which is of particular importance and may be demanded by the immigration officer is a valid passport with a photograph or some other means of establishing identity and nationality. The immigration officer is entitled to detain the passport until either leave to enter is given or the applicant is about to depart, having been refused entry (1971 Act, Sched 2, para 4(2A) as amended by the 1988 Act). In addition, an immigration officer may ask to see documents of 'any description appearing to an immigration officer to be relevant for the purposes of carrying out the examination'. Such documents need to be genuine ones by necessary implication (*Chan v S of S* [1992] Imm AR 233). In order to see if a person is carrying relevant documents the immigration officer may search that person's luggage. If any documents are found he may be detained for up to seven days

by the immigration officer. If it seems likely that any such document may be required for an appeal under the Act, the officer may keep it until it appears no longer to be necessary. Finally, under the Immigration (Landing and Embarkation Cards) Order 1975 (SI No 65), passengers who:
(a) are over 16;
(b) are leaving and entering the UK;
(c) do not have the right of abode;
(d) are not travelling within the Common Travel Area
may be required to produce embarkation and landing cards to the immigration authorities. Such provision will not apply to EC nationals.

Guidelines have been issued to immigration officers requiring them to follow the Police and Criminal Evidence Act 1984 (PACE) Codes of Practice when conducting examinations pursuant to their power under the 1971 Act. However, a person does not have a right to have a legal representative present at an interview. The immigration officer's discretion to permit legal representation at an interview must be exercised on proper and relevant grounds (*Ex p Vera Lawson* [1994] Imm AR 58). In many cases the immigration officer may be interested in establishing whether or not the person he is interviewing is an illegal entrant. He will be bound by PACE codes where he is investigating offences. Moreover, he is bound by the administrative guidelines referred to above when he is not conducting investigations into offences. A variety of views have been expressed. In *Ex p Ogunlande* [1992] COD 46, it was doubted whether the Codes applied. However, in *Ex p Okusanya* [1993] Imm AR 13 Macpherson J acknowledged that the S of S has decided that immigration officers will apply the relevant aspects of the codes in investigations. He proposed a solution to the apparent difficulty that in any interview a charge may potentially be brought in respect of illegal entry in *Ex p Eid Mohammed Ibrahim* [1993] Imm AR 125. He stated:

> the fact is that the immigration officers were considering immigration questions but they were also investigating an offence because, to come into this country by deception and to be an illegal entrant, does constitute a criminal offence for which a charge can be levelled. So that the Code and [PACE] plainly, in my judgment applied to the interview.

Evidence obtained as a result of a breach of the PACE codes may be excluded. The test is whether the particular investigations relate to a matter in respect of which 'a charge can be levelled', and not whether there is an intention on the part of the immigration officers to level such a charge (see (1993) LAG Bulletin, p 21).

(a) Notice of leave or refusal

When a person is examined he is to be told of the outcome within 24 hours of the end of the examination. However, an examination may continue for a long period and in *R v Chief Immigration Officer, Manchester Airport, ex p Insah Begum* [1973] 1 All ER 594 the CA held that it was not concluded until all the necessary information has been gathered (see also *Perera v Immigration Officer, London (Heathrow) Airport* [1979–80] Imm AR 58). An examination is ended when it is concluded by the immigration officer that a second interview is not necessary (*Ex p V* [1988] Imm AR 561).

If no notice refusing leave to enter is given within 24 hours of the conclusion of the examination, the entrant is to be deemed to have been granted six months' leave to enter subject to a condition prohibiting employment (1971 Act, Sched 2, para 6(1), as amended by the Immigration Act 1988, Sched, para 8). Indefinite leave to remain is obtained if the stamp was made before 1 August 1988, when para 6(1) was amended. There must be an examination of the person for the benefit of para 6(1) to be claimed (*Ex p Balwinder Kumar* [1990] Imm AR 265). Such leave is not obtained where an entrant is mistakenly waived through without inspection, even where the person behaves with no impropriety personally and where the immigration officer had no knowledge or thought of the need for a decision to be made on the person's entry (*Ex p Rehal* [1989] Imm AR 576). Where the immigration officer concludes that the person does not need leave to enter, whether or not that conclusion is the result of a mistake, negligence, or due to deception, the person entering is an illegal entrant and cannot claim the benefit of Sched 2, para 6(1) (*Ex p Bagga* [1990] 3 WLR 1013). Further, the examination must have been concluded for the paragraph to apply (*S of S v Sittampalam Thirukumar* [1989] Imm AR 402). If a notice is withdrawn as procedurally incorrect, the examination to which the 1971 Act refers is deemed to continue from the moment the notice loses its effect until a further decision is taken. Thus the person does not obtain six months' leave to enter from the moment the first notice is withdrawn (*Ex p Siddique* [1992] Imm AR 127).

Illegible stamps Where an entry stamp is ambiguous because it is illegible the stamp does not constitute effective notice in writing for the purposes of the 1971 Act, s 4(1) (*Ex p Betancourt* [1988]

Imm AR 78). Accordingly, a person was deemed by virtue of para 6(1) to have been given six months' leave to enter, 24 hours after the illegible stamp was made (see also *R v IAT, ex p Lakhani* [1988] Imm AR 474 and *Ex p Minton* [1990] Imm AR 199). If the illegible stamp was made before 1 August 1988 its effect is to grant the entrant indefinite leave to remain 12 hours after the stamp was made. The notice may be defective for other reasons, and where no statement of appeal rights appears on a notice, the applicant may rely on para 6(1) (*Ex p Lateef* [1991] Imm AR 334). Where a stamp contains two dates, either of which may be that from which a leave period runs, any ambiguity is resolved in favour of the applicant (*S of S v Behrooz* [1991] Imm AR 82).

(b) Removal of illegal entrants and persons refused leave (1971 Act, Sched 2, para 9)

Immigration officers are empowered to make arrangements for the removal of illegal entrants and persons who are refused leave to enter. This they may do by giving directions to the captain of the ship or aircraft on which the passenger arrived or to the owners or agents of any ship or aircraft (*R v Immigration Officer, ex p Shah* [1982] 1 WLR 544), or to the concessionaires of the Channel Tunnel. Paragraph 9 provides that the power to remove arises where the person is an illegal entrant, and is not given leave to enter.

The power therefore arises where the person is an illegal entrant, is known to be such, and is not given leave to enter. Leave to enter given at a time when it is not known whether a person is a legal or illegal entrant or not is irrelevant for the purposes of the exercise of the removal power, despite the fact that para 9 requires that the person is an illegal entrant and is not given leave to enter and the words of Lord Bridge in *Khawaja* (above) that the words 'illegal entrant' are not capable of qualification (*Ex p Lapinid* [1984] 3 All ER 257). The power to remove arises where a person has entered unlawfully and is not thereafter given leave to remain (*Ex p Razak* [1986] Imm AR 44).

Such directions must be issued within two months of the date upon which leave was refused when they are issued by an immigration officer; after that time they are ineffective (*Parshotam Singh v S of S* [1989] Imm AR 469). In any case in which the S of S considers it to be impracticable for directions to be given by an immigration officer, he may give directions himself. The same applies if such directions if given would be ineffective. He must do so in any case if two months have expired since the entrant was refused leave. These directions must specify the country to which the entrant is to be removed (paras 10(1) and 8(1)(*c*)). In the normal case, the entrant will be removed to his country of citizenship. The S of S pays the costs of complying with a removal direction which he issues. Before removal from the UK a person should be given an opportunity to contact friends and relations in the UK, or his High Commission or consul (para 88).

Asylum seekers Asylum seekers are protected from removal while their applications are being considered and during the period in which they either appeal or may appeal (1993 Act, s 6 and Sched 2, paras 7 and 8; and see ministerial statements referred to in Chapter 20).

2 Detention of persons liable to examination or removal

The 1971 Act, Sched 2, para 16 gives wide powers of detention to immigration officers in two circumstances. The first is that if a person is liable to examination, he may be detained under the authority of an immigration officer until he is examined and until the result of the examination is notified. The second is that any person in respect of whom directions for removal may be made may be detained until those directions are given and once they are given, until he is removed pursuant to them. A person may be removed from a ship or aircraft in order to be detained under para 16. At the same time, an entrant may be ordered by an immigration officer to be detained on board a ship or aircraft if he has been refused leave to enter.

Any person who is thus liable to detention may be arrested without a warrant by an immigration officer or a police constable. Justices of the peace have wide powers to issue warrants authorising a police constable to enter into and search premises where such persons are thought likely to be and to arrest them.

While detained a detainee may be photographed and measured by an immigration officer, constable or prison officer and any other steps necessary to establish his identity may be taken in relation to him. Such a person may be conveyed in the custody of a constable or immigration officer from place to place in order to establish his nationality. Under the 1993 Act an asylum seeker may be fingerprinted irrespective of whether he is in detention, and may be detained if he fails to attend in order to be fingerprinted (see Chapter 19).

Under Sched 2, para 19 the owners or agents of the ship or

aircraft on which the person arrives may be liable, if he is refused leave to enter and directions for his removal are given, to pay to the S of S on demand any expenses of detaining that person in the UK. There is no such liability if the detainee was the holder of a certificate of entitlement, current entry clearance, or work permit, unless these are patent forgeries. Detention is an instrument of last resort. In the debates on the 1993 Act in the HL, Earl Ferrers stated the government's policy in relation to the detention. He said in relation to an amendment:

> The amendment would provide that a person could only be detained if there were reasonable grounds for believing that he would not comply with the requirement to report to an immigration officer. That is essentially what happens already. It is our practice when considering detention in all immigration cases. The specific power to detain in Clause 7 of the Bill will only be exercised if we do not believe that the person would in fact keep in touch with the immigration authorities, and that unless he were detained, it would be impossible to enforce that departure. That is what happens.
>
> I can assure noble Lords that there is no intention whatever to exercise the powers of detention when there is a practical alternative. Apart from the obvious effect on the detainee, detention is costly. The Home Office has no wish to tie up limited detention accommodation unnecessarily (see HL Debs Vol. 543 No 104, 2 March 1993, col 631).

3 Temporary admission and release

(a) Temporary admission of a person liable to be detained

A person who is liable to detention or in fact detained may nevertheless be temporarily admitted to the UK. An immigration officer may authorise this in writing. He will then be released from detention. The immigration officer may make temporary admission subject to conditions such as reporting and as to residence, or prohibiting employment or occupation (1971 Act, Sched 2, para 21 as amended by the 1988 Act, Sched, para 10). Where temporary admission is refused, the decision may be challenged in judicial review proceedings (*Vilvarajah v S of S* [1990] Imm AR 457). A person who is temporarily admitted has not entered the UK (1971 Act, s 11(1)) and if he absconds he becomes an illegal entrant. Save in the case of asylum seekers such absconding persons have no right of appeal whilst present in the UK (see *Bugdaycay v S of S* [1987] AC 514).

(b) Bail for examination detainees

If a person is detained for examination under Sched 2, para 16(1), and not released by the immigration authorities, he may, if seven days have elapsed, apply for bail to an adjudicator. He should be notified of his right to apply after seven days. The adjudicator may release him on bail upon his entering into a recognisance (Sched 2, para 22). That recognisance may be subject to any conditions which seem likely to result in the appearance of the person and may be subject to sureties. The adjudicator may, instead of taking the bail, specify its amount and conditions in order that it be taken by another person such as a police officer. The same principles apply to bail for asylum seekers who are appealing against a decision to remove or exclude them from the UK under the 1993 Act, s 10.

(c) Sureties

In a circular the Chief Adjudicator indicated that it would be rare for an adjudicator to release an applicant without sureties of less than £1,000 each being available, and that frequently the total value of the sureties will be £5,000 (reproduced in (1991) 5 INL&P 123). In any event a recognisance will be demanded of an applicant in a nominal sum (eg £5).

If a recognisance is forfeited by reason of the failure of the person to appear, the adjudicator may order the persons bound by the recognisance to pay the sums they are bound to pay under it, or part of those sums. The order must specify a magistrates' court which will deal with the collection, enforcement and remission of the sums as if it had forfeited the sums in question.

Immigration officers and police constables have wide powers of arrest in relation to a person thus temporarily released or bailed. They may arrest him without a warrant if they believe on reasonable grounds that such a person is likely to break, is breaking, or will break a condition of his recognisance by failing to appear or otherwise. They may also arrest him without a warrant if they are notified in writing by a surety that he believes that the person bailed is unlikely to appear and that the surety wishes to be relieved of his obligations as surety (Sched 2, para 24(1)).

A person who is thus arrested should be brought before an adjudicator within 24 hours, or if this is not practicable, he should be brought before a magistrate within 24 hours. He may instead be brought before an immigration officer within 24 hours if it was a condition of the recognisance under which he was originally released that he appear before an immigration officer within that time limit.

When a person is brought before an adjudicator or magistrate under these provisions, they may adopt one of three courses. If they are of the opinion that no breach has occurred, and is not likely, they must release the person under his original recognisance. If, however, they take the view that there has been a breach, they may release him on a new recognisance or order his detention under the authority of the person by whom he was arrested (Sched 2, para 24(2) and (3)).

4 Bail pending an appeal

When an appeal is pending, an appellant may be released on bail by a chief immigration officer, a police inspector, an adjudicator, or the IAT. The appellant may be released on his entering into a recognisance subject to conditions, one of which is that he will appear before an adjudicator or the IAT at a stated time and place. An adjudicator or the IAT must grant bail to a person who has filed a notice of appeal from the adjudicator's decision in certain circumstances (see below). There must be an appeal pending for the power to arise. Where, for example, an appeal against removal directions was made but no alternative destination was referred to, the appeal was not properly constituted and was therefore not pending, so that the adjudicator had no power to grant bail (*R v An adjudicator, ex p Umeloh* [1991] Imm AR 602).

(a) Restrictions on the power to grant bail pending appeal

The consent of the S of S is required if directions for removal have been made in respect of the appellant, or there is a power to make such directions in respect of him. In fact however where an appeal is pending, any directions for removal have no effect, and so the S of S's consent will not be required (*R v IAT, ex p Alghali* [1984] Imm AR 106).

The power of the IAT or adjudicator to release on bail a person who has lodged an appeal against the adjudicator's decision is limited to where:

(a) no leave to appeal to the IAT is required; or
(b) he has granted leave to appeal to the IAT; and in either case;

(c) the appellant has entered into proper recognisances; and
(d) if required, the sureties are sufficient;
(e) none of the following apply:
   (i) the appellant has failed to comply with previous bail;
   (ii) he is likely to commit offences if released on bail;
   (iii) he is likely to cause a danger to public health;
   (iv) he suffers from a mental disorder and continued detention is in his own interests or for the protection of any other person;
   (v) he is under 17 and arrangements ought to be made for his care in the event of release, and no satisfactory arrangements can be made (1971 Act, Sched 2, para 30(2)(a)–(e)).

The IAT may release on bail a person to whom it has granted leave where the above conditions are observed.

Adjudicators and the IAT have similar powers of forfeiture in relation to recognisances when they release a person on bail under Sched 2, para 22. Immigration officers and constables have similar powers of arrest in relation to persons released pending an appeal as they do of persons released under para 22.

(b) Judicial review (see also Chapter 27)

Where a person is refused leave to enter, or is an illegal entrant, the High Court may grant bail if the adjudicator has no power to grant it. When an application for leave for judicial review or the substantive hearing is pending, the High Court has an inherent jurisdiction to grant bail. If the High Court makes an order which is unappealable, for example because it is a refusal of leave to apply for judicial review, the court is thereafter *functus officio*, and only the CA can grant bail (*Ex p Turkoglu* [1988] QB 398). In *Swati v S of S* [1986] 1 WLR 477 at 485, the CA observed that bail would only exceptionally be granted when leave to apply for judicial review was not granted. However, it may be granted where an application for leave to apply for judicial review is adjourned (*Thamathirampillai v S of S* [1987] Imm AR 47).

The High Court has perhaps unnecessarily limited the principles on which bail may be granted in these circumstances. In order to grant bail it must effectively find that the decision of the S of S not to grant temporary admission was unreasonable or erroneous in law (see *Vilvarajah v S of S* [1990] Imm AR 457 in which no cases were cited). This sets a very high standard, in which broad considerations may justify a refusal to grant temporary admission and therefore bail, such as the fact that a person may sometimes go into hiding if he is released on temporary admission (see eg *R v Governor of Haslar Prison, ex p Egbe* (1991) *Times*, 4 June, and also *Dhillon v S of S* [1987] Imm AR 222). It is not open to the applicant to pick the forum for his application for bail. The *forum non conveniens* rule applies to such applications. It is not therefore possible to lodge the application in Scotland merely because there is more chance of obtaining bail there (*Sokha v S of S* [1992] Imm AR 14).

The writ of *habeas corpus* is another route to release from detention under the Act (see Chapter 28).

Chapter 22

Procedure on Deportation

1 Orders for deportation by the S of S

This is governed by the 1971 Act, s 5, and HC 395 Part 13 (paras 362–395). A deportation order is an administrative requirement that the person in respect of whom it is made should leave the UK and not return. Its effect is to cancel any antecedent leave which the deportee had to enter, or remain in, the UK. It also invalidates any leave to enter or remain given to the deportee after the order is made and for so long as it is still in force. Thus if the person in respect of whom a deportation order has been made returns to the UK through immigration control and obtains unlimited leave to enter and remain, that leave is of no effect. He is a person entering in breach of a deportation order and therefore an illegal entrant (1971 Act, s 33(1)). He may simply be removed.

(a) Decision to deport

There are two stages before a person may be deported. The first is that the S of S decides to make the order, or a criminal court recommends it. A decision to deport may be taken by an immigration officer of the rank of inspector or above (*Oladehinde v S of S* [1990] 3 All ER 393). The decision to deport is made under the 1971 Act, s 3(5), the recommendation of the criminal court is made under s 3(6). At that stage, the person against whom the order is to be made can appeal. A person in respect of whom the S of S has decided to make an order is notified in writing of that decision provided his whereabouts are known (see *Islam v S of S* [1975] Imm AR 106; *R v IAT, ex p Ekrem Mehmet* [1978] Imm AR 46; *Rehman v S of S* [1978] Imm AR 80; and *Rhemtulla v IAT* [1979–80] Imm AR 168). It is usual in cases where the proposed subject cannot be found for the Home Office to try to trace him. If he is found the deportation decision is served upon him dated contemporaneously.

The notice must state the grounds relied upon in the decision to deport, and the destination to which the person is to be deported. He may appeal against it through the statutory appeals machinery unless he is being deported on the basis that deportation is conducive to the public good, on political grounds, when there is no appeal whatsoever. A person who is recommended to be deported by the court can appeal through the criminal appeals machinery. While appeals are pending in both cases the S of S may not make a deportation order (1971 Act, ss 6(6) and 15(2)).

(b) Signing the order

The second stage is if there is no appeal in time or if the appeals are unsuccessful the S of S may make a deportation order. This is done by signing the deportation order. However, there are limitations on this power. A deportation order may not be made on grounds of family membership if it is more than eight weeks since the deportation of the member of the family on which the proposed order would be based. A 'family' deportation order ceases to have effect if the person against whom it is made ceases to be a member of the family on which the order was based through divorce or, if a child, through reaching the age of 18. Lastly, a person may not be deported if the only country to which he could be removed is one to which he is unwilling to go from a well-founded fear of persecution because of his race, religion, nationality, membership of a particular group, or political opinion (para 380 see Chapter 19). If a person is liable to deportation on any ground, the S of S under the 1971 Act, s 5(6) may make payments, in his discretion, to defray the expenses of the potential deportee's departure from the UK. These expenses may include those of the person's family or household. However, two conditions must be met. The first is that no deportation order must have been made. The second is that the potential deportee must leave the UK to live permanently abroad. The result is that as no deportation order has been made it may be easier to re-enter the UK in the future.

At present the practice is to delegate to senior immigration staff the power to make decisions to deport in 'straightforward' cases. These are cases in which there is no long and complicated history, and no significant compassionate circumstances. Immigration inspectors are required to record the facts that were made known to them, and upon which they based their decision. The powers delegated likewise extend to issuing notices of intention to deport, detention, and authorising supervised departure in cases 'where deportation action against those found to have overstayed a leave or to be in breach of a condition attached to a leave is justified' (Letter, 18 December 1990 to JCWI, reproduced in full at (1991) 5 INL&P 26).

There may sometimes be a considerable gap between the decision to deport and the signing of the deportation order. It may be unreasonable for the Home Office not to review the decision in order to permit the person who is to be deported to show the circumstances prevailing at the time at which consideration is being given to signing the order (*Bashirotyo v IAT* [1990] Imm AR 461).

2 Recommendations by the criminal courts

A recommendation for deportation (see 1971 Act ss 3(6), 6) may be made by a court in respect of a person over the age of 17 convicted of an imprisonable offence. Any court which has power to sentence the offender may make a recommendation for deportation unless the offender is committed to be sentenced to another court. The defendant's lawyer should be asked to address the court specifically on whether it is appropriate to make a recommendation.

A court may not make a recommendation for deportation unless the defendant has been given seven days' notice in writing of certain matters. The procedure is to be strictly observed; the 1971 Act, s 3(6) is clear and precise. If the procedure is not observed any recommendation may be appealed (*R v Omojudi* [1992] Imm AR 104). The matters to be notified are:
  (*a*) that a British citizen is not liable to deportation;
  (*b*) a description of what it is to be a British citizen;
  (*c*) that the burden of proving British citizenship lies on the person who asserts it; and
  (*d*) that certain residents, though not British citizens, are not liable to deportation by the 1971 Act, s 7.

Once the court has convicted an offender it may adjourn for seven days to enable the notice to be given: or if the notice was given before the date of conviction, in order to allow the seven days to elapse.

If a court recommends deportation, the S of S then considers whether or not to make an order. He should take into account every relevant factor including, for example, age, length of residence in the UK, the nature of the offence, the defendant's record and compassionate circumstances. Representations on the defendant's behalf will be considered, and can be of crucial importance at this stage. The S of S may make a deportation order on the recommendation of the court, although this deprives the deportee of a right of appeal via the Immigration Appellate authorities (*Ex p Kusi Boahem* [1988] Imm AR 540).

3 Effect of a deportation order

Once a deportation order has been made by the S of S, he has power to issue directions for removal of the deportee (1971 Act, Sched 3). These directions may be issued to the captain of a ship or aircraft which is about to leave the UK or the owners or agents of any ship or aircraft. Alternatively, the S of S may make arrangements for removal himself. The directions should specify the country to which the deportee is to be removed. This must be a country of which he is a citizen, or one which is likely to admit him. Although there is a limited statutory right of appeal against these directions, the Divisional Court held in *R v Immigration Officer, ex p Shah* [1982] 1 WLR 544 that in addition an immigrant had sufficient *locus standi* to challenge directions given to an airline by way of an application for judicial review.

A deportee in respect of whom directions for removal have been made may be placed on board the ship or aircraft on which he is to be removed under the authority of the S of S. Once the deportee is on board the ship or aircraft he must be prevented by its captain from disembarking, if the S of S so requires. The S of S may use the deportee's monies to pay for the cost of maintaining him before departure and the cost of his departure. Otherwise, the S of S must defray these expenses.

4 Detention of persons before deportation

If a court makes a recommendation for deportation and does not at the same time sentence the offender to imprisonment, and the offender has not been released on bail, he is to be detained pending the making of the deportation order. The only exceptions to this are that the S of S may order his release pending further consideration of his case, or the court which made the recommendation for deportation may order him not to be detained.

In addition, Sched 3 further provides that where a person has been notified under the notice regulations, of a decision to make a deportation order against him, and he is neither detained in pursuance of a sentence or order of a court nor on bail, the S of S may authorise his detention pending the making of the deportation order. Alternatively, the person may be placed under residence or reporting restrictions. The S of S may lawfully detain a young person who has been released on bail by a court which had no knowledge of the decision to make a deportation order or which released the offender on bail before the decision to make the deportation order was notified (*Ex p Giambi* [1982] 1 All ER 434).

Once the deportation order has been made, the S of S may authorise the deportee's detention pending his removal from the UK. If he is already detained by virtue of the provisions discussed above, his detention is to continue unless the S of S orders otherwise.

In *R v Hardial Singh* [1983] Imm AR 198, Woolf J held that the power to detain was impliedly limited to a period reasonably necessary for the purpose, and that the S of S had to exercise reasonable expedition to ensure that all reasonable steps were taken for removal within a reasonable time. If there was unreasonable delay, the court would issue a writ of *habeas corpus*, or make an order for release.

A person who is liable to detention under any of these powers may be arrested without a warrant by a police constable or an immigration officer. A justice of the peace may issue a warrant authorising the entering (if necessary by force) and searching of any premises in which there are reasonable grounds for suspecting such a person may be found. The warrant also authorises the arrest of such a person.

A person who is detained under these powers may be detained where the S of S directs. Such a person may be photographed and measured. He may be conveyed from place to place in the custody of a constable, or some other person authorised by an immigration officer.

5 Revocation of deportation orders

Application for revocation of a deportation order may be made to an entry clearance officer or direct to the Home Office (HC 395, paras 390–395).

Part VI
Remedies

Chapter 23

Appeal Procedures I

1 HC 395, Part 12

Paras 353 to 361 of HC 395 make provision for the procedures relating to rights of appeal.

PART 12

RIGHTS OF APPEAL

Notice of refusal of leave to enter

353. Where refusal of leave to enter is confirmed, the person concerned should be handed a notice informing him of the decision and of the reasons for refusal. This notice will also inform him whether he has a right of appeal under Section 13 of the 1971 Act and, if so, how the right of appeal might be exercised. If he has difficulty in understanding the notice its meaning should be explained to him.

Rights of appeal in relation to a person claiming to have the right of abode

354. A person who claims to have the right of abode is not entitled to appeal against a decision that he requires leave to enter unless he holds either a United Kingdom passport describing him as a British citizen or as a citizen of the United Kingdom and Colonies having the right of abode in the United Kingdom, or a certificate of entitlement duly issued to him by or on behalf of the Government of the United Kingdom certifying that he has such a right of abode.

Rights of appeal in relation to a person who holds an entry clearance or work permit

355. Subect to Section 13(5) of the Immigration Act 1971, a person in possession of a valid United Kingdom entry clearance or named in a current work permit who is entitled to appeal against refusal of leave to enter the United Kingdom may exercise his right of appeal before removal from the United Kingdom. If such a person sought entry through the

Channel Tunnel he may, upon giving notice of appeal, be brought through the tunnel to enable him to pursue his appeal.

Rights of appeal exercisable from abroad

356. Except in cases involving an asylum application to which paragraph 348 applies and cases described in paragraphs 354 and 355 above, a person entitled to appeal against refusal of leave to enter, irrespective of his national status, may exercise that right only after he has left the United Kingdom.

Rights of appeal against a time limit or condition

357. A person aggrieved by the imposition on entry of a time limit or condition may apply to the Home Office for variation of his leave. Subject to paragraph 358 below, he will have a right of appeal if variation is refused.

Rights of appeal against variation of leave to enter or refusal to vary it

358. A person may appeal against any variation of his leave to enter or any refusal to vary it except:
   (i) when a refusal is on one of the grounds specified in Section 14(2A) of the 1971 Act; or
   (ii) if the case comes within Section 14(3) of the 1971 Act following a decision taken personally by the Secretary of State and not by a person acting under his authority; or
   (iii) when a variation of leave is made by statutory instrument; or
   (iv) if leave is curtailed under Section 7(1) of the Asylum and Immigration Appeals Act 1993.

Notice of appeal rights

359. Where an application for variation of leave to enter is refused; or a variation is made otherwise than on the application of the person concerned, or is less favourable than that for which he applied, notice of the decision and, if an appeal lies, of his right of appeal will normally be handed to the person concerned or sent to his last known address. Alternatively it may be so given or sent to a person who has either made the application on behalf of another, or has subsequently been appointed to act on another's behalf in connection with an application.

Explanatory statement

360. If notice of appeal is given within the period allowed, an explanatory statement summarising the facts of the case on the basis of which the decision was taken will normally be prepared and be sent to the independent appellate authorities, who will notify the appellant of the arrangements for any appeal to be heard.

Rights of appeal in asylum cases

361. Rights of appeal in asylum cases are covered in paragraph 348 above.

COMMENTARY

(a) Introduction

Sections 13-17 of the 1971 Act and s 10 of the 1993 Act set out the circumstances in which there is or is not a right of appeal in non-asylum cases. Para 353 states that the applicant should, on refusal, be handed a notice informing him of the decision and of the reasons for it. The notice also tells him whether he has a right of appeal or not. Such a notice cannot give or deprive a person of a right of appeal. Since rights of appeal are purely statutory, these Acts are a comprehensive statement of those rights. The first step is to see if there is a right of appeal. An appeal can be launched if the is a dispute as to whether the appellant is entitled to appeal. Under the Immigration Appeals (Procedure) Rules (SI 1984 No 2041: 'the 1984 Appeal Rules'), the existence of a right to appeal will be taken as a preliminary point by the respondent and at the hearing of the appeal it will be determined as a preliminary issue (see rr 8 and 11).

In cases where the appellant is entitled to be notified of an appealable decision the decision is deemed to have been taken on the date the notification is posted to, or served on, the appellant (see 4 below). Unless otherwise stated, the appeal lies in the first instance to the adjudicator. Leave to appeal is not required for any appeal, to an adjudicator or to the IAT if the IAT is sitting at first instance. There is an appeal pending for the purposes of the 1971 Act when there is a notice of appeal duly given (s 33(4)).

(b) Circumstances in which there is a right of appeal

Whether there is a right to appeal may be determined as a preliminary issue at the hearing. It is not a question which the S of S has the power to determine even if a notice of appeal has to be lodged with him. The S of S may not declare that a person has no right of appeal, or has forfeited that right (*S of S v Ken'aan* [1990] Imm AR 544).

A person may only appeal against a refusal of entry whilst in the UK where:

(*a*)   he is an asylum seeker (see Chapter 19); or
(*b*)   he was refused leave at the port of entry, and held a current

entry clearance or was named in a current work permit (s 13(3)).

Under HC 395 the right of appeal is to be exercised only after the person has left the UK except in the following cases:

(a) asylum cases (para 348 and see Chapter 19);
(b) cases where a person claims to have the right of abode and he has either a UK passport describing him as a British citizen or as a CUKC having the right of abode, or a certificate of entitlement (para 354);
(c) cases where a person is in possession of a valid entry clearance or is named in a current work permit; save that a person may not appeal if the S of S certifies that directions have been given by him personally for the appellant not to be given entry to the UK on the ground that his exclusion is conducive to the public good (para 355).

A person who is refused entry to the UK may make further applications for leave to enter before his removal from the UK. A refusal of that second application (in some other capacity) will attract a right of appeal under s 13 of the 1971 Act and will only be exercisable outside the UK, save where it is an appeal under s 8 of the 1993 Act on asylum grounds. Where a second application is made after a first application has been refused, no entry clearance conferring a right to appeal on the applicant while he is in the UK exists. The second appeal can only be made from abroad. If the second application is made before the decision on the first application has been determined, both decisions will attract an in-country right of appeal (*Ashraf v IAT* [1989] Imm AR 234 and *Moussavi* [1986] Imm AR 39).

There is no right of appeal against a refusal of entry clearance or leave to enter if the refusal is based upon the failure of the applicant to have a relevant document or to satisfy a requirement of the immigration rules as to age or nationality or citizenship, or if the person seeks entry for a period exceeding that permitted under the immigration rules (1971 Act, s 13(3B) as inserted by 1993 Act). A person who seeks entry to the UK as a visitor, or in order to follow a course of study of not more than six months' duration for which he has been accepted, or who has the intention of studying but has not been accepted on a course, or who is a dependant of a person in one of these categories may not appeal against a refusal of entry clearance. He may only appeal against refusal of leave to enter if he has a current entry clearance (s 13(3A), 1971 Act).

(c) Exclusion: refusal of entry clearance, visa and of entry to the UK (s 13)

Under s 13 of the 1971 Act, there are rights of appeal in the following circumstances:

(1) A person is refused leave to enter the UK.
(2) A person is refused an entry clearance or certificate of entitlement to the right of abode.
(3) A person who, it has been decided, requires leave to enter.
(4) A person who is refused entry, and who holds a passport stating that he has a right of abode in the UK, or is a British citizen, or bears a certificate of entitlement to the right of abode in the UK (he may appeal on the grounds that he has a right of abode in the UK). A person who holds a current entry clearance or is named in a current work permit may appeal against a refusal of leave to enter. If he is refused entry whilst trying to enter through the Channel Tunnel system, he may (upon giving notice of appeal) be brought through the tunnel to enable him to pursue his appeal (HC 395, para 355).

Destination There is a right of appeal where directions are given under the 1971 Act for a person's removal from the UK either:

(a) on his being refused leave to enter; or
(b) on a deportation order being made against him; or
(c) on his having entered the UK in breach of a deportation order.

Such a person may appeal to an adjudicator against the directions on the ground that he ought, if at all, to be removed to a different country or territory specified by him (s 17(1)) (see below, p 423).

If the person appeals on being refused leave to enter and before he appeals directions have been given for his removal from the UK to any other country, or the S of S or an immigration officer serves on him a notice stating that any directions which may be given for his removal will be for his removal to a country specified in the notice, he may appeal both against the refusal of leave to enter and against the destination in the same proceedings (s 17(2) of the 1971 Act). In all cases, if either the adjudicator is satisfied that the appellant was an illegal entrant at the time he was refused entry, or there was a deportation order in force against the appellant at the time he was refused entry, the adjudicator must refuse the appeal.

A person who makes a claim for asylum may appeal against

a refusal of that claim and against any refusal of leave to enter in the same proceedings. He appeals to the special adjudicator. He may appeal to the special adjudicator at any time on asylum grounds. In particular where he arrived in the UK and applies for leave to enter on a non-asylum ground but is refused, he is entitled to make a further application while still in the UK on an asylum ground. Such an application is a valid application for leave to enter and will now attract an in-country right of appeal (cf *R v IAT, ex p S of S* [1990] Imm AR 652 (see Chapter 20)).

Time limits: Rule 4 of the Immigration Appeals (Procedure) Rules 1984 The following time limits apply to s 13 appeals:
 (1) Where the appeal is against refusal of leave to enter or the decision that leave to enter is required, then the time limit is 28 days after the person departs from the UK if the refusal was either not at the port of entry, or the person refused did not carry a current entry clearance.
 (2) If the appeal does not have to be made from outside the UK, it can be made at any time before or after departure from the UK, but must be made before 28 days from the date of departure at latest.
 (3) If the appeal is against the refusal of a certificate of entitlement to the right of abode, and the application for the certificate was made to the ECO, the appeal may be lodged up to three months after the decision.
 (4) If the appeal against the refusal of the certificate of entitlement arises from an application to the S of S, the appeal must be lodged within 14 days from the date of the decision.
 (5) If the appeal is against the refusal of an entry clearance the time limit is three months from the date of the decision.
(See further on time limits pages 418 and 422–424 below).

The effect of these provisions is that where the application is refused while the person is still abroad, there is generally a three-month period in which to appeal, whereas if the decision is made after the person has come to the UK, there are the shorter time limits of either 14 or 28 days.

(d) Conditions on limited leave (s 14)

Where a person has limited leave to enter the UK, he may appeal to the adjudicator against a variation of his leave, or against a refusal to vary his leave. He may appeal whether the variation relates to the conditions of his leave or the length of his leave.

Thus where an applicant applied for indefinite leave to remain and was granted a limited leave, he could appeal under s 14 for the removal of the limitation on his leave (*S of S v Behroooz* [1991] Imm AR 82 (IAT)). The appeal must be made while the appellant has limited leave. Under the Immigration (Variation of Leave) Order 1976 as amended by the 1993 Order (VOLO) if a person has limited leave to enter and applies before the expiry of that leave for a variation of leave, the duration of his leave is extended to the date of the decision on the application for variation. Thus if an appeal is lodged in the course of the 28 days given under the VOLO rules, it attracts the s 14 right of appeal, but if the appeal is made 29 days or later after the decision refusing the variation, there is no right of appeal (see *ex p Selo Wa-Selo* [1990] Imm AR 76, and *Akhtar* [1991] Imm AR 232).

While an appeal under s 14 is pending, the *status quo* is maintained, and the variation which it is sought to impose shall not take effect. The appellant is not to be required to leave the UK during that time merely because his leave expired (s 14(1)). If, however a deportation order is made against a person whose appeal is pending, then his appeal lapses (s 14(5)). Where a person who is appealing under s 14 leaves the country, he has no right to re-enter (*R v Immigration Officer, ex p Nikhat Ali* [1982] Imm AR 1). Under s 8 categories of persons can be exempt from the provisions of the 1971 Act; those who are members of diplomatic missions are also exempt. Where a person ceases to have this immunity, or ceases to be a British citizen, and is given limited leave to remain, he may appeal to the adjudicator against any provision which limits his leave, and likewise is protected from removal.

Para 358 of HC 395 provides that a person may appeal against any variation of leave to enter or refusal to vary it except where:

(*a*) the refusal is on the ground that:
    (i) a relevant document required by the immigration rules has not been issued;
    (ii) the person does not satisfy a requirement of the immigration rules as to age, nationality or citizenship;
    (iii) the variation would result in the duration of the person's leave exceeding that permitted by the immigration rules; or
    (iv) any fee required by or under any enactment has not been paid (s 14(2A), 1971 Act as inserted by the 1993 Act) (see below)).

(b) the S of S certifies that the departure of the person is conducive to the public good, or in the interests of national security, or relations of the UK to another country;
(c) a variation of leave results from a statutory instrument;
(d) the leave is curtailed under s 7(1) of the Asylum and Immigration Appeals Act 1993.

Time Limits, Rule 4 The time limit under s 14 is 14 days from:
(a) the variation of leave or refusal to vary (s 14(1)); or
(b) the grant of limited leave after the cessation of exempt status (s 14(2)).

2 Deportation orders (s 15)

Section 3(5) of the 1971 Act permits a deportation order to be made in the following circumstances:
(a) Where the person has a limited leave to enter or remain, and does not observe a condition (eg prohibition on work) which is attached to the leave, and remains beyond the time limited by the leave;
(b) Where the S of S deems that the person's deportation is conducive to the public good; or
(c) where there is another member of the person's family who is or has been ordered to be deported.

The right of appeal contained in s 15 is a right to appeal against either a decision to make a deportation order, or a decision to refuse to revoke a deportation order. There is a distinction to be drawn between a decision to deport and the signing of a deportation order (see above, p 404). The order itself cannot be made so long as an appeal may be brought against the decision to make the deportation order. Likewise where an appeal has been duly brought and lodged in proper form, no order may be signed whilst the appeal is pending (s 15(2)). Where the decision to deport or the refusal to revoke the deportation order is made on the grounds that deportation would be conducive to the public good there is no right of appeal to the adjudicator, but there is a right of appeal to the IAT at first instance. Where however the decision to deport or the refusal to revoke is made on the grounds that it is in the national interest, for political reasons, or for national security reasons, there is no right of appeal at all. The refusal to revoke for these reasons may only be taken by the S of S and not a person acting under his authority (s 15(3)). Where a decision of this nature is made on these special grounds, there is merely an opportunity for the person to state that he disagrees with the decision in front of the advisers under the special procedure which the Home Office has adopted in these cases (see below p 431). There is no right of appeal against a refusal to revoke a deportation order whilst the person is still in the UK, or where he has entered the UK while the deportation is in force.

If the decision to deport (or refusal to revoke) is made on the grounds that another member of the person's family is or has been ordered to be deported, the appellant is barred from disputing statements made with a view to obtaining leave to enter or remain, for the purpose of showing that he does not or did not belong to the family of the principal deportee. He may however dispute such statements if he can show that the statement was not made by him or anyone acting with his authority for the purposes of gaining leave to enter or remain. He must also show that when he took the benefit of the leave he did not know that any such statement had been made to obtain it. Where a child under 18 years of age knows that a statement was made on his behalf to obtain entry or leave to remain, he may still dispute the statement, and appeal on the basis that he is not a member of the principal deportee's family. Certain decisions to deport attract a right of appeal direct to the IAT.

Limits on the right to argue merits   Section 5 of the Immigration Act 1988, has severely reduced the right of appeal to the adjudicator. Any person who was last given leave to enter the UK less than seven years before the date of the decision to deport is not entitled to appeal against the merits of a decision to make a deportation order against him if the decision is based on either:

(*a*) a breach of limited leave (under s 3(5)(*a*) of the 1971 Act); or

(*b*) the fact that the person is a member of the family of a person who is or has been ordered to be deported (under s 3(5)(*c*)).

It is presumed that an appellant was last given leave to enter less than seven years before the decision to deport was made, unless the appellant can prove on the balance of probabilities that he was last given leave to enter more than seven years before the decision (1988 Act, s 5(4)). A person may still appeal against the decision to deport even if falling within (*a*) or (*b*) above, if on the facts of his case there is no power in law to make the deportation order for the reasons stated in the notice of the decision to make the deportation order.

Under the Immigration (Restricted Right of Appeal against Deportation) (Exemption) Order 1993 SI 1993 No 1656, there are two further categories of person who may argue the merits of their case:
  (a) any person whose limited leave to enter or remain in the UK has been curtailed by the S of S under s 7(1) of the 1993 Act; and
  (b) any person who would have last been given leave to enter the UK seven years or more before the date of the decision to make a deportation order against him, but for his having obtained a subsequent leave after any absence from the UK within the period limited for the duration of the earlier leave.

Such leave on return within the period of an earlier leave will normally be for the remainder of the earlier leave. Leave to argue that an earlier Exemption Order (SI 1988 No 1203) was *ultra vires* because it was arbitrary in its effect was granted by the Court of Appeal in *Fuller* (cf [1993] Imm AR 177). Where a person argues that he is a refugee, he may argue the merits of that point, or that there is no power to make the decision to deport for the reasons set out in the decision to deport, but may not argue other merits of the claim. Otherwise there is a full right of appeal under s 15 of the 1971 Act for those who returned within the period of an earlier leave, with the benefit of s 3(3)(b), or those whose last leave to enter was more than seven years before the decision to deport.

In considering an appeal under s 15 the adjudicator may take account of facts which were not known to the S of S, but which existed at the time of the decision to make a deportation order (*R v IAT, ex p El Hassanin* [1986] 1 WLR 1448 (CA)). However in a case not falling within the exceptions above the adjudicator is confined to considering whether the S of S had power in law to make the decision. The appellate authorities may not examine whether the decision is invalid because of the invalidity of the decision making process leading up to the decision to deport (*Ex p Mahli* [1990] 1 WLR 932, *R v IAT, Ex p S of S* [1992] Imm AR 554, *Sasiharan v Secretary of State* [1993] Imm AR 253, and also *Aujla* (6459)). Such matters relate to the exercise of power, and not to the existence of the power to make the decision, and are properly the subject of judicial review (*Oladehinde and Alexande* [1990] 3 All ER 393). There is no power to make a decision to deport where the appellant remains in the UK with authority. Such authority may exist where the appellant is subject to the order of one of the organs of state (eg a prisoner) and cannot therefore leave the country (*Makinde v S of S* [1991] Imm AR 469). Section 5 has effect at the time the decision is made, and it does not matter that the period of overstaying started before the 1988 Act came into force (*Ex p Panchan* (1991) *Times*, 7 May), or that the period of overstaying commenced at a time when the person appealing would have had rights under the now repealed s 1(5) of the 1971 Act (*Ex p Ouakkouche* [1991] Imm AR 5). It is sufficient if the written notice of the decision to deport was given after the Act was in force (*Mundowa v S of S* [1992] Imm AR 80). The adjudicator in other immigration cases will have the jurisdiction to investigate procedural matters relating to the claim (*Ex p Bakhtaur Singh* [1986] Imm AR 352).

The IAT as a first-instance tribunal The IAT sits as a tribunal of first instance in certain deportation cases. The adjudicator has no jurisdiction for this reason in the following cases:

(*a*) the ground of the deportation decision was that it was conducive to the public good (s 15(7)(*a*));

(*b*) the appeal is against a decision to make a deportation order against a person as a family member;

(*c*) the appeal is against the refusal to revoke a deportation order on the grounds of family membership (s 15(7)(*b*));

(*d*) in 'pending related appeal' cases (s 15(7)(*c*)).

Pending Related Appeals (s 15(8) and (9)) There is a pending appeal, for the purposes of the 1971 Act when there is a notice of appeal duly given (s 33(4)). A related appeal is one against a deportation order made on family membership grounds against another member of the family of the person whose appeal is pending. Where:

(*a*) an appeal by X to the adjudicator is pending; but

(*b*) the adjudicator has not begun to hear it; and

(*c*) an appeal is brought by Y, a member of X's family, against a decision to deport him on the basis of membership of X's family,

The appeal lies in the first instance to the IAT and the adjudicator has no jurisdiction to hear X's appeal, or that of his family (s 15(8)). If the decision to deport was made on other grounds against the family member that would not affect his right to appeal to the adjudicator.

Criminal court recommendations The recommendation of the criminal court for deportation is part of the sentence of the court, and may be appealed in the same way as any other part of the sentence with the time limits applicable to the forum in which the sentence was passed (s 6(5)(*a*) of the 1971 Act and s 50 of the Criminal Appeals Act 1968). Where there is an appeal (or further appeal) through the criminal appeals system pending, no deportation order may be made.

Time Limits The time limit for an appeal against the S of S's decision to make a deportation order is 14 days from the date of the decision (Appeal Rules, r 4(7)). The time limit for appealing a refusal to revoke a deportation order is 28 days from the refusal (Appeal Rules, rule 4(8)). The time limit for appealing against a refusal of asylum, in a case which the S of S has certified as without foundation, is two working days (see Chapter 20); and the time limit for appealing against any other refusal of asylum is ten working days.

Appeals out of time Difficulties may arise where notice of the decision to order deportation is not communicated to the person concerned within the time limits set out under rule 4 of the Appeals rules. This may occur because the Home Office does not know of his whereabouts. If the person is missing, the Home Office usually dates the decision to deport from the date he is traced, but it is not unreasonable for the S of S to serve the notice of deportation on the person's last known address even where it is apparent that the person no longer lives at that address (*Pargan Singh v S of S* [1993] 1 WLR 1052). There is a mechanism under the Appeal Rules for all appeals which fail to be lodged within the time limits set down by r 4 of the Appeals Rules. If the S of S alleges that the appeal is out of time, the point must be taken as a preliminary point. The adjudicator has power to allow the appeal to be heard out of time. Special circumstances must exist (Appeal Rules, r 11(4)). In *R v IAT, ex p Ekrem Memhet* [1977] 2 All ER 602 it was held that 'special circumstances' should be liberally construed and may include the merits of a case as well as an explanation for the delay in appealing. Separate considerations apply in asylum cases which are dealt with in Chapter 20.

(a) Directions for removal (s 16)

Under paras 8–10 of Sched 2 to the 1971 Act immigration officers and the S of S have powers to give directions for the removal from the UK of persons refused leave to enter and of illegal entrants refused leave to enter. In addition there are special powers of removal in relation to crew members of ships and aircraft, contained in paras 12–15 of the same schedule. Removal is normally to the country where the person boarded the vessel (aircraft, hydrofoil or train) which brought him to the UK (see also *Mustafa v S of S* [1979-80] Imm AR 32 and *Kelzani v S of S* [1978] Imm AR 193).

There is a right of appeal in both kinds of case. The appeal is limited to a challenge as to the validity of the directions. Under s 16 the appellant can only appeal on the basis that there is no power in his case to make directions for removal. The appeal cannot normally be made in the UK. There is one exception. If the directions for removal are based on entry in breach of a deportation order and the appellant claims he is not the person named in the deportation order, then he may appeal while still in the UK. On any appeal under this section, the appellant is precluded from challenging the validity of any deportation order on which the directions for removal are based. If the appellant appeals successfully against directions made against him as the member of the crew of a ship or aircraft, his appeal is nevertheless to be dismissed by the adjudicator, if the adjudicator is satisfied that there was power to give further directions for removal based on the fact that the appellant was, in any event, an illegal entrant.

Time limits If the appellant is not entitled to appeal while still in the UK, his appeal must be lodged not later than 28 days after his departure from the UK. In any other case, the appeal must be given not later than 28 days after the appellant's departure, but may be made at any stage before his departure (Appeal Rules, r 4(9), above).

(b) Objections to destination (s 17)

When directions are made for the removal of an entrant he may in certain circumstances appeal against them because he objects to the destination named in them. If such directions are made on a refusal of leave to enter, or on a deportation order being made against the entrant, or when the entrant enters the UK in breach of a deportation order, the entrant may appeal on the basis that the directions (if they are to be made at all) should name a different country specified by the appellant.

On an appeal against refusal of entry under s 13(1), if, before the appeal against refusal is launched, directions for removal are given, or if at any stage the S of S or an immigration officer notifies the appellant that if directions are made, they will specify one or more particular countries, the appellant may in the course of the appeal against refusal of leave to enter object to the country or countries specified. Similarly, if a person appeals under s 15 against the decision to make a deportation order against him and he is at any stage notified by the S of S of the country or countries to which he will be removed by direction, he may on that appeal object to the destination(s) notified.

The consequence of those two provisions is that if an objection to the destination for removal is challenged on an appeal under ss 13 or 15, and the appeal fails, or if no appeal is mounted in respect of destination in those proceedings, the question of destination cannot be reopened on a further appeal, if the directions are ultimately made and specify the same destination.

It should be noted that the right to object to the destination for removal on the refusal of leave to enter is limited. Such an appeal can only be made in two circumstances: first, if the appellant is appealing against the decision that he requires leave to enter at all; second, if the appellant, though holding a current entry clearance or work permit, was refused leave at a port of entry. The majority of persons who are refused leave to enter, therefore, may not object to the destination chosen for them.

Whenever an appeal is made, whether under this section, or under s 13(1), or s 15, in which objection is taken to the destination specified in the directions for removal, the appellant must, with his notice of appeal, serve a supplementary statement. This must be in writing and must support his objection to the destination specified and his claim to be removed to an alternative destination (see *Kroohs v S of S* [1978] Imm AR 15 and *S of S v Croning* [1972] Imm AR 51 for some relevant considerations). In the normal case, a person is removed to his country of citizenship. Where the alternative destination is not set out in the notice of appeal, the appeal is nullity (*R v An adjudicator, ex p Chuks Umeloh* [1991] Imm AR 602, *Ex p Omishore* [1990] Imm AR 582 and *Ex p Durali Tuglaci* [1993] Imm AR 47).

Time limits Where the directions have been given on the refusal of leave to enter, the appeal may be made at any stage before the appellant's departure, but not thereafter. In any other case the appeal must be made before the appellant's departure, and not later than 14 days after the directions are given (Appeal Rules 1984, r 4(10)).

3 Circumstances in which there is no right of appeal

(a) Exclusion from the UK (s 13)

There is no right of appeal against a refusal of entry if the entrant does not hold a passport describing him as a British citizen, or as a CUKC, with the right of abode in the UK, or a certificate of entitlement and seeks to appeal on the ground that he has the right of abode in the UK. However, there is a right of appeal if the entrant claims to have the right of abode and is able to produce a UK passport describing him either as a British citizen or as a CUKC with the right of abode in the UK, or produces a certificate of entitlement.

Equally, a woman may appeal in this situation if she claims to be a British citizen by virtue of her Commonwealth citizenship and her marriage to a British citizen who holds or held that citizenship by virtue of birth, adoption, naturalisation or registration in the UK or by virtue of descent from a parent who so held that citizenship. Such a woman must show that immediately before the commencement of the 1981 Act, she was a CUKC, and had the right of abode in the UK by virtue of her marriage as described above.

There is no right of appeal at all against the refusal of an entry clearance or of entry if it is certified by the S of S that the appellant should not be given entry to the UK on the ground that the exclusion of the appellant is conducive to the public good and that directions to that effect have been given by the S of S himself, and not by someone acting on his behalf. Nor is there any right of appeal if the leave to enter or the entry clearance was refused pursuant to such directions.

Visitors, short-term and prospective students and their dependants   A person who seeks entry to the UK or entry clearance to travel to the UK on the following grounds:

(a) as a visitor (see paras 40–56, pages 82 ff above);

(b) in order to follow a course of study of not more than six months' duration for which he has been accepted (paras 57–62, pages 96 ff above);

(c) with the intention of studying but without having been accepted for any course (paras 82–87, pages 112 ff above); or

(d) as a dependant of a person in (b)–(c) (paras 79–81 and page 111);

is not entitled to appeal against a refusal of leave to enter unless he holds a current entry clearance. He is not entitled to appeal against a refusal of an entry clearance (1971 Act, s 13(3A) inserted by 1993 Act s 12). Further, a person may not appeal against either a refusal of entry or of entry clearance if the refusal is based upon any of the following grounds, namely that:

(a) he does not hold a relevant document (see page 427 below);
(b) he does not satisfy a requirement of the immigration rules as to age or nationality or citizenship; or
(c) he seeks entry for a period exceeding that permitted by the immigration rules (1971 Act, s 13(3B) as inserted by 1993 Act, s 13).

The effect of these provisions is draconian, and is discussed below at page 428.

(b) Conditions (s 14)

A person has no right of appeal against a variation of leave which narrows its time limit, or against a refusal to enlarge or remove that limit, if the S of S makes the requisite declaration in relation to the appellant. The S of S must certify, first, that the appellant's removal from the UK would be conducive to the public good. The S of S must also certify that the grounds are the interests of national security or the relations between the UK and any other country or for other reasons of a political nature. Similarly, there is no appeal if the S of S certifies that the decision appealed from was taken by himself (and not by a functionary) on those grounds.

There is no appeal against any variation in the conditions attached to a person's leave to enter and remain if that variation is affected by any statutory instrument. By the same token, there is no appeal under s 13 against the refusal of the S of S to make a statutory instrument.

If a deportation order is made against a person, any appeal against a refusal to vary or extend leave which is pending at that time shall lapse (1971 Act, s 14(5)).

There is no right of appeal against a refusal to vary leave to enter or remain if the refusal is based on any of the following grounds:

(a) a relevant document required by the immigration rules has not been issued; or
(b) the person, or a person whose dependant he is, does not satisfy a requirement of the immigration rules as to age or nationality or citizenship; or

(c) the variation would result in the duration of the person's leave exceeding what is permitted under the immigration rules; or
(d) any fee required by or under any enactment has not been paid (1971 Act, s 14(2A)).

If a person with limited leave seeks asylum and the S of S has considered the claim and given the person notice in writing of his rejection of that claim for asylum, he may, by notice given at the same time as the notice of rejection of the asylum claim, curtail the duration of his limited leave to remain (1993 Act s 9(1)). In such circumstances the person may not bring an appeal against the curtailment of the leave under s 14 of the 1971 Act, or under s 10(2) of the 1993 Act which deals with asylum appeals and mixed appeals. Although the person may appeal against the refusal to grant him refugee status under s 10(2), he may not appeal against the decision to curtail his leave. His remedy will be to bring proceedings for judicial review if the decision to curtail is one which no reasonable decision maker could come to, or which is procedurally flawed (for example, because the person has not been given an opportunity to make representation as to whether the S of S should exercise his discretion to curtail) or is based on an error of law of some sort.

(c) Refusals which are mandatory under the immigration rules: Relevant documents

A person who has been refused leave to enter or entry clearance, and a person who has had an application for variation of leave refused on the grounds that he does not possess relevant documents, may not appeal under the 1971 Act. For these purposes 'relevant documents' means:
(a) entry clearances;
(b) passports or other identity documents; and
(c) work permits (1971 Act, ss 13(3C) and 14(2B)).

The obvious remedy of a person refused a variation or leave to enter will be to apply for judicial review. In that context it is important to note the scheme which the S of S proposes for the consideration of applications for entry clearances. Those refused visas will receive a more detailed refusal notice than they did under the old system. It will set out the reason for the refusal of the visa. The applicant ought to be told by the notice:
(a) the reason for the refusal; and

(b) what points of information are lacking;
(c) that a previous refusal will not prejudice any subsequent application; and
(d) that there is no right of appeal.

The notice is to be provided to the person seeking entry clearance on the same day as the interview takes place, wherever that is possible (Charles Wardle, Official Report of Standing Committee A, 8 December 1992, col 667). The grounds of refusal which are to be treated as mandatory and against which no appeal will lie relate to refusals of entry clearance or of leave to enter, and those relating to applications for a variation of the leave of a person already in the UK.

Thus a visa national who arrives at a port without a visa may not appeal against a refusal of entry, nor may a person who arrived seeking entry for a purpose of which a prior entry clearance is required, such as marriage, or establishment in business, or settling as a dependant relative. However, not all documents required by the immigration rules are included in the definition of 'relevant documents'. Thus a person applying for leave to remain as a businessman will have a right of appeal if the reason for the refusal is that he did not produce audited accounts.

Those who are already in the UK in one capacity, for example as students, and who then apply for leave to remain in another capacity for which they should, under the rules, have obtained an entry clearance before coming to the UK, such as setting up in business, will not be able to appeal against a refusal of that variation application. The position is similar to that relating to the refusal of approval of work by the Department of Employment. Such a refusal may be amenable to judicial review (see *Ex p Barry Allan*). However, the effect of the wording of the section is that the genuineness of such documents is now properly a matter for judicial review, because failure to possess the relevant documents is a precedent fact for the S of S being able to treat the person he alleges does not have the relevant documents as a person who does not have a right of appeal, and as a person who in particular does not have a pending appeal under s 33(4) of the 1971 Act. If a person has a pending appeal, removal directions and deportation proceedings against him are suspended. Thus a person who is accused of possessing false documents may in certain circumstances be entitled to review any attempt to treat him as a person without appeal rights, and without the protection of a pending appeal.

A person who marries a person settled in the UK, after entering in another capacity will remain entitled to appeal, as will a person who entered in one capacity, but sought to remain as a dependant relative of a person settled in the UK. Such applications if refused are not refused on the basis of the absence of an entry clearance on entry, but because the application fails in substance.

The second circumstance giving rise to a mandatory refusal under the current immigration rules, and in which a person will not have a right of appeal, is where a person does not meet a requirement as to age or nationality or citizenship under the rules. Thus au pairs and working holidaymakers must be between the ages of 17 and 27 (paras 89(ii) and 95(ii)). Similarly under paras 186 (exception to the work permit rule on the grounds of UK ancestry) and 95 (working holidaymakers) there is a requirement that the applicant should be a Commonwealth citizen. Anyone failing to fulfil those criteria will not have a right of appeal. Powers of removal may be challenged by way of judicial review if there is a factual dispute over the age of a person, or over questions of his nationality in these circumstances. If as a result of those proceedings it was established that he did have the right of appeal he would then be able to challenge the refusal through the appeals system.

The third ground of mandatory refusal is that a person seeks entry for, or a variation of stay which would result in his being in the UK for, a period in excess of that permitted by the immigration rules. Thus a visitor may not seek entry for a period of more than six months, and an au pair or working holidaymaker may not stay for more than two years.

Finally if any fee required by or under any enactment has not been paid, no appeal against a refusal to vary leave to enter or remain is possible. Under s 9 of the 1988 Act indefinite leave to remain is not granted if a fee in connection with the grant has not been paid. Regulations under s 9 for the charging of fees have not been made, although it is the present government's intention to introduce fees for indefinite leave to remain. It is clear however that the power is broader by virtue of the way in which it is worded, and would seem to permit immigration officials to refuse a variation of leave to remain on the basis that any fee required under any Act has not been paid, without that decision being challenged by way of appeal.

When promoting the 1993 Act in the House of Lords, Earl Ferrers set forth the safeguards against low standards of decision making by ECOs (HL Debs 16 February 1993 Vol 542 No 96 cols 1041–1042):

(1) The leaflets to be made available to visitors and their sponsors are to be amplified and added to, in order to show what can be done to facilitate initial applications; such forms will be available from the IND.
(2) Where a person is refused he will receive a more detailed notice setting out the reasons for the decision (see above).
(3) The notice will make clear that the refusal will not prejudice a further claim.
(4) If any exceptional compassionate circumstances, illogicalities or procedural errors are raised with the FCO in the UK, they will ask the diplomatic post concerned to review the decision.
(5) Wherever possible the review will be carried out by a more senior officer.
(6) If further information is put forward in that application, it will be considered wherever possible by a different ECO.
(7) In larger posts where entry clearance work is overseen by entry clearance managers, those managers will conduct a daily review of all refusal decisions. Where the senior officer reverses the decision of the ECO, the applicant will be contacted and the visa will be issued. It will occur in every case (in a larger post) which has been reviewed.

It is quite clear however that this internal review system will not constitute an alternative appeal mechanism, so that time for the purposes of judicial review will run from the date of the original decision. Lord Ackner speaking from the cross benches in the House of Lords said of the above safeguards:

'As I understand it, the decision will have been made initially by a junior official on the issue of credibility. I do not see how an office manager, when the applicant has gone home, can confirm an issue on credibility, having never seen the party. If that is not rubber stamping, I do not know what is.' (HL Debs 16 February 1993 col 1045).

The intention of the internal review system is in some way to make applications for judicial review more difficult in that it is supposed to be more difficult to obtain judicial review if the applicant has already gone through two suits before applying for judicial review. The system proposed at present is clearly procedurally flawed in that the applicant will not be given a right to make representations to the reviewing officer in those places at which such reviews are to take place. Further, the system of review will not be treated as an alternative appeal which would prevent an applicant from reviewing the initial decision. Such powers of review are common in areas such as social security law already, and do not have that effect.

The S of S is to appoint a person, not a civil servant, to monitor, in such manner as the S of S may determine, refusals of entry clearance where there is no right of appeal by reason of s 13(3A) of the 1971 Act. The person, who will carry out an audit of ECO's decisions shall make an annual report, on the discharge of his functions to the S of S who shall lay it before each House of Parliament (1971 Act s 13(3AA)). Thus the S of S seeks to put a quality control on the decisions of ECOs. What is envisaged is a periodic review by an independent person who has been appointed for the purpose of a sample of cases where entry clearance has been refused. It is unlikely that such a review will provide any adequate remedy for the individual.

(d) Deportation orders (s 15)

National Security If a decision is made to deport a person and the basis of the decision is that deportation would be conducive to the public good, on the limited grounds of the interests of national security or relations between the UK and another country, or for other reasons of a political nature, there is no right of appeal or review whatsoever, so long as the decision has been reached following the correct procedure (*Ex p H* [1988] Imm AR 389). There exists a non-statutory advisory procedure only. This was considered by the CA in *ex p Hosenball* [1977] 3 All ER 452, and more recently in *ex p Cheblak* [1991] 2 All ER 319. The court, quite apart from the advisory procedure is necessarily restricted by the nature of the subject matter (see also *Ex p B* (1991) *Independent,* 29 January). Such supervision as the court allows itself will be very limited indeed.

The procedure was set up as a result of an undertaking given by the S of S to the House of Commons during the passage of the 1971 Act. The deportee is permitted to call witnesses before, and make representations to, three advisers appointed by the S of S. He is not entitled to legal representation, but may, at the advisers' discretion, be represented by a friend. Mr Hosenball attempted to quash a deportation order made after the advisory procedure had been invoked on the ground of breaches of the rules of natural justice in that he had not been given sufficient particulars of the allegations against him. The CA declined to intervene, in essence because it took the view that the interests of national security took precedence over the individual's interest in natural justice. However,

Lord Denning MR and Cumming-Bruce LJ did indicate that the court retained a vestigial supervisory jurisdiction over the advisory procedure.

Such supervisory jurisdiction was considered in *Ex p Chahal* [1994] Imm AR 107. The S of S must consider the Geneva Convention on Refugees, the ECHR and the Convention against Torture when considering deportation on these grounds, and must carry out a balancing exercise balancing the rights of the individual against the threat to national security.

Similarly, there is no right of appeal from a refusal to revoke a deportation order, if the S of S certifies that the appellant's exclusion from the UK is conducive to the public good. If the S of S personally refused to revoke the order on that ground, there is no right of appeal either.

(e) Miscellaneous

There are some types of decision which are outside the statutory appeals machinery. One such type concerns the issue of special vouchers in East Africa (see page 191). A further example of an unappealable decision is a refusal to depart from the immigration rules. In *Tosir Khan v ECO Dacca* [1974] Imm AR 55 the appellant sought to question a refusal of an entry certificate on the basis, *inter alia*, that other applicants in his position had been granted certificates on a discretionary basis because of the civil disturbances in Bangladesh. The IAT held that it was precluded from allowing an appeal on that basis because it was a request for the S of S to depart from the rules. The language of s 19(2) of the 1971 Act, therefore precludes such an appeal, provided the discretion exercised by the S of S does not actually conflict with the immigration rules. The same is true of a discretionary amnesty (*Purwal v ECO New Delhi* [1977] Imm AR 98). Equally, the refusal to issue a work permit is not appealable under the 1971 Act (*Pearson v IAT* [1978] Imm AR 212; see also *Latiff v S of S* [1972] Imm AR 76 in relation to training schemes operated by the DoE). However, where there is no applicable rule and a discretion is exercised outside the rules there is power to hear an appeal relating to the exercise of that discretion (*Jinnah Rahman v S of S* [1989] Imm AR 325). Where there is a request to depart from the rules the appellate authorities have jurisdiction to decide whether or not the decision of the S of S was in accordance with the law under s 19 (*Saemian v Immigration Officer Heathrow* [1991] Imm AR 489). This jurisdiction includes the whole of UK and EC law and in particular may include points of public law in cases which are not governed by s 5(1) of the 1988 Act (deportation), see *Andereh* (91331)).

In *Andereh* the IAT stated that the jurisdiction of the appellate authority is not discretionary in the sense that there is no provision for a refusal to exercise jurisdiction if it exists under the 1971 Act. The IAT went on: 'It is stated quite clearly in s 19 that an appeal must be allowed if it is not in accordance with the law, and it seems to us that that provision imposes a duty to consider that issue however that issue may arise.' Thus where a decision is made outside the rules it may be challenged on appeal by reference to s 19(1)(*a*)(i). However, the appellate authorities cannot review the factual merits of a refusal to depart from an applicable immigration rule (*Somasundaram v ECO Colombo* [1990] Imm AR 16).

Chapter 24

Appeal Procedures II: Instituting and Conducting an Appeal to the Adjudicator

1 Notification of rights of appeal

Section 18 of the 1971 Act empowers the S of S by regulations to provide for a potential appellant to be notified in writing of his rights of appeal. This power was exercised by the Immigration Appeals (Notices) Regulations 1984 (SI 1984 No 2040) ('1984 Notice Regs'). The regulations follow the requirements stipulated in s 18. The notice is to be given to the appellant 'as soon as practicable' (1984 Notice Regs, Reg 3). Where the decision is to give limited leave to enter, or to refuse leave to enter, it is 'practicable' to give notice of rights of appeal at the same time as the notice of the decision itself. Under para 6 of Sched 2 to the 1971 Act, the notice is to be given within 24 hours of the making of the decision, and if it is not, the entrant is deemed to have received six months leave to enter, with a condition prohibiting employment. Where a notice is given under para 6 of Sched 2, the notice is to be treated as satisfying the regulations. In every case the notice should inform the person of the decision, the reasons for the refusal, and whether he has a right of appeal under s 13 of the 1971 Act. If he does have a right of appeal the notice should explain how that right may be exercised. The notice should be explained to the person if he appears not to understand it (para 352). The right for a person to communicate with friends, relations, a legal adviser, his consul or High Commission if he wishes, in order to assist him in deciding whether to appeal in para 91 of HC 251, does not appear in HC 395.

Note that the notice issued under these regulations is conclusive both of the identity of the person who made the decision and of the grounds upon which that decision was made (s 18(2) of the 1971 Act). The result is that such a notice is the authorities' last word on the identity of the decision maker and the grounds on which the decision is made. Thus, for instance, if the notice records that the S of S has certified that directions have been given by the S of S for the appellant to be refused entry to the UK on the ground that his exclusion is conducive to the public good, then that is the end of the matter. The appellant has no right of appeal in that situation (1971 Act, s 13(5)) and the notice cannot be challenged as it could be, for example, if some one other than the S of S has so certified. There may, however, be grounds for an application for judicial review.

It is open to the respondent to an appeal before the adjudicator to rely on a ground for his decision different to that which was given in the notice, provided the appellant is given proper notice of the case which he has to meet on appeal and provided that the adjudicator does not seek to go behind a finding of fact of the S of S which is favourable to the applicant (*R v IAT ex p Hubbard* [1985] Imm AR 110 especially at 118-19 (approved in *Nadeem Tahir v IAT* [1989] Imm AR 98), *Dagdalen v S of S* [1988] Imm AR 425, and *Parsayian v Visa Officer Karachi* [1986] Imm AR 155, but see *Swati v S of S* [1986] Imm AR 88, per Sir John Donaldson MR at 93-4).

Notice complying with the regulations need not be given in two circumstances. The first is when the officer or authority concerned has no knowledge of the whereabouts or address of the potential appellant. There is then no requirement to give a notice at all. This rule was considered in *R v IAT, ex p Mehmet* [1977] Imm AR 56 and in *Rhemtulla v IAT* [1970-80] Imm AR 168. It was argued that the rule was *ultra vires* s 18(1)(a) of the 1971 Act. The argument was rejected in both cases. The second situation where notice is not required is where the decision relates to an application for variation of leave and the outcome is favourable to the appellant. In that case, the notice need only inform the appellant of the outcome and need not give reasons, or information, as to rights of appeal and their method of exercise.

2 Methods of service

Notices may be served either by personal service or by post.

(a) Service of notices by post (Notice Regs, reg 6)

Notices may be served under the regulations by post. Registered post or recorded delivery must be used. There is no requirement of personal service: postal service by the above two methods to the appellant's last known or usual address suffices or to the address given by him for the service of notice. If a person makes an application to the authorities on behalf of another person, the former and not the latter may be notified under the regulations of the result of the application (Notices Regs, reg 3(3)). A typical example of this is where solicitors act for an applicant. A notice addressed to the solicitors, and not the applicant, would be sufficient. In *R v Chief Immigration Officer of Manchester Airport, ex p Insah Begum* [1973] 1 All ER 594 the CA held that the service of a notice on an illiterate entrant's solicitor was sufficient in circumstances where it could be presumed he had authority to act for her.

Where a person subject to immigration control fails to advise the Home Office of a change of address, the Home Office can effect good service of notices by sending them to the individual's last known address (*Ex p Yeboah* [1987] 1 WLR 1586), even where the knowledge of that address came to the S of S's attention via a third party (*Ex p Kamara* [1991] Imm AR 423). Time for the appeal starts to run from the date the notice was posted (Appeals Rules, r 4(11)(a)).

(b) Effect of serving notice

The effect of service of a notice under the regulations is that for the purposes of the time limits for appealing, the decision of which the notice informs the appellant is deemed to have been made on the date of sending or service of the notice (Appeal Rules, r 4(11)). The document is sent at the time it is despatched in the post and not at the time it is received (*Ex p Yeboah* [1987] 1 WLR 1586). Time starts to run from that point. Sir Nicholas Browne-Wilkinson VC, regretted the consequence that 'an immigrant who in fact never receives notice of a decision is deprived of his right of appeal' (at p 1594). The question of the date of the S of S's decision to deport a person is a question of fact. It cannot be inferred as a matter of law that the requirement that notice be served 'as soon as practicable' after the decision, that the date of the decision is the date of the notice (*Rehman v S of S* [1978] Imm AR 80).

If the immigration officer does not know the person's whereabouts he need not serve notice on him (Notice Regs, reg 3(4)). Nor does the S of S need to ensure that he serves a notice while he knows of the person's whereabouts (*Al-Anbari v S of S* [1988] Imm AR 567). The Notice regulations apply at the date that the S of S's decision is taken, so that if at that time the whereabouts of the person are not known, the S of S may rely on reg 3(4).

(c) Contents of notice (Notice Regs, reg 4)

A notice under the regulations must contain certain information. If it does not, it is invalid. This can be important, because time for appealing runs from the service of the notice in many cases. If an invalid notice is served, time arguably should not run. The information which must appear in the notice is:

(a) a statement of the reasons for the decision or action notified;
(b) if the decision is to remove a person from the UK, a statement of the country to which he is to be removed;
(c) a statement of the rights of appeal (if any) under the 1971 Act;
(d) how the rights are to be exercised;
(e) the address to which the appeal should be sent;
(f) the time limit for appealing; and
(g) the facilities available for advice and assistance in connection with appeals.

The notice must, then, contain a statement of the reasons for the decision or action to which it relates. If it does not, it is invalid. The potential appellant is not, however, entitled to a written statement of the facts relating to the decision or action in question. He is only entitled to such a statement on giving notice of appeal. The notice need only give sufficient information for the applicant to be able to decide whether or not to appeal (*Swati v S of S* [1986] 1 All ER 717). There is no obligation to give reasons for the reasons in the notice (*Ex p Khushi Mohammed and Khawaja* [1990] Imm AR 439), and the notice need only contain the conclusions of the decision maker which led to the decision made.

A notice which is invalid because it does not comply with the Immigration Appeals (Notices) Regulations 1984 will sometimes invalidate the decision to which it relates, but not always. The appellant will be left without a remedy if he has suffered no prejudice by an irregularity in the notice (*Labiche v S of S* [1991] Imm AR 263, where a notice of a refusal was not accompanied by a statement of the right of appeal and was held to be valid). However, it is possible for the invalidity of a notice to be cured by waiver, including waiver by conduct (*Mawji v S of S* [1986] Imm AR 290).

The notice need not be very specific as to the type of decision of which it informs the potential appellant. In *R v IAT, ex p Ahluwalia* [1979-80] Imm AR 1 the wife of a Commonwealth citizen was served with a notice of intended deportation which referred to s 3(5) of the 1971 Act without specifying which sub-paragraph was relied upon. Lord Widgery CJ said that provided the facts of the case fell within two or more of the sub-paragraphs, the S of S need not rely on one exclusively. Furthermore it has been held that the appellate authorities have jurisdiction to permit amendments to the notice of refusal (see p 441 below). A notice should give the legal basis for the decision. It should identify the basis of the S of S's authority, and also indicate the reason why he proposes to exercise it (*R v IAT, ex p Dukobu* [1990] Imm AR 390). Thus where a notice relates to a person who has overstayed his leave the notice should give details of the date of the original leave, its length, and the extent to which the person has overstayed it. Where the notice relates to a deportation under s 3(5)(*b*) it should state why the deportation is conducive to the public good, and should recite the offence or conduct of which complaint is made (*R v IAT, ex p Razaque* [1989] Imm AR 451).

A notice must be served even if, on the facts of his particular case, a person does not have a right of appeal.

3 Launching an appeal

(a) Written notice (Appeal Rules, r 6)

Generally, an appeal is launched (or 'given' in the words of the appeal rules) by serving a notice of appeal containing the particulars described in the rules:
  (*a*) name, address, date of birth and nationality of the appellant;
  (*b*) particulars of the decision or action to which the decision relates; and
  (*c*) the grounds of appeal on which the appellant intends to rely (1984 Appeal Rules, r 6(3)(*c*)).

The notice must be signed by the appellant or his duly authorised representative. The notice must be served on the appropriate officer. If the action or decision appealed against is that of an immigration officer, he is the appropriate officer. If the decision is a refusal to grant an entry clearance or a certificate of entitlement, the notice of appeal should be served on the ECO who made it. In the case of any other decision, the notice should be served on the S of S (1984 Appeal Rules, Rule 6(2)). In the case of an appeal against the first two types of decision, the S of S, if he is satisfied that because of special circumstances it is impossible or impracticable for the appropriate officer to be served, may designate another appropriate officer instead or may designate himself. An obvious example where this substitution would be necessary would be if the immigration officer who had refused the appellant entry had died after the refusal and before notice of appeal could be served. Time limits should constantly be borne in mind. A notice of appeal must be received within the relevant time limit; its mere posting is insufficient (*R v IAT, ex p Rocha* [1982] Imm AR 12).

The regulations make it clear that the notice of appeal need not set out the grounds of appeal in a detailed, final form. The grounds may be varied or amplified at any stage during the course of the appeal. In addition, the appellate authorities have powers to require either party to the appeal to furnish any particulars which seem necessary to the determination of the appeal. This is just as well, since the time limits for appealing (in some cases as little as 14 days) do not give appellants opportunity to formulate lengthy and sophisticated grounds of appeal. The possibility of amendment during the progress of the proceedings and the powers to require particulars mean that advisors should in the first instance concentrate on complying with the applicable time limits rather than on elaborating grounds of appeal. Thus short grounds of appeal may be submitted. However, the contention that the decision appealed against is either not in accordance with the law or with any applicable immigration rule, or, if it is a decision involving the exercise of a discretion by the S of S or an officer, that the discretion should have been exercised differently, should at least be included. In circumstances where short grounds are submitted, they should be supplemented by further grounds submitted shortly after by way of amendment. If the appellant has submitted short grounds, which are sufficient to constitute a notice of appeal, together with a statement that further grounds are to follow, the appellate authorities may act unfairly if they do not wait for these grounds or at least indicate that they should be submitted by a certain date (*R v IAT, ex p Pollicino* [1989] Imm AR 531, dealing with appeals to IAT).

(b) Oral Notice of Appeal (r 6(1))

In certain circumstances an appeal may be launched without service of a notice of appeal. If the appellant is refused leave to enter, and either wishes to appeal against that refusal, or against the decision that he requires leave to enter (s 13 of the 1971 Act) he may do so simply by telling an immigration officer that he desires to appeal. The immigration officer need not be the officer who made the decision. This right may be exercised either by the appellant or by someone duly authorised to act on his behalf (for example, a relative or a solicitor). This right may only be exercised if the appellant is in the UK. Furthermore, this right cannot be exercised by a person who is not entitled to appeal while he is still in the UK (s 13(3) of the 1971 Act).

4 Interlocutory matters before hearing of appeal

(a) Respondent's Explanatory Statement (1984 Appeal Rules, r 8)

As soon as practicable after a notice of appeal is given, the respondent to the appeal (whether an immigration officer, ECO or the S of S) must prepare a written statement. This must deal with the facts on which the decision appealed from is based, and must give reasons for that decision, and must take account of the illiteracy of the appellant (*ex p Dinesh* [1987] Imm AR 131). The statement should be referred to the adjudicator (or IAT, as the case may be) and a copy should be sent to the appellant. There is no absolute requirement that this should be done. If the immigration officer concerned considers it impracticable in view of the lack of time before the appeal is due to be heard to do so, he may instead notify the authority and the appellant that the statement will be given orally at the hearing of the appeal (r 8(2)). Similarly, if the respondent intends to take a preliminary point his statement need only contain that allegation.

The respondent may, in any event, amplify the written statement at the hearing In *Bhagat v S of S* [1972] Imm AR 189 the IAT emphasised that it was not permissible for the immigration authorities to rely on and argue on appeal any ground which, though contained in the explanatory statement, was not in the notice of the decision.

However, *Bhagat's* case was distinguished in *Immigration Officer, Ramsgate v Cooray* [1974] Imm AR 38. In that case the IAT held that the adjudicator had jurisdiction to give leave to amend the notice of refusal so that it corresponded with the explanatory statement, in order to arrive at the real issue between the parties. The appellate authority is to consider the immigration authority's decision in the round, and not just in the light of the reasons given for it at the time. *Bhagat's* case is therefore likely to be treated as confined to its own facts. (See *R v IAT, ex p Hubbard* [1985] Imm AR 110, 151).

An explanatory statement can be prepared by the Home Office in concert with the immigration officer concerned, even if the Home Office is not a respondent to the appeal (*Akhtar Jan v ECO, Islamabad* [1977] Imm AR 107). The adjudicator may hear an appeal once the notice of appeal is lodged, even if no explanatory statement is lodged (*Lokko v S of S* [1990] Imm AR 111). However, both parties should be given an opportunity to be heard (*ECO Islamabad v Mohammad Ishfaq* [1992] Imm AR 289).

(b) Amendment, particulars and directions

The appeal rules expressly permit the amplification or variation of the grounds of appeal at any time during the course of the appeal. The IAT held, in *Francis v S of S* [1972] Imm AR 162, that amendments are permissible if they 'vary slightly' the grounds of appeal but not if they are 'a material alteration'. A material alteration should form the basis of a fresh application. A similar conclusion was reached by the IAT in *Muthulakshmi v S of S* [1972] Imm AR 23. An amendment may be made at any stage, however drastic, if it is simply a change in the legal basis on which the appeal is to be argued. If, on the other hand, it is an amendment which fundamentally alters the factual basis of the initial application, then it would fall within the principles enunciated in *Francis* and *Muthulakshmi*.

There is no equivalent express facility for the respondent: he may simply amplify his written statement at the hearing. However, in *Tambimuttu v S of S* [1979-80] Imm AR 91, the IAT held that the respondent could amend the notice of refusal, providing the amendment did not change 'the legal basis' of the refusal. The IAT was reluctant to lay down a 'hard and fast rule applicable to every case' (see also *R v IAT, ex p Ekrem Mehmet* [1978] Imm AR 46). If the amendment is only 'an amplification, correction or clarification of the original notice' it should be allowed. The appellant must be notified: if need be an adjournment should be granted.

Particulars Under r 25 of the appeal rules the appellate authority may at any time require any party to an appeal to supply particulars. However, if such particulars appear necessary they should be requested from the other party prior to appeal; if the other party does not comply, the appellate authority should be requested to give directions on the matter. The appellate authority may at any stage give directions relating to the appeal to any party who requests them (r 37(b)). The power to give directions can only be exercised by the appellate authority which is seised of the appeal. Thus the IAT has no jurisdiction to give directions in a matter which is part-heard before the adjudicator (*Hussain v S of S* [1972] Imm AR 264). The power to order particulars does not permit an adjudicator to order documents (*R v an adjudicator, ex p S of S* [1989] Imm AR 423).

(c) Discovery and inspection of documents (1984 Appeal Rules, r 10 and 30)

Rule 10 provides that the appellate authority is responsible for ensuring that copies of all notices and other documents required for an appeal are supplied to every party to an appeal. By virtue of r 30, the appellate authority is required, when it takes into consideration any documentary evidence, to give every party to the appeal an opportunity of inspecting that evidence and taking copies of it. There is an exception to this general rule in the case of an appeal in which it is alleged that the appellant relies on a forged travel document, if it would be against the public interest for the method of detection of the forgery to be disclosed, and supplying the document will involve such disclosure (r 30(2)). There is no provision in the rules for automatic discovery, for parties to request discovery, or for the appellate authorities to order discovery of their own motion (*R v an adjudicator, ex p S of S* [1989] Imm AR 423). If in any case the appellate authority did not comply with rule 30 well in advance of the hearing and disclosure only took place at the hearing, no doubt an application by the appellant for an adjournment, if time is needed to consider the documents would be sympathetically received. Further, it is open to the adjudicator to order a witness to attend with documents in his custody or under his control which may relate to any matter in question in the appeal (Appeal Rules 1984 r 27 and see *R v an adjudicator ex p S of S* (above)).

(d) Service of documents (1984 Appeals Rules, r 44)

Under the Appeals (Notices) Regulations service may be effected by a registered letter or by the recorded delivery service directed to a person's last known or usual place of abode (reg 6). Thus in *Ex p Abassi* [1992] Imm AR 349 the notice was delivered to the ship on which the appellant worked as his last known address. Personal service is also clearly contemplated by the regulations.

Under the Appeal Rules, service may be effected in the same ways (r 44). Documents intended for the IAT may be served on the Secretary to the IAT; for the adjudicator, on his clerk; for the S of S, on the IND (Appeals Section) of the Home Office; for the immigration officer or ECO, on the address specified in the refusal notice. The HL in *Pargan Singh v S of S* [1993] 1 WLR 1052 held that r 3(4), which has the effect of dispensing with the need for service where the appellate authorities do not know the whereabouts of the appellant, was *intra vires* the 1971 Act. So if an appellant in these circumstances does not receive notice of refusal, that does not prevent time from running against him for the purposes of appealing.

5 Preliminary points and further opportunity to appeal

(a) Preliminary points (1984 Appeals Rules, rr 8 and 11)

In four situations rules 8 and 11 provide that the respondent to an appeal may take a preliminary point. These are:
- (a) if it is alleged that the appellant has no statutory right of appeal (for example, where no destination is specified in a destination appeal (*S of S v Omishore* [1990] Imm AR 582);
- (b) if he relies on a travel document which is a forgery;
- (c) if he has not signed the notice of appeal; or
- (d) if he has submitted his notice of appeal outside the limit prescribed by r 4.

If a preliminary point is taken, the respondent's statement need only advert to that point. The appellate authority is only obliged to determine the point as a preliminary issue if the respondent insists. It should be noted that there is no obligation to hold a hearing. If the preliminary issue is determined in the appellant's favour, the appellate authority will then give directions for the preparation of a full written statement by the respondent.

Time limits If the preliminary point is that the application is out of time, the question (if raised by the Respondent) must be taken before considering the substantive issues of the case (*Ogunde v S of S* [1990] Imm AR 257). It is not an interlocutory application, and an appeal to the IAT is available (*S of S v Ibrahim* [1994] Imm AR 1). The appellate authority has a discretion whether to allow the appeal to proceed: it may allow it if 'it is of the opinion that by reason of special circumstances it is just and right to do so'. (rr 8(3) and 11). There is no such discretion if there is a deportation order currently in force against the appellant.

The Home Office will normally not take the limitation point if the appeal is put in before a person who has applied for a variation of leave and has been refused lodges the appeal within his 'packing up' time. Thus the time limit for such an appeal is 14 days, but the S of S may in his discretion not take a limitation point if the application is lodged within 28 days of the decision.

Extending time The 'special circumstances' rule has been considered in many cases. In *Rhemtullas's* case (above) the CA refused to interfere with the appellate authorities' exercise of their discretion. The facts were that the appellant had not been served with notice of refusal because he had changed his address and had not notified the authorities. This was not a 'special circumstance' case. *Rhemtulla's* case underlines the importance of appellants keeping the authorities informed of changes of address. That case is to be contrasted with another decision of the CA in *Cheema (MA) v S of S* [1982] Imm AR 46, in which it was held that a mistake on the part of the appellant's legal advisers was capable of constituting 'special circumstances'. The court also indicated that the substantive merits of the appeal were a factor which the appellate authority could take into account in deciding whether or not there were 'special circumstances'. The discretion to allow an appeal out of time should be used liberally (*R v IAT, ex p Mehta (VM)* [1976] Imm AR 174). 'Special circumstances' may include the merits of the case as well as an explanation for the delay in appealing (*R v IAT, ex p Ekrem Mehmet* [1977] Imm AR 56). No special circumstances will be found where the appellant receives notice of refusal after the expiry of his leave because he did not advise the Home Office of his change of address (*Selo Wa Selo v S of S* [1990] Imm AR 76), nor where the application for variation originally was out of time, due to the fault of the adviser. There the applicant has no right of appeal.

(b) Further opportunity to appeal (1984 Appeal Rules, r 5)

Rule 5 provides an alternative course for an appellant if his appeal is submitted out of time. This is the procedure of petitioning the appropriate officer in writing for a further opportunity to appeal. The petition is referred to the appellate authorities, who may give a further opportunity to appeal if they are 'of opinion that by reason of special circumstances it is just and right to do so'. This procedure is not available to persons in respect of whom there is a deportation order currently in force.

There is no advantage at all in following this procedure rather than submitting the appeal out of time and waiting for the respondent to take a preliminary point. The reason is that the petition procedure is a cul-de-sac. In *Ex p Bahadur Singh* [1976] Imm AR 143 the Div Ct decided that if a petition is made and considered by the adjudicator with a result that is adverse to the appellant, there is no further right of appeal to the IAT.

6 Other interlocutory matters

(a) Bail

Rule 23 makes provision for the grant of bail while persons are detained under Sched 2 to the 1971 Act and while appeals are pending. Under Sched 2 to the 1971 Act the authorities have wide powers to detain persons who are liable to examination or removal. They may detain a person for examination under para 16(1) and they may also detain a person pending removal under para 16(2). Under paras 22 and 29 of that Schedule, adjudicators and immigration officers are empowered to release persons who are being detained for the purposes of examination or pending appeal on bail.

The chief immigration officer has no power to grant bail where the person is being detained pending removal (*Re Serif Maybasan* [1991] Imm AR 89). If an appellant is granted leave to appeal to the IAT (or does not require leave and has appealed) he must, if he requests, be released on bail (see Sched 2, para 29(4)).

Applications for bail to chief immigration officers or police officers of the rank of inspector or above may be made orally: applications to the appellate authorities may be made orally or in writing. The appellant must enter into a recognisance. The authorities may require sureties to be taken. Once those having custody of the appellant are satisfied that all required recognisances have been taken, they are to release the appellant. (See Sched 2, para 29(6)).

At some hearing centres bail applications and applications for extensions of bail go into a 'floating list'. They are listed early and can go to any available adjudicator. Notices for bail hearings are being dispensed with in favour of telephone calls from the applicant's representatives. On receipt of a request for a bail hearing, the clerk will take down particulars of the applicant, particulars of the sureties, and particulars of the sums offered by way of recognisances. These details may then be faxed to the Home Office so that checks can be made. (Full details of the procedure appear in a letter from the Chief Adjudicator to ILPA, the text of which appears in (1991) 5 INL&P, 122.) The speed of the process requires early preparation of the application for bail. The whole process should take between three to five working days once full information is received by the appellate authority.

(b) Procedure at an adjudicator's bail hearing

The adjudicator will confirm that jurisdication exists for a bail application. The adjudicator does not have jurisdiction in cases where the decision is that the person should not be admitted to the UK at all. An application for judicial review of the S of S's decision not to grant temporary admission is appropriate in those circumstances (*Vilvarajah v S of S* [1990] Imm AR 457). If the person is detained pending examination, or is appealing, the adjudicator has jurisdication to grant bail. The adjudicator will then check whether there are any objections to bail from the Home Office. If there are not, he will grant bail subject to satisfactory sureties. If there are objections the Home Office Presenting Officer will be invited to oppose bail, and the applicant will have an opportunity to reply.

When considering whether or not to grant bail, in opposed applications, the adjudicator will consider the following factors:

(*a*) whether the applicant will answer bail;
(*b*) whether he has previously failed to comply with bail conditions;
(*c*) whether he is likely to commit offences if released on bail;
(*d*) whether his release will be likely to cause danger to public health;
(*e*) the period of time he has been and is likely to remain in custody pending a decision or appeal;
(*f*) whether he is suffering from a mental disorder necessitating his detention in his own interests or the protection of the public;
(*g*) whether he is younger than 17 and whether arrangements have been made for his care on release if he is (1971 Act, Sched 2, para 30).

If the adjudicator is minded to grant bail, consideration will then be given to sureties. The Home Office will be invited to examine or check the sureties offered if they have not already done so. If the Presenting Officer can state that the sureties are fit and proper persons to stand, that the sums offered are adequate in all the circumstances, and that the sureties are good for the recognisances offered the adjudicator will generally grant bail and accept the sureties. The amount of the recognisances is entirely a matter for the discretion of the adjudicator, and the Presenting Officer is merely invited to express a view.

Where the Presenting Officer is not satisfied as to the factors listed above, the adjudicator hears his objections and the applicant has the opportunity to reply. If bail is granted the Presenting Officer may request that conditions be imposed which are additional to the two that appear in form APP 6, namely the sum of the recognisances and the date and place of the next hearing. The adjudicator may then impose those conditions. The adjudicator may direct that the recognizance be taken by the Police or the Governor of the detention centre at which the applicant is held. Finally he will stress to the sureties the personal nature of the liabilities attaching to the offer of surety.

(c) Summoning Witnesses (Rule 27)

Under r 27 of the 1984 Appeal Rules, the appellate authorities have power to summon witnesses to attend at the hearing of the appeal to give evidence and produce documents in their custody or control. It is clear from r 27 that a summons may be made at the request of a party to the appeal. A witness is not obliged to attend if it involves travelling more than 16 kilometres and his expenses are not paid, or offered to him, by the relevant party, if the summons issues at the request of a party. If a person disobeys a witness summons, without reasonable excuse, he is guilty of an offence and liable on summary conviction to a maximum fine of £200 (1971 Act, s 22(6)).

(d) Transfer and consolidation of proceedings (rr 33 and 36)

Transfer of proceedings rule 33 of the 1984 Appeal Rules provides for the transfer of proceedings between adjudicators by the chief adjudicator before they have been determined. This could be necessary, for example, if one adjudicator is taken ill in the course of proceedings: it would not then be 'practicable' for the proceedings to be completed by the first adjudicator 'without undue delay'. There is no power to transfer where the proceedings may be dealt with without undue delay (*ECO Dhaka v Rayful Bibi* [1993] Imm

AR 63). The adjudicator can himself transfer an appeal to another adjudicator if there are better facilities elsewhere for medical examination, or the adjudicator has a personal connection with, or interest in, the appeal.

Consolidation of proceedings If two or more appeals raise common issues of law or fact, or relate to members of the same family or it is for some other reason desirable that they be consolidated, the appellate authority may decide to hear them together (Rule 36). The consent of the parties is necessary.

(e) Notification of hearing (r 24)

Under r 24 of the 1984 Appeal Rules the appellate authority is to notify the parties in writing of the time and place of hearing as soon as is practicable after the notice of appeal is served. If the appellant is detained under para 16 of Sched 2 the authorities may instead orally inform an immigration officer, who is to ensure the parties are present. Similarly, notice of adjournment hearings must be given to the parties unless a party has been absent throughout the proceedings, or it is impracticable to notify him.

(f) Withdrawal of appeal (r 6(6)(a))

The 1984 Appeal Rules provide that after notice of appeal has been given to the appropriate officer, it may be withdrawn by a written notice of withdrawal addressed to that officer. In *Saleh v S of S* [1975] Imm AR 154 the IAT held that an appellant has an inherent right to withdraw his appeal notwithstanding that r 6(6)(a) is not complied with. So it was decided in that case that the adjudicator was not entitled to refuse an oral application to withdraw an appeal made right at the start of the hearing before the adjudicator. The IAT did not say at what stage the right to withdraw would be lost, although it noted Lord Goddard's remarks in *R v Hampstead and St Pancras Rent Tribunal, ex p Goodman* [1951] 1 All ER 170 at p 172 that an appeal could be withdrawn up to any time before an IAT gives its decision.

It appears that counsel can withdraw a case on behalf of an absent client (*Fauzia Khan v S of S* [1987] Imm AR 543 (CA)). Where solicitors withdraw an appeal without instructions they have no authority to do so, and the IAT will review the case (*Nachtar Singh v S of S* [1991] Imm AR 195). Where someone who does not have the right of audience before the appellate authorities but who does have the authority of the appellant withdraws the appellant's appeal, the withdrawal is effective (*Tamakloe v S of S* [1991] Imm AR 661).

Once an appeal has been withdrawn it cannot be reinstated or resuscitated. If an appeal has been withdrawn from the adjudicator, the IAT has no jurisdiction to entertain a further appeal or application for leave (*Ancharaz v Immigration Officer, London (Heathrow) Airport* [1976] Imm AR 49).

(g) Costs

There are no powers to award costs under the rules. If a case is adjourned, for example, because an interpreter has not been provided by the Home Office, despite a request by the appellant, or because the Presenting Officer does not have the file because the appellate authority's staff failed to notify the hearing date to the Home Office, or because documents required for the hearing have not been verified, the Lord Chancellor's department will authorise payment of costs thrown away due to the fault of the appellate authority. It will not make such payments where the Home Office have asked for an adjournment in advance and have been granted it, and the appellate authority bears no responsibility for the circumstances leading to the request. This is an informal concession, and will have limited application. However, if the adjudicator indicates that the fault for the adjournment lies with the appellate authority, such costs thrown away may be recovered on an application in writing either to the Chief adjudicator or to the senior civil servant dealing with the appellate authority.

(h) Appeals on interlocutory matters

Finally, it should be noted that there is no right of appeal against a decision on an interlocutory (as opposed to a preliminary) point. This emerges from *R v IAT, ex p Lila* [1978] Imm AR 50. In that case it was attempted to appeal against an adjudicator's refusal to admit certain documentary evidence. The Div Ct held that there was no right of appeal on an interlocutory point since it was not a 'determination' on an appeal by an adjudicator. The court observed that if the decision on the interlocutory point affected the outcome of the substantive appeal, then it could, of course, be challenged as part of a substantive appeal. Decisions relating to jurisdiction which can be taken as preliminary issues are amenable to appeal, and the IAT does have power to rule upon them (*Lokko v S of S* [1990] Imm AR 111).

7 The hearing

(a) Circumstances in which the appeal may be determined without a hearing or in the absence of a party (r 12)

The appellate authority at first instance has a discretion to determine an appeal without a hearing under r 12 of the 1984 Appeal Rules. Rule 12 contains a restricted category of cases. Only those falling within r 12 may be determined in this way (*ECO Islamabad v Mohammad Ishfaq* [1992] Imm AR 289). A case may be determined without a hearing:

- (*a*) if neither party has asked for a hearing, having been given the opportunity to state whether or not an oral hearing is requested (*ECO Islamabad v Thakurdas* [1990] Imm AR 288);
- (*b*) if the authority decides to allow the appeal on written representations. If the case turns on documentary evidence the parties must have sight of it, and the opportunity to comment on it (*Immigration Officer Heathrow v Ekinci* [1989] Imm AR 346);
- (*c*) if the appellant is outside the UK, or cannot be contacted and has authorised no representative to act in his stead (*R v Diggines, ex p Rahmani* [1986] AC 475);
- (*d*) if the only issue on appeal is an objection to destination for removal, and the matters put forward in support of the appeal do not in the opinion of the authority warrant a hearing;
- (*e*) if the appeal involves a preliminary issue and the appellant has either failed to put forward a written rebuttal of the respondent's allegation under r 8(3) or that rebuttal does not appear to warrant a hearing.

If the appellant is abroad and wishes to attend the hearing, he may seek entry clearance to visit for that purpose. Provided there are no other reasons for refusing, he should be granted it. In particular a visit for that purpose should not be treated as a visit for an unascertainable period (*Chhaganbhai Patal v Visa Officer, Bombay* [1991] Imm AR 97 and *Aiyub Patel v ECO Bombay* [1991] Imm AR 273).

The IAT may dispense with the hearing of an appeal from an adjudicator (r 20). It can do so if neither side has requested a hearing, or the appellant is outside the UK or cannot be contacted, and has authorised no representative to act for him. Where a person has an automatic right to appeal to the IAT because he is appealing against a refusal of leave to enter when he has arrived with entry clearance and the IAT is of the opinion, after giving the appellant an opportunity of responding to any evidence submitted in writing by the respondent, that the matters put forward in support of the appeal do not warrant a hearing, it may refuse a hearing (r 20(c)). This rule is only appropriate, however, in those cases where it is plain that no advantage could be gained by a hearing. (*R v IAT, ex p Boss Wayne Jones* [1986] Imm AR 496 affd [1987] Imm AR 210).

Summary disposal Under rule 35 the appellate authority may dispose summarily of an appeal, without a hearing, if certain conditions are met. The issues raised by the appeal must have been previously decided by an appellate authority co-ordinate or superior in jurisdiction to that before which the appeal has been presented. The appellant must have been a party to that determination. The facts must not have been materially different from those on which the instant appeal is based.

Before an appeal is determined in this way, an opportunity must be given to the parties to make representations to the contrary. If an appeal is determined, the parties must be notified in writing. The notice must specify what issues were raised in the appeal and in what previous proceedings they had been determined.

In *Ramzan v Visa Officer, Islamabad* [1978] Imm AR 111, the respondent to the appeal invoked the summary procedure at the outset of the hearing before the adjudicator. The adjudicator assented and determined the case summarily. It was argued before the IAT on appeal that the procedure could not be used after the case had been listed for a full hearing. The IAT concluded that it could be invoked at any stage. Rule 35 does not envisage only a pre-hearing written procedure. Two previous IAT decisions, *Ahmed v ECO Islamabad* and *Taj Bibi v ECO Islamabad* [1977] Imm AR 25 were followed. (See also *Sae-Heng v Visa Officer, Bangkok* [1979–80] Imm AR 69.)

Lastly, the appellate authorities may hear an appeal in the absence of the appellant. They may do so if the appellant is not in the UK, or is suffering from a communicable disease or mental disorder, or is unable through illness or accident to attend the hearing, or where the authority is satisfied that it is impracticable to give him notice of the hearing and that no person is authorised to represent him at the hearing. Furthermore, the hearing may take place in the absence of any party who has been notified of its time and place. However, if that party has explained his absence, the hearing should only proceed without him if it appears proper in the circumstances of the case. Notice of a pre-hearing review may be given. Such a hearing is an intermediate step before hearing. An appeal should not be dismissed if the applicant fails to attend (*Sing and Kaur v S of S* [1993] Imm AR 382). Notice of hearing is deemed to have been given if it has been posted not later than seven days before the date of the hearing. In one situation the hearing must take place in the absence of the appellant. Under s 22(4) of the 1971 Act if it is alleged that the appellant relies on forged documents and disclosure of the method of detection would be against the public interest, the appellant and his representatives must be absent while that allegation is investigated.

(b) Procedure at oral hearings

At the hearing the parties may address the appellate authority, give evidence, call witnesses and question persons giving evidence before the authority. The parties may at the conclusion of the evidence make representations on the effect of the evidence. In most other respects the appellate authority determines its own procedure. However, it is obliged by rr 8(4) and 11(3) of the 1984 Appeal rules to give the respondent an opportunity to amplify the explanatory statement (see rule 28). This procedure does not apply in asylum or mixed appeals.

The appellate authority is not entitled to adopt a procedure which results in a denial of natural justice. Such a decision is outside the IAT's jurisdiction, and therefore amenable to the supervisory jurisdiction of the High Court to quash proceedings. However, where the applicant is denied an opportunity to have a fair hearing, not because of the fault of the adjudicator, but because of his advisers, the decision of the adjudicator will not be amenable to judicial review (*Ex p Al-Mehdawi* [1990] Imm AR 140). In such circumstances the applicant could ask the S of S to exercise his powers under s 21 of the 1971 Act to refer any matter which was not put before the adjudicator, back to the adjudicator. Thus the facts of *R v Diggines, ex p Rahmani* [1985] QB 1109, in which the appellant's advisers mistakenly informed the adjudicator that they had no instructions and asked the adjudicator to determine the matter on the basis of the material before him, would not now give rise to judicial review of the adjudicator's decision.

In *Oberoi v S of S* [1979–80] Imm AR 175 the adjudicator decided an appeal on the basis that had not been relied upon by the Home Office either in its notice, or at the hearing. The adjudicator had not indicated that he saw it as important. The result was that the appellant had no chance to address him on it. The IAT allowed the appeal. It held that although the adjudicator could have decided the case on a ground not put forward by the Home Office, he should have given the appellant the opportunity to address him on it; if necessary by granting an adjournment. In *Wadia v S of S* [1977] Imm AR 92 the appellate authority's discretion to regulate procedure was also considered. It was held that the adjudicator was entitled to exclude witnesses from the room in which the hearing was being held while evidence was being given, until the time came for them to give evidence. There is however no inherent power to control procedure in the interests of fairness (see *R v An Adjudicator ex p S of S* [1989] Imm AR 423; the adjudicator is limited to power vested in him by statute and subordinate legislation). The public may be excluded from a hearing under r 32, although the general rule is that hearings are to be held in public. If the appellant is excluded under s 22(4) of the 1971 Act, so must the public be. A member of the public may also be excluded at the request of a party or because he is behaving disruptively or because evidence is being given which in the interests of a party should not be heard in public. However, any member of the Council on Tribunals may attend a hearing at any time.

A party may be represented (1971 Act s 22(3) and 1984 Appeal Rules, r 26). The appellant may appear in person or may, as of right, be represented by counsel, a solicitor, a consular official (or equivalent), or a person appointed by a voluntary organisation receiving a grant from the S of S under s 23 of the 1971 Act. With leave, he may be represented by anyone else, such as a member of the Free Representation Unit. While such leave is discretionary, reasons for refusing it should be given, and the representative as well as the appellant should be given the opportunity to appear before the adjudicator to argue why the representative should be permitted to appear and to state the consequences of a refusal of representation (*Iqbal v ECO Islamabad* [1992] Imm AR 255 (IAT)). The S of S (or other officer) may be represented by counsel, a solicitor or any Home Office official.

The appellate authority is obliged by r 40 of the 1984 Appeal Rules to ensure that there is a record of the proceedings. This may be a manuscript summary or a record kept by way of shorthand notes or mechanical methods. In *S of S v Sidique* [1976] Imm AR 69 it was emphasised that the parties' submissions should be summarised in the adjudicator's notes. Further it is desirable that adjudicators record their impressions of witnesses (*Asfaw* (5339) and also *R v IAT, ex p Iram Iqbal* [1993] Imm AR 270).

Where an appellate authority does not reserve its decision the 1984 Appeal Rules, r 39 provides that it shall pronounce the determination and reasons for the decision at the conclusion of the hearing, and then send to the parties a record of that determination. However if the appellate authority does reserve its determination, the rule provides that it shall as soon as is practicable notify every party to the appeal of its determination and send them a copy of the document recording it. Thus an indication by an adjudicator made at the end of a hearing, that he was intending to allow an appeal but that the written determination would follow, does not constitute a determination (*R v IAT, ex p Rasiah Kandiah* [1991] Imm AR 431). A determination should indicate how the adjudicator came to his conclusions. It should set out such parts of the evidence as influenced his views adversely or otherwise (*ECO Islamabad v Ajaib Khan* [1993] Imm AR 68 and also *Raja Zia v S of S* [1993] Imm AR 404). The appellant should be able to see why he was not believed, if that is the reason for the failure of the appeal (*Jagtar Saini v S of S* [1993] Imm AR 96).

Irregularities in proceedings before the appellate authorities, which occur before a decision has been reached, and arise from a failure to comply with the rules, do not by themselves render the proceedings void. The authorities have a wide discretion to cure irregularities, for example by the amendment of documents (1984 Appeal Rules, r 38).

(c) Burden of proof (r 31)

The burden of proof on an appeal is upon the appellant. The 1984 Appeal Rules, r 31 provides that if on appeal the appellant asserts that a decision under the 1971 Act should not have been taken against him because he is not a person to whom the provisions apply, he must prove that assertion. Equally, if on appeal a fact is put forward of the existence of which it would have been for the appellant to satisfy the immigration authorities in the first instance, the appellant must prove that fact.

The stringency of this rule is shown by the facts of *Visa Officer, Islamabad v Channo Bi* [1978] Imm AR 182. In that case the IAT said that a previous successful application for entry to the UK did not raise an estoppel against the immigration authorities. On a second application, the applicant has to prove all the facts again. However, the IAT did indicate that although the burden of proof

APPEAL PROCEDURES II   455

was unaffected by the previous application, the fact of that application was an important part of the evidence in the applicant's favour on the second application. The S of S cannot be estopped by representations made by officials (*Deen v S of S* [1987] Imm AR 543, *Paet v S of S* [1979–80] Imm AR 185), nor by a long delay before initiating proceedings (*Deen*, above).

There is no reference in the appeal procedure rules to standard of proof, but it is assumed throughout the reported cases that it is the civil standard: that is to say, proof on the balance of probabilities and, in *R v IAT, ex p Mehra* [1983] Imm AR 156, an IAT decision was quashed because the IAT had applied a higher standard of proof (see also *Nadeem Tahir v IAT* [1989] Imm AR 98). (For the burden of proof in political asylum cases see Chapter 19).

(d) Evidence (Appeal Rules 1984, r 29)

By virtue of rule 29, the appellate authority is entitled to admit any evidence in whatever form, whether or not it would be admissible in an ordinary court, so long as it is evidence of any fact which appears to be relevant to the appeal. Thus the Civil Evidence Act 1968 does not apply to proceedings before the adjudicator or IAT. Notes of an interview are admissible without the need for them to be produced by the immigration officer who made them (*Giri Poudel v S of S* [1991] Imm AR 567). The authorities have a judicial discretion to exclude irrelevant evidence (*R v IAT, ex p Lila* [1978] Imm AR 50 (documentary evidence) and *Wadia v S of S* [1977] Imm AR 92 (oral evidence)). Oral evidence may be given on oath or affirmation. The authority has narrower powers to compel persons to give evidence or produce documents than are possessed by civil courts. So an appellate authority cannot compel a witness to give an answer which is self-incriminatory, or to produce a document which is privileged (for example, a communication between solicitor and client relating to the appeal). However, evidence derived from a search of baggage conducted in a manner of which the adjudicator does not approve cannot be excluded on that basis if it is relevant (*Immigration Officer Heathrow v Neil Mirani* [1990] Imm AR 132). It is arguable however that evidence which is derived from a search conducted in breach of the PACE codes, which the S of S has instructed immigration officers to observe could be excluded by an adjudicator exercising his judicial discretion.

Fresh evidence The question of admissibility of evidence

frequently arises in the course of appeals. A significant point often is what evidence of facts, not before the immigration authorities, the appellate authorities should receive. In *R v IAT, ex p El-Hassanin* [1986] Imm AR 502, the CA held that on any appeal where the question is whether a discretion of the S of S or an officer should have been exercised differently, evidence of any facts which existed at the time the relevant decision was made is admissible, even though those facts were not known to the decision maker at the time. The credibility of the evidence and weight to be attached to it are different matters.

In *Visa Officer, Cairo v Ashraf* [1979–80] Imm AR 45 the IAT held that evidence of events occurring after the decision of a visa officer to refuse an application for an entry clearance as a visitor was properly admissible. In that case the ground of refusal was that the applicant's *bona fides* was suspected. The evidence admitted by the adjudicator was that after the visa officer's decision the applicant had embarked on a course of study in Egypt, and the applicant's father had emigrated to the USA. This evidence strongly supported the applicant's contentions as initially declared to the visa officer and so was rightly admitted by the adjudicator. This should be contrasted with the IAT's decision in *Yosef v S of S* [1979–80] Imm AR 72.

The IAT in *Yosef* referred to the principles set out in *Visa Officer, Karachi v Hassan Mohammed* [1978] Imm AR 168. These are that fresh evidence should always be received on appeal provided it is relevant evidence of facts already in existence at the time of the decision under appeal. If the evidence is documentary, it matters not that it bears a date later than the decision, provided it concerns facts existing at the date of the decision. So where the applicant for an entry clearance as a visitor tendered at the appeal documentary evidence, which was not available to the visa officer, that he owned land in Pakistan, this was held to be admissible. This followed the approach of the Div Ct in *R v IAT, ex p Abdul Rashid* [1978] Imm AR 71. In *Mohammed*'s case the IAT observed that evidence of facts occurring after the decision should normally form the basis of a fresh application, not an appeal. If this seems likely to lead to injustice, it is open to the adjudicator dealing with the appeal so to indicate to the S of S.

The adjudicator cannot admit evidence going to facts that came into existence subsequent to the decision of the authority (*R v IAT, ex p Weerasuriya* [1982] Imm AR 23). A similar conclusion was reached in *R v IAT, ex p Kotecha* [1982] Imm AR 88 and the guidelines laid down in *Hassan Mohammed*'s case (above) were approved. However, in *R v IAT, ex p Amirbeaggi* (1982) *Times,* 25 May, these cases were explained as not laying down any rigid rule that fresh evidence which is relevant to the issue before the authority will not be admitted. *Amirbeaggi* itself was explained by the CA in *Mohammed Ashraf v IAT* [1988] Imm AR 101. Where the relevant decision of the immigration authority is based on a view of a state of affairs in existence at the time the decision was made, fresh evidence should, on the whole, not be admitted. Where, however, the authority had based its decision upon a forecast, for example as to the future prospect of a business, the admission of fresh evidence as to the performance of the business is appropriate. Evidence of funding may be admitted where there is a question of whether funding will be available to a couple (*ECO Islamabad v Bashir Ahmed* [1991] Imm AR 130). However, evidence of a subsequent pregnancy was considered irrelevant in *Ex p Prajpati* [1990] Imm AR 513. The IAT is not bound to grant leave to appeal on the basis that there is fresh evidence to support evidence which the adjudicator rejected (*Ex p Jasmine Miah* [1991] Imm AR 184).

Hearsay evidence An interesting case on the admissibility of hearsay evidence is *Visa Officer, Islamabad v Moh'd Altaf* [1979–80] Imm AR 141. In that case the respondent applied for settlement as a dependant of his sponsor. The application was refused, partly on the basis of information gathered by an ECO on a field visit to the respondent's village in Pakistan. The officer showed photographs of the applicant and his relations to the villagers and was satisfied as a result that the applicant was not who he claimed to be. The IAT, following an unreported CA decision, *Mod'd Ejaz v S of S for the Home Department* (21 December 1978), held that the adjudicator had not attributed sufficient weight to this evidence and had, accordingly, wrongly allowed the appeal. The CA decision is itself authority that the S of S is entitled to take into account hearsay evidence from informers in reaching a determination. It may be dangerous, however, to rely on hearsay alone (*R v IAT, ex p Lulu Miah* [1987] Imm AR 143).

Oral evidence In *Kassam v S of S* [1976] Imm AR 20 the IAT considered what attitude an adjudicator should adopt towards oral evidence by appellants. The IAT observed that even if there are inherent implausibilities in that evidence, it should not properly be discounted unless it has been challenged in cross-examination before the adjudicator and rebutting evidence, even if only by way of affidavit, has been tendered. It was perhaps significant to the

IAT's approach in that case that the Home Office had advance notice of the nature of the evidence to be given by the appellants. Although the immigration officer, if he is the respondent to the appeal, is not obliged to attend and give evidence, this is clearly desirable in the light of the observations in *Kassam*. Indeed, in *Padmore v S of S* [1972] Imm AR 1 the IAT emphasised that the officer should attend, if it is practicable, so that he can be questioned both by the appellant and by the adjudicator. On an appeal from a decision of an ECO, where the adjudicator does not see or hear the applicant, and the ECO has had that advantage, the IAT have recommended that adjudicators should not usually interfere with the ECO's findings of fact concerning the applicant (*ECO Karachi v Zafar Ahmed* [1989] Imm AR 254). In such cases further evidence should be made available. Conversely, where an appeal has been remitted from the IAT to a different adjudicator, it is an error of law to fail to consider the evidence afresh whilst taking note of the previous adjudicator's hearing, and the hearing in the IAT. The adjudicator is not entitled to accept the earlier adjudicator's assessment of the credibility of the witnesses without proper consideration of the evidence (*ECO Bombay v Vali Patel* [1991] Imm AR 147).

It is clear from the cases on evidence and the rules as to burden of proof, that an appeal is very much a re-hearing of the facts and matters on which the decision of the S of S or the immigration official was based. It is not a re-hearing on the documents, but closer to a re-trial, since evidence may be called as to all facts which are relevant to the grounds of the decision, even if those facts were not before the immigration authorities. This should be borne in mind when appeals are being prepared.

If the adjudicator can consider the merits of an appeal against deportation, he should consider all the compassionate circumstances that could be put and were put before him. These include any that have been considered in relation to another earlier appeal (*Anima Umarji v S of S* [1989] Imm AR 285). It is also open to the adjudicator, in considering whether or not the discretion of the S of S has been exercised properly, to reach findings of fact which are at variance with those of the S of S, without allowing the appeal for that reason (*R v IAT, ex p Kalsoom Razaque* [1989] Imm AR 451). In considering marriage a compassionate circumstance in a deportation appeal, the question of the primary purpose of the marriage should be approached in accordance with the *Hoque* guidelines (see page 208). If it is found that the primary purpose of the marriage was not to obtain settlement that might lessen the weight to be given to any overstaying that has taken place (*Ex p Rakesh Arora* [1990] Imm AR 89).

(e) Duties and powers of adjudicator on appeal (1971 Act, s 19)

The primary source of an adjudicator's duties on appeal is s 19 of the 1971 Act. This provides that an adjudicator must allow an appeal in two cases. First, if he considers that the decision questioned was not in accordance with law or any applicable immigration rule; and second, if, in relation to a decision which involves the exercise of discretion, he considers that the S of S or the officer involved should have exercised his discretion differently.

In any other case, the adjudicator must dismiss an appeal. The only other express statutory fetters on the adjudicator's discretion have been noted. The IAT has identical powers and duties when it sits as the court of first instance.

Section 19 makes it clear that the adjudicator is entitled to investigate the factual basis of the immigration authority's decision. (Also see *R v IAT, ex p Khan (SGH)* [1975] Imm AR 26.) It also provides that a decision made in accordance with the immigration rules is not to be treated as a decision involving the exercise of a discretion if the S of S has been invited to depart from the rules and has refused. However, the adjudicator may look to see whether the decision is in accordance with the law in general. The adjudicator is not confined to the rules and the various Immigration Acts. If an adverse decision relies on the rules, it is treated as a refusal to depart from the rules. A decision not to depart from the rules is unappealable. However the decision under the S of S's residual discretion may still be scrutinised to see if it is in accodance with the law (*Dawood Patel v S of S* [1990] Imm AR 478). Principles of the law on children, such as that the interests of the child are paramount, may not apply to immigration cases (*R v IAT ex p Girishkumar Patel* [1990] Imm AR 153 and *In Re A (a minor)* [1991] Imm AR 606 where an attempt to make a child, whose father was an illegal entrant, a ward of court was struck out as an abuse of process). Clearly where a child's welfare is involved, the S of S must take it into account in deciding whether or not to take or continue enforcement action (see page 273).

In *S of S v Purushothaman* [1972] Imm AR 176 the IAT held that the adjudicator's task on appeal is to take the immigration authority's decision as the starting point. In deciding whether the decision conforms with the law and immigration rules, the adjudicator is to take into consideration all the evidence, including further evidence, and review any conclusions of fact on which the decision was based. (See (*d*) above).

The appellate authority has a duty to consider the applicability of all relevant parts of a rule under consideration in a case, even if a particular part of a rule has not been drawn to its attention by either party (*R v IAT, ex p Tohur Ali* [1988] Imm AR 237) or in situations where the rule could be relied upon by the applicant in two different ways but is relied upon in only one (*Hawa Uddin v IAT* [1991] Imm AR 134). It is the duty of the applicant to present to the ECO the factual basis upon which he relies, and the ECO should then apply all the relevant rules to the facts before him. If he does not, the appellate authority may consider rules not applied by the ECO (*Shabir Hussain v ECO Islamabad* [1991] Imm AR 483). Where there is a close connection between two rules, and the factual basis put forward by the applicant could fall under either, the appellate authorities can apply either rule (*Ach-Charki v ECO Rabat* [1991] Imm AR 162). However, an adjudicator cannot review an application made on a particular ground, on another ground which is inconsistent with it (see *Tahir* [1992] Imm AR 157 and *Shabir Hussain* (above)).

Where an appellant does not challenge an allegation of fact, there is no duty or obligation on the appellate authority to make an enquiry into that allegation of its own volition (*R v IAT, ex p Martinez Tobon* [1987] Imm AR 536). Where an adjudicator considers that an appeal should be determined on an issue not argued before him, he should afford the parties an opportunity to make submissions to him on that issue (*Moussavi v S of S* [1987] Imm AR 39. See also *R v IAT, ex p Hubbard* [1985] Imm AR 110 and *Tahir* (above)). There is no requirement for the case to be remitted to the S of S for reconsideration in those circumstances, if the adjudicator takes a view of the basis of the decision which differs from that of the S of S on the facts (see *Tahir* above).

In *R v Peterkin (Adjudicator), ex p Soni* [1972] Imm AR 253 the Div Ct emphasised that the adjudicator's task is to exercise his own discretion on the facts. The adjudicator is not confined to intervening only in cases where it can be shown that the immigration authority's exercise of a discretion is plainly wrong or perverse. (See, also, *R v IAT, ex p Desai* [1987] Imm AR 18.) Furthermore, the adjudicator is not restricted to considering the case under the rules applied to it by the immigration authorities as evidenced by the notice of refusal (*R v IAT, ex p Tong* [1981]

Imm AR 214). However, if the adjudicator does decide the case under a rule not relied upon by the immigration authorities, and under that rule the immigration authorities have a discretion, the adjudicator has no jurisdiction to exercise that discretion in their stead. The case must, in effect, be remitted to the statutory authorities for them to decide it (*R v IAT, ex p Malik* (1981) *The Times*, 18 November). He must however decide the case under the rules and not under his own concept of natural justice (*S of S v Glean* [1972] Imm AR 84), nor under his own amalgam of rules (*R v IAT, ex p Martin* [1972] Imm AR 275). The adjudicator is limited to the rules applicable to the case before him. He cannot therefore deal with an application to enter as a wife on the basis that it is an application (outside the rules) to enter as a cohabitee, which has been refused (*Hawa Uddin v IAT* [1991] Imm AR 134). In considering rules other than those taken into account by the S of S the appellate authorities are only required to do what is reasonable, and not to construct ingenious arguments. The adjudicator should not embark upon 'any roving expedition among the rules to see if there is anything which might be of assistance to one side or another' (*Hawa Uddin* per McCowan LJ at p 144).

Findings on evidence The adjudicator is obliged to make findings on the evidence, but it is not possible to infer from the fact that he has not referred to certain specific matters that he had not taken them into account (*R v IAT, ex p Gondalia* [1991] Imm AR 519). The adjudicator's determination should deal with every issue which has been identified by the deciding officer as leading to the refusal of the application (*ECO Islamabad v Mohammed Hussain* [1991] Imm AR 476). The adjudicator must also take care to avoid language which would suggest that the wrong standard was being used to assess the S of S's decision. Thus the adjudicator should not suggest that he is considering the S of S's decision purely on the basis of administrative law principles instead of considering the case on its merits (*Clifford Ofoajoku v S of S* [1991] Imm AR 68); or use language which suggests that a non-civil standard is being used such as that some evidence is 'unconvincing' or that he was 'satisfied certainly' (*Abdul Azid v ECO Dhaka* [1991] Imm AR 578). An adjudicator is entitled to make adverse findings on a person's credibility even if that person's evidence was not challenged before him (*R v IAT, ex p Jasmine Miah* [1991] Imm AR 184). Conversely, the adjudicator is not obliged to refer to matters contained in notes of interview if they are not raised by the parties before him (*R v IAT, ex p Sumeina Masood* [1991] Imm AR 283).

The adjudicator's determination should make clear what approach he adopts to the consideration of the relevant factors. Thus where the merits of a decision to deport are considered, the adjudicator should start from the proposition that deportation will normally be the proper course where a person has failed to comply with a condition of his leave, or remained without authority, and then take account of all the relevant factors listed in para 364, balancing those factors. It is merely desirable, not essential, that the adjudicator should refer to the relevant rule explicitly (*Adaah v S of S* [1993] Imm AR 197).

Interpreters The Home Office have recognised that difficulties are caused by interpreters who are not of the highest quality or trained in the appropriate dialects. The S of S is currently reviewing the requirements for interpreters; however, he has rejected the idea that interpreters should be approved by the Institute of Linguists. The interpreter's qualifications should nevertheless be put before the adjudicator. Where an allegation of bias is made against an interpreter used at an interview, the suspicion of bias raised by the applicant may be dispelled by something less than persuasive evidence that the allegation is untrue. A reasonable suspicion of bias however, if not disproved, is a basis upon which the decision based on the translated answers may be quashed (*Saichon Chomsuk* [1991] Imm AR 29). Where the allegation against the interpreter is incompetence rather than bias, it has to be shown that the S of S knew that the interpeter was incompetent to conduct the interview. The court cannot simply judge the competence of the interpreter (*R v Mayor and Burgesses of the London Borough of Tower Hamlets, ex p Jalika Begum* [1991] Imm AR 86).

Power to give directions If the adjudicator allows the appeal, he is empowered to give such directions for giving effect to that determination as he thinks proper at any stage, including after the promulgation of the determination. Such directions should only be given however if a party requests them (*Mohammed Yousuf v ECO Karachi* [1990] Imm AR 191). The adjudicator may also make recommendations with respect to any other action which he considers should be taken in the case under the Act. He may hear evidence on an application for directions (*Yousuf* (above)). An adjudicator may not give directions where the merits of the application on which the directions are to be based, have not been considered by the S of S (*S of S v Razaq Abdel* [1992] Imm AR 152). The authorities are obliged to implement directions. However, they need not do so while an appeal may be brought against the adjudicator's decision, and, if such an appeal is brought, for so long as it is pending. In *Visa Officer, Aden v Thabet* [1977] Imm AR 75 the IAT examined the adjudicator's powers to give directions and concluded that they were narrow. So the adjudicator had no power to impose stringent conditions on the successful appellant's entry clearance, such as conditions as to place of residence and length of stay, and a condition prohibiting a subsequent application for a variation of status. The adjudicator was entitled only to give a direction that the appellant be granted a visitor's entry clearance. Conditions were for the immigration authorities alone. This power should not be confused with the power to give procedural directions in the course of an appeal under r 33 of the procedure rules (*S of S v Fardy* [1972] Imm AR 192).

If, after directions have been given, the ECO attempts to prevent entry by pursuing further enquiries seeking to circumvent the adjudicator's decision, his decision would be amenable to judicial review (*Ex p Mohammed Yousuf* [1989] Imm AR 554). However, where no directions are given, the ECO has a duty to make further enquiries and is not limited to a right of appeal against the adjudicator's decision, if he finds that there has been a change of circumstances (*Mohammed Yousuf* (above)).

When an appeal is dismissed there is no statutory power to make recommendations and the adjudicator is not under a duty to consider making one if the applicant does not request that one should be made (*Ex p Kumar* [1993] Imm AR 401). The adjudicator will occasionally make comments which the S of S may take or ignore. They do not raise a legitimate expectation that they will be carried out by the S of S (*Fozlu Miah v S of S* [1991] Imm AR 581). Also, there is no basis for an appeal against a failure to make a recommendation when the adjudicator dismisses an appeal, nor can an adjudicator who comes to reconsider the decision of the first adjudicator be obliged to make a recommendation merely because the first one did (see *Fozlu Miah* and *Grenda Gillegao* [1989] Imm AR 174).

In *Visa Officer, Islamabad v Hussain* [1987] Imm AR 39, the IAT stated that in most cases it was inadvisable for an adjudicator to dictate his determination at the end of the hearing, since errors could easily creep in.

Chapter 25

Appeal Procedures III: Appeal to the IAT and CA

A Appeals to the IAT (1971 Act, s 20)

The 1971 Act, s 20 provides that any party to an appeal to an adjudicator may appeal to the IAT if dissatisfied with the outcome. Thus the immigration authorities as well as the appellants are entitled to appeal from the adjudicator. Appeals consisting of, or containing, an issue of asylum are dealt with in Chapter 20. The IAT's jurisdiction is fixed by statute, and may not be extended by agreement (*O v Immigration Officer, Heathrow* [1992] Imm AR 584). The IAT may confirm the adjudicator's conclusion or reach any other decision which could have been reached by him. In reaching its decision the IAT duly notes matters of principle laid down in previous IAT decisions, but more emphasis is placed on the facts of the case before it (*Entry Certificate Officer, New Delhi v Bhambra* [1973] Imm AR 14). The IAT may alter or add to any recommendations made by the adjudicator, or replace them altogether. It may also remit a case to the adjudicator for him to determine it in accordance with the IAT's directions, or for him to take further evidence with a view to a determination by the IAT (1971 Act, s 22(2)(*a*); and r 21).

Where a case is referred to an adjudicator for a hearing *de novo*, he is fully entitled to have regard to the record of the evidence given in previous proceedings. He should then apply his mind afresh to the issues, the law and the evidence involved, without regard to the previous adjudicator's determination (*Mohammed Karim v Visa Officer, Islamabad* [1986] Imm AR 224). He should make his own assessment of the credibility of the witnesses, and not rely on the assessment made by the previous adjudicator (*ECO Bombay v Vali Patel* [1991] Imm AR 147).

There is an indication in s 20(1) that the 1971 Act contemplates that leave to appeal may be necessary. However, the Act does not lay down the circumstances in which leave to appeal is required. These requirements are contained in the 1984 Appeal Rules, r 14 which states that an appeal in all cases will lie only with the leave of the adjudicator or of the IAT. The IAT has no power to determine whether an appeal against a decision of the S of S is out of time (*ECO Antananviro v Hansa Popat* [1990] Imm AR 598).

1 Criteria to be satisfied before leave will be granted (1984 Appeal Rules, r 14)

Under r 14(2) there are various circumstances in which leave to appeal must be granted. First, there are cases under the 1971 Act, s 22(5):

(*a*) where there is an appeal against a decision that the appellant required leave to enter the UK and the appellate authority is satisfied that the appellant held a current entry clearance or certificate of entitlement; and

(*b*) where the appeal is against refusal of leave to enter and the appellate authorities are satisfied that at the time of the refusal the appellant held an entry clearance (and that dismissal of the appeal is not required because the appellant was an illegal entrant).

Second, there are those cases set out in the 1984 Appeal Rules, r 14. These were considered by Simon Brown J in *R v IAT, exp Rashida Bi* [1990] Imm AR 348. Leave is required in all cases and involves an element of discretion. If one of the grounds submitted is that the adjudicator misdirected himself in law, the IAT has to reach a preliminary view as to that ground. If that ground is arguable, the IAT must decide whether, without error of law, the adjudicator could have properly come to the conclusion he arrived at. If he could, there is no requirement to grant leave. In such a case the IAT should look at the case and exercise its discretion as to whether, considering the facts, it would itself have come to the same conclusion (in which case leave should be refused), otherwise leave should be granted.

By the 1993 Asylum Appeals (Procedure) Rules, r 13, in an asylum appeal, or an appeal containing an asylum element, leave to appeal from the special adjudicator is required (see Chapter 20). Under the law before the 1993 Act, the IAT was required to grant leave where the applicant had a well-founded fear of persecution, but was entitled to see if the fear was well founded before granting leave. There is no obligation to hear the applicant for leave before making a decision (*R v IAT, ex p Bouchtaoui* [1992] Imm AR 433).

(a) Arguable point of law

An 'arguable point of law' is a fairly strict requirement. In many cases leave to appeal will be refused because although there may be two views on the facts, the view taken by the adjudicator does not give rise to an 'arguable point of law'. A clear example of a case in which leave was refused under the rule is *Harmail Singh v IAT* [1978] Imm AR 140. In that case the point was whether the applicant's 'whole family' was being admitted for settlement when an elder brother was staying in India. In essence it was a question of fact, not law, whether or not the elder brother was still a member of the family unit. Leave was therefore refused. This is a harsh result, but is one which is within the rules. However, if the adjudicator reaches what is apparently a determination of fact on the evidence before him, but the determination is entirely unsupported by that evidence, or he apparently directs himself correctly in law but reaches a conclusion which offends common sense, then it is submitted that this would give rise to an arguable point of law. In that situation, the appellant would be entitled to leave to appeal. Both types of error are errors of law (see *Edwards v Bairstow* [1956] AC 14, *per* Viscount Simmonds at p 29 and *per* Lord Radcliffe at p 36). In *R v IAT, ex p Khan* [1975] Imm AR 26 the Divisional Court applied such a test to determine whether the applicant should have been granted leave to appeal. In *R v IAT, ex p Kirimetiyane* (1982) *Times*, 17 June, the Divisional Court suggested that the *Wednesbury* test (*Associated Provincial Picture Houses v Wednesbury Corp* [1948] 1 KB 223) was appropriate for determining whether there was an arguable point of law entitling the appellant to leave to appeal. (See also *R v IAT, ex p Ahmud Khan* [1982] Imm AR 134 on the need for the appellate authority to give reasons for its decision.)

The statute and rules provide, in addition, that there are two circumstances in which leave to appeal must be granted. They involve exclusions from the UK. First, if an entrant appeals against a decision that he requires leave to enter the UK and the appellate authority is satisfied that he held a certificate of entitlement at the time of the decision, he must be given leave to appeal. This is so even if the appellant freely admits that his entry certificate was obtained by a false representation (*Williams v Immigration Officer, Heathrow* [1986] Imm AR 186). Second, if the appellant was excluded from the UK at a time when he held an entry clearance, he must have leave unless he was either an illegal entrant at the time of the exclusion, or there was a deportation order in force against him at the time of the exclusion.

There is a curious disparity between the criteria governing the grant of leave to appeal and the nature of the IAT's appellate jurisdiction. As we have seen, with a few exceptions, leave will only be granted if it is shown that the appeal turns on an arguable point of law. However, the IAT can intervene and overturn an adjudicator's decision on a pure question of fact. It seems, at the least, unfair, that a more difficult hurdle has to be overcome in obtaining leave than has to be overcome in appealing successfully.

This point emerges very clearly from *Alam Bi v IAT* [1979–80] Imm AR 146. In that case the CA held that the IAT did not err in law in rejecting the adjudicator's assessment of the credibility of a witness whom he had seen and the IAT had not, and preferring the entry clearance officer's assessment instead. The CA noted that the officer, who had conducted an interview in a non-judicial atmosphere, was probably in a better position to assess the credibility of a witness than the adjudicator. The CA was anxious to stress that this was an unusual case, but the principle seems plain enough. The IAT is entitled to overturn adjudicators' decisions on what are essentially questions of fact: but most appeals cannot reach the IAT unless they turn on an arguable point of law. The IAT will generally be wary of interfering with the adjudicator's assessment of the credibility of witnesses and the findings of fact reached by him (*R v IAT, ex p Mahendra Singh* [1984] Imm AR 1). However, they may reverse the adjudicator's findings without hearing evidence (*R v IAT, ex p Hussain* [1989] Imm AR 382). If a case should turn on the assessment of two factors, on one of which the adjudicator heard evidence and assessed the witness, it might be a reviewable or appealable error if the IAT were to reverse the adjudicator without hearing from the witness.

2 How to appeal to the IAT

The first step in appealing to the IAT is to obtain leave if it is a case in which leave is required. There are three ways of obtaining leave:
  (*a*) by applying to the adjudicator orally (usually at the hearing of the appeal);
  (*b*) by applying to the adjudicator in writing;

(c) by applying to the IAT itself.

If application is made to the adjudicator, it must be made 'forthwith' after his determination. Time runs from the pronouncement of the decision if it is announced orally, or the date it is posted to or served on the appellant if the decision is reserved. Where the decision is given orally, then the application for leave must be made at the end of the hearing; where the decision is reserved, the application must be made immediately on receipt of the written decision. If application is made to the IAT, it must be made within 14 days of the adjudicator's determination, except that where the appellant is not in the Common Travel Area the time limit is 42 days. This time limit goes to the jurisdiction of the IAT (*R v IAT, ex p Samaraweera* [1974] 2 All ER 171; *R v IAT, ex p Armstrong* [1977] Imm AR 80.) If an application for leave has already been made to the adjudicator and been refused, it is submitted that time ought to run from that refusal, and not from the initial decision of the adjudicator to dismiss the appeal. However, the Divisional Court in *Samaraweera*'s case thought otherwise.

If the adjudicator allows an oral application, notice of appeal must be served on the adjudicator 'as soon as practicable' after that decision. These words were held in *Samaraweera*'s case to mean that notice of appeal should be served within the time limit applying to service (seven days under the rules then in force: 14 days now) and 'as soon as practicable'.

This limit should therefore be borne well in mind in submitting notices of appeal when leave has been granted orally by the adjudicator. If the adjudicator allows a written application, notice of appeal must be served on the IAT within 14 days. If the IAT allows an application for leave to appeal, the written application is treated as a notice of appeal. In any case where leave is not required, notice of appeal must be served on the IAT within 14 days of the adjudicator's decision. Time runs from the time when the appellant or his representatives first learned or ought to have learned of the adjudicator's decision (*R v IAT, ex p Suleman* [1976] Imm AR 147). The IAT has no power to extend the time limit for serving an application for leave to appeal, and it is irrelevant if an appellant seeks, but fails, to serve in time (*R v IAT and An Adjudicator, ex p S of S* [1990] Imm AR 166).

An application for leave to appeal to the adjudicator or the IAT is normally to be dealt with on the documents. However, the appellate authority may hold a hearing if 'special circumstances render such a hearing desirable'. In *Mehta (BKD) v IAT* [1979–80]

Imm AR 16 the CA emphasised that if a hearing is desired, it is up to the appellant to request it. The CA also said that in such a case the appellant must indicate in his grounds of appeal the 'special circumstances', which must be relevant to the grounds of appeal, rendering a hearing desirable.

Applications for leave to the IAT may be, and usually are, dealt with by the President or a chairman alone. A notice of appeal or a notice of application for leave must contain:
 (a) the full name, address, date of birth, nationality or citizenship of the appellant;
 (b) particulars of the relevant determination of the adjudicator; and
 (c) the grounds on which the appellant intends to rely. The grounds may be amplified or varied at the hearing.

3 Refusal of leave to appeal and grounds of appeal

There is no right of appeal from a refusal of leave to appeal to the IAT. A refusal may be amenable to judicial review if, for example, the IAT has failed to give proper reasons for the refusal. Decision-making bodies are normally obliged to give proper and adequate reasons for their decisions (*R v Criminal Injuries Compensation Board, ex p Cummins* (1992) *Times*, 21 January; *R v IAT, ex p Khan* [1983] Imm AR 134). The IAT's decisions on leave may accordingly be brief, but should give reasons which are sufficient to show the party against whom they determine leave, why he lost.

Where an application for leave has been sent to the IAT, consideration should be given to the grounds of appeal before the leave application is determined. If short grounds were put in, to preserve the appellant's right of appeal, there is an opportunity to put in full grounds when the IAT notifies the parties that the leave application is to be determined by a particular date. Plainly the IAT's reasons for refusing leave will be considered to be more or less adequate on a review depending on whether the grounds of appeal were more or less full. The full grounds should therefore be submitted before the date upon which the IAT have notified that the determination of leave will take place. The IAT can reconsider the refusal of leave if additional grounds in support of the appeal are brought to their attention, which were not before them when the application for leave was first made. However, they will only do so where an administrative error on the IAT's part had prevented all the grounds submitted in support being considered earlier (*ECO Bombay v Khalid Patel* [1991] Imm AR 553).

4 Evidence and documents on appeal to the IAT (1984 Appeal Rules, r 18)

The basic evidence which the IAT is obliged to consider on appeal is the evidence received by the adjudicator as contained in the record of proceedings before the adjudicator (r 18). If a party wishes to adduce further evidence before the IAT, he must notify the IAT in writing. This notice must be served either with the notice of appeal, or as soon as is practicable thereafter. If it is the respondent who wishes to rely on further evidence, he must notify the IAT as soon as is practicable after he has been notified of the appeal. The notice must indicate the nature of the further evidence.

If the notice is not served, it would seem, on the wording of r 18, that the IAT has no discretion to admit further evidence at the request of a party. If the notice requirement is complied with, the IAT may admit the evidence in its discretion. In addition, the IAT may of its own motion request further evidence to be furnished in order to enable it to arrive at a proper determination of the appeal. In any case in which the IAT decides to admit further evidence, it may either direct it to be given orally, before it or before an adjudicator, or it may direct that it be submitted in writing.

Except in a case which involves forgery of documents, it is for the IAT to ensure that all notices and other documents required for an appeal, other than those already supplied to the parties, are supplied to the parties. It is therefore the IAT's responsibility to ensure that the parties receive, in particular, copies of the adjudicator's record of proceedings since this is pre-eminently a document required for an appeal.

B Reference of cases to the S of S for further consideration (1971 Act, s 21)

There is a final avenue of 'appeal' provided for in the statute. The 1971 Act, s 21 gives the S of S power to refer any case to the appellate authorities for further consideration. If an adjudicator has dismissed an appeal and leave to appeal to the IAT has been refused, or there has been no further appeal, or if the IAT has affirmed the adjudicator's dismissal of an appeal, or reversed an adjudicator's decision to allow an appeal, the S of S may at any stage refer the case either to the adjudicator or the IAT. This is a procedure expressly designed to bring to the appellate authority's attention an aspect of the case which was not previously before it. The authority is then required to report its opinion on the case to the S of S. This procedure is not available as of right to parties to the appeal. There would be nothing to prevent an unsuccessful appellant from requesting the S of S to invoke the procedure. However, whether or not the S of S invokes it is wholly within his discretion. If the S of S refuses to use the procedure, there can be no challenge to, or appeal from, that decision (*R v IAT, ex p Nathwani* [1979-80] Imm AR 9; and see *Ex p Uddin* [1990] Imm AR 181, and *R v IAT, ex p Ali* [1990] Imm AR 531). This power has been discussed in the context of proving blood relationships (see page 222).

C Appeals to the CA

The 1993 Act introduces a new right of appeal in all immigration cases, whether involving an asylum element or not, to appeal with leave to the CA. Where the IAT has made a final determination of an appeal any party to the appeal may bring a further appeal to the CA (or the Court of Sessions in Scotland) on any question of law material to that determination (1993 Act, s 9). An appeal may only be brought with the leave of the IAT, or where such leave has been refused, with leave of CA (1993 Act, s 9(2)).

(a) Asylum or mixed cases

In asylum or mixed cases an application for leave to appeal to the CA must be made not later than ten working days after the receipt of the written notice or the determination. The President or a chairman of the IAT determines the application and must notify the parties to the proceedings of the determination and the reasons therefor not later than ten working days after the IAT has received the application (Asylum Appeals (Procedure) Rules 1993, r 21(5)). Where the IAT fails to determine any application for leave within the prescribed time, the application for leave is deemed to be granted (1993 Appeal Rules, r 30). Where the application is refused, and an application to the CA has failed, the refusal may be amenable to judicial review.

(b) Non-asylum cases

Where there is no question of asylum involved in the appeal, the appellant must rely on the rules contained in the 1984 Rules, Part IIIA, as inserted by the Immigration Appeals (Procedure) (Amendment) Rules 1993 (SI 1993 No 1662). An application to the IAT for leave must be made not later than 14 days after the party seeking to appeal has received notice of the determination (1984 Appeal Rules, r 21B). The application for leave is made by serving on the IAT a notice of the application for leave to appeal prescribed in the Rules (1984 Appeal Rules, Sched, Form 4), and may be determined by the President or Chairman acting alone, and without a hearing, unless the IAT considers that there are special circumstances making a hearing necessary or desirable.

The section was introduced as a late amendment by the government during the Committee Stage in the House of Lords. There was debate over whether the words 'any question of law material to that determination' restricted consideration to matters of immigration law. Earl Ferrers stated that this was not the intention behind the words.

The court can look at any issue of law which is involved in the tribunal decision, including any other kind of law such as European Community law. Any part of the law in which the tribunal decision was made can be included. Therefore it does not only refer to immigration law. (HL Debs, 2 March 1993, Vol 543 No 105, cols 649–650).

Further, he stated, in response to a request for an assurance that any part of the law relating to the basis on which the original decision was made included issues relating to administrative law, that administrative law is covered if that was a matter which the IAT considered (col 650).

It has been long recognised that certain principles of administrative law will found successful appeals in appeals from industrial tribunals under the similarly worded s 136 of the Employment Protection (Consolidation) Act 1978. Thus where the industrial tribunal has misdirected itself in law or misunderstood the law, or where there was no evidence to support a finding of fact or conclusion, or where the decision was perverse, the EAT will allow an appeal. Further, a failure to give reasons will be an error of law, as will the exercise of a discretion on wrong principles. Similarly, where the decision of the S of S is flawed according to administrative law principles, and the IAT refused to overturn the decision on that basis, that would be an error of law.

Chapter 26

The Impact of the European Convention on Human Rights

1 Introduction

The UK ratified the European Convention for the Protection of Human Rights and Fundamental Freedoms (ECHR) in 1950 (the main text, which has been supplemented by protocols, is to be found in Cmnd 8969 of 1953). In 1966 the UK recognised the compulsory jurisdiction of the European Court of Human Rights (ECt.HR) and accepted the right of an individual to petition the court. The UK's obligations under the Convention are treaty obligations in international law. However, the Convention has not been expressly incorporated in statutory form into domestic law; nor is it a European treaty for the purposes of the European Communities Act 1972. Nevertheless, there are two principal ways in which the Convention affects the law and practice of immigration. The first is that the British courts may have regard to the Convention in their interpretation of domestic legislation. The second is that an individual who is aggrieved by the operation of the immigration legislation may petition the court for redress.

There are a number of articles of the Convention which may be relevant in the immigration context; for example, art 3 (the right not to be subjected to inhuman or degrading treatment or punishment), art 5 (the right to liberty), arts 8 and 12 (the right to respect for family life and the right to marry respectively), art 13 (the right to an effective remedy before a national authority) and art 14 (the right to enjoy the freedoms set out in the Convention without discrimination).

2 The Convention as an interpretative guide

Perhaps the most definitive evidence of the role of the Convention in statutory interpretation is to be found in *Waddington v Miah* [1974] 1 WLR 683. In that case Lord Reid, referring to art 1 of the Convention (which proscribes the retrospective creation of criminal offences) said: '... it is hardly credible that any government department would promote or that Parliament would pass retrospective criminal legislation'. However, in *R v Chief Immigration Officer, London (Heathrow) Airport, ex p Salamat Bibi* [1976] 3 All ER 843, the CA was quite clear that the Convention is not part of UK domestic law. *Dicta* in earlier cases which supported the view that immigration officers were bound to have regard to the provisions of the Convention were disapproved. Their sole function is as a means of interpretation in the case of ambiguous statutory provisions. The limited application of the Convention in English law was stressed again by Taylor J in *R v IAT, ex p Chundawadra* [1987] Imm AR 227 (and see *R v IAT, ex p Patel* [1990] Imm AR 153 and *Ex p Jibril* [1993] Imm AR 308). There is no legitimate expectation that the Convention on its own will be taken into account in immigration cases (*Chundawadra v IAT* [1988] Imm AR 161). However, the House of Lords said in *Ex p Brind* [1991] 1 AC 696, that interference with human rights should be given close scrutiny, and in *Bugdaycay v S of S* [1987] AC 514 that where the result of a flawed administrative decision would be to imperil life or liberty of a person, the court should require the utmost fairness in the decision-making process.

Brind concerned restrictions on freedom of speech, the justification for which was the combating of terrorism. The court asked whether the decision maker could reasonably have concluded on the material before him that there was a competing interest which was sufficient to warrant interference with the human right (see pp 750, 751, and 757–758 and 765; and *Ex p Cox* [1992] COD 72). Principles of the Convention on Human Rights may be invoked in conjunction with policy statements made by the government when promoting the 1993 Act which may give rise to a legitimate expectation that they will be honoured. Charles Wardle stated (Official Report, Standing Committee A, 12 November 1992, cols 52–53):

> A number of hon Members have referred to exceptional leave to remain. This is, by definition, outside the immigration rules. The essence of exceptional leave to remain is flexibility, and it provides the ability to respond to individual circumstances. It cannot be spelt out in legislation. As I have said we use exceptional leave to remain to respond to cases that are outside the 1951 Convention but within the terms of our other

obligations, including the European Convention on Human Rights and the UN Convention on Torture. That will remain the case under the Bill.

We have no intention of removing exceptional leave to remain in genuine humanitarian cases . . . .

These remarks were made in the context of a proposed amendment, the purpose of which was include the European Convention on Human Rights, the UN Convention Against Torture, and the UN Convention on the Rights of the Child in the definition of 'convention' in the 1993 Act. It would seem to be a clear statement of policy, and would appear to require the grant of exceptional leave to remain to the parent of a child who is to be deported, as being the only way in which the right of the child to family life (under art 8) may be preserved whilst at the same time preserving the child's right to education (art 2). There is clear authority that the European Convention on Human Rights will be interpreted as imposing an obligation on the UK to preserve the child's rights in these circumstances (*Berrehab v The Netherlands* (1988) 11 EHRR 322) and *Moustaquim v Belgium* (1991) 13 EHRR 802). Thus in such circumstances it should be possible to challenge removal directions or a deportation order by means of judicial review of the S of S's refusal to grant exceptional leave to remain to the parent (see also IND guidelines, page 273). A person may be granted entry to exercise rights of access to a child (see page 190).

3 The Convention as a remedy

Since 1966 an individual aggrieved by the action of the UK has been able to petition the ECtHR for redress. The procedure is lengthy and complicated, but it may represent a valuable recourse when all other appeals fail.

The first stage in the procedure is that the individual petitions the Commission. This body investigates the complaint and then issues a report. First, the Commission has to decide if a *prima facie* case of violation of the Convention has been made out: if the case is 'admissible'. The petitioner must also overcome two hurdles: he must have exhausted all domestic remedies, and he must bring his petition within six months of the last effective domestic decision. The way in which the criterion of exhaustion has been applied may be gauged from two decisions of the Commission. In *Kamal v UK* (1982) 4 EHRR 244, the applicant had not pursued judicial review after his appeal was dismissed by the IAT. The Commission nevertheless held he had exhausted his remedies because his complaint related to a dispute of fact with the immigration authorities for which judicial review would afford no remedy. However, in *Caprino v UK* (1982) 4 EHRR 97 the applicant whose complaint related to deportation, was held not to have exhausted his domestic remedies. He had not applied for a writ of *habeas corpus*. On the facts of the case the Commission held that it could not find a violation unless the applicant had invoked the remedy (and failed) or could show why it did not apply to him (see page 510 below).

If the complaint is found to be admissible it is fully investigated by the EC Commission which then attempts to achieve an agreed settlement between the parties. If no settlement is reached, the case is referred to the Committee of Ministers. They may deal with it themselves, or it may be referred to the ECtHR within three months by the Commission or by the state concerned. The Court may award 'just reparation' to the individual, including damages. Few cases actually reach the stage of being the subject of a determination by the Court. Many are settled long before that point.

The most celebrated case relating to immigration pursued under the Convention is probably that of the 31 East African Asians who claimed that their exclusion from the UK under the Commonwealth Immigrants Act 1968 was a violation of the Convention, arts 3, 8 and 14. The Commission reported to the Committee of Ministers on 14 December 1973 that art 3 had been violated in relation to the 25 Asians who were citizens of the UK and Colonies but not in relation to the six who were British protected persons, and that arts 8 and 14 had been violated in relation to three of the applicants. The Committee of Ministers finally issued a resolution on 21 October 1977 (reported at [1981] 3 EHRR 16) to take no further action, since by then all 31 claims had been settled by administrative action.

In *Uppal v UK* (1981) 3 EHRR 391 the Commission declared admissible a claim that the deportation of the applicant and his family was a violation of arts 8 and 14 read together. This claim was eventually settled on a 'friendly basis'.

In *Berrehab v The Netherlands* (1988) 11 EHRR 322 the deportation of a father was challenged by the father and his minor daughter. The father and mother had been separated and the child had lived with the mother. The father, however, saw his daughter regularly. The deportation was held to threaten the father and child's rights to respect for their family life. Although travel was possible between the father's country of origin and that of the child, the possibility of maintaining family relationships was theoretical in a situation in which regular contacts were essential in view of the very young age of the child.

The derogations in art 8(2) (in favour of public policy) are less likely to apply in the case of a proposed deportation of one who had lived in a country lawfully for several years, and against whom the government has no complaint. Thus the deportation of an innocent overstayer with a family in the UK could be challenged on this ground. Even where the government does have a complaint against the proposed deportee, the deportation can be challenged if it represents a disproportionate means to achieve the legitimate aim pursued under the derogation. The ECtHR will make allowance for a margin of discretion left to the state (*W v UK* (1988) 10 EHRR 29).

In *Soering v UK* (1988) 11 EHRR 439 the ECtHR dealt with the question of whether judicial review is an effective remedy under art 13, holding that the death row phenomenon was a breach of art 3 which was relevant to the question of whether to deport or not and would render a decision to extradite unreasonable. The applicants accepted that where the facts of the case are not in dispute, judicial review is an effective remedy. However, in *Vilvarajah v UK* (1991) *The Independent*, 5 November (45/1990/236/302–306) the applicants argued that where the facts of a case are in dispute, judicial review, which only examines the reasoning process, is not an effective remedy. The Court did not consider that there was a material difference between *Vilvarajah*'s case and *Soering*'s case. They based their decision on the fact that it was not disputed that in asylum cases the courts in the UK can review the refusal to grant it. The court recognised that there are limitations on the powers of the national court, but took the view that judicial review provided an effective degree of control over the decisions of the administrative authorities in asylum cases.

It is noteworthy that in *Uppal v Home Office* (1978) *The Times*, 20 October, whose facts gave rise to the application to the ECtHR referred to above, an application in the national court for a declaration that Uppal's deportation order should not be enforced pending the outcome of the case before the ECtHR was refused. A petition to the ECtHR does not, as a matter of law, operate as a stay on further action by the Home Office. However, it would seem that as a matter of administrative procedure, it often has that effect in practice.

The best example of the effect which the European Convention on Human Rights has had on the state of immigration law in this country comes from the case of *Abdulaziz, Cabales and Balkandali v UK* [1984] EHRR 451. In that case, the ECtHR held that the old rules discriminated against women because they made it easier for a husband settled in the UK to be joined by his wife than for a wife to be joined by her husband. This decision precipitated the amendments to the immigration rules relating to fiancés and spouse, introduced by HC 503 in 1985. (See page 201 ff, above.) Predictably, perhaps, the effect of the amendments was restrictive, making it as difficult for fiancées and wives to enter the UK as it had previously been for fiancés and husbands.

It can thus be seen that the Convention has had an important impact on the state of immigration law in this country. However, the present state of affairs is unsatisfactory: the procedure is lengthy and costly. What is required is that the Convention should be expressly incorporated into English law. Only then will it provide an effective remedy and as such make a distinct and valuable contribution to the better protection of human rights in general.

4 The Convention under EC law

The principles on which the European Convention on Human Rights is based should be taken into account in a case involving the application of EC law (*Johnston v Chief Constable of RUC* [1987] QB 129). The Convention forms an integral part of the principles of EC law. The European Court of Justice will not permit measures which are incompatible with the fundamental rights recognised and guaranteed by constitutions (*Hoechst v EC Commission* (Cases 46/87, 227/88) [1989] ECR 2859). The Convention, to which member states are parties, can also supply indications of the principles to be taken into account in EC law. Derogations from EC rights may not infringe its provisions unless based on objective factors (*Nold v EC Commission* (Case 4/73) [1974] ECR 491 para 14, and *The State v Watson and Belmann* ([1976] ECR 1185). The European Court will take the provisions of the Convention as the general principles stemming from the constitutional traditions of the member states. The public policy derogations from the freedom of movement articles must be construed strictly, and in the light of the provisions of the Convention, art 2, Protocol 4 (*Rutili v Minister of the Interior* [1975] ECR 1219 para 32; see also the Advocate General in *Henn and Darby v DPP* (C 34/79) on ECHR art 10, and *ERTAE v Kouvelas* (C 260/89). The European Court has power to safeguard the protection of the Convention rights when acts of the EC authorities may have an effect upon them (*Procureur de la Republique v Waterkyn* (Case 314-6/81). However, the European Court cannot examine the compatibility of national legislation outside the scope of EC law, with the provisions of the Convention (*Demirel v Stadt Schwabisch Gmund* (Case 12/86) [1989] 1 CMLR 421). Where the national law is within the field of EC law it has an obligation to comply with the provisions of the Convention in its compliance with the provisions of EC law (*SPUC v Grogan* (Case 159/90), (1991) *The Independent*, 15 October).

5 Procedure for making an application to the ECHR Commission

The first step in the procedure for bringing a claim before the ECtHR is to make an application to the ECHR Commission. An application should be made on a form available from the Commission for Human Rights, 67006 Strasbourg Cedex, France (tel 88 614961). The form is called *Application under Article 25 of the European Convention on Human Rights and Rules 37 and 38 of the Rules of Procedure of the Commission*. When completed, it forms the petition under art 25, and is the basis for the Commission's examination of the case. A full statement of the case should therefore be enclosed with it. By the Commission's Rules of Procedure (CPR), r 37, the application must be in writing and signed by the applicant or his duly authorised representative, or the person authorised to represent a group of persons in multiple applications.

The application must contain the name, age and the occupation, if any, of the applicant, together with details of his representative including the basis of his authority. It must identify the Contracting Party against whom complaint is made. As far as possible, the purpose of the application and the provision of the Convention breached should be stated, together with a full statement of the facts and arguments involved (CPR, r 38). The documents in the case must be attached to the application and if there is a judicial act or judgment involved in the case, a copy of it should be sent with the application. The application should contain sufficient information to show that the domestic remedies are exhausted, and that the final decision was made not more than six months before the date of the first communication from the applicant to the Commission in which the purpose of the application was set out, even in summary form.

If there was another appeal or domestic remedy which was available, the applicant should state why he has not used it, giving full details. The Article which is alleged to have been breached may contain derogations permitting interference with the rights conferred. These may be, for example, acts done in the interests of:

(*a*) national security;
(*b*) public safety;
(*c*) the economic well-being of the country;
(*d*) the prevention of crime; or
(*e*) the protection of public morals or the rights of others.

Where the applicant relies on such an article (for example, art 8) an explanation of why the derogation does not apply should be given.

Because a complaint may be rejected by the Commission on a preliminary examination the importance of giving detailed information as soon as possible cannot be stressed too highly.

Legal aid If the commission finds the complaint admissible it may grant legal aid to cover the proceedings. If the ECtHR thinks fit it may grant legal aid to cover representation before the European Court of Human Rights where the applicant has not obtained it from the Commission.

Chapter 27

Judicial Review

It is possible to appeal against a decision of the S of S or an immigration officer acting on his behalf to the adjudicator, and from the adjudicator to the IAT with leave in most cases. It is now possible to appeal from a decision of the IAT, with leave, to the CA, and from there to petition the HL. Such appeal rights are not available, however, for many immigration decisions relating to entry, in the light of the abolition of appeal rights for certain categories of person under the 1993 Act, and may cease to be available where the IAT or CA refuse to grant leave to appeal. An application for judicial review may be brought before the Divisional Court, and thence to the CA and HL. The Divisional Court will be unwilling to entertain a claim for judicial review if any statutory machinery for appeal has not been exhausted.

Where there is doubt as to which judicial review remedy is appropriate the remedies should be pleaded in the alternative (RSC Ord 53, r 2). In relation to all of the remedies the essentially discretionary nature of the jurisdiction should not be overlooked.

1 The remedy of judicial review

The High Court retains a jurisdiction to supervise inferior courts, tribunals and decision makers exercising public law functions. The rules relating to the exercise of this jurisdiction are contained in the Supreme Court Act 1981, s 31, and in Ord 53 of the Rules of the Supreme Court. The court is concerned with reviewing not the merits of the decision in respect of which the application for judicial review is made, but the decision-making process itself (*Chief Constable of the North Wales Police v Evans* [1982] 3 All ER 141; *R v ECO Bombay, ex p Amin* [1983] 2 AC 818). The process of review differs from an appeal in that the court will not substitute its own view for that of the decision maker, as an appellate body might. Where particular types of criticism can be made of the manner in which a decision was arrived at, the court will grant relief by either quashing the decision or directing the decision maker in a particular regard. The grounds upon which administrative action is subject to control by judicial review have been classified as threefold. The first ground is 'illegality': the decision maker must understand correctly the law that regulates his decision-making power, and must give effect to it. The second is 'irrationality', namely *Wednesbury* unreasonableness. The third is 'procedural impropriety' (see *Bugdaycay v S of S* [1987] AC 514). The principal remedies are *certiorari, mandamus* and *prohibition* (see page 499 ff below). In appropriate circumstances the court may in addition grant injunctive and declaratory relief (Supreme Court Act 1981, s 34).

2 The nature of immigration decisions amenable to judicial review

In an immigration law context there are a number of areas of decision-making which may be subject to judicial review. Where a decision is made in the exercise of a prerogative power, it is *prima facie* amenable to judicial review (*R v Foreign and Commonwealth Office, ex p Everett* [1989] 2 WLR 224). There is no right of appeal in the following cases:

(a) a decision not to grant a special voucher (*R v ECO Bombay, ex p Amin* [1983] AC 818);

(b) a decision of the IAT or a refusal of the Department of Employment to issue a work permit (*R v Department of Employment, ex p Allan* [1991] Imm AR 336);

(c) questions of the proper approach to evidence by an adjudicator, or where leave to appeal is refused by the IAT (*R v IAT, ex p Kalsoom Razaque* [1989] Imm AR 451) or the CA;

(d) a decision to refuse a person entry clearance for a visit, or leave to enter for the purposes of being a student or visitor or a dependant of a student or visitor (see pages 82, 96); and

(e) the exercise of the S of S's discretion in relation to the operation of certain concessions (such as those relating to long residence). Where the extra-statutory discretion is in loose terms or not well defined, the court will rarely intervene. Thus where the decision under review is one taken in response to letters written on behalf of the applicant by an MP, the court will only rarely review it (*Asiedu v S of S* [1988] Imm AR 186, *per* Woolf LJ at p 188-9). Where, however, there is a publicly stated policy which is clear, such as the concession relating to ten years of lawful residence or 14 years' residence (pages 263-264) it will be easier to obtain a review of a decision made under it (*Miah v S of S* [1992] Imm AR 106, and see *Hussain v IAT* [1991] Imm AR 413).

There are decisions where, although there is a right of appeal, there are exceptional circumstances which make judicial review the more appropriate vehicle of redress (*R v Chief Immigration Officer, Gatwick Airport, ex p Kharrazi* [1980] 3 All ER 373). Decisions concerning the procedural powers of the adjudicator (*R v An Adjudicator (Care), ex p S of S* [1989] Imm AR 423) are amenable to judicial review. More radically still, immigration rules said to be *ultra vires* the 1971 Act (*R v IAT, ex p Manshoora Begum* [1986] Imm AR 385 and *Ex p Ounejma* [1989] Imm AR 75) may be declared to have no effect on a judicial review application. Decisions by the S of S involving the need to establish a precedent fact, are amenable to judicial review; for example, that a person is an illegal entrant. In all other cases it is only open to the court to grant judicial review on the basis of illegality, irrationality, or procedural impropriety (see below, *Swati v S of S* [1986] Imm AR 88; *Ex p Bugdaycay* [1987] AC 514.) Thus it is possible to review a decision to deport (*R v IAT, ex p Bakhtaur Singh* [1986] Imm AR 352); or a 'port refusal' of leave to enter (*R v IAT, ex p Lulu Miah* [1987] Imm AR 143), or a refusal to grant temporary admission (*Vilvarajah v S of S* [1990] Imm AR 457).

In deciding whether a decision is amenable to judicial review it is necessary to distinguish between errors of fact and errors of law, for it is only in respect of the latter that the court will exercise its discretion. Where fact finding is left to the decision maker and the complaint is about a fact which the decision maker has found, the court will be unlikely to intervene. Where the decision has been taken perversely, the court may intervene on the facts (*R v Hillingdon London BC, ex p Puklhoffer* [1986] AC 484). Where the decision maker makes the decision as to the facts on the basis of no evidence at all, there is an error of law (*Edwards v Bairstow* [1956] AC 14). On the other hand, the weight to be attached to a particular piece of evidence is for the decision maker (*Mohammed Jaifrey v S of S* [1990] Imm AR 6), and the court will not interfere where it is felt that not enough weight has been attached to a piece of evidence. The court will intervene if the evidence relates to a fact which is the basis for the power of the decision maker or the administrative action taken, and goes to prove that the facts were not such as to give rise to that jurisdiction (*Ex p Khawaja* [1984] AC 74).

(a) Threats to life and liberty, and interference with human rights

When considering a decision which it is said is reviewable and involves questions of life and liberty, the principle is that rigorous examination should be given to the decision to ensure that it is in no way flawed, in accordance with the gravity of the issue which the decision determines.

The most fundamental of all human rights is the individual's right to life and when an administrative decision under challenge is said to be one which may put the applicant's life at risk, the basis of the decision must surely call for the most anxious scrutiny. (*Ex p Bugdaycay* [1987] 1 All ER 940, *per* Lord Bridge).

Lord Templeman spoke of a similar special responsibility 'where the result of a flawed decision may imperil life or liberty'. In *Bugdaycay* Lord Templeman stated that all questions of fact on which the discretionary decision whether to grant or withhold leave to enter or remain depends must necessarily be determined by the immigration officer or the S of S. The question whether an applicant for leave to enter is or is not a refugee is only one, if a particularly important one, of a multiplicity of questions which immigration officers must determine daily. Determination of such questions is now open to challenge in the appeals system on the merits of the claim.

Interference with human rights Decisions which involve interference with human rights should be subjected to close scrutiny (*Ex p Brind* [1991] 1 AC 696). Where the person has relied on issues which do not raise questions under the 1954 Convention on Refugees, but nevertheless raise issues of human rights in which life or liberty are at risk, such fundamental scrutiny by means of judicial review is appropriate. The court should ensure that the decision-making process has been wholly fair throughout (*Gaima v S of S* [1989] Imm AR 205). Where a refusal of leave to enter is based on facts disclosing a criminal offence, the S of S is not required to establish that these are precedent facts (*Ex p Mohammed Fazor Ali* [1988] Imm AR 274). The existence of an allegation of human rights violation does not require the court to consider the state of the facts, but merely to give close scrutiny to the decision-making process.

(b) Precedent facts: illegal entrants, and claims 'without foundation'

Certain facts must be shown to exist for particular powers to be available to the S of S. Thus the S of S may only claim that an asylum claim which is appealed to the special adjudicator later than two days after the decision is out of time if in fact the claim is without foundation according to the 1993 Act, Sched 2, para 5(3). The fact that a person does not hold a relevant document for the purposes of having a right of appeal against a refusal of entry, is a precedent fact for the purposes of the question of whether he has a right of appeal under the 1971 Act. Similarly, a person may only be detained and removed as an illegal entrant if in fact he is an illegal entrant. A person entering in breach of the immigration laws is an illegal entrant no matter what his state of knowledge is at the time of entry (*Mokuolu v S of S* [1989] Imm AR 51). The S of S is not obliged to show how the entrant entered the UK (*Ex p Musawwir* [1989] Imm AR 297), but where it is alleged that entry was effected by deception the HL in *Ex p Khawaja* [1984] AC 74 has held that the courts have greater powers to review decisions which concern illegal entrants. A person who is detained pending removal as an illegal entrant may apply for judicial review or *habeas corpus*. In such an application the burden falls on the S of S or the immigration authorities to satisfy the court to a high standard on a balance of probabilities that the facts on which their powers depend (ie that the person entered in breach of the immigration laws) did in fact exist at the time the power was exercised. If the facts are not shown to exist the exercise of the power was outside the Act and illegal. If the facts are shown to exist the court can go on to consider in the usual way whether there has been any illegality, irrationality or procedural impropriety in the decision-making process. The exercise of the administrative power requires the existence of certain facts, entitling the court to exercise a wider power of review especially where it involves questions of a person's liberty. The power to remove illegal entrants under the 1971 Act, Sched 2, para 9 only arises where the entrant is in fact an illegal entrant. By contrast, a decision as to whether to grant leave to enter the UK is one in respect of which the court will only consider the reasoning process. That reasoning process may be challenged as illegal, irrational or procedurally unfair without considering whether in reality certain facts existed.

In such decisions factual issues are determined by the immigration officer or the S of S in the exercise of discretion vested in them by the 1971 Act, s 4(1), and it is purely the factual situation known to the immigration officer that will be of concern to the court. The court will not hold a decision to be unreasonable on *Wednesbury* principles if it can only be shown to be so on evidence which was not before the immigration officer at the time of the decision (*Ex p Johny Suarez* [1991] Imm AR 54). Even where a person claims that a threat to life or liberty is involved, the information must be before the S of S before it can form part of a challenge to his decision (eg *Zibrilla Alassini v S of S* [1991] Imm AR 367).

3 Grounds for judicial review

In *CCSU v Minister for Civil Service* [1985] AC 374, three heads of challenge were identified. These were illegality, irrationality and procedural impropriety. A further head, lack of proportionality, was recognised, and is considered below under 'irrationality' (page 488). In *Nottinghamshire CC v S of S for the Environment* [1986] AC 240 this analysis was said to be classical, but not exhaustive.

(a) Illegality

Where the decision-maker is charged with a public duty, and makes a decision based on an erroneous proposition of law, he exceeds his jurisdiction and the decision may be judicially reviewed (*Anisminic Ltd v Foreign Compensation Commission* [1969] 2 AC 147). Where the decision made was one which the terms of the empowering statute or regulation did not permit the decision maker to make, there is an error of law amenable to judicial review. Thus questions of construction of terms of the statute empowering administrative action will be properly brought before the court on a judicial review, since the scope of the power is determined by the scope of the term. Similarly, the immigration rules are capable of construction to show the extent of the discretionary power vested in the immigration officer (*R v Immigration Officer Gatwick, ex p Kharrazi* [1980] 3 All ER 373, *R v IAT, ex p Akhtar* [1991] Imm AR 326). However, the powers conferred on the immigration officer include such powers as are reasonably incidental to the performance of his duties.

Many of the powers granted to immigration officers are

discretionary. Decisions made pursuant to those powers may be illegal if any of the following have taken place:
(a) fettering of the discretion of the immigration officer by his imposing limits on his future freedom to make decisions, or willingness to hear an applicant (*BOC Ltd v Ministry of Technology* [1971] AC 610; *Ex p Tarrant* [1985] QB 251);
(b) taking account of irrelevant matters or failing to take into account relevant matters (*R v IAT, ex p Bakhtaur Singh* [1986] 1 WLR 910);
(c) unlawful subdelegation of his decision-making power; however, an immigration officer is expressly permitted to delegate some of his powers to agents, such as the power to detain a person.

Judicial review may be the only way in which a practice or a policy of the S of S may be challenged. Since the powers conferred on the S of S under the 1971 Act are broad it will be difficult to argue that a policy or rule fetters the discretion of immigration officers illegitimately. In *Ex p Samya Ounejma* [1989] Imm AR 75, the immigration rules which provide for mandatory refusal of certain persons arriving who have not obtained entry clearance in advance were challenged as fettering the discretion vested in the immigration officer under the 1971 Act. If an instruction is issued which is inconsistent with the immigration rules (under the 1971 Act, Sched 2, para 1(3)) it can be challenged as an illegitimate fetter on the discretion of the immigration officer. Although it is a fetter on the power of the immigration officer the 1971 Act permitted the S of S to give directions as to how the immigration officers are to exercise their discretion.

Illegality may arise where the S of S has delegated a power. In *Oladehinde v IAT* [1990] 3 All ER 393 the HL held that immigration officers were not holders of a statutory office, but civil servants within the Home Office. The S of S was entitled to delegate the exercise of his statutory powers. The 1971 Act did not expressly or impliedly limit his powers of delegation in relation to deportation decisions.

Oral decisions of a decision maker may be reviewed where there is a discernable error of law contained in the reasons for the decision (*R v Crown Court at Knightsbridge, ex p International Sporting Club (London) Ltd* [1982] QB 304). Thus if an immigration officer gives a reasoned oral decision it will be amenable to review and should be noted down.

(b) Irrationality

In *Associated Provincial Picture Houses Ltd v Wednesbury Corp* [1948] 1 KB 223, it was held that a decision will be amenable to judicial review if the decision maker

(a) has taken into account matters which ought not to be taken into account, or has refused to take into account matters which ought to have been taken into account;

(b) although observing (a), the decision maker has nevertheless come to a conclusion so unreasonable that no reasonable decision maker properly directing itself on the law could ever have made it.

The court needs to be persuaded that it is not merely substituting its own discretion for that of the decision maker (*Swati v S of S* [1986] 1 WLR 477 and *Hukan Said v IAT* [1989] Imm AR 372) before it will grant relief on this basis. Consideration of whether the decision is unreasonable will be weighed against the needs of good administration. The courts are particularly reluctant to interfere with questions of the weight given to evidence (*Mohammed Jaifrey v S of S* [1990] Imm AR 6).

Relevant and irrelevant considerations A factor may be rendered irrelevant by reliance being placed upon it, or by undue prominence being given to it in relation to factors which might counterbalance it (*R v Police Complaints Board, ex p Madden* [1983] 1 WLR 447). However, if there is information on the basis of which the immigration officer could legitimately have concluded as he did, the court is likely to hold that the decision is not reviewable on this ground (see eg *Nkiti v Immigration Officer, Gatwick* [1989] Imm AR 585).

More often the complaint will be that some relevant piece of information was not taken into account. Relevance will be dictated by the framework provided by the rules, and the nature of the decision being made. Thus Ralph Gibson LJ in *Mowla* [1991] Imm AR 210 stated (p 86 H) that a decision could be open to challenge if it could be shown to have been made in disregard of the facts known to the immigration officer as to the applicant's conduct or history while in the UK for the purposes of consideration under para 60. In a deportation case it is possible to argue that the known effects of a deportation order, which have an unacceptable consequence, should be taken into account when considering compassionate circumstances. Thus in *Ex p Alavi Veigho* [1989] *Times*, 22 August, the existence of the death penalty for drug smuggling in the proposed country of return should have been taken into account in considering compassionate circumstances. In *Re Musisi* [1987] AC 514 the HL held that the S of S should consider a third country's policy of repatriation if the facts require him to do so in an asylum case.

Unreasonable decisions In *CCSU v Minister for the Civil Service* [1985] AC 374 at 410, Lord Diplock stated the principle of irrationality:

By 'irrationality' I mean what can now succinctly be referred to as '*Wednesbury* unreasonableness' .... It applies to a decision which is so outrageous in its defiance of logic or of accepted moral standards that no sensible person who had applied his mind to the question to be decided could have arrived at it.

Where the S of S is being challenged on the basis of a failure to adhere to a policy statement, it will be necessary to show that the facts of the case satisfied the terms of that policy before the applicant can show that the decision not to observe it was inconsistent and so unreasonable (*Ex p Steve Ken Amoa* [1992] Imm AR 218). The assertion that a decision is illogical or in outrageous contravention of accepted moral principles will be weighed against the needs of good administration, as seen by the court. The court will weigh the assertion of the decision maker that he has taken into account all relevant circumstances against consideration of whether a reasonable decision maker properly aware of his duties and powers could have reached the same decision. Thus where leave to move for judicial review had been granted, the S of S withdrew the decision under review. He gave the same reasons for a second refusal as for the first. The court refused to find that this automatically resulted in an unreasonable decision on the second occasion (*Ex p Nzamba-Liloneo* [1993] Imm AR 225).

Proportionality In the *CCSU* case [1985] AC 374 it was accepted that there was a head of challenge whereby a decision of the S of S may be irrational because the means used by him to achieve an aim (eg, of immigration control) is disproportionate to that aim, having regard to less drastic alternatives open to him. Such considerations may apply where the S of S has announced a concession which provides in a given case a less drastic alternative to the strict application of the immigration rules. However, the HL in *Ex p Brind* [1991] 1 AC 696 held that the principle of proportionality was not a distinct ground of challenge in English law. A decision may be unreasonable because it bears no reasonable relation to the objectives of the principles under which it was taken, and the circumstances of the case, ie that it is a disproportionate decision (*CCSU v Minister for Civil Service* (above)). Proportionality will be recognised as an aspect of irrationality in that total lack of proportionality would lead to a decision which no reasonable decision maker could make, but unless it leads to the conclusion that the decision was irrational it requires a consideration of the merits of the claim, and is therefore not an aspect of UK judicial review (see Lord Ackner in *Brind*, above, at p 762). However, if the court is asked to consider the application of EC law, the principle of proportionality may be applied (*Thomas v Chief Adjudication Officer* [1991] 2 QB 164). Under EC law it is a recognised separate head of challenge. The action proposed by a decision maker must be necessary for the achievement of an accepted goal in EC law, and bear a reasonable relation to that objective.

(c) Procedural impropriety

Where the decision maker is supposed to follow a procedure and does not, the court will look to the effect of that non-compliance, and will have to be convinced that a procedural impropriety made no difference before refusing to act on it (*Ali Celik v S of S* [1991] Imm AR 8). If the procedural breach had no effect on the applicant, judicial review may in the court's discretion not be granted (*Ali Celik*). Breaches of procedure are regarded seriously where the consequences of a breach of procedure are serious for the applicant, such as in cases where there is a threat to life or liberty.

Where the decision maker is not obliged to give reasons by a statutory scheme, he is still obliged to give proper and adequate reasons for the decision (*R v Criminal Injuries Compensation Board, ex p Cummins* (1992) *Times*, 21 January; *R v IAT, ex p Khan* [1982] Imm AR 134, *R v Civil Service Appeal Board, ex p Cunningham* [1991] 4 All ER 310). However, after being notified of a challenge by way of judicial review the S of S may supply full reasons for the decision. In *Ex p Ul-Haq* [1993] Imm AR 144 Hutchison J refused to restrict consideration of the S of S's reasons to those given at the date of the original decision where new material has been placed before the S of S after that time.

Duty to be fair Natural justice should be observed in immigration matters as much as in other administrative decisions. Thus an immigration officer, although acting other than in a judicial capacity, is under a duty to act fairly in carrying out the decision-making process (*Re HK* [1967] 2 QB 617; *O'Reilly v Mackman*

[1983] 2 AC 237 at 275 *per* Lord Diplock). The court will focus on the activities of the decision maker as a whole and ask whether with regard to those activities something has 'gone wrong' in nature and degree to warrant the intervention of the court, and whether it has resulted in real injustice. If it has the court has to intervene, because a decision maker is not entitled to confer on itself the power to inflict injustice on those subject to its control (see Woolf LJ in *R v Panel on Takeovers and Mergers, ex p Guiness plc* [1990] 1 QB 146 at 193-4). Lord Denning MR in *Ex p Santillo* [1981] QB 778 said at p 795: 'The rules of natural justice—or fairness—are not cut and dried. They vary infinitely'. What they demand depends on the character of the decision-maker and the kind of decision being made in the statutory framework of the 1971 or 1993 Acts. Thus regard is to be had to the immigration rules and the Appeal Rules, together with the requirements of the Acts and the consequences of the decision, before deciding what are the requirements of fairness in the particular case.

Fairness includes the right to a fair hearing (*Ridge v Baldwin* [1964] AC 40) which is 'of universal application' (*per* Lord Reid, p 69). This requirement will be implied into a procedure under a statute where it is clear that the statutory procedure alone is insufficient to achieve justice, and that to require additional steps would not frustrate the apparent purpose of the legislation (*Wiseman v Borneman* [1971] AC 297, *per* Lord Reid at p 308). Thus under the 1993 Act, s 13(3AA) provision is made for the 'auditing' of ECO's refusals of applications for leave to enter (see page 431). The statute is clearly aiming to provide a review of the ECO's decision. The provisions of the 1993 Act do not in relation to any individual case provide a procedure sufficient to achieve justice in any particular case. The courts will be likely to infer that the rules of fairness are to be observed in relation to any review of the ECO's decision on a particular application: the applicant should have the right to be heard (see in particular the non-statutory scheme of review which is proposed under the 1993 Act (page 429). Moreover, it is clearly not the intention of the 1993 Act to preclude such principles from being applied save in cases where under statutory instruments, hearings are not required (see, eg, the 1993 Asylum Appeal Rules).

The duty to act rationally entails a duty to treat like cases alike (*HTV Ltd v Price Commission* [1976] ICR 170; *R v IRC, ex p Preston* [1985] AC 835). The essence of an allegation of procedural impropriety is that the applicant has been deprived of a fair hearing, a chance to state a case properly or at all.

Procedural fairness The rule against procedural unfairness may be invoked where a person is deprived of the right to what a reasonable person in the circumstances would call a fair hearing. Natural justice requires that a person should know the case against him, and should have a fair opportunity of answering the case against him (*Kanda v Government of Malaya* [1962] AC 322 at 337, *Fairmount Investments Ltd v S of S for the Environment* [1976] 1 WLR 1255; and, eg, *Afful v S of S* [1983] Imm AR 236). This entails that the person should have notice of the allegations sufficiently far in advance of a decision being made so as to be able to have the opportunity of making representations on them. If the decision maker is minded to proceed on the basis of a matter which has not been aired with the applicant, the applicant should be alerted to the possibility of the decision maker taking the point into account, so that he may have the opportunity to put forward any argument which might persuade the decision maker on that point (*R v Mental Health Review Tribunal, ex p Clatworthy* [1985] 3 All ER 699). The breach of natural justice arises from the default of the decision-maker in notifying the applicant of the point on which the decision is to turn. If he does not receive such notice due to the default of his solicitors, or representatives, there is no breach of natural justice by the decision maker (*S of S v Al-Mehdawi* [1990] 1 AC 876). The applicant should have the opportunity of dealing with the real basis of a refusal (*Ex p Awuku* [1988] Imm AR 606).

In relation to most decisions in an immigration context the burden is on the applicant to present the relevant information to the immigration officer, but the latter must act with fairness, and give a real opportunity of satisfying him on any point about which he is suspicious (*Ex p Mughal* [1974] QB 313). Decisions which are taken on the basis of inadequate information given by the applicant will generally not be reviewable on this ground, even if the true facts are more favourable to the applicant and come to light later. There is an exception to the rule that judicial review of a decision will consider only the information available to the decision maker at the time of making the decision, in cases where it is necessary to establish a fact before a power to act arises in the decision maker (*Ex p Muse* [1992] Imm AR 282). However, where there has been a significant change in the applicant's circumstances between the time of the making of a decision to deport and the upholding of that decision, the S of S may review the original decision in the light of any additional material put before him. He is not restricted to considering matters as they stood at the time of the original decision in those circumstances (*S of S for the Home Department, Exp Ul-Haq* [1993] Imm AR 144).

Legitimate expectation Where a person is subject to a decision which either (*a*) deprives him of a benefit which he has had in the past, and which he can legitimately expect to continue to enjoy unless he is permitted to comment on the reasons for withdrawal, or (*b*) which deprives him of a benefit which he has been assured by the decision maker will not be withdrawn without first giving him the opportunity for advancing reasons why it should not be, he may obtain judicial review of the decision unless there has been communicated to him some rational grounds for withdrawing the benefit, on which he has been given the opportunity to comment (*CCSU v Minister for Civil Service* [1985] 1 AC 374 at 408G, *per* Lord Diplock). The legitimate expectation doctrine has been applied in certain circumstances in immigration cases. So, for example, a legitimate expectation of entry was raised where a foreign child for adoption satisfied four criteria set out in the relevant Home Office circular, and where the prospective adoptive parents had followed the procedures set out in the circular. A new policy could only be adopted against the recipient of the circular after considering whether the overriding public interest demanded it. As a result the S of S was permitted to refuse entry only if he offered interested persons a hearing (*Khan (Asif) v IAT* [1984] Imm AR 68).

It should be noted that Home Office customary practices and procedures will not give rise to a legitimate expectation in every case (*Exp Yusufu* [1987] Imm AR 366). In *R v IAT, exp Anilkumar Patel* [1988] AC 910 the CA held that the mere fact that a person held a re-entry visa did not give rise to a legitimate expectation of this sort (see also *Exp Bolanle Balogun* [1989] Imm AR 603). Ministerial statements may give rise to a legitimate expectation that the policy they set forth will be honoured. In *Domfeh Gyeabou* [1989] Imm AR 94 an overstayer acquired a legitimate expectation that he would not be deported following a statement in Parliament by the Home Secretary that ten years' residence would be *prima facie* a reason to permit a person to remain. On the other hand in *Mohammed Hussain v IAT and S of S* [1991] Imm AR 413, the CA considered the case of an overstayer who for half his residence of in excess of ten years, had known he was the subject of a deportation order; the court held his contention that he had a reasonable expectation that he would not be deported to be unarguable. Where rights are changed by operation of law it is unlikely that there will be a legitimate expectation that the previous rights will continue (*Vun Liew v S of S* [1989] Imm AR 62 (IAT)).

Where the Home Office changes its policy an applicant can have no legitimate expectation that the old policy will be followed where the terms of the new policy have been communicated to immigrants' advisory services (*Dawood Patel v S of S* [1990] Imm AR 478). A legitimate expectation was said to arise in the GCHQ case, above where a specific representation has been made to the applicant, or where a specific course of conduct has been followed which gives rise to a legitimate expectation that a particular course is to be followed (*Manjit Singh v S of S* [1990] Imm AR 124, CA).

A number of cases have considered whether stamps in passports can create legitimate expectations of a right to enter or re-enter the UK. In *Oloniluyi v S of S* [1989] Imm AR 135 the applicant held a passport which prior to the expiry of her leave to remain was endorsed with further leave, a s 3(3)(*b*) stamp, and a visa exempt stamp. She also received oral assurances from an official at Lunar House that she could return without any difficulties prior to the expiry of her earlier leave. The CA held that she had a legitimate expectation that she would be given leave to enter on her return, although the extension of leave in itself did not give rise to such an expectation. In *Ex p Mowla* [1992] 1 WLR 70, the CA considered a number of cases relating to the stamps themselves, and held that such stamps either singly or together do not give rise to a legitimate expectation. The CA held that oral assurances given on the basis of full knowledge of the immigrant's situation had founded the legitimate expectation in *Oloniluyi*'s case. The CA also considered the extent of the legitimate expectation that can arise in these circumstances. The only legitimate expectation is that the applicant will be permitted to re-enter if the full facts be known and if there is no change of circumstances in the meanwhile (see also *Ex p Fida Bhatti* [1989] Imm AR 189). Finally, an adjudicator's recommendation does not give rise to a legitimate expectation that the S of S will follow it (*Ex p Sakala* [1994] Imm AR 143).

Even where a legitimate expectation is created, the court will consider whether there has been a detriment to the applicant when that expectation is not fulfilled. If there is no injustice to the applicant, a breach of natural justice will not have occurred (*Nkiti v Immigration Officer, Gatwick* [1989] Imm AR 585).

4 Restrictions on judicial review

(a) Locus standi

In order to be able bring a claim for judicial review, the applicant must have sufficient *locus standi* (ie standing) before the court. The applicant in an immigration matter will have such standing; so will anyone who has a sufficient interest in the outcome of the case. For example, a wife has sufficient *locus* to bring a judicial review of the IAT's decision to refuse her husband leave to appeal (*R v IAT, ex p Sumeina Masood* [1991] Imm AR 283), and similarly the sponsor of a visitor who is refused entry clearance or leave to enter will have *locus*. The concept has been interpreted widely by the courts, and it is arguable that those who would be affected by a decision (eg the congregation of a place of worship in relation to a religious leader) would have sufficient standing (see *Covent Garden Community Association v GLC* [1981] JPL 183). The problem can arise both at the leave stage (RSC, Ord 53, r 3(7)), and at a full hearing. Leave may be granted on the basis of a *prima facie* view of the applicant's standing, but at the full hearing regard is to be had to the whole of the complaint; it is necessary to consider the powers and duties in law of those against whom relief is sought, and the position of the applicant in relation to them (*Inland Revenue Commission v National Federation of Self-employed and Small Businesses Ltd* [1982] AC 617).

(b) The existence of alternative remedies

A claim for judicial review will fail if there is an alternative appeals procedure which should have been used (*R v Chief Constable of Merseyside, ex p Calveley* [1986] 2 WLR 144). If either at the leave stage or at the full hearing the court finds that there was an alternative appeal machinery, that is sufficient to dispose of the case (*Ex p Su-san Chong* [1990] Imm AR 397). That factor will also incline the court not to exercise its discretion in favour of the applicant if, even on legal advice, he has abandoned an appeal which could have dealt with the issue before the court (*Ex p Allegret* [1989] Imm AR 211), and will only permit an application by way of judicial review in such cases to proceed where there are exceptional circumstances (*Ex p Attivor* [1988] Imm AR 109).

The test of whether an appeal machinery is an alternative remedy, such as to provide a basis for refusal of relief, was considered in *Johny Suarez v S of S* [1991] Imm AR 54. In that case on a renewed application for leave before the CA, the applicant argued that the proper test was whether judicial review was the most convenient and effective of two alternative remedies. In dismissing the application, the court said *obiter* that there was no distinction proved between that test and the one set out in *Swati v S of S* [1986] Imm AR 88, namely that the jurisdiction of judicial review would not be exercised where there was an alternative remedy by way of appeal, save in exceptional circumstances. More recently, in *Soon Ok Ryoo v S of S* [1992] Imm AR 59, the CA held that it need not be shown that the alternative remedy was as effective or as convenient as judicial review, where the case turns on the credibility of the applicant. Russell LJ stated that judicial review is not geared to the exercise of assessing the credibility of the applicant. In *Ex p Hindjou* [1989] Imm AR 24, Schiemann J held that the proper test was whether the decision maker misapplied the criteria applicable to the decision to be made. Where all relevant information is contained in the documents and such an error is found, the court will consider the existence of an alternative appeals procedure as a factor in deciding whether or not to quash the decision. Generally where a tribunal has misunderstood its functions and therefore not exercised them in the correct manner, judicial review is the correct avenue (see eg *R v Windsor Licensing Justices, ex p Hodes* [1983] 1 WLR 685). However, in *Doorga v S of S* [1990] Imm AR 98, the CA, without expressly overruling *Hindjou*, indicated that the alternative appeal argument should prevail save in exceptional circumstances. These circumstances are very tightly drawn.

'Exceptional circumstances' In considering whether exceptional circumstances exist, regard should be had to the following factors among others (*R v Hallstrom, ex p Waldren* [1986] 1 QB 824, *per* Glidewell LJ):

(a) whether the alternative statutory remedy would resolve the question at issue fully and directly;

(b) whether the statutory remedy would be quicker or slower than review; and

(c) whether the case depends upon some particular or technical knowledge which was more readily available to the appellate body.

The CA has indicated that to take a case outside the general rule in *Swati*, the circumstances must be germane to the decision as to whether or not the applicant ought to follow the normal rule and make an appeal (in that case from abroad) (*Jorge Grazales v S of S* [1990] Imm AR 505; *Hassan Khan* [1991] Imm AR 174). Applicants must therefore show that some feature of the case distinguishes it from one in which an appeal is appropriate. There may be particular circumstances in which a right of appeal from abroad will be worthless. This was the case in *R v Chief Immigration Officer, Gatwick Airport, ex p Kharrazi* [1980] 1 WLR 1396, where an Iranian would have been obliged to exercise his right of appeal from that country, which had imposed a ban on any children of his age leaving. Thus where even if successful, the appeal would not result in the applicant being able to enter the country, it is arguable that there is no other effective remedy.

The courts have not been consistent in their approach to the question of when alternative appeal rights must be exhausted. In *Ex p Hindjou* [1989] Imm AR 24 Schiemann J held that *Swati* did not require that the applicant must show that there is no appeal procedure available to him, but he had to show that the decision maker misapplied the criteria for granting leave to enter. In *Doorga* ([1990] Imm AR 98) however, this case was confined to its own facts. Some guidance can perhaps be gained from *Re Preston* [1985] AC 835 in which Lord Scarman indicated in relation to a taxpayer that it would be unfair in certain circumstances to require him to initiate appeal procedures. Those circumstances were where the conduct of the commissioners in initiating the action taken against him was such that, had they not been a public authority, their action would have amounted to either breach of contract or breach of representation giving rise to an estoppel (at p 852 F-H). Thus it may be that cases in which a legitimate expectation may be alleged can be challenged by way of judicial review, notwithstanding that there may be a right of appeal.

The guidance that can be obtained from the cases is rather more negative than positive guidance. Thus the threat of imminent removal from the UK is not *per se* a special circumstance (*Ex p Su-san Chong* [1990] Imm AR 397); the fact of having to exercise the appeal from abroad when that would be inconvenient to the applicant is not an exceptional circumstance (*Grazales* and *Soon Ok Ryoo* (above); *Ex p Pulgarin* [1992] Imm AR 59); nor is the length of time a person spends in custody (*Re Balasingham* (1987) *Times*, 22 July). There were no exceptional circumstances where there was no practical obstacle and no danger to a person returning to his own country and appealing the decision from there despite the fact that he would be put to domestic and professional inconvenience (*Ex p Salamat* [1993] Imm AR 239). The trend of recent decisions has been to refuse to grant judicial review where there is an alternative remedy by way of appeal which has not been exhausted. Further, where on advice a person abandons an appeal in favour of judicial review, he will only be permitted in exceptional circumstances to apply for leave (*Ex p Attivor* [1988] Imm AR 109) and his application for leave may be rejected in the court's discretion (*Ex p Allegret* [1989] Imm AR 211).

(c) Delay and time limits

The Supreme Court Act 1981, s 31(6) directs that the court may refuse leave if it considers that there has been undue delay and that the application for relief sought 'would be likely to cause substantial hardship to or substantially prejudice the right of any person or would be detrimental to the interests of good administration.' Rules of court therefore provide that an application for judicial review must be made promptly. In any event it must be made within three months of the decision or action being complained of (RSC, Ord 53, r 4; and see *Bagga Khan v S of S* [1987] Imm AR 543).

Time runs from the decision and not from the exhaustion of any appeal against the decision if there is an appeal machinery. It is likely that the time limit cannot be sidestepped by seeking a review by the Home Office of the decision which in reality it is sought to review before the court, and upon refusal of that review by the Home Office, taking the matter to the court promptly (*Ex p Hindjou* [1989] Imm AR 24).

Guidance on time limits was given by the HL in *R v Dairy Produce Quotas Tribunal, ex p Caswell* [1990] 2 AC 738. The fact that the application is lodged within three months does not mean it has been made 'promptly' and an application for leave may be refused on the basis that it is out of time even though the three-month period has not elapsed (*Re Friends of the Earth Ltd* [1988] JPL 93). It is a factual question whether there is good reason to grant an extension of time. 'Undue delay' is determined objectively, and failure to comply with RSC Ord 53, r 4 in failing to be prompt or to be within the three months is undue delay. Having established that there has been undue delay, it is a matter for the court's discretion whether to extend time under r 4 or refuse leave to apply or leave consideration of s 31 matters of undue delay to the full hearing, at which they may again be raised. The HL stated further that leave should be refused if the application is not made promptly or within three months unless the applicant shows good reason, when an extension can be granted. Leave should be refused even where otherwise it would be granted if the court believes that granting relief would cause substantial hardship or be detrimental to good administration. If good reason is shown the court should normally grant leave and the question of detriment to good administration should be heard at the main hearing. Where delay has been caused by obtaining legal aid, that may be good reason (*R v Stratford on Avon DC, ex p Jackson* [1985] 1 WLR 1319). Detriment to good administration is nowhere defined, but in *Caswell* the HL suggested that mere inconvenience is not enough, there must be some foreseeable harm to the administration. There must be evidence from which detriment can be inferred. If there has been delay it should be dealt with in detail when drafting the application (see page 501 below).

(d) Discretion

Judicial review is a discretionary remedy. In the exercise of that discretion judicial review may be refused on the basis of the undeserving conduct of the applicant (*Ex p Ketowoglo* [1992] Imm AR 268, *R v Williams, ex p Phillips* [1914] 1 QB 608, *Ex p Pushpaben Patel* [1993] Imm AR 392—the applicant had stated that she would not apply for a visa which she could have obtained). In *Ketowoglo* the CA expressed concern at the length of time a case may take to come to a full hearing, and stated that any failure to make full disclosure at the *ex parte* stage may be such misconduct on the part of the applicant as to affect the exercise of its discretion, unless an explanation for the lack of full disclosure.

(e) National security

One area in which the court has in the past taken a highly restrictive view is that of national security. In *Ex p Hosenball* [1977] 3 All ER 452 the CA refused to find that the S of S was obliged by the principles of natural justice to give reasons for deportation on national security grounds (see also *Ex p NSH v S of S* [1988] Imm AR 389, and *Ex p Cheblak* [1991] 2 All ER 319).

5 Remedies

(a) Certiorari

Certiorari brings decisions of an inferior court, tribunal or authority before the High Court for review so that they may be quashed because the inferior body has exceeded its power or is acting contrary to law.

The grounds of the application are to be considered at the date of the judgment order, or other proceedings complained of (RSC Ord 53, r 4(2)). If leave is granted it operates as a stay on the proceedings to which the application relates until disposal or further order (RSC, Ord 53, r 3(10)(*a*)). Such a stay is binding on the Minister concerned (*S of S for Education, ex p Avon County Council* [1991] 2 WLR 702 and see *Ex p Muboyayi* [1992] 1 QB 244).

(b) Prohibition

Where the action of the Crown servant complained of is continuing or prospective, and is an abuse of jurisdiction or natural justice (see below), prohibition is the appropriate remedy, preventing the carrying out of the action. The grant of leave operates as a stay of the proceedings complained of.

(c) Mandamus

This is an order of the court requiring a public duty to be performed, and which has powers of enforcement attached to it under RSC Ord 45, r 5 and Ord 52, r 1. Such an order would be appropriate to challenge a policy statement refusing to consider some category of person.

(d) Injunctions

Injunctions are a remedy in judicial review, but are not available against the Crown (*R v S of S for Transport, ex p Factortame Ltd* [1990] 2 AC 85) except where there is a point of EC law involved (*Factortame* [1991] 1 All ER 70), (ECJ preliminary ruling). Thus a person exercising an EC right may seek an injunction to prevent him being removed by way of an interlocutory or final order. An injunction in such a case would be granted if it were just and convenient, having regard to the respondent, the nature of the matters in respect of which relief can be granted by a prerogative order, and the other circumstances of the case (Supreme Court Act 1981, s 31(2)). The grounds for an injunction are the same as those for the substantive remedies sought under the judicial review procedure (ie, *certiorari, prohibition,* and *mandamus*).

6 Procedure for applying for judicial review

Where the applicant is likely to be removed from the jurisdiction of the court, and it is not possible to obtain an undertaking from the Home Office that he will not be removed until the outcome of the application for leave (which has been issued) is known, consideration should be given to an application for *habeas corpus* (*Ex p Muboyayi* [1992] 1 QB 244; and see page 510). Where a person is removed from the jurisdiction in breach of an undertaking consideration should be given to the bringing of contempt proceedings against the civil servants involved. Where the individual civil servant or Minister has interfered with the course of justice in failing to ensure that the person is returned he may be liable for contempt and the court will grant an interim injunction to prevent removal before leave is obtained and [1992] 2 WLR 73(CA), (see *M v Home Office and Baker* (1993) *Times*, 28 July HL).

(a) Application for leave

It is always necessary to obtain leave to apply for judicial review (RSC Ord 53, r 3). The purpose of this stage is to weed out hopeless, frivolous or vexatious cases. The first stage in an application is always an *ex parte* application for leave, which is made on Form 86A and by swearing an affidavit verifying the facts relied upon. Criticism of vague grounds has been expressed, and submissions which do not define the issues but which are so broad as to cover any ground should be avoided, eg the decision is against the immigration laws and rules and against natural justice, (*Ex p Fauzia Bagga Khan* [1987] Imm AR 543). Despite the fact that many of these applications have to be made with utmost speed, a full application will ensure that the application is more likely to be taken seriously.

The form must in any event give sufficient detail to identify the order or proceeding in respect of which relief is sought, and to identify the purpose of the relief sought; it should also show the basis of the argument. The application is made to a High Court judge by filing the form in the Crown Office. As a result of a *Practice Direction* [1979] 2 All ER 880 special forms have been devised for immigration cases which are available from the Chief Clerk of the Crown Office. The form should be accompanied by an affidavit verifying the facts relied upon. Since the affidavit is in interlocutory proceedings, it may contain hearsay if the deponent states the sources and grounds of the belief (RSC, Ord 41, r 5(2)). It should be as full as the circumstances of the case allow, given that any further affidavits are limited by Ord 53, r 6(2) to those dealing with new matters arising out of an affidavit of another party to the proceedings. The judge can consider the matter on the papers, without a hearing, unless one is requested by the applicant. In either case the need for full information cannot be too highly stressed.

The applicant's representatives have an obligation to lodge the application for judicial review expeditiously and to place before the court at the earliest opportunity all material documents including those that have come into existence after the application for leave to move for judicial review had been lodged with the court (*Ex p Nwosu* [1993] Imm AR 206). Since the application is *ex parte* there is a duty of full and frank disclosure to the court, and any failure to observe this duty will be viewed with utmost seriousness. The court may refuse an application on these grounds alone (*R v Kensington Commissioners, ex p Polignac* [1917] 1 KB 486). The Home Office will frequently send a letter containing an outline of its case to the applicant on learning that an application is being made to the court for judicial review. The letter will normally end with a request to the recipient to place it before the court, and failure to refer to the existence of this letter or to put it before the court will generally result in the legal adviser responsible paying the costs of the application, and the application being dismissed (*Ex p William Bekro* [1991] Imm AR 127, *per* Popplewell J applying RSC, Ord 62, r 11.) Counsel who fail to exhibit such a letter or to ensure that the court sees it, while knowing of its existence and contents, may find that they or their instructing solicitors are ordered to pay the costs (*Sushma Lal v S of S* [1992] Imm AR 303), and may face disciplinary action. In *Ex p Ketwoglo*, it was said to go to the court's discretion in relation to the applicant. If the applicant is distanced from his advisers' fault and there is any risk that the applicant will be prejudiced, it is unlikely that the court will refuse to exercise its discretion. Where the evidence before the court shows that the grounds for the application were misleading, this will be drawn to the attention of the taxing master or the legal aid authority. Where the conduct of the case falls below proper standards the bills of the defaulting party are likely to be disallowed (*Ex p Guiled* [1993] Imm AR 236). Conduct such as the late withdrawal of a case without informing the Crown Office or the S of S will result in costs being awarded against the representative in certain circumstances (*Ex p Mudzengi* [1993] Imm AR 320). If the applicant's case is hopeless he may have costs awarded against him (*Ex p Atrvinder Singh* [1993] Imm AR 450 and see *Ifzal Ali v S of S* [1994] Imm AR 69).

Standard for leave At the leave stage of an application the applicant must show that he has an arguable case, and that there is no alternative remedy available (see eg *Tadimi v S of S* [1993] Imm AR 90). Normally this will involve the judge in a quick perusal of the available material to see if it discloses an arguable case on the heads of judicial review, and not going into the matter in any depth (*Inland Revenue Commissioners v National Federation of Self-employed* [1982] AC 617). If on such a perusal the court considers that the material discloses what might on further consideration turn out to be an arguable case, it ought to give leave.

In immigration cases a trend has arisen to encourage *inter partes* leave applications. If the court is not sure whether or not an arguable point of law has been disclosed, because for example the facts are not clear, the respondent may be invited to attend and make representations (*Ex p Angur Begum and Rukshanda Begum* [1990] Imm AR 1). In *Doorga v S of S* [1990] Imm AR 98 at p 101, Lord Donaldson MR set out the principles to be followed on these applications:

(1) Where there are *prima facie* reasons for granting judicial review, leave should be granted.
(2) Where the application is wholly unarguable, leave should be refused.
(3) Where the judge is left with an uneasy feeling as to whether on a weak case leave should be refused, or on a stronger looking case, that there might be a quick and easy answer to the points raised so that leave should in fact be refused, then the proper course is to adjourn for the leave application to be heard *inter partes*. At the *inter partes* leave hearing the respondent does not have to put forward his full argument, but if he can produce some totally knock-out point which makes it clear that there is no basis for the application at all, then leave will be refused.

More recently the CA in *Mehmet Oral v S of S* [1991] Imm AR 208 held that where on consideration of an *ex parte* application it was apparent that there might be a dispute on evidence, it would be desirable for the S of S to have the opportunity to put in evidence, which could be done by directing that the matter of leave be heard *inter partes*. Where the court has directed that an *inter partes* leave application should take place, although there is no formal statement of the duties of the applicant, he should serve the respondent with the papers in the case. A refusal to do so on request by the respondent will result in an order being made, possibly incurring a penalty in costs (*Ex p Dyfan* [1993] Imm AR 180).

At the leave stage, issues of fact may be determined on the basis of the affidavits, and there is no necessity for leave to be granted merely because issues of fact are raised on the affidavits (*Ex p Fawehimi* [1990] Imm AR 1). The need to have an arguable case is not affected by the burden on the Home Office to prove that the applicant is in fact an illegal entrant, or the requirement to scrutinise precedent facts with care in illegal entrance cases where liberty is at issue. *Khawaja* does not oblige the court to grant leave in every case concerning an illegal entry by deception, including a concealed intention (*Ubakanwa Uche v S of S* [1991] Imm AR 252), nor to permit strong identification evidence to be tested at a full hearing (*Irawo-Osan v S of S* [1992] Imm AR 337: fingerprints).

Evidence The normal rule is that only the evidence which was before the decision-maker at the time of the decision will be admitted, as it forms the pool of information on the basis of which the decision was or ought to have been made. There are exceptions to this rule, where the jurisdiction of the decision maker depends upon the existence of a precedent fact (such as in illegal entrant cases); or where there is a dispute over the procedure observed, or misconduct of the proceedings by the decision maker, such as bias (see *Ex p Muse* [1992] Imm AR 282).

The documents for an application for leave should be bundled. The bundle should be paginated and supplied with an index to conform to *Practice Direction (Evidence: Documents)* [1983] 1 WLR 922. Failure to do this may result in the application being struck out.

Where counsel has advised that there is no merit in a claim and the client is legally aided, when the application for leave is dismissed, if the legal aid certificate is still operative, the applicant has 14 days to persuade the area director that his case has merit. The order of the court will not be drawn up for 28 days in such circumstances (*Ex p Olokodana* [1992] Imm AR 499).

(b) Renewal of application for leave

If the judge refuses the paper application or grants it on terms, the applicant may renew the application for leave before a single judge sitting in open court, lodging notice of intention to renew with the Crown Office within ten days on Form 86B (RSC Ord 53, r 3(5)). An oral application can be the first stage in the process (see page 501 above). The court may at this stage direct that the leave application be heard by a single judge sitting in open court or Divisional Court. If the single judge refuses the application, there is no further renewal except before the CA.

An applicant refused leave by the single judge in open court may on an *ex parte* application on notice renew the application before the CA. The renewed application must be made within seven days of the single judge's refusal. When leave to move has been refused after an *inter partes* hearing of an application for leave to move for judicial review, it is inappropriate for the court to grant leave to appeal, renewal being the proper channel (*Soon Ok Ryoo v S of S* [1992] Imm AR 59).

In addition to the increase in judicial review applications, there has been an increase in such renewals, and several points have now been established in relation to them. First, the CA regards itself as bound by its previous reasoned judgments in *ex parte* renewal applications (*David Thevarajah v S of S* [1991] Imm AR 371). Second, a point which was not raised below cannot be taken on the renewal (*Fozlu Miah v S of S* [1991] Imm AR 581). Third, if the CA refuses leave to apply for judicial review there is no appeal to the HL (*Re Poh* [1983] 1 WLR 2). Finally, where the application for leave has been refused by the High Court, a renewal should not be made to the CA where the S of S has written clarifying his reasons for the decision, and demonstrating that the initial application was meritless (*Mahtab Ahmed v S of S* [1992] Imm AR 538).

The CA has a system for the identification of renewed applications in immigration cases. Generally, if there is any urgency it is possible to have a case renewed within a matter of days.

By the Supreme Court Act 1981, s 51(6) as amended, a legal representative may be ordered to meet the whole or part of any costs which may be wasted by a frivolous appeal. This power will be exercised where the court regards the appeal as an abuse of process and an example of irresponsible conduct on the part of those acting for the applicant; they owe a duty both to the client and the court. Bringing an appeal which has no possible prospect of success is inconsistent with such a duty (*Saleem Abassi v S of S* [1992] Imm AR 349). Further, although it is permissible to raise doubts about the *bona fides* of the Home Office (*Irawo-Osan v S of S* [1992] Imm AR 387), if unsubstantiated and scandalous allegations are made it is possible that counsel will be made to bear the costs (*Mutengu v S of S* [1992] Imm AR 419). Where an applicant is legally aided, if costs are wasted by a failure to conduct proceedings with reasonable competence, the court may invite the taxing authorities to consider whether any of the costs should be disallowed (*Oladehinde v S of S* [1992] Imm AR 443).

(c) Setting aside leave

Once leave has been granted *ex parte*, the respondent may apply for it to be set aside under Ord 32, r 6. The respondent should apply promptly, and cannot leave it to the full hearing, by which time it is pointless. Leave should only be set aside in very special circumstances, such as where the proceedings were fundamentally misconceived either in law or fact, or where there has been either fraud on the part of the applicant or non-disclosure of material facts. Where there is an application for leave to be set aside, the court should go through the same sort of process as on the application for leave (*Ex p Begum* [1989] Imm AR 302). In *Ex p Sholola* [1992] 135 the court considered the question of the circumstances in which the grant of leave should be set aside when leave was granted *ex parte*. The power should only be exercised in an extremely plain case. It is not enough to show that the application for judicial review is very likely to fail, nor that the judge hearing the application would not himself have granted the leave application if it had been made before him. It is necessary to show that there is something almost amounting to a quasi-jurisdictional bar to review, such as the plain existence of an alternative appeal mechanism which should be used. If some 'bald point of statutory construction upon which the applicant's case was founded' is manifestly unarguable or if leave was granted in ignorance of some leading authority, the application for leave to be set aside will be granted. Similarly, if the application was based upon factual premises which can shortly be shown not to exist, leave will be set aside. Finally, if there has been a serious non-disclosure leave will be set aside.

Should leave be granted, it is possible to obtain a stay of the action complained of, where prohibition or *certiorari* have been applied for by Ord 53, r (10)(a). Where the applicant is in detention and bail (see page 507 below) has been denied or has not yet been applied for, a request should be made for an expedited hearing (ie that the case be included in Part D of the Crown Office List). If granted, a further application should be made that time for service of the respondent's affidavit be abridged in accordance with *Practice Note (QBD)(Judicial Review: Affidavit in Reply)* [1989] 1 WLR 358. Application should be made at this stage to make amendments to the Form 86A (RSC, Ord 53, r 3(6)). New grounds may be added, or new relief sought, and if not done at this stage may be applied for as a separate interlocutory matter. On granting leave or permitting amendment, the judge may impose terms of a general nature, such as that counsel review matters on sight of the affidavit of the respondent.

(d) Interlocutory applications and bail

Order 53, r 8 deals with interlocutory applications which may be made, and which include an application for leave to cross-examine the deponent of a affidavit, discovery and inspection. The court may direct on granting leave that deponents attend to be cross examined (*Ex p Fawehimi* [1990] Imm AR 1). In *Re H* (1990) *Guardian*, 17 May, Roch J stated that discovery would not be ordered except as necessary for disposing fairly of the case or saving costs. There could be no discovery on a contingent basis in the hope that it will show the contents of affidavits to be untrue or inaccurate, but where there is some matter which suggests that the affidavits are not accurate, discovery will be permitted of documents which will clarify the position. Moreover, in relation to discovery of interview notes in particular, it is necessary to depose to what the applicant remembers was said at the interview. It is only if the applicant's memory of the interview is different from that of the immigration officers that discovery of the notes may be possible (*Yadvinder Singh v S of S* [1988] Imm AR 480). The standard to be applied when deciding whether discovery should be made is no higher than that applied when considering whether or not to grant leave (*R v Governor of Pentonville Prison, ex p Herbage (No 2)* (1986) *The Times*, 29 May). Discovery will be limited to the issues arising out of the affidavits, but should not be ordered unless reasonable grounds on the merits are disclosed (*Inland Revenue Commissioners v National Federation of Self-employed and Small Businesses Ltd* [1982] AC 617).

Bail The court has an inherent jurisdiction to grant bail. The principles in immigration cases on which that jurisdiction will operate were considered in *Ex p Turkoglu* [1987] Imm AR 484. The court held that it has power to grant bail when an application for leave to apply for judicial review has been made but not disposed of, and where leave was granted but the full hearing has not occurred; but there is no jurisdiction where leave to move has been refused. Where the applicant is refused admission and is in custody pending removal, the court will only grant bail when it considers that the

S of S has committed an error of law in failing to grant temporary admission pending the outcome of the judicial review, or that his decision was unreasonable on *Wednesbury* principles (*Re Vilvarajah* [1990] Imm AR 457). The same approach has been adopted by the Court of Sessions in Scotland (*Jaswant Singh v S of S* [1993] Imm AR 4).

(e) The hearing

Once leave has been granted, certain documents must be served on the respondent and any other person directly affected within 14 days of leave being granted; these documents are the notice of motion, a copy of the affidavit in support and a copy of Form 86A (RSC, Ord 53, r 6(1)). An affidavit of service must be filed before the motion is entered for hearing which accords with r 5(6). The motion for judicial review must be entered for hearing by filing a copy of the notice of motion in the Crown Office within 14 days of leave being granted, but after filing the affidavit of service (RSC, Ord 53, r 5(5)).

The respondent has 56 days after the service of the notice in which to file an affidavit in reply, unless time has been abridged (*Practice Note (Judicial Review Affidavit in Reply*) [1989] 1 WLR 358). The time limit is strict, and extensions will only be granted in wholly exceptional circumstances. Any further affidavits may only be filed if they deal with new matters arising out of the affidavit of the other party. Notice of intention to use a further affidavit must be given to the respondent by an applicant.

At the full hearing legal argument is heard on the basis only of Form 86A and the evidence on affidavit (and, when ordered, evidence arising from cross-examination on the affidavit). Counsel should ensure that the court is provided with a skeleton argument in accordance with the Rules of Court (*R v IAT, ex p Islam* [1992] Imm AR 452; *R v IAT, ex p Amin* [1992] Imm AR 367). As a rule the court will not permit fresh evidence which was not in existence at the time of the decision, but will admit fresh evidence to determine a precedent fact, or as to whether there was a procedural breach (see *Marchano Singa v S of S* [1992] Imm AR 160).

(f) Appeals

Interlocutory appeals The appeal is to the Divisional Court, but otherwise follows Ord 58, and is treated as an appeal from a Queen's Bench judge in chambers. The appeal is by way of a rehearing of the interlocutory application, at which fresh evidence may be adduced as of right. A further appeal on interlocutory matters lies to the CA, with leave either of the Court or the Court of Appeal. On appeal to the CA no fresh evidence may be adduced save at the discretion of the CA.

Appeals from full hearings   Appeals are governed by the Supreme Court Act 1981 s 16(1), and are initially to the CA, whose powers are governed by RSC, Ord 59. There is a time limit of four weeks from the date of judgement. By Ord 59, r 10 the CA has the same powers and duties as the High Court. There is a discretion to admit fresh evidence on such an appeal, which is wider than in other civil matters. In *Ex p Momin Ali* [1984] 1 WLR 663, the majority of the CA observed that public law required finality in litigation save in the interests of justice. The specific rules in *Ladd v Marshall* [1954] 3 All ER 745 do not apply in full, but the presumption remains against admitting fresh evidence.

(g) Legal aid

Many of the preliminary steps in an immigration case may be covered by the Green Form scheme. In a case where judicial review is contemplated, assistance may be obtained to cover preliminary steps such as the obtaining of counsel's opinion on the merits of the claim, and legal aid thereafter if so advised. Where an application for leave has been made and refused, it is possible to renew the application to the CA. However, if the case is legally aided, counsel should not sign an opinion supporting an application for an extension of legal aid to cover the renewed application unless he expresses that opinion on full information, and where he believes that there is a reasonable chance of success (*Marchano Singa v S of S* [1992] Imm AR 160).

Chapter 28

Habeas Corpus

Where a person is detained it may be possible to challenge the lawfulness of the detention by applying for a writ of *habeas corpus* in accordance with the procedures set out in RSC, Ord 54. An *ex parte* application is made, usually to a High Court judge, although it may be directed to be made to a Divisional Court of the Queen's Bench Division. The application must be supported by an affidavit sworn by the person detained, which states that he instigated the application and describes the nature of his detention. If the detainee is unable to make the affidavit it may be made by his representative.

On an *ex parte* application the court may issue the writ immediately or make directions for an *inter partes* hearing. The court may direct the writ to issue in the meantime, or adjourn the application for the writ. If the writ is issued, the return (ie the reply) must set out the reasons for the applicant's detention. At the hearing there is an inquiry into the legality of the applicant's detention. Note that where the appellate authorities have power to deal with bail and have refused it, judicial review and not *habeas corpus* is the appropriate remedy (*Re Serif Maybasan* [1991] Imm AR 89).

In the past the effectiveness of *habeas corpus* as a remedy for those detained under the 1971 Act has been rather less than impressive. The cases on applications for *habeas corpus* by detained immigrants have shown a pronounced executive-mindedness in the courts (see *Ex p Choudhary* [1978] 3 All ER 790 (overruled by *Khawaja*); also *Ex p Phansopkar* [1975] 3 All ER 497, *per* Lord Denning MR, at p 508; *Ex p Zamir* [1980] AC 930; *Re Olusanya (Olugbenga)* [1988] Imm AR 117).

However, in *Ex p Khawaja* [1984] AC 74 the HL emphasised that on an application for judicial review or for a writ of *habeas corpus*, the facts on which the Home Office has reached a decision

had to be carefully reviewed by the court. Lord Wilberforce (at p 340) stated the respective functions of the immigration authorities and of the courts to be as follows:
(1) The immigration authorities have the power and the duty to determine and to act upon the facts material to the detention as illegal entrants of persons prior to removal from the UK.
(2) Any person whom the S of S proposes to remove as an illegal entrant, and who is detained, may apply for a writ of *habeas corpus* or for judicial review. Upon such an application the S of S or the immigration authorities if they seek to support the detention or removal (the burden being on them) should depose to the grounds on which the decision to detain or remove was made, setting out essential factual evidence taken into account and exhibiting documents sufficiently fully to enable the courts to carry out their function of review (see also *Ex p Choudhary* (1981) *The Times*, 16 December).
(3) The court's investigation of the facts is of a supervisory character and not by way of appeal. It should appraise the quality of the evidence and decide whether it justifies, for example, a conclusion that the applicant obtained permission to enter by fraud or deceit. If the court is not satisfied with any part of the evidence it may remit the matter for reconsideration or itself receive further evidence. It should quash the detention order where the evidence was not such as the authorities should have relied on or where the evidence received does not justify the decision reached or, of course, for any serious procedural irregularity.
(4) Where the power of an officer or the S of S to make a decision affecting a person's liberty is dependent on the existence of certain facts, the court has to be satisfied on a civil standard of proof to a high degree of probability that those facts did in fact exist at the time the power was exercised.

Further, in *Re Hardial Singh* [1983] Imm AR 198, Woolf J held that the power of the S of S to detain persons pending removal was limited to a period reasonably necessary for his purpose. If there was unreasonable delay before removal, the court would issue a writ of *habeas corpus*.

An application for *habeas corpus* is only appropriate where the facts justifying the detention are challenged. If the underlying decision which gives rise to the power to detain is challenged, the proper challenge is by way of judicial review (*Ex p Muboyayi* [1992] 1 QB 244). In *Muboyayi* the S of S advanced the argument that the practical effect of issuing a writ of *habeas corpus* would be to enjoin the Crown contrary to the principles in *R v S of S for Transport, ex p Factortame* [1990] 2 AC 85. The CA stated that it was their duty to uphold the classic statement of the rule of law in Chapters 39 and 40 of Magna Carta which provide that no freeman shall be arrested or imprisoned or exiled except by lawful judgment of his peers and by the law of the land. The CA held that *Factortame* did not prevent *habeas corpus* issuing against the Crown for that reason. A writ of *habeas corpus* will issue where someone is detained without any authority or the purported authority is beyond the powers of the person authorising detention and is therefore unlawful. Judicial review should be used where the decision sought to be opposed is within the powers of the person taking it, but due to procedural error or a misapplication of the law, a failure to take account of relevant matters, taking account of irrelevant matters, or because the decision is fundamentally unreasonable, the decision should not have been taken at all. Where that is the case the decision is lawful, until it is set aside by a court. In the case of detention, if the warrant or underlying decision to deport is set aside but the detention continues, then *habeas corpus* will issue (*Ex p Cheblak* [1991] 1 WLR 890 at p 894, *per* Lord Donaldson MR). However it was accepted in *Ex p Muboyayi* (above) that the 1971 Act, Sched 2, para 18(4) does not have the object of ousting *habeas corpus* in favour of judicial review of detentions in immigration cases, but permits a person detained to be kept in detention at any place, not only in a lawful prison, even if at the time of the order for detention no place is specified in it. Where the S of S refuses to give an undertaking that a person will not be removed from the UK before the conclusion of proceedings, where judicial review proceedings have been issued to challenge the decision underlying a detention, a writ of *habeas corpus* may be issued (*Muboyayi*, above and see also *Akhtar v Governor of Pentonville Prison* [1993] Imm AR 424).

The Home Office stated their practice in relation to judicial review proceedings where removal is planned in the course of the *Muboyayi* case as follows:

(1) Where leave to move is granted they will not remove until the case is disposed of in the High Court.
(2) If removal takes place notwithstanding the grant of leave

either because the application is made extremely late or because of a mistake, the S of S will do his best to return the applicant to the jurisdiction.

(3) In all cases removal directions are made in advance of removal and the person is given notice. In cases where applications for leave to the High Court or CA are pending, adequate notice will be given to enable the appropriate application to be made (see *Muboyayi* at page 259).

Part VII

Criminal Offences

Chapter 29

Criminal Offences

1 Criminal offences under the Immigration Act 1971

There are four classes of offence created by the 1971 Act. Section 24 creates the offence of illegal entry and other generic offences. Section 25 makes it an offence to assist illegal entry and to harbour illegal entrants. Section 26 provides that failure or refusal to comply with certain administrative directions under the Act are to be offences. Section 21 makes criminal certain acts committed in connection with the ownership of ships and aircraft or the management of ports. Some of these offences are subject to an extended time limit for prosecutions provided by s 28(1). An information may be laid within three years of the commission of the offence, as long as it is laid within two months from the date on which evidence on which a prosecution could be based became available to a police oficer. The offences created by the 1971 Act are not retrospective and accordingly a person cannot be convicted under the Act as a result of something done before the Act came into force (*Waddington v Miah* [1974] 1 WLR 683).

2 Illegal entry and similar offences

Section 24 is concerned with breaches of immigration control before and after entry committed by persons who are not British citizens. All the offences are summary offences, and the maximum punishment on conviction is a fine of not more than the current amount at level 4 on the standard scale, presently £1,000 and/or six months' imprisonment. They are arrestable offences (s 24(2)): immigration officers as well as constables are given power of arrest. The only exception is an offence under s 24(1)(*d*)(refusal to submit to a medical examination).

517

(a) Entry in breach of a deportation order or without leave

Under s 24(1)(a) it is an offence knowingly to enter the UK in breach of a deportation order, or to enter without leave. The offence is not committed if a person enters with leave, but with leave obtained by deception; such circumstances may give rise to an offence under s 26(1)(c), below. The extended time limit applies to this offence but the offence is only committed on the day of entry (*Grant v Borg* [1982] 1 WLR 638, below). In proceedings for the offence of entering without leave any date stamp apparently made by an immigration officer on the defendant's passport or travel documents is to be presumed to be a proper stamp unless the contrary is proved (s 24(4)). If proceedings are begun within six months of the alleged illegal entry (but not if proceedings are begun under the extended time limit) the onus of proving that the defendant had leave to enter is on the defendant. This means that if proceedings are begun more than six months after the alleged illegal entry, the defendant is in a more favourable position than if they had been begun within six months, since he does not then have what may be the difficult task of proving positively that he had leave to enter. In *Lamptey v Owen* [1982] Crim LR 42 the Divisional Court held that a defective stamp in the entrant's passport, which did not show, as the prosecution contended, that the entrant only had leave to remain for six months, did not amount to proof that he had committed a s 24(1)(b) offence (see below).

(b) Overstaying or breach of condition of leave

Section 24(1)(b) makes it an offence for a person who has limited leave to enter or remain in this country, either knowingly to overstay the time limit, or knowingly to breach a condition of that leave. The offence of overstaying, but not breaching a condition, is subject to the extended time limit. So if a person had leave to stay for six months and stayed for seven, it would be an offence if he was aware that he was overstaying. But it is not a strict liability offence. It might therefore be thought that he would have a good defence if it could be shown that he has mislaid or lost the relevant papers and believed that time would expire later than it did. However, in *R v Bello* (1978) 67 Cr App Rep 288 the Court of Appeal held that if the defendant once knew the relevant facts, so that they were capable of being revived in his memory, he was guilty of the offence. In *Grant v Borg* [1982] 1 WLR 638 the House of Lords held that the s 24(1)(b)(i) offence of overstaying can only be committed on the day after the limited leave expires and on no other day. The knowledge required to constitute the offence is knowledge of the material facts, not of the relevant law. The offence of knowingly remaining beyond the time limited by the leave is committed on the day when the defendant first knows that the time limited by his leave has expired, and he continues to commit the offence throughout any period during which he is in the UK thereafter (1971 Act, s 24(119)). This provision only applies where leave expired after 10 July 1988. The principle in *Grant v Borg* for leave expiring after 10 July 1988 has been displaced by the 1988 Act. However, a person cannot be prosecuted more than once in respect of the same limited leave. The position is different with regard to the s 24(1)(*b*)(ii) offence of breaching a condition of leave. In *Manickavsager v Metropolitan Police Commissioner* [1987] Crim LR 50, the Divisional Court held that the offence of breach of conditions was a continuing one. In *Grant v Borg* Lords Russell and Bridge made interesting observations about the effect on *mens rea* of an immigrant's ignorance. There is a distinction between lack of knowledge and ignorance of the law. Lord Russell said (at p 642F):

An immigrant unfamiliar with the language and perhaps illiterate, may, by a misunderstanding of what is written in his passport, genuinely think as a fact that he has leave to remain; I give this as a possible example of a case in which he would lack the knowledge in point of fact that he was remaining after the expiration of his leave.

Lord Bridge observed (at p 646C):

It would be unusual but by no means impossible for an immigrant (as, for example, one who was wholly illiterate) to remain beyond the time limited for his leave but nevertheless to be honestly mistaken in believing that his leave had not expired.

(c) Overstaying after entry under s 8(1)

Section 24(1)(*c*) deals with the position of persons who have entered the country legally under s 8(1). Section 8 allows a person who is a member of a crew of a ship or aircraft who is employed on terms that he will leave the country on the ship or plane that brought him here (or on another ship or plane within seven days of his entry) to enter this country without leave. He is only prevented from entering if he is already subject to a deportation order or was refused entry on his last attempt to enter the UK, or an immigration officer requires him to submit to an examination under

Sched 2 to the Act. If such a person, after entering in this way, subsequently fails to leave on his ship or aircraft when that leaves or on another one within seven days of entry, he is guilty of an offence. This offence is subject to the extended time limit, and liability is strict.

(d) Medical examination

It is an offence under s 24(1)(*d*) not to comply with a requirement imposed under Sched 2 to the Act to report to a medical officer of health or to undergo a medical test or examination required by such an officer. Under Sched 2, para 1, an immigration officer has power to require an entrant to whom leave is given to enter the country to report his arrival to a medical officer of health and submit to any such examination as that officer may require. This requirement can only be made on the advice of a medical inspector appointed by the S of S under Sched, para 1(2) or, if he is not available, on the advice of a fully qualified medical practitioner. Furthermore, it can only be made if the immigration officer is of the opinion as a result of that advice that such an examination is required in the interests of public health.

It should not be an offence under s 24(1)(*b*) to fail to comply with a direction made by an immigration officer in the absence of the necessary medical advice. It is not enough for an immigration officer, simply because an entrant looks unhealthy, to require him to undergo such an examination. The power is clearly aimed at scrutiny of real public health dangers. For example, if someone was diagnosed by a medical practitioner as a possible sufferer from tuberculosis, that would be a proper case for a requirement under para 7. Clearly, clarification of the position would be in the interests of public health. However, if the entrant was merely diagnosed as suffering from a cold, a requirement to undergo a medical examination would not be in the interests of public health. An offence under this subsection, unlike the others created by s 24, is not an arrestable offence. Furthermore, it is a defence to show that there is a reasonable excuse for the breach.

(e) Breach of conditions by persons liable to detention or removal

Under s 24(1)(*e*) it is an offence to breach any restriction imposed by virtue of Scheds 2 or 3 with regard to either residence, employment, or reporting to the police or to an immigration officer. It is a defence if there is a reasonable excuse for the breach. Under Sched 2, para 16 some persons are liable to detention or removal under the authority of an immigration officer. These are persons refused entry and illegal entrants, and persons who have arrived in the UK and are subject to examination by an immigration officer under para 2. By virtue of Sched 2, para 21(1), an immigration officer may give a written authority permitting such persons to be admitted temporarily without being detained, or to be released from detention. Paragraph 21(2) provides that such persons shall be subject to such conditions as to residence, reporting to the police or to an immigration officer as the immigration officer may notify in writing.

Under Sched 3, if a deportation order is in force against a person he may be detained by a court or by the S of S. If he is not detained he is to be subject to such restrictions as to residence and reporting to the police as the S of S may from time to time notify him of in writing (para 2(5)).

(f) Ships and aircraft

Section 24(1)(*f*) makes it an offence to disembark in the UK from a ship or aircraft after having been placed on board in order to be removed from the UK. Under Sched 2, para 8, an immigration officer has power to direct various persons (for example, ships' captains and ships' owners) to remove any person who has been refused entry: the S of S has a similar but wider power under para 10. If such directions have been made, an immigration officer may, under para 11, authorise the would-be entrant to be placed on board the relevant ship or aircraft. If that person then disembarks from the ship or aircraft, he is guilty of an offence. Liability for this offence is strict.

(g) Leaving the UK in breach of an Order in Council

By virtue of s 24(1)(*g*) it is also a strict liability offence to leave the UK in contravention of an Order in Council made under s 3(7). This section is a tit-for-tat provision. If any country restricts the right of British citizens to leave that country an Order in Council may be made prohibiting or restricting citizens of that country who are not British citizens from leaving the UK. This power has not yet been exercised, and presumably will not be exercised except in a serious crisis of international relations.

3 Assisting illegal entry and harbouring

Section 25 creates two separate offences of assisting illegal entry into the UK and of harbouring illegal entrants.

(a) Assisting illegal entry

Under s 25(1) it is an offence knowingly to be concerned in arrangements for illegal entry into the UK. The defendant must know, or have reasonable cause to suspect, that the person whose entry he is effecting or assisting is an illegal entrant. The offence is indictable. If it is tried summarily the maximum penalty is a fine of £2,000 and/or six months' imprisonment. On conviction on indictment the maximum penalty is a fine and/or seven years' imprisonment. This is an arrestable offence (immigration officers have powers of arrest in respect of it), and the extended time limit applies.

Acts falling within s 25(1) are an offence even if done outside this country, if they are committed by a British person belonging to any of the categories of 'British' citizenship under the 1981 Act; see s 4, and Chapter 3.

There are provisions, if a defendant is convicted on indictment, and he is the owner or captain of the ship, aircraft or vehicle used in connection with the offence, for the ship, aircraft or vehicle to be forfeited, subject to certain restrictions (s 25(6), (7)).

A person is not an 'illegal entrant' for the purposes of s 25(1) if:

(a) he is an asylum seeker; and
(b) he does not attempt to seek entry otherwise; or
(c) he does not obtain entry by fraud, such as by the use of false documents; or
(d) he does not obtain entry without documents.

If a person merely disembarks and does not leave the area of the port designated for disembarkation, he is not an illegal entrant (*R v Nallie* [1992] Imm AR 395).

In *R v Singh and Meeuwsen* [1972] 1 WLR 1600 the Court of Appeal considered whether this offence could be committed despite the fact that the defendants' acts of assisting the illegal entrants were intended to be carried out at a time when the entrants had passed into an area outside the control of the immigration authorities. The entrants had been smuggled in on a ship, hidden inside boilers which were then transported outside the area of the port controlled by the immigration authorities. One of the defendants had intended to drive the immigrants away from the port, and the other defendant was equipped to release them from the boilers. The Court of Appeal held that on the true construction of s 25(1), 'entry into the UK' included helping the entrants to get away from their disembarkation point, so that the defendants had been rightly convicted.

Where the person convicted of an offence of assisting illegal entry is the captain or owner of a ship, aircraft or vehicle used or intended to be used in the carrying out of the arrangements for the illegal entry, the ship, aircraft or vehicle concerned may be forfeited (s 25(6)). This provision also applies where the convicted person is a director or manager of a company which owns the ship, aircraft or vehicle in question.

(b) Harbouring illegal entrants or persons in breach of conditions of entry

Under s 25(2), it is a summary offence knowingly to harbour someone whom the defendant believes or has reasonable cause to believe is either an illegal entrant, or someone who has committed an offence under s 24(1)(*b*) or (*c*). The maximum penalty is a fine of £2,000 (level 5 on the standard scale) and/or six months' imprisonment. The extended time limit applies to this offence. 'Harbouring' means 'giving shelter' (*R v Mistry, R v Asare* [1980] Crim LR 177). Merely being present when the illegal entrant was sheltered, and engaging him in conversation, is not sufficient to amount to harbouring (*Darch v Weight* [1984] 1 WLR 659). The subsection creates two offences. The first is harbouring a person knowing or believing him to be an illegal entrant. The second is harbouring a person knowing or believing him to be an overstayer. An information which fails to specify which offence is alleged will be bad for duplicity (*Rahman v Qadir* [1993] Crim LR 874).

4 General offences in connection with the administration of the 1971 Act

Section 26 creates a series of summary offences connected with the administration of the 1971 Act. They are all punishable by a maximum fine of £1,000 (level 4 on the standard scale) and/or six months' imprisonment.

(a) Failure to submit to examination

Under s 26(1)(a) it is an offence not to submit to an examination under Sched 2 to the Act. The relevant parts of Sched 2 are para 2, which empowers immigration officers and medical inspectors to examine entrants, and para 3, which empowers immigration officers to examine persons seeking to leave the country in order to establish whether they are British citizens and, if not, who they are.

(b) Failure to provide information or documents

This subsection makes it an offence not to produce information or documents which a person has, if he is requested to produce them in an examination under these provisions. It is a defence both to a charge under this subsection and to one under subs (1)(a) that there was a reasonable excuse for the refusal or failure.

(c) Misrepresentation

Section 26(1)(c) makes it an offence to make, or cause to be made, any misrepresentation to an immigration officer or other person acting lawfully in the execution of the 1971 Act. This would include knowingly making a false statement in an application form under the Act, making an oral statement, for example, to an immigration officer which the maker did not believe to be true, or presenting a document such as a passport which the person knew contained false information. It covers a statement which is in fact true, but which the maker did not believe to be true. This subsection does not only apply to statements made in the course of examinations under Sched 2. It is wide enough to cover tacit representations by conduct. However, it does not go so far as to impose a positive duty of disclosure. The subsection should now be read in conjunction with the offences created by the 1981 Act, s 46 (see page 526 below). The extended time limit for prosecutions applies to an offence under this subsection.

The scope of the phrase 'or other person acting lawfully in the execution of this Act' was considered by the HL in *R v Clarke (Ediakpo)* [1985] AC 1037. It was held that the phrase did not apply to a police officer, even where the officer was investigating a suspected offence under the Act. The 1971 Act confers no duty or power upon a police officer to investigate criminal offences committed in contravention of the Act: the police officer's duty to investigate suspected offences arises from the common law.

CRIMINAL OFFENCES 525

Accordingly, an offence under s 26(1)(c) can be committed only by a misrepresentation to a medical officer or some other person (such as a medical inspector), with functions to perform under Sched 2 itself which will, or may, involve the obtaining of relevant information.

(d) Alteration of, and possession of altered, documents

Under s 26(1)(d) it is an offence either to alter any official document issued under the Act (for example, a certificate of entitlement or entry clearance) or to possess any such document or passport which its possessor knows or has reasonable cause to believe is false. It is a defence to a charge under the first limb of this subsection that the alteration was made with lawful authority. The extended time limit for prosecutions applies to the offence. It is also an offence to possess for use a genuine passport with false entries (*R v Zaman* (1975) 6 Cr App Rep 227, CA). A document is false in this context if it falls within the test in the Forgery and Counterfeiting Act 1981, s 9 (broadly, that it was made or authorised by the wrong person: *R v S of S, ex p Patel* [1986] Imm AR 208).

(e) Failure to complete and produce documents

Under Sched 2, para 3 to the 1971 Act the S of S is given power by statutory instrument to make provision for the production of landing and embarkation cards. This power is exercised under the Immigration (Landing and Embarkation Cards) Order 1975 (SI 1975 No 65). Section 26(1)(e) makes it an offence, without reasonable excuse, not to complete and produce such a card.

(f) Failure to comply with regulations

Under s 26(1)(f) it is an offence without reasonable excuse to fail to comply with regulations made by the S of S under the 1971 Act, s 4(3), as to registration with the police and under s 4(4) of that Act, as to providing information for hotel records.

(g) Obstruction of relevant officers

Section 26(1)(g) creates the offence of obstructing an immigration officer (or other person) acting lawfully in the execution of his duties under the Act. For example, it would be an offence to obstruct a medical inspector acting under Sched 2, para 2(2). It is a defence that there is a reasonable excuse for the action under question. (see *R v Clarke (Ediakpo)* [1985] AC 1037).

5 Offences by persons connected with ships, aircraft, ports or with the Channel Tunnel

Section 27 creates further summary offences which can be committed by captains, owners or agents of ships or aircraft. These are all punishable by a maximum of six months' imprisonment and/or a fine of £1,000.

Under the 1971 Act, Scheds 2 and 3, various detailed provisions are made as to the requirements or directions which can be given to captains of ships and aircraft, and their owners or agents, by immigration officers and the S of S. These requirements or directions concern, for instance, the removal of seamen and aircrews who are not British citizens (Sched 2, paras 12 and 13). Schedule 2 also imposes duties on such persons. For instance, para 27 directs captains of ships and aircraft to ensure that passengers do not disembark without being subject to immigration control.

Section 27(a)(i) and (ii) set out the offences which can be committed by captains of ships and aircraft in this context. Section 27(b)(i), (ii) and (iii) provide for offences which can be committed by aircrafts' and ships' owners and agents. These include, for example, failure to supply passengers with embarkation cards (s 27(b)(iii)). Section 27(c) creates an offence of failing to comply with Sched 2, para 26, in connection with 'control areas'. This offence can only be committed by owners or agents of ships or aircraft, or by persons concerned with managing ports or the Channel Tunnel concessionaires. The latter commit an offence if they fail without reasonable cause or excuse to make arrangements for the removal of a person from the UK when required to do so by directions given under the 1971 Act. They also commit an offence if they fail without reaonable excuse to observe any condition or restriction notified to them under the 1971 Act in relation to a control area (see 1971 Act, s 27(d), inserted by Channel Tunnel (Fire Services, Immigration and Prevention of Terrorism) Order 1990).

6 Criminal offences under the British Nationality Act 1981

Section 46 of the 1981 Act creates two summary offences. The first, under s 46(1)(a) and (b), is similar to that created by s 26(1)(c) of the 1971 Act. It concerns the making of a false statement. The difference is that the statement must be made with the object of procuring something to be done, or not to be done, under the

CRIMINAL OFFENCES

1981 Act, whereas the offence under the 1971 Act concerns any statement made to persons acting lawfully under the 1971 Act. Two types of statement are caught by the 1981 Act: those made which are known by the maker to be false in a material particular and those which are made recklessly and are in fact false. This is a better-drafted provision than that creating the equivalent offence under the 1971 Act, which makes it criminal to make a true statement if the maker does not believe it to be true (1971 Act, s 26(1)(c)).

This offence is punishable with a maximum of three months' imprisonment and/or a fine not exceeding £2,000. The extended time limit described above in relation to offences under the 1971 Act applies in respect of this offence also.

The second offence is a failure to comply, without reasonable excuse, with requirements as to certificates of naturalisation. Under the 1981 Act, s 41(1)(f), the S of S may make provision by regulations for the cancellation and registration of certificates of naturalisation of persons deprived of citizenship under the 1981 Act. He may also specify requirements for the delivery up of such certificates. This power has not yet been exercised.

Section 46(2) makes it an offence to fail to comply with these regulations as to the delivering up of certificates of naturalisation. The maximum penalty is a fine of £1,000.

7 Liability to deportation

(a) Under the Immigration Act 1971

Chapter 14 contains a wider discussion of this topic. This section is concerned with liability to deportation for criminal offences. Liability to deportation is provided for under the 1971 Act, Part I. British citizens are not liable to deportation. There are two categories of liability to deportation. The first is under s 3(5): a person is liable to deportation if he has entered with limited leave and either breaches a condition of that leave, or overstays. He is also liable if the Secretary of State deems his deportation to be conducive to the public good, or he is a member of the same family as someone else in respect of whom a deportation order is or has been made. The second is under s 3(6), which provides for a further head of liability in the case of conviction for certain offences. The offender must have attained the age of 17, the offence must be one punishable with a sentence of imprisonment, and his deportation must be recommended by the court at the time of conviction. Detailed provision as to the procedure to be followed in these cases is made by s 6 of the Act and is dealt with in Chapter 14.

Section 5 of the Act makes detailed provisions as to the making of deportation orders. Schedule 3 sets out the manner in which persons are to be removed from the UK on deportation and makes provision for the detention and control of persons under deportation orders.

(b) Under the Prevention of Terrorism (Temporary Provisions) Act 1976: removal and exclusion orders

It should be noted that while British citizens are not liable to deportation, they may be liable to removal or exclusion from England, Scotland and Wales (Great Britain) or from Northern Ireland under the provisions of the Prevention of Terrorism (Temporary Provisions) Act 1976, and its successors. This is the successor to the 1974 Act of the same name, passed after the IRA bombings in Birmingham. The purpose of this Act is to enable the authorities to arrest and question persons who are thought to be terrorists and to exclude them from parts of the UK. Under the Act the relevant S of S may make an order excluding a person from the UK entirely, or from part of it. There is no right of appeal against an exclusion order, although the person on whom it is served may make representations to the Home Secretary within 96 hours. Statutory instruments made under the Act make provision for strict controls at ports of entry.

8 Criminal offences under the Housing Act 1985 and the 1993 Act

A person commits an offence under the Housing Act 1985, s 74 where he:

(*a*) has the intention of inducing a local authority to believe in connection with the exercise of its function in relation to homelessness under the Housing Act 1985 that he or another person
  (i) is homeless or threatened with homelessness;
  (ii) has priority need; or
  (iii) did not become homeless or threatened with homelessness intentionally; and
(*b*) knowingly or recklessly makes a statement which is false in a material particular; or
(*c*) knowingly withholds information which the authority have reasonably required of him to give in connection with those functions.

Persons who fail to notify a material change in their circumstances also commits an offence under the Housing Act 1985, s 74(3). The offences are punishable by a scale 4 fine. The 1993 Act applies these provisions to statements made or information withheld with the intention of inducing the housing authority to believe that a person is or is not an asylum seeker or a dependant of an asylum seeker (1993 Act, Sched 1, para 5).

9 Police station interviews

Interviews will be conducted under caution. If, however, the person has been detained and is being questioned in connection with immigration matters his silence may be construed as lack of co-operation, and may affect the administrative decision as to temporary admission or bail. The provisions of the PACE codes should be observed both by police officers who may interview the detainee, and also by immigration officers if they are investigating a potential offence.

Appendix

The Immigration (European Economic Area) Order 1994 SI No 1895

The Agreement on the European Economic Area, signed at Oporto on 2 May 1992 and adjusted by the Protocol signed at Brussels on 17 March 1993, forms part of the legal order of the EC and now the EU. The EEA Order 1994 is the means by which the UK implements the Agreement. The Order extends freedom of movement and residence under nine Directives from EC nationals to nationals of Austria, Finland, Iceland, Norway and Sweden.

The Directives in question are:
 (a) 64/221, on grounds for exclusion or removal of an EC national;
 (b) 68/360, on free movement for workers;
 (c) 72/194, on residence rights for workers;
 (d) 73/148, on the right of establishment;
 (e) 73/34, on residence rights for the self employed;
 (f) 75/35, on the application of the grounds for removal or exclusion to the self employed;
 (g) 90/364, on residence rights;
 (h) 90/365, on residence rights for the retired self employed;
 (i) 93/96, on the right of residence for students.

Note that where there is a conflict between (a) the provisions of the Order and (b) those of the EEA Agreement, and the various provisions of EC law upon which an applicant may rely, the provisions of the EEA Agreement and Directives prevail. The Order came into effect on 20 July 1994. On the same day s 7 of the 1988 Act came into force, which provides that a person does not require leave to enter or remain in the UK in any case in which he is entitled to do so by virtue of an enforceable Community right or any provision made under s 2(2) of the European Communities Act 1972 as amended by the European Economic Area Act 1993. Article 21 provides that s 8 of the Asylum and Immigration Appeals

Act 1993 dealing with appeals to a special adjudicator extends to persons to whom the 1994 Order applies, as it does in relation to a person who requires leave to enter or remain in the UK. Appeals by asylum seekers are thus the same regardless of their status under the EEA Order (see Chapter 20). Under the Order, on arrival in the UK, the EEA national must produce a valid EEA passport or national identity card. The EEA national is processed by a separate EEA immigration channel at most airports. No stamp or endorsement is placed in his passport, which is inspected to confirm his identity and nationality. Once he enters he may work in employment or self-employment. He may study and he may retire or reside in the UK.

The Order

Definitions

Article 2 sets out the definitions used in the Order. The EEA agreement is defined as above. 'EEA national' is defined as a national of a state which is a contracting party to the Agreement, save nationals of Liechtenstein which has not yet brought the Agreement into force. 'EEA family permit' means an entry clearance, issued free of charge, to a family member who wishes to locate himself in the UK with a person known as a 'qualified person'. 'Family member' in relation to an EEA national means:

(a) that national's spouse;
(b) a descendant of that national or his spouse who is under 21 years of age or is their dependant;
(c) a dependant relative in the ascending line of the EEA national or his spouse. A residence permit and residence document is a permit or document issued by the S of S as proof of the holder's right of residence in the UK.

Marriages of convenience Article 2(2) of the Order states that (in Article 2(1) of the Order) the term 'spouse' does not include a party to a marriage of convenience. In a letter to the S of S dated 30 March 1994, the Clerk to the Joint Committee on Statutory Instruments questioned the *vires* of the Order. Community instruments relating to free movement confer rights on the spouses of EEA nationals. None of these instruments contains a definition of 'spouse'. It is questionable whether the Order is *intra vires* the various Directives and Regulations it purports to implement. The

APPENDIX 533

S of S replied to that letter by a Memorandum of 12 April 1994 in which he stated:

the word spouse in these Community provisions cannot include those who have merely entered into the formalities of a marriage. In particular it cannot include a person who is a party to a marriage contracted for the sole purpose of acquiring a right of residence conferred by Community law. Otherwise the purpose of Community law (namely facilitating the free movement of persons by conferring rights of residence on family members) would be defeated.

The memorandum goes on to say that the primary purpose test will not be applied to the spouses of EEA nationals relying on Community law, but that 'a ground of disqualification can be the fact that the marriage is a "paper marriage" designed solely to acquire Community rights to which the party to the marriage would not otherwise be entitled'. On 12 July 1994 Earl Ferrers wrote to Lord MacIntosh, the Opposition spokesman on Home Affairs, expressing the intention behind the term 'marriage of convenience'. He said that the S of S will not regard as a marriage of convenience the case of a couple who are living apart for work reasons or where there has been a breakdown leading to separation in a genuine marriage. He went on:

Furthermore, although it is an important principle that parties to a marriage of convenience should not benefit from Community law, *we would make further enquiries into a marriage application only when there were reasonable grounds for suspecting that the marriage is a sham – for example a marriage involving a non-European Area national who was on the point of deportation and where there was no evidence of any relationship prior to the marriage.*

When the motion to approve the draft Order came before the House of Lords on 18 July 1994, Earl Ferrers repeated the part of the above statement italicised. He also stated 'I would like to make it quite clear that the provision [Article 2(2)] has been included to deal with marriages which are entirely bogus, the purpose of which is simply to circumvent immigration control.' (HL Debs Vol 557 No 120, Col 116).

Earl Ferrers confirmed that the primary purpose test was not to be applied to EEA marriage cases (Col123). However, considering these ministerial statements, the S of S must prove that the sole intention of the couple was to circumvent the immigration rules. A much higher test is envisaged than that used in primary purpose cases. The position adopted by Earl Ferrers was not that envisaged by earlier formulations of the S of S's position, which referred to marriages of convenience in terms of a 'settled and genuine relationship'. For the purposes of EC law a settled and genuine relationship is not necessary (*Datta v Land Berlin*). It is not necessary, for example, that the parties should intend to live together. If, at the time of the decision, the parties are separated with a view ultimately to divorce the marriage may still form the basis for the exercise of Community rights. The case of *Kwong* (10661) is currently before the Court of Appeal and a reference to the ECJ is likely on the concept of a marriage of convenience.

Carriers' liability

The Immigration (Carriers' Liability) Act 1987 applies to a visa national who is required to hold a family permit as it applies to a person required to hold a visa under the 1971 Act. It is likely that such a person will be checked by the carrier before arrival in the UK.

Entry

Articles 3 and 4 of the Order set out the principal rights of EEA nationals. By Art 3, an EEA national must be admitted to the UK if he produces, on arrival, a valid national identity card or passport issued by another EEA state. A family member of an EEA national must also be admitted to the UK if he produces, on arrival, a valid national identity card issued by an EEA state or a valid passport He may also be required to produce proof that he is a member of the EEA national's family. If he is not an EEA national himself, and is a visa national, he must also have an EEA family permit (Art 3). The rights in Art 3 apply to all EEA nationals and their family members. In particular, it is not necessary for the EEA national to be 'qualified person'.

Residence

The right to residence may be enjoyed by a qualified person and members of his family (Art 4). The right is conferred on the qualified person as long as he remains a qualified person, and on the family members of a qualified person for as long as they remain members of his family. Qualified persons, and the members of their families, may reside and pursue an economic activity in the UK. They may do this whether or not any application for a residence permit or residence document that the Order requires them to make, has been determined by the S of S (Art 4(3)).

Qualified person (Art 6) A 'qualified person' is an EEA national undertaking the activities set out below in the UK. Article 6 is intended to implement the rights of the persons under the directives and regulations of the EC upon which EEA nationals may rely. The activities are those of:

(a) a worker as covered by Art 48 of the Treaty of Rome;
(b) a self-employed person, including a person intending to pursue such an activity;
(c) a provider of services, including a person who seeks to provide services within Art 60 of the EC Treaty;
(d) a recipient of services, including a person who seeks to receive services within the meaning of Art 60 of the EEC Treaty;
(e) a self-employed person who has ceased economic activity in the UK;
(f) a self-sufficient person;
(g) a retired person;
(h) a student.

Workers and unemployment

The residence permit to be granted to a worker takes the form set out in Directive 68/360 EEC. By that Directive, as proof of the right residence, the national must be given a document entitled *Residence permit for a National of a Member State of the EEC.* The document must include a statement in the following form:

This permit is issued pursuant to Regulation (EEC) No 1612/68 of the Council of the European Communities of 15 October 1968 and to the measures taken in implementation of the Council Directive of 15 October 1968. In accordance with the provisions of the above mentioned Regulation, the holder of this permit has the right to take up and pursue an activity as an employed person in [UK] territory under the same conditions as [UK] workers (Art 11(1)).

A worker does not cease to be a qualified person on the ground of unemployment, if he is either temporarily incapable of work as a result of illness or accident, or he is involuntarily unemployed. In the latter case, the fact of his involuntary unemployment must be recorded by the relevant employment office (Art 7(1)). In other words, the person must sign on, and must be involuntarily unemployed for the purpose of unemployment benefit law. The conditions for disqualification from receiving unemployment benefit are set out in s 28 of the Social Security Contributions and Benefits Act 1992. However, on the occasion of the first renewal of a residence permit, the validity of the permit may be limited to one year if the worker has been involuntarily unemployed in the UK for more than one year (Art 13(2)).

Self-employed person who has ceased economic activity in the UK

A self employed person who has ceased economic activity in the UK is defined as a person who satisfies one of the following set of conditions:
(1) On terminating his economic activity in a self-employed capacity, he has reached the age at which he is entitled to a state pension. He must also satisfy the following requirements: (i) he must have pursued an activity in a self-employed capacity in the UK for at least 12 months before ceasing his self employed activity; (ii) he must have resided in the UK for more than two years.
(2) (i) he has resided in the UK for more than two years, and (ii) he has terminated his activity in a self employed capacity as a result of a permanent incapacity to work.
(3) (i) he has been continuously resident and continuously active in a self-employed capacity in the UK for three years, and (ii) he is active in a self-employed capacity in the territory of another EEA state, but resides in the UK and returns to his residence at least once a week.

When considering the requirements relating to length of residence in the UK, or to the length of time a self-employed activity has been pursued, periods of absence from the UK not exceeding three months in any year, or any period of absence from the UK due to military service, are not taken into account in calculating that period. Periods of inactivity caused by circumstances outside the control of the self-employed person and periods of inactivity caused by illness or accident are taken into account, and are treated as periods of activity in a self-employed capacity (Art 6(3)). A self-employed person does not cease to be a qualified person if he is temporarily incapable of work as a result of illness or accident (Art 7(2)).

A family member of a self-employed person (who has ceased economic activity) is a qualified person. If the self-employed person dies the family member continues to be a qualified person if the following conditions are satisfied: the family member must have resided with the self-employed person before the latter's death; alternatively if the death took place before the retirement of the self-employed person, the self-employed person had resided continually in the UK for at least two years. Further, a family member of a self-employed person whose death was the result of an accident at work or occupational disease will continue to be a qualified person for the purposes of the Order (Art 8).

Self sufficient person

'A self sufficient person' is defined in Article 6 as being one who does not enjoy a right of residence under any provision of EC law, other than Directive 90/364 which provides for the admission and residence of persons who have sufficient means to avoid them becoming a burden on the social security system. Such a person must, for the purpose of the Order, have sufficient resources to avoid him becoming a burden on the social assistance system of the UK. The term social assistance is nowhere defined. However, for these purposes a person's resources or income shall be regarded as sufficient if they exceed the level in respect of which the recipient of those resources or income would qualify for social assistance (Art 6(4)). The calculation will require the immigration officer to consider the applicant's capital and income, so as to be able to calculate whether his requirements exceeded his resources for the purposes of being able to claim any of the types of social assistance available in the UK.

Retired persons

'A retired person' is defined as a person who has pursued an activity as an employed or self-employed person, who is covered by sickness insurance in respect of all risks in the UK. He must also be in receipt of one of the following benefits:

(*a*) an invalidity or early retirement pension;
(*b*) old age benefits;
(*c*) survivor's benefits;
(*d*) a pension in respect of an industrial accident or disease.

The amount payable under any of these benefits is paid to the applicant and must be sufficient to avoid him becoming a burden on the social security system of the UK (Art 6(2)(*g*)). In contrast to the provisions relating to 'social assistance' referred to in the definition of self sufficient persons, the retired person need only avoid becoming a burden on the social security system of the UK.

Students

A student is defined as a person who is enrolled at a recognised educational establishment in the UK for the principal purpose of following a vocational training course. He must have sufficient resources to prevent him becoming a burden on the social assistance system of the UK, and he must be covered by sickness insurance which covers him for all risks in the UK (Art 6(2)(*h*)). The only persons who are treated as the family members of a student are his spouse and dependent children (Art 9).

The Joint Committee of both Houses of Parliament appointed to scrutinise Delegated Legislation in its fifteenth report drew special attention to the EEA Order on the ground that there is doubt whether it is *intra vires*. The doubt concerns Art 6(2)(*h*). Article 1 of the Council Directive 93/96 EEC requires only that the student 'assures the relevant national authority by means of a declaration or by such alternative means as the student may choose that are at least equivalent, that he has sufficient resources to avoid becoming a burden on the social assistance system of the host member state'. The Committee suggested that the requirement of the Order may be more onerous than the Directive intended. In order to satisfy the requirement it should be sufficient for a student to produce a declaration giving details of his resources which on the face of it are not clearly inadequate. Also he may under the Directive produce a letter from his funding body confirming his financial position. The S of S sought to reply by means of a Memorandum dated 12 April 1994. The S of S stated that the Order '*does not specify by what means the student is to prove that he has sufficient resources: indeed it does not place any burden of proof on him. It is submitted that the question whether his resources are sufficient is one of fact*'. The Memorandum went on to state that Art 1 of the Directive requires the assurance of the national authority that the student has sufficient resources, and that a mere statement would be insufficient. The S of S stated:

> It cannot, for example, be the case that a student who misrepresents the sufficiency of his resources in a declaration thereby automatically becomes entitled to a right of residence under the Directive (and possibly a burden on public funds) without the risk of removal from the United Kingdom. Resources must in fact be sufficient and this is provided for in the Order.

Arguably the Government's view is at variance with the clear wording of the Directive. Having seen the Memorandum, the Committee concludes '... but the Committee believes that it is doubtful whether the Order does in this respect implement the Directive. There is therefore doubt whether the Order is *intra vires*.' Earl Ferrers stated in the debate on the Order of 18 July 1994:

> We will only require applicants for student residence permits to show

APPENDIX

reasonable evidence of funds, such as bank statements. A declaration, consisting of a letter indicating financial support from parents or other sponsors would generally be regarded as sufficient. Our clear view remains that it cannot be right that a student should be able to acquire a right of residence – possibly also thereby becoming a burden on public funds – by misrepresenting the adequacy of his resources through a false declaration
(HL Debs Vol 557 No 120, 18 July 1994 Col 118).

However, the Directive makes a requirement merely about how the student may be required to assure the national authority. The *vires* of the Order therefore remains in question.

Residence Permits

Grant of residence permits

The S of S must grant a residence permit when a qualified person applies for a residence permit, and (*a*) produces a valid identity card or passport issued by an EEA state and (*b*) proves that he is a qualified person (Art 5(1)). If he is a worker, he may only prove that he is a qualified person by means of confirmation of his engagement from his employer or a certificate of employment (Art 5(3)). If a member of the qualified person's family applies, the S of S must grant a residence permit or a residence document to him, provided that he produces:

(*a*) a valid identity card issued by an EEA state or a valid passport; and

(*b*) proof that he is a family member of a qualified person.

If the person applying for the residence permit or residence document is not an EEA national and requires a family permit for admission to the UK, he must, instead of satisfying the requirement that he produce proof that he is a family member of a qualified person, produce the permit (Art 5(2)). A residence document issued to a family member who is not an EEA national may take the form of a stamp in his passport (Art 11(2)).

The S of S is not obliged to issue a residence permit in the circumstances set out below, regardless of whether a person satisfies the above requirements.

The S of S is not obliged to grant a residence permit to a person other than a qualified person. He is also not obliged to issue a residence permit to the following persons:

(*a*) a worker whose employment in the UK is limited to three months and who either holds a document from his employer

certifying that his employment is limited to three months, or who is a person whose employment is within the scope of the Directive of 25 February 1964 on the freedom to provide services as an intermediary in commerce, industry and small craft industries, or the provisions of Directive 68/360;
- (b) a worker who is employed in the UK, but who resides in another EEA state, returning to that residence at least once a week;
- (c) a seasonal worker whose contract of employment has been approved by the DoE;
- (d) a person who provides or receives services if the services are to be provided for no more than three months.

Art 10).

The S of S may also refuse to grant a residence permit or document to a qualified person or a member of his family if the refusal is justified on grounds of public policy, public security or public health (Art 16).

A residence permit is valid for at least five years (Art 12). However, there are a number of exceptions to this rule. In all cases the validity of the residence permit is not affected by the absence of the holder from the UK for no more than six consecutive months or absence of whatever length for military service (Art 12(7)). The S of S is obliged to renew the residence permit on application, save that certain limitations apply in the case of workers and students (Art 13(1)).

The permit may be limited to the duration of the employment of:
- (a) a worker who is to be employed in the UK for less than twelve, but more than three, months (Article 12(2));
- (b) a seasonal worker who is to be employed for more than three months. The duration of the employment must be indicated in the document confirming the worker's engagement or certificate of employment.

The residence permit may be limited to the period for which services are to be provided in the case of a provider or recipient of services (Art 12(4)). In the case of a student the residence permit may be limited in the following ways:
- (a) to the duration of the course;
- (b) one year if the course lasts longer than a year (Art 12(5)).

In the case of a student whose residence permit is limited

to one year in this way, renewal of the permit may be for periods limited to one year.

The residence permit may be limited to two years in the case of a self sufficient person, or a retired person. The initial period of two years may be extended for a further three years (Art 12(6)).

The family member of an EEA national is entitled to a residence permit or residence document of the same duration as the residence permit granted to the qualified person of whose family he is a member. The permit or document is subject to the same terms as to renewal as apply to the EEA national's permit (Art 14).

Appeals against refusal or withdrawal of a residence permit or residence document

An EEA national or the family member of an EEA national who is refused a residence permit or residence document, or has it withdrawn by the S or S, may appeal against the refusal. He is treated as a person who has a limited leave under the 1971 Act who is appealing against a refusal to vary that leave. The refusal or withdrawal shall not take effect whilst there is an appeal pending, nor shall a person be required to leave the UK during that time. His right to appeal is subject to Art 20 of the Order which applies the following sections of the 1971 Act (the effect of which is considered below):

(a) section 5 (procedure for deportation);
(b) section 13(5) (exclusion conducive to the public good);
(c) section 14(3) (departure conducive to the public good);
(d) section 15(3) (deportation conducive to the public good);
(e) Schedule 2 (examination).

Exclusion and removal of an EEA national from the UK

The provisions of the Order relating to exclusion and removal are designed to implement the provisions of Directive 64/221.

Exclusion

Under Art 15 a person is not entitled to be admitted to the UK by virtue of Art 3 if his exclusion is justified on grounds of public policy, public security or public health. A person who is excluded may appeal against the refusal of admission as if he had been refused leave to enter, and was entitled to appeal by virtue of s 13(1) of the 1971 Act. He may not appeal while he is in the UK. The right to appeal thus conferred is subject to Art 20(2) of the Order. This states that the procedure for deportation under s 5 of the 1971 Act shall apply. Further, the appellant will be treated as if he is not entitled to appeal if the S of S has certified that directions have been given by him personally (and not a person acting under his authority) for the appellant not to be given entry. The direction must be given on the basis that his exclusion is conducive to the public good (1971 Act, s 13(5)). Such a person is also subject to Sched 2 to the 1971 Act which makes provision for the administration of control on entry. In the Order Sched 2's scope is summarised as relating to examination. However, Sched 2 includes provisions relating to removal of illgal entrants (para 8), detention of persons liable to examination (para 16), the effects of appeals, and bail pending appeal (Part II).

Removal

An EEA national and a member of his family may be removed from the UK according to the Order when the EEA national ceases to be a qualified person. A family member may also be removed if he ceases to be a member of the qualified person's family. The EEA national, or the member of his family, may also be removed if his removal is justified on the grounds of public policy, public security or public health (Art 15(2)).

A right of appeal against removal is also conferred by Article 15(2). A person who ceases to be a qualified person or the member of the family of a qualified person is deemed to be a person in respect of whom the S of S has decided to make a deportation order and who is entitled to appeal by virtue of s 15(1)(a) of the 1971 Act. This provides for a right of appeal by a person who the S of S intends to deport under s 3(5) of the 1971 Act either:

(*a*) for having breached a condition of his limited leave or overstaying; or

(*b*) because the S of S deems his deportation to be conducive to the public good; or

(*c*) because another person to whose family he belongs is or has been ordered to be deported.

A person who is to be removed because he has ceased to be a member of an EEA national's family is treated as if he is entitled to appeal under the 1971 Act (Art 15(2)(ii)). There are however further requirements and procedures to be satisfied or followed in his case. He is subject to the procedures for deportation under s 5 of the 1971 Act. In addition he is not entitled to appeal against a *variation* of his leave which reduces its duration, or against any refusal to enlarge or remove the limit on its duration where the

S of S certifies that the appellant's departure from the UK would be conducive to the public good, as being in the interests of national security or of the relations between the UK and any other country or for other reasons for a political nature. He will not be able to appeal where the decision against which he seeks to appeal was taken on one of those grounds by the S of S personally, and not by a person acting under his authority (Art 20(2) applying the 1971 Act, s 14(3)). There is no appeal against a decision to make the *removal order* if the ground of the decision is that his deportation is conducive to the public good as in the interests of national security or of relations between the UK and any other country or for other reasons of a political nature (Art 20(2) applying the 1971 Act s 15(3)). Article 15(2)(ii) also applies s 15(7). Thus a person who has ceased to be a member of an EEA national's family is entitled to appeal to the IAT in the first instance if a deportation order has been made and the ground for making that order was either (*a*) that deportation is conducive to the public good or (*b*) the ground of the deportation order is that he belongs to the family of another person. He must also appeal to the IAT if there is a pending related appeal.

The scheme is to say the least confused. First, the appeal is against a decision to remove him as a person in respect of whom removal is justified on the grounds of public policy public security or public health. These terms have a specific meaning under EC law and refer to the grounds in EC Directive 64/221. However, the circumstances in which there is or is not a right of appeal make reference to grounds 'conducive to public good'. Such considerations limit the right of appeal to which a person is entitled under the Directive, and may breach EC law. Second, the requirement that the person be out of the UK at the time of appeal also acts practically as a (albeit temporary) exclusion and to that extent may be in breach of EC law.

Public policy, public security and public health

Article 17 of the Order attempts to set out the principles upon which decisions taken on the grounds of public policy, public security and public health are to be taken. They are as follows:

(*a*) the relevant grounds shall not be invoked to secure economic ends;
(*b*) a decision taken on one or more of the relevant grounds shall be based exclusively on the personal conduct of the individual in respect of whom the decision is taken;

(c) a person's previous criminal convictions shall not, in themselves, justify a decision on grounds of public policy or public security;
(d) a decision to refuse admission to the United Kingdom or to refuse to grant the first residence permit to a person on the grounds that he has a disease or disability shall be justified only if the disease or disability is of a type specified in council Directive 64/221 EEC;
(e) a disease or disability contracted after a person has been granted a first residence permit shall not justify a decision to refuse to renew his residence permit or a decision to remove him;
(f) a person shall be informed of the grounds of public policy, public security or public health upon which the decision taken in his case is based unless it would be contrary to the interests of national security to do so.

Treatment of persons ceasing to be qualified persons or members of a qualified person's family

Upon ceasing to be a qualified person, an EEA national who is in the UK and the family member of an EEA national in the UK are both to be treated as if they were persons who require leave to enter or remain in the UK under the 1971 Act.

Index

Ability—
 student, leave to enter as, 98–99
Abode, right of—
 acquisition, methods of, 10
 after 1981 Act, 13
 proof of—
  burden of proof, 66–67
  certificate of entitlement, 66–67
  generally, 65–66
  passport, 66
Absence of party—
 asylum appeal, 385–387
Access—
 child, to, person exercising rights of, 190–191
Accommodation—
 business, person intending to establish himself in, 170
 primary purpose test, 211–213
 undertaking relating to, 79
 variation of leave to enter or remain, refusal of, 257
Acquisition of British citizenship. *See* British citizenship—
Adjudicator—
 bail hearing, procedure at, 446–447
 duties and powers of, 459–463
 See also Appeal
Adoption—
 acquisition of British citizenship from 1 January 1983, 30
 foreign child, 233–235
 indefinite leave to enter or remain, 230–233
Afghanistan—
 transit visa, citizen requiring, 92
Agricultural camp—
 seasonal worker at, 122–124

Aircraft—
 criminal offences relating to, 521 526
Airlines—
 Immigration (Carriers' Liability) Act 1987, 37–41
 overseas-owned, airport-based operational ground staff of,
  extension of stay, 157
  indefinite leave to remain, 158
  leave to enter, 156–157
 return air fare, possession of, 88
Algeria—
 co-operation agreement between EC and, 322–325
Aliens—
 Eire, citizens of, 28
 meaning, 29
Ancestry. *See* United Kingdom ancestry
Appeal—
 adjudicator—
  bail hearing, procedure at, 446–447
  duties and powers of, 459–463
Asylum—
 asylum and Immigration Appeals Act 1993, 50
 claim without foundation, 378–381
 Court of Appeal, appeal to, 471
 detention of asylum seeker, 388–390
 determination of, 377–378
 frivolous appeal, 379–380
 from IAT, 383
 general procedure under 1993 Rules,
  absence of party, 385–387
  disclosure, 384–385

545

Appeal—*contd*
  asylum—*contd*
    general procedure under 1993
      Rules—*contd*
        generally, 383–384
        time, 387
        national security, relating to,
          380–381
        removal of asylum seeker, 388–390
        right of appeal, 346, 372–375, 413
        rules, 375–377
        special adjudicator, from,
          full hearing, 381–382
          leave, 381
          special procedure case, 381
        special appeals procedure, 378–381
        to IAT—
          full hearing, 381–382
          leave, 381
          special procedure case, 381
        vexatious appeal, 379–380
  bail—
    adjudicator's hearing, procedure
      at, 446–447
    generally, 445–446
  bail pending—
    generally, 401
    judicial review, 402–403
    restrictions on power to grant,
      401–402
  consolidation of proceedings, 448
  costs, 449
  Court of Appeal, to—
    asylum case, 471
    generally, 471
    mixed case, 471
    non-asylum case, 472
  deportation, against—
    appeal out of time, 422
    criminal court recommendations,
      421–422
    destination, objections to, 423–424
    generally, 418–419
    hearing, 280
    IAT as first instance tribunal, 421
    merits, limits on right to argue,
      419–421
    pending related appeals, 421
    remaining rules, 278–279
    removal, directions for, 422–423
    revocation of order, 283–284
    time limits, 422
  documents—
    appeal to IAT, 470
    discovery of, 442

Appeal—*contd*
  documents—*contd*
    inspection of, 442
    service of, 442–443
  EEA national, relating to, 314–316
  entry clearance, refusal of, 261
    415–416
  frivolous, 379–380
  further opportunity to appeal,
    444–445
  hearing—
    absence of party, 450–452
    adjudicator, duties and powers of,
      459–463
    appeal determined without,
      450–452
    burden of proof, 454–455
    evidence, 455
    notification of, 448
    oral, procedure at, 452–454
  Immigration Appeal Tribunal—
    asylum appeal. *See* asylum, *above*
    criteria to be satisfied—
      arguable point of law, 466–467
      generally, 465–466
    documents, 470
    evidence, 470
    first instance tribunal, as, 421
    generally, 464–465
    grounds of appeal, 469–470
    how to appeal to, 467–469
    refusal of leave to appeal, 469–470
  interlocutory matters before
    hearing—
    adjudicator's bail hearing,
      procedure at, 446–447
    amendment, 441–442
    bail, 445–446
    consolidation of proceedings, 448
    costs, 449
    directions, 441–442
    discovery of documents, 442
    generally, 449–450
    inspection of documents, 442
    notification of hearing, 448
    particulars, 441–442
    respondent's explanatory
      statement, 440–441
    service of documents, 442–443
    summoning witnesses, 447
    transfer of proceedings, 447–448
    withdrawal of appeal, 448–449
  judicial review, application for—
    full hearing, appeal from, 509
    interlocutory appeal, 508–509

INDEX

Appeal—*contd*
  launching—
    oral notice, 439–440
    written notice, 438–439
  leave to enter, refusal of, 261
    415–416
  notice—
    contents of, 437–438
    oral, 439–440
    post, service by, 435–436
    service of, 435–438
    written, 438–439
  notification of rights of, 434–435
  oral hearing, 452–454
  oral notice, 439–440
  out of time, 422
  preliminary points, 443–444
  rights of—
    asylum case, 346, 372–375, 413
    circumstances in which there is none,
    conditions, 426–427
    deportation order, 431–432
    exclusion from UK, 424–426
    generally, 413–414
    mandatory refusal, 427–431
    miscellaneous, 432–433
  exclusion, 415–416
  generally, 15–16 413
  HC 395 Part 12, 411–418
  limited leave, conditions on, 416–418
  notification of, 434–435
  Secretary of State, reference of case to, 470–471
  service of notice,
    contents of notice, 437–438
    effect of, 436–437
    post, by, 435–436
  summoning witnesses, 447
  transfer of proceedings, 447–448
  vexatious, 379–380
  withdrawal of, 448–449
  written notice, 438–439
Approved exchange scheme—
  language assistant coming to UK under, 124–126
  teacher coming to UK under, 124–126
Arrival—
  entry to UK compared with, 65
  meaning, 65

Artist—
  extension of stay, 184–186
  indefinite leave to remain, 185–186
  leave to enter, 184
Associations—
  variation of leave to enter or remain, refusal of, 257
Asylum—
  appeal—
    Asylum and Immigration Appeals Act 1993, 50
    claim without foundation, 378–381
    Court of Appeal, appeal to, 471
    detention of asylum seeker, 388–390
    determination of, 377–378
    frivolous, 379–380
    from IAT, 383
    general procedure under 1993 Rules,
      absence of party, 385–387
      disclosure, 384–385
      generally, 383–384
      time, 387
    national security, relating to, 380–381
    removal of asylum seeker, 388–390
    right of, 346, 372–375, 413
    rules, 375–377
    special adjudicator, from,
      full hearing, 381–382
      leave, 381
      special procedure case, 381
    special appeals procedure, 378–381
    to IAT—
      full hearing, 381–382
      leave, 381
      special procedure cases, 381
    vexatious, 379–380
  application—
    asylum applicant, meaning, 335 336–337
    cessation of status, 343–344
    construing convention, 337–338
    exclusion of status, 344
    generally, 335–336, 338–339
    grant of asylum, 336, 339–343
    owing to well founded fear,
      meaning, 341
    previously rejected application, 345–346, 352
    race, persecution for reasons of, 341–342

Asylum—*contd*
  application—*contd*
    refugee, meaning, 340–341
    refusal of asylum, 339–340
    religion, persecution for reasons
      of, 341–342
    social group, 342–343
    status—
      cessation of, 343–344
      exclusion of, 344
  Asylum and Immigration Appeals Act
    1993, 50
  child—
    dependant, 363–364
    unaccompanied, 363
  consideration of cases,
    credibility, 360–362
    generally, 352–353
    paras 340–344, 358–360
    preparation of asylum claim,
      353–358
  deception, entry by, 20
  deportation of person who has
    claimed, 280–281
  detention of asylum seeker, 388–390
  Dublin Convention, 367–370
  EU law—
    Dublin Convention, 367–370
    generally, 367
    responsible state, duties of,
      370–371
  exceptional leave to remain, 365
  fingerprinting of asylum seeker,
    358–360
  generally, 260
  grant of, 336, 339–343
  housing provision, 366–367
  preparation of claim—
    asylum seeker's statement,
      354–358
    background materials, 354
    generally, 353
    in country cases, 358
    initial interview, 353–354
    port application, 354
  refugee, meaning, 340–341
  refusal of—
    appeal, right of, 346
    generally, 339–340, 344–345
    previously rejected application,
      345–346, 352
    third country case, 345

Asylum and Immigration Appeals Act
  1993—*contd*
  refusal of—*contd*
    without consideration,
      former Yugoslavia, statement
        on refugees from, 351–352
      safe third country, 346–350
      substantial links with UK,
        350–351
  removal of asylum seeker, 388–390
  settlement and, 365–366
  social security provision, 366–367
  statement of asylum seeker, 354–358
Au pair placement—
  extension of stay as, 116–117
  leave to enter as, 115–116
  meaning, 115
Aunt—
  exceptional compassionate circumstances relating to, 243

BDTCs. *See* British Dependent
  Territories citizens (BDTCs)—
BNOs. *See* British Nationals
  (Overseas)—
BOCs. *See* British overseas citizens
  (BOCs)—
BPP. *See* British protected persons
  (BPP)—
Bail—
  adjudicator's bail hearing, procedure
    at, 446–447
  appeal, interlocutory matters before
    hearing, 445–446
  examination detainee, for, 399–400
  judicial review, application for—
    507–508
  pending appeal—
    generally, 401
    judicial review, 402–403
    restrictions on power to grant,
      401–402
Birth—
  acquisition of British citizenship
    from 1 January 1983, 29–30
Blood relationship—
  proof of, 222–224
British citizenship—
  acquisition from 1 January 1983,
    adoption, by, 30
    birth, by, 29–30
    descent, by, 30–31
    generally, 29

INDEX 549

British citizenship—*contd*
  acquisition from 1 January
    1983—*contd*
      naturalisation, by,
        general requirements, 34
        generally, 33-34
        spouses of British citizens,
          34-35
      registration, by, 31-33
  loss of—
    deprivation, by, 35-36
    generally, 35
    renunciation, by, 35
  meaning, 25
  spouses of British citizens, 34-35
British Dependent Territories citizens
  (BDTCs)—
  general background, 4
  meaning, 25-26
  registration, application for, 32-33
British Nationality Acts—
  1948,
    CUKC, 5
    general background, 5
  1981,
    acquisition of British citizenship
      from 1 January 1983,
      adoption, by, 30
      birth, by, 29-30
      descent, by, 30-31
      generally, 29
      naturalisation, by—
        general requirements, 34
        generally, 33-34
        spouses of British citizens,
          34-35
      registration, by, 31-33
    aliens, 29
    British citizens, 25
    British dependent Territories
      citizens, 25-26
    British Nationals (Overseas)(Hong
      Kong), 26
    British overseas citizens, 26-27
    British protected persons, 27
    British subjects, 27
    categories of citizenship defined
      by—
        aliens, 29
        British citizens, 25
        British Dependent Territories
          citizens, 25-26

British Nationality Acts—*contd*
  1981—*contd*
    categories of citizenship defined
      by—*contd*
        British Nationals (Overseas)
          (Hong Kong), 26
        British overseas citizens, 26-27
        British protected persons, 27
        British subjects, 27
        Eire, citizens of, 28
        EU citizens, 28-29
        other relevant categories, 27-29
    EU citizens, 28-29
    general background, 6-7, 24
    loss of British citizenship,
      deprivation, 35-36
      generally, 35
      renunciation, 35
    Hong Kong. *See* Hong Kong
British Nationals (Overseas)—
  Hong Kong, 26
  registration, application for, 32-33
British overseas citizens (BOCs)—
  general background, 4
  meaning, 26-27
  registration, application for, 32-33
British protected persons (BPP)—
  general background, 3
  meaning, 27
  registration, application for, 32-33
British subjects—
  categories, 3-4
  meaning, 27
  registration, application for, 32-33
Broadcasting organisation,
  representative of—
  extension of stay, 144-145
  leave to enter, 143-144
Burden of proof. *See* Proof
Business—
  EC Association Agreement, under,
    extension of stay, 178-181
    Hungary, national of, 177-178
    indefinite leave to remain, 178-181
    leave to enter, 175-177
    Poland, national of, 177-178
  existing, taking over or joining,
    171-172
  free movement of EC nationals,
    299-300
  new, establishment of, 172

Business—*contd*
person intending to establish himself
in—
accommodation, 170
disguised employment, 170-171
establishing new business, 172
extension of stay, 173-174
his own money, 169-170
indefinite leave to remain, 174
joining existing business, 171-172
lawyers, concession relating to, 172
leave to enter, 166-172
maintenance, 170
meeting liabilities, 171
taking over existing business, 171-172
visitor, 85-86

CUKC. *See* Citizenship of UK and Commonwealth (CUKC)—
Carrier—
Immigration (Carriers' Liability) Act 1987, 37-41
Certificate of entitlement—
abode, proof of right of, 66-67
Certiorari—
judicial review, remedy for, 499-500
Change of circumstance—
entry clearance, refusal of, 253
leave to enter, refusal of, 253
Channel Islands—
common travel area, 67-68
Channel Tunnel—
criminal offences relating to, 526
person arriving in UK or seeking entry through, 63
Character—
variation of leave to enter or remain, refusal of, 257
Child—
access to, person exercising rights of, 190-191
adopted—
foreign child, 233-235
indefinite leave to enter or remain, 230-233
settlement as, leave to enter or remain for, 235-237
adoption—
after entry, 234-235
foreign child, 233-235

Child—*contd*
asylum—
dependant, 363-364
unaccompanied child, 363
blood relationship, proof of, 222-224
born in UK who is not British citizen, 228-230
British Nationality (Hong Kong) Act 1990, application under, 48, 49
deportation and, 275
foreign, adoption of, 233-235
indefinite leave to enter or remain—
adopted child, 230-233
both parents present and settled in UK, 225
child born in UK who is not British citizen, 228-230
compelling family or other considerations, 226-228
concession relating to child under 12, 226
generally, 218-222, 224, 228
serious family or other considerations, 226-228
settlement, on same occasion admitted for, 225
sole responsibility, 225-226
parent. *See* Parent
person with limited leave to enter or remain, of, 132-134 163-165 188-190 198-200
polygamous marriage, of, 222
resident in UK, person with rights of access to, 190-191
student, of, 111-112
unaccompanied, asylum and, 363
under 12, concession relating to, 226
working holidaymaker, of, 121-122
See also Minor
Citizenship of UK and Commonwealth (CUKC)—
British Nationality Act 1948, 5
general background, 3-4
patrials distinguished from non-patrials, 4
Cohabitant—
primary purpose test, 213-214
Common travel area—
immigration authorities, acceptability of refusal to enter to, 247
meaning, 67-68

INDEX

Commonwealth citizens—
    patrials distinguished from non-patrials, 4
    settled in UK in 1973, immigration rules and, 52
    See also Citizenship of UK and Commonwealth (CUKC)
Commonwealth Imigrants Acts 1962 and 1968—
    general background, 5
Composer—
    extension of stay, 184–186
    indefinite leave to remain, 185–186
    leave to enter, 184
Concession—
    child under 12, relating to, 226
    established marriage, intervening devotion in, 211
    lawyers, relating to, 172
Conduct—
    variation of leave to enter or remain, refusal of, 257
Control of immigration. *See* Immigration control—
Costs—
    appeal, of, 449
Course of study—
    full time, 99–100
    intention to leave at end of, 105–106
Court of Appeal—
    appeal to, 471–472
Creative artist—
    extension of stay, 184–186
    indefinite leave to remain, 185–186
    leave to enter, 184
Credibility—
    asylum, application for, 360–362
Crew member—
    leave to remain, refusal of, 255
Criminal conviction—
    entry clearance, refusal of, 251
    leave to enter, refusal of, 251
Criminal court—
    deportation, recommendation relating to, 269–271, 279, 406–407, 421–422
Criminal offences—
    1993 Act, under, 528–529
    aircraft, relating to, 521, 526
    British Nationality Act 1981, under, 526–527
    Channel Tunnel, relating to, 526
    deportation, liability to, 527–528

Criminal offences—*contd*
    illegal entry,
        assisting, 522–523
        generally, 517–521
        harbouring illegal entrant, 523
    Immigration Act 1971,
        administration of, general offences in connection with, 523–525
        under, 517
    police station interview, 529
    port, relating to, 526
    ship, relating to, 521, 526

Daughter—
    exceptional compassionate circumstances relating to, 243
Deception—
    entry by, 19–22
    obtaining previous leave by, 249
Declaration—
    duration of stay, as to, 257
Delay—
    judicial review, restrictions on, 498–499
Dentist—
    post-graduate, leave to enter as, 109–110
Department of Employment. *See* Employment, Department of—
Dependent relative—
    indefinite leave to enter or remain, 237–242
Deportation—
    appeal against—
        appeal out of time, 422
        criminal court recommendations, 421–422
        destination, objections to, 423–424
        generally, 418–419
        hearing, 280
        IAT as first instance tribunal, 421
        merits, limits on right to argue, 419–421
        pending related appeals, 421
        remaining rules, 278–279
        removal, directions for, 422–423
        revocation of order, 283–284
        time limits, 422
    appendix, 285–286
    child and, 275
    criminal court, recommendations of, 269–271, 279, 406–407, 421–422
    detention of person before, 407–408

Deportation—*contd*
  detriment to community, 270
  EEA national, of—
    EC provision, 312–313
    national security, 313–314
  European Convention on Human
    Rights and Deportation, 270–271
  family member, of, 275–278
  generally, 262–263
  liability to, 527–528
  long residence policies,
    fourteen years, 264
    generally, 263
    ten years, 263–264
  marriage and, 273–275
  national security, in interest of,
    313–314, 431–432
  order—
    appeal. *See* appeal against, *above*
    asylum, person claiming, 280–281
    breach of conditions, 266–267
    child, case involving, 275
    considerations to be taken into
      account, 272–273
    criminal court, recommendations
      by, 269–271, 279 406–407,
      421–422
    effect of, 407
    entry clearance, refusal of, 246
    generally, 265–266
    leave to enter, refusal of, 246
    marriage, case involving, 273–275
    public good, deportation
      conducive to, 267–269, 279–280
    revocation of, 283–284, 408
    Secretary of State, by—
      decision to deport, 404–405
      generally, 404
      signing order, 405–406
    student working in breach of, 267
    unauthorised stay, 266–267
  procedure—
    arrangements for removal,
      281–282
    generally, 281, 282–283
    order. *See* order, *above*
    returned deportees, 282
    returned family member, 282
    supervised departure, 282
  public good, conducive to, 267–269
    279–280
Deprivation—
  loss of British citizenship by, 35–36

Descent—
  acquisition of British citizenship
    from 1 January 1983, 30–31
  patriality by virtue of, 11–12
Destination—
  appeal, right of, 415–416
  objections to, 423–424
Detention—
  asylum seeker, of, 388–390
  bail for examination detainee,
    399–400
  breach of conditions by person liable
    to, 520–521
  deportation, before, 407–408
  examination, person liable to,
    398–399
  removal, person liable to, 398–399
  temporary admission of person
    liable to be detained, 399
Diplomatic household
  private servant in—
    extension of stay, 149–151
    leave to enter, 148–149
Directions—
  adjudicator's power to give, 462–463
Disciplined services—
  British Nationality (Hong Kong) Act
    1990, application under, 48
Disclosure—
  asylum appeal, 384–385
  material facts, failure to disclose,
    249–250
  material non-disclosure, 250, 253
Discretion—
  judicial review, restrictions on, 499
Divorce—
  deportation and, 274–275
Doctor—
  post-graduate, leave to enter as,
    109–110
Documents—
  appeal. *See* Appeal
  criminal offences, 524, 525
  failure to produce, 246–247
  variation of leave to enter or remain,
    refusal of, 257–258
Domestic work—
  work permit holder, 136
Duration of stay—
  declaration as to, 257

EC. *See* European Community (EC)

INDEX

ECHR. *See* European Convention on Human Rights—
EEAA. *See* European Economic Area Agreement—
EU. *See* European Union (EU)—
Eire—
  citizens of, 28
  common travel area, 67–68
  Dublin Convention, 367–370
Employee—
  overseas government—
    extension of stay, 151–152
    indefinite leave to remain, 152
    leave to enter, 151
Employment—
  disguised, person intending to establish himself in business, 170–171
  EEA undertaking, third country national employed in, 325
  meaning, 88–89
  person in, right to residence permit, 307
  retirement after, EEA worker, 298–299
  student, leave to enter as, 102–103
  work permit. *See* Work permit
Employment, Department of—
  approved training or work experience—
    extension of stay, 129–131
    leave to enter for, 126–127
    requirements, 127–129
  work permit, requirements relating to, 138–141
Enforcement—
  EC law, of, 328–332
  EEA law, of, 328–332
Entrepreneurs—
  British Nationality (Hong Kong) Act 1990, application under, 48
Entry—
  arrival compared with, 65
  Channel Tunnel, through, 63
  clearance—
    asylum. *See* Asylum
    generally, 72–74
    meaning, 73
    refusal of—
      appeal, right of, 261, 415–416
      general grounds for, 244–246

Entry—*contd*
  clearance—*contd*
    refusal of—*contd*
      mandatory grounds—
        common travel area immigration authorities, acceptability to, 247
        deportation order, currently subject to, 246
        documents, failure to produce, 246–247
        visa national, 247
        medical reasons, 247–248
      non-mandatory grounds—
        criminal conviction, 251
        deception, previous leave obtained by, 249
        false representation, 249–250
        information, failure to furnish, 248
        material facts, failure to disclose, 249–250
        material non-disclosure, 250
        parent's consent, 250–251
        passport not recognised, 249
        public good, discretionary exclusion conducive to, 251–252
        returning residents, 248–249
        time limit or conditions, failure to observe, 249
        undertaking, sponsor's refusal to give, 249
    person in possession of entry clearance—
      change of circumstance, 253
      false representation, 253
      generally, 252–253
      non-disclosure, 253
      restricted returnability, 254
      public good, exclusion conducive to, 247–248
    visa national, 74–75
  deception, by, 19–22
  extension of stay. *See* Extension of stay
  illegal. *See* Illegal entry
  indefinite leave to remain. *See* Indefinite leave to remain
  leave to enter UK—
    agricultural camp, seasonal worker at, 122–123
    appeal, right of, 261, 415–416

Entry—*contd*
  leave to enter UK—*contd*
    arrival, meaning, 65
    artist, 184
    asylum. *See* Asylum
    au pair placement, 115–116
    broadcasting organisation, representative of, 143–144
    business, person intending to establish himself in, 166–169
    Channel Tunnel, through, 63
    child. *See* Child
    composer, 184
    creative artist, 184
    curtailment of, 254–258
    diplomatic household, private servant in, 148–149
    DoE approved training or work experience, 126–127
    EC Association Agreement, person establishing himself in business under, 175–177
    EEA national, 260
    fiance(é), 216–218
    general provisions, 62–65
    identity, evidence of, 63
    independent means, retired person of, 194, 195–196
    investor, 181–182
    language assistant under approved exchange scheme, 124–125
    minister of religion, 152–154
    missionary, 152–154
    nationality, evidence of, 63
    news agency, representative of, 143–144
    overseas firm, sole representative of, 145–146
    overseas government employee, 151
    overseas newspaper, representative of, 143–144
    overseas-owned airlines, airport-based operational ground staff of, 156–157
    police, registration with, 258–260
    private servant in diplomatic household, 148–149
    refusal of—
      curtailment of leave, 254–258
      entry clearance, person in possession of, change of circumstance, 253

Entry—*contd*
  leave to enter UK—*contd*
    refusal of—*contd*
      non-mandatory grounds—*contd*
        false representations, 253
        generally, 252–253
        non-disclosure, 253
        restricted returnability, 254
      exercise of power to refuse, 63
      general grounds, 244–246
      mandatory grounds—
        common travel area immigration authorities, acceptability to, 247
        deportation order, currently subject to, 246
        documents, failure to produce, 246–247
        visa national, 247
      medical reasons, 247–248
      non-mandatory grounds,
        criminal convictions, 251
        deception, obtaining previous leave by, 249
        false representation, 249–250
        information, failure to furnish, 248
        material facts, failure to disclose, 249–250
        material non-disclosure, 250
        parent's consent, 250–251
        passport not recognised, 249
        public good, discretionary exclusion conducive to, 251–252
        returning resident, 248–249
        time limit or conditions, failure to observe, 249
        undertaking, sponsor's refusal to give, 249
    para 323, 258
    public good, exclusion conducive to, 247–248
    variation of leave to enter or remain, 254–258
    religious order, member of, 153–154
    retired person of independent means, 194, 195–196
    returning residents, 69–71
    seasonal worker at agricultural camp, 122–123
    sole representative, 145–146

INDEX

Entry—*contd*
  leave to enter UK—*contd*
    spouse of person present and settled in UK, 204–205
    spouse of person with limited leave to remain, 131–132, 161–163, 186–188, 196–198
    student. *See* Student
    teacher under approved scheme, 124–125
    UK ancestry, on grounds of, 158–159
    variation of, 75–78
    visitor. *See* Visitor
    withdrawn application, 78–79
    work permit holder, 137–138
    working holidaymaker, 117–118
    writer, 184
  returning resident, as, 69–71
Establishment—
  right of, 291–292
European Commission—
  procedure for making application to, 479–480
European Community (EC)—
  admission, right of,
    business, 299–300
    residence, 302
    retired person, 303
    self-employed person, 299–300
    services, provision or receipt of, 299–300
    students, 301
    workers, 294–299
  Association Agreement, person intending to establish himself in business under,
    extension of leave, 178–181
    Hungary, national of, 177–178
    indefinite leave to remain, 178–181
    leave to enter, 175–177
    Poland, national of, 177–178
  employment, person in, 307
  European Convention on Human Rights under law of, 478–479
  external frontiers of Member States, agreement on, 325–327
  free movement—
    admission, right of,
      business, 299–300
      residence, 302
      retired person, 303
      self-employed person, 299–300

European Community (EC)—*contd*
  free movement—*contd*
    admission, right of—*contd*
      services, provision or receipt of, 299–300
      student, 301
      workers, 294–299
    Algeria, co-operation agreement with, 322–325
    application of law, 328–332
    EEA undertaking, third country nationals employed in, 325
    EEAA. *See* European Economic Area Agreement
    enforcement of law, 328–332
    external frontiers of Member States, agreement on, 325–327
    generally, 289–290
    injunction, 331
    Morocco, co-operation agreement with, 322–325
    permitted derogation, nature of,
      deportation of EEA national, 303–305
      public health, 305
      public policy, 303–305
      public security, 303–305
      refusal of entry, 303–305
    personal scope of right to,
      EEA national, 293–294
      family member, 293–294
    preliminary rulings—
      generally, 331–332
      procedure for applying, 332
    third country agreements, 320–327
    Tunisia, co-operation agreement with, 322–325
    Turkey, Association Agreement with, 320–322
    UK implementation of, 316–319
    UK provisions, 305–306
  third country agreements,
    Algeria, with, 322–325
    EEA undertaking, national employed in, 325
    external frontiers of Member States, 325–327
    generally, 320
    Morocco, with, 322–325
    Tunisia, with, 322–325
    Turkey, with, 320–322
  treaties, UK nationals for purposes of, 33

European Convention on Human
Rights
EC Commission, procedure for
making application to, 479–480
EC law, under, 478–479
generally, 473
interpretative guide, as, 473–475
remedy, as, 475–478
European Economic Area Agreement
Act of 1993, 292–293
admission, rights of—
business, 299–300
residence, 302
retired person, 303
self-employed person, 299–300
services, provision or receipt of,
299–300
students, 301
workers, 294–299
deportation of national—
EC provision, 312–313
national security, 313–314
EEA national, meaning, 62
employment—
person in, 307
retirement after, 298–299
family permit—
issue of, 317
meaning, 317
public health, exclusion on
grounds of, 319
public policy, exclusion on
grounds of, 319
public security, exclusion on
grounds of, 319
qualified person, meaning, 319
refusal of application for, 317
free movement—
annex V, 291
annex VIII, 292
application of law, 328–332
enforcement of law, 328–332
establishment, right of, 291–292
generally, 290–291
injunction, 331
personal scope of right to,
293–294
preliminary rulings—
generally, 331–332
procedure for applying for, 332
public health, exclusion on
grounds of, 303–304, 319

European Economic Area
Agreement—*contd*
free movement—*contd*
public policy, exclusion on
grounds of, 303–304, 319
public security, exclusion on
grounds of, 303–304, 319
self-employed person, 291
services, 292
UK implementation of, 316–318
Immigration (European Economic
Area) Order 1994, 292–293
nationals—
appeal relating to, 314–316
deportation of, 303–304
families, and, 194
meaning, 62
police, registration with, 260, 318
refusal of entry to, 303–305
objectives, 290
police, registration of national with,
260, 318
principles, 290
residence—
admission, rights of, 302
appeal, right of, 314–316
deportation and, 312–314
Directive 68/360, 307–308
employment, person in, 307
generally, 307
incapacitated person, 310–312
other rights, 309–310
retired person, 310–312
rights of, 307–308
services, in relation to, 308–309
students, 309
retirement after employment,
298–299
undertaking, third country national
employed in, 325
European Union (EU)—
asylum law—
Dublin Convention, 367–370
generally, 367
responsible state, duties of,
370–371
citizens, 28–29, 135–136
spouse, 201–202
student, 103–104
Evidence—
appeal—
adjudicator, duties and powers of,
461–462

INDEX

Evidence—*contd*
  appeal—*contd*
    hearing, 455–459
    to IAT, 470
    findings on, 461–462
    fresh, 456–457
    hearsay, 457
    intervening devotion, of, 210–211
    judicial review, application for, 504
    oral, 457–459
    primary purpose case, 213
Examination—
  bail for detainee, 399–400
  detention of person liable to, 398–399
  immigration authorities, by, generally, 393–396
  illegal entrant, removal of, 397–398
  notice of leave or refusal, 396–397
  person refused leave, removal of, 397–398
  satisfactory progress, student required to make, 106
Exceptional leave to remain—
  asylum and, 365
  See also Indefinite leave to remain
Extension of stay—
  agricultural camp, seasonal worker at, 123–124
  artist, 184–186
  au pair placement, 116–117
  broadcasting organisation, representative of, 144–145
  business, person intending to establish himself in, 173–174
  composer, 184–186
  creative artist, 184–186
  diplomatic household, private servant in, 149–151
  DoE approved training or work experience, 129–131
  EC Association Agreement, person establishing himself in business under, 178–181
  fiance(é), 217
  independent means, retired person of, 195
  investor, 182
  language assistant under approved exchange scheme, 125–126
  minister of religion, 155–156
  missionary, 155–156

Extension of stay—*contd*
  news agency, representative of, 144–145
  overseas firm, sole representative of, 146–148
  overseas government employee, 151–152
  overseas newspaper, representative of, 144–145
  overseas-owned airline, airport-based operational ground staff of, 157
  postgraduate dentist, 109–110
  postgraduate doctor, 109–110
  primary purpose test, 215–216
  private medical treatment, visitor for, 94–95
  private servant in diplomatic household, 149–151
  prospective student, 113
  religious order, member of, 155–156
  retired person of independent means, 195
  seasonal worker at agricultural camp, 123–124
  sole representative, 146–148
  spouse of person present and settled in UK, 205–206
  student , 104–105
  student nurse, 107–109
  teacher under approved exchange scheme, 125–126
  training, 129–131
  UK ancestry, on grounds of, 159–160
  visitor , 90–91
  visitor in transit, 91
  work experience, 129–131
  work permit employment, 141–142
  working holidaymaker, 118–119 120–121
  writer, 184–186

False representation—
  entry clearance, refusal of, 249–250 253
  leave to enter, refusal of, 249–250
Family member—
  aunt, 243
  child. *See* Child
  daughter, 243
  dependent relative, 237–242
  deportation of, 275–278 282–283

INDEX

Family member—*contd*
　EEA family permit—
　　issue of, 317
　　meaning, 317
　　public health, exclusion on grounds of, 319
　　public policy, exclusion on grounds of, 319
　　public security, exclusion on grounds of, 319
　　qualified person, meaning, 319
　　refusal of application for, 317
　grandparent, 237-242
　parent, 222, 237-242
　primary purpose test. *See* Primary purpose test
　son, 243
　spouse. *See* Spouse
　uncle, 243
Fear—
　asylum, application for, 341
Fiance(é)—
　extension of stay, 217
　leave to enter, 216-218
Finance—
　primary purpose test, 211-213
Fingerprinting—
　asylum seeker, of, 358-360
Firm—
　overseas, sole representative of,
　　extension of stay, 146-148
　　indefinite leave, 147, 148
　　leave to enter, 145-146
Free movement. *See* European Community (EC); European Economic Area Agreement—
Full time course of study—
　student, leave to enter as, 99-100

General background—
　British Dependent Territories citizens, 4
　British Nationality Acts. *See* British Nationality Acts
　British overseas citizens, 4
　British protected persons, 3
　citizenship of UK and Commonwealth, 3-4, 5
　Commonwealth Immigrants Acts 1962 and 1968, 5
　Immigration Acts. *See* Immigration Acts
　parliamentary materials, use of, 7-8

General occupational class—
　British Nationality (Hong Kong) Act 1990, application under, 47
Goods—
　production of, visitor not intending to engage in, 88-89
Government—
　overseas government employee,
　　extension of stay, 151-152
　　indefinite leave to remain, 152
　　leave to enter, 151
Grandparent—
　indefinite leave to enter or remain, 237-242

Habeas corpus—
　application for, 510-513
Harbouring—
　illegal entrant, of, 523
Head of household—
　British Nationality (Hong Kong) Act 1990, application under, 47
Hearing—
　appeal. *See* Appeal
　judicial review, 508
Holder of special voucher—
　indefinite leave to enter, 191-194
Holidaymaker. *See* Working holidaymaker—
Home Office—
　concessions, 54-55
　policies, 54-55
Hong Kong—
　British Nationality (Hong Kong) Act 1990,
　　children, 48, 49
　　consequences of registration, 49-50
　　disciplined services, 48
　　entrepreneurs class, 48
　　exceptions to registration, 49
　　general occupational class, 47
　　generally, 43
　　head of household, 47
　　qualification, 43-46
　　scheme, 46-47
　　sensitive service class, 48
　　spouses, 48, 49
　　third country citizenship, 48
　British nationals (Overseas), 26
　registration—
　　children, 48, 49
　　consequences of, 49-50

INDEX

Hong Kong—*contd*
  registration—*contd*
    disciplined services, 48
    entrepreneurs class, 48
    exceptions to, 49
    general occupational class, 47
    generally, 43
    head of household, 47
    qualification, 43–46
    scheme, 46–47
    sensitive service class, 48
    spouses, 48, 49
    third country citizenship, 48
Housing—
  asylum seeker, provision for, 366–367
Human rights—
  interference with, judicial review, 484–485
  See also European Convention on Human Rights
Hungary—
  agreement between EC states and, 177–178

Illegal entrant—
  harbouring, 523
  judicial review, 485–486
  removal of, 397–398
Illegal entry—
  assisting illegal entry, 522–523
  criminal offences, 517–521
  deception, entry by, 19–22
  generally, 16–18
  harbouring illegal entrant, 523
  illegal entrant, meaning, 16, 17
  mistake, effect of, 18–19
  proof of, 22–23
Illegality—
  judicial review, grounds for, 486–487
Immigration (Carriers' Liability) Act 1987—
  summary of provisions, 37–41
Immigration Acts
  1971—
    abode, right of—
      acquisition, methods of, 10
      after 1981 Act, 13
      before 1981 Act, 10
      appeal, rights of, 15–16
      general background, 6
      generally, 9

Immigration Acts—*contd*
  1971—*contd*
    illegal entry,
      deception, entry by, 19–22
      generally, 16–18
      illegal entrant, meaning, 16, 17
      mistake, effect of, 18–19
      proof of, 22–23
      ordinary residence, 14–15
    patriality—
      abode, right of, 10
      burden of proving, 10–12
      concept of, 9–12
    proof—
      illegal entry, of, 22–23
      patriality, of, 10–12
    settlement—
      aspects to being settled, 13
      generally, 13–14
      meaning, 13
      ordinary residence, 14–15
  1988, summary of provisions, 41–43
Immigration Appeal Tribunal. *See* Appeal
Immigration authorities—
  examination by, 393–398
Immigration control—
  artist—
    extension of stay, 184–186
    indefinite leave to remain, 185–186
    leave to enter, 184
  assimilating citizenship to, 4–5
  broadcasting organisation, representative of,
    extension of stay, 144–145
    leave to enter, 143–144
  business—
    EC Association Agreement, under, extension of stay, 178–181
    Hungary, national of, 177–178
    indefinite leave to remain, 178–181
    leave to enter, 175–177
    Poland, national of, 177–178
    person intending to establish himself in—
      accommodation, 170
      disguised employment, 170–171
      establishing new business, 172
      extension of stay, 173–174
      his own money, 169–170
      indefinite leave to remain, 174

560 INDEX

Immigration Control—*contd*
  business—*contd*
    penson intending to establish himself in—*contd*
      joining existing business, 171–172
      lawyers, concession relating to, 172
      leave to enter, 166–172
      maintenance, 170
      meeting liabilities, 171
      taking over existing business, 171–172
  child. *See* Child
  composer—
    extension of stay, 184–186
    indefinite leave to remain, 185–186
    leave to enter, 184
  deportation. *See* Deportation
  entry. *See* Entry
  extension of stay. *See* Extension of stay
  family member. *See* Family member
  general background, 3–5
  indefinite leave to remain. *See* Indefinite leave to remain
  investor—
    extension of stay, 182
    indefinite leave to remain, 182–183
    leave to enter, 181–182
    maintenance, 183
    money of his own under his control, 183
  minister of religion—
    extension of stay, 155–156
    indefinite leave to remain, 155–156
    leave to enter, 153–154
    meaning, 152
  missionary—
    extension of stay, 155–156
    indefinite leave to remain, 155–156
    leave to enter, 153–154
    meaning, 152
  news agency, representative of—
    extension of stay, 144–145
    leave to enter, 143–144
  overseas government employee—
    extension of stay, 151–152
    indefinite leave to remain, 152
    leave to enter, 151
  overseas newspaper, representative of—
    extension of stay, 144–145

Immigration control—*contd*
  overseas newspaper, representative of—*contd*
    leave to enter, 143–144
  overseas-owned airlines, airport-based operational ground staff of,
    extension of stay, 157
    indefinite leave to remain, 158
    leave to enter, 156–157
  primary purpose test. *See* Primary purpose test
  religious order, member of,
    extension of stay, 155–156
    indefinite leave to remain, 155–156
    leave to enter, 153–154
    meaning, 153
  rules. *See* Immigration rules
  sole representative of overseas firm,
    extension of stay, 146–148
    indefinite leave, 147, 148
    leave to enter, 145–146
  spouse. *See* Spouse
  UK ancestry—
    extension of stay on grounds of, 159–160
    indefinite leave to remain on grounds of, 160
    leave to enter on grounds of, 158–159
  work permit. *See* Work permit
  writer—
    extension of stay, 184–186
    indefinite leave to remain, 185–186
    leave to enter, 184
Immigration Law Practitioners' Association (ILPA)
  functions, 54
Immigration rules
  1994, 51–52, 59–81
  abode, proof of right of, 65–67
  accommodation, undertaking relating to, 79
  application, 60
  certain British passport holders, admission of, 68–69
  common travel area, 67–68
  commonwealth citizens settled in UK in 1973, 52
  concessions, 54–55
  decisions taken outside, 54–55
  EEA national, meaning, 62
  entry—
    clearance, 72–75

INDEX

Immigration rules—*contd*
1994—*contd*
leave to enter UK. *See* leave to enter UK, below
visa national, 74–75
generally, 51 59
implementation, 59–60
interpretation, 61–62
judicial review, 55
leave to enter UK—
arrival, meaning, 65
Channel Tunnel, through, 63
general provisions, 62–65
identity, evidence of, 63
nationality, evidence of, 63
refusal of, 63
returning residents, 69–71
undertakings, 79
variation of, 75–78
withdrawn application for variation, 78–79
maintenance, undertaking relating to, 79
medical, 80–81
parent, meaning, 61–62
passport—
certain British passport holders, admission of, 68–69
restricted, holder of, 71–72
policies, 54–55
public funds, meaning, 61
restricted travel documents and passports, holders of, 71–72
returning residents, 69–71
settled in UK, meaning, 61
status of, 52–54
transitional provisions, 59–60
undertaking—
accommodation, relating to, 79
maintenance, relating to, 79
variation of leave to enter or remain in UK, 75–78
visa national, meaning, 62
withdrawn application for leave to remain in UK, 78–79
Incapacitated person—
residence, right of, 310–312
Indefinite leave to remain—
artist, 185–186
broadcasting organisation, representative of, 144–145
business, person intending to establish himself in, 174

Indefinite leave to remain—*contd*
child. *See* Child
composer, 185–186
creative artist, 185–186
crew member, 255
diplomatic household, private servant in, 150
EC Association Agreement, person establishing himself in business under, 178–181
holder of special voucher, 191–194
independent means, retired person of, 195
investor, 182–183
minister of religion, 155–156
missionary, 155–156
news agency, representative of, 144–145
overseas government employee, 152
overseas newspaper, representative of, 144–145
overseas-owned airline, airport-based operational ground staff of, 158
primary purpose test, 215–216
private servant in diplomatic household, 150
religious order, member of, 155–156
retired person of independent means, 195
sole representative, 147, 148
special voucher holder, 191–194
UK ancestry, on grounds of, 160
work permit holder, 141–142
writer, 185–186
Information—
failure to furnish, 248
failure to provide, 524
Injunction—
EC law, enforcement of, 331
judicial review, remedy for, 500
Intention—
student, leave to enter as, 98–99 100–102
Interpreter—
requirements for, 462
Interview—
asylum claim, preparation of, 353–354
failure to attend, 257–258
police station interview, 529
Investor—
extension of stay, 182
indefinite leave to remain, 182–183

Investor—*contd*
  leave to enter, 181–182
  maintenance, 183
  money of his own under his control, 183
Iran—
  transit visa, citizen requiring, 92
Irish Republic. *See* Eire
Irrationality—
  judicial review, grounds for, 488–490
Isle of Man—
  common travel area, 67–68

Joint Council for Welfare of Immigrants (JCWI)
  functions, 54
Judicial review—
  application for,
  appeal—
    full hearing, from, 509
    interlocutory, 508–509
  bail, 507–508
  generally, 500–501
  hearing, 508
  interlocutory application, 507–508
  leave—
    application for, 501–504
    evidence, 504
    renewal of application for, 504–506
    setting aside, 506–507
    standard for, 502–503
  legal aid, 509
  procedure for, 500–509
  setting aside leave, 506–507
  bail pending appeal, 402–403
  certiorari as remedy, 499–500
  claim without foundation, 485–486
  generally, 481
  grounds for—
    generally, 486
    illegality, 486–487
    irrationality—
      generally, 488
      irrelevant considerations, 488–489
      proportionality, 489–490
      relevant considerations, 488–489
      unreasonable decisions, 489
    procedural impropriety—
      generally, 490–491
      legitimate expectation, 493–494
      procedural fairness, 492–493

Judicial review—*contd*
  human rights, interference with, 484–485
  illegal entrant, 485–486
  immigration rules, of, 55
  injunction as remedy, 500
  mandamus as remedy, 500
  nature of immigration decisions amenable to, 482–486
  precedent facts, 485–486
  prohibition as remedy, 500
  remedy of, 481–482
  restrictions on—
    alternative remedies, existence of, 495–498
    delay, 498–499
    discretion, 499
    locus standi, 495
    national security, 499
    time limits, 498–499
  threat to life and liberty, 484

Language assistant—
  approved exchange scheme, coming to UK under, 124–126
Lawyer—
  concession relating to, 172
Leave to enter UK. *See* Entry
Leave to remain—
  exceptional, asylum and, 365
  indefinite. *See* Indefinite leave to remain
Lebanon—
  transit visa, citizen requiring, 92
Legal aid—
  judicial review, application for, 509
Legitimate expectation—
  judicial review, grounds for, 493–494
Liabilities—
  business, person intending to establish himself in, 171
Liberty—
  threat to, judicial review, 484
Libya—
  transit visa, citizen requiring, 92
Life—
  threat to, judicial review, 484
Locus standi—
  judicial review, restrictions on, 495
Long residence policies—
  fourteen years, 264
  generally, 263
  ten years, 263–264

# INDEX

Loss of British citizenship. *See* British citizenship

Maintenance—
  adequate means, 103–104
  business, person intending to establish himself in, 170
  investor, of, 183
  public funds, visitor maintaining himself without recourse to, 89
  student, leave to enter as, 103–104
  undertaking relating to, 79
  variation of leave to enter or remain, refusal of, 257
  See also Public funds
Mandamus—
  judicial review, remedy for, 500
Marriage—
  deportation and, 273–275
  established, intervening devotion in, 211
  intervening devotion—
    established marriage, in, 211
    evidence of, 210–211
  patriality, burden of proving, 11
  polygamous, 203–204
  primary purpose, cases on, 209–210
Material facts—
  failure to disclose, 249–250
Material non-disclosure—
  entry clearance, refusal of, 250
  leave to enter, refusal of, 250
Medical examination—
  criminal offences, 520, 524
Medical inspector—
  role of, 80–81
Medical reasons. *See* Public health
Medical treatment. *See* Private medical treatment
Minister of religion—
  extension of stay, 155–156
  indefinite leave to remain, 155–156
  leave to enter, 153–154
  meaning, 152
Minor—
  British Nationality (Hong Kong) Act 1990, application under, 48 49
  registration, acquisition of British citizenship by, 31–32
  See also Child
Misrepresentation—
  criminal offences, 524–525

Missionary
  extension of stay, 155–156
  indefinite leave to remain, 155–156
  leave to enter, 153–154
  meaning, 152
Mistake—
  illegal entry, effect on, 18–19
Money—
  business, person intending to establish himself in, 169–170
  investor, of, 183
Morocco—
  co-operation agreement between EC and, 322–325

National security—
  asylum appeal, 380–381
  deportation of EEA national, 313–314
  deportation order, appeal against, 431–432
  judicial review, restrictions on, 499
Naturalisation—
  acquisition of British citizenship by, general requirements, 34
  generally, 33–34
  spouses of British citizens, 34–35
News agency, representative of
  extension of stay, 144–145
  leave to enter, 143–144
Newspaper—
  overseas, representative of,
    extension of stay, 144–145
    leave to enter, 143–144
Non-disclosure—
  material, 250, 253
  variation of leave to enter or remain, refusal of, 256
Non-disclosure—
Notice of appeal. *See* Appeal
Nurse—
  student. *See* Student

Offences. *See* Criminal offences
Ordinary residence—
  concept of, 14–15
  patriality, burden of proving, 11
Overseas—
  airlines, airport-based operational ground staff of—
    extension of stay, 157
    indefinite leave to remain, 158
    leave to enter, 156–157

Overseas—*contd*
  firm, sole representative of,
    extension of stay, 146–148
    indefinite leave, 147 148
    leave to enter, 145–146
  government employee—
    extension of stay, 151–152
    indefinite leave to remain, 152
    leave to enter, 151
  newspaper, representative of—
    extension of stay, 144–145
    leave to enter, 143–144

Parent—
  both parents present and settled in UK, 225
  consent to child seeking leave to remain, 250–251, 258
  indefinite leave to enter or remain, 237–242
  meaning, 61–62, 222
Parliamentary materials
  use of, 7–8
Passport—
  abode, proof of right of, 66
  certain British passport holders, admission of, 68–69
  eligibility to hold, 11
  entry clearance, refusal of, 249
  leave to enter, refusal of, 249
  restricted, holder of, 71–72
Patriality—
  abode, right of, 10
  burden of proving, 10–12
  concept of, 4, 9–12
  descent, by virtue of, 11–12
  marriage, by virtue of, 11
  ordinary residence, by virtue of, 11
  patrials distinguished from non-patrials, 4
Persecution—
  asylum, application for, 341–342
  meaning, 341
Poland—
  agreement between EC state and, 177–178
Police
  police station interview, 529
  registration with—
    EEA national, 260, 318
    leave to enter UK, 258–260
Polygamous marriage
  spouse, 203–204

Port
  asylum claim, preparation of, 354
  criminal offences relating to, 526
Preliminary ruling—
  EC law, application of, 331–332
  procedure for applying for, 332
Primary purpose test—
  accommodation, 211–213
  cohabitants, 213–214
  extension of stay, 215–216
  finance, 211–213
  generally, 207–209
  intervening devotion—
    established marriage, in, concession on, 211
  evidence of, 210–211
  marriage, cases on, 209–210
Private medical treatment—
  extension of stay as visitor for, refusal of, 94
  requirements for, 94–95
  visitor seeking to enter for, refusal of leave to enter, 93
  requirements for leave to enter, 92–94
Private servant—
  diplomatic household, in, extension of stay, 149–151
  leave to stay, 148–149
Procedural impropriety—
  judicial review, grounds for, 490–493
Procedure—
  asylum. *See* Asylum
  bail. *See* Bail
  detention. *See* Detention
  examination. *See* Examination
  temporary admission and release, bail for examination detainee, 399–400
  person liable to be detained, 399
  sureties, 400–401
Prohibition—
  judicial review, remedy for, 500
Proof—
  abode, right of—
    burden of proof, 66–67
    certificate of entitlement, 66–67
    generally, 65–66
    passport, 66
  blood relationship, of, 222–224
  burden of—
    abode, right of, 66–67
    appeal, 454–455

INDEX 565

Proof—*contd*
  illegal entry, of, 22–23
  patriality, of, 10–12
Proportionality—
  judicial review, grounds for, 489–490
Prospective student—
  exclusion from UK, 425
  leave to enter as, requirements for, 112–114
Public funds—
  free movement of EEA nationals, 304–305
  meaning, 61, 89
  visitor maintaining himself without recourse to, 89
Public good—
  deportation conducive to, 267–269 279–280
  discretionary exclusion conducive to, 251–252
  exclusion conducive to, 247–248
Public health—
  free movement of EEA nationals, 305, 319
  public good, exclusion conducive to, 247–248
Public policy—
  free movement of EEA nationals, 303–304, 319
Public security—
  free movement of EEA nationals, 303–304, 319

Race—
  persecution for reasons of, 341–342
Refugee—
  asylum. *See* Asylum
  former Yugoslavia, from, statement on, 351–352
  meaning, 340–341
Registration—
  acquisition of British citizenship from 1 January 1983, 31–33
  British Nationality (Hong Kong) Act 1990,
    children, 48, 49
    consequences, 49–50
    disciplined services, 48
    entrepreneurs class, 48
    exceptions, 49
    general occupation class, 47
    generally, 43
    head of household, 47

Registration—*contd*
  British Nationality (Hong Kong) Act 1990—*contd*
    qualification, 43–46
    scheme, 46–47
    sensitive service class, 48
    spouses, 48, 49
    third country citizenship, 48
  police, with—
    EEA national, 260, 318
    leave to enter UK, 258–260
Religion—
  member of religious order. *See* Religious order, member of
  minister of. *See* Minister of religion
  missionary. *See* Missionary
  persecution for reasons of, 341–342
Religious order, member of—
  extension of stay, 155–156
  indefinite leave to remain, 155–156
  leave to enter, 153–154
  meaning, 153
Remedies—
  appeal. *See* Appeal
  European Convention on Human Rights as, 475–478
  habeas corpus, 510–513
  judicial review. *See* Judicial review
Removal—
  asylum seeker, of, 388–390
  breach of conditions by person liable to, 520–521
  detention of person liable to, 398–399
  directions for, 422–423
  illegal entrant, of, 397–398
  person refused leave, of, 397–398
Renunciation—
  loss of British citizenship by, 35
Republic of Ireland. *See* Eire
Residence—
  EEA nationals,
    admission, rights of, 302
    appeal, 314–316
    deportation, 312–314
    Directive 68/360, 307–308
    family permit, 317, 319
    free movement, UK implementation of, 316–318
    generally, 307
    incapacitated person, 310–312
    other rights, 309–310
    person in employment, 307

Residence—*contd*
  EEA nationals—*contd*
    retired person, 310–312
    services, relating to, 308–309
    student, 309
    free movement of EC nationals, 302
  ordinary. *See* Ordinary residence
  services, relating to, 308–309
  Restricted returnability—
    entry clearance, refusal of, 254
    leave to enter, refusal of, 254
Retired person—
  free movement of EC national, 303
  independent means, of,
    extension of stay, 195
    indefinite leave to remain, 195
    leave to enter, 194, 195–196
    residence, right of, 310–312
Retirement—
  employment, after, EEA worker, 298–299
Returning resident—
  entry as, 69–71
  entry clearance, refusal of, 248–249
  leave to enter, refusal of, 248–249
  restricted returnability, 257
Rules. *See* Immigration rules

Seasonal worker—
  agricultural camp, at, 122–124
Secretary of State—
  deportation order made by,
    decision to deport, 404–405
    generally, 404
    signing order, 405–406
  further consideration, reference of case for, 470–471
Self-employed person—
  European Economic Area Agreement, 291
  free movement of EC nationals, 299–300
Sensitive service class—
  British Nationality (Hong Kong) Act 1990, application under, 48
Separation—
  deportation and, 274–275
Servant—
  private, in diplomatic household,
    extension of stay, 149–151
    leave to enter, 148–149
Services—
  meaning, 292

Services—*contd*
  production of, visitor not intending to engage in, 88–89
  receipt of, EC, 300
  residence in relation to, 308–309
Settlement—
  aspects to being settled, 13
  asylum, application for, 365–366
  free movement, UK implementation of, 316–317
  generally, 13–14
  meaning, 13
  ordinary residence, 14–15
  settled in UK, meaning, 61
Ship—
  criminal offences relating to, 521, 526
Social group—
  asylum, application for, 342–343
Social security—
  asylum seeker, provision for, 366–367
Somalia—
  transit visa, citizen requiring, 92
Son—
  exceptional compassionate circumstances relating to, 243
Special voucher holder—
  indefinite leave to enter, 191–194
Sponsor—
  undertaking, refusal to give, 249, 257
Spouse—
  British citizen, of, 34–35
  British Nationality (Hong Kong) Act 1990, application under, 48, 49
  extension of stay, 205–206
  generally, 201–203
  leave to enter, 204–205, 206–207
  person with limited leave to enter or remain, of, 131–132, 161–163, 186–188 196–198
  polygamy, 203–204
  student, of, 110–111
  under 16, 203
Sri Lanka—
  transit visa, citizen requiring, 92
Student—
  children of, 111–112
  course of study,
    full time, 99–100
    intention to leave at end of, 105–106

INDEX 567

Student—contd
  deportation order, working in breach of, 267
  European Union (EU), 103-104
  free movement of EC nationals, 301
  generally, 96
  leave to enter as—
    ability, 98-99
    adequate means, 103-104
    course of studies, intention to leave at end of, 105-106
    employment, 102-103
    extensions, 104-105
    full time course of study, 99-100
    intention, 98-99
    intention to leave, 100-102
    postgraduate doctor or denist, 109-110
    refusal of, 97
    requirements for, 96-98
    satisfactory progress, 106
    student nurse, 106-109
  nurse—
    extension of stay as—
      refusal of, 108
      requirements for, 107-109
    leave to enter as—
      refusal of, 107
      requirements for, 107
    meaning, 106-107
    postgraduate doctor or dentist, 109-110
  prospective—
    exclusion from UK, 425
    extension of stay as, generally, 113
    refusal of, 113
    leave to enter as—
      refusal of, 113
      requirements for, 112-114
  residence, right of, 309
  short-term, exclusion from UK, 425
  spouse of, 110-111
  visitor not intending to engage in study, 88-89
Sureties—
  temporary admission and release, 400-401

Teacher—
  approved exchange scheme, coming to UK under, 124-126
Terrorism, prevention of—
  deportation, liability to, 528
  deportation of EEA national, 313-314

Third country—
  agreements. *See* European Community (EC)
  asylum, refusal of, 345
  safe, 346-350
Threat—
  life and liberty, to, judicial review, 484
Time limits—
  appeal, right of, 418
  asylum appeal, 387
  deportation order, appeal against, 422
  failure to observe, 249
  judicial review, restrictions on, 498-499
  preliminary points, 443-444
Training—
  DoE approved,
    extension of stay, 129-131
    leave to enter for, 126-127
    requirements, 127-129
Transit—
  visitor in, 91-92
Travel documents—
  restricted, holder of, 71-72
Tunisia—
  co-operation agreement between EC and, 322-325
Turkey—
  Association Agreement between EC and, 320-322
  transit visa, citizen requiring, 92

Uganda—
  transit visa, citizen requiring, 92
Uncle—
  exceptional compassionate circumstances relating to, 243
Undertaking—
  accommodation, relating to, 79
  EEA, third country national employed in, 325
  maintenance, relating to, 79
  sponsor's refusal to give, 249, 257
United Kingdom ancestry—
  extension of stay on grounds of, 159-160
  indefinite leave to remain on grounds of, 160
  leave to enter on grounds of, 158-159

United Kingdom national—
  Community treaties, for purposes of, 33
Visa national—
  appeal, right of, 415–416
  entry clearance—
    generally, 74–75
    refusal of, 247
  leave to enter, refusal of, 247
  meaning, 62
Visitor—
  business visitor, 85–86
  employment, meaning, 88–89
  exclusion from UK, 425
  extension of stay as—
    refusal of, 90
    requirements for, 90–91
  goods, production of, 88–89
  in transit—
    extension of stay as, 91
    leave to enter as, 91
    refusal of leave to enter as, 91
    requirements for admission as, 91–92
  intends to leave UK at end of his visit, meaning, 86–88
  leave to enter as—
    business visitor, 85–86
    period of admission, 83–84
    purpose of visit, 84–86
    refusal of, 83
    requirements for, 82–83
  period of admission, 83–84
  private medical treatment, leave to enter for—
    extension of stay,
      refusal of, 94
      requirements for, 94–95
    refusal of, 93
    requirements for, 92–95
  public funds—
    meaning, 89
    recourse to, 89
  purpose of visit, 84–86
  services, production of, 88–89
  study, entry for, 88–89

Witness—
  summoning, 447
Work experience—
  DoE approved,
    extension of stay, 129–131
    leave to enter, 126–127
    requirements, 127–129
Work permit—
  details to be supplied, 139–141
  domestic work, 136
  EU citizen, position of, 135–136
  employment—
    DoE requirements, 138–141
    extension of stay, 141–142
    leave to enter for, 137
    refusal of leave to enter for, 137
    requirements—
      DoE, 138–141
      generally, 137–138
      excluded categories, 139
      generally, 135
  holder—
    domestic work, 136
    EU citizen, 135–136
    generally, 135
    keyworkers, 138–139
    possession of, 135
Workers—
  admission under law governing EEA, right of, 294–299
Working holidaymaker—
  child of, 121–122
  extension of stay as, 118–119
    120–121
  generally, 119–120
  leave to enter as, 117–118
Writer—
  extension of stay, 184–186
  indefinite leave to remain, 185–186
  leave to enter, 184

Yugoslavia—
  former, statement on refugees from, 351–352

Zaire—
  transit visa, citizen requiring, 92